Supperstone and O'Dempsey on Immigration and Asylum

4th Edition

Michael Supperstone QC, MA, BCL (Oxon)

of the Middle Temple, Barrister

and

Declan O'Dempsey MA (Cantab), Dip Law

of the Middle Temple, Barrister

LAW & TAX

© Pearson Professional Limited 1996

ISBN 0752 002856

Published by
FT Law & Tax
21–27 Lamb's Conduit Street
London WC1N 3NJ
A Division of Pearson Professional Limited

Associated Offices
Australia, Belgium, Canada, Hong Kong, India, Japan,
Luxembourg, Singapore, Spain, USA

First Edition 1983
Second Edition 1988
Third Edition 1994

A CIP catalogue record of this book is available from the British
Library.

Printed in Great Britain by
Bell and Bain Ltd, Glasgow

Consulting Editor

Michael Supperstone QC of 11 Kings' Bench Walk specialises in immigration law, judicial review and employment law. He sits as a Recorder and he is Chairman of the Administrative Law Bar Association.

General Editor

Declan O'Dempsey is a Barrister at 4 Brick Court, specialising in immigration, employment and administrative law.

Contributors:

Fiona Lindsley is a solicitor at BM Birnberg & Co specialising in immigration and asylum law.

Naomi Cunningham is a Barrister and a member of Inner Temple. She is currently a Case Worker at the North Kensington Law Centre.

Tim Pitt Payne is a Barrister at 11 Kings' Bench Walk specialising in employment, commercial, public and asylum law.

Rajeev Thacker is a Barrister at 4 Brick Court, specialising in immigration law, employment law, public law and housing.

Helen Curtis is a Barrister at 4 Brick Court practising in all areas of criminal law.

Contents

Part II   The Immigration Rules: HC 395

Part III   Procedure

Part VI   Asylum

Part VII   Criminal Offences

Preface

The Asylum and Immigration Appeals Act 1993 represented a dramatic change in the treatment of asylum seekers in the UK. A right of appeal was introduced and assurances were given that the asylum seeker would be able to appeal while in the UK. The Asylum and Immigration Act 1996 changes the scope of the 'manifestly unfounded' procedures for asylum claims, introducing the concept of 'designated country of destination'. This is a country in which, in the opinion of the Secretary of State there is in general no serious risk of persecution. The 1996 Act also permits asylum seekers to be removed before lodging an appeal to 'designated safe third countries' or to member states of the EU. This represents part of a movement in the EU to harmonise refugee procedures.

Other changes in the 1996 Act are more welcome, such as the right in illegal entrant cases to apply for bail to the adjudicator, or when appealing to the Court of Appeal.

In practice the most significant change has been the introduction of draconian curbs on the right of refused asylum seekers to claim social welfare benefits. The history of the death and resurrection of the Social Security (Persons from Abroad) Miscellaneous Amendment Regulations 1996 (SI No 30) perhaps should be set out. The regulations were declared to be *ultra vires* by the Court of Appeal in *Ex p B*. Within two weeks they were revivified by Sched 1 to the 1996 Act when the government relied on the votes of hereditary peers to force through the addition of Sched 1 to the 1996 Act. The full repercussions of this piece of legislation are still to be realised. Recently Collins J (*R v Hammersmith & Fulham BC, Ex p M* (1996) *The Times*, 10 October) ruled that local authorities may have to provide the necessities of life for asylum seekers.

The introduction of the asylum appeals system has led to a proliferation of decisions concerning the law of asylum. To reflect this the title of the book has changed. The book continues to use the analysis of the Immigration

Rules HC 395 (as amended) as its core. Having established the book firmly in the Practitioners' Series, Michael Supperstone QC is now consulting editor, and a team of contributors have helped to write this fourth edition. I am very grateful to him and to that team, Naomi Cunningham, Helen Curtis, Fiona Lindsley, Timothy Pitt Payne and Rajeev Thacker for their work, although I am responsible should any mistakes remain. I would like to thank the Home Office and the JCWI for their assistance. In addition I would like to thank Sue Shutter, Vicki Guedella, Susan Belgrave, Meena Gill, Melanie Lewis, Mark Phillips, Julia Onslow-Cole, Katie Ghose, Jonathan Glasson and Clare Cozens variously for help and encouragement. Clare Cozens deserves a further mention for obtaining materials for the book, often at short notice. Britha Parekh, Pauline Callow and the production team on this edition have been extremely patient and understanding of the delays which became inevitable after the Secretary of State decided to introduce a requirement of maintenance and accommodation to the majority of the temporary stay categories in mid-November 1996.

I have attempted to ensure that the law is stated as at 19 November 1996, although any materials which we were able to include in the text after that date have been introduced.

Declan O'Dempsey
4 Brick Court, Temple

Table of Abbreviations

References to paragraph numbers without more are references to the Immigration Rules HC 395.

Where a case name commences 'R v Secretary of State for the Home Department, ex parte', this has been abbreviated to 'Ex p' throughout. Cases referred to in the style 'Akbar (8670)' are unreported Immigration Appeal Tribunal cases.

Table of UK Cases

Table of Statutes

xlv

Table of Statutory Instruments

Table of Immigration Rules

Table of ECJ and Other non-UK Cases

Table of EC Legislation

Table of Treaties, Conventions etc

Part I

Background

Chapter 1

Introduction

The Immigration Act 1971 and the British Nationality Act 1981 are authority for, and the main sources of, the network of subordinate legislation and administrative discretion which is the basic law of immigration control. In addition significant modifications to rights of appeal and immigration control have been effected by the Immigration Act 1988, the Asylum and Immigration Appeals Act 1993 and the Asylum and Immigration Act 1996. The ramifications of the rule-making powers given to the S of S by these Acts are extensive.

Immigration control results from a few substantive rights granted by statute and subordinate legislation, and from procedural rules governing the grant and refusal of leave to enter and remain. As a result of the large areas of discretion granted to the S of S, substantive rights have to be derived from the procedural mechanism governing that discretion.

The 1971 Act is concerned with the control of travel to and from the UK, and the control of settlement within the UK. Before the British Nationality Act 1948 the basic distinction (which still remains today) was between those persons with and those without the right of entry. They were divided broadly into British subjects who had that right, and aliens and British Protected Persons (BPPs) who were born in or had a connection with a British Protectorate, who did not.

The 1948 Act made a division within the category of British subjects. It created three categories: citizens of the UK and Commonwealth (CUKCs), citizens of independent Commonwealth countries (such as India, Ghana or Jamaica), and British subjects without citizenship. All these had the right of entry. By the time of the 1971 Act further distinctions had been made within these categories. Certain persons who previously had the right of entry lost it. British subjects without citizenship lost the right of entry, ironically being called 'British subjects' thereafter.

The 1971 Act removed the right of entry by means of the concept of patriality. Within the categories of those who had previously had the right of entry, it made the distinction between 'patrials' who were not subject to immigration control, and 'non-patrials' who were. This distinction remains in the separation of those who have and those who do not have the right of abode. It further split the category of CUKC, into 'patrial' CUKCs (those

CUKCs with the right of abode), and 'non-patrial' CUKCs (without the right of abode). The category of citizens of independent Commonwealth countries was similarly split. They were thereafter known as 'patrial Commonwealth citizens' and 'non-patrial Commonwealth citizens'.

By the 1981 Act, citizenship rights were equated with freedom from immigration control. Thus CUKCs with the right of abode (patrial CUKCs) became known as British citizens. Patrial Commonwealth citizens became known as 'Commonwealth citizens patrial on 31 January 1982'. Both these categories were free from immigration control and could enter the UK after any length of absence. Non-patrial CUKCs became further subdivided into British Dependent Territories citizens (BDTCs) and British overseas citizens (BOCs). Commonwealth citizens who were non-patrial became known as 'Commonwealth citizens not patrial on 31 January 1982'. Before the 1981 Act the right of abode in the UK was defined by reference to the concept of patriality. Since the 1981 Act the right of abode is determined by reference to the categories of citizenship which were created at that time (see Chapter 3). It is characteristic of this area of law that what seems to be a substantive right of citizenship in fact flows from a person's relation to immigration control, and not *vice versa*.

The illogical process of assimilating citizenship to immigration control is the result of a gradual retreat by successive British governments from the imperial stance which recognised all citizens of the Empire as British subjects. Various pressures have led governments to withdraw some of the full rights of citizenship (ie the right freely to enter and settle in the UK) from members of the Commonwealth. At the same time governments have been reluctant to renounce symbolic labels such as 'citizen of the UK and colonies' and 'Commonwealth citizen'. The 1981 Act finally acknowledged the hypocrisy of offering a citizenship which entails subjection to immigration control inconsistent with the titular status of that citizenship.

For reasons of space, the account which follows of the various Acts is necessarily schematic. In particular, for a fuller account of matters relating to Citizenship see Fransman, *British Nationality Law*, 2nd edn.

1   The British Nationality Act 1948

Until the BNA 1948, everyone who owed allegiance to the Crown was a British subject. All others were aliens. The BNA 1948 divided the category of British subject (which was interchangeable with 'Commonwealth citizen' under that Act) into two categories, CUKCs and persons who had citizenship of independent Commonwealth countries (s 1).

Citizenship of the United Kingdom and Colonies (CUKC)
A person acquired the status of CUKC either by birth in the UK and colonies, or by descent from a father who was born there (ss 4 and 5). The intention seems to have been that as the remaining colonies gradually

became independent, a large number of CUKCs would lose that citizenship on acquiring the citizenship of their newly independent country. The position would eventually be reached where the CUKC category would be reduced to citizens of the UK. All other former members of that category would be citizens of independent Commonwealth countries, and therefore British subjects (or Commonwealth citizens).

2 The Commonwealth Immigrants Acts 1962 and 1968

Not all British colonies became independent. Some persons, particularly Asians living in East Africa, did not automatically acquire the citizenship of the country in which they lived when it became independent, and they remained CUKCs. The result was that persons who had strong ties with the UK shared the same citizenship status as those who did not. Some critics believed that this was anomalous. Consequently the gradual effect of legislation since 1948 has been to subdivide the category of CUKC by subjecting its members to differential immigration control. This in turn has come to seem anomalous. The 1981 Act dispersed the category of CUKC to the four winds. The first steps on this road were taken by the 1962 Act, the first Act to impose immigration control on British subjects. One group that had not been subject to that control, the East African Asians, were subsequently caught in the expanding net of control by the 1968 Act.

3 The Immigration Act 1971

The structure of the 1971 Act is relatively simple. It has four parts and six schedules. The key parts of the Act are Parts I–III. Part I provides for the control of entry into and stay within the UK. The effect of this Part and the rules made under it are examined in Part II of this book. Part II of the Act sets up the statutory appeals machinery examined in Chapters 18 ff. Part III of the Act deals with criminal offences, which are discussed in Part VII of this book.

The pivotal sections of the Act are ss 1–3. Section 1 sets out the travellers and the journeys which are subject to immigration control. The right of abode in the UK (previously known as patriality) is defined in s 2. This section was substantially amended by the 1981 Act so that the right of abode is defined by reference to the categories of citizenship set up under the 1981 Act, instead of by reference to the concept of patriality. Section 3 of the Act makes general provision as to immigration control, with subs 3(2) being the source of the S of S's power to make the crucial immigration rules.

4 The British Nationality Act 1981

The pattern of the 1981 Act is superficially simple. There are five parts. The first four create four new categories of citizenship: British citizenship, British Dependent Territories Citizen (BDTC), British Overseas Citizen, and

British subject. These new categories and their consequences are discussed in Chapter 3. Part V is a miscellany, which among other things makes, by s 39, amendments to the 1971 Act.

In the case of British citizenship and BDTCs the 1981 Act sets out how these categories of citizenship may be acquired: both at the commencement and after commencement of the Act. As to BOCs and British subjects, there are only limited statutory mechanisms for the acquisition of citizenship after commencement, since it was intended that these categories would die out. The Act makes provision for the loss of citizenship.

The main change to the pre-existing law made by the 1981 Act in connection with citizenship was that it was no longer possible to acquire the citizenship which is crucial to freedom from immigration control simply by being born in the UK. Before the 1981 Act anyone who was born in the UK became a CUKC and had the right of abode (ie was patrial), simply by virtue of place of birth. Since the 1981 Act, however, birth in the UK is not sufficient and the clearest traditional means of acquiring citizenship (*jus soli*) is abolished.

The apparently simple structure of the 1981 Act is complicated by the necessity of cross-reference to earlier nationality laws. The question of who belongs to the four categories of citizenship under the 1981 Act cannot be determined simply by looking at that Act. It is necessary first to look at the categories of citizenship which preceded those set out in the 1981 Act: they are the foundation upon which that Act is built.

5 Use of parliamentary materials

In general, reference to parliamentary materials has not been permitted as an aid to the construction of statutes, but there are a number of exceptions to this rule. It is permissible when construing primary or secondary legislation to use the reports of Commissions and to refer to White Papers solely to ascertain the mischief which a provision is intended to cure (*Assam Railways & Trading Co Ltd v Commissioners of Inland Revenue* [1935] AC 445 at 457–8). In *R v S of S for Transport, ex p Factortame Ltd* [1990] 2 AC 85, the HL was prepared to look at a Law Commission Report for the purpose of drawing an inference as to the intention of Parliament from the fact that Parliament had not implemented one of its recommendations. The HL, in *Pickstone v Freemans plc* [1989] AC 66, [1988] 3 CMLR 221, departed from the general rule when construing a statutory instrument, to ascertain the intention of Parliament at the time the instrument had been presented to Parliament by the responsible Minister.

The general prohibition on reference to parliamentary materials stems from the view that such reference might infringe art 8 of the Bill of Rights 1689, prohibiting the questioning of proceedings in Parliament in any other place. However, in *Pepper v Hart* [1993] AC 593; [1992] 3 WLR 1032, the HL held that the use of clear ministerial statements by the courts as a guide to the construction of ambiguous legislation would not infringe the Bill of Rights. Lord Browne-Wilkinson said (at p 1056) that reference to 'parliamentary materials should only be permitted where such material clearly discloses the mischief aimed at or the legislative intent behind the ambiguous or obscure words'. He thought it unlikely that any statement other than the statement of the Minister or other promoter of a Bill would meet these criteria.

It is therefore possible to use *Hansard* as a guide to the interpretation of legislation in the following circumstances:

(a) where the legislative provision is ambiguous or obscure or leads to absurdity;

(b) where the materials which are relied upon consist of one or more statements by Ministers or other promoters of a Bill;

(c) where other parliamentary materials are needed to understand the statements of the Ministers and their effects.

Where words in a statute are capable of bearing more than one meaning, and Parliament considered what interpretation should be placed upon those words, the court should look at parliamentary materials in appropriate cases regardless of the practical difficulties that may be created by such a practice. Where the interpretation previously given to ambiguous words by a court conflicts with that expressed by the Minister at the time of the promotion of a Bill, the Minister's interpretation should in the future prevail. It is possible to refer to statements made by way of a concession by a Minister in Parliament in addition to such interpretive references.

Practice Direction (Hansard extracts)
Practice Direction (Hansard extracts) [1995] 1 WLR 192; [1995] 1 All ER 234 provides that the following practice is to be followed if a passage from parliamentary debates is to be referred to under the principles in *Pepper v Hart* and *Pickstone v Freemans plc* (above) or otherwise. The practice direction applies to passages which are relied on to show the S of S's policy in an area of immigration law, outside the *Pepper v Hart* principles. The practice direction applies to both final and interlocutory hearings.

Unless the judge directs otherwise, the party intending to refer to any extract from *Hansard* must serve on all parties and the court:

(a) copies of the extract, together with

(b) a brief summary of the argument intended to be based on such report.

Service of the extract and summary of arguments must be effected not less than five clear working days before the first day of the hearing, whether or not there is a fixed date. Service on the court is effected by sending (in the Crown Office) two copies to the Head of the Crown Office, Room C312, Royal Courts of Justice.

If a party fails to comply with the practice direction the court may make such order, relating to costs and otherwise, as was in all the circumstances appropriate.

Chapter 2

The Immigration Act 1971

The 1971 Act distinguishes between those categories of person who are subject to immigration control and those who are not. The key phrase used by the 1971 Act is 'right of abode in the UK'. This is not a phrase which appears in the passport of a person who is not subject to immigration control. The 1971 Act, s 1(1) provides that all those who have a right of abode in the UK shall be free to live in and to come and go into or from the UK without let or hindrance except in so far as may be necessary to establish that right. Section 2 defines who is to have a right of abode and provides that such persons are to be described as 'patrials'. This section was amended by the British Nationality Act 1981, s 39 and Sched 4. The right of abode remains the crucial factor which distinguishes those who are and those who are not subject to immigration control. However, the 1981 Act also redefined, by reference to the categories of citizenship, the persons who do or do not have a right of abode in the UK.

The 1971 Act also introduces the concepts of 'illegal entry' and 'settlement'. These continue to have relevance, and are discussed below.

1   The concept of patriality and right of abode before the 1981 Act

Patriality was a characteristic of CUKCs and citizens of independent Commonwealth countries only. Once a person had established his patriality to the satisfaction of the authorities and obtained his passport, in which was stamped the phrase 'holder has right of abode in the UK', he was free to come and go as he pleased. In practical terms, he would have been subject to immigration control in the sense that he would probably have been asked to show his passport when he entered and left the country. There were, however, no restrictions on how long he could stay and or on his right to work. There was no requirement to undergo examination or register with the police. The practice of stamping the passport in this way has now ceased, because the holder would have those rights automatically as a British citizen.

(a) The right of abode (patriality)
Methods of acquisition   Patriality is now known as the right of abode in the UK. After the 1971 Act a CUKC or Commonwealth citizen either had the

right of abode (was patrial) or did not have it (was non-patrial). Before 1983 patriality was acquired by various routes:

(1) The first and most obvious route to patriality was to have been born, adopted, naturalised or registered (with some exceptions) in the UK and Islands (Channel Islands or the Isle of Man).

(2) The second way was by descent from or adoption by a father who was born etc in the UK and Islands, or was himself descended from or adopted by a father who was born etc in the UK or Islands.

(3) A third method of acquiring patriality was by being a CUKC who was settled at any time in the UK and Islands, and having been at that time ordinarily resident in the UK for five years or more.

(4) Patriality could be acquired by being a Commonwealth citizen born to or adopted by a parent who was a CUKC by virtue of his or her birth in the UK or Islands.

(5) The 1971 Act, s 2 made provision for certain women to be patrials by virtue of their marriage, namely, those women who were Commonwealth citizens and married to, were the widows of, or the ex-wives of men who were patrials by virtue either of birth in the UK and Islands, or were adopted, naturalised or registered in the UK, or had patriality by any of the other means. Widows and ex-wives of British subjects under the pre-BNA 1948 law, who would have been patrials either because they were born etc in the UK or were descended from a patrial, were also patrials.

(b) The burden of proving patriality

Under the 1971 Act, s 3(8), if any question arises as to whether a person does or does not have the right of abode (is or is not a patrial), the burden of proving that fact is on the person who asserts that he has the right. In the past a passport which said 'holder has right of abode in the UK' would have been sufficient proof. Difficulties arose in the case of a person who did not hold such a passport. The case of *S of S v Lakdawalla* [1972] Imm AR 26 underlines the problems experienced by persons who did not possess the appropriate passport. The IAT accepted that there was no entitlement as of right to a passport: the issue of passports is within the royal prerogative. However, the refusal to issue a new passport is amenable to judicial review (*R v S of S for the Foreign and Commonwealth Office, ex p Everett* [1989] QB 811). *Lakdawalla* was a case under the Commonwealth Immigrants Acts 1962–68, but the principle is the same today. The IAT reached the conclusion, under the immigration rules in force at the time, that 'eligible to hold a passport' did not (and presumably could not) mean 'legally eligible to hold a passport'. The IAT then directed itself in accordance with the administrative practices followed in passport offices in deciding whether or not the respondent was 'eligible' to hold a passport.

The 1971 Act, s 3(9), provided that persons who claimed patriality either by virtue of ordinary residence (route (3)) or marriage (route (5)) should prove it by means of a certificate of patriality. He needed no certificate if his claim was made by his spouse, who was a patrial either by virtue of birth in the UK or Islands, or by virtue of descent (routes (1) and (2)). Changes were introduced to this by the 1981 Act (see Chapter 3 below).

The cases on patriality show a tendency to deny patriality to potential holders. In *R v IAT, ex p De Sousa* [1977] Imm AR 6, the appellant was refused entry to the UK. She appealed on the basis that she was naturalised in the UK and so did not require leave to enter at all. She was a BPP resident in Kenya who was granted a certificate of naturalisation by the Kenyan Governor. The certificate bore the signature of a Colonial Office functionary in London, and was registered at the Home Office. However, the Divisional Court held that she was not 'naturalised in the UK', and so not a patrial. A similar conclusion was reached in *Keshwani v S of S* [1975] Imm AR 38 in relation to an appellant naturalised by virtue of a certificate granted by the Ugandan Governor.

In *Hussein v S of S* [1975] Imm AR 69 it was held that patriality by virtue of descent (route (2) above) could not be acquired unless the grandparent from whom citizenship was traced had that citizenship by virtue of his own birth, adoption or naturalisation or registration in the UK. The appellants, one of whose maternal great-grandfathers had been born in Derby, were not patrials because their grandfather, although a British subject, was born in Madras, and their mother in Bombay.

In summary, before the 1981 Act came into force, there were two main categories for the purposes of nationality law: British subjects (or Commonwealth citizens), and aliens. This was, however, a superficial division, since most Commonwealth citizens were for the purposes of immigration control in almost the same position as aliens, as most of them were non-patrial and therefore had no right of entry. The same patrial/non-patrial division existed within the CUKC category. CUKCs, and Commonwealth citizens who were not patrial, BPPs and aliens were subject to immigration control and required leave to enter and remain.

Limited exceptions to this wide general rule were provided for in the 1971 Act, s 8. In summary, there were exemptions from immigration control under that section in favour of seamen and aircrews in certain circumstances, anyone in whose favour the S of S had made an order, members of diplomatic missions, their families and households, and members of certain armed forces. (The position of nationals of EEA countries and of the Republic of Ireland is different from that of other aliens: see Chapters 16 and 17 below.)

The result was that before the commencement of the 1981 Act non-patrial CUKCs and other Commonwealth citizens, despite the ties of their citizenship with the UK, were not free to enter and remain as they chose as the 1971 Act makes clear. Section 3 provided that non-patrials could not enter the UK without leave to enter. They could be given limited or indefinite leave to enter and remain; and such leave might be given subject to conditions such as restrictions on employment. Non-Commonwealth citizens could also be required to register with the police.

This meant that a large number of persons seeking to enter and stay in the UK had no right or entitlement to do so. They could do so only as the result of an administrative discretion which is vested by the 1971 Act in the S of S (who makes the rules) and the immigration officers (who administer those rules). Section 4 provides that the power of giving or refusing leave to enter the UK is to be exercised by immigration officers. Leave, once given, can be varied. This power is vested in the S of S (s 4).

2   The right of abode after the 1981 Act

The 1981 Act amended the 1971 Act, s 2. The definition of who is to have the right of abode was changed.

The 1981 Act, s 39(2), provides that for s 2 of the 1971 Act there shall be substituted:

> A person is under this Act to have the right of abode in the UK if—
> (a)   he is a British citizen; or
> (b)   he is a Commonwealth citizen who—
>   (i)   immediately before the commencement of the British Nationality Act 1981 was a Commonwealth citizen having the right of abode in the UK by virtue of s 2(1)(d) or s 2(2) of this Act as then in force; and
>   (ii)   has not ceased to be a Commonwealth citizen in the meanwhile.

The new categories of citizenship under the 1981 Act are discussed in Chapter 3.

The 1981 Act, s 39(3) amends the 1971 Act, s 3(9), and provides for certificates of patriality to be replaced by certificates of entitlement where such certificates may be required under the 1981 Act. The documentation that may be necessary to obtain entry is discussed in Chapter 6.

3   Settlement

'Settlement' was first defined in the 1971 Act, and s 50(2)–(5) of the 1981 Act largely repeat the effect of the provisions of the 1971 Act. Clearly cases decided under the 1971 Act and cases decided under the 'returning residents' rule (see p 70 below) will be authoritative in relation to the concept. There are two aspects to being settled:

(1)   A person is not settled until he is free of any restriction under the immigration laws as to the length of his stay in the UK.

(2)   He must be ordinarily resident in the UK.

Reference may also be made to the interpretation sections of the immigration rules, para 6 (see p 58). A person who is settled is no longer bound by the particular purpose for which he was admitted. So, for example, a person who had entered on a work permit to take up a particular job, may take up a completely different type of work when settled. Persons who are settled are also described as having 'indefinite leave to remain' or as having been granted 'permanent stay'. A person with this kind of leave may have a stamp in his passport stating that he has 'indefinite leave to remain in the

UK'. Under the immigration rules there is a qualifying period of leave to remain, after which an entrant may apply for indefinite leave to remain.

Ordinary residence

Ordinary residence is partially defined in the 1981 Act, s 50(5). A person cannot be ordinarily resident if he is in the UK in breach of the immigration laws (see *Ex p Margueritte* [1983] 2 AC 309). 'Immigration laws' includes past immigration laws (see the 1981 Act, s 50(1) and *Lui v S of S* [1986] Imm AR 287). Clearly if he has committed an offence under the 1971 Act or the 1981 Act he is in breach; but the concept of breach is wider than that, and embraces presence in the UK as an illegal entrant. Breach of the immigration laws also includes breaches of administrative directions under the legislation, such as a deportation order, and conditions of leave to enter or remain in the UK. It is irrelevant that such a breach is innocent and inadvertent (*IAT v Chelliah* [1985] Imm AR 192).

Ordinary residence is a concept used in other areas such as tax legislation and the Education Acts. It refers to a person's abode in a particular place or country which he has adopted voluntarily, or for settled purposes (which can include education), as part of the regular order of his life for the time being, whether of short or long duration (*R v Barnet LBC, ex p Shah* [1983] 2 AC 309, *per* Lord Scarman at p 343). A person can be ordinarily resident in the UK while absent for not insignificant periods, so long as he maintains some tie or connection with the UK. There must be 'an element of having a home here' (*Ex p Abu Bakar* (1981) unreported, *per* Woolf J). However, a person may be ordinarily resident in two places at once (*Britto v S of S* [1984] Imm AR 93). It is a question of fact in every case. The decided cases give broad guidance, but are not to be regarded as decisive precedents (see, for example, *IRC v Lysaght* [1928] AC 234 and *Levene v IRC* [1928] AC 217).

Exceptions to the general rule about settlement are contained in the 1981 Act, s 50(3), (4). A person who would otherwise fall to be regarded as settled, is not in fact settled for the purposes of the legislation if he is subject to an exemption under the 1971 Act, s 8(2), (3), (4)(*b*) and (*c*). That section confers exemption from immigration control on various categories of person, such as those in respect of whom the S of S has made an order, diplomatic agents (and members of their families and households) and members of visiting Commonwealth forces. A person who falls within one of these exemptions is not 'settled' in the UK, even if he meets all the other requirements of settlement. There is an exception to this rule in the case of a person to whom a child is born while he or she is apparently settled, but subject to a s 8 exemption unless the person is entitled to diplomatic immunity.

4 Rights of appeal

Until 1969 there was no statutory machinery for appeals in connection with immigration. The 1971 Act, s 12 continued the existence of the IAT and of the adjudicators first set up under the Immigration Appeals Act 1969. Schedule 5 to the 1971 Act makes provision for the appointment, administration and organisation of these appellate bodies. Adjudicators and the members of the IAT are now appointed by the Lord Chancellor. Further changes have been made to rights of appeal by the Asylum and Immigration Appeals Act 1993, according a right of appeal to the CA provided that the IAT has granted leave, but withdrawing rights of appeal from persons entering as visitors or short-term students and from persons whose applications for leave must, under the immigration rules, be refused, either because they do not have the correct documentation or because they do not fulfil mandatory requirements of the immigration rules (see Part V). Yet further changes to the appeals machinery are made by the Asylum and Immigration Act 1996 (see Chapter 26).

Part II of the 1971 Act sets out the rights of appeal to these bodies. An appeal is usually in the first instance to the adjudicator, and then to the IAT. Exceptionally, the adjudicator may be leapfrogged (for instance under s 15(7)). It is to be noted that there is generally no right of appeal against a decision to deport made on the grounds of national security (see p 359 below).

Appeals may be made against

(a) refusal of entry clearance;

(b) refusal of leave to enter;

(c) conditions of leave to enter and remain;

(d) a decision to make a deportation order;

(e) the validity of directions for removal;

(f) refusal to revoke a deportation order; and

(g) treatment as an illegal entrant.

Under s 18, the S of S may by regulations make provision for written notice of a decision which is amenable to appeal under the 1971 Act to be given to the potential appellant. This power was exercised by the Immigration Appeals (Notices) Regulations 1984 (SI 1984 No 2040). The notice must give reasons for the decision, but it is conclusive of the person by whom and the reasons for which the decision has been taken. The notice must also inform the person concerned of his rights of appeal under the Act. It must contain enough information to identify the basis of the decision made by the S of S. The sufficiency of the information will vary with the type of decision being taken. In a notice of a decision to deport based on the allegation that it would be conducive to the public good, more information (such as the offence for which the deportee is being deported, or the conduct complained of by the S of S) is required, than if the decision is based upon a breach of a condition of leave, such as overstaying (*R v IAT, ex p Kalsoom Razaque* [1989] Imm AR 451).

5 Illegal entry

An 'illegal entrant' is defined in the 1971 Act, s 33(1) as a person:

(a) unlawfully entering or seeking to enter in breach of a deportation order, or of the immigration laws,

(b) entering or seeking to enter by means which include deception by another person,

and includes a person who has entered as mentioned in paragraph (a) or (b) above.'

Under the 1971 Act, the S of S is entitled to order the detention and removal of an immigrant who entered the UK under an apparently valid permission only if the immigrant is in fact an illegal entrant.

In *Ex p Khawaja* [1984] AC 74, the HL decided that on an application to the court for judicial review of an immigration officer's order detaining a person in the UK as an illegal entrant, the court had a duty to enquire whether there had been sufficient evidence to justify the immigration officer's belief that the entry had been illegal. It is not enough for the immigration officer reasonably to believe that the person is an illegal entrant: if the S of S cannot prove that on the balance of probabilities the facts relied upon by the immigration officer show that the entrant is an illegal entrant, he has no power to remove him on that basis. The burden of proving that the person is an illegal entrant falls on the S of S, provided that the applicant can produce evidence of leave to enter having been granted. This will usually take the form of a genuine passport stamp. It is enough for the S of S to prove the facts which establish that entry was not in accordance with the immigration laws. For example, if the stamp in the passport is not genuine, it is not necessary for the S of S to prove how the person entered the country (*Ex p Mussawir* [1989] Imm AR 297 and *Ifzal Ali v S of S* [1994] Imm AR 69).

A British citizen does not require leave to enter and may enter, and remain under the 1971 Act, ss 1(1) and 2(1). Anyone who does not have the right of abode in the UK requires leave to enter under s 3(1) of that Act. The onus is on a person who asserts that he is a British citizen to prove that he is (s 3(8); and see *In Re Bamgbose* [1990] Imm AR 135).

The definition of 'illegal entrant' is broad, and the categories of illegal entrants are not closed. Three categories may be identified:

(a) those who enter the UK clandestinely; or

(b) those who obtain leave to enter either by themselves practising fraud, or by someone practising fraud on their behalf, or by concealing material facts; or

(c) those who obtain leave to enter by the use of a materially false document (*R v Naillie* [1993] Imm AR 462).

Under the 1971 Act, s 11, provision is made for persons who disembark to be deemed not to have entered the UK if they remain within an area approved by an immigration officer for persons to remain pending a decision on their entry. A person does not enter the UK merely by disembarking, so that a person who disembarks without a right of entry is not automatically an illegal entrant. Asylum seekers, who may arrive with forged documents or no documents at all, are not considered to have entered if they remain in such an area before making an application for asylum. In *Naillie* the HL held that as long as a person disembarking is an asylum seeker, and does not attempt otherwise to seek entry or obtain entry by fraud, such as by the use of false documentation or without any documentation at all, but remains within a designated area when he claims asylum, he is not an illegal entrant.

Anyone who is subject to British immigration control and does not have leave to enter and enters the UK will be an illegal entrant, however innocent that entry may be (*Keung v S of S* [1992] Imm AR 201). It includes those who enter clandestinely; those who have entered by deception (see (b) below and *Ex p Khawaja* [1984] AC 14); and a person who has absconded having been granted temporary admission, for such a person has not been granted leave to enter (*Ex p Taj Mohammed Khan* [1985] Imm AR 104 and *Ex p Awais Butt* [1994] Imm AR 11). It also includes a person who has broken a condition of temporary admission (*Ex p Mohammed Mustafa* [1994] Imm AR 18).

The definition includes a person who requires leave under the immigration laws to enter and enters without it. He is an illegal entrant whether or not he intended to enter by deception, or was aware that he was entering illegally (*Ex p Abdul Khaled* [1987] Imm AR 67, following *R v Governor of Ashford Remand Centre, ex p Bouzagou* [1983] Imm AR 69 (CA)). No element of *mens rea* is involved.

In *Abdul Khaled* a 13-year-old boy was brought into the country by British citizens who falsely claimed that he was their son. Their deception rendered the entry illegal. In *Bouzagou* a person was held to be an illegal entrant, when, having overstayed his limited leave and travelled to the Republic of Ireland, he entered the UK by the port of Liverpool at which no immigration control operated (and see *Akin Ali v S of S* [1994] Imm AR 489). A person who was naturalised by registration or by issue of a certificate cannot, however, be declared an illegal entrant unless deprived of his status as a British citizen under s 40 of the 1981 Act (*Ex p Ejaz* [1994] 2 WLR 534).

(a) Mistake
The general principle is that those who require leave to enter, but enter without leave, are illegal entrants. It is not necessary for the S of S to prove that a deception has occurred where there has been a breach of some statutory provision (*R v Immigration Officer, ex p Chan* [1992] 1 WLR 541 and see *Kuet v S of S* [1995] Imm AR 274). In *Mokuolo v S of S* [1989] Imm AR 51, two Nigerian sisters were held to be illegal entrants when they were admitted without the grant of leave because their passports mistakenly stated that they were British citizens. Further, an entrant may be an illegal entrant where the passport clearly gives the correct status of the entrant, shows that he requires leave to enter, and the immigration officer mistakenly believes that the entrant does not require leave to enter. In *Rehal v S of S* [1989] Imm AR 576 the immigration officer failed to grant leave to enter, because he believed the entrants to be British citizens, while their passports clearly stated that they were BOCs. The applicants were guilty of no mis-

representation of any kind, but nevertheless were illegal entrants because they lacked leave to enter when they needed to have it (see also *Ex p Mohan* [1989] Imm AR 436).

Where the entrant (and any other person) is innocent of any deception, and the immigration officer places a stamp in his passport granting him leave to enter, the position is different. In *Ex p Ram* [1979] 1 WLR 148 the immigration officer, in the mistaken belief that the entrant had the right to indefinite leave to remain, stamped his passport to that effect. The effect of that stamp was that the entrant did receive indefinite leave to remain (and would now receive six months' leave), as the immigration officer was acting within his powers. The entry was not therefore illegal (see also *R v IAT, ex p Coomasaru* [1983] 1 WLR 14).

Where the immigration officer puts a stamp in a person's passport which is illegible, the person obtains six months' leave to enter (Immigration Act 1988, Sched, para 8). Such leave is deemed to be subject to a condition prohibiting employment. In *Minton v S of S* [1990] Imm AR 199 the length of a visit could not be determined from the stamp in the passport. The CA took the view that the statutory provisions should be construed strictly. Extrinsic evidence as to the meaning of the stamp could not be introduced, so as to avoid six months' leave being deemed to have been granted. Unsurprisingly a person who absconds from detention before enquiries can be completed does not obtain such leave, on the grounds that his examination is not completed in accordance with Sched 2 (*Ex p Awais Butt* [1995] Imm AR 11).

(b) Entry by deception

Section 33 of the 1971 Act is amended by Sched 2, para 4 of the Asylum and Immigration Act 1996. The term 'illegal entrant' covers a person entering or seeking to enter by means which include deception by another person. A deception may occur either at the stage of securing entry clearance or at the time the would-be entrant presents himself to the immigration officer at the port of entry. Thus where, between the consideration of entry clearance and presentation for leave to enter, a person became married and did not reveal that fact because he thought it might jeopardise his application for leave to enter, it was permissible to treat him as an illegal entrant (*Ex p Nazmul Miah* [1994] Imm AR 279 and [1995] Imm AR 24). Deceptive concealment of a person's immigration history, such as breach of a condition attached to an earlier leave, will justify treatment as an illegal entrant (*Ex p Samuel Anjorin* [1994] Imm AR 276). The deception may be that of the entrant or of another person. In *Ex p Khan* [1977] 3 All ER 538 a husband produced an incorrect passport on behalf of his wife. The deception, of which she was ignorant, vitiated her leave. In *Chan* [1992] 1 WLR 541, the entrant innocently produced false documents of a kind required under the 1971 Act. In that case the documents which were produced were invalid. Entry pursuant to invalid documents is unlawful entry. So, on the face of it, if a person produces a passport which is in fact a forgery, it does not matter whether he knows that it is a forgery or not. The leave obtained by means of its production is vitiated (*Hamid v S of S* [1993] Imm AR 216). However, the Court of Appeal, in *Kuet v S of S* [1995] Imm AR 274, limited the *ratio decidendi* of *Chan*. They stated that *Chan* was expressly decided on the basis that the work permit with which the court was concerned was invalid. *Kuet* involved the issue of inappropriate (but not invalid) work permits. Unlike in *Chan*, the application for the documents had been made directly to the correct department, and there was no false information in the applications. Ordinarily, entry would not have been granted, and if an immigration officer had investigated the position before granting leave to enter, leave would have been refused. The court in *Kuet* did not regard itself as bound by *Chan* in these circumstances (see *Kuet*, p 280). The amendment to s 33 of the 1971 Act has the effect of nullifying *Kuet*, as the civil servant involved in issuing the work permits perpetrated a deception (that the work permits were properly issued) by which the applicants entered the UK. Thus the distinction between invalid documents and inappropriate documents may have no relevance where deception is involved. However, where the immigration officer, by mistake, gives leave which is inappropriate, but is not rendered invalid, the entrant will not be an illegal entrant. In any event, deception must be a material deception. The facts involved in the deception must be decisive to the grant of leave to enter, in that if they were disclosed to the immigration officer he would in all probability refuse entry. Thus a deception operates to vitiate consent if it is in relation to material facts and leave would in all probability not have been granted but for the deception (*Ex p Jayakody* [1982] 1 WLR 405). However, the entrant may not gain leave to enter on the basis of deceptive information, and thereafter admit his true purpose and claim that he could have obtained leave on the basis of the true facts (see p 247).

The question whether or not facts are material must be seen in the context of the leave sought. An entrant must not give a version of his intentions which is in fundamental respects at variance with his true intention (*Bugdaycay v S of S* [1987] AC 514). Thus in *Jayakody*, the CA asked itself whether the Home Secretary would have been bound to refuse entry or whether he would in all probability have refused entry to a man who had applied for leave to remain for two months as a visitor. He had failed to disclose that he was married to a woman who was on a nursing course in the UK, and after he had obtained leave, he applied for leave to remain until she completed the course. The CA held that even if the immigration officer had known about the marriage he might still have granted leave to enter as a visitor, so that the deception was not material. In *Bugdaycay*, the deception was that the entrant maintained that he wanted leave to enter the UK for a short period, whereas the true facts were that he wanted to apply for asylum. Thus if the entrant obtains leave to enter in one capacity, but secretly intends to remain in another capacity, the deception used to obtain leave is likely to be material, and it does not matter that had the truth been told, leave might have been granted (see *Ex p C F Ming* [1994] Imm AR 216). In *Ex p Nazmul*

Miah [1995] Imm AR 24 the CA held that in deciding whether deception had been practised in order to secure entry clearance, it was the applicant's circumstances at the time of the issue of the entry clearance, and not on the date of the application for entry clearance, that were relevant. The correct test of materiality therefore would appear to be whether the decep-tion was likely to influence the immigration officer's decision (see *Ex p Durojaiye* [1991] Imm AR 307 at 313–14).

In *Sukhjinder Kaur* (12480) a sponsorship declaration gave the impression that the sponsor was living in a house, when he was in fact in prison. This was material to the issue of whether the sponsor could support his wife. A refusal of entry clearance on this basis was justified.

A person seeking asylum who has entered the UK illegally will not be removed from the UK before he has had the opportunity to appeal against any refusal of asylum save where the case is being dealt with under the special appeals procedure (see p 506). A person enters illegally if he is an asylum seeker whose journey has been arranged by an agent who has practised a deception on his behalf (see s 33(1) as amended).

In *Adesina v S of S* [1988] Imm AR 442, the entrant sought leave to enter as a visitor, but in fact intended to study in the UK. Likewise in *Ex p Chomsuk* [1991] Imm AR 29 a concealed intention to work vitiated leave to enter granted for the purpose of studying. More generally, untruths which are told to an immigration officer and lead to the avoidance of further questions will be material deceptions (*Ex p Ghulam Yasin* [1996] Imm AR 62). In *Mohammed Tadimi v S of S* [1993] Imm AR 90, the CA held that the applicant had deceived the immigration officer where he had entered as a student, was a student, but was also a chef. His nominal role as a student was not his real role or occupation.

In *Zamir v S of S* [1980] AC 930, the HL decided that apparently legal entry through the system of immigration control could be rendered illegal by non-disclosure of material facts. The case concerned an entrant who married after obtaining entry clearance for settlement to join his parents on the basis that he was unmarried. He did not disclose his marriage on entry. He was not asked about marriage at that time. He was detained with a view to removal when his marriage was discovered by the S of S. The HL held that he had entered by deception, and his entry was illegal. This decision suggested that there was a duty of candour on entrants amounting to a requirement of utmost good faith to disclose all material facts. However, the facts which are material to the immigration authorities may not be appreciated as being important by the entrant. In *Ex p Khawaja* [1984] AC 74 the HL decided that there is no duty of candour on an entrant amounting to a duty of utmost good faith. However, the HL accepted that silence as to a material fact is capable of amounting to deception so as to render entry illegal. Actions such as the presentation of a passport known to contain false information may amount to deception (*Ex p Patel* (1987) *The Times*, 24 October). Thus in *Durojaiye v S of S* [1991] Imm AR 307 an extension of leave was obtained after entry by deception. The stamp resulting from that was later relied on when the passport holder presented his passport on re-entry. Presentation of the passport alone amounted to deception. Knowledge of a family member's concealed motive for seeking entry as a visitor (to seek asylum for the whole family) may amount to a deception (*Ex p Al Zahrany* [1995] Imm AR 283 and (CA) 510).

If the S of S cannot prove that the entrant or his agent concealed a materially deceptive intention at the time he obtained entry, he will be unable to show that the entry was vitiated by deception (see eg *Sorraseakh Monomai* [1991] Imm AR 29 (note)). However, if the entrant was given leave to enter for one purpose, but intended to follow another purpose if that was possible, he will be taken to intend to pursue that other purpose. Thus in *Ex p Brakwah* [1989] Imm AR 366 the entrant obtained leave to enter as a visitor, but intended to study if the conditions were favourable to that course of action. Glidewell LJ sitting in the Divisional Court stated that the basic question was:

> Has the Home Office proved to the required standard that the Applicant lied when he said that he wished to enter for a few weeks as a visitor and was that lie the effective means of obtaining leave to enter?

The CA, in *Saffu-Mensah v S of S* [1992] Imm AR 185, stated that those who apply for leave to enter are required to tell the truth in the statements they make to the immigration officer which are material to their application. The critical date for consideration of whether the representation made by the entrant is true or not is the date on which the representation is made, and there is nothing in the rules to suggest that the S of S should consider only whether the representation is true or false at the date of the application to enter (*Ex p Salim* [1990] Imm AR 316).

If the entrant made no representations at all, but fails to correct something said by someone else, which he may or may not have known about, he may in certain circumstances not be treated as an illegal entrant by reason of deception. Thus, in *Ex p Dordas* [1992] Imm AR 99, Kennedy J held that a Filipino servant, entering with her employer, who harboured an intention at the time of entry to run away from her employer but did not disclose this, made no representation on this basis. She had not been asked to make any representations, and had played no real part in the preparations for coming to the UK.

When the entrant entered before the coming into force of the 1971 Act, and his entry was secured by a third party's deception, he is entitled to be treated as settled in the UK by virtue of the returning residents rule. After his settlement, later deceptions on re-entry, although possibly criminal offences, would not alter his status as a legal entrant (*Hiran Khan v S of S* [1990] 1 WLR 798). However, if he is not lawfully settled, the position is different. The CA has held that if a minor entered the UK before the coming into force of the 1971 Act by virtue of a third party's deception (of which he knew) that entry was not lawful (*Rahim Miah v S of S* [1989] 1 WLR 806). Subsequent re-entries were not lawful where he relied on the same deception, even if he satisfied para 56 of HC 169.

(c) Proving illegal entry

The S of S must prove that the entry is illegal. The standard of proof remains a civil one, but where there is an allegation that entry was obtained by means of a deception, a high degree of probability is necessary for the S of S to succeed (*Ex p Miah* [1983] Imm AR 91). Since a person declared an illegal entrant is liable to detention as such, the court must be satisfied that the facts of the case are as stated by the immigration officer. The S of S must prove to a high degree of probability that the facts leading to the conclusion that the entrant was an illegal entrant were in existence at the time that conclusion was reached by the immigration officer. A statement by the immigration officer that there were reasonable grounds for believing that the entrant was an illegal entrant does not by itself satisfy the burden of proof. The court must look at the evidence relied on by the immigration officer to see whether or not it satisfied the burden of proof (*Khawaja v S of S* [1984] AC 74). The court will look at all the evidence, and not merely that which was available at the time of the decision of the S of S (see *Ex p Mahoney* [1992] Imm AR 275 and *Ex p Muse* [1992] Imm AR 282). Such evidence can arise from interview for a variation of leave (*Ex p Zenaat Bibi* [1994] Imm AR 550).

If a person asserts his right of entry on the basis of being a British citizen, the burden of proof that he is a British citizen falls on him by the 1971 Act, s 3(8). By s 3(9) of the Act a person entering the UK and claiming to have the right of abode must prove that he has that right, by means of a UK passport describing him as a British citizen or as a CUKC having the right of abode, or by means of a certificate of entitlement certifying that he has the right. An immigration officer may be satisfied that a would-be entrant is a British citizen on evidence other than a passport. That evidence may be oral or documentary (*Minta v S of S* [1992] Imm AR 380). If, however, the entrant produces a passport describing him as a British citizen, the immigration officer must accept that as proof. If the immigration officer does not accept that the passport is genuine, the burden is on the S of S to prove that it is a false passport, but the burden of showing that he is a British citizen remains on the entrant. A British Visitor's passport will not qualify under s 3(9) as conclusive proof that the bearer is a British citizen, because it is not one of the documents specified under that subsection.

(d) Further consequences of illegal entry

As a result of the decision of the CA in *R v S of S for the Environment, ex p LB Tower Hamlets* [1993] QB 632, a local authority may determine whether a person is an illegal entrant for the purposes of s 33(1) of the 1971 Act. If it concludes that he is, it must notify the Home Office. The *Homelessness Code of Guidance* indicates that local authorities' enquiries need not be limited to housing matters. However, 'Immigration decisions are for the immigration authorities' (*per* Sir Thomas Bingham MR at p 643).

When the application of the Housing Act 1985 may depend of the immigration status of a person, that status can be finally determined only by the S of S. This does not prevent the housing authority from making its own decision, which may be overtaken by a subsequent decision of the S of S. The correct procedure for a local authority in a disputed case is not clear. EU nationals entering the UK pursuant to rights under the EC Treaty are lawfully in the UK and are owed a duty to be housed (*R v City of Westminster, ex p Castelli and Anor* (1996) *The Independent*, 23 February; *The Times*, 27 February 1996).

(e) Concessionary policy concerning enforcement
The concessionary policy whereby enforcement action is stayed in certain illegal entry cases is dealt with in Chapter 14. A person liable to be removed as an illegal entrant may be detained pending removal (see Chapter 15). Enforcement action is initiated in relation to an illegal entrant when notice that he is an illegal entrant is served on him (*Ramesh Kumar* [1996] Imm AR 190). Finally, the S of S is entitled to require conclusive proof of long residence (*Ex p Mannan* [1996] Imm AR 215).

Chapter 3

The British Nationality Act 1981

By virtue of the 1981 Act, CUKCs are divided into three groups: British citizens, British Dependent Territories citizens (BDTCs) and British Overseas Citizens (BOCs). Residual classes of British subjects under the Act and British protected persons continue to exist. The label of Commonwealth citizen is also continued: it applies to all categories of citizen created by the 1981 Act, to British subjects under the Act and to all citizens of the countries listed in Sched 3 to the Act. It is a citizenship of little more than symbolic value.

The 1981 Act changes the definition of right of abode in the UK. Further, it ends the equation between right of abode and the description 'patrial'. That ungainly word now disappears from immigration law. The distinction between 'patrial' and 'non-patrial' no longer exists. However, there is still a distinction between those who have and those who do not have the right of abode.

It might have been thought logical that right of abode would be determined under the 1981 Act simply by the fact of British citizenship. However, the concept of 'patrial' under the unamended 1971 Act did not quite coincide with that of 'British citizen' under the 1981 Act. In the same way there is no total identity between 'British citizenship' and 'right of abode' under the 1981 Act. Those who have a right of abode under the 1981 Act are British citizens and those Commonwealth citizens who were patrials under the 1971 Act. This means that no nominally 'British' citizenships under the 1981 Act entail freedom from immigration control, apart from British citizenship itself. By contrast, certain Commonwealth citizens, who are not even nominally 'British', are free from immigration control altogether. These, on the whole, are citizens of 'white' Commonwealth countries whose parents were born in the UK and Islands.

1 Categories of citizenship under the Act

(a) British citizens
Broadly speaking, British citizens are those who, under the 1971 Act, were CUKCs and patrials. There are two exceptions to this generalisation:

    (a) persons who were registered as CUKCs under the British Nationality (No 2) Act 1964. These were stateless persons registered on the ground that their mothers were CUKCs at the time of their birth. They are not British citizens unless either

      (i) their mothers became (or if alive would have become) British citizens at the commencement of the Act; or

      (ii) they were patrials by virtue of being a CUKC settled at any time in the UK or Islands, ordinarily resident there for five or more years, at the commencement of the 1981 Act;

    (b) persons excluded from patriality under the 1971 Act, s 2 apparently by mistake. They are British subjects without any citizenship who, on commencement of the BNA 1948, would have become CUKCs but for their citizenship of (or potential citizenship of) a Commonwealth country.

Under the 1948 Act, s 12(6) they could apply to be registered as CUKCs and the S of S could in his discretion accept or refuse the application. If the application was made in an independent Commonwealth country the UK High Commissioner was to exercise the powers of the S of S. Under the 1981 Act persons became British citizens if they were registered under the BNA 1948, s 12(7), and were so registered by virtue of their descent by the male line from someone who was born or naturalised in the UK or colonies.

The wording of the 1948 Act is strictly interpreted and the status of a person under the Act depends on his status under s 12 at the date of commencement of the Act (*Ross-Clunis v S of S for the Foreign and Commonwealth Office* [1991] Imm AR 595).

(b) British Dependent Territories citizens (BDTCs)

The second category of 'British' citizen created by the 1981 Act on the abolition of CUKC status is that of BDTC. This is a class of CUKC who have some form of connection with a dependent territory, for example by birth, descent, naturalisation or registration. Those territories are listed in the 1981 Act, Sched 6. They include Gibraltar. Initially the Falkland Islands were included in the list, but in 1985 citizens of the Falklands were made British citizens (British Nationality (Falklands Islands) Act 1983).

The methods by which this citizenship is acquired are laid down in the 1981 Act, s 23. The first group of persons who hold this citizenship are CUKCs who are such by virtue of their birth, naturalisation or registration in a dependent territory; CUKCs who are born to a parent who at the time of the birth was a CUKC by virtue of birth, naturalisation or registration in a dependent territory, or were themselves born to a parent who held such citizenship; and women who were CUKCs and have at some time been married to men in either of the above categories. Those who were CUKCs by virtue of a connection with a British Dependency (such as Hong Kong at 31 December 1982) became BDTCs on 1 January 1983.

The second group of persons who are BDTCs are, broadly, those who were registered as CUKCs under the BNA 1948, s 7 or s 12(6), and have some form of connection by descent with a dependent territory.

Since 1 January 1983, a BDTC can pass on that status to a child at birth if the child is born after that date in the dependent territory. Likewise the child of a person who is settled in a dependent territory will be a BDTC. If he is not, he will have to register or be registered.

(c) British Nationals (Overseas) (Hong Kong)

A person who, but for a connection with Hong Kong, would not be a BDTC, will lose his citizenship on 1 July 1997, when the territory passes to China (Hong Kong (British Nationality) Order 1986, SI 1986 No 948). The Order creates a new form of citizenship: British Nationals (Overseas), for persons connected with Hong Kong. If, but for a connection with Hong Kong, a person would not be a BDTC, he may, before 1 July 1997, register as a British National (Overseas). This category is an illusory category of citizenship; the Chinese do not recognise it. The system whereby Hong Kong BDTCs can acquire the right of abode is described in Chapter 4.

(d) British Overseas citizens (BOCs)

Those CUKCs who are neither British citizens nor BDTCs are BOCs. This is the residual class of 'British' citizenship. It is not defined in the 1981 Act, except negatively in s 26. It covers those persons who, when the colony in which they lived became independent, did not acquire citizenship of that new country, but retained their CUKC status. They are therefore in the odd position of not really belonging anywhere. They are not citizens of the country in which they live, and yet their citizenship is of a type which gives them no right to enter the UK, the country which gives them nominal citizenship.

(e) British subjects

There is a further category of citizenship under the 1981 Act, that of 'British subject under the Act'. This does not coincide with the class of British subject under the BNA 1948, but was the new name for the category of British subjects without citizenship. Under the 1981 Act, British subjects without citizenship, women who registered as British subjects under the BNA 1965 and Irish citizens born before 1949 who chose to retain their status as British subjects, continue as 'British subjects under the Act' (ss 30 and 31).

(f) British Protected Persons (BPPs)

The final category of citizenship under the 1981 Act is that of BPP. Under s 38, the Queen may by Order in Council declare, in relation to any territory which has at any time been a protectorate or protected state for the purposes of the BNA 1948 or a UK Trust Territory under that Act, that any group of persons in that territory shall be BPPs. This is subject to the proviso that they are not citizens of any Commonwealth country which consists of, or includes, the territory in question. Most BPPs currently live in Brunei. BPPs are not included in the definition of Commonwealth citizenship (see the 1981 Act, s 37(1)). They are in a citizenship limbo because they are not aliens either.

2 Other categories of citizenship

There are two other categories of citizenship which, although not defined in the 1981 Act, are relevant for immigration purposes. These are citizenship of an EU country, and of the Republic of Ireland. Such persons are aliens. They have, however, many advantages over the persons categorised as 'British' citizens above, apart from British citizens themselves. They are not subject to immigration control under the rules or the 1971 Act.

(a) Citizens of the Republic of Ireland

Citizens of Eire are aliens. However, by virtue of the Ireland Act 1949, s 2 they are not to be regarded as such. Thus an Irish citizen may vote in a UK parliamentary election.

Citizens of Eire born before 1948 were British subjects. The BNA 1948, s 2 enabled them, if they wished, to opt formally to remain British subjects. The 1981 Act, s 31(2) enables them to remain British subjects even if they live in Eire. Irish citizens who had been settled in the UK since before 1 January 1973 could register as British citizens under the 1981 Act before 31 December 1987 (s 7). Citizens of Eire are liable to deportation. However, their liability is affected by the fact that they are EU nationals, and may be deported only in accordance with EC Directive 64/221 ([1964] OJ 056/850; see Chapter 16). In any event, Irish citizens who were ordinarily resident in the UK on the day the 1971 Act came into force are not liable to deportation (1971 Act, s 7).

(b) EU citizens

The UK, as a result of its accession to the European Community, is obliged by the Treaty on European Union to allow freedom of movement to EU citizens, and to permit them to work, study, reside, and establish themselves in self-employment without restriction in the UK (European Communities Act 1972, s 2 and the Treaty on European Union, arts 3(c), 48). Although there is no reflection of this in any amendment to either the 1971 Act or 1981 Act, special provision in the immigration rules has been made for the admission of EU nationals and their dependants. It is arguable that even this provision contravenes the Treaty on European Union. The Immigration Act 1988, s 7 provides that EU nationals do not require leave to enter under UK domestic law. The EC provisions discussed in Chapter 16 may be relied on to override any provision of UK law with which they are incompatible.

EU nationals can be refused entry to a member state on the ground of personal unacceptability (EC Directive 64/221). Examples of this are that the presence of the person is a threat to public policy, national security, or public health. In *Van Duyn v Home Office* [1974] 3 All ER 178, the plaintiff, who was Dutch, was refused entry to the UK on the basis that she wanted to take a job as a secretary with the Church of Scientology. The European Court of Justice accepted that her exclusion was valid because the terms of EC Directive 64/221 were satisfied, even though the organisation in that case, which the government described as 'socially harmful', was not actually illegal.

The power to deport EC nationals who, under the Treaty of Rome, have the right to live in the country where they are workers or self-employed persons, has been considered in *R v Bouchereau* [1978] 2 WLR 251 and *Ex p Santillo* [1981] 2 All ER 897. In both cases the court emphasised that a deportation order should not be lightly made, and that the court should inquire carefully into all the circumstances. The order should be made only if the court is satisfied that the person in question represents a real threat to society. (The same rules apply to EEA nationals exercising free movement rights; see, generally, Chapter 16.)

(c) Aliens

Aliens are all those persons who do not fall into any of the categories of British nationality and are not citizens of any other Commonwealth country. No elaborate definition is necessary. They have no claim or right to enter or remain in the UK unless they fall into one of the two privileged classes discussed above. However, in practice they may be given unlimited leave to remain, as may any member of the categories of British nationality. Aliens are as much potential victims or beneficiaries of the discretionary system of control as are the holders of other kinds of British nationality, that is, of course, apart from British citizens themselves.

3   Acquisition of British citizenship from 1 January 1983

There are four ways in which British citizenship may be acquired under the 1981 Act. These are by birth or adoption, by descent, by registration and by naturalisation. Birth in the UK from 1 January 1983 by itself is no longer an automatic route to citizenship.

(a) By birth or adoption

Birth   A child born in the UK to a parent, living or dead, who is either a British citizen or settled in the UK, is a British citizen. 'Settled' is defined at some length in s 50(2), (3), (4) and (5) of the Act and is discussed in Chapter 2. Where the parents are not married, only the mother counts as a 'parent' for these purposes (see s 50(9)(a) and *Ex p Crew* [1982] Imm AR 94). Where there is a suggestion that the child may be legitimated by some rule of foreign law, the legitimacy of the child is determined by the father's domicile (*Lake* (3393)).

There is a rebuttable presumption, in the case of a child abandoned in the UK, that one of his parents satisfies the requirements necessary to confer British citizenship by birth. A child born in the UK whose parents are known not to satisfy the requirements is nevertheless entitled to register as a British citizen if one of his parents subsequently meets one of the requirements and an application is made so to register him.

A child born in the UK to parents who at no time satisfy the requirements is nevertheless entitled to apply to be registered as a British citizen after the age of ten if, in each year of his life, he has not been absent from the UK for more than 90 days. The S of S may in his discretion register any person who has been absent for longer.

Adoption   If an adoption order is made by a British court in respect of a minor who is not a British citizen, he will be a British citizen if his adopter, or one of his adopters, is a British citizen. He retains that citizenship even if subsequently the adoption order ceases to have effect.

(b) By descent

A person born outside the UK may be a British citizen if when he is born one of his parents is a British citizen, in three situations. The first is if one parent is a British citizen otherwise than by descent (see British Nationality Act 1981, s 14). The second is when one parent is a British citizen serving abroad either in Crown service or in any service designated by the S of S (ie working at a British Embassy etc, or serving in the armed forces abroad, or in one of a number of listed jobs such as working for the British Council or the Medical Research Council). Recruitment for that service must have taken place in the UK. The third occurs when one parent is serving in an institution of the EC; recruitment for that service must have taken place in a country which was at the time of recruitment a member of the EC.

Whether or not citizenship by descent arises will be determined by the status of the relevant parent at the time of the birth (the father only if the birth was before 1983). In *R v IAT, ex p Uddin* [1990] Imm AR 104, the CA held that where the father of the applicant, for leave to enter registered as a CUKC after the birth of the applicant, the applicant had become a citizen of Pakistan, and therefore did not obtain British citizenship on his father's registration. The fact that his father had been issued with a British Seaman's identity card and National Registration card was irrelevant.

The principal disadvantage suffered by a British citizen by descent, in comparison with British citizens by any other means, is that he will not automatically pass his citizenship on to a child born abroad. It will be possible, however, for the child to obtain British citizenship by registration (see below).

(c) By registration

It has been noted above that the 1981 Act, s 3, provides that in two cases children born in this country can be registered as British citizens. Registration is a method of acquiring citizenship by administrative grant. In most instances, provided that statutory conditions are met, there is a right to registration. This is not to be confused with naturalisation, which is a wholly discretionary grant of citizenship. There is thus a right to challenge a refusal of registration in the courts, whereas there is no such right to appeal from the withholding of naturalisation. British citizens who acquire their citizenship by registration or naturalisation can be deprived of it by the S of S (British Nationality Act 1981, s 40).

Acquisition of citizenship by registration is governed by ss 3, 4 and 5 of the Act. Sections 7–10 make provision for transitional cases. There are four main areas to be considered:

Minors   Under s 3, the S of S has a discretion to register a minor as a British citizen if an application for registration is made on his behalf. In addition to this broad discretion, s 3 confers certain entitlements to registration as a British citizen on children born outside the UK.

The first such entitlement is in the case of a child born outside the UK on whose behalf an application is made within 12 months of his date of birth. One of the child's parents, or the mother if the parents are not married, must be a British citizen by descent (defined in s 14). In turn, one of the grandparents must have been a British citizen otherwise than by descent at the date of birth, or is now such a citizen (or would be if alive). Finally, the child's parent must have spent a period of three years in the UK before the date of birth, and during that period must not have been absent from the UK for more than 270 days. In other words, the entitlement to registration accrues only if a child's parent has ties of both descent and residence with the UK. The S of S may, in his discretion, consider an application made up to six years from the date of birth. Once registered, the child will become a British citizen by descent.

There is a further entitlement to registration in the case of a child born outside the UK if an application is made while he is a minor and the following statutory requirements are met:

(*a*)   one parent must be a British citizen by descent at the date of birth;

(*b*)   the child and his parents (or parent if the marriage has ended or led to a legal separation, or one of the parents is dead) must have lived in the UK for three years preceding the application, and not have been absent from the UK for more than 270 days in that period;

(*c*)   the consent of the parents (or parent) to the registration must have been signified in the prescribed manner.

Thus, if one parent to a subsisting marriage objects to the application on well-founded grounds, the registration cannot go through. Equally, if the parents are living apart, in different countries, but there has been no formal divorce or legal separation, the child is not entitled to be registered, unless both parents have been in the country for the stipulated three-year period (with permitted absences). If the parents are not married the requirements must be met by the mother. Again, once he is registered, the child will become a British citizen by registration.

BDTCs and others   Section 4 applies to applications for registration by BDTCs, BNOs, BOCs, British subjects under the 1981 Act and BPPs. If the conditions laid down by the section are met, the applicant is entitled to be registered a British citizen.

Under the 1981 Act, s 4(2), to qualify the applicant must have been in the UK at the beginning of the period of five years ending with the date of the application, and the number of days on which he was absent from the UK must not exceed 450. In addition he must not have been absent in the 12 months leading up to the application for more than 90 days. In that latter period he must have been free from restrictions on the period of his stay under the immigration laws. Lastly, he must not have been in breach of the immigration laws in the five-year period.

In the case of such applications the S of S has a discretion to register even if the requirements as to length of absence from the UK are not met. Equally, he may disregard restrictions on the period of stay if they are not in force at the date of the application. Finally, he may even disregard breaches of the immigration laws. The S of S also has a discretion to register applicants under this section who have served in Crown service under the government of a dependent territory or in paid or unpaid service in other government institutions established by law in a dependent territory.

UK nationals for the purposes of Community treaties   On accession to the EC the UK defined 'UK national' for the purposes of the Community treaties in a unilateral declaration which is annexed to the Treaty of Accession. The legal status of this declaration is uncertain. The definition is framed in such a way as to include citizens of the UK and Colonies by virtue of birth, registration or naturalisation in Gibraltar, as well as patrial CUKCs. Under the 1981 Act, s 5, the former are entitled to registration as British citizens without needing to have lived in the UK at all, and for a nominal fee. For the purposes of EC law nationality is determined by the domestic law of each member state. In certain cases nationality is defined by ethnicity and may include persons with no other connection with the member state (see Chapter 16).

Transitional provisions   There are cases in which persons are entitled to registration if they applied, in most instances, within five years of commencement of the 1981 Act. In essence this applies to persons who had acquired a right under previous legislation to be registered: but if they do not exercise this right in time, they will lose it. The 1981 Act came into force on 1 January 1983 and the five-year period ended on 31 December 1987.

Section 7   One case under s 7 is that of Commonwealth and Irish citizens settled in this country on 1 January 1973 (the date of commencement of the 1971 Act). Provided they had been settled since that date, they were entitled to registration if they applied before 1 January 1988, though the S of S had a discretion in any particular case to entertain an application before

1 January 1991. Commonwealth citizens settled in the UK before 1 January 1973, except those under 18 on 1 January 1983, who retained this right had five years after their 18th birthday to register. The right finally expired at the end of 1995.

(d) By naturalisation

The final way of acquiring British citizenship is by naturalisation. This is entirely discretionary. Naturalisation is governed by the 1981 Act, s 6 and Sched 1. The S of S may in his discretion grant a certificate of naturalisation to a person of full age and capacity if he considers that he satisfies the conditions set out in Sched 1 (see p 416 below).

The major change reflected in s 6 was that all spouses of British citizens became eligible to apply for naturalisation. Before the 1981 Act, wives of patrial CUKCs were entitled to registration as such citizens. Wives have now lost that right. They must now apply, like husbands, for naturalisation. Sex equality has been achieved by withdrawing a right from one sex rather than by extending it to the other.

The requirements in Sched 1 differ according to whether the application is made under s 6(1) or (2). The requirements to be met by a spouse of a British citizen are less stringent than those affecting other applicants for naturalisation. The members of the latter group must have a sufficient knowledge of English, Welsh or Scots Gaelic and be of good character. They must intend either to live mainly in the UK if they are naturalised, or to enter or continue in Crown service, service in an international organisation of which the UK is a member, or employment in a company or association established in the UK. They must also have been in the UK for five years before the application, and absent for less than 450 days in that period. They must not have been absent from the UK for more than 90 days in the 12 months immediately before the application, nor in that period can they have been subject under the immigration laws to any restriction on their length of stay. In the five years leading up to the application, they must not have been in breach of the immigration laws. The S of S has a discretion to waive or modify all or any of the foregoing conditions except those relating to linguistic ability, good character and intention to remain in the UK. However, the S of S may, at his discretion, refuse to grant naturalisation to a person who is subject to a restriction on his length of stay at the date of application for naturalisation. In a letter of 14 September 1995 to Simmons & Simmons, the IND set out its expectation as to the relationship between an applicant and a UK established company:

(1) there is or will be an express or implied contract of employment with the UK established company; and either
(2) the applicant is or will be in the direct employment of the company concerned; or
(3) is or will be employed by an unregistered associate company (parent or subsidiary) but is or will be regarded by the seconding company as one of its own career staff.

The IND does not insist that the employee is paid direct from the UK office or that there is tax or national insurance liability. The above details would need to be documented by the UK company. The length of employment must satisfy the qualifying period. If the applicant is absent for more than 450 days in the five-year period, the S of S has a discretion to waive that absence depending on the circumstances of the case. In all cases, the applicant must demonstrate that he had made his home in the UK by establishing his home, family and a substantial part of his estate in the UK. Consideration may also be given to the applicant's residence before the five year period, and the reasons for any absences and their precise extent. The greater the period of absence to be disregarded, the more exceptionally compelling the reasons for the absence would have to be.

Spouses of British citizens   The requirements affecting the spouse of an existing British citizen are similar to those outlined above. However, the residence requirement is only three years (with not more than 270 days' absence in that period). In the year before the application the applicant must not be absent for more than 90 days; the couple must be settled by the date of the application. There are no language qualifications for such applicants, nor need they intend to reside in the UK or enter or continue in Crown service. They need only be of good character. The S of S again has a discretion to waive or modify the conditions, except that relating to good character.

4   Loss of British citizenship

There are two ways in which British citizenship may be lost under the 1981 Act. The first is by renunciation—this is an act of the citizen himself. The second is by deprivation—this is an act of the S of S. The first can be exercised by all persons who have acquired British citizenship by whatever method. The second affects only British citizens who acquired their citizenship by registration or naturalisation. Under s 42(5) of the 1981 Act a certificate of naturalisation confers the status of citizenship from its date of issue. The holder is a British citizen whether or not he belongs to one of the categories of persons identified by s 6 of the 1981 Act and can be deprived of that status only under the procedures laid down by s 40(1) (*Ex p Naheed Ejaz* [1994] 2 WLR 534).

(a) Renunciation
British citizenship can be renounced only by a declaration of renunciation made in the prescribed manner. Under the 1981 Act, s 12, the renunciation is not effective unless and until it is registered by the S of S. The S of S must refuse to register the declaration unless he is satisfied that the person concerned will have, or will acquire, an alternative citizenship. If a registration is made, and it transpires that the person concerned has no alternative citizenship at the date of registration, and did not acquire one within six months of that date, he is to be deemed always to have been a British citizen,

despite the registration of his declaration. The S of S also has a discretion to refuse to register declarations made in time of war.

If a renunciation is made in order to acquire a different citizenship, the person concerned has a right to resume his British citizenship subsequently by registration under s 13(1). However, he may do so only once. Anyone who has made a declaration of renunciation for whatever reason may apply by registration to resume his British citizenship; such registration is in the S of S's discretion.

(b) Deprivation

British citizens who have acquired their citizenship by registration or naturalisation may be deprived of their citizenship by the S of S. Broadly, there are two statutory justifications for this: either that the citizen acquired his status by deception, or that while holding that citizenship he has acted in a way which is thought to make him unfit to hold it any longer.

The S of S may deprive of citizenship anyone who has exhibited disloyalty or disaffection towards Her Majesty, or anyone who has unlawfully traded, or communicated with or assisted the enemy in time of war, or has, within five years of his acquisition of citizenship, been sentenced anywhere in the world to a year's imprisonment or more. The S of S's discretion to make an order of deprivation is subject to two overriding considerations. First, the order must not be made unless it is 'not conducive to the public good' for the person concerned to remain a citizen. Secondly, no one is to be deprived of British citizenship if, as a result, he becomes stateless. The person concerned has the right to be notified if the S of S intends to make an order and has a right to an inquiry before a committee appointed by the S of S. The S of S's power in relation to 'unfit' citizens extends to all those registered or naturalised under the 1981 Act and all those naturalised under previous legislation.

The S of S may also make an order of deprivation under s 40(1) in respect of anyone whom he is satisfied obtained his registration or naturalisation by fraud, false representation or the concealment of a material fact. This wide power makes it crucial for an applicant for citizenship to be completely honest in his application. Any false representation may mean that the applicant finds his status is abruptly changed. Section 40(1) applies not only to citizens registered or naturalised under the 1981 Act, but also to those registered under the British Nationality Acts 1948–1964 and anyone naturalised before the commencement of the 1981 Act.

Chapter 4

Statutory Developments Since 1981

The chief statutory developments since the 1981 Act are the Immigration (Carriers' Liability) Act 1987, the Immigration Act 1988, the British Nationality (Hong Kong) Act 1990, and, finally, the Asylum and Immigration Appeals Act 1993.

1 The Immigration (Carriers' Liability) Act 1987

The Immigration (Carriers' Liability) Act 1987 sets out a system for levelling fines against airlines carrying persons without proper documentation. The fine currently stands at £2,000 per person arriving without the proper documentation (Immigration (Carriers' Liability Prescribed Sum) Order 1991, SI 1991 No 1497). If a person who requires leave to enter the UK arrives in the UK by ship or aircraft, the owners or agents of the ship or aircraft shall be liable to pay the S of S on demand £2,000 in respect of that person (CLA 1987, s 1(1)) if he fails to produce the following documents when required to do so by an immigration officer:

(a) a valid passport with photograph or some other document satisfactorily establishing his identity and nationality or citizenship; and

(b) in the case of a visa national, a valid entry or transit visa.

However, no liability is incurred if the carrier can show that the person produced to the carrier the above documents when embarking on the aircraft or ship for the journey to the UK. Nor is the carrier liable if shown a document which purports to be one of the appropriate documents unless its falsity is reasonably apparent. The Channel Tunnel concessionaires are exempt from fines (see HL Debates, 1 April 1993 cols 1003–6).

The IND pursues an active role in training airlines and shipping companies to ensure that passengers arriving in the UK are properly documented. Airline staff have to act as informal immigration filters for the UK. Schiemann J made the point in *Ex p Yassine* [1990] Imm AR 359 that the 1987 Act, together with requirements imposed by the S of S relating to visas, pose substantial obstacles in the path of refugees wishing to come to the UK, in that a visa national needs a visa before travelling to the UK; refugee visas are not available in the country of persecution as a person needs to be outside his country of habitual residence or origin before claiming that status; and carriers are disinclined to carry those without visas in the light of the 1987 Act. The refugee therefore has the following options:

    (a) lying to the UK authorities in his own country to obtain, eg a visitor's or student's visa;

    (b) obtaining a credible forgery of a passport;

    (c) obtaining a ticket to a third country with a stopover in the UK.

Under the Asylum and Immigration Appeals Act 1993, the S of S may by order require persons of any description who, on arrival in the UK, intend to pass through to another country or territory without entering the UK, to hold a visa for that purpose. The order may specify a description of persons by reference to nationality, citizenship, origin or other connection with any particular country or territory, but not by reference to race, colour or religion (1987 Act, s 1A(2)(*a*), as inserted by the 1993 Act, s 12). The order shall not, however, permit the requirement of a transit visa to apply to any person who has the right of abode under the 1971 Act. Further, any category of person may be exempted from the operation of the order. From 22 July 1993, citizens of Afghanistan, Iran, Iraq, Lebanon, Libya, Somalia, Sri Lanka, Turkey, Uganda and Zaire required transit visas; other visa nationals did not, if there was less than 24 hours between their flights (Immigration (Transit Visas) Order 1993, SI 1993 No 1678). The Immigration (Transit Visa) (Amendment) Order 1996 (SI 1996 No 2065), made under the Immigration (Carriers' Liability) Act 1987, s 1A(1), (2), in force from 1 September 1996, amends the transit visa list by adding Eritrea and Ethiopia so that the current list is Afghanistan, the People's Republic of China, Eritrea, Ethiopia, Ghana, Iran, Iraq, Libya, Nigeria, Somalia, Sri Lanka, Turkey, Uganda and Zaire.

Guidelines for the operation of the 1987 Act have been issued by the Home Office in order to afford a greater degree of discretion in the operation of the Act to local immigration officers at ports of entry. The guidelines explain the procedure for dealing with passengers with inadequate documentation on arrival, for notifying a carrier that it is liable for a charge, for making representations against the charge, and for recovering the charge. The guidelines also explain the criteria applied by the immigration service for waiving the charge. (See Immigration (Carriers' Liability) Act 1987; and *Charging Procedures: A Guide for Carriers*.)

Carriers are expected to ensure:

    (a) that a passport or travel document presented by a passenger is acceptable for entry to the UK;

    (b) that the passenger is the rightful holder;

    (c) that it is valid;

    (d) if the passenger needs a visa, that the visa is valid for the holder and any other accompanying passengers named in the passport.

The IND provides guidance on UK document requirements and on forgery detection. A forgery is reasonably apparent for the purposes of the 1987 Act if it is of a standard which a trained representative of a carrying company, examining it carefully but briefly and without the use of technological aids, could reasonably be expected to detect. A trained representative is expected to have a basic level of knowledge of how to identify fraudulent documents, but not to be expert nor to have the resources for a highly detailed examination.

If a passenger has no documents on arrival, the carrier is liable unless it can show that the passenger presented proper documents on embarkation. In any case where the documents presented raise doubts in the carrier's mind, the IND takes the view that it is generally advisable to take all possible steps to resolve those doubts before deciding to carry the passenger. If it is not possible to resolve the doubts (eg by reference to the UK immigration service or embassy), a contemporaneous record of the document and details of the steps taken to check it is recommended. The carrier is advised to photocopy the document, showing the pages containing the holder's personal details, photograph and visa. The carrier is expected to keep a record of the details on those pages. If the carrier can show a proper system, has a record of relatively few inadequate document cases, and the record or photocopy does not reveal an obvious forgery, the charge may be waived. If the passenger arrives with insufficient or false documents, and is detected by the immigration service, the carrier is notified, and given the opportunity to examine the documentation and interview the passenger if the passenger agrees. At this stage the port inspector may decide that there is no liability. If he decides that there is, Form IS80(b) is sent to the carrier, indicating that a charge will be levied. The port inspector will consider the standard of the forgery, or any exceptional circumstances (such as whether the flight was diverted). Once the carrier receives the notification, it has 30 days in which to make representations to the port inspector, who may allow further time if it is difficult to obtain evidence in that time, and there is good cause for the delay.

The carrier may make representations as to the standard of the forgery, or give details of exceptional circumstances at the time of the embarkation which prevented a full document check, or make representations concerning the endorsements. A non-exhaustive list of cases in which the inspectors will normally be prepared to waive a charge is given in the guidance note. The charge may be waived in the case of visa national passengers if the visa is not endorsed as valid for the number of persons travelling and included in the same document. However, if the visa is endorsed 'holder only' a charge will be levied in respect of any other person travelling with the holder and included in the document. The charge may also be waived if the visa is used and the immigration officer's endorsement was not placed on the same page, or placed so that no more than one page of the document need be turned either way in order to see the endorsement. If the endorsement is unclear or obscure the charge may also be waived. However, if the visa itself has expired the charge will be levied.

Finally, the charge may be waived where the visa national passenger arrives by air, and the carrier genuinely believed that the passenger's sole purpose in the UK was transit, and that he qualified for a visa waiver under the International Civil Aviation Organisation's terms, ie at the time of booking in he was in possession of a confirmed onward booking by air within 24 hours of scheduled arrival, and the necessary documentation, such as a genuine valid visa for his destination.

Nationals of Iraq and Sri Lanka are not entitled to the concession of transit without a visa. Nationals of Iran, Lebanon, Libya, Somalia, Syria and Turkey may transit through the UK only if they remain in airport transit areas. Liability may also be incurred if they approach and apply to immigration control. The carrier is warned that many UK airports do not allow passengers to remain in transit areas overnight. More countries have been added to the list of transit visa countries under regulations made under the Asylum and Immigration Appeals Act 1993.

Where the port inspector waives the charge, formal notification is sent; if the charge is maintained, a Notification of Formal Demand (IS80(d)) is issued. This informs the carrier that there are 30 days in which to pay. Further representations may then be made to the immigration inspectors at the Carriers' Liability Section at the immigration service headquarters within 30 days.

The carrier should mention all relevant information and explain why it believes the decision is wrong. The port inspector may reconsider at this preliminary stage, but if the decision is again maintained, the representations are forwarded to the Carriers' Liability Section. Time may be extended to obtain necessary information.

There is no right of appeal against the notice. However, the immigration service cannot enforce the prescribed sum as a fine, but only as a civil debt. The Act provides no means of enforcement. The carrier's remedy in respect of a charge may take the form solely of a judicial review of the decision to impose the charge. Alternatively, the 1987 Act may be viewed as creating a statutory duty. The court would then have some scope for intervention as to the sum payable.

2   The Immigration Act 1988

The Immigration Act 1988 introduced further restrictions on the rights of Commonwealth citizens, restricted rights of appeal in deportation cases, and amended the 1971 Act. The 1988 Act, s 1, repealed s 1(5) of the 1971 Act, which provided that the immigration rules should be so framed that Commonwealth citizens settled in the UK on 1 January 1973, their wives and children were not less free to come into and go from the UK by virtue of those rules than if the 1971 Act had not been passed. If the application for entry clearance to come to the UK for settlement by the wife or child was made before the date on which the section came into force (1 August 1988) the right was not affected.

A woman with a right of abode by virtue of marriage to a man to whom she is or was polygamously married, and who was a CUKC with a right of abode at the commencement date of the 1981 Act, and who has not since her marriage been in the UK before 1 August 1988, is not entitled to enter the

UK in certain circumstances. She is not entitled if there is another woman living who is the wife or widow of that husband who:

    (a) is or has been in the UK at any time since marrying the husband; or

    (b) has a certificate of entitlement in respect of the right of abode as his wife; or

    (c) has an entry clearance to enter the UK as the wife of the husband (1988 Act, s 2(2)).

If since her marriage she has been in the UK, and at that time there was no other wife of the husband satisfying the above conditions, she is not precluded from re-entering the UK (s 2(4)). The woman has the burden of proving she had been in the UK before 1 August 1988, and since her marriage. However, only the legal presence of a woman in the UK other than as a visitor will affect the rights of a woman claiming to be able to enter (s 2(7)).

The 1988 Act, s 5, restricted the right of appeal against deportation in cases where the applicant had broken the terms of his limited leave, or was a family member of such a person's family. In those cases a person could appeal against the decision to make a deportation order only on the ground that, on the facts of his case, there is in law no power to make the deportation order for the reasons stated in the notice of the decision. The restriction applied only to a person who was last given leave to enter the UK less than seven years before the date of the decision, and does not apply to persons whose leave to enter or remain has been curtailed under the Asylum and Immigration Appeals Act 1993, s 7(1) or (1A), alleging that their deportation would breach the UK's obligations under the Convention and Protocol relating to the Status of Refugees of 1951 (Immigration (Restricted Right of Appeal Against Deportation) (Exemption) Order 1993, SI 1993 No 1656, as amended by SI 1996 No 2145). Unless the person proves that he had not been given leave to enter less than seven years before the decision, it is presumed that he was given leave within seven years (see Chapter 18).

The 1988 Act, s 7(1), provides that a person shall not require leave to enter or remain in any case in which he is entitled to do so by virtue of an enforceable Community right or of any provision made under the European Communities Act 1972, s 2(2). Until this provision is brought into operation, such persons may rely on the various free movement rights granted under the Treaty of Rome as amended by the Single European Act of 1986, and under the Treaty on European Union 1993. EEA nationals exercising rights to free movement require no leave to enter (see Chapter 16).

Section 8 provides for the examination of passengers before their arrival in the UK. Where a person arrives in the UK with a passport or travel document bearing a stamp placed there by an immigration officer before his departure, or on or during his journey to the UK, and the stamp states that he may enter the UK, he is deemed to have been given, on arrival in the UK, the leave specified in the stamp, subject to such conditions (if any) as are imposed by its terms. Such a person is not subject to examination on arrival, save to establish that he satisfies these conditions (s 8(4)). However, the leave may be cancelled by notice in writing from the immigration officer refusing him leave to enter. The leave may be cancelled in this way at any time before the end of a period of 24 hours from his arrival at the port of entry, or the conclusion of the examination conducted to verify that he carries the appropriate stamp. The port of entry includes the terminal area of the Channel Tunnel system in the UK, and the service and maintenance area of the system in the UK. The provision applies only to the first occasion that the person arrives in the UK after his passport is stamped, where that arrival is not later than seven days after the stamping of his passport.

The Schedule to the 1988 Act provides for the continuation of limitations and conditions on a leave which is granted to a person who has leave, but who obtains a subsequent leave within the period of the earlier leave (para 1). Where a deportation order is made against a person appealing in respect of a limited leave, any appeal pending in respect of that limited leave lapses (para 3). Immigration officers are given the power to detain any passport or other document produced by a person pursuant to an examination until the person is either given leave to enter, or is about to depart or be removed following a refusal of leave to enter (para 6). The time limit for giving or refusing or cancelling leave to enter has been extended to 24 hours, and the default leave obtained by the person entering, if a decision was not made within that time, was reduced from indefinite leave to remain to six months' leave to remain with a condition prohibiting employment (paras 7 and 8).

3   The British Nationality (Hong Kong) Act 1990

The British Nationality (Hong Kong) Act 1990 provided a scheme for registration which operated by a points system, enabling Hong Kong heads of households, their spouses and children to register as British citizens. It favoured those with education, special skills, necessary skills, or those who have done voluntary service for the community. The scheme also provided for entrepreneurs and members of the sensitive services to be invited to register as British citizens.

(a) Qualification
Selection is in accordance with a scheme set out in the schedule to the British Nationality (Hong Kong) (Selection Scheme) Order 1990 (SI 1990 No 2292). By the 1990 Act, Sched 1, para 4, to qualify for registration an applicant must:
   (a) be settled in Hong Kong by reason of being ordinarily resident and lacking any restriction on the duration of his stay; and
   (b) fall within one of the following categories:
      (i)   a BDTC by virtue of a connection with Hong Kong; or
      (ii) a BN(O); or
      (iii) a BOC; or
      (iv) a BPP; or
      (v)   a British subject; or

(vi) a person who is not a British national who applied for naturalisation or registration as a BDTC in Hong Kong before 26
July 1990, and whose application for registration as a BDTC is
ultimately successful; and

(c) where the application is made under the General Occupational Class
or the Disciplined Services Class (police, etc), the applicant is
engaged in one of the occupations covered by those classes.

Under the 1990 Act, the Governor may make recommendations that
persons in the various categories mentioned above be registered as having
the right of abode.

The British Nationality (Hong Kong) Act 1990, s 1, is concerned with the
decision of the S of S in relation to the grant or refusal of an application for
British citizenship. The Governor and the S of S are not required to give
reasons for decisions made in the exercise of a discretion vested in either of
them by the Act. Further, 'no such decision shall be subject to appeal or
liable to be questioned in any court' (s 1(5)). Some commentators take the
view that these words exclude an application for judicial review of any such
decision. This is arguably not so. Ouster clauses of this kind do not prevent
the court from intervening in the case of excess of jurisdiction (*Anisminic Ltd
v Foreign Compensation Commission* [1969] 2 AC 147). Action in contravention of the principles of natural justice amounts to an excess of
jurisdiction. Thus in *Attorney General v Ryan* [1980] AC 718, where a
Minister refused an application for citizenship without giving the applicants
a fair hearing, the Privy Council held his decision invalid, notwithstanding
the relevant statute providing that it 'shall not be subject to appeal or review
in any court'. Moreover, as every error of law is jurisdictional, all 'shall not
be questioned' clauses are arguably ineffective. (But see *Pearlman v Harrow
School Governors* [1979] QB 56 and *Re Racal Communications* [1981] AC
374 in relation to decisions of judicial bodies.) Where it is a judicial
act which is in issue, an ouster clause may be effective, particularly where it
is a decision of an inferior court that is involved; but in relation to an
administrative decision which, arguably, a grant of citizenship would be, the
Anisminic approach would still prevail.

The supervisory powers of the court may be restricted only by the most
clear and explicit words (*R v Medical Appeal Tribunal, ex p Gilmore* [1957]
1 QB 574 at 583, *per* Denning LJ). Nevertheless, where a statute lays down
the way in which a measure may be challenged and the grounds on which
this may be done, and expressly prohibits any other form of legal challenge,
a court may decide that it has no jurisdiction to entertain claims on grounds
or in a manner not set out in the statute (see for example *R v Cornwall CC,
ex p Huntingdon* [1992] 3 All ER 566, DC). The critical distinction between
that type of situation and that under the 1990 Act is that in the latter the
legislation gives no opportunity of questioning the validity of the decision in
the High Court at all. Where there is no statutory right of appeal to the
courts, judicial review should not be excluded. However, the extent of the
review is likely to be limited to procedural as opposed to substantive grounds

(*CCSU v Minister for the Civil Service* [1985] AC 374; and *R v S of S for Foreign and Commonwealth Affairs, ex p Everett* [1989] 2 WLR 224, CA).

Under s 3(3) the Governor appoints a committee to advise him on matters arising under the scheme for registration of applicants, and may authorise public officers to exercise functions in respect of applications, but no recommendation can be made except by the Governor. It is thus possible that the decisions taken by the committee, or the advice given by such a committee, could be susceptible to judicial review even where the advice given relates to a decision which is ultimately within the discretion of the Governor.

Decisions taken by public officers exercising the Governor's discretionary decision-making function are not susceptible to appeal or liable to be questioned by a court (1990 Act, s 3(4)). This provision is subject to the qualifications mentioned above in relation to such ouster clauses. Public officers involved in administering the scheme may be applicants themselves, and therefore the Order provides, under art 29, that they, along with committee members and staff members on the establishment of Government House, may not deal in an official capacity with their own application, or any application in which they have a personal interest. The Governor is under a duty to provide an annual report on the discharge of his duties under the 1990 Act to the S of S, but there is no requirement for the publication of the report beyond that.

(b) The scheme

The 1990 Act, Sched 1, provides for the scheme for the selection of persons to be recommended by the Governor for registration under s 1(1). The scheme prescribes criteria or quotas for persons of different classes or descriptions, selection methods as between persons of different classes or descriptions, and areas of discretion. The scheme also permits recommendations on the basis of special contributions by a person to the economy of Hong Kong. For the system of allocation of points see the third edition of this work.

(c) Consequences of registration

When the applicant is registered as a British citizen under the 1990 Act, s 1(1), he is treated as a British citizen otherwise than by descent, and thus his children born after registration will be British citizens. Those who are registered under the children and spouses scheme in the 1990 Act, Sched 2 are to be treated as British citizens by descent, so that unless their children are born in the UK they will not be British citizens. Those whose status before registration was that of a BDTC cease to be BDTCs if they become British citizens under the 1990 Act. Persons registered become subject to the scheme of the British Nationality Act 1981 relating to Commonwealth citizenship, deprivation of citizenship, legitimated and posthumous children, evidence and offences.

4   The Asylum and Immigration Appeals Act 1993

The Asylum and Immigration Appeals Act 1993 came into force on 26 July 1993. It introduced the following changes:
  (1) It gave primacy to the Convention and Protocol on the Status of Refugees.
  (2) It made provision for the treatment of asylum seekers.
  (3) It provided asylum seekers with a right of appeal in all cases.
  (4) It removed the right of appeal from persons seeking to come as visitors and short term students, from those whose appeal would have to be refused under the immigration rules, and from those who do not have certain documents required under the immigration rules.
  (5) It provided a right of appeal (with leave) to the CA in all immigration cases, save asylum applications certified to be without foundation.
  (6) It provided for an abbreviated appeal process in cases which are certified to be without foundation. Persons whose cases are so certified may appeal to the special adjudicator.
  (7) It amended the Immigration (Carriers' Liability) Act 1987 so as to extend the liability of carriers in respect of persons who are required to have transit visas, and who are specified by Order.

The 1993 Act provided for the introduction of amendments to the immigration rules which dealt with asylum claims. The subject is discussed in detail in Chapters 25 and 26, and the right of appeal to the CA is dealt with in Chapter 20.

5   The Asylum and Immigration Act 1996

The controversial Asylum and Immigration Act 1996 introduces a range of changes to immigration law in the UK:
  (1) It expands the special appeals procedure in Sched 2, para 5 to the 1993 Act (see p 506) to cases to which, broadly, the following apply:
      (a) the country or territory to which the appellant is to be sent is designated in an Order as a country in which it appears to the S of S that there is in general no serious risk of persecution. Such countries are on a so-called 'white list'. For a discussion of this provision see p 469 at (d);
      (b) on being required by an immigration officer to produce a valid passport, the appellant failed either to produce one or to give a reasonable explanation for his failure to do so; or he produced a passport which was not in fact valid, but failed to inform the officer of that fact. For a discussion of this provision see p 472 et seq;
      (c) the appellant's claim: (i) does not show a fear of persecution by reason of his race, religion, nationality, membership of a particular social group or political opinion; or (ii) shows such a

fear, but that fear is manifestly unfounded, or the circumstances which gave rise to that fear no longer subsist; or (iii) is made after refusal of leave to enter, or a recommendation for deportation by a court has been made, or notification of a decision to make a deportation order by the S of S or after notification of his liability to be removed; or (iv) is manifestly fraudulent, or any of the evidence adduced in support of it is manifestly fraudulent; or, finally, (v) is frivolous or vexatious.

There is an exception where the evidence adduced in any of these cases establishes a reasonable likelihood that the appellant has been tortured in the territory of proposed return.

(2) The 1996 Act makes provision for the removal of asylum claimants to safe third countries. For a discussion of this provision see Chapter 27. The S of S must be satisfied that the person is not a national of the country of proposed return, and that his life and liberty would not be threatened in that country for Convention reasons (see Chapter 27); and finally that the government of that country would not send the person to another country in which life and liberty would be threatened.

(3) The 1996 Act establishes an appeals mechanism against certificates issued pursuant to (2) above. For a discussion of this nominal appeal structure see Chapter 27. In cases where the person is to be returned to a 'white list' or EU country the appeal cannot be exercised while the appellant is in the UK.

(4) The 1996 Act creates the offences of obtaining leave to enter or remain in the UK by means including deception; and of assisting asylum claimants and persons seeking to obtain leave by deception. It also increases penalties for illegal entry and other and similar offences. It grants powers of arrest and search to constables or immigration officers in respect of illegal entry; obtaining leave to enter or remain by means including deception; remaining beyond the time limited by leave ('overstaying'); and breaching a condition of leave. For a discussion of these provisions see Chapter 27.

(5) The 1996 Act introduces the offence of employing a person over 16 who is subject to immigration control, who has not been granted leave to enter or remain in the UK, or whose leave is not valid or subsisting or is subject to a condition precluding the person from taking up the employment. These provisions are discussed in Chapter 27. There is a defence for the employer, where he kept or recorded a document produced to him before the employment began which appeared to him to relate to the employee and to be of a description specified in Orders to be made by the Secretary of State. Potentially, the new offence creates a dilemma for employers: on the one hand the employer must not commit a criminal offence; on the other he must avoid contravening the provisions of the Race Relations Act 1976 (see Chapter 27).

(6) In line with other provisions introduced over the last three years, the 1996 Act limits entitlement to housing accommodation and assistance by housing authorities, and to child benefit (see p 61 *et seq*).

(7) Schedule 2 amends s 3 of the 1971 Act. A person who is not a British citizen, if given limited leave to enter or remain in the UK, may be given leave subject to all or any of the following: (i) a condition restricting his employment or occupation in the UK; (ii) a condition requiring him to maintain and accommodate himself and any of his dependants without recourse to public funds; (iii) a condition requiring him to register with the police. The 1971 Act introduces a criminal offence of knowingly breaching a condition of leave (s 24(1)(*b*)). By turning maintenance and accommodation into a *condition* of leave, the 1996 Act ensures that a person who does not maintain or accommodate himself and any of his dependants without recourse to public funds commits a criminal offence (see Chapter 27).

(8) A person who obtains leave to remain by deception becomes liable to deportation, and has a right of appeal limited to the issue of whether the S of S had power in law to make the deportation order (see p 350). The 1996 Act also amends the 1971 Act regarding membership of a person's family for the purposes of deportation as a member of the family. Under the new provision, for the purposes of deportation, X is regarded as a member of Y's family, if (a) Y is a woman and X is her husband; or (b) if X is Y's child and under the age of 18. Technically this equalises the position between the sexes. However the previous power was rarely used.

(9) The 1996 Act amends the 1971 Act by providing that a person shall not be entitled to appeal against any variation of leave, or refusal to vary his leave, if the refusal is on the ground that a relevant document which is required by the immigration rules has not been issued. Work permits or *equivalent documents issued after entry* are included in the list of relevant documents. This will now include documents issued granting an approval to work.

(10) The 1996 Act clarifies the definition of 'illegal entrant' to include persons entering or seeking to enter by means which *include* deception by another person (see p 14 above), and provides that an appeal is to be treated as abandoned by reason of the appellant's leaving the UK. After that point, an appeal will no longer be treated as pending for the purposes of the 1971 Act.

(11) Paragraph 4(2)(*b*) of Sched 2 to the 1971 Act provided that a person who is being examined by an immigration officer must, if required by the officer, declare whether or not he is carrying or conveying documents which appear to the officer to be relevant for the purpose of the examination. The officer may conduct a search. The 1996 Act adds the requirement for the person to declare whether or not he has

carried or conveyed such documents in the past. The purpose of the search is broadened to include checking to see whether the person has carried or conveyed the documents (see p 284).

(12) Under the 1971 Act, where an illegal entrant was not given leave to enter or remain in the UK, an immigration officer could give directions for his removal to the owners or captain of the ship or aircraft on which he arrived. The directions could also specify the destination of return. The 1996 Act adds a stipulation that any leave to enter the UK which is obtained by deception shall be disregarded for the purposes of considering whether the illegal entrant was given leave to enter. Under the 1971 Act the power to remove only arose where the illegal entrant had not been given leave to enter or remain. The HL decided, in *Ex p Khawaja* [1984] AC 74, that leave obtained by deception is not vitiated. The amendment in effect reverses the effect of *Khawaja* for the purposes of the power of the immigration officer to make removal directions.

(13) If a person is on temporary admission and fails at any time to report as required to an immigration officer, the immigration officer may direct that his examination shall be treated as concluded at that time. However, the usual requirement that the notice giving or refusing leave to enter the UK should be given to the person within 24 hours after that time shall not apply (see p 289 below).

(14) The 1996 Act extends bail provisions to those refused leave to enter and illegal entrants pending removal. It provides a method other than judicial review to secure the release of such persons pending their removal.

(15) The third Schedule to the 1996 Act provides for the curtailment provisions under the 1993 Act (see p 245) to apply to the limited leave granted to any dependant of the person whose leave has been curtailed. Such persons will have no right of appeal against such curtailment and may be detained pending the making of deportation orders against them.

(16) The 1996 Act amends s 8(3) of the 1993 Act. It permits an appeal on the basis both that a deportation order was made, and that the S of S has refused to revoke a deportation order (see Chapter 14). However, a person may not appeal against the refusal of the S of S to revoke a deportation order where he had the right to appeal against a deportation order, whether or not he exercised that right.

(17) The 1996 Act introduces a right to apply for bail pending appeal to the Court of Appeal from the IAT (see p 401).

(18) Finally, the 1996 Act deals with some ambiguity that existed under the 1993 Act, and brings into clear legislative effect the undertakings given by Earl Ferrers at HL Debs, 2 March 1993, vol 543, no 104 at col 620, and HL Debs, 11 March 1993, vol 543, no 110, col 1188, relating to the concept of a pending appeal under s 33(4) of the 1971 Act.

6   The Hong Kong (War Wives and Widows) Act 1996

By the Hong Kong (War Wives and Widows) Act 1996, the S of S may register as a British citizen any woman who, before the passing of the Act, was the recipient (or intended recipient) of a 'UK settlement letter'. The following conditions must be satisfied:

(a)   she has her residence or principal residence in Hong Kong; and

(b)   where she is no longer married to the man in recognition of whose service the assurance was given, she has not remarried (s 1).

A 'UK settlement letter' is defined as a letter written by the S of S which:

(a)   confirmed the assurance given to the intended recipient that in recognition of her husband's service, or her late or former husband's service, in defence of Hong Kong during the Second World War, she could come to the UK for settlement at any time;

(b)   was sent by the S of S to the Hong Kong Immigration Department for onward transmission to the intended recipient (whether or not she in fact received it) (s 1(2)).

A woman who is registered as a British citizen under the Act is treated for the purposes of the 1981 Act as a British citizen otherwise than by descent. Section 2 also applies sections of the 1981 Act to such a woman; these sections include those relating to the deprivation of citizenship (see Chapter 3).

This Act makes provision for a limited category of persons only. See also the Hong Kong (Occupational Categories) Act 1995.

Chapter 5

The Immigration Rules

1 Introduction

The immigration rules are not, like most delegated legislation under Acts of Parliament, statutory instruments. They take the form of statements placed by the S of S before Parliament, and take effect subject to a negative resolution by either House within 40 days of the date they are laid before Parliament.

The system of control is very much an administrative, discretionary one, and the language of the rules underlines this. It is an area in which legal principles are difficult to formulate. The first tier of the statutory appeal procedure, too, exhibits many of the characteristics of an administrative rather than a judicial process. Adjudicators are appointed by the Lord Chancellor, and paid by his department. Adjudications are not reported. IAT decisions are retained in the library at Thanet House, London, and copies are held in the Supreme Court Library at the Royal Courts of Justice. The Immigration Appeal Reports (Imm AR) are published by HMSO in volumes which are known, for the obvious reason, as 'Green Books'. Unreported decisions of the High Court and the IAT are often summarised in *Tolley's Immigration and Nationality Law and Practice* (INL&P), the journal of the Immigration Law Practitioners Association (ILPA) and the Legal Action (LAG) Bulletin. The latter has a quarterly updating article, which is probably the easiest way of keeping up to date. The Joint Council for the Welfare of Immigrants (JCWI) also produces a quarterly bulletin which provides useful updating information and reports of mainly unreported IAT cases. Finally, practitioners may find the editor's twice-yearly update articles in the *Solicitors' Journal* of assistance.

2 The 1994 rules

The 1971 Act, s 3(2) requires the Home Secretary to make rules:

> as to the practice to be followed in the administration of this Act for regulating the entry into and stay in the United Kingdom of persons required by this Act to have leave to enter, including any rules as to the period for which leave is to be given and the conditions to be attached in different circumstances.

The current rules are contained in the *Statement of Changes in Immigration Rules* (HC 395) which took effect on 1 October 1994. They cover control on and after entry in respect of all persons required by the Act to have leave to enter. The provisions relating to asylum were substantially amended by Cm 3365 as of 1 September 1996.

3   Commonwealth citizens settled in the UK in 1973

The rules in operation before 1989 were framed so that Commonwealth citizens settled in the UK at the coming into force of the 1971 Act, and their wives and children, were not, by virtue of anything in the rules, any less free to enter and leave the UK than if the 1971 Act had not been passed. This protection derived from s 1(5) of the 1971 Act, but the subsection was repealed by the 1988 Act, s 1. Since 8 July 1989 wives and children of Commonwealth citizens have had to show that they can maintain and accommodate themselves in accordance with the current immigration rules.

4   Status of the rules

In *R v Chief Immigration Officer, London (Heathrow) Airport, ex p Salamat Bibi* [1976] 3 All ER 843, Roskill LJ observed (at p 848) that the immigration rules 'are just as much delegated legislation as any other form of rule making activity or delegated legislation which is empowered by Act of Parliament ... they are just as much part of the law of England as the 1971 Act itself'. However, all three members of the CA in *R v S of S, ex p Hosenball* [1977] 3 All ER 452 disapproved of this observation; and in *R v IAT, ex p Bakhtaur Singh* [1986] Imm AR 352; [1986] 1 WLR 910, Lord Bridge, at p 359, said:

> Immigration rules ... are quite unlike ordinary delegated legislation ... The rules do not purport to enact a precise code having statutory force. They are discursive in style, in part merely explanatory and, on their face, frequently offer no more than broad guidance as to how discretion is to be exercised in different typical situations. Insofar as they lay down principles to be applied they generally do so in loose and imprecise terms ...

In *Hosenball's* case (above) Lord Denning MR said (at p 459) that the immigration rules were not rules of law but were 'rules of practice laid down for the guidance of immigration officers and tribunals who are entrusted with the administration of this Act'. He recognised that to some extent the courts must have regard to them because there are provisions in the Act itself, particularly in s 19, which show that in appeals to an adjudicator, if the immigration rules have not been complied with, then the appeal is to be allowed. In addition the courts always have regard to the rules, not only in matters where there is a right of appeal, but also in cases under prerogative writs where there is a question whether the officers have acted fairly.

It follows from the present approach to the rules that the strict canons of construction applicable to statutes cannot properly be applied to the rules.

They are not statutory instruments but are designed under the 1971 Act, s 3(2), to be 'rules as to the practice to be followed in the administration of the Act'. Thus, in interpreting the rules, regard must be had to the purpose for which they were made (*Chauda v ECO Bombay* [1978] Imm AR 40). They must be construed sensibly according to the natural meaning of the language which is employed (*R v IAT, ex p Alexander* [1982] 1 WLR 1076 and *R v IAT, ex p Manshoora Begum* [1986] Imm AR 385). In particular, where several paragraphs deal with the same matter, those paragraphs are to be read together (*ECO Bombay v Stanley de Noronha* [1995] Imm AR 341). Although they are to be given a commonsense construction looking at the rules altogether, it is not proper to disregard a requirement in a rule which is specific and expressed in plain and unambiguous language (*R v IAT, ex p Rahman* [1987] Imm AR 313).

As the Convention on Human Rights and Fundamental Freedoms is not formally part of the law of England, immigration officers are under no duty to bear in mind the principles stated in the Convention when exercising their powers under the rules (but see Chapter 21). Their decisions are to be made solely in accordance with the rules (*R v Chief Immigration Officer, London (Heathrow) Airport, ex p Salamat Bibi* [1976] 3 All ER 843, *per* Lord Denning MR at p 847; and *dicta* of Lord Denning MR in *R v S of S for Home Affairs, ex p Bhajan Singh* [1975] 2 All ER at p 873 and of Scarman LJ in *R v S of S, ex p Phansopkar* [1975] 3 All ER at p 511 disapproved). However, the Convention is usually a background to a complaint of irrationality. The fact that a decision-maker failed to take account of Convention obligations when exercising an administrative discretion is not of itself a ground for impugning that exercise of discretion (see Chapter 21 and *R v MOD, ex p Grady* [1996] 2 WLR 305). Further, the court conceives it to be its duty, when free to do so, 'to interpret the law in accordance with the obligations of the Crown under this treaty' (*Attorney-General v Guardian Newspapers Ltd (No 2)* [1990] 1 AC 109 at 283–4). The Convention may be resorted to in order to help resolve some uncertainty or ambiguity in municipal law (*per* Lord Ackner in *R v S of S, ex p Brind* [1991] 1 AC 696, 761).

The S of S retains a residual discretion in these matters, and may be requested by an appellant to depart, or to authorise an officer to depart, from the rules (see ss 4(1) and 19(2) of the Act). The appellate authorities are able to review the exercise of the S of S's discretion in relation to a decision taken outside the rules. A restrictive interpretation of the rules should not be employed so as to exclude a person from appealing (*R v IAT, ex p Takeo* [1987] Imm AR 522).

5   Decisions taken outside the rules: concessions and policies

Where the proper course under the immigration rules would be to refuse an application for leave either to enter or to remain, the Home Office may make an exception to the rules and grant leave. Certain practices have been defined in parliamentary answers or MPs' correspondence and are consistently applied. The Joint Council for the Welfare of Immigrants, the Immigration Law Practitioners' Association and other organisations have in the past been able to assist in the clarification of such practices by requesting information from the Home Office, who then set out the concession in letters to them. Adjudicators can, however, allow an appeal only where the decision is not in accordance with the law or the immigration rules applicable (1971 Act, s 19). In all other cases they must dismiss the appeal.

The effect of a concession on an appeal In *Ex p Abdi* [1996] Imm AR 148, the CA proceeded on the basis that if it can be shown that the S of S failed to act in accordance with established principles of administrative or common law, for example if he did not take account of or give effect to his own published policy, that was not 'in accordance with the law'. (See also *R v IAT, ex p Bakhtaur Singh* [1986] 2 All ER 721; [1986] Imm AR 352, *per* Lord Bridge at p 360, and *Ex p Malhi* [1991] 1 QB 194; [1990] Imm AR 275 at p 283.)

The first issue is the precise terms of the relevant concession. The applicant will have to fit into the letter of the concession, not merely its spirit, to qualify.

Second, whether the S of S had regard to a particular policy or concession may be raised with an adjudicator on an appeal. If an extra-regulatory concession is not properly taken into account, the S of S has not acted in accordance with the law, and the appeal should be allowed (s 19(1)(a)(i)). In addition, the adjudicator is entitled, under s 19(2), to review any determination of fact on which the decision was based. Thus, if a finding by the S of S that the applicant did not have the necessary status for the application of a concession is raised before the adjudicator, the adjudicator may resolve that issue. Where the S of S proceeded on a misapprehension of the material facts, the S of S does not properly take the concession into account and there is an error which makes the decision not in accordance with the law for the purpose of s 19(1)(a)(i). An example of such a fact was the fact of dependency, which was crucial to the applicability of the final sentence of para 8.1.1 of the 1990 'Somali family reunion concession' (*Ex p Dhudi Abdi* [1996] Imm AR 148. In relation to the '10 year concession' (p 254), see also *Arokianathan* (11497) JCWI B Vol 5 No 8 Spring 1995 p 10).

Unless it is inevitable that the applicant will be given entry clearance if the S of S reconsiders the application on the correct facts, the matter must be remitted to the S of S for him to reconsider the application in the light of those true facts (*Dhudi Abdi* [1996] Imm AR 142; see also *Evon* (p 239) and *Ko* (p 106)).

In a series of decisions of the IAT, the correct position has been adopted (see for example, *Gautam* (10985)). In *Umujakporue* ((12448) and see JCWI B Vol 5 No 10, Autumn 1995 p 10), the appellant had been a student for over ten years. However, he spent two years in Sligo, Eire, although during that time he maintained his rented accommodation in London, frequently went there for long weekends, and met his girlfriend in England. The IAT held that the absence of the applicant in Ireland for studies did not destroy his residence in the UK, and stated 'there is no ground on which the Secretary of State could refuse the application for indefinite leave and maintain the policy which he has promulgated'. In *Arokianathan* (above), the matter was referred back to the S of S for reconsideration on the basis of the facts found by the adjudicator.

Where an appeal is dismissed, it remains open to the adjudicator (or, at a later stage, the IAT) to make a recommendation that the S of S should exercise his discretion outside the rules. In certain circumstances it is possible to apply for judicial review of a decision not to depart from the rules, whether by applying a recognised concession or otherwise (see Chapter 22). Recommendations are normally followed, and failure to follow a recommendation can give rise to grounds for judicial review: (eg) *Ex p Alakesan* CO/3774/94; but see *Ex p Sakala* [1994] Imm AR 143. A recommendation will not normally be appropriate where the applicant has not given oral evidence (*Akinpelumi v Immigration Officer* (12963)).

Where the Home Office's concessions are less well defined or are not consistently applied, they are more likely to be known as either policies or principles. The more important of these concessions are mentioned in the text at the appropriate place. They relate to:

(a) private domestic servants (see p 150);

(b) foreign nationals liable to removal or deportation married to a person settled in the UK (DP 3/96; see Chapter 14);

(c) indefinite leave to remain based on long residence of ten or 14 years, and sponsored students' long residence (see Chapter 14);

(d) entry clearance or leave to remain for children under 12 applying to join a lone parent (see p 221);

(e) exceptional leave concessions;

(f) policies on third safe countries;

(g) bringing children for adoption;

(h) Somali family reunion (withdrawn by Parliamentary Written Answer of 29 February 1996);

(i) deportation in cases involving families and children (DP 4/96, DP 5/96) (see Chapter 14);

(j) adoptive children of EEA nationals (see p 338);

(k) returns to Bosnia to 'test the waters';

(l) absences from the UK by investors (see p 179);

(m) overseas carers (BDI 2/95) (see p 99);

(n) unaccompanied children (see p 486);

(o) public funds and maintenance and accommodation in marriage (see p 207);

(p) naturalisation concession;

(q) concession relating to EC Association Agreements (see p 173);

(r) AIDS and HIV positive cases (BDI 3/95) (see p 98).

An applicant's awareness of a relevant concession may give rise to a legitimate expectation on his part that he will be treated in accordance with it. Some of the concessions relate purely to the practice of the Home Office and may change rapidly. The JCWI, 115 Old Street London EC1V 9JR, and ILPA are the best sources of information on concessions and information relating to Home Office practices. Both issue bulletins and newsletters, providing the practitioner with a good way of keeping up to date with developments. (For the useful discussion of such concessions see *Home Office discretion outside the Immigration Rules* by F Webber in *Legal Action*, February 1994, p 18. However, all concessions are currently under review.)

Where an application for settlement is made by a person whose leave to enter was granted in a category under HC 251 which was significantly changed under HC 395 (such as retired persons of independent means (see p 188) or sole representatives (see p 143)), if the person satisfies the requirements of HC 251 regarding settlement, he will be regarded as satisfying those of HC 395. (For the text of a letter dated 9 November 1994, setting out this policy, see *Butterworth's Immigration and Nationality Law Service* at D[101]). This applies only in respect of retrospective requirements. HC 395 would also be regarded as modified appropriately in respect of entry clearances granted under the previous rules in respect of persons of independent means. Otherwise the applicant must meet the requirements of HC 395. In the case of persons of independent means who entered under HC 251, the IND may be prepared to waive the requirement of an income of £25,000 pa, as long as the requirement under HC 251 of an income of £20,000 is met.

6   Judicial review

Since the immigration rules are made by the S of S pursuant to powers granted to him by the Immigration Act 1971, the rules themselves may be subject to judicial review. They may be struck down as *ultra vires* if they are unreasonable on the test laid down in *Associated Provincial Picture Houses Ltd v Wednesbury Corporation* [1948] 1 KB 223. In *R v IAT ex p Manshoora Begum* [1986] Imm AR 385, Simon Brown J struck down as unreasonable, thus *ultra vires*, a requirement in the rules that in considering whether there were exceptional compassionate circumstances justifying the admission of relatives aged under 65 of persons settled in the UK, the immigration officer should satisfy himself that the applicant had a standard of living substantially below that of his own country, as well as being financially dependent on someone in the UK. (See also *R v S of S, ex p Ounejma* [1989] Imm AR 75; *Rajput v IAT* [1989] Imm AR 350; *R v An adjudicator, ex p S of S* [1989] Imm AR 423, and Chapter 22.)

Part II

The Immigration Rules: HC 395

Chapter 6

Introduction, Interpretation and Part 1: General Provisions

1 Introduction

1. The Home Secretary has made changes in the Rules laid down by him as to the practice to be followed in the administration of the Immigration Acts for regulating entry into and the stay of persons in the United Kingdom and contained in the statement laid before Parliament on 23 March 1990 (HC 251) (as amended). This statement contains the Rules as changed and replaces the provisions of HC 251 (as amended).

2. Immigration Officers, Entry Clearance Officers and all staff of the Home Office Immigration and Nationality Department will carry out their duties without regard to the race, colour or religion of persons seeking to enter or remain in the United Kingdom.

3. In these Rules words importing the masculine gender include the feminine unless the contrary intention appears.

Implementation and transitional provisions

4. These Rules come into effect on 1 October 1994 and will apply to all decisions taken on or after that date save that any application made before 1 October 1994 for entry clearance, leave to enter or remain or variation of leave to enter or remain other than an application for leave by a person seeking asylum shall be decided under the provisions of HC 251, as amended, as if these Rules had not been made.

COMMENTARY

The current immigration rules are contained in HC 395 as amended. These make a number of substantive changes to the earlier version, presenting the rules in a format in which the 'on entry' and 'after entry' rules are grouped together. Thus, in respect of visitors, for example, the requirements for entry and for an extension of leave are all to be found in the same place. This part of this work contains a restatement of the amended rules and commentary on them as at 1 September 1996.

The rules explain the practice to be followed in the administration of the Immigration Acts for regulating entry into and the stay in the UK of persons who do not have the right of abode in the UK. Immigration officers and entry clearance officers must carry out their duties without regard to the race, colour or religion of persons seeking to enter the UK (para 2). In the rules, words importing the masculine gender include the feminine, unless the contrary intention appears (para 3). The rules came into effect on 1 October 1994. They apply to all decisions taken on or after that date, except where the application for entry clearance, leave to enter, or leave to remain was made before 1 October 1994. Applications made before that date are decided under the provisions of HC 251 as amended.

The words 'other than an application for leave by a person seeking asylum' were inserted in HC 395 by Cm 3365. An application for asylum made after 1 September 1996, whether for leave to enter or remain or variation of leave to enter or remain for this purpose, is determined under the provisions of HC 395 as amended in the light of the 1996 Act (see Chapter 26). Otherwise, the rules represent a codification of many of the pre-existing practices of the Home Office. Refusal of leave to enter or remain under the new rules is in many cases mandatory unless certain conditions are met. Cutting down the area of the immigration officer's discretion creates perhaps too rigid a framework. The Home Office has not published the various concessions and policies by which immigration officers in fact operate so as to make them part of the immigration rules. This is particularly unfortunate as the rules are intended to represent the S of S's guidelines for the exercise of the immigration officer's discretion. As a result, concessions remain important, although they are the less satisfactory method of decision-making.

Application

5. Save where expressly indicated, these Rules do not apply to a European Economic Area (EEA) national or the family member of such a national who is entitled to enter or remain in the United Kingdom by virtue of the provisions of the Immigration (European Economic Area) Order 1994. But an EEA national or his family member who is not entitled to rely on the provisions of that Order is covered by these Rules.

COMMENTARY

The European Economic Area is dealt with in Chapter 16. If a conflict were to arise between the UK legislation and that of the EU, including any treaties with non-EU countries, the law of the EU would prevail. This principle would not be affected by the apparent reservation in para 5. Further, the last sentence of the paragraph does not alter this principle. For the scope of 'family' in the context of adoption by EEA nationals see p 338.

2 Interpretation

By para 6 of the rules the following interpretations apply:

'the Immigration Acts' mean the Immigration Act 1971 and the Immigration Act 1988.
'the 1993 Act' is the Asylum and Immigration Appeals Act 1993.
'the 1996 Act' is the Asylum and Immigration Act 1996.

'the 1994 EEA Order' is the Immigration (European Economic Area) Order 1994.

'United Kingdom passport' bears the meaning it has in the Immigration Act 1971.

'Immigration Officer' includes a Customs Officer acting as an Immigration Officer.

'public funds' means

(a) housing under Part II or III of the Housing Act 1985, Part I or II of the Housing (Scotland) Act 1987, Part II of the Housing (Northern Ireland) Order 1981 or Part II of the Housing (Northern Ireland) Order 1988;

(b) attendance allowance, severe disablement allowance, invalid care allowance and disability living allowance under Part III, income support, family credit, council tax benefit, disability working allowance and housing benefit under Part VII and child benefit under Part IX of the Social Security Contribution and Benefits Act 1992;

(c) attendance allowance, severe disablement allowance, invalid care allowance and disability living allowance under Part III, income support, family credit, disability working allowance, housing benefit under Part VII and child benefit under Part IX of the Social Security Contributions and Benefits (Northern Ireland) Act 1992; and

(d) income-based jobseeker's allowance under the Jobseekers Act 1995.

'Department of Employment' [means the Department for Education and Employment and includes, where appropriate, the equivalent Government Department for Northern Ireland.]

'settled in the United Kingdom' means that the person concerned:

(a) is free from any restriction on the period for which he may remain save that a person entitled to an exemption under Section 8 of the Immigration Act 1971 (otherwise than as a member of the home forces) is not to be regarded as settled in the United Kingdom except in so far as Section 8(5A) so provides; and

(b) is either:
   (i) ordinarily resident in the United Kingdom without having entered or remained in breach of the immigration laws; or
   (ii) despite having entered or remained in breach of the immigration laws, has subsequently entered lawfully or has been granted leave to remain and is ordinarily resident.

'a parent' includes

(a) the stepfather of a child whose father is dead;

(b) the stepmother of a child whose mother is dead;

(c) the father as well as the mother of an illegitimate child where he is proved to be the father;

(d) an adoptive parent but only where a child was adopted in accordance with a decision taken by the competent administrative authority or court in a country whose adoption orders are recognised by the United Kingdom (except where an application for leave to enter or remain is made under paragraphs 310–316);

(e) in the case of a child born in the United Kingdom who is not a British citizen, a person to whom there has been a genuine transfer of parental responsibility on the ground of the original parent(s)' inability to care for the child.

'visa nationals' are the persons specified in the Appendix to these Rules who need a visa for the United Kingdom.

'employment', unless the contrary intention appears, includes paid and unpaid employment, self-employment and engaging in business or any professional activity.

'EEA national' means a national of a State which is a Contracting Party to the European Economic Area Agreement other than the United Kingdom, but until the EEA Agreement comes into force in relation to Liechtenstein does not include a national of the State of Liechtenstein.

'family member' in relation to an EEA national has the same meaning as in the 1994 EEA Order.

COMMENTARY

Public funds The words in square brackets were substituted by the Statement of Changes in Immigration Rules, HC 31 of 1996, altering the definition of 'public funds'. Persons admitted on a limited leave are generally subject to a requirement that there should be no resort to public funds. The following categories are affected:

(a) spouses (para 281(v) and (vi) and 284(viii) and (ix)); see p 207;

(b) fiancés (paras 290(vi) and (vii) and 293(iv));

(c) children (paras 297, 298, 301, 310 and 311);

(d) dependants (para 317).

Section 3(1)(c) of the 1971 Act provides that if a person is given limited leave to enter or remain in the UK, it may be given subject to all or any of the following conditions:

(a) restricting his employment or occupation;

(b) requiring him to maintain and accommodate himself and any dependants of his without recourse to public funds; and

(c) requiring him to register with the police.

The general rule is that there should not be any direct or indirect reliance on public funds by persons in the categories in respect of which such reliance is prohibited. Indirect reliance may take the form of relying on savings made from benefits received by another person from public funds. In *IAT ex p Chhinderpal Singh* [1989] Imm AR 69, Kennedy J held that there would be (indirect) recourse to public funds where the sponsor had saved money out of his supplementary benefit. There must, however, be some evidence of reliance or prospective reliance. In *Memoona Shah* (12444) the IAT found that a couple living with parents who were reliant on public funds could support themselves. The IAT stated that since the couple would 'make a proper contribution to the outgoings of the accommodation, any question of indirect reliance on public funds would be negatived'. In a letter dated 5 October 1994 to the UK Council for Overseas Student Affairs (UKCOSA) the Home Office stated that there is no objection to other residents in the same household receiving public funds to which they are entitled in their own right: 'The question is whether additional recourse to public funds would be necessary on the applicant's arrival here. The sponsor's means, including any public funds to which they are entitled in their own right, must therefore be sufficient to provide adequate maintenance and accommodation for the applicants and their dependants (if any)' (see JCWI Bulletin, vol 5, no 7, Winter 1994, p 1). Savings from invalidity benefit were held not to be public funds (*Azam* (11704)). In *Yousaf* (9190) the IAT held that whether an applicant had recourse to public funds was an issue of fact, and there needs to be causation between the provision of the public funds and the applicant's admission. Clearly as a matter of fact there will be no such causal link where there is no *additional* recourse to public funds. However, in law there will be no causation even if there is additional recourse to public funds, but it is too remote from the admission in factual causation, or it is too insignificant. The IAT adopted reasoning similar to that in the Home Office's letter of 5 October 1994, applying a construction whereby the rules require the applicant to show that his admission would not give rise to recourse to public funds. Thus if a house was provided to the sponsor because he was homeless, regardless of the admission of his spouse, the house was not provided because of the admission of the spouse. However, in *Ex p Bibi & Begum* [1995] Imm AR 157, Hidden J stated 'If a person in fact is maintained out of public funds which are paid to and intended for someone else, there is recourse to public funds as was found in *Chhinderpal Singh*.' This prompted a statement of policy in a letter from Nicholas Baker dated 2 October 1995 that the judgment ran counter to the Home Office's more generous interpretation of the rules relating to maintenance and accommodation, and because the Home Office operated a more generous policy, it was not bound to follow the judgment. Despite this, in *Iqbal* (12528) the IAT held that the letter of 5 October 1994 was merely a comment on a particular set of facts and was not a change to the rules. The IAT considered itself bound by *Bibi & Begum* to hold that indirect reliance without any increase in the sponsor's (or another person's) reliance on public funds was prohibited. It is clear, however, that neither *Singh*, nor *Bibi & Begum*, suggests that there is reliance on public funds merely because the sponsor is reliant on public funds. There must be some evidence that the applicant is likely to be maintained out of those funds. The only sense in which indirect reliance becomes an issue is if the sponsor intends to maintain the applicant out of funds which have a sufficiently close link to public funds (for example because they are savings out of such funds) that it can be said that the applicant is to be maintained from public funds. For an interesting discussion of reliance on public funds see INLP vol 10, no 2, 1996, p 50. In *Scott* (TH/65485/91), the IAT appears to have adopted what is clearly the correct approach: there should as a matter of fact be additional recourse to public funds caused by the admission of the applicant. (See also p 207.)

Entitlement to housing and family credit of persons subject to immigration control Sections 9 and 10 of the 1996 Act deal with the entitlement to housing accommodation and assistance (s 9) and to family credit (s 10) of persons who are subject to immigration control. By s 13, 'a person subject to immigration control' means a person who, under the 1971 Act, requires ▶

leave to enter or remain in the UK, whether or not such leave has been given (s 13(2), 1996 Act). There are separate provisions on income support which relate to asylum seekers (see Appendix B).

Under s 9 of the 1996 Act, a housing authority must secure that, so far as practicable, no tenancy of, or licence to occupy, housing accommodation provided under Parts II and III of the Housing Act 1985 is granted to a person subject to immigration control unless he is of a class specified in an order made by the S of S. A person is subject to immigration control if he does not have the right of abode (s 1, 1971 Act). A person has the right of abode if he is a British citizen, or is a Commonwealth citizen who had the right of abode before the 1981 Act and has not ceased to be a Commonwealth citizen in the meanwhile (see Chapter 3). This concept is distinct from settlement or indefinite leave to remain. A person is subject to immigration control when settled, and may, for example, be deported (see p 259). A person who is settled in the UK may apply to become a British citizen (1981 Act, ss 4 and 6). On the face of it, the provisions apply to settled persons as well as those with limited leave. Under the Housing Accommodation and Homelessness (Persons Subject to Immigration Control) Order 1996 (SI 1996 No 1982), however, the following persons are entitled to housing and accommodation in the ordinary way (art 3):

(a) a person recorded by the S of S as a refugee within the meaning of art 1 of the 1951 Convention (see Chapter 25) (Class A persons);

(b) a person:
   (i) who has been granted exceptional leave to remain in the UK outside the provisions of the immigration rules within the meaning of the 1971 Act; and
   (ii) whose leave is not subject to a condition requiring him to maintain and accommodate himself and any of his dependants without recourse to public funds (Class B persons);

(c) a person who has a current leave to enter or remain in the UK which is not subject to any condition or limitation (Class C persons. These are persons with indefinite leave to enter or remain in the UK);

(d) an overseas student where the housing accommodation which is or may be provided to him is let by a housing authority to a specific educational institution for the purposes of enabling that institution to provide accommodation for students attending a full-time course at the institution and which would otherwise be difficult for that authority to let on satisfactory terms (Class D persons).

By art 1 the following definitions apply: 'Full time course' means a course normally involving not less than 15 hours attendance a week in term time for the organised day time study of a single subject or related subjects (see p 103); and 'overseas student' means a person who is attending a full-time course at a specified education institution. A 'specified education institution' means one of the following:

(a) a university or other institution within the higher education sector within the meaning given by s 91(5) of the Further and Higher

Education Act ('FHEA') 1992 or s 4(4), Education Act 1996 (or s 56(2) of the Further and Higher Education (Scotland) Act 1992);

(b) an institution within the further education sector within the meaning given by s 91(3) of the FHEA 1992 or s 4(3), Education Act 1996;

(c) a board of governors managed college of further education in Scotland or a central institution (s 135(1), Education (Scotland) Act 1980);

(d) an institution which provides a course qualifying for funding under Part I of the Education Act 1994 (art 2, Housing Accommodation and Homelessness (Persons Subject to Immigration Control) Order 1996).

To be a university or other institution within the higher education sector the institution must fall within s 91(5) of the FHEA 1992. Thus institutions within the higher education sector are:

(a) universities receiving financial support under s 65, FHEA 1992;

(b) institutions conducted by higher education corporations, and

(c) institutions designated for the purposes of Part II of the FHEA 1992 (defined in s 72(3) of the FHEA 1992).

'Exceptional leave to remain' is mentioned in no statute, although the expression appears in various SIs such as regulations relating to job seekers, council tax, and income support. However, the concept of exceptional leave to remain outside the provisions of the immigration rules within the meaning of the 1971 Act clearly recognises that there is a power to grant such leave.

By s 9(2) of the 1996 Act, a person subject to immigration control is not entitled to relief from homelessness. Such a person is not eligible for accommodation or assistance under Part III of the Housing Act 1985, and is to be disregarded in determining whether another person is homeless or has a priority need for accommodation (s 9(2)(*a*)&(*b*)). By art 4 of the 1996 Order, Classes A–C are exempted from the effect of s 9(2). However, for obvious reasons, overseas students in accommodation which is difficult to let (see above, Class D) are not. In addition there are Classes E and F. Class E consists of any:

(e) person who has made a claim for asylum which is recorded by the S of S as having been made either:

(i) on his arrival (other than on his re-entry) in the UK from a country outside the 'common travel area' (see p 69); or

(ii) within three months from the day on which the S of S makes a declaration to the effect that the country of which he is a national is subject to such a fundamental change in circumstances that he would not normally order the return of a person to that country (art 4).

The exemption lasts while the asylum claim is being determined (art 4). If the claim is recorded as having been abandoned the exemption ceases. If the applicant is recorded by the S of S as being a refugee, he will remain exempt by virtue of being in Class A. If he obtains exceptional leave to remain he will probably be exempt by virtue of being in Class B. If it is determined that he is not a refugee and exceptional leave is not granted the local authority will cease to owe him a duty under Part III of the Housing Act 1985.

Finally, there is Class F which applies to a person (unless he is an asylum claimant within class E) who, on or before 4 February 1996, made a claim for asylum and was on that date entitled to benefit under the Housing Benefit (General) Regulations 1987 and:

(a) his claim has not been recorded by the S of S as having been determined or abandoned; or

(b) there was on that date an appeal pending in respect of that claim if such an appeal is made within the time limits specified in rules of procedure made under s 22 of the 1971 Act (see p 502).

In either case the S of S must not have recorded, since that date, either the abandonment of the appeal or its determination (art 4).

These provisions apply to the legislation governing Northern Ireland and Scotland.

Section 10 of the 1996 Act inserts s 146A into the Social Security Contributions and Benefits Act 1992 (and the equivalent provision in Northern Ireland). This provides that a person subject to immigration control is not entitled to child benefit for any week unless he satisfies conditions which are to be prescribed. As at 11 August 1996 no such provision has been made.

The use of welfare benefits as a form of immigration screening mechanism is of increasing importance. The effect of Sched 1 to the 1996 Act is set out in Appendix B.

Other provisions   The Immigration (EEA) Order 1994 was intended to give effect to EC law relating to the European Economic Area. Under it, rights to free movement are granted to citizens of the EEA states (see Chapter 16).

'Housing' under Part III of the Housing Act 1985, and similar provisions for Scotland and Northern Ireland, is the provision of local authority housing to a person classed as homeless.

Settlement   Section 33(2A) of the 1971 Act defines 'settlement' as being ordinarily resident in the UK without being subject to any restriction on the period for which the person may remain. In the context of admission for the purposes of marriage, a person with a right of abode in the UK can be admitted for settlement, although not subject to immigration control if he intends to take up ordinary residence (*Kouchalieva v S of S* [1994] Imm AR 147). The concepts of settlement and ordinary residence are dealt with in more detail at pp 12 and 13.

3   Part 1: General provisions regarding leave to enter or remain in the United Kingdom

Leave to enter the United Kingdom

7. A person who is neither a British citizen nor a Commonwealth citizen with the right of abode nor an EEA national or the family member of such a national who is entitled to enter or remain in the United Kingdom by virtue of the

provisions of the Immigration (European Economic Area) Order 1994 requires leave to enter the United Kingdom.

8. Under Sections 3 and 4 of the Immigration Act 1971 an Immigration Officer when admitting to the United Kingdom a person subject to control under that Act may give leave to enter for a limited period and, if he does, may impose all or any of the following conditions:

(i)   a condition restricting employment or occupation in the United Kingdom;

(ii) a condition requiring the person to maintain and accommodate himself and any dependants of his, without recourse to public funds; and

(iii) a condition requiring the person to register with the police.

He may also require him to report to the appropriate Medical Officer of Environmental Health. Under Section 24 of the 1971 Act it is an offence knowingly to remain beyond the time limit or to fail to comply with such a condition or requirement.

9. The time limit and any conditions attached will be made known to the person concerned by a written notice which will normally be given to him or be endorsed by the Immigration Officer in his passport or travel document.

Exercise of the power to refuse leave to enter the United Kingdom

10. The power to refuse leave to enter the United Kingdom is not to be exercised by an Immigration Officer acting on his own. The authority of a Chief Immigration Officer or of an Immigration Inspector must always be obtained.

Requirement for persons arriving in the United Kingdom or seeking entry through the Channel Tunnel to produce evidence of identity and nationality

11. A person must, on arrival in the United Kingdom or when seeking entry through the Channel Tunnel, produce on request by the Immigration Officer:

(i)   a valid national passport or other document satisfactorily establishing his identity and nationality; and

(ii) such information as may be required to establish whether he requires leave to enter the United Kingdom and, if so, whether and on what terms leave to enter should be given.

COMMENTARY

A person whose passport records that he is a British citizen should have no difficulty in entering the UK. Problems arise in the case of persons who are British citizens but have no passport evidencing the fact, and persons who are not British citizens and seek entry under the discretionary powers vested in the immigration authorities.

A person must on arrival in the UK produce, on request by an immigration officer, a valid national passport or other document satisfactorily establishing his identity and nationality (1971 Act, Sched 2, para 4(1)). Anyone arriving in the UK is liable to be examined and must furnish an immigration officer with such information as may be required for the purpose of deciding whether he requires leave to enter, and if so on what terms leave should be given. An immigration officer is under a duty to act fairly at all times (*Re HK (an infant)* [1967] 2 QB 617 and especially at 630). The rules make clear that the power to refuse leave to enter may be exercised by an immigration officer only with the consent of a Chief Immigration Officer. A person seeking entry to the UK and claiming to have a right of abode may prove that he has that right by producing a UK passport describing him as a British citizen or as a CUKC with the right of abode (1971 Act, s 3(9)(*a*), as amended by the Immigration Act 1988, s 3). Use of the British Visitor's Passport has been discontinued. It was not sufficient to discharge the burden under s 3(9) because it did not describe the bearer as a British citizen (see *Minta v S of S* [1992] Imm AR 380). While the immigration officer may be satisfied by other evidence of citizenship, he is bound to accept only a valid full British passport or certificate of entitlement as proof of citizenship under s 3(9).

Of course, EEA nationals, diplomats immune under the provisions of the 1971 Act, crew members and Commonwealth citizens with the right of abode do not require leave to enter the UK. EU nationals can be required to produce only a valid identity document; and, under art 8a of the Treaty of European Union, such border controls as there are for travellers between member states are of doubtful validity (but see *Flynn v S of S* [1995] Imm AR 594 (CA)). Again, the express provision in para 7 restricting entry to those who do not require leave under the EEA Order will be of no effect if the provisions of the EEA Order conflict with EC law on free movement.

Paragraph 8 was amended by Cm 3365. The only alteration is to add that a condition of maintenance and accommodation without recourse to public funds may be imposed on the admission of persons who are subject to immigration control (see p 61). Persons being admitted for settlement may not have this condition imposed on their leave.

The time limit and any condition attached, for example a condition restricting employment, is made known to the passenger by a written notice. This is normally given to the passenger or endorsed by the immigration officer in the passenger's passport or travel document. Any ambiguity in such an endorsement should be resolved in favour of the passenger. Where a notice contains two dates, either of which might denote the date from which leave might run, the later date will be taken if it is more favourable to the passenger (*Behrooz v S of S* [1991] Imm AR 82 (IAT)). The rules specify that it is an offence under s 24 of the 1971 Act for a person knowingly to remain beyond the time limit or to fail to comply with a condition or requirement imposed on his leave (see Chapter 27; such conditions now include those in respect of maintenance and accommodation).

Leave to enter must be given by an immigration officer. The fact that a person may be examined by a police officer on arrival does not give rise to any leave being granted, for police officers in such situations cannot be treated as having the implied authority to grant leave to enter (*R v S of S, ex p Mohan* [1989] Imm AR 436).

The issue of a passport by the UK government is a matter within the Royal Prerogative. It is a question of discretion, and the government cannot be compelled to grant a passport to a person even if he is apparently eligible to hold one (*S of S v Lakdawalla* [1972] Imm AR 26). However, the CA has held that refusal to issue a new passport, though part of the prerogative power, is amenable to judicial review (*R v Foreign & Commonwealth Office, ex p Everett* [1989] 1 All ER 655).

Under para 6 of the Schedule to the Immigration Act 1988, the immigration officer has the power to detain a passport or other document establishing the identity and nationality or citizenship of the holder until the holder is given leave to enter, or is about to depart following refusal of leave.

'Arrival' in the UK is not the same as entry to the UK. A person arriving in the UK on a ship or aircraft is deemed not to have entered the UK until he has disembarked and left any area approved by an immigration officer for persons to remain pending a decision on entry, or while he is on temporary admission to the UK pending the decision (1971 Act, s 11 and Sched 2). There may be some debate whether a person's rights under international law, such as the law relating to asylum, arise where he is in the UK but has not been granted leave to enter. The scope of a Treaty obligation may be co-extensive with the geographical jurisdiction of the signatory unless a contrary intention is indicated in the treaty or can be derived from international practice (see the principle now embodied in art 29 of the Vienna Convention On The Law Of Treaties Signed At Vienna 23 May 1969, but note art 4. The Vienna Convention itself is applicable to Treaties signed on or after 27 January 1980). Where a person comes to the UK via the Channel Tunnel system he is deemed not to have entered the UK unless and until he leaves the Channel Tunnel system (1971 Act, s 11(1A)).

Requirement for a person not requiring leave to enter the United Kingdom to prove that he has the right of abode

12. A person claiming to be a British citizen must prove that he has the right of abode in the United Kingdom by producing either:

(i)   a United Kingdom passport describing him as a British citizen or as a citizen of the United Kingdom and Colonies having the right of abode in the United Kingdom; or

(ii)   a certificate of entitlement duly issued by or on behalf of the Government of the United Kingdom certifying that he has the right of abode.

13. A person claiming to be a Commonwealth citizen with the right of abode in the United Kingdom must prove that he has the right of abode by producing a certificate of entitlement duly issued to him by or on behalf of the Government of the United Kingdom certifying that he has the right of abode.

14. A Commonwealth citizen who has been given limited leave to enter the United Kingdom may later claim to have the right of abode. The time limit on his stay may be removed if he is able to establish a claim to the right of abode, for example by showing that:

(i)   immediately before the commencement of the British Nationality Act 1981 he was a Commonwealth citizen born to or legally adopted by a parent who at the time of the birth had citizenship of the United Kingdom and Colonies by his birth in the United Kingdom or any of the Islands; and

(ii)   he has not ceased to be a Commonwealth citizen in the meanwhile.

COMMENTARY

Burden of proof Where a person claims a right to enter by reason of citizenship or the right of abode, the burden of proof, on the balance of probabilities, rests with him (1971 Act, s 3(8) and *Bamgbose* above), and remains on him throughout (*Fawehinmi v S of S* [1991] Imm AR 1 and see *R v S of S, ex p Ali* [1988] Imm AR 274 and *Visa Officer Islamabad v Channo Bi* [1978] Imm AR 182). The immigration officer is not bound to accept proof by production of a copy birth certificate (*Re Bamgbose* [1990] Imm AR 135). Where, however, a person presents a passport or certificate of entitlement, the evidential burden shifts, and it is for the S of S to prove that the document has been forged or fraudulently obtained or that the person is for some other reason an illegal entrant (*R v S of S, ex p Khawaja* [1984] AC 74; see, eg Lord Fraser at 97F). In *Mokuolu v S of S* [1989] Imm AR 51 it was held that despite *Khawaja* the legal burden of proof does not shift where the ground on which the applicant seeks to rebut an allegation that he is an illegal entrant is that he has a right of abode or British citizenship. Section 3(8) requires proof, on the balance of probabilities, and the mere production of a birth certificate may not discharge it if there are any discrepancies in the applicant's case which render it unlikely that he is a British citizen or has the right of abode.

Passport (see p 70).

Certificate of entitlement A person who seeks to enter the UK and claims to have the right of abode proves that right by means of a certificate of entitlement issued by or on behalf of the government of the UK certifying that he has such a right of abode (1971 Act, s 3(9)(*b*) as amended by 1988 Act, s 3, and see *Minta v S of S* [1992] Imm AR 380). A statement in a UK passport that the holder of a passport has a right of abode can constitute a certificate of entitlement (*Wong* (5991)). A certificate of entitlement to the right of abode is invalid when it is issued on production of a forged passport (*Ex p Saira Begum* [1995] Imm AR 406).

A person who claims to be a British citizen because he was, on 31 December 1982, a CUKC with a right of abode under s 2(1)(*c*) or 2(2) of the 1971 Act as then in force, must, however, prove that he has the right of abode by producing the certificate of entitlement duly issued to him by a British government representative overseas or by the Home Office, unless he can meet the requirements of s 3(9) of the 1971 Act as amended.

A Commonwealth citizen who is not a British citizen but has a right of abode must prove that he has the right of abode by producing a certificate of entitlement duly issued to him by a British government representative overseas or by the Home Office (para 8).

As in the case of entry certificates, the queues for certificates of entitlement were very long. The problems caused by the length of queues in India were considered by the CA in *R v S of S, ex p Phansopkar* [1976] QB 606. The appellant was married to a patrial and wished to join him in the UK. The issue of certificates of entitlement was subject to a 14–21-month delay. She sought entry without one and was refused. On being detained she sought *habeas corpus* and judicial review of the decision. The CA granted these remedies and ordered the S of S to grant her application for a certificate of patriality in the UK as opposed to India. The court observed that patrials had the right to leave and enter the UK without let or hindrance subject only to the question of proof of patriality. That right could not be taken away by delaying the issue of the certificate without good cause. Since 1985 the queues in the Indian subcontinent have been divided into four groups, with those claiming the right of abode having the shortest time to wait.

The common travel area

15. The United Kingdom, the Channel Islands, the Isle of Man and the Republic of Ireland collectively form a common travel area. A person who has been examined for the purpose of immigration control at the point at which he entered the area does not normally require leave to enter any other part of it. However certain persons subject to the Immigration (Control of Entry through the Republic of Ireland) Order 1972 (as amended) who enter the United Kingdom through the Republic of Ireland do require leave to enter. This includes:
(i) those who merely passed through the Republic of Ireland;
(ii) persons requiring visas;
(iii) persons who entered the Republic of Ireland unlawfully;
(iv) persons who are subject to directions given by the Secretary of State for their exclusion from the United Kingdom on the ground that their exclusion is conducive to the public good;
(v) persons who entered the Republic from the United Kingdom and Islands after entering there unlawfully or overstaying their leave.

COMMENTARY

The 1971 Act establishes what is called the 'common travel area', defined above. A person who does not have leave to enter or remain in the UK does not benefit from this paragraph. A person who enters from the Republic of Ireland does not pass through immigration control. The Immigration (Control of Entry through the Republic of Ireland) Order 1972 provides, in art 4, that such a person may remain for a period of not more than three months from the date on which he entered the UK. A person entering the UK from the Republic of Ireland does not require, and is not given, leave by the order, but he is automatically put under a restriction as to the length of permitted stay; if he disregards that restriction, he will become an overstayer (*Tahira Kaya v S of S* [1991] Imm AR 572). The provision spells out the categories of person requiring leave to enter from the Republic, by means of an inclusive list. The absence of a category from that list will not render lawful an entry which was otherwise unlawful. A person who breaches a condition of his leave (that does not relate to the length of his stay) and then travels to the Republic does not require leave if he returns within his period of leave. Although agreements such as the Schengen Agreement exist and permit 'borderless' movement between a limited number of member states, it may be that in due course areas of free movement such as these will be declared unlawful if it can be shown that they may have the effect of undermining the internal market of the EU by creating unlawful differences in the quality of free movement between the member states.

Admission of certain British passport holders

16. A person in any of the following categories may be admitted freely to the United Kingdom on production of a United Kingdom passport issued in the United Kingdom and Islands or the Republic of Ireland prior to 1 January 1973, unless his passport has been endorsed to show that he was subject to immigration control:

(i)   a British Dependent Territories citizen;
(ii)   a British National (Overseas);
(iii) a British Overseas citizen;
(iv)   a British protected person;
(v)   a British subject by virtue of Section 30(a) of the British Nationality Act 1981 (who, immediately before the commencement of the 1981 Act, would have been a British subject not possessing citizenship of the United Kingdom and Colonies or the citizenship of any other Commonwealth country or territory).

17. British Overseas citizens who hold United Kingdom passports wherever issued and who satisfy the Immigration Officer that they have, since 1 March 1968, been given indefinite leave to enter or remain in the United Kingdom may be given indefinite leave to enter.

COMMENTARY

A BDTC, a BOC, a BNO, a BPP or a British subject by virtue of s 30(a) of the 1981 Act who holds a UK passport should be admitted freely on production of a British passport which was issued in the common travel area before 1 January 1973. He will not be admitted freely if the passport is endorsed to show that he is subject to immigration control. The effect of demanding the production of the passport issued before the introduction of the 1971 Act is that persons falling within this category must have the out-of-date passport with them on entering the UK, in addition to their current passport. The Home Office has indicated that only the production of the expired passport will establish the right not to be subjected to immigration control. BOCs who hold UK passports, whenever issued, and who satisfy the immigration officer that since 1 March 1968 they have been granted indefinite leave to enter or remain in the UK will be given indefinite leave to enter.

4   Returning residents

18. A person seeking leave to enter the United Kingdom as a returning resident may be admitted for settlement provided the Immigration Officer is satisfied that the person concerned:

(i)   had indefinite leave to enter or remain in the United Kingdom when he last left; and
(ii)   has not been away from the United Kingdom for more than 2 years; and
(iii) did not receive assistance from public funds towards the cost of leaving the United Kingdom; and
(iv)   now seeks admission for the purpose of settlement.

19. A person who does not benefit from the preceding paragraph by reason only of having been away from the United Kingdom too long may nevertheless be admit-ted as a returning resident if, for example, he has lived here for most of his life.

20. The leave of a person whose stay in the United Kingdom is subject to a time limit lapses on his going to a country or territory outside the common travel area. Such a person who returns after a temporary absence abroad within the period of this earlier leave has no claim to admission as a returning resident. His application to re-enter the United Kingdom should be considered in the light of all the relevant circumstances. The same time limit and any conditions attached will normally be reimposed if he meets the requirements of these Rules, unless he is seeking admission in a different capacity from the one in which he was last given leave to enter or remain.

COMMENTARY

Under the earlier immigration rules, HC 251, the following factors were considered:

(a) the length of the original residence in the UK of the person;

(b) the length of time that he had been out of the UK;

(c) the reasons for the absence exceeding two years; was it at the applicant's wish or through no fault of his own;

(d) the nature of any family ties in the UK, how close they are and the extent to which the person has maintained those family members during his absence from the UK;

(e) the purpose and intent of the person returning to the UK at the time he returned (it had to be at least for the purposes of settling in the UK);

(f) whether the person had a home in the UK, and if he was admitted to the UK, whether he intended to live in that home (see *Ex p Ademuyiwa* [1986] Imm AR 1, and *S of S v Agyen-Frempong* [1986] Imm AR 108).

The underlying principle of the earlier rule was that if a person could not establish that he had not been away from the UK for longer than two years, he had to show strong connections with the UK, by a combination of length of residence and family or other ties. Paragraph 19 permits the immigration officer to exercise his discretion about the readmission of a person. The only example it gives of a factor to be taken into account in the exercise of that discretion is that the person has lived in the UK for most of his life. Other factors may be taken into account, and the factors listed under the previous rules are all clearly relevant in determining whether a person is a resident primarily of the UK who is returning to settle here.

The returning resident must have been settled in the UK on the last occasion that he was in the UK. 'Settlement' (see Chapter 2) requires the applicant to be ordinarily resident (*ECO Bombay v Joshi* [1975] Imm AR 1) in the UK without any conditions attached to his stay and without having entered or remained in breach of the immigration laws (*Bashir v Immigration*

Officer, Dover [1976] Imm AR 96). A person with indefinite leave to remain may lose the right to settle under the provisions of the returning residents rule if he returned to the UK and was granted limited leave at any stage before making the application to enter as a returning resident. *S of S v Akinrujomu* [1988] Imm AR 590 was authority under the previous set of rules for the proposition that was incorporated into HC 395. Where a person enters the UK and is granted leave as a visitor for the purposes of a short visit he will not be able to rely on the returning residents rule thereafter.

The person entering must have a present intention to settle in the UK. Returning resident status must therefore be claimed on entry (echoing *R v IAT ex p Coomasaru* [1983] 1 WLR 14 under earlier rules). However, if a person seeks admission only as a visitor or as a student for a limited period, there is no obligation on an immigration officer to advise him of his right to be admitted for settlement (*Ex p Tolba* [1988] Imm AR 78). The status of returning resident does not extend to a person who has already returned in a different capacity (*Goodison v S of S* [1979–80] Imm AR 122, *R v IAT, ex p Aisha Khatoon Ali* [1979–80] Imm AR 195). It is a question of the entrant's current intentions. In this regard some guidance as to 'an intention to settle' may be had from Simon Brown J in *R v IAT, ex p Rafique* [1990] Imm AR 235, a 'primary purpose' case (see p 205), where he stated that if there is uncertainty about the duration of a person's stay, but a claim is made to enter for the purposes of marriage, it is proper to consider the application as an application for settlement as if ordinary residence is contemplated. If a person seeks entry as a returning resident, but expresses uncertainty about the duration of his stay, it would be appropriate similarly to consider him as intending ordinary residence sufficient for settlement. Where a person ordinarily resident in the UK returned within the two-year period to preserve his right to remain in the UK he sought admission for the purpose of settlement. That purpose encompassed the purpose of being able to remain ordinarily resident in the UK for the purposes of paras 18 and 19 (*Ex p Chugtai* [1995] Imm AR 559).

The addition of the words 'by reason only' in para 19 emphasises that the discretion in para 19 can be exercised only where the time condition alone is not fulfilled. There is no discretion where the applicant has indefinite leave to remain but leaves the UK, re-enters on a limited leave, and subsequently seeks to re-enter as a returning resident more than two years after his last departure while on indefinite leave (see *ECO Bombay v Noronha* [1995] Imm AR 341). Thus in *Bhajan Singh & Avtar Kaur* (11350) the appellants had settled in the UK, but had then returned to India. Much later, in 1992, they came to the UK as visitors. They then applied for leave to remain as returning residents. The husband had made another visit which placed him firmly outside the returning residents rule. The wife had indefinite leave to remain on her last stay in the UK. She was a visa national and therefore there was a mandatory requirement that she have prior entry clearance for the purpose for which she sought entry (as she was returning more than two years after her last visit). In the case of visa nationals the intention made known to the ECO before entry is the relevant intention.

5 Holders of restricted travel documents and passports

21. The leave to enter or remain in the United Kingdom of the holder of a passport or travel document whose permission to enter another country has to be exercised before a given date may be restricted so as to terminate at least two months before that date.

22. If his passport or travel document is endorsed with a restriction on the period for which he may remain outside his country of normal residence, his leave to enter or remain in the United Kingdom may be limited so as not to extend beyond the period of authorised absence.

23. The holder of a travel document issued by the Home Office should not be given leave to enter or remain for a period extending beyond the validity of that document. This paragraph and paragraphs 21–22 do not apply to a person who is eligible for admission for settlement or to a spouse who is eligible for admission under paragraph 282 or to a person who qualifies for the removal of the time limit on his stay.

COMMENTARY

Under earlier immigration rules a person could be refused entry on the grounds that he would not be admitted to his country of normal residence if he stayed more than a certain period. HC 395 retains that power where the person holds a document which requires entry to another country in less than two months. Otherwise the current rule merely permits a limitation on the leave which can be granted. Under para 282 a person seeking leave to enter the UK as the spouse of a person present and settled in the UK, or who is being admitted on the same occasion for settlement, may be admitted for an initial period of up to 12 months. Such a person must have an entry clearance for this purpose. In such a case, the fact that his travel documents may indicate that his permission to enter another country has to be exercised before a certain date does not permit the S of S to terminate his leave at least two months before that date. Further, if his passport permits him to remain outside his country of normal residence only for a limited period, his leave cannot be limited so as not to extend beyond the period of the absence authorised by his country of normal residence.

6 Entry clearance

24. A visa national and any other person who is seeking entry for a purpose for which prior entry clearance is required under these Rules must produce to the Immigration Officer a valid passport or other identity document endorsed with a United Kingdom entry clearance issued to him for the purpose for which he seeks entry. Such a person will be refused leave to enter if he has no such current entry clearance. Any other person who wishes to ascertain in advance whether he is eligible for admission to the United Kingdom may apply for the issue of an entry clearance.

25. Entry clearance takes the form of a visa (for visa nationals) or an entry certificate (for non-visa nationals). These documents are to be taken as evidence of the holder's eligibility for entry into the United Kingdom, and accordingly accepted as 'entry clearances' within the meaning of the Immigration Act 1971.

26. An application for entry clearance will be considered in accordance with the provisions in these Rules governing the grant or refusal of leave to enter. Where appropriate, the term 'Entry Clearance Officer' should be substituted for 'Immigration Officer'.

27. An application for entry clearance is to be decided in the light of the circumstances existing at the time of the decision, except that an applicant will not be refused an entry clearance where entry is sought in one of the categories contained in paragraphs 296–316 solely on account of his attaining the age of 18 years between receipt of his application and the date of the decision on it.

28. An applicant for an entry clearance must be outside the United Kingdom and Islands at the time of the application. An applicant for an entry clearance who is seeking entry as a visitor must apply to a post designated by the Secretary of State to accept applications for entry clearance for that purpose and from that category of applicant. Any other application must be made to the post in the country or territory where the applicant is living which has been designated by the Secretary of State to accept applications for entry clearance for that purpose and from that category of applicant. Where there is no such post the applicant must apply to the appropriate designated post outside the country or territory where he is living.

29. For the purposes of paragraph 28 'post' means a British Diplomatic Mission, British Consular post or the office of any person outside the United Kingdom and Islands who has been authorised by the Secretary of State to accept applications for entry clearance. A list of designated posts is published by the Foreign and Commonwealth Office.

30. An application for an entry clearance is not made until any fee required to be paid under the Consular Fees Act 1980 (including any Articles or Orders made under that Act) has been paid.

30A. An entry clearance may be revoked if the Entry Clearance Officer is satisfied that:

(i)   whether or not to the holder's knowledge, false representations were employed or material facts were not disclosed, either in writing or orally, for the purpose of obtaining the entry clearance; or

(ii)   a change of circumstances since the entry clearance was issued has removed the basis of the holder's claim to be admitted to the United Kingdom, except where the change of circumstances amounts solely to his exceeding the age for entry in one of the categories contained in paragraphs 296–316 of these Rules since the issue of the entry clearance; or

(iii) the holder's exclusion from the United Kingdom would be conducive to the public good.

COMMENTARY

Paragraph 30A was inserted from 1 November 1996. The term 'entry clearance' is defined in s 33(1) of the 1971 Act. Entry clearances are visas, entry certificates (for non-visa Commonwealth citizens) or other documents which, in accordance with the immigration rules, are to be taken as evidence or the requisite evidence of a person's eligibility for entry into the UK, although he is not a British citizen. Other documents may not be treated as such evidence of eligibility to enter (see *R v S of S, ex p Balogun* [1989] Imm AR 603). Documents such as work permits (s 33(1)) or special quota vouchers (*Amin v ECO Bombay* [1983] 2 All ER 864) are not entry clearances. A previous leave stamp is not the equivalent of an entry clearance (*R v Immigration Officer, ex p Valentine Oyo* [1995] Imm AR 553). A stamp on a passport showing an earlier leave to remain, which has not expired but has lapsed by reason of the applicant's intervening departure, is not an entry clearance (*R v S of S, ex p Oyeleye* [1994] Imm AR 268 and *Ex p Katoorah* [1996] Imm AR 482.) 'Visa exempt' stamps issued under s 3(3)(*b*) of the 1971 Act are not entry clearances. They are no longer issued, but they are in any event merely a declaration of the provision of the immigration rules that in certain circumstances citizens of some countries do not require visas. They do not confer any greater rights than were granted to the bearer at the time the extension of his leave is granted (*Balogun* (above)).

Entry clearance officers are not mentioned in the 1971 Act, but no significance has been attached to that omission (*R v S of S, ex p Ounejma* [1989] Imm AR 75). HC 359 makes clear that the term 'Entry Clearance Officer' should be substituted for 'Immigration Officer' in the rules governing the grant of leave to enter, as these govern the grant of entry clearance.

An application for an entry clearance is not considered to have been made until all the appropriate fees have been paid (para 30).

An application for entry clearance need not be made in any prescribed form, but there must be a request in quite unambiguous terms for entry clearance to be issued to a particular person (*Prajapati v IAT* [1982] Imm AR 56). A letter from a solicitor stating 'we would be grateful if you would review our client's case and authorise the Entry Clearance Officer to grant entry clearance' was held by Kennedy J not to constitute an application, in *R v IAT, ex p Jaifor Ali* [1990] Imm AR 531. He held that an application had to follow a prescribed form. *Prajapati* was not cited to him. In *Banjoko* (12427), however, the IAT, considering *Prajapati*, held that a request made to the Home Office to permit the appellant to remain in the UK so that she could 'stay and grow up with the rest of her family', was not an application, actual or implied, for settlement.

Visa nationals   Nationals of certain countries are required to produce to the immigration officer a passport or other identity document endorsed with a UK visa issued for the purpose for which the individual seeks entry. Such nationals, known as 'visa nationals', may be either foreign nationals, or Commonwealth citizens specified in the Appendix to HC 395; see p 541. They must produce to the immigration officer a passport or other identity document endorsed with a UK entry clearance issued for the purpose for which they seek entry. They must be refused leave to enter if they have no such current entry clearance. Holders of refugee travel documents issued under the 1951 Convention relating to the Status of Refugees by countries who signed the Council of Europe Agreement of 1959 on the Abolition of Visas for Refugees do not need visas if they are visiting the UK for three months or less. Paragraph 2 of the Appendix to the rules exempts such persons from the requirement of a visa. There is no discretion to grant leave to enter to a visa national if he does not have a current visa (*Walid* (1662)). A visa national needs a visa even if he is a transit passenger (*Immigration Officer, Heathrow v Yuvraj Kapoor* [1991] Imm AR 357). Where an EEA national is accompanied by a non-EU family member, the family member may be required to show a visa (art 3(2), Directive EC 68/360; see p 300). Every facility must be provided to such a person to enable him to obtain the necessary visa, and impediments put in the way of such a family member, such as a requirement that the visa be obtained in the country of the person's origin, are a breach of the directive. Such a non-EU family member will also need a family permit under the EEA Order (see p 335).

Paragraph 30A represents a substantial increase in the powers of ECOs. It is not clear that such revocation carries a right of appeal under s 13 of the 1971 Act. If it does not, the only remedy is by judicial review.

7   Variation of leave to enter or remain

31. Under Section 3(3) of the 1971 Act a limited leave to enter or remain in the United Kingdom may be varied by extending or restricting its duration, by adding, varying or revoking conditions or by removing the time limit (whereupon any condition attached to the leave ceases to apply). When leave to enter or remain is varied an entry is to be made in the applicant's passport or travel document (and his registration certificate where appropriate) or the decision may be made known in writing in some other appropriate way.

32. After admission to the United Kingdom any application for an extension of the time limit on or variation of conditions attached to a person's stay in the United Kingdom must be made to the Home Office before the applicant's current leave to enter or remain expires.

33. Where the application is in respect of employment for which a work permit or a permit for training or work experience is required or is in respect of the spouse or child of a person who is making such an application, the application should be made direct to the Department of Employment Overseas Labour Service.

With the exception of applications made under paragraph 33 (work permits), paragraphs 255 to 257 (EEA nationals) and Part 11 (asylum), all applications for variation of leave to enter or remain must be made using the form prescribed for the purpose by the Secretary of State, which must be completed in the manner required by the form and be accompanied by the documents and photographs specified in the form. An applicant for such a variation made in any other way is not valid.

COMMENTARY

For an application for variation of leave to be made for the purposes of the 1971 Act, the applicant must prove not only that he sent it that the Home Office received the application (*S of S v Peters* [1993] Imm AR 187). The question of whether an application is an application for a variation of leave to remain is a question of fact, incomplete applications being relevant to that question (*Soyemi v S of S* [1989] Imm AR 564). Merely sending a passport without any covering letter will not generally be sufficient to qualify as an application for a variation of leave (*Elu v S of S* [1989] Imm AR 568 and *Ex p Ijitoye*, 21 November 1995, CA (cf *Adepoju* (12573) (IAT) and *Ex p Oyeleye* [1994] Imm AR 268 (QBD), *contra* and not cited in *Ijitoye*). The application must not be too vague: it must be reasonably clear that the communication is an application for leave (*Dial v S of S* [1987] Imm AR 36). The application must be in unambiguous terms (*Prajapati v IAT* [1982] Imm AR 56), but if the Home Office acts upon the sending of a passport, it will be difficult for it to argue that no application has been made (see *Soyemi*). The application must be made to the correct S of S. Unless the rules indicate otherwise, as in the case of applications for extensions of work permits, which are made to the Department of Education and Employment, the correct S of S will be the S of S for the Home Department. No valid application will be made if an application is sent to another department (*Naved Masud v IAT* [1992] Imm AR 129).

An attempt was made to require all applications for extension or variation of leave made on or after 3 June 1996 to be on standard application forms, but the measure introducing them was declared *ultra vires*. The position at the time of writing is that the S of S intends to re-introduce compulsory forms from 25 November 1996. They are available from a direct line telephone service, (0181) 760 2233. The forms will not apply to EEA nationals or asylum seekers. The effect of the successful introduction of these forms is unclear. The Home Office has, however, indicated that applications will be rejected as invalid on any of the following grounds:

- (*a*) the application has been made on the wrong form;
- (*b*) the applicant has failed to answer all the relevant questions, or to sign and date the form;
- (*c*) the applicant has failed to submit all relevant documents with the form;
- (*d*) the form is not as prescribed, or has been altered.

Applicants whose current leave is about to expire may submit their application forms in person at the Public Enquiry Office, where validity will be determined while they wait. Where the necessary information to support an application may take any substantial time to compile, therefore, applicants will be well advised to apply well before the expiry of their current leave in order to allow for possible rejection of their first attempt.

Extension of leave: the rule in Suthendran's case   There is one very important point to be borne in mind when applications for a variation of leave are made. This arises from the decisions of the CA and the HL in *R v IAT, ex p Subramaniam* [1977] QB 190 and in *Suthendran v IAT* [1977] AC 359. Applications must be made before the current leave, which it is sought to vary, expires. If this is not done, rights of appeal against refusal are lost (see also *R v IAT, ex p Bastiampillai* [1983] 2 All ER 844). The strictness of the decision in *Suthendran*'s case was mitigated by the operation of the Immigration (Variation of Leave) Order 1976 (SI 1976 No 1572).

In *Suthendran*'s case the majority of the HL, following *Subramaniam*, held that if an application for variation of leave is made after that leave expires, there is no right of appeal against refusal. Section 14(1) of the 1971 Act gives a right of appeal only to someone who has limited leave to remain. The majority also held that if an application is made before a person's leave expires, but it is not refused until after the expiration of leave, there is no right of appeal either (see also *R v IAT, ex p Bhanji* [1977] Imm AR 89, considered in *Halil v Davidson* [1979–80] Imm AR 164).

The 1976 Order provided that if an application for variation is made before leave expires but is dealt with after expiration, that person's leave is to continue until 28 days after the refusal of the variation. From 8 July 1989, where a person has applied for a variation of a current leave and withdraws that application, his leave must be extended for a period of 28 days after the withdrawal (Immigration (Variation of Leave) (Amendment) Order 1989 (SI 1989 No 1005)).

The date of the decision for the purposes of the 28-day period is either:

(a) the date on which notice of the decision is posted;

(b) the date on which the notice of the decision is otherwise served (art 3(3)).

The 1976 Order has been considered in several cases. In *S of S v Petrou* [1978] Imm AR 87 the IAT held that if a person's leave expires on a Sunday and an application for a variation is not made until the following Monday, that person is not protected by the provisions of the 1976 Order. However, an application for a variation of leave is to be deemed to be made on the date it is posted (*Lubetkin v S of S* [1979–80] Imm AR 162). So where an application was posted on the day leave expired, the applicant was protected by the 1976 order. This is a broad interpretation of the order, but a just one, in view of the delays which can be experienced in the postal system.

The position of a person who is enjoying extended leave under the operation of the order and makes a fresh application for an extension of leave on new grounds is complicated. The relevant principles have been summarised in *Moussavi v S of S* [1986] Imm AR 39:

(i) Article 3(1) of the order extends the duration of an applicant's leave when he makes an application during the currency of leave granted to him otherwise than by virtue of the order.

(ii) Such extension operates so that a further application made during the period of the extension will be made during the currency of leave.

(iii) By virtue of art 3(2)(*c*), the order does not apply to the further application so as to extend yet again the appellant's leave because of the further application.

(iv) In consequence of the decision in *Suthendran* and the non-extension of the appellant's leave because of the further application, a right of appeal against a refusal of the further application accrues only if that refusal is made during the extension of the leave operating by the order because of the first application.

(v) The extension of leave conferred by art 3(1) of the order terminates 28 days after an application which causes that extension to come into operation is withdrawn.

It is not possible for a person to extend his leave indefinitely by making successive applications for variation and consequent appeals. During the course of an extension under the variation of leave provisions, the conditions attached to the original grant of leave continue to be attached (*R v S of S, ex p Lapinid* [1984] 1 WLR 1269, *Rajendran v S of S* [1989] Imm AR 512 and *Ofoajoku v S of S* [1991] Imm AR 68).

The order does not apply where:

(a) the date of the decision is more than 28 days before the end of the period of leave;

(b) the leave expired before the order came into operation;

(c) there is no other concurrent period of leave save that granted by an operation of the order;

(d) the duration of a person's leave has been curtailed by the S of S under s 7(1) of the 1993 Act (art 3(2) as amended).

By art 4 (inserted by the Immigration (Variation of Leave) (Amendment) Order 1993 (SI 1993 No 1657)), where the duration of a person's leave has been extended by art 3, and the duration of his leave has been curtailed under s 7 of the 1993 Act, the extension has no effect after the date on which leave is curtailed.

Withdrawn applications for leave to remain in the United Kingdom

34. Where a person whose application for variation of leave to enter or remain is being considered requests the return of his passport for the purpose of travel outside the common travel area, the application for variation of leave shall, provided it has not already been determined, be treated as withdrawn as soon as the passport is returned in response to that request, and the provisions of the Immigration (Variation of Leave) Order 1976 (as amended) will apply.

COMMENTARY

On departure from the common travel area the limited leave held by an entrant lapses. The entrant must satisfy the authorities each time of his right to enter the UK (*Channo Bi* [1978] Imm AR 182, *Ghassemian v Home Office* [1989] Imm AR 42 and *Kuku v S of S* [1990] Imm AR 27). The S of S cannot be estopped from refusing entry on a second or subsequent occasion. If the applicant requests the return of his passport for the purposes of travel outside the common travel area, any application he has pending before the immigration service will be taken to be withdrawn (although the Home Office has no power unilaterally to cancel the application, see *Dungarwalla v S of S* [1989] Imm AR 476). Woolf LJ, in *Kuku*, thought that it would be desirable for the Home Office to issue documents dealing with the effects of leaving the common travel area during the currency of leave to remain. Stamps issued under s 3(3)(*b*) of the 1971 Act do not give rise to a legitimate expectation that the person whose passport bears the stamp will be readmitted if he leaves the common travel area and returns before the expiration of his leave (*S of S v Mowla* [1991] Imm AR 210). The stamps are merely an attempt to set out the effects of the 1971 Act (Sched 2, para 14); they do not grant any extra rights.

The leave of a person who withdraws his application for an extension will be extended for 28 days after the withdrawal, by the Immigration (Variation of Leave) Order 1976 (as amended). He will have 28 days in which to travel, but as soon as he leaves the common travel area, he must obtain fresh leave to re-enter whether or not he returns within that 28-day period. Leave also lapses when a person's application has been treated as withdrawn because his passport has been returned in response to his request for it.

8 Undertakings

35. A sponsor of a person seeking leave to enter or variation of leave to enter or remain in the United Kingdom may be asked to give an undertaking in writing to be responsible for that person's maintenance and accommodation for the period of any leave granted, including any further variation. Under the Social Security Administration Act 1992 and the Social Security Administration (Northern Ireland) Act 1992, the Department of Social Security or, as the case may be, the Department of Health and Social Services in Northern Ireland may seek to recover from the person giving such an undertaking any income support paid to meet the needs of the person in respect of whom the undertaking has been given.

COMMENTARY

A relative or friend of an applicant for variation of leave may be asked to give an undertaking to be responsible for that person's maintenance and accommodation. Under the Social Security Act 1986 or the Social Security (Northern Ireland) Order 1986, the Department of Social Security, or the Department of Health and Social Services in Northern Ireland, may recover from the person who gave the undertaking any income support subsequently paid to the applicant. The undertaking must be written before such enforcement action can be taken against the relative or friend. The Social Security (Persons from Abroad) Miscellaneous Amendments Articles 1996 (SI 1996 No 30) withdrew entitlement to income support, housing benefit and council tax benefit from persons living in the UK in respect of whom such an undertaking has been signed. The prohibition lasts for five years or until the sponsored person has come to the UK, whichever is the longer period.

9 Medical examination

36. A person who intends to remain in the United Kingdom for more than 6 months should normally be referred to the Medical Inspector for examination. If he produces a medical certificate he should be advised to hand it to the Medical Inspector. Any person seeking entry who mentions health or medical treatment

as a reason for his visit, or who appears not to be in good mental or physical health, should also be referred to the Medical Inspector; and the Immigration Officer has discretion, which should be exercised sparingly, to refer for examination in any other case.

37. Where the Medical Inspector advises that a person seeking entry is suffering from a specified disease or condition which may interfere with his ability to support himself or his dependants, the Immigration Officer should take account of this, in conjunction with other factors, in deciding whether to admit that person. The Immigration Officer should also take account of the Medical Inspector's assessment of the likely course of treatment in deciding whether a person seeking entry for private medical treatment has sufficient means at his disposal.

38. A returning resident should not be refused leave to enter on medical grounds. But where a person would be refused leave to enter on medical grounds if he were not a returning resident, or in any case where it is decided on compassionate grounds not to exercise the power to refuse leave to enter, or in any other case where the Medical Inspector so recommends, the Immigration Officer should give the person concerned a notice requiring him to report to the Medical Officer of Environmental Health designated by the Medical Inspector with a view to further examination and any necessary treatment.

39. The Entry Clearance Officer has the same discretion as an Immigration Officer to refer applicants for entry clearance for medical examination and the same principles will apply to the decision whether or not to issue an entry clearance.

Students

39A. An application for a variation of leave to enter or remain made by a student who is sponsored by a government or international sponsorship agency may be refused if the sponsor has not given written consent to the proposed variation.

COMMENTARY

Under para 37, the role of the medical inspector is to advise whether a person seeking entry is suffering from a specified disease or condition which may interfere with his ability to support himself or his dependants. The immigration officer has discretion, on the basis of that advice, to admit the person.

A person who satisfies the rules relating to returning residents is not to be refused entry on medical grounds alone, but may be required to report to the Medical Officer of Environmental Health with a view to further examination and any necessary treatment.

Immigration officers are to refer EEA nationals (when they are exercising rights of free movement) to a medical inspector only if they show 'obvious signs of mental or physical ill-health'. They may be refused leave to enter only if the medical inspector certifies that they are suffering from one of the diseases listed in the annex to EC Directive 64/221. Similarly, members of the family of an EEA national may be refused leave to enter for medical reasons only if they are suffering from such a disease.

Paragraph 39A was added, by HC 329, with effect from 4 April 1996. The effect of this paragraph is that government sponsored students, or those sponsored by an international sponsorship agency, may be refused a variation if the sponsor has not given consent in writing to the proposed variation.

Chapter 7

Part 2: Visitors

Part 2 of the immigration rules deals with the general requirements applying to those who seek to enter or remain in the UK for six months or less, for any purpose not dealt with by another part of the rules (*Yi Fan Xu* [1993] Imm AR 519). It covers those in transit, and persons coming to the UK for private medical treatment and for the purpose of transacting business during their visits.

EEA nationals wishing to visit are not subject to the requirement of leave to enter when they are exercising an EEA right of free movement. Such persons may be subject to passport controls at the border (see *Flynn v S of S* [1995] Imm AR 594).

Visitors who wish to switch to another immigration category cannot switch to be a trainee or au pair, or to a working holiday. Only non-visa nationals may switch to being a student or a student nurse. Nationals of Hungary, Poland, Bulgaria, the Czech Republic, Romania and Slovakia, attempting to establish themselves in business may switch from being a visitor. Other visitors may not remain as investors or in the other temporary categories dealt with in the following chapters. Provision is made for prospective students to obtain a prospective student visa before travelling.

1 Leave to enter or remain

Requirements for leave to enter
40. For the purpose of paragraphs 41–46 a visitor includes a person living and working outside the United Kingdom who comes to the United Kingdom to transact business (such as attending meetings and briefings, fact finding, negotiating or making contracts with United Kingdom businesses to buy or sell goods or services). A visitor seeking leave to enter or remain for private medical treatment must meet the requirements of paragraphs 51 or 54.

41. The requirements to be met by a person seeking leave to enter the United Kingdom as a visitor are that he:
(i)   is genuinely seeking entry as a visitor for a limited period as stated by him, not exceeding 6 months; and
(ii) intends to leave the United Kingdom at the end of the period of the visit as stated by him; and

(iii) does not intend to take employment in the United Kingdom; and

(iv) does not intend to produce goods or provide services within the United Kingdom, including the selling of goods or services direct to members of the public; and

(v) does not intend to study at a maintained school; and

(vi) will maintain and accommodate himself and any dependants adequately out of resources available to him without recourse to public funds or taking employment; or will, with any dependants, be maintained and accommodated adequately by relatives or friends; and

(vii) can meet the cost of the return or onward journey.

Leave to enter as a visitor

42. A person seeking leave to enter the United Kingdom as a visitor may be admitted for a period not exceeding 6 months, subject to a condition prohibiting employment, provided the Immigration Officer is satisfied that each of the requirements of paragraph 41 is met.

Refusal of leave to enter as a visitor

43. Leave to enter as a visitor is to be refused if the Immigration Officer is not satisfied that each of the requirements of paragraph 41 is met.

COMMENTARY

For the general grounds for refusal of leave see Chapter 13.

From July 1993, visitors have no right of appeal against refusal of entry clearance (s 13(3A)(a), 1971 Act and see p 354). Many of the IAT decisions referred to below may be of assistance when contemplating judicial review of the ECO's decision. In *Ex p Nauranga Kaur* [1994] Imm AR 180, Schiemann J held that following the removal of the right of appeal from abroad such cases are not affected by the principle in *Ex p Swati* [1986] Imm AR 88 because there is no alternative appeal structure. However, he went on to say that because that case turned on the resolution of disputes of fact, judicial review is not an appropriate procedure (for a further discussion of this view see Chapter 22). Clearly, if this approach is correct, very few judicial review applications concerning refusal of visits will be successful. Where a visitor obtains entry clearance but is then refused entry there is a right of appeal provided that the visitor does not seek leave to enter for a period in excess of six months (see para 44 HC 395, and s 13(3)(c), 1971 Act as amended).

The requirements of para 41 are mandatory, and leave to enter is to be refused if they are not all met (para 43). They do not set out an exhaustive list of the purposes for which leave to enter as a visitor may be granted, nor do they provide any restriction on the kind of purpose which will suffice, beyond the specific prohibitions in subparas (iii), (iv) and (v). Leave to enter as a visitor may be granted for any legitimate temporary purpose provided it does not fall foul of any of those prohibitions.

2 'is genuinely seeking entry as a visitor for a limited period as stated by him not exceeding 6 months'

(a) Period of admission

A visitor and any dependants accompanying him will normally be given leave to enter for a period of six months, although the rules leave the period to the immigration officer's discretion. The applicant must state the length of the intended visit (see *ECO Nicosia v Georgiou* [1976] Imm AR 151), and the immigration officer must be satisfied that the applicant will genuinely seek entry for that period alone. The applicant must satisfy the immigration officer that he will be able to maintain and accommodate himself for that period. The immigration officer is not obliged to consider whether he could grant leave to enter for a period shorter than that stated by the applicant (*Immigration Officer, London (Heathrow) Airport v Schonenburger* [1975] Imm AR 7, and *Ex p Harnaik Singh* [1989] 2 All ER 867). The immigration officer may not refuse an application because the applicant is likely to apply for an extension of leave once admitted (*Ex p Arjumand* [1983] Imm AR 123). The immigration officer is entitled to consider whether the stated period for which leave is sought is the period for which the applicant genuinely seeks to be in the UK. However, if the entrant genuinely seeks entry for a shorter period, but there is a chance that his purposes may not be completed within that time and he will need to seek an extension, leave to enter should not be refused on that basis. In *Ah Chong Wong* (11979) the appellant had stayed for five months as a visitor and was then granted two years' leave as a working holiday maker. He then applied for a further three months' extension as a visitor. This was refused because the Home Office stated that 'any further extensions' would lead to more than six months as a visitor. If this was correct there would be no right of appeal. The IAT, however, held that there was a right of appeal because the Home Office could have considered a shorter extension of leave which would have kept the total within the original six months (cf *IAT ex p Sam* [1996] Imm AR 272). In *Chirenje v Immigration Officer, Heathrow* [1996] Imm AR 321, the CA held that where the period of entry sought is more than six months, leave to enter is not sought as a visitor.

(b) Purpose of visit

The only requirement is that the person genuinely seeks entry as a visitor. An immigration officer, when considering whether or not an applicant is a genuine visitor, takes into consideration the circumstances of the person seeking entry. Thus a person of means and position in his country of origin may well be accepted as a genuine visitor even if his declared intention is 'only to visit the maze at Hampton Court'. However, when a considerable sum of money is to be expended by a family with limited resources, the reasons for the expenditure will be scrutinised closely (*Manmohan Singh v ECO New Delhi* [1975] Imm AR 118). In *Gusai* (12037), the IAT held that a refusal on the basis of an intention not to leave, which was based on the behaviour of the appellant's brother, was unlawful. A refusal thus based on speculation and suspicion rather than evidence will be unlawful. In *Kokumo* (11503) the applicant had applied for two weeks' leave. On arrival she was, in accordance with the practice observed by immigration officers almost as a matter of course, granted six months' leave to enter. She stayed three months. It was this that caused the ECO to doubt her intentions. The IAT stated that it did not think that her staying longer than she originally said she wanted to stay amounted to a breach of trust, and her appeal against a later refusal of leave to enter was allowed.

A person who does not fall into the other categories in the immigration rules may seek entry as a visitor. Where an applicant has a wish to study if a place becomes available to him, that may be seen as an intention to study. Leave to enter as a visitor will be refused (*Ex p Brakwah* [1989] Imm AR 366). However, it is the *current* intention of the applicant which must be assessed (see *ECO Hong Kong v Lai* [1974] Imm AR 98). On the other hand, there is no category in the rules of persons visiting the UK 'for family reasons'. Such a visit may be permissible, depending on the substantive purpose of the visit. A visit for the purposes of maintaining family relationships while the applicant's children are being educated in the UK is to be dealt with under the rules governing visitors (*Sehan Kelada v S of S* [1991] Imm AR 400). In *Syad Riaz Ussain* (10037), the ECO refused a visitor's visa on the basis that the applicant's income was disproportionate to the cost of the journey. The IAT held that an applicant does not expect any other benefit from a visit than seeing his family. A person entering for the purposes of attending his own appeal will also be dealt with under the visitor rules (*Patel v ECO Bombay* [1991] Imm AR 273). It is, however, important to distinguish between, on the one hand, an application to visit with a view to assisting relatives in times of illness, or a mother with the care of her children so as to enable her to attend a course of training or study (*Hamilton v ECO Kingston, Jamaica* [1974] Imm AR 43, and *ECO Lagos v Samanda* [1975] Imm AR 16), which is acceptable; and on the other hand, an application to enter as a visitor to relieve the mother of the care of her children so that she can be gainfully employed (*Obeyesekere v S of S* [1976] Imm AR 16), which is not acceptable. An application for a work permit should have been made in this latter type of case (see also *ECO Manila v Magalso* [1993] Imm AR 293). Otherwise, the reasons for entry may be unimportant, or even frivolous.

Persons entering for private medical treatment must satisfy the conditions set out in para 51, and those seeking an extension of stay should satisfy the conditions in para 54 (see p 97). A person who is in the UK in any temporary capacity who seeks leave to remain to care for another person suffering from a terminal illness may be granted exceptional leave to remain for three months to make arrangements for the patient's care (see p 99 and the IND B Division instruction, 'Carers', BDI 2/95). A distinction is also drawn between persons entering to transact business as visitors and those seeking to establish themselves in the UK in business. The latter have to satisfy the conditions set out at paras 200–10.

Business visitors   A business visitor is a person based and employed outside the UK who comes to the UK to transact business (such as attending meetings and briefings, observing or checking facts and negotiating or making contracts with UK businesses to buy or sell goods or services), and who then leaves the UK.

Where a person bought an 'off-the-shelf' company and registered it to process goods, he was regarded as having ceased merely to transact business, and to be engaging in business (*Ex p Ayoola* [1992] Imm AR 170). In *Hossain v Immigration Officer, Heathrow* [1990] Imm AR 520, the IAT held that a person with a multiple visit stamp in his passport who set up a company in the UK, and was the driving force behind it, was engaged in business rather than merely transacting it on each of the visits he made on the stamp.

The rules are to be operated in accordance with established Home Office practice. Whether a visitor is engaging in business or merely transacting business is a matter of fact and degree. A person will be regarded as transacting business if he is attending meetings, signing contracts, arranging deals, or undertaking activities of a similar nature, and not taking a job which could be done by a resident worker or doing any 'productive work' (Home Office letter to ILPA in (1991) 5 INL&P No 1).

The Home Office has published the basic requirements used to identify a *bona fide* business visitor:

(1) The person should live and work abroad, and should not be attempting to base himself in the UK, even temporarily. The visit should therefore be short.

(2) He should continue to be paid by his overseas employer.

(3) He should not be providing a service to a UK firm, but his work should arise from his employment for the overseas employer.

(4) He must not do a job which might otherwise be taken by an EU worker and if his work entails a product of some kind (goods or services), it should at all times be produced abroad, otherwise he will be doing 'productive work'. Productive work means work which is capable of producing goods or services which have a monetary or exchange value, and can include attending a meeting if it involves preparing a report, collecting and analysing data, and making recommendations to the UK company.

The nature of the work to be done determines whether a visitor is transacting business or should seek entry under the rules relating to business persons. Thus a person providing a service for a fee would have to gain admission under the business rules, whereas a person attached temporarily to a UK company in an advisory capacity only would be admitted as a business visitor (see Anne Balcombe, *Business visitors: Home Office Practice* (1993) 7 INL&P 19).

3 'intends to leave the United Kingdom at the end of his visit'

The immigration officer must be satisfied that the applicant intends to leave the UK at the end of his visit (see *Swati v S of S* [1986] 1 WLR 4772). It is the applicant's intentions at the time of seeking leave to enter, not intentions no longer held by him, that are relevant (see *ECO Hong Kong v Lai* (above)). If there are doubts about the applicant's intention to leave the UK, leave to enter must be refused (see HC 395 para 43). The fact that a sponsor is willing to give an undertaking that the applicant will leave will not resolve those doubts (*ECO New Delhi v Kumar* [1978] Imm AR 185, but see *Ikiliagwu* (below)). However, unsuccessful applications to enter the UK may be taken into account in deciding whether the applicant will leave at the end of his visit, as may successful past visits.

Factors taken into account

Any factor may be considered. However, mere suspicion that a person will not return to his country at the end of his visit is not a sufficient ground for refusal of leave to enter (*R v Lympne Airport Chief Immigration Officer, ex p Amrik Singh* [1968] 3 All ER 163, and see *Gusai* (above)). Suspicions should be supported by tangible evidence (*Baig* (1886) and *Qaiser* (11502)). Thus, in *Bhagat Singh v ECO New Delhi* [1978] Imm AR 134 (IAT), the only matter which aroused suspicion about the intention of the applicant, a 74-year-old widower, was his reply to repeated questions as to whether he would apply to remain with his son; he said that he would see what the position was when he arrived and then he might apply. The ECO should, however, have weighed that factor against the fact that he was financially independent, that he had three brothers and sisters living in his home village, that he had returned from the UK previously, and that his health would suffer if he lived in a cold climate. Had he done so, he would not have found that the applicant was not a genuine visitor. In *Jawad* (12039), the appellant was refused entry clearance because the Jordan ECO was suspicious about the fact that he did not know the immigration status of one of his brothers in the UK. There was no evidence to suggest that the appellant should have known that his brother was allegedly seeking asylum. There was therefore no basis for the ECO to find that the application was not in good faith.

In the absence of any bad faith, the fact that the person is the holder of a UK passport issued outside the UK should not lead to the presumption that he would not leave at the end of the visit (*Mohammed Din v ECO Karachi* [1978] Imm AR 56), but it is a factor which may be taken into account among other factors (*Patel (MR) v ECO Bombay* [1978] Imm AR 154).

The mere lack of incentive to leave the UK at the end of the visit is an insufficient reason for not being satisfied that the applicant intends to leave the UK at the end of the visit (*Blair* (1797)). The so-called 'economic incentive' for an applicant to leave his country and 'better himself' in the UK may, though, be taken into account by immigration officers. In *ECO Colombo v Hanks* [1976] Imm AR 74, one applicant was granted an entry certificate to enable her to visit the UK, but her son and daughter were refused entry certificates. By reason of her age and the expectation that she would inherit a family house in her country of origin, the mother was said not to have the same incentive as her children to leave Sri Lanka permanently. The daughter's previous applications to enter the UK had failed, and she had applied to emigrate to Australia. The son had been practically unemployed save for casual work for a period of nearly four years. These matters were held to disclose a strong intention on their part not to return to Sri Lanka. On the other hand, the existence of an economic incentive cannot be assumed or given much weight. In *Osibarnowo* (12116), the appellant produced a forged Nigerian income tax certificate. In addition, her financial arrangements were very unclear. However, this was not sufficient, on the balance of probabilities, to indicate that she was not intending to leave at the end of her visit. The IAT, in *Qaiser* (11502), stated that it was 'spurious' for the ECO to suggest that there was no pressing reason for the visit, and granted an appeal against a decision based on the suspicion that a young single man would have no incentive to return to Pakistan. Clearly such decisions can be regarded as taking account of irrelevant factors, or as '*Wednesbury*' unreasonable (see Chapter 22).

In *Patel v ECO Bombay* [1973] Imm AR 30, an elderly widow was granted an entry certificate to visit her son, daughter and grandchildren. Various factors pointed to the genuine nature of the visit. It was cheaper for her to visit her relatives than the other way round. She had lived in India all her life, and spoke no English. She was of an age at which it was unlikely she would want to uproot herself and settle in a country with a different climate. She would not gain very much financially by coming to the UK, and she had a return air fare, paid for by her son who lived in India. He had saved for five years to pay for it.

The mere possession of a return air fare, on the other hand, is not by itself conclusive evidence that the passenger will leave the UK at the end of his stay (*Immigration Officer Birmingham v Mohammed Sadiq* [1978] Imm AR 115). Similarly the fact that a person has told lies on a past attempt to enter the UK should not be over-emphasised; it is the merit of the *current* claim that the immigration officer has to consider. Moreover, the fact that a person could qualify for settlement in the UK if he so wishes should not be given excess weight (see *Sodhi Singh* (12249)). In *Joga Singh* (10139), the IAT held that it was not justifiable to base an assessment of an applicant's credibility on this issue on a few discrepancies concerning the ages of his sponsor's children, when no weight is given to the fact that the applicant has previously visited the UK and returned to his own country after his visit. Refusal of entry clearance on this basis is likely to be unreasonable. The case has to be looked at as a whole, and all the factors must be considered. Thus in *Ikiliagwu* (11795), a 64-year-old grandmother lied that her sponsor's wife was pregnant (she was 55) in order to assist her application for a visit visa. The IAT found that the adjudicator had been correct in making positive findings on the credibility of the sponsor concerning the likelihood of the appellant's overstaying. The adjudicator was correct in finding that the appellant could not overstay without the active connivance of the sponsor and his wife, who would not countenance her doing so. In those circumstances it was reasonable to take account of the involvement of the sponsor in determining the likelihood of the appellant's overstaying.

Persons of limited means, without substantial positions, may have more difficulty in persuading an immigration officer that they have a real intention to leave at the end of their stay (*Manmohan Singh* (above)). The presence of relatives in the home country, and evidence that the applicant is or will be employed in that country, are other factors taken as a guide to whether the applicant will leave (*Huda v ECO Dacca* [1976] Imm AR 109). The undertaking of a person to maintain and accommodate a person of limited means may assist in removing the suspicion that he will not leave at the end of the visit.

Refusal to answer questions put by the ECO or immigration officers, for example in relation to family details, gives reasonable grounds for the immigration officer not to be satisfied that the applicant intends to leave at the end of the proposed visit (*Immigration Officer Birmingham v Mohammad Sadiq* [1978] Imm AR 115, and *Abid Hussain v ECO Islamabad* [1989] Imm AR 46). An accumulation of suspicious matters may justify refusal (*In Re Olusanya (Olugbenga)* [1988] Imm AR 117). However, even in cases of persons of limited means, the issue will be whether there is a genuine intention to seek entry as a visitor in compliance with the rules. Advisors should ensure that an applicant provides detailed, preferably documentary, evidence on the state of his finances and their circumstances. In *Manjit Singh* (12235), 18 items of evidence on these points were supplied, which, if considered properly, showed that on the balance of probabilities the appellant was seeking entry as a visitor.

4   'does not intend to take employment in the United Kingdom'

Paragraph 6 defines 'employment' as including paid and unpaid employment, self-employment and engaging in any business or any professional activity, unless a contrary intention appears in rules. Visitors must not intend to engage in any of those activities. If the applicant intends to take employment, whether paid or unpaid, or to engage in business or professional activity, leave to enter as a visitor will be inappropriate, and the requirements relating to those seeking to enter for employment or to engage in business or professional activity should be satisfied (see p 165). Entry will be refused if the applicant comes to the UK with the definite purpose of seeking employment, even if that purpose is secondary to the main purpose of the visit (*Baldachino v S of S* [1972] Imm AR 14).

An employer who employs a person subject to immigration control, aged 16 or over, is guilty of an offence if the following conditions apply:

(*a*) the employee has not been granted leave to enter the UK, or to remain in the UK; or

(*b*) the employee's leave is not valid and subsisting, or it is subject to a
        condition precluding him from taking up employment (s 8(1), 1996
        Act)

Further conditions may be made by order. None have been made yet, and
there is no date for this section to come into force. For further discussion see
Chapter 27, but note that there is a restricted definition of 'employment' for
the purposes of this criminal offence. It is committed only where there is a
contract of employment, which is defined in s 8(8) as a contract of service or
apprenticeship, whether express or implied, and, if it is express, whether it is
oral or written. Thus contracts for services or casual contracts, and
independent contractors, are outside the definition of 'employment' in s 8(8),
which is the same as under the Employment Rights Act 1996.

The test for a contract of employment for tax and employment law pur-
poses is to be found in a line of cases derived from *Ready Mixed Concrete
(South East) Ltd v Minister of Pensions & National Insurance* [1968] 1
All ER 433, among others;

A contract of service exists if the following three conditions are fulfilled:

(*a*) the servant agrees that in consideration of a wage or other
        remuneration he will provide his own work and skill in the
        performance of some service for his master;
(*b*) He agrees, expressly or impliedly, that in the performance of that
        service he will be subject to the other's control in a sufficient degree
        to make that other master;
(*c*) the other provisions of the contract are consistent with its being a
        contract of service.

An obligation to do work subject to the other party's control is a necessary,
though not always a sufficient, condition of a contract of service. In this
context 'control' means the lawful authority to command (*Zuijus v Wirth
Brothers Pty Ltd* (1955) 93 CLR 561). Freedom to do a job either by one's
own hands or another's is inconsistent with a contract of service, though a
limited or occasional power of delegation may not be. Cooke J, in *Market
Investigations Ltd v Minister of Social Security* [1968] 3 All ER 732 (a case
concerning part-time interviewers for a market research organisation), stated:

> ... the fundamental test to be applied is this: 'Is the person who has engaged
> himself to perform these services performing them as a person in business on his
> own account?'. If the answer to that question is 'Yes', then the contract is a
> contract for services. If the answer is 'No' then the contract is a contract of
> service. No exhaustive list has been compiled and perhaps no exhaustive list can
> be compiled of considerations which are relevant in determining that question,
> nor can strict rules be laid down as to the relative weight which the various
> considerations should carry in particular cases. (at p 737).

In *O'Kelly v Trusthouse Forte plc* [1983] IRLR 369, the CA upheld an
industrial tribunal's decision that the nature of the employment relationship
required a mutuality of obligation between the parties. In a contract of

service, the employee was under a continuing obligation not just to do the work given to him but to take work when it was offered by the employer. An employer under a contract of service was bound not just to pay for work done, but also to continue to make work available. In that case, casual employees taken on by a hotel for functions as regular casuals were held to be self-employed.

Applying these tests to the definition of 'contract of employment' in s 8(8) of the 1996 Act, it is difficult to see that many convictions could be secured. Further, the burden of proving that there was a contract of employment will be on the prosecution, and the standard is that the existence of a contract of employment should be proved beyond a reasonable doubt. For the employer's defence see Chapter 27.

5   'will maintain and accommodate himself and any dependants out of the resources available to him, without working or recourse to public funds'

'Public funds' means (see para 6):
   (a) housing under Part II or III of the Housing Act 1985, Part I or II of the Housing (Scotland) Act 1987, Part II of the Housing (Northern Ireland) Order 1981 or Part II of the Housing (Northern Ireland) Order 1988;
   (b) attendance allowance, severe disablement allowance, invalid care allowance and disability living allowance under Part III, income support, family credit, council tax benefit, disability working allowance and housing benefit under Part VII and child benefit under Part IX of the Social Security Contribution and Benefits Act 1992;
   (c) attendance allowance, severe disablement allowance, invalid care allowance and disability living allowance under Part III, income support, family credit, disability working allowance, housing benefit under Part VII and child benefit under Part IX of the Social Security Contributions and Benefits (Northern Ireland) Act 1992; and
   (d) income-based jobseeker's allowance under the Jobseekers Act 1995.
A relative or friend may be asked to give an undertaking in writing to be responsible for the person's maintenance and accommodation for the period of any leave granted, including any variation (para 35, see p 79). They are rarely sought in practice, but any income support paid to an entrant may be recovered from the person giving the undertaking. If the relative or other sponsor of a person seeking entry to the UK refuses to give, when requested to do so, an undertaking in writing to be responsible for that person's maintenance and accommodation for the period of leave granted, leave may be refused to the person seeking entry on the ground that he cannot maintain himself without recourse to public funds (HC 395, para 35). The phrase 'available to him' should include monies other than the applicant's own. In HC 251, the rule relating to business persons joining UK businesses required

the applicant to show that he would be bringing money 'of his own'. No similar requirement is contained in this rule.

Where the immigration officer is not satisfied as to the above, leave to enter as a visitor must be refused under the immigration rules (para 43).

6 Extensions of stay

Requirements for an extension of stay as a visitor

44. Six months is the maximum permitted leave which may be granted to a visitor. The requirements for an extension of stay as a visitor are that the applicant:
(i)   meets the requirements of paragraph 41(ii)–(vii); and
(ii) has not already spent, or would not as a result of an extension of stay spend, more than 6 months in total in the United Kingdom as a visitor.
Any period spent as a seasonal agricultural worker is to be counted as a period spent as a visitor.

Extension of stay as a visitor

45. An extension of stay as a visitor may be granted, subject to a condition prohibiting employment, provided the Secretary of State is satisfied that each of the requirements of paragraph 44 is met.

Refusal of extension of stay as a visitor

46. An extension of stay as a visitor is to be refused if the Secretary of State is not satisfied that each of the requirements of paragraph 44 is met.

COMMENTARY

An applicant for an extension of leave may appeal against refusal of the extension if the extension applied for would have resulted in the total period of leave not exceeding six months (ss 14(1) and 2(A)(c), 1971 Act as amended).

A person seeking an extension of leave to remain as a visitor must satisfy the immigration officer that he intends to leave the UK at the end of his visit, and that he does not intend to take paid or unpaid employment or engage in business or professional activity. He must also satisfy the immigration officer that he will maintain and accommodate himself and any dependants out of the resources available to him, without working or recourse to public funds. He must show that he can meet the cost of his return or onward journey. Once the applicant has been admitted, any application for an extension must be considered under these paragraphs. The aggregate stay may not exceed six months (para 44). However, where an application is made for a period which would bring the aggregate to more than six months, it may be treated as an application for an extension for the remainder of the six-month period if it relates to some specific event, such as seeing the Christmas lights (*S of S v Riaz* [1987] Imm AR 88). It is not necessary for the applicant to specify a further limited period, as he is not required to satisfy para 41(i), although he would be well advised to specify such a period so as to satisfy the immigration officer that he intends to leave the UK at the end of the visit. The application must be refused if the result of an extension would be that the aggregate period of the visit exceeds six months. Extensions may be granted to non-visa nationals to remain in some other temporary capacity, such as a student or working holiday maker, or on marriage, or as a dependant (*Nisa v S of S* [1979–80] Imm AR 20).

The Home Office has issued instructions (BDI 2/95) for immigration officers considering applications from persons in the UK for temporary purposes for leave to remain to care for a friend or relative who is ill or disabled. In such cases leave will normally be restricted to a period of three months, on the understanding that if longer term care is needed the applicant will arrange for its provision by a person who does not require leave to remain. Leave to remain to care for a friend will normally be refused, except in emergencies; and will be extended beyond three months only in 'wholly exceptional' circumstances.

7   Visitors in transit

Requirements for admission as a visitor in transit to another country
47. The requirements to be met by a person (not being a member of the crew of a ship, aircraft, hovercraft, hydrofoil or train) seeking leave to enter the United Kingdom as a visitor in transit to another country are that he:
(i)   is in transit to a country outside the common travel area; and
(ii)   has both the means and the intention of proceeding at once to another country; and
(iii) is assured of entry there; and
(iv)   intends and is able to leave the United Kingdom within 48 hours.

Leave to enter as a visitor in transit
48. A person seeking leave to enter the United Kingdom as a visitor in transit may be admitted for a period not exceeding 48 hours with a prohibition on employment provided the Immigration Officer is satisfied that each of the requirements of paragraph 47 is met.

Refusal of leave to enter as a visitor in transit
49. Leave to enter as a visitor in transit is to be refused if the Immigration Officer is not satisfied that each of the requirements of paragraph 47 is met.

Extension of stay as a visitor in transit
50. The maximum permitted leave which may be granted to a visitor in transit is 48 hours. An application for an extension of stay beyond 48 hours from a person admitted in this category is to be refused.

COMMENTARY

The S of S made orders under s 1A(2)(*a*) of the Immigration (Carriers' Liability) Act 1987 requiring that citizens of Afghanistan, Iran, Iraq, Lebanon, Libya, Somalia, Sri Lanka, Turkey, Uganda, and Zaire have transit visas for all entries to the UK. Other visa nationals require them only if there are more than 24 hours between their arrival and departure flights (The Immigration (Transit Visa) Order 1993, SI 1993 No 1678). The list is amended from time to time. Most recently, the Immigration (Transit Visa) (Amendment) Order 1996 (SI 1996 No 2065), made under the Immigration

(Carriers' Liability) Act 1987, s 1A(1), (2), and in force from 1 September 1996, amended the transit visa list by adding Eritrea and Ethiopia. The complete list is now Afghanistan, the People's Republic of China, Eritrea, Ethiopia, Ghana, Iran, Iraq, Libya, Nigeria, Somalia, Sri Lanka, Turkey, Uganda and Zaire.

If he does not leave the transit lounge, a transit passenger will be deemed not to have entered the UK (1971 Act, s 11). A transit visitor must have the means and the intention of proceeding at once to another country. 'Means' is not confined to financial means. Where no airline will carry a transit passenger, he does not have the means of proceeding to another country (*R v S of S, ex p Caunhye* (1988) *The Independent*, 20 April).

A visa national in transit to another country requires a current visa in order to be given leave to enter the UK (*Immigration Officer, Heathrow v Yuvraj Kapoor* [1991] Imm AR 357).

A person who is granted leave to enter as a transit visitor should have the appropriate stamp in his passport. If he does not, it should be assumed that he has been granted leave to enter as a visitor (see *Fui-Chun Low v S of S* [1995] Imm AR 435).

8   Private medical treatment

Requirements for leave to enter as a visitor for private medical treatment
51. The requirements to be met by a person seeking leave to enter the United Kingdom as a visitor for private medical treatment are that he:
(i)   meets the requirements set out in paragraph 41(iii)–(vii) for entry as a visitor; and
(ii)   in the case of a person suffering from a communicable disease, has satisfied the Medical Inspector that there is no danger to public health; and
(iii) can show, if required to do so, that any proposed course of treatment is of finite duration; and
(iv)   intends to leave the United Kingdom at the end of his treatment; and
(v)   can produce satisfactory evidence, if required to do so, of:
    (a)   the medical condition requiring consultation or treatment; and
    (b)   satisfactory arrangements for the necessary consultation or treatment at his own expense; and
    (c)   the estimated costs of such consultation or treatment; and
    (d)   the likely duration of his visit; and
    (e)   sufficient funds available to him in the United Kingdom to meet the estimated costs and his undertaking to do so.

Leave to enter as a visitor for private medical treatment
52. A person seeking leave to enter the United Kingdom as a visitor for private medical treatment may be admitted for a period not exceeding 6 months, subject to a condition prohibiting employment, provided the Immigration Officer is satisfied that each of the requirements of paragraph 51 is met.

Refusal of leave to enter as a visitor for private medical treatment
53. Leave to enter as a visitor for private medical treatment is to be refused if the Immigration Officer is not satisfied that each of the requirements of paragraph 51 is met.

COMMENTARY

There is no requirement in the immigration rules that the visitor be genuinely seeking to enter for a period not in excess of a specified period, such as six months, where a visitor's purpose in seeking entry is to obtain private medical treatment. This is because the private medical visitor does not have to satisfy the requirements of para 41(i) (see p 83).

For the general grounds for refusal see Chapter 13. The IND has instructed immigration officers that the fact that a person is HIV positive or has AIDS is not a ground for refusing (or sufficient by itself for granting) entry clearance or leave to remain if the person otherwise qualifies under the immigration rules (see IND B Division Instruction BDI 3/95—*AIDS and HIV Positive cases*, p 98 below). Refusal of leave to enter is mandatory if the immigration officer is not satisfied about any one of the conditions specified in para 51 (para 53).

The evidential requirements of para 51(v) should be noted when making any application. The applicant must not intend to take paid or unpaid employment or engage in business or professional activity. He must maintain and accommodate himself and any dependants out of the resources available to him, without taking work and without recourse to public funds. He must not intend to study at a maintained school. He must be able to meet the cost of the return or onward journey. It is not necessary for the applicant to show that he can meet the cost of his medical treatment out of personal funds (*Foon v S of S* [1983] Imm AR 29), but he must be able to show that he can meet the cost of the treatment from funds which are available to him. The availability of treatment in the person's country is not a ground for refusal of entry (*Mohan* [1973] Imm AR 9).

The likely costs of the treatment are assessed by the medical inspector, and the immigration officer is obliged to take account of that assessment when considering whether the applicant's means are adequate (para 37). The length of the visit sought before or on entry may exceed six months. However, initially the applicant is likely to receive six months' leave to enter (para 52). After entry, if further medical treatment is necessary, an extension may be sought. A person seeking entry for the purposes of private medical treatment need not show that he intends to leave the UK at the end of the period stated by him for his visit. He must, however, show that he intends to leave the UK at the end of his course of treatment. He does not have to be precise about the length of his visit (see *Foon* (above), and *Onofriou* (2704)). However, treatment must be of finite duration, so an applicant must have some information on the likely duration of his treatment. It is not clear from the rule whether a provisional duration is sufficient for this requirement. In practice, a provisional duration should suffice. During the first six months the applicant may receive treatment from a general practitioner, or practitioner of alternative medicine. However, he will require the support of an NHS consultant to obtain an extension (see para 54).

Extension of stay

Requirements for an extension of stay as a visitor for private medical treatment

54. The requirements for an extension of stay as a visitor to undergo or continue private medical treatment are that the applicant:

(i) meets the requirements set out in paragraph 41(iii)–(vii) and paragraph 51(ii)–(v); and

(ii) has produced evidence from a registered medical practitioner who holds an NHS consultant post of satisfactory arrangements for private medical consultation or treatment and its likely duration; and, where treatment has already begun, evidence as to its progress; and

(iii) can show that he has met, out of the resources available to him, any costs and expenses incurred in relation to his treatment in the United Kingdom; and

(iv) has sufficient funds available to him in the United Kingdom to meet the likely costs of his treatment and intends to meet those costs.

Extension of stay as a visitor for private medical treatment

55. An extension of stay to undergo or continue private medical treatment may be granted, with a prohibition on employment, provided the Secretary of State is satisfied that each of the requirements of paragraph 54 is met.

Refusal of extension of stay as a visitor for private medical treatment

56. An extension of stay as a visitor to undergo or continue private medical treatment is to be refused if the Secretary of State is not satisfied that each of the requirements of paragraph 54 is met.

COMMENTARY

There is no requirement in the immigration rules that a visit for private medical treatment should not exceed any specified time. Therefore, a person refused an extension may appeal under s 14 of the 1971 Act, even though the duration of the visit will exceed six months.

HC 395 introduced a restriction on the scope of the rule relating to extensions of leave to remain by a person undergoing private medical treatment. An application for an extension of stay for medical treatment must now be supported by a registered medical practitioner who holds an NHS consultant post. A person seeking an extension of leave for the purposes of private medical treatment must not intend to take paid or unpaid employment or engage in business or professional activity. He must maintain and accommodate himself and any dependants out of the resources available to him, without taking work and without recourse to public funds (see p 60). He must be able to meet the cost of the return or onward journey. If the medical disorder is a communicable disease he must have satisfied the medical inspector that there is no danger to public health. He must be able to show the course of treatment he is to undergo is of finite duration. It is unlikely that an extension will be granted 'until treatment is concluded' where there is no known date for that event (*Hyrapiet* (2232)).

The rule provides for the granting of an extension of stay for private medical treatment at the discretion of the S of S. The discretion will not be exercised if:

(a) the applicant does not produce evidence from a registered medical practitioner who holds an NHS consultant post of satisfactory arrangements for private medical consultations or treatment and its likely duration. Where treatment has begun, he must also give evidence of its progress;

(b) there is reason to believe that the treatment would be at the public expense.

The S of S may, in the exercise of his discretion, take account of the fact that the treatment is available in the applicant's country (*Aviva Ganu v S of S* [1993] Imm AR 20).

The duration of the treatment, particularly whether or not, it is finite, is a factor. In *Athar Ul Haq* (10062), the IAT departed from the approach adopted in *Ganu* and *Foon* (above) concerning whether the applicant needs to show that the proposed treatment is of finite duration. Since the introduction of para 51 there is now only a requirement that the applicant show, *if required*, that the treatment is of finite duration. In *Afzalan* (11565) the treatment (for infertility) was taking much longer than originally anticipated. The appellants were not using the treatment to prolong their visit unnecessarily, and did show an intention to leave when the treatment was finished. Clearly also, the fact that the duration of treatment is uncertain does not mean that the duration is not finite.

AIDS and HIV positive cases

IND instruction BDI 3/95 advises IND staff on how to proceed in cases involving AIDS or HIV positive sufferers. The instruction applies to all categories, including EEA nationals and their families. As noted above, the fact that an applicant is suffering from AIDS or is HIV positive does not constitute grounds for granting or refusing entry clearance or leave to remain (para 2). A distinction is drawn between HIV and AIDS. In the former the person may still be asymptomatic, and a serious case for exceptional treatment is unlikely to arise. Applications for entry clearance from persons who disclose that they are HIV positive or suffering from AIDS may be referred to the Home Office by the ECO. The applicant will still have to meet the requirements of the immigration rules (para 3.1), but if there is evidence to suggest that he is in need of regular medication or treatment, he should provide evidence that he can meet the costs of such medication during his stay, in addition to the usual requirements concerning maintenance and accommodation. Where there is perceived to be a risk to public health, the IND staff should seek advice from the Department of Health international relations unit (para 3.2). When the person arrives in the UK (ie on entry), the immigration officer will examine whether the provisions of the immigration rules are satisfied. If the applicant is found to have AIDS, the advice of the

Port Medical Inspector will be sought to determine whether the applicant can satisfy the rules (see p 80). If he does not, entry is to be refused (para 4.1).

If, after entry and on an application for leave to remain, there is evidence that the applicant is suffering from AIDS or is HIV positive, the application should nonetheless be determined under the rules. An application can be made for leave to remain outside the rules where there are strong compassionate circumstances justifying the exercise of discretion outside the rules. Leave may be granted despite the fact that treatment will be provided under the NHS (para 5.1). A consultant's letter confirming the following will be required:

(a) that the applicant has AIDS or is HIV positive;

(b) his life expectancy;

(c) the nature and location of the treatment he is receiving;

(d) his fitness to travel if required to leave the UK (para 5.2).

The availability of treatment in the applicant's country will be checked (para 5.3). The fact that that country's services are not as advanced as in the UK does not constitute a reason for allowing someone with AIDS or who is HIV positive to remain in the UK. Where there are no facilities for treatment in the applicant's country and the evidence suggests that this will significantly shorten his life expectancy, it is normally appropriate to grant leave to remain (para 5.4).

A person with AIDS or an HIV positive person will not be removed if he is not fit to travel, or has only a few months to live. Consideration will be given to allowing the person to remain for a limited period on compassionate grounds (para 5.5). EEA nationals should have a certificate confirming that their parent state will bear the costs of the treatment. They cannot be refused entry on the basis of having AIDS or being HIV positive alone (para 6). In *Davoren v S of S* [1996] Imm AR 307, the CA held on the facts of that case that the application of the Home Office policy was not irrational.

Those caring for HIV/AIDS sufferers A person who wishes to come to the UK for a short period to care for a friend or relative may be admitted as a visitor, provided the requirements of the immigration rules are met. The provision of care must not constitute employment. The maximum time allowed is six months, but it may be appropriate to allow a short extension in exceptional circumstances (see below and BDI 2/95).

Carers

There are no provisions in the immigration rules for overseas carers to be granted leave to remain for that purpose. Such applications are considered outside the immigration rules. However, it is normal policy to grant overseas carers leave to stay for three months only. Any further application for leave to remain on the same basis is considered on its merits at the time (letter to the Independent Immigration Support Agency from IND, 7 May 1996). The IND B Division Instructions BDI 2/95 give guidance to IND staff on how to proceed in cases involving applications from persons in the UK in a temporary capacity seeking leave to remain to care for a friend or relative who is suffering from a terminal disease or has a mental or physical disability.

The policy is that applications for leave to remain in order to care for a sick or disabled relative should normally be granted for a period of three months, on the strict understanding that during that period arrangements will be made for the future care of the patient by a person who does not require leave to remain outside the immigration rules.

The Disability Discrimination Act 1995, Part III, prohibits discrimination for a reason relating to a person's disability in the context of the provision of goods and services. Cases on race and sex discrimination legislation suggest that the Disability Discrimination Act 1995 will not apply to the consideration of immigration cases (see *Amin v ECO Bombay* [1983] 2 AC 818). However, the authorities were decided before the introduction of the Citizen's Charter and it may be that the courts would consider that the IND is providing a service to the public or a section of the public. If so, the IND may not, for a reason relating to his disability, treat a disabled person less favourably than it treats or would treat a person to whom that reason does not apply. Note that such discrimination may be justified by a material and substantial reason relating to the circumstances of the individual's case. In due course, a right to have reasonable adjustments made to policies and practices of a service provider is to be introduced. (For a full treatment of this topic, see *Disability Discrimination: The Law and Practice,* FT Law and Tax, 1st edn, 1996.)

Chapter 8

Part 3: Students

1 Leave to enter or remain

Part 3 of the rules makes provision for persons seeking to enter or remain in the UK for studies. HC 395 provides that all students are expected to be enrolled for at least 15 hours a week of full-time daytime study. The only exception relates to students enrolled on a full-time degree course at a publicly funded institution of further or higher education. Students are allowed to enrol on a variety of part-time courses in order to make up the 15 hours. Enrolment must be for a single subject or a number of directly related subjects at a single institution. A child under 16 who seeks leave to enter or remain for studies must be in full-time education, which meets the requirements of the Education Act 1944 (now the Education Act 1996), at an independent fee paying school. Children under 16 may not therefore enrol on secretarial courses, for example. Practitioners should stress to the client his personal responsibility to ensure his immigration status is correct, as clients are frequently let down by the administration of the institution they seek to attend.

Requirements for leave to enter as a student

57. The requirements to be met by a person seeking leave to enter the United Kingdom as a student are that he:
(i) has been accepted for a course of study at:
    (a) a publicly funded institution of further or higher education; or
    (b) a *bona fide* private education institution which maintains satisfactory records of enrolment and attendance; or
    (c) an independent fee paying school outside the maintained sector; and
(ii) is able and intends to follow either:
    (a) a recognised full-time degree course at a publicly funded institution of further or higher education; or
    (b) a weekday full-time course involving attendance at a single institution for a minimum of 15 hours organised daytime study per week of a single subject or directly related subjects; or
    (c) a full-time course of study at an independent fee paying school; and
(iii) if under the age of 16 years is enrolled at an independent fee paying school on a full-time course of studies which meets the requirements of the Education Act 1944; and
(iv) intends to leave the United Kingdom at the end of his studies; and

(v) does not intend to engage in business or to take employment, except part-time or vacation work undertaken with the consent of the Secretary of State for Employment; and

(vi) is able to meet the costs of his course and accommodation and the main-tenance of himself and any dependants without taking employment or engaging in business or having recourse to public funds.

Leave to enter as a student

58. A person seeking leave to enter the United Kingdom as a student may be admitted for an appropriate period depending on the length of his course of study and his means, and with a condition restricting his freedom to take employment, provided the Immigration Officer is satisfied that each of the requirements of paragraph 57 is met.

Refusal of leave to enter as a student

59. Leave to enter as a student is to be refused if the Immigration Officer is not satisfied that each of the requirements of paragraph 57 is met.

COMMENTARY

For the general grounds for refusal of leave, see Chapter 13. Section 8 of the Asylum and Immigration Appeals Act 1993 provides that if a person is refused entry as a student for a period of study up to six months, and he does not have a prior entry clearance for the purpose or is refused entry as a prospective student, he may not appeal against the decision to refuse him entry. Where he seeks an entry clearance in order to follow a course of study of not more than six months' duration for which he has been accepted, or seeks an entry clearance with the intention of studying, but without being accepted for any course of study, he may not appeal against a refusal of that entry clearance. Such decisions are now amenable to judicial review (see further Chapter 22). The period of leave granted under the entry rules may be any appropriate period depending on the length of the course of study and the student's means.

Educational establishments   It is necessary for the course to be at a *bona fide* educational establishment (*R v IAT, ex p Idiaro* [1991] Imm AR 546, an example of one that was not). Whether the establishment is a *bona fide* establishment is a question of fact, and the immigration officer should consider whether the educational establishment can conceivably provide what it claims to provide for students. The individual establishment should be considered, and general assumptions about the character of particular educational establishments should not be made (*Oke* (8557)). The educational establishment is required by para 57 to keep satisfactory records of enrolment.

(a) 'able and intends to follow'

In assessing the ability of the applicant to follow the course, it is likely that the intellectual abilities of the applicant will be considered as under the old rules; however, the express mention of consideration of the applicant's 'qualifications' has disappeared. The immigration officer will consider whether the applicant's knowledge of English is sufficient for the type of course on which he is enrolled (*ECO Karachi v Ahmed* [1989] Imm AR 254). A poor knowledge of English will indicate an inability to follow a computer course (*Goffar v ECO Dacca* [1975] Imm AR 142), and the need for an interpreter will indicate inability to follow a highly technical course (*R v IAT, ex p Ozkurtulus* [1986] Imm AR 80). Where the applicant clearly does not appear to understand sufficient English, or, for example, mathematics, to attend a course of studies at a college of further education, the immigration officer may contact the college to make sure that they will accept the applicant (*R v Chief Immigration Officer, Bradford Airport, ex p Ashiq Hussain* [1969] 3 All ER 1601). The requirement of ability is not satisfied by the student's showing only that he could achieve the qualification sought by dogged persistence over a long period (*S of S v Mensah* (10855)).

Lack of ability may be taken to be evidence of lack of intention to follow the course. However, there must be evidence, and not mere suspicion, that the applicant cannot and/or does not intend to follow the course (*ECO New Delhi v Bhambra* [1973] Imm AR 14). Ability, conversely, does not indicate that a person's intention, for example to study English, is any less realistic (*Dagdar* (2101)).

(b) 'full time course of study'
This concept covers a 'coherent and definite educational proposal which the student could reasonably be expected to complete' (*R v Chief Immigration Officer, Gatwick Airport, ex p Kharrazzi* [1980] 1 WLR 1396). Thus it can include, as in that case, ten years of education including 'O' and 'A' levels and the attainment of a university degree, even before the student has been guaranteed or accepted for a place at university. The phrase 'full-time course of study' may include more than one course, provided that they are specific parts of a coherent whole (*ibid, per* Waller LJ at p 1406). Each case depends on its own facts and the ability of the individual concerned (*Myeen Rashid v ECO Dacca* [1976] Imm AR 12). A three-year-old, however, may not be a student (*Issa* (4011)).

In *Patel v IAT* [1983] Imm AR 76, the CA stated, *obiter*, that the wider meaning given to 'studies' in *Kharrazzi* should include 'the gaining of experience' and 'any activity which is related to the studies' (*per* Lawton LJ at 81). Paragraph 57 now requires that if the studies involve more than one course, the subjects studied must consist of 'directly related' subjects.

In *Awosika v S of S* [1989] Imm AR 35, the IAT held that where a course comprised organised classes which did not take up the whole or a substantial part of the student's time, but were supplemented by private study which did, the rule may be satisfied. Thus two part-time courses can constitute a full-time course of daytime study for the purposes of this rule (*Shomali* (3451)). However, the rule requires attendance for 15 hours. The discretion under the earlier HC 251 has been removed by the requirement that leave must be refused if any of the requirements of para 57 is not satisfied.

'*Organised*' When considering the general rule that there must be 15 hours of organised study per week, consideration must be given to whether the study is organised. In *R v IAT, ex p Idiaro* [1991] Imm AR 546, Henry J held that to be 'organised' study there must be both (a) an organiser making the rules, and (b) the organised, who adhere to those rules, have tasks set for them, do them at specific times and places and under supervision. A course which was not structured in this way might nevertheless satisfy the paragraph, which merely sets out a general rule. Certain *obiter dicta* in *Durojaiye v S of S* [1991] Imm AR 307 suggest that 'organised daytime study' encompasses more than merely formal teaching time at an institution. However, the 15 hours referred to in the paragraph are those hours which are compulsory under the course and for which the applicant must attend and study. Merely attending for 15 hours may not result in fulfilling the conditions in the paragraph.

(c) Intention to leave

Occasionally there is direct evidence of an intention not to leave. For example, where the applicant firmly states that he intends to remain in the UK after the course and take employment, entry will be refused (*ECO Lagos v Sobanjo* [1978] Imm AR 22).

In most cases the intention of the applicant will be ascertained by indirect evidence and by looking at all the circumstances surrounding the application. It is a question of fact (*Patel v IAT* [1983] Imm AR 76). Lack of plans by an applicant to take up employment in his home country after completion of his course of training, and complete vagueness on the subject of future employment anywhere, may suggest to an immigration officer that the applicant will not leave the UK after he has concluded his studies. However, on the authority of *R v Lympne Airport Chief Immigration Officer, ex p Amrik Singh* [1968] 3 All ER 163, such a suspicion would not form a valid reason for refusing to grant an entry certificate or to grant admission for present study (*Puri v S of S* [1972] Imm AR 21).

Although the immigration officer may refuse entry if satisfied that the applicant intends not to leave at the end of the course, the fact that the applicant has in mind the possibility, among other things, of being allowed to stay in the UK after his course, should not affect his right of entry, provided that the course of study is the primary purpose of entry to the UK (*R v IAT, ex p Perween Khan* [1972] 3 All ER 297). Thus the fact that the applicant expresses a hope of being able to remain after completion of his studies does not necessarily nullify the applicant's intention, at the time of entry, to leave at the end of his studies (*R v IAT, ex p Shaikh* [1981] 1 WLR 1107). On the other hand, if the intention to undergo a course of studies is a mere device to gain entry so as to be able to stay in circumstances in which he knows he would be unlikely to be permitted to remain, he should not be permitted to enter (*Perween Khan* (above) at 273, *per* Bridge J). An intention to leave is not exhibited if the applicant intends to leave only if he cannot avoid doing so by lawful means (*Patel v IAT* (above)). The immigration officer may also take account of the applicant's immigration history, and the fact that he has failed to complete his study plans on previous visits (*Ex p Fernando* [1987]

Imm AR 377). Similarly, a history of examinations failed or unattempted may be evidence of lack of ability and/or lack of intention to leave the UK after study terminates (*Ex p Gomez,* CA, unreported, 17 January 1991). Where an applicant was asked where he would go after his religious studies, and said 'God would choose', in so far as the matter is a decision to be taken by him, he had an intention to leave the UK at the end of his studies (*Olatoye* (11963)).

Lack of realism is not a proper ground for refusing entry clearance or admission. The Divisional Court, in *R v Khan (Sett)* [1975] Imm AR 26, allowed an application for *certiorari* where an ECO refused an entry certificate to a Pakistani citizen who applied to attend a short computer course. The officer took the view that it was unrealistic that the applicant should have involved his first cousin in expenditure for the course fees plus the cost of his return air ticket, particularly as there were local computer operator schools in Karachi, whose courses were much cheaper than in the UK. The applicant had not made any specific inquiries of companies about employment on his return. However, the officer misdirected himself. May J said, at p 30:

> that it might in the circumstances have been foolhardy, and certainly less than thrifty to come all the way from Karachi to London for the course without making inquiries may be so and perhaps this may be said to be unrealistic, but in my judgment it in no way follows that it was dishonest or that the applicant was not genuine.

Nevertheless, in assessing whether an application is genuine, it is often necessary to take into account factors which would also be reviewed when considering whether an application is realistic. On an application to attend a computer operator's course, such factors as the applicant's background, and whether he had made inquiries about suitable courses and employment prospects in the computer field in his home country, may well be material in determining whether the applicant intended to leave the UK on completion of his course (*Goffar v ECO Dacca; Dey v ECO Dacca* [1975] Imm AR 142). The absence of any inquiries about job opportunities locally, or concern about material benefits to be gained by taking a short vocational course, coupled with such matters as a large expenditure of money by a poor family to enable an applicant to attend a course in the UK, will be highly relevant when considering whether the applicant will leave the UK on completion of his course (*Khan (SGH) v ECO Karachi* [1975] Imm AR 64 at 68). Thus an application by a rickshaw puller to study the Egyptian scarabs in the British Museum would be likely to create an immediate doubt about the applicant's intentions, which would be for the applicant to dispel. A university graduate making the same application would not have such difficulty (*Islam v ECO Dacca* [1974] Imm AR 83 at p 86).

Save in so far as doubts are raised as to the intention to leave the UK after completion of study, as long as the immigration rules are complied with, the nature of the study proposed is a matter of indifference. So too is the use to which the applicant proposes to put the knowledge thereby gained (*Islam* at p 85).

The IAT, in *Ghosh v ECO Calcutta* [1976] Imm AR 60, held that there was nothing objectionable in the ECO's request that the applicant obtain written confirmation from his present employers (whom he claimed had given him leave of absence) that the qualifications he would acquire from attendance at a 16-week course in computer programming would be 'acceptable' to them for employment in that field. Such a request was considered to be very different from asking an applicant for an assurance that he would be employed as a computer programmer after his proposed training (*S of S v Virdee* [1972] Imm AR 215). Moreover, when substantial sums of money are paid for a short vocational course, the source of those funds is 'clearly not an irrelevant matter and one not to be disregarded' (*Ghosh*, at p 65). For cases on 'genuine and realistic intentions' in the context of finances, see p 204.

(d) Long residence and the intention to leave

There is a policy that where a person has been in the UK for ten years continuously with leave, he may apply for indefinite leave to remain (see p 254). It would not be in accordance with the law to refuse an application which fell within the strict letter of the policy (see *Gautam* (10985)). The fact that a student whose stay is approaching this period makes an application for indefinite leave to remain, for administrative convenience, does not necessarily indicate that he does not intend to leave at the end of his studies. In *Ko* (11440), the student still had several more years post-graduate studies to complete and the grant of indefinite leave to remain would save making annual applications for extensions. However, in *Egbulefu* (11884), it was recognised that such applications for indefinite leave to remain and extensions of limited leave must raise doubts as to the applicant's future intentions, which are likely to be displaced only by cogent and credible evidence. As the ten-year policy is applied very strictly, applications should be made at the ten-year period, rather than before. In *Umujakporue* (12448) the student spent his last two years in the Republic of Ireland, maintaining and visiting his home in the UK on many long weekends. The IAT held that it could review the merits of any discretion contained in a policy if the effect of the policy is to waive the rules in regard to a class of applicants. As the absence in the Republic did not destroy the student's residence in the UK, the S of S could not maintain his policy and refuse the application for indefinite leave to remain.

(e) Employment

Students are admitted subject to a condition prohibiting or restricting their freedom to take employment. With the consent of the Department of Education and Employment, *bona fide* students may work in their free time. If the course involves employment, the educational establishment should agree with the local Jobcentre that all its overseas students on that course should be permitted to engage in the employment required for the course. The educational establishment may also ask the student's employer to obtain a permit for him.

Where a student wishes to take a job which is not integral to the course in this way, the student should apply to the Department of Education and Employment to obtain a variation of any prohibition on his taking employment. If the student cannot show that he does not need to take employment to finance his studies, a variation is unlikely to be granted.

Where the condition stamped on the passport is a restriction on working, the student should apply for permission from his local Jobcentre, which will need to see the passport stamp, and will give the student form OSS1. The student should ensure that the form is properly completed by himself, his educational establishment and the prospective employer. Permission is more likely if the job has been advertised and is in some way relevant to his course. Employment taking up more than 20 hours is very unlikely to be permitted.

The student's earnings from free-time employment are not to be taken into account in deciding whether his means are adequate (see below).

Students are not allowed to engage in business (*Ex p Ayoola* [1992] Imm AR 170). It may be that a student, who is not expressly prohibited from doing so, may transact business (see *Strasburger v S of S* [1978] Imm AR 165).

(f) Adequate means

The applicant must be able to meet the costs of his course and accommodation and the maintenance of himself and any dependants, without working or having recourse to public funds. It is a question of fact whether the applicant can meet these costs. Detailed documentary evidence is important, including communications from banks, and bank statements showing that funds are available and, where appropriate, can be transferred to the UK (*Murgai v ECO New Delhi* [1975] Imm AR 86). Letters of sponsorship and other documentary evidence must be specific and unambiguous. In *Ayettey v S of S* [1972] Imm AR 261, neither a letter from the applicant's father stating that he was financially responsible for his son and was able to bear the costs of the course, nor one from a solicitor testifying that the father was of substance who owned property abroad was held to be sufficient (see also *Bhagat v S of S* [1972] Imm AR 189). There must be evidence showing how the total costs can be met. The (non-dependent) spouse of a student may be able to work (see p 114). In those circumstances the student can use evidence of earnings from such work to show that he can meet the costs of his course and accommodation and the maintenance of himself and any dependants without recourse to public funds (see p 60 and para 57(vi)).

(g) EU students

The position of students who are EU citizens is governed by the freedom of movement provisions (art 48 of the Treaty of Rome), which take precedence over the immigration rules. The position of students under the Treaty has been dealt with by Directive 93/96, OJ 1993 L317/59. This gives nationals of member states who have been accepted on a vocational training course the right to pursue that course. The right of free movement is also given to the spouse and children of a person pursuing such a course. The student must have sickness insurance, and satisfy the national authority that he will not place a burden on the national social assistance scheme during his period of residence. The right of residence is restricted to the period of study. Members of his family who are not EU nationals will receive visas for the same duration as the course of the student, and may engage in employment or self-employment in the host state. This directive is discussed in detail in Chapter 16.

2   Extensions

Requirements for an extension of stay as a student
60. The requirements for an extension of stay as a student are that the applicant:
(i)   was admitted to the United Kingdom with a valid student entry clearance if he is a person specified in the Appendix to these Rules; and
(ii)   meets the requirements for admission as a student set out in paragraph 57(i)–(vi); and
(iii)   has produced evidence of his enrolment on a course which meets the requirements of paragraph 57; and
(iv)   can produce satisfactory evidence of regular attendance during any course which he has already begun, or any other course for which he has been enrolled in the past; and
(v)   can show evidence of satisfactory progress in his course of study including the taking and passing of any relevant examinations; and
(vi)   would not, as a result of an extension of stay, spend more than 4 years on short courses (ie courses of less than 2 years duration, or longer courses broken off before completion); and
(vii)   has not come to the end of a period of government or international scholarship agency sponsorship, or has the written consent of his original sponsor for a further period of study in the United Kingdom and satisfactory evidence that sufficient sponsorship funding is available.

Extension of stay as a student
61. An extension of stay as a student may be granted, subject to a restriction on his freedom to take employment, provided the Secretary of State is satisfied that the applicant meets each of the requirements of paragraph 60.

Refusal of extension of stay as a student
62. An extension of stay as a student is to be refused if the Secretary of State is not satisfied that each of the requirements of paragraph 60 is met.

COMMENTARY

The wording of para 62 makes clear that the requirements of the rule are mandatory. This mirrors the position under HC 251, para 111: a person who entered the UK without clearance as a student or prospective student must be refused an extension for the purposes of study (*Okello v S of S* [1995] Imm AR 269). A person applying for an extension of his leave as a student must continue to satisfy the admission criteria above, and must also satisfy all the requirements of para 60, failing which his application must be refused. However, a person who had been properly admitted to the UK as a student and received extensions as such for studies at a technical college on an HND course in business studies, lost his student status when he subsequently entered into a four-year training contract with a firm of chartered accountants (*Yeong Hoi Yuen v S of S* [1977] Imm AR 34). To fulfil the requirement that the applicant for an extension of leave be enrolled, it is sufficient that the applicant is entitled to an unconditional, confirmed place on a course which satisfies the rules (*Chinwo v S of S* [1985] Imm AR 74 and *Yovsani* (3181)). Extensions of stay are not normally granted to a sponsored student without evidence that the sponsor does not object to his staying longer. Regular attendance is a mandatory requirement of the rule, showing the good faith of the student. It does not require the student to attend without absences, but there must be satisfactory explanations for any absences (*Pour* (1479)). If the requirement is not satisfied the application must be refused (*S of S v Durojaiye* [1991] Imm AR 248). If an application for an extension has been properly refused by reason of the applicant's unsatisfactory attendance record, the applicant cannot succeed on appeal against the refusal by showing that his attendance since that refusal has improved (*Juma v S of S* [1974] Imm AR 96). It is for the S of S to decide whether to accept certificates of attendance from an educational establishment as evidence of regular attendance (*Kpoma v S of S* [1973] Imm AR 25). The IAT stated that it would be better for the Home Office to notify the appellant if there is no response from the college regarding his attendance record. Such a procedural failure can be rectified if there is an appeal, and the appellant should produce evidence of his attendance, or an explanation for the lack of it, to the adjudicator.

The Statement of Changes to the Immigration Rules, HC 797 of 1995, provides: 'paragraph 60(i) does not apply to any application for an extension of stay for the purpose of studying made by a national of Gambia whose current leave to enter or remain was granted before 27 October 1995'. Cm 3073 of 1996 and HC 274 of 1996 make similar provision in respect of nationals of Tanzania and Kenya whose current leave to enter or remain was granted before 5 January 1996 and 8 March 1996 respectively. HC 329 of 1996 provides that para 60(i) of HC 395 does not apply to any application for an extension of stay for the purpose of studying made by a national of Bahrain, the Dominican Republic, Fiji, Guyana, Kuwait, the Maldives, Mauritius, Niger, Papua New Guinea, Peru, Qatar, Surinam, United Arab Emirates or Zambia whose current leave to enter or remain was granted before 4 April 1996. The effect of these exceptions is that such nationals are not prevented from obtaining extensions because they were not admitted with valid student entry clearances before the relevant dates.

(a) Intention to leave at the end of the course of studies

This requirement applies both on entry and on applications for extensions. Thus a student who deliberately ignored the time limit and conditions subject to which he was admitted was refused an extension of his stay (*Lee v S of S* [1975] Imm AR 75). Where a student entrusted his passport to a college on the understanding that they would look after his immigration matters, and it failed to do so, the S of S was entitled to take account of the student's own inertia (*Ex p Animashaun* [1990] Imm AR 70). Similarly a student who had taken ordinary full-time employment in breach of the conditions of his admission was refused an extension to remain as a student (*S of S v Thaker* [1976] Imm AR 114), as was an applicant who had falsely represented herself as only a holiday visitor when she applied for an entry certificate, whereas her intention was to pursue a course of study (*Owusu v S of S* [1976] Imm AR 101), and a student who deceived the immigration authorities as to his examination history (*Ex p Adebodun* [1991] Imm AR 60). These cases would now probably be considered under the general grounds for refusal (see Chapter 13). An applicant does not have the necessary intention to leave if he intends to leave only if he cannot avoid doing so by lawful means (*Patel v IAT* [1983] Imm AR 76). In assessing whether the student has an intention to leave the UK at the end of his leave the immigration officer is entitled to take into account all the circumstances, including the applicant's academic record (*Ex p Chandana Mohotty* [1996] Imm AR 256).

The rules make clear that where a period of government or international scholarship agency sponsorship has ended, no further extensions may be granted. Under HC 251, if the same course of study was being followed after the end of the period of sponsorship, the S of S could exercise his discretion to extend leave.

(b) Satisfactory progress

A prolonged lack of examination success will be taken into account. Thus an appellant's total lack of success in his four years' study in the UK justified the doubts of the S of S that he intended to return to his own country on the completion of his studies (*Mahendran v S of S* [1988] Imm AR 492). Likewise even if the applicant could obtain the qualification sought, but only by 'dogged persistence' over a lengthy period, the immigration officer will be entitled to conclude that satisfactory progress is not being made (*Mensah* (10855)). Further, if the person has not taken any exams over a three-year period, the S of S may take that into account (*Adebodun* [1991] Imm AR 60). Moreover, there is no obligation on the S of S to warn a student that a lack of academic success can be taken into account in considering his application for extension of leave (*Ofoajoku v S of S* [1991] Imm AR 68). On the other hand, where there is evidence that the student is moving from one course to another, to obtain qualifications in a specific branch of a profession, the immigration officer may not conclude that the applicant is moving from course to course with no intention of bringing his studies to an end (*Alonga* (10919)).

A visa national will be granted an extension only if he was admitted to the UK with an entry clearance for the purposes of studying.

3   Student nurses

Definition of student nurse

63. For the purposes of these Rules the term student nurse means a person accepted for training as a student nurse or midwife leading to a registered nursing qualification; or an overseas nurse or midwife who has been accepted on an adaptation course leading to registration as a nurse with the United Kingdom Central Council for Nursing, Midwifery and Health Visiting.

Requirements for leave to enter as a student nurse

64. The requirements to be met by a person seeking leave to enter the United Kingdom as a student nurse are that the person:
(i)   comes within the definition set out in paragraph 63 above; and
(ii)   has been accepted for a course of study in a recognised nursing educational establishment offering nursing training which meets the requirements of the United Kingdom Central Council for Nursing, Midwifery and Health Visiting; and
(iii) did not obtain acceptance by misrepresentation; and
(iv)   is able and intends to follow the course; and
(v)   does not intend to engage in business or take employment except in connection with the training course; and
(vi)   intends to leave the United Kingdom at the end of the course; and
(vii) has sufficient funds available for accommodation and maintenance for himself and any dependants without engaging in business or taking employment (except in connection with the training course) or having recourse to public funds. The possession of a Department of Health bursary may be taken into account in assessing whether the student meets the maintenance requirement.

Leave to enter the United Kingdom as a student nurse

65. A person seeking leave to enter the United Kingdom as a student nurse may be admitted for the duration of the training course, with a restriction on his freedom to take employment, provided the Immigration Officer is satisfied that each of the requirements of paragraph 64 is met.

Refusal of leave to enter as a student nurse

66. Leave to enter as a student nurse is to be refused if the Immigration Officer is not satisfied that each of the requirements of paragraph 64 is met.

Requirements for an extension of stay as a student nurse

67. The requirements for an extension of stay as a student nurse are that the applicant:
(i)   was admitted to the United Kingdom with a valid student entry clearance if he is a person specified in the Appendix to these Rules; and
(ii)   meets the requirements set out in paragraph 64(i)–(vii); and
(iii) has produced evidence of enrolment at a recognised nursing educational establishment; and
(iv)   can provide satisfactory evidence of regular attendance during any course which he has already begun; or any other course for which he has been enrolled in the past; and

(v) would not, as a result of an extension of stay, spend more than 4 years in obtaining the relevant qualification; and

(vi) has not come to the end of a period of government or international scholarship agency sponsorship, or has the written consent of his original sponsor for a further period of study in the United Kingdom and evidence that sufficient sponsorship funding is available.

Extension of stay as a student nurse

68. An extension of stay as a student nurse may be granted, subject to a restriction on his freedom to take employment, provided the Secretary of State is satisfied that the applicant meets each of the requirements of paragraph 67.

Refusal of extension of stay as a student nurse

69. An extension of stay as a student nurse is to be refused if the Secretary of State is not satisfied that each of the requirements of paragraph 67 is met.

COMMENTARY

HC 395 defines a student nurse. A person seeking leave to remain in the UK as a student nurse must satisfy the immigration officer or ECO that he intends to leave the UK at the end of his studies. Student nurses are not allowed to switch to work permit employment once they have qualified. They must qualify under the Training and Work Experience Scheme provisions if they wish to take post-registration courses. This change, brought about by HC 395, is a result of the Department of Education and Employment's no longer regarding nursing as a shortage occupation.

For the general grounds for refusal, see Chapter 13. An application for leave to enter or for an extension must satisfy the requirements of paras 64 and 67 respectively. In either case, if the requirements are not all satisfied, refusal is mandatory. When applying for an extension of leave to remain as a student nurse, the applicant must satisfy the immigration officer that he falls within the definition of 'student nurse'. He must be accepted for training as a student nurse leading to a registered nursing qualification. If a qualified nurse or midwife, he must be accepted on an adaptation course leading to registration as a nurse with the UK Central Council for Nursing, Midwifery and Health Visiting. He must be accepted for a course of study in a nursing educational establishment and must not have obtained that acceptance by misrepresentation. He must be able and intend to follow the course. He must not intend to take employment except in connection with a training course. He must intend to leave the UK at the end of the course. He must have sufficient funds available for accommodation and maintenance for himself and any dependants without doing work other than in connection with the training course, and without having recourse to public funds (see p 60). The student nurse's means include funds awarded under a Department of Health bursary. He must not, as a result of the extension, spend more than four years obtaining the relevant qualification.

Prospective student nurses will now be able to apply under the rules relating to prospective students. For the position under HC 251, see *Namubiru* (11636) and *Agyemang* (10385).

4 Post-graduate doctors and dentists

Requirements for leave to enter as a postgraduate doctor or dentist

70. The requirements for leave to enter the United Kingdom for the purpose of training as a postgraduate doctor or dentist are that the applicant:

(i)   (a)   is a graduate from a United Kingdom medical school intending to undertake Pre-Registration House Officer employment for up to 12 months, as required for full registration with the General Medical Council; and

      (b)   has not spent more than 12 months in aggregate in Pre-Registration House Officer employment; or

(ii)   (a)   is a doctor or dentist eligible for full or limited registration with the General Medical Council or with the General Dental Council who intends to undertake postgraduate training in a hospital; and

      (b)   has not spent more than 4 years in aggregate in the United Kingdom as a postgraduate doctor or dentist, excluding any period spent in Pre-Registration House Officer employment;

(iii) intends to leave the United Kingdom on completion of his training period; and

(iv) is able to maintain and accommodate himself and any dependants without recourse to public funds.

Leave to enter as a postgraduate doctor or dentist

71. A person seeking leave to enter the United Kingdom to study as a postgraduate doctor or dentist may be admitted for a period not exceeding 12 months provided the Immigration Officer is satisfied that each of the requirements of paragraph 70 are met.

Refusal of leave to enter as a postgraduate doctor or dentist

72. Leave to enter as a postgraduate doctor or dentist is to be refused if the Immigration Officer is not satisfied that each of the requirements of paragraph 70 is met.

Requirements for extension of stay as a postgraduate doctor or dentist

73. The requirements for an extension of stay as a postgraduate doctor or dentist are that the applicant:

(i)   (a)   meets the requirements of paragraph 70(i)(a); and

      (b)   would not, as a result of an extension of stay, spend more than 12 months in aggregate in Pre-Registration House Officer employment; or

(ii)   (a)   is a doctor or dentist who can provide satisfactory evidence of limited or full registration with the General Medical Council or registration with the General Dental Council and intends to undertake postgraduate training in a hospital; and

      (b)   would not, as a result of an extension of stay, spend more than 4 years in aggregate in the United Kingdom as a postgraduate doctor or dentist excluding any period spent in Pre-Registration House Officer employment;

(iii) intends to leave the United Kingdom on completion of his training period; and

(iv) is able to maintain and accommodate himself and any dependants without recourse to public funds.

Extension of stay as a postgraduate doctor or dentist

74. An extension of stay as a postgraduate doctor or dentist may be granted for a period not exceeding 12 months provided the Secretary of State is satisfied that each of the requirements of paragraph 73 is met.

Refusal of extension of stay as a postgraduate doctor or dentist

75. An extension of stay as a postgraduate doctor or dentist is to be refused if the Secretary of State is not satisfied that each of the requirements of paragraph 73 is met.

5   Spouses

Requirements for leave to enter or remain as the spouse of a student or prospective student

76. The requirements to be met by a person seeking leave to enter or remain in the United Kingdom as the spouse of a student are that:

(i)   the applicant is married to a person admitted to or allowed to remain in the United Kingdom under paragraphs 57–75; and

(ii) each of the parties intends to live with the other as his or her spouse during the applicant's stay and the marriage is subsisting; and

(iii) there will be adequate accommodation for the parties and any dependants without recourse to public funds; and

(iv) the parties will be able to maintain themselves and any dependants adequately without recourse to public funds; and

(v)   the applicant does not intend to take employment except as permitted under paragraph 77 below; and

(vi) the applicant intends to leave the United Kingdom at the end of any period of leave granted to him.

Leave to enter or remain as the spouse of a student or prospective student

77. A person seeking leave to enter or remain in the United Kingdom as the spouse of a student may be admitted or allowed to remain for a period not in excess of that granted to the student provided the Immigration Officer or, in the case of an application for limited leave to remain the Secretary of State, is satisfied that each of the requirements of paragraph 76 is met. Employment is to be prohibited except where the period of leave being granted is 12 months or more.

Refusal of leave to enter or remain as the spouse of a student or prospective student

78. Leave to enter or remain as the spouse of a student is to be refused if the Immigration Officer or, in the case of an application for limited leave to remain, the Secretary of State is not satisfied that each of the requirements of paragraph 76 is met.

COMMENTARY

For the general grounds for refusal see Chapter 13. The spouse of a student should not have their freedom to work restricted where the student's course is longer than 12 months. However, a person must show that he can maintain and accommodate himself without recourse to public funds and without working in order to gain admission as a spouse of a student.

The Home Office parliamentary under-secretary wrote to Tony Banks MP on 26 July 1995 confirming the policy that a student's dependant who is granted less than 12 months' leave to remain will not usually be permitted to take up employment save where the student would have qualified for 12 months' leave at the time of the application, but, because of the administrative delays at the IND, is granted a period of less than 12 months. In such circumstances, discretion may be used not to impose a prohibition on employment on the spouse (see *Legal Action*, November 1995, p 23). HC 31, from 1 November 1996, extended these provisions to prospective students and introduced the maintenance and accommodation requirement for post-graduate doctors and dentists.

6 Children

Requirements for leave to enter or remain as the child of a student

79. The requirements to be met by a person seeking leave to enter or remain in the United Kingdom as the child of a student are that he:
(i) is the child of a parent admitted to or allowed to remain in the United Kingdom as a student under paragraphs 57–75 or 82–87; and
(ii) is under the age of 18 or has current leave to enter or remain in this capacity; and
(iii) is unmarried, has not formed an independent family unit and is not leading an independent life; and
(iv) can, and will, be maintained and accommodated adequately without recourse to public funds; and
(v) will not stay in the United Kingdom beyond any period of leave granted to his parent.

Leave to enter or remain as the child of a student or prospective student

80. A person seeking leave to enter or remain in the United Kingdom as the child of a student may be admitted or allowed to remain for a period of leave not in excess of that granted to the student provided the Immigration Officer or, in the case of an application for limited leave to remain, the Secretary of State is satisfied that each of the requirements of paragraph 79 is met. Employment is to be prohibited except where the period of leave being granted is 12 months or more.

Refusal of leave to enter or remain as the child of a student or prospective student

81. Leave to enter or remain in the United Kingdom as the child of a student is to be refused if the Immigration Officer or, in the case of an application for limited leave to remain, the Secretary of State is not satisfied that each of the requirements of paragraph 79 is met.

COMMENTARY

HC 31 extended these provisions to a prospective student's children. For the general grounds for refusal see Chapter 13. A student's child who is under 18 will be granted entrance for the period of the student's authorised stay if he can be maintained and accommodated without recourse to public funds. His freedom to take employment will not be restricted. It must be shown that he has not formed an independent family unit, and that he is not leading an independent life. He must be maintained and accommodated adequately without recourse to public funds. He must be admitted with his parent who is the spouse of the student. The exceptions to this rule are where the student is the only parent still alive, or the parent is allowed to remain has sole responsibility for the child's upbringing; or there are serious and compelling family or other considerations which make exclusion undesirable. Suitable arrangements must have been made for his care.

The maximum period of his leave must not exceed the maximum period granted to the student parent.

7   Prospective students

Requirements for leave to enter as a prospective student
82. The requirements to be met by a person seeking leave to enter the United Kingdom as a prospective student are that he:
(i)   can demonstrate a genuine and realistic intention of undertaking, within 6 months of his date of entry, a course of study which would meet the requirements for an extension of stay as a student set out in paragraphs 60 or 67; and
(ii)   intends to leave the United Kingdom on completion of his studies or on the expiry of his leave to enter if he is not able to meet the requirements for an extension of stay as a student set out in paragraphs 60 or 67; and
(iii) is able without working or recourse to public funds to meet the costs of his intended course and accommodation and the maintenance of himself and any dependants while making arrangements to study and during the course of his studies.

Leave to enter as a prospective student
83. A person seeking leave to enter the United Kingdom as a prospective student may be admitted for a period not exceeding 6 months with a condition prohibiting employment, provided the Immigration Officer is satisfied that each of the requirements of paragraph 82 is met.

Refusal of leave to enter as a prospective student
84. Leave to enter as a prospective student is to be refused if the Immigration Officer is not satisfied that each of the requirements of paragraph 82 is met.

Requirements for extension of stay as a prospective student
85. Six months is the maximum permitted leave which may be granted to a prospective student. The requirements for an extension of stay as a prospective student are that the applicant:
(i)   was admitted to the United Kingdom with a valid prospective student entry clearance if he is a person specified in the Appendix to these Rules; and
(ii)   meets the requirements of paragraph 82; and
(iii) would not, as a result of an extension of stay, spend more than 6 months in the United Kingdom.

Extension of stay as a prospective student
86. An extension of stay as a prospective student may be granted, with a prohibition on employment, provided the Secretary of State is satisfied that each of the requirements of paragraph 85 is met.

Refusal of extension of stay as a prospective student

87. An extension of stay as a prospective student is to be refused if the Secretary of State is not satisfied that each of the requirements of paragraph 85 is met.

COMMENTARY

The course of study must be at either an independent fee paying school or a college outside the maintained sector. It must be a recognised full-time degree course at a publicly funded institution of further or higher education; or a weekday daytime course involving attendance for a minimum of 15 hours' organised study per week of a single subject or directly related subjects; or a full-time course of study at an independent fee paying school or college. Also, if the applicant is under 16, he must be enrolled on a full-time course of studies which meets the requirements of the Education Act 1996. The prospective student must satisfy the immigration officer that he intends to leave the UK on completion of his studies or on the expiry of his leave to enter the UK if he cannot satisfy the requirements for an extension of stay as a student.

The maximum period of leave as a prospective student is six months. Thus, if he cannot produce evidence of enrolment on a suitable course, or has failed regularly to attend the course if it has started, or if he cannot show that he has regularly attended past courses for which he was enrolled, his application for an extension must be refused. Also, if he cannot show evidence of satisfactory progress in his course of study, or if the extension would result in his undertaking more than four years of courses of less than two years, or courses which are longer, but which have been broken off before completion, the application must be refused. If he has come to the end of a period of government or international scholarship agency sponsorship, again, the application must be refused. He must also be able to meet the costs of his intended course and accommodate and maintain himself and his dependants while making arrangements to study and during the course of his studies, without working or having recourse to public funds.

Chapter 9

Part 4: Au Pairs, Working Holidaymakers, Training or Work Experience

1 Au pairs

Definition of an au pair placement

88. For the purposes of these Rules an au pair placement is an arrangement whereby a young person:
(a) comes to the United Kingdom for the purpose of learning the English language; and
(b) lives for a time as a member of an English speaking family with appropriate opportunities for study; and
(c) helps in the home for a maximum of 5 hours per day in return for a reasonable allowance and with two free days per week.

Requirements for leave to enter as an au pair

89. The requirements to be met by a person seeking leave to enter the United Kingdom as an au pair are that he:
(i) is seeking entry for the purpose of taking up an arranged placement which can be shown to fall within the definition set out in paragraph 88; and
(ii) is aged between 17–27 inclusive or was so aged when first given leave to enter in this capacity; and
(iii) is unmarried; and
(iv) is without dependants; and
(v) is a national of one of the following countries: Andorra, Bosnia-Herzegovina, Croatia, Cyprus, Czech Republic, The Faroes, Greenland, Hungary, Macedonia, Malta, Monaco, San Marino, Slovak Republic, Slovenia, Switzerland, or Turkey; and
(vi) does not intend to stay in the United Kingdom for more than 2 years as an au pair; and
(vii) intends to leave the United Kingdom on completion of his stay as an au pair;
(viii) if he has previously spent time in the United Kingdom as an au pair, is not seeking leave to enter to a date beyond 2 years from the date on which he was first given leave to enter the United Kingdom in this capacity; and
(ix) is able to maintain and accommodate himself and any dependants without recourse to public funds.

Leave to enter as an au pair

90. A person seeking leave to enter the United Kingdom as an au pair may be admitted for a period not exceeding 2 years with a prohibition on employment except as an au pair, provided the Immigration Officer is satisfied that each of the requirements of paragraph 89 is met. (A non-visa national who wishes to ascertain in advance whether a proposed au pair placement is likely to meet the

requirements of paragraph 89 is advised to obtain an entry clearance before travelling to the United Kingdom).

Refusal of leave to enter as an au pair

91. An application for leave to enter as an au pair is to be refused if the Immigration Officer is not satisfied that each of the requirements of paragraph 89 is met.

Requirements for an extension of stay as an au pair

92. The requirements for an extension of stay as an au pair are that the applicant:
(i)   was given leave to enter the United Kingdom as an au pair under paragraph 90; and
(ii)   is undertaking an arranged au pair placement which can be shown to fall within the definition set out in paragraph 88; and
(iii)   meets the requirements of paragraph 89(ii)–(ix); and
(iv)   would not, as a result of an extension of stay, remain in the United Kingdom as an au pair to a date beyond 2 years from the date on which he was first given leave to enter the United Kingdom in this capacity.

Extension of stay as an au pair

93. An extension of stay as an au pair may be granted with a prohibition on employment except as an au pair, provided the Secretary of State is satisfied that each of the requirements of paragraph 92 is met.

Refusal of extension of stay as an au pair

94. An extension of stay as an au pair is to be refused if the Secretary of State is not satisfied that each of the requirements of paragraph 92 is met.

COMMENTARY

HC 31, from 1 November 1996, adds a prohibition on reliance on public funds (see Chapter 27 for the effect of this). HC 329 removed Liechtenstein from the list of countries whose nationals may enter as au pairs, with effect from 4 April 1996. HC 395 removed the discrimination against men under HC 251. HC 395 requires that au pairs have two free days per week and their maximum period of leave (two years) is not an aggregate but a continuous period. The requirements under para 89 must be satisfied, and if they are not the immigration officer has no discretion to grant leave under the rules. The arrangement must be the sole reason that the person wishes to visit the UK. If it appears at interview that his ultimate intention is to take up full-time employment, he will be refused entry (*Ramjane v Chief Immigration Officer Gatwick Airport* [1973] Imm AR 84). Evidence should be produced to satisfy the immigration service that the arrangement has been made. A letter from the host family, confirming the arrangement, and describing the au pair's duties, should be provided. It should indicate that he will have to study English, and how much pocket money he will be paid.

EU citizens may work as au pairs exercising their right to free movement. They do not need leave to enter for this or any other purpose. Nationals of states which are parties to the European Economic Area Agreement do not require leave to enter (or to remain in) the UK when exercising rights of free movement. The EEA countries are listed on p 298.

Extensions   A woman whose current leave to enter or remain was granted before 5 July 1992 may be granted an extension of leave as an au pair even if she did not enter in that capacity. Similarly, under Co-operation Agreements in the Field of Labour which are directly effective between the EU and several countries (Turkey, Morocco, Algeria and Tunisia) the rule may discriminate against workers from those countries wishing to continue in employment as au pairs (see *ONEM v Kziber* C18/90 [1991] ECR I-199).

2   Working holidaymakers

Requirements for leave to enter as a working holidaymaker
95. The requirements to be met by a person seeking leave to enter the United Kingdom as a working holidaymaker are that he:
(i)   is a Commonwealth citizen; and
(ii)   is aged 17–27 inclusive or was so aged when first given leave to enter in this capacity; and
(iii)   is unmarried or is married to a person who meets the requirements of this paragraph and the parties to the marriage intend to take a working holiday together; and
(iv)   has the means to pay for his return or onward journey; and
(v)   is able and intends to maintain and accommodate himself without recourse to public funds; and
(vi)   is intending to take employment incidental to a holiday but not to engage in business, provide services as a professional sportsman or entertainer or pursue a career in the United Kingdom; and
(vii)   does not have dependent children any of whom are 5 years of age or over or who will reach 5 years of age before the applicant completes his working holiday; or commitments which would require him to earn a regular income; and
(viii) intends to leave the United Kingdom at the end of his working holiday; and
(ix)   if he has previously spent time in the United Kingdom as a working holidaymaker, is not seeking leave to enter to a date beyond 2 years from the date he was first given leave to enter in this capacity; and
(x)   holds a valid United Kingdom entry clearance for entry in this capacity.

Leave to enter as a working holidaymaker
96. A person seeking leave to enter the United Kingdom as a working holidaymaker may be admitted for a period not exceeding 2 years with a condition restricting his freedom to take employment, provided he is able to produce to the Immigration Officer, on arrival, a valid United Kingdom entry clearance for entry in this capacity.

Refusal of leave to enter as a working holidaymaker
97. Leave to enter as a working holidaymaker is to be refused if a valid United Kingdom entry clearance for entry in this capacity is not produced to the Immigration Officer on arrival.

Requirements for an extension of stay as a working holidaymaker
98. The requirements for an extension of stay as a working holidaymaker are that the applicant:

(i) entered the United Kingdom with a valid United Kingdom entry clearance as a working holidaymaker; and

(ii) meets the requirements of paragraph 95(i)–(viii); and

(iii) would not, as a result of an extension of stay, remain in the United Kingdom as a working holidaymaker to a date beyond 2 years from the date on which he was first given leave to enter the United Kingdom in this capacity.

Extension of stay as a working holidaymaker

99. An extension of stay as a working holidaymaker may be granted with a condition restricting his freedom to take employment, provided the Secretary of State is satisfied that the applicant meets each of the requirements of paragraph 98.

Refusal of extension of stay as a working holidaymaker

100. An extension of stay as a working holidaymaker is to be refused if the Secretary of State is not satisfied that each of the requirements of paragraph 98 is met.

COMMENTARY

HC 395 introduced a mandatory requirement for entry clearance. A person who entered in another capacity cannot switch to the category of working holidaymaker. A person who does not have an entry clearance may not appeal against refusal of entry under this category (s 13(3B) of the 1971 Act as amended by the 1993 Act, s 11). For the definition of 'Commonwealth citizen' see pp 4–5. The rule permits married couples to take a working holiday together, but a dependent spouse must qualify independently as a working holidaymaker.

'Incidental to a holiday' A working holidaymaker may not engage in business, pursue a career, or provide services as a professional sportsman or entertainer. The employment must be incidental to the holiday. The requirement under the former HC 251 that the holiday be taken before the person 'settled down' no longer applies. Thus the holiday can be taken for any purpose, including obtaining experience in a trade, as long as the employment is incidental to it. In *Rani* (9987), the purpose of the holiday was in part to cope with bereavement, and in part to obtain such experience. Such purposes were permissible. The main purpose must be a holiday, with employment only incidental to that purpose. The leave granted under this rule is different from leave granted for the purpose of taking employment, and different considerations apply (*S of S v Pope* [1987] Imm AR 10). An intention to obtain a full-time job, rather than to take on a job or jobs which would be occasional and subordinate to the holiday, would not be acceptable (*Gunatilake v ECO Colombo* [1975] Imm AR 23).

The Home Office has indicated that working holidaymakers may work part-time for the whole of the holiday, or full-time for part of the holiday According to the Home Office information leaflet on working holidaymakers, full-time work is work for more than 25 hours per week. The Home Office states that out of the two years, only one could be spent working, otherwise a work permit should be sought. The rule does not, however, preclude the applicant from taking full-time work provided it is not for the duration of the holiday, nor does it specify what kind of employment is acceptable. The IAT gave a broader interpretation to the paragraph as worded in HC 251 than the Home Office. Full-time work, such as being a director of a company on a fixed contract lasting more than 12 months, may be consistent with the rule (*Kenneth De Clive Lowe v Immigration Officer, Heathrow* [1992] Imm AR 91). The rule as it appears in HC 395 provides that the applicant must not have 'commitments' which would require him to earn a regular income, and specifically mentions dependent children who will attain five years of age during the period of the working holiday. The immigration officer will refuse leave to enter if the person does not have the means to pay for his return journey or if the immigration officer has reason to believe that recourse to public funds is likely. For 'public funds' see p 60. To be a genuine working holidaymaker, a person must initially have some resources with which to finance his holiday, augmenting his resources from time to time by taking employment (*S of S v Grant* [1974] Imm AR 64). There is no obligation, however, on an intending working holidaymaker to show that he will work at all during his holiday (*Bari v IAT* [1986] Imm AR 264 (QBD); [1987] Imm AR 13 (CA)), but he must show that he has an intention to take employment incidental to a holiday. Thus, an intention to assist a relative with child care arrangements will not suffice (*Vdofia* (10829)). Where the applicant admitted that he could not find a job in his country of origin it was open to the immigration officer to find that the applicant's real intention was primarily to take employment (*Mulligan* (6022)).

Extensions   In addition to satisfying the requirements for applications for entry, a person applying to extend his leave as a working holidaymaker must show that he entered with a valid entry clearance as a working holidaymaker. Where a visitor had no funds with him on arrival and had been working for his sponsor more or less full-time, it appeared that his holiday was not incidental to his work and he did not therefore meet the requirements of the rules (*S of S v Grant* [1974] Imm AR 64). If a similar case were to arise under HC 395, the issue would be whether the working holidaymaker had worked part-time for the whole of the holiday or full-time for part of the holiday. Either would now be acceptable. Out of the two years one could be spent working, otherwise a work permit should be sought. The IAT dismissed an appeal on facts which indicated that the freelance work in the textile industry taken by an appellant could not, by reason of her high earnings on commission, be accepted as an employment only incidental to her holiday (*Baijal v S of S* [1976] Imm AR 34). Nor, where on the evidence it was plain that an appellant had been a hard working full-time member of the staff of a department store, could 'her work properly be described as employment which was only incidental to a holiday' (*Munasinghe v S of S* [1975] Imm AR 79). On extension, periods of full-time work are permitted, as is ownership of a limited company in certain circumstances (*De Clive*

Lowe v Immigration Officer, Heathrow [1992] Imm AR 91). Conversely, as noted above, the rules do not require the person to work at all for the duration of his leave as a working holidaymaker. He must not, however, become a charge on public funds (*Badrul Bari v IAT* [1987] Imm AR 13). The maximum period of two years' leave to remain as a working holidaymaker is continuous, not aggregated.

3   Children of working holidaymakers

Requirements for leave to enter or remain as the child of a working holidaymaker

101. The requirements to be met by a person seeking leave to enter or remain in the United Kingdom as the child of a working holidaymaker are that:

(i)   he is the child of a parent admitted to or allowed to remain in the United Kingdom as a working holidaymaker; and

(ii)   he is under the age of 5 and will leave the United Kingdom before reaching that age; and

(iii)   he can and will be maintained and accommodated adequately without recourse to public funds or without his parent(s) engaging in business or taking employment except as provided by paragraph 95 above; and

(iv)   both parents are being or have been admitted to or allowed to remain in the United Kingdom save where:

     (a)   the parent he is accompanying or joining is his sole surviving parent; or

     (b)   the parent he is accompanying or joining has had sole responsibility for his upbringing; or

     (c)   there are serious and compelling family or other considerations which make exclusion from the United Kingdom undesirable and suitable arrangements have been made for his care; and

(v)   if seeking leave to enter, he holds a valid United Kingdom entry clearance for entry in this capacity or, if seeking leave to remain, was admitted with a valid United Kingdom entry clearance for entry in this capacity.

Leave to enter or remain as the child of a working holidaymaker

102. A person seeking leave to enter or remain in the United Kingdom as the child of a working holidaymaker may be admitted or allowed to remain for the same period of leave as that granted to the working holidaymaker provided that, in relation to an application for leave to enter, a valid United Kingdom entry clearance for entry in this capacity is produced to the Immigration Officer on arrival or, in the case of an application for leave to remain, he was admitted with a valid United Kingdom entry clearance for entry in this capacity and is able to satisfy the Secretary of State that each of the requirements of paragraph 101(i)–(iv) is met.

Refusal of leave to enter or remain as the child of a working holidaymaker

103. Leave to enter or remain in the United Kingdom as the child of a working holidaymaker is to be refused if, in relation to an application for leave to enter, a valid United Kingdom entry clearance for entry in this capacity is not produced to the Immigration Officer on arrival or, in the case of an application for leave to remain, the applicant was not admitted with a valid United Kingdom entry

clearance for entry in this capacity or is unable to satisfy the Secretary of State that each of the requirements of paragraph 101(i)–(iv) is met.

COMMENTARY

Paragraph 101 provides that the child must not, during the holiday, attain five years. Note the definition of 'parent' in para 6 (p 59). Both parents must be admitted or have been admitted, save where only one parent survives and the child accompanies that parent. He may also accompany a single parent or join a single parent where the parent he is accompanying has sole responsibility for his upbringing (see p 221). The child may also accompany one parent where there are serious and compelling family or other considerations which make exclusion from the UK undesirable and suitable arrangements have been made for his care (see p 222). He may be maintained by recourse to employment which is incidental to the holiday.

4   Seasonal workers at agricultural camps

Requirements for leave to enter as a seasonal worker at an agricultural camp

104. The requirements to be met by a person seeking leave to enter the United Kingdom as a seasonal worker at an agricultural camp are that he:
- (i)   is a student in full-time education aged between 18–25 years inclusive, except if returning for another season at the specific invitation of a farmer; and
- (ii) holds a valid Home Office work card issued by the operator of a scheme approved by the Secretary of State; and
- (iii) intends to leave the United Kingdom at the end of his period of leave as a seasonal worker;
- (iv) does not intend to take employment except in the terms of this paragraph; and
- (v)   is able to maintain and accommodate himself and any dependants without recourse to public funds.

Leave to enter as a seasonal worker at an agricultural camp

105. A person seeking leave to enter the United Kingdom as a seasonal worker at an agricultural camp may be admitted with a condition restricting his freedom to take employment for a period not exceeding 3 months or until 30 November of the year in question, whichever is the shorter period, provided the Immigration Officer is satisfied that each of the requirements of paragraph 104 is met.

Refusal of leave to enter as a seasonal worker at an agricultural camp

106. Leave to enter the United Kingdom as a seasonal worker at an agricultural camp is to be refused if the Immigration Officer is not satisfied that each of the requirements of paragraph 104 is met.

Requirements for extension of stay as a seasonal worker at an agricultural camp

107. The requirements for an extension of stay as a seasonal worker at an agricultural camp are that the applicant:
- (i)   entered the United Kingdom as a seasonal worker with a valid Home Office work card under paragraph 105; and
- (ii) meets the requirements of paragraph 104(iii)–(v); and

(iii) can show that there is further farm work available under the approved scheme; and

(iv) would not, as a result of an extension of stay, remain in the United Kingdom as a seasonal worker for longer than 6 months in aggregate or beyond 30 November of the year in question, whichever is the shorter period.

Extension of stay as a seasonal worker at an agricultural camp

108. An extension of stay as a seasonal worker may be granted with a condition restricting his freedom to take employment for a further period not exceeding 3 months or until 30 November of the year in question, whichever is the shorter period, provided the Secretary of State is satisfied that the applicant meets each of the requirements of paragraph 107.

Refusal of extension of stay as a seasonal worker at an agricultural camp

109. An extension of stay as a seasonal worker at an agricultural camp is to be refused if the Secretary of State is not satisfied that each of the requirements of paragraph 107 is met.

COMMENTARY

HC 31, from 1 November 1996, adds para 104 (v) (see Chapter 27 for the consequences). A person applying for an extension must have been granted leave to enter as a seasonal worker at an agricultural camp. He will therefore be a student of between 18 and 25 years, or returning for another season at the specific invitation of a farmer. He will have to provide evidence of such an invitation. He must also hold a valid Home Office camp card issued by the operator of the scheme, which must have been approved by the S of S. He must intend to leave the UK at the end of his period of leave as a seasonal worker, and must not intend to take other work. He must also have been given leave for a period of three months or until 30 November of the year in question, whichever is the shorter period. He must be able to show that there is further farm work available under the approved scheme. A letter from the person organising the camp should be sufficient evidence of this. Leave must in any event expire on 30 November of the year in question or after a further three months, so that the maximum period of leave is six months (para 107(iv)).

5 Teachers and language assistants

Requirements for leave to enter as a teacher or language assistant under an approved exchange scheme

110. The requirements to be met by a person seeking leave to enter the United Kingdom as a teacher or language assistant on an approved exchange scheme are that he:

(i) is coming to an educational establishment in the United Kingdom under an exchange scheme approved by the Education Departments or administered by the Central Bureau for Educational Visits and Exchanges or the League for the Exchange of Commonwealth Teachers; and

(ii) intends to leave the United Kingdom at the end of his exchange period; and

(iii) does not intend to take employment except in the terms of this paragraph; and

(iv) is able to maintain and accommodate himself and any dependants without recourse to public funds; and

(v) holds a valid United Kingdom entry clearance for entry in this capacity.

Leave to enter as a teacher or language assistant under an exchange scheme
111. A person seeking leave to enter the United Kingdom as a teacher or language assistant under an approved exchange scheme may be given leave to enter for a period not exceeding 12 months provided he is able to produce to the Immigration Officer, on arrival, a valid United Kingdom entry clearance for entry in this capacity.

Refusal of leave to enter as a teacher or language assistant under an approved exchange scheme
112. Leave to enter the United Kingdom as a teacher or language assistant under an approved exchange scheme is to be refused if a valid United Kingdom entry clearance for entry in this capacity is not produced to the Immigration Officer on arrival.

Requirements for extension of stay as a teacher or language assistant under an approved exchange scheme
113. The requirements for an extension of stay as a teacher or language assistant under an approved exchange scheme are that the applicant:

(i) entered the United Kingdom with a valid United Kingdom entry clearance as a teacher or language assistant; and

(ii) is still engaged in the employment for which his entry clearance was granted; and

(iii) is still required for the employment in question, as certified by the employer; and

(iv) meets the requirements of paragraph 110(ii)–(iv); and

(v) would not, as a result of an extension of stay, remain in the United Kingdom as an exchange teacher or language assistant for more than 2 years from the date on which he was first given leave to enter the United Kingdom in this capacity.

Extension of stay as a teacher or language assistant under an approved exchange scheme
114. An extension of stay as a teacher or language assistant under an approved exchange scheme may be granted for a further period not exceeding 12 months provided the Secretary of State is satisfied that each of the requirements of paragraph 113 is met.

Refusal of extension of stay as a teacher or language assistant under an approved exchange scheme
115. An extension of stay as a teacher or language assistant under an approved exchange scheme is to be refused if the Secretary of State is not satisfied that each of the requirements of paragraph 113 is met.

COMMENTARY

There is a mandatory requirement for an entry clearance for the purpose of this category. A person without an entry clearance may not appeal against refusal of leave to enter (s 13(3B) of the 1971 Act as amended by s 11 of the 1993 Act).

A person seeking an extension of leave as a teacher or language assistant must have entered the UK with a valid UK entry clearance in that category. He must still be in the employment for which the entry clearance was granted, although the rule would appear to envisage a person's being granted leave where the establishment at which he was still employed had ceased to be approved for exchanges since his original leave was granted. He must produce a certificate from his employer stating that he is still required for the employment in question. He must intend to leave the UK at the end of the exchange period. He must not intend to take employment other than under the exchange. The aggregate total of his leave in this capacity, including the extension, should not exceed two years. A person who did not have an entry clearance for the purpose may not appeal against a refusal to extend his leave under this category (s 14 of the 1971 Act as amended by s 11 of the 1993 Act).

6   Approved training or work experience

Requirements for leave to enter for Department of Employment approved training or work experience

116. The requirements to be met by a person seeking leave to enter the United Kingdom for Department of Employment approved training or work experience are that he:

(i)   holds a valid work permit from the Department of Employment issued under the Training and Work Experience Scheme; and

(ii)   is not of an age which puts him outside the limits for employment; and

(iii) is capable of undertaking the training or work experience as specified in his work permit; and

(iv)   intends to leave the United Kingdom on the completion of his training or work experience; and

(v)   does not intend to take employment except as specified in his work permit; and

(vi)   is able to maintain and accommodate himself and any dependants adequately without recourse to public funds.

Leave to enter for Department of Employment approved training or work experience

117. A person seeking leave to enter the United Kingdom for approved training may be admitted to the United Kingdom for a period not exceeding 3 years and a person seeking entry for approved work experience may be admitted for a period not exceeding 12 months, provided the Immigration Officer is satisfied that each of the requirements of paragraph 116 is met. Leave to enter is to be subject to a condition permitting the person to take or change employment only with the permission of the Department of Employment.

Refusal of leave to enter for Department of Employment approved training or work experience

118. Leave to enter the United Kingdom for Department of Employment approved training or work experience is to be refused if the Immigration Officer is not satisfied that each of the requirements of paragraph 116 is met.

COMMENTARY

Although HC 395 refers to the 'Department of Employment', these references are now to be taken as references to the Department for Education and Employment.

The applicant must have a permit from the Department for Education and Employment issued under the Training and Work Experience Scheme. If the Department does not approve the training, the applicant will need a work permit and has no right of appeal against refusal of leave under this category (*Malikebu* (12195)). Application for a training and work experience permit is made on form WP2. The Department for Education and Employment requirements are set out below, including those relating to age for each of work experience and training. The maximum leave to enter available for a person seeking training is three years. The maximum leave to enter available to a person seeking approved work experience is 12 months. HC 395 prohibits visitors switching to the training and work experience Scheme after arrival. However, those granted leave to enter as students may switch.

Department for Education and Employment requirements   The post must genuinely be for training and work experience. If the application is in fact to employ an overseas national in a vacant post, application for a work permit should be made on form WP1. Permits are not required for:

(*a*)   business persons and the self-employed, including writers and artists;
(*b*)   ministers of religion;
(*c*)   representatives of overseas newspapers, news agencies and broadcasting organisations;
(*d*)   private servants of diplomatic staff;
(*e*)   sole representatives of overseas firms;
(*f*)   teachers and language assistants under approved schemes;
(*g*)   employees of an overseas government or international organisation;
(*h*)   seamen under contract to join a ship in British waters;
(*i*)   operational ground staff of overseas owned airlines;
(*j*)   seasonal workers at agricultural camps under approved schemes;
(*k*)   doctors and dentists in postgraduate training;
(*l*)   business visitors.

Permission is given to enable a national of any country to come to the UK for training towards a professional or specialist qualification, or to undertake a short period of work experience. The applicant must have a sufficient command of English to enable him to benefit from the training or work experience. The applicant must return overseas at the end of the training. The Department for Education and Employment will not approve a transfer to ordinary employment in the UK. The applicant must work abroad, usually for a minimum of two years, before an application can be made for approval of further training or work experience. He will normally have to work abroad for a period of at least two years before applying for a work permit.

Training   The training should lead to a professional or specialist qualification. The trainee must be 18 or older. He must have qualifications equivalent to UK degree level or NVQ level 4 or higher. The employer must be able to show that the training is relevant to the qualifications of the trainee. The training period must be agreed in advance. If qualifications take a number of years to obtain, approval will be given for an initial period. That period will be extended if the trainee is making satisfactory progress. The trainee will be allowed a maximum of three attempts (or chances) to take any one examination before the Department for Education and Employment approval will be affected. The trainee should be training for a minimum of 30 hours per week. No approval will be given for supplementary qualifications to be taken once the agreed course of training is completed. The trainee must be subject to the same terms and conditions, and receive the same salary, as UK or EU trainees. If the qualification is a professional one, the employer must be registered or approved by the appropriate professional body.

Work experience The overseas national should be aged 18 to 25. He must be employed in a supernumerary capacity, and should not be filling a job which would otherwise be available to a UK or EU national. In those cases an application for a work permit should be made. An exception is made for recognised exchange arrangement exchanges. The person must have the appropriate experience or the appropriate academic qualifications to enable him to benefit from the proposed work experience. Only in very exceptional circumstances will a period longer than 12 months be approved by the Department for Education and Employment. Under para 117, the maximum period of leave on entry is 12 months. The work experience must be of a level acceptable to the Department for Education and Employment. It must be at least NVQ 4 or higher, and should last 30 or more hours per week.

Any payment made to the overseas national should be a modest personal spending allowance only. A person working under an exchange agreement where rates of pay are reciprocal may be paid a full wage. Where a person is transferred from an overseas branch of a company to the UK for the purposes of work experience, he may receive a full wage. If he is employed in a senior position, an application for a work permit should be made on Form WP1.

If an application for a training and work experience position with the employer in question has not been made in the previous four years, the employer should send to the Department copies of the latest audited accounts and the latest annual report, or any publicity or marketing material. If these are not available, evidence of the tenure of the business premises, details of staff employed in the UK, and a copy of the company's documents of incorporation should be sent.

The company must show that it is already providing goods or services, or is contractually committed to doing so. Applications for approval of training and work experience schemes are made on Form WP2, and are dealt with at the Overseas Labour Section, the Employment Department, W5 Moorfoot, Sheffield S1 4PQ. They are generally dealt with within six to eight weeks of receipt.

Extensions

Requirements for extension of stay for Department of Employment approved training or work experience

119. The requirements for an extension of stay for Department of Employment approved training or work experience are that the applicant:

(i)   entered the United Kingdom with a valid work permit under paragraph 117 or was admitted or allowed to remain in the United Kingdom as a student; and

(ii) has written approval from the Department of Employment for an extension of stay in this category; and

(iii) meets the requirements of paragraph 116(ii)–(vi); and

(iv) would not as a result of an extension of stay spend more than 2 years in the United Kingdom for Department of Employment approved work experience.

Extension of stay for Department of Employment approved training or work experience

120. An extension of stay for approved training may be granted for a further period not exceeding 3 years; and an extension of stay for approved work experience may be granted for a further period not exceeding 12 months provided the Secretary of State is satisfied that each of the requirements of paragraph 119 is met. An extension of stay is to be subject to a condition permitting the applicant to take or change employment only with the permission of the Department of Employment.

Refusal of extension of stay for Department of Employment approved training or work experience

121. An extension of stay for Department of Employment approved training or work experience is to be refused if the Secretary of State is not satisfied that each of the requirements of paragraph 119 is met.

COMMENTARY

The maximum period a person may remain in the UK on approved training is three years. The maximum period a person may remain in the UK on approved work experience is two years. If the person wishes to change employer, or the employer wishes to change the type of work the person is doing, permission must be obtained. It will be given to a new employer only if he offers the same training or work experience as the first employer. The new employer must apply separately. Applications for extensions should be made well in advance. The employer should explain why he wishes to keep the overseas national.

Training The employer should give details of the dates and number of attempts at each examination taken by the trainee, together with his results and future examination dates.

Work experience Extensions beyond 12 months are not usually approved without agreement at the commencement of the work experience period. Exceptionally, an extension may be granted if a fully reasoned application is made. A programme of further work should be sent to the Department for Education and Employment.

The application must show that the trainee is continuing on a training and work experience scheme, and is making satisfactory progress (*S of S v Brizmohun* [1972] Imm AR 122). An extension will be refused without the appropriate approval from the Department for Education and Employment (see *Yeong Hoi Yueng v S of S* [1977] Imm AR 34 and *Roy v S of S* [1988] Imm AR 53).

7 Spouses

Requirements for leave to enter or remain as the spouse of a person with limited leave to enter or remain in the United Kingdom under paragraphs 110–121

122. The requirements to be met by a person seeking leave to enter or remain in the United Kingdom as the spouse of a person with limited leave to enter or remain in the United Kingdom under paragraphs 110–121 are that:

(i) the applicant is married to a person with limited leave to enter or remain in the United Kingdom under paragraphs 110–121; and

(ii) each of the parties intends to live with the other as his or her spouse during the applicant's stay and the marriage is subsisting; and

(iii) there will be adequate accommodation for the parties and any dependants without recourse to public funds in accommodation which they own or occupy exclusively; and

(iv) the parties will be able to maintain themselves and any dependants adequately without recourse to public funds; and

(v) the applicant does not intend to stay in the United Kingdom beyond any period of leave granted to his spouse; and

(vi) if seeking leave to enter, the applicant holds a valid United Kingdom entry clearance for entry in this capacity or, if seeking leave to remain, was admitted with a valid United Kingdom entry clearance for entry in this capacity.

Leave to enter or remain as the spouse of a person with limited leave to enter or remain in the United Kingdom under paragraphs 110–121

123. A person seeking leave to enter or remain in the United Kingdom as the spouse of a person with limited leave to enter or remain in the United Kingdom under paragraphs 110–121 may be given leave to enter or remain in the United Kingdom for a period of leave not in excess of that granted to the person with limited leave to enter or remain under paragraphs 110–121 provided that, in relation to an application for leave to enter, he is able, on arrival, to produce to the Immigration Officer a valid United Kingdom entry clearance for entry in this capacity or, in the case of an application for limited leave to remain, was admitted with a valid United Kingdom entry clearance for entry in this capacity and is able to satisfy the Secretary of State that each of the requirements of paragraph 122(i)–(v) is met.

Refusal of leave to enter or remain as the spouse of a person with limited leave to enter or remain in the United Kingdom under paragraphs 110–121

124. Leave to enter or remain in the United Kingdom as the spouse of a person with limited leave to enter or remain in the United Kingdom under paragraphs 110–121 is to be refused if, in relation to an application for leave to enter, a valid United Kingdom entry clearance for entry in this capacity is not produced to the Immigration Officer on arrival or, in the case of an application for limited leave

to remain, if the applicant was not admitted with a valid United Kingdom entry clearance for entry in this capacity or is unable to satisfy the Secretary of State that each of the requirements of paragraph 122(i)–(v) is met.

COMMENTARY

The spouse of a person on approved training or work experience, or the spouse of a person who has leave as a teacher or language assistant under an approved exchange scheme, must satisfy the requirements of para 122. The first of these is that the couple are married. They must intend to live together as spouses during the applicant's stay, and the marriage must be subsisting. Some evidence that the marriage is subsisting should therefore be available. The requirements of para 122 are mandatory, as is possession or production of an entry clearance.

8   Children

Requirements for leave to enter or remain as the child of a person with limited leave to enter or remain in the United Kingdom under paragraphs 110–121

125. The requirements to be met by a person seeking leave to enter or remain in the United Kingdom as the child of a person with limited leave to enter or remain in the United Kingdom under paragraphs 110–121 are that:

(i)   he is the child of a parent who has limited leave to enter or remain in the United Kingdom under paragraphs 110–121; and

(ii) he is under the age of 18 or has current leave to enter or remain in this capacity; and

(iii) he is unmarried, has not formed an independent family unit and is not leading an independent life; and

(iv) he can, and will, be maintained and accommodated adequately without recourse to public funds in accommodation which his parent(s) own or occupy exclusively; and

(v)   he will not stay in the United Kingdom beyond any period of leave granted to his parent(s); and

(vi) both parents are being or have been admitted to or allowed to remain in the United Kingdom save where:

    (a) the parent he is accompanying or joining is his sole surviving parent; or

    (b) the parent he is accompanying or joining has had sole responsibility for his upbringing; or

    (c) there are serious and compelling family or other considerations which make exclusion from the United Kingdom undesirable and suitable arrangements have been made for his care; and

(vii) if seeking leave to enter, he holds a valid United Kingdom entry clearance for entry in this capacity or, if seeking leave to remain, was admitted with a valid United Kingdom entry clearance for entry in this capacity.

Leave to enter or remain as the child of a person with limited leave to enter or remain in the United Kingdom under paragraphs 110–121

126. A person seeking leave to enter or remain in the United Kingdom as the child of a person with limited leave to enter or remain in the United Kingdom

under paragraphs 110–121 may be given leave to enter or remain in the United Kingdom for a period of leave not in excess of that granted to the person with limited leave to enter or remain under paragraphs 110–121 provided that, in relation to an application for leave to enter, he is able, on arrival, to produce to the Immigration Officer a valid United Kingdom entry clearance for entry in this capacity or, in the case of an application for limited leave to remain, he was admitted with a valid United Kingdom entry clearance for entry in this capacity and is able to satisfy the Secretary of State that each of the requirements of paragraph 125(i)–(vi) is met.

Refusal of leave to enter or remain as the child of a person with limited leave to enter or remain in the United Kingdom under paragraphs 110–121
127. Leave to enter or remain in the United Kingdom as the child of a person with limited leave to enter or remain in the United Kingdom under paragraphs 110–121 is to be refused if, in relation to an application for leave to enter, a valid United Kingdom entry clearance for entry in this capacity is not produced to the Immigration Officer on arrival or, in the case of an application for limited leave to remain, if the applicant was not admitted with a valid United Kingdom entry clearance for entry in this capacity or is unable to satisfy the Secretary of State that each of the requirements of paragraph 125(i)–(vi) is met.

COMMENTARY

The applicant must be the child of a person who has limited leave as a person on approved training or work experience, or a person who has leave as a teacher or language assistant under an approved exchange scheme. The child must be under 18. He must not have formed an 'independent family unit'. He must not be married. He must not be living an independent life. The child must be maintained and adequately accommodated without recourse to public funds. For the definition of 'public funds' see p 60. There is no requirement that the parents themselves maintain the child. However, there is a requirement that he is maintained and accommodated in accommodation which his parent(s) own or occupy exclusively. Thus the parent(s) must either own the accommodation exclusively, or occupy it exclusively. No definition of 'accommodation' is offered. Both parents must be admitted or have been admitted, unless the conditions set out in para 125(vi) apply. For 'sole responsibility' see p 221, and for 'serious and compelling family or other considerations', see p 222.

Chapter 10

Part 5: Employment

1 Introduction

Possession of a work permit does not automatically result in leave to enter, nor can it be treated as the same thing (*S of S v Gomes* [1990] Imm AR 576). If the Department for Education and Employment ('DfEE') refuses to grant a permit, there is no appeal against the decision (*Pearson v IAT* [1978] Imm AR 212). It may be possible to apply for judicial review of a decision to refuse a work permit in appropriate circumstances. Thus a decision of the DfEE regarding the grant of a work permit may be reviewed if the DfEE does not take account of the latest information available to it at the time of the decision, but merely that available at the time of the application (*R v Department of Employment, ex p Barry Allan* [1991] Imm AR 336); but not, it seems, on the basis that the grant or refusal of a work permit is an act of discrimination under the Sex Discrimination Act 1975 (*R v IAT, ex p Bernstein* [1987] Imm AR 182). Moreover, where a policy statement is issued, it may give rise to a legitimate expectation on the part of the entrant that its terms will be observed until the Department announces a change in its policy (for judicial review, see Chapter 22).

EEA citizens The position of EEA citizens and their dependants is dealt with in detail in Chapter 16. An EU citizen is permitted to enter without obtaining leave, by virtue of the free movement provisions of the Treaty of Rome, Regulation 1612/68 and directives made pursuant to that treaty. Further, freedom of movement may apply to non-EU citizens employed by undertakings from an EU state while it is carrying out a project in the UK (*Rush Portuguesa LDA v Office National d'Immigration* [1990] ECR I-1417. Thus a requirement that the non-EU national employee of an EU undertaking must be in possession of a work permit cannot be imposed on such employees.

Domestic work No rule covers the position of those who do domestic work for persons of independent means. Frequently they are given a visitor stamp, which, as the Home Office knows, does not reflect what they are actually doing. The Home Office produces a leaflet, which is given to the worker and his employer, explaining a concession. This formalises the earlier practice of the Home Office. The following requirements need to be fulfilled for the concession to apply:

(*a*) the domestic servant must be 17 years or older;

(*b*) in the case of an employer visiting the UK, the servant must have been employed by him for at least 12 months before entry to the UK;

(*c*) in any other case the employment must have been for at least 24 months;

(*d*) the domestic servant must have entry clearance.

When considering whether to grant or refuse entry clearance, the ECO will investigate the sort of work the servant will do, and the hours involved. The servant will be asked whether he wishes to go to the UK. The servant is told, and it is stressed in the leaflet, that he will not be permitted to change employment after entry. The servant's leave will be granted in line with that of his employer. The practice of granting visitor's stamps in these circumstances was criticised by the IAT in *Memi v S of S* [1992] Imm AR 122, where it was said that such stamps failed to make clear, as they are required to by the 1971 Act, the terms of the grant of leave. Where a domestic worker had been admitted to the UK pursuant to this concession, and her application for an extension was refused because she was trying to change from one employer to another, the adjudicator and the IAT had jurisdiction to consider whether the decision was in accordance with the law. If the domestic worker's legitimate expectation under the concession has been infringed, the appellate authorities may find that the decision is not in accordance with the law. However, a domestic worker's legitimate expectation under this concession can only be that he will be allowed to remain in the UK as long as the employer with whom he arrived remains (*Regina* (8973)). The Home Office issue a leaflet (*Information about Domestic Servants Travelling to the UK*, ISBN 1858 93 50 67), dealing with the rights of domestic workers while in the UK, including whether they may change employer, and what they should do if they are ill treated.

2   Work permit holders

Requirements for leave to enter the United Kingdom for work permit employment

128. The requirements to be met by a person coming to the United Kingdom to seek or take employment (unless he is otherwise eligible for admission for employment under these Rules or is eligible for admission as a seaman under contract to join a ship due to leave British waters) are that he:

(i)   holds a valid Department of Employment work permit; and

(ii)   is not of an age which puts him outside the limits for employment; and

(iii) is capable of undertaking the employment specified in the work permit; and

(iv) does not intend to take employment except as specified in his work permit; and

(v)   is able to maintain and accommodate himself and any dependants adequately without recourse to public funds; and

(vi) in the case of a person in possession of a work permit which is valid for a period of 12 months or less, intends to leave the United Kingdom at the end of his approved employment.

Leave to enter for work permit employment

129. A person seeking leave to enter the United Kingdom for the purpose of work permit employment may be admitted for a period not exceeding 4 years (normally as specified in his work permit), subject to a condition restricting him to employment approved by the Department of Employment, provided the Immigration Officer is satisfied that each of the requirements of paragraph 128 is met.

Refusal of leave to enter for employment

130. Leave to enter for the purpose of employment is to be refused if the Immigration Officer is not satisfied that each of the requirements of paragraph 128 is met (unless he is otherwise eligible for admission for employment under these Rules or is eligible for admission as a seaman under contract to join a ship due to leave British waters).

COMMENTARY

The requirements for a work permit are set out below. The person must not be of an age which puts him outside the limits for employment. Where a person is not eligible under any of the following categories he must meet the requirements of para 128 before entering the UK to work.

The categories are:

(a) post graduate doctor or dentist;

(b) working holidaymakers;

(c) seamen;

(d) seasonal workers at agricultural camps;

(e) training or work experience;

(f) representatives of overseas newspapers, news agencies and broadcasting organisations;

(g) sole representatives of overseas firms;

(h) private servants of diplomatic staff;

(i) overseas government employees;

(k) ministers of religion etc;

(l) airport based operational ground staff of overseas airlines;

(m) exceptions based on UK ancestry.

(a) DfEE requirements

Form WP1 must be filled in by the prospective employer as soon as the person is identified for a post. The application should be made not more than six months before the date on which the employer wishes to bring the employee to the UK, or three months before the person's current leave expires. Permits will be issued only for posts requiring either recognised degree level or equivalent professional qualifications, with, normally, two years' post qualification experience. Time spent in the UK in a permit-free capacity (see above) will not normally be taken into account for the purposes of calculating length of experience. Where a worker is employed under a work permit the employer must take responsibility for the employee's pay, tax and national insurance. The terms and conditions relating to the employment must be equal to those offered to UK employees for similar work. The current policy of the DfEE is to grant 18-month permits for first-time applications from employers. Thereafter longer periods may be granted.

Key workers   Key workers are persons having technical or specialised skills and expertise essential to the day-to-day running of the company. A key worker must have specialised skills, knowledge or experience not readily available in the EU, and the jobs of others must depend on him. Permits are issued for short periods only. Catering and hotel specialists may also be key workers. If the worker has extensive knowledge of languages and cultures which is not readily available in the UK or EU, he may be processed as a key worker if at least 60 per cent of his time is spent in contact work using his cultural or linguistic knowledge. The employer has to show that he has vigorously tested the local labour market before appointing a key worker from overseas, and that the key worker will be able to train a resident worker who can take over once he leaves the UK. It will assist the application if it can be shown that the presence of the key worker will prevent job losses.

Work permits will not be issued for certain categories of employment. Thus, no permits will be issued for manual, craft, clerical, secretarial or similar work, or for resident domestic workers, such as nannies or house-keepers.

Employers seeking work permits for persons to fill the following categories of post need fill in only the first part of WP1:

(*a*)   a senior post in an international company which requires an existing employee to transfer from abroad, or a post designed to develop the career of an existing employee;

(*b*)   a post at board level or equivalent for which there is no other suitable candidate;

(*c*)   a new post essential to an inward investment project bringing jobs and capital to the UK;

(*d*)   a post in an occupation acknowledged by the industry or profession concerned as subject to an acute shortage of personnel nationally and likely to be so within the EC. The DfEE may vary the 'shortage occupations' in accordance with the changing labour market, and inquiries should be addressed to the Department at the time of the application.

Part 1 of Form WP1 asks for details of the following:

(*a*)   the person to be employed;

(*b*)   the UK employer;

(*c*)   the employment offered, including how long the person is expected to be employed in the UK (specifying a period). If a period of more than four years is specified, reasons for the longer period must be given. The form must specify the duties involved in the job, the pay and hours;

(*d*) the qualifications of the employee, including any bodies with whom the person is registered, and the qualifications required by the job;

(*e*) the employee's employment record, including whether the person has held a training and work experience scheme permit within two years;

(*f*) the reasons for recruiting from outside the EU, including whether it is a transfer within an international company, and the reasons for making the offer to the person in terms of heads (*a*) to (*d*) above;

(*g*) if it is said that the occupation is one requiring high level skills, qualifications and experience acknowledged to be in acute short supply within the EU, and the employer has had difficulty in recruiting, evidence to show that there is no suitable candidate available in the EU, and details of any recruitment methods tried by the employer.

In all other cases, Part II of the Form WP1 must be filled in, and in particular where the person:

(*a*) has held a training and work experience scheme permit in the last two years; or

(*b*) has held a permit for a career development post in the last six months; or

(*c*) is already in the UK; or

(*d*) is a key worker.

The whole of the form must be filled in. Thus, the following details must be given:

(*a*) evidence of the need to recruit from outside the EU:
   (i) why training or transfer cannot fill the need;
   (ii) why the job cannot be filled by an EU worker;

(*b*) in relation to key workers:
   (i) special skills, experience or qualifications which make the worker uniquely qualified to do the job;
   (ii) the way in which the jobs of workers in the UK, and the success of the business, depend on the recruitment of the person;
   (iii) the relevant knowledge of language or cultural skills which are not readily available in the EU, together with reasons why these skills are essential for the job.

The prospective employer must supply:

(*a*) evidence of the qualifications of the person;

(*b*) original references, on letter headed paper, covering the last two years;

(*c*) copies of all advertisements, showing the name and date of publication;

(*d*) if the person is in the UK and not in approved employment, his passport.

If no application for a work permit has been made in the last four years the following must also be supplied:

(*a*) the employer's latest audited accounts with the accountant's name clearly shown;

(*b*) a copy of the latest annual report or publicity or internal marketing.
In default of the above, evidence of the tenure of the business premises,
the staff employed in the UK, and copies of any company incorporation
documents should be provided.

Advertisements should identify a specific post and must have been placed,
within the last six months before the application, in a quality newspaper with
national or EU circulation, or in a trade journal. For key worker posts the
advertisement must be available in all EU countries.

(b) Extension of stay for work permit employment

Requirements for an extension of stay for work permit employment

131. The requirements for an extension of stay to seek or take employment
(unless the applicant is otherwise eligible for an extension of stay for employment under these Rules) are that the applicant:

(i)   entered the United Kingdom with a valid work permit under paragraph 129;
       and

(ii)   has written approval from the Department of Employment for the con-
       tinuation of his employment; and

(iii) meets the requirements of paragraph 128(ii)–(v).

Extension of stay for work permit employment

132. An extension of stay for work permit employment may be granted for a
period not exceeding the period of approved employment recommended by the
Department of Employment provided the Secretary of State is satisfied that each
of the requirements of paragraph 131 is met. An extension of stay is to be
subject to a condition restricting the applicant to employment approved by the
Department of Employment.

Refusal of extension of stay for employment

133. An extension of stay for employment is to be refused if the Secretary
of State is not satisfied that each of the requirements of paragraph 131 is
met (unless the applicant is otherwise eligible for an extension of stay for
employment under these Rules).

Indefinite leave to remain for a work permit holder

134. Indefinite leave to remain may be granted, on application, to a person
admitted as a work permit holder provided:

(i)   he has spent a continuous period of 4 years in the United Kingdom in this
       capacity; and

(ii)   he has met the requirements of paragraph 131 throughout the 4 year period;
       and

(iii) he is still required for the employment in question, as certified by his
       employer.

Refusal of indefinite leave to remain for a work permit holder

135. Indefinite leave to remain in the United Kingdom for a work permit holder
is to be refused if the Secretary of State is not satisfied that each of the requirements of paragraph 134 is met.

COMMENTARY

A person who holds a work permit may apply for an extension of leave to remain as a work permit holder. He must be in possession of a valid permit. He must not intend to take employment except as specified in the permit. He must be able to maintain and accommodate himself and any dependants without recourse to public funds (see p 60). The DfEE must approve the continuation of the employment, and must have issued an 'approval to work'. If the DfEE refuses to approve a change of employment, there is no right of appeal, as the 1996 Act makes an 'approval to work issued after entry' a document which the appellant must have under s 14(2B) of the 1971 Act (see p 356), thus overturning *Kwai Nin Pang* (12083). The only remedy will be judicial review (see Chapter 22).

A work permit is issued in relation to a specific job with a specific employer, so that if the person wishes to change employers, the new employer must apply for a work permit and satisfy the above requirements. In any event, changes of employer are allowed only if the employee continues in the kind of work for which the original permit was issued. If the employer wishes the person to change jobs within the company, a fresh permit application must be made.

Applications for extensions of work permits are made on Form WP5. The passport must be sent, and the DfEE will need to be satisfied that the employer needs to keep the overseas national and that efforts have been made to fill the post with an EU national. The employer must state the results of those efforts; and the period of the employer's need for the overseas national. An application should not be made earlier than three months before the permit expires, but before the permit does expire. Form WP5 also seeks details of why training or transfer will not fill the employer's need during the extended period.

Under Co-operation Agreements in the Field of Labour, between the EU and Turkey, Morocco, Algeria, and Tunisia, workers from those countries may not need an extension of a work permit to remain working in the UK (see Chapter 16).

An applicant who has leave for four years and whose employer wishes to continue to employ him will probably be granted indefinite leave to remain (para 134). The applicant must show that he has spent a continuous period of four years in the UK as a work permit holder. He must show that he is still required for the employment in question. Indefinite leave to remain is not now automatic after service of the four-year period. Where the claim for indefinite leave is based on approved employment, all four years must be approved (*R v IAT, ex p Inovejas* [1983] Imm AR 204).

3   Representatives of overseas newspapers, news agencies and broadcasting organisations

Requirements for leave to enter as a representative of an overseas newspaper, news agency or broadcasting organisation

136. The requirements to be met by a person seeking leave to enter the United Kingdom as a representative of an overseas newspaper, news agency or broadcasting organisation are that he:

(i)   has been engaged by that organisation outside the United Kingdom and is being posted to the United Kingdom on a long-term assignment as a representative; and

(ii) intends to work full-time as a representative of that overseas newspaper, news agency or broadcasting organisation; and

(iii) does not intend to take employment except within the terms of this paragraph; and

(iv) can maintain and accommodate himself and any dependants adequately without recourse to public funds; and

(v)   holds a valid United Kingdom entry clearance for entry in this capacity.

Leave to enter as a representative of an overseas newspaper, news agency or broadcasting organisation

137. A person seeking leave to enter the United Kingdom as a representative of an overseas newspaper, news agency or broadcasting organisation may be admitted for a period not exceeding 12 months provided he is able to produce to the Immigration Officer, on arrival, a valid United Kingdom entry clearance for entry in this capacity.

Refusal of leave to enter as a representative of an overseas newspaper, news agency or broadcasting organisation

138. Leave to enter as a representative of an overseas newspaper, news agency or broadcasting organisation is to be refused if a valid United Kingdom entry clearance for entry in this capacity is not produced to the Immigration Officer on arrival.

COMMENTARY

The rules require the person entering to have an entry clearance as a representative. He will have no right of appeal without one. If a representative of an overseas newspaper, news agency or broadcasting organisation is on a long-term assignment to the UK, he will not require a work permit. The Home Office interpret the word 'newspaper' broadly to include magazines concerned with news (see INL&P October 1986, p 92).

Requirements for an extension of stay as a representative of an overseas newspaper, news agency or broadcasting organisation

139. The requirements for an extension of stay as a representative of an overseas newspaper, news agency or broadcasting organisation are that the applicant:

(i)   entered the United Kingdom with a valid United Kingdom entry clearance as a representative of an overseas newspaper, news agency or broadcasting organisation; and

(ii) is still engaged in the employment for which his entry clearance was granted; and

(iii) is still required for the employment in question, as certified by his employer; and

(iv) meets the requirements of paragraph 136(ii)–(iv).

Extension of stay as a representative of an overseas newspaper, news agency or broadcasting organisation

140. An extension of stay as a representative of an overseas newspaper, news agency or broadcasting organisation may be granted for a period not exceeding 3 years provided the Secretary of State is satisfied that each of the requirements of paragraph 139 is met.

Refusal of extension of stay as a representative of an overseas newspaper, news agency or broadcasting organisation

141. An extension of stay as a representative of an overseas newspaper, news agency or broadcasting organisation is to be refused if the Secretary of State is not satisfied that each of the requirements of paragraph 139 is met.

Indefinite leave to remain for a representative of an overseas newspaper, news agency or broadcasting organisation

142. Indefinite leave to remain may be granted, on application, to a representative of an overseas newspaper, news agency or broadcasting organisation provided:

(i) he has spent a continuous period of 4 years in the United Kingdom in this capacity; and

(ii) he has met the requirements of paragraph 139 throughout the 4 year period; and

(iii) he is still required for the employment in question, as certified by his employer.

Refusal of indefinite leave to remain for a representative of an overseas newspaper, news agency or broadcasting organisation

143. Indefinite leave to remain in the United Kingdom for a representative of an overseas newspaper, news agency or broadcasting organisation is to be refused if the Secretary of State is not satisfied that each of the requirements of paragraph 142 is met.

COMMENTARY

Where an application for indefinite leave is based on permit-free employment, the applicant must have been 'on call' for duties for his employers for a period of time for it to count towards settlement (*Marwah* (7422)).

4   Sole representatives

Requirements for leave to enter as a sole representative

144. The requirements to be met by a person seeking leave to enter the United Kingdom as a sole representative are that he:

(i) has been recruited and taken on as an employee outside the United Kingdom as a representative of a firm which has its headquarters and principal place of business outside the United Kingdom and which has no branch, subsidiary or other representative in the United Kingdom; and

(ii) seeks entry to the United Kingdom as a senior employee with full authority to take operational decisions on behalf of the overseas firm for the purpose of representing it in the United Kingdom by establishing and operating a registered branch or wholly-owned subsidiary of that overseas firm; and

(iii) intends to be employed full-time as a representative of that overseas firm; and

(iv) is not a majority shareholder in that overseas firm; and

(v) does not intend to take employment except within the terms of this paragraph; and

(vi) can maintain and accommodate himself and any dependants adequately without recourse to public funds; and

(vii) holds a valid United Kingdom entry clearance for entry in this capacity.

Leave to enter as a sole representative

145. A person seeking leave to enter the United Kingdom as a sole representative may be admitted for a period not exceeding 12 months provided he is able to produce to the Immigration Officer, on arrival, a valid United Kingdom entry clearance for entry in this capacity.

Refusal of leave to enter as a sole representative

146. Leave to enter as a sole representative is to be refused if a valid United Kingdom entry clearance for entry in this capacity is not produced to the Immigration Officer on arrival.

COMMENTARY

The sole representative should be able to produce evidence relevant to the above requirements, such as his contract of employment with the overseas firm and information relating to its trading circumstances.

The firm must be *bona fide*, and a person will be regarded as a representative of an overseas firm only if there is an active trading concern in existence outside the UK. If there is not, the applicant will probably be viewed as entering to set up business (*Certilan* (4689)). If the base office has effectively ceased trading, the applicant will need a work permit (*R v IAT, ex p Lokko* [1990] Imm AR 111 (IAT); [1990] Imm AR 539 (QBD)).

Sole representative Paragraph 144(ii) defines 'sole representative' as a senior employee with authority to take operational decisions on behalf of the overseas firm for the purpose of representing it in the UK by establishing and operating a registered branch or wholly owned subsidiary of that overseas firm. This encapsulates the effect of a series of cases under previous rules. Thus, a sole representative will generally have considerable plenipotentiary powers and will be fully versed in all aspects of the company's activities and policies. He will have responsibility for making important decisions on behalf of the firm (*Hope* (832)). Such plenipotentiary powers are not, however, necessary in the light of modern communications. The firm's affairs should occupy a visible part of the applicant's time and effort, and his duties should be essential to the proper functioning of the firm (*Baydur* (5442)). He must intend to be employed full-time as a representative of the overseas firm, and it is not clear whether being 'on call' for the firm would be enough. The decision in *Lokko*, in so far as it suggests that a majority shareholder in an overseas organisation may enter as its sole representative, is overturned by para 144(iv).

'Oversea company'   Section 744 of the Companies Act 1985 defines 'oversea companies' to mean companies incorporated elsewhere than in Great Britain, which establish a place of business in Great Britain after the commencement of the Act, or had done so before the commencement of the 1985 Act and continued to have an established place of business in Great Britain after its commencement. An overseas company which establishes a place of business in Great Britain must comply with the requirements of Part XXIII of the Companies Act 1985, and The Oversea Companies and Credit and Financial Institutions (Branch Disclosure) Regulations 1992 (SI 1992 No 3179), which implement the Eleventh Company Law Directive 89/666, adopted on 21 December 1989 (OJ 30.12.89 L 395), concerning the disclosure of branches established within the European Union of companies incorporated in countries outside the European Union. The requirement under the immigration rules that the branch should be 'registered' is a reference to such disclosure.

Branch   Section 698(2) of the Companies Act 1985 defines 'branch' as 'a branch within the meaning of the Eleventh Company Law Directive'. Article 2 of the directive deals with the activities of a company opening a branch in a member state. A company may open a branch in a member state to conduct activities from an address there, through permanent representatives. The term 'branch' occurs also in the Convention on Jurisdiction and the Enforcement of Judgments in Civil and Commercial Matters (s 2, art 5(5)), incorporated into English law by the Civil Jurisdiction and Judgments Act 1982, although the term is not defined here. In the context of the Convention, the ECJ, in *Blanckaert & Willems v Trost* [1981] ECR 819, approved the following passage from *Somafer SA v Saar-Ferngas AG* [1978] ECR 2183:

> The term 'branch, agency or other establishment' implies a place of business which has the appearance of permanency, such as the extension of a parent body, has a management and is materially equipped to negotiate business with third parties so that the latter, although knowing there will if necessary be a legal link with the parent body the head office of which is abroad, do not have to deal directly with such parent body but may transact business at the place of business constituting the extension.

Thus an independent commercial agent who negotiates business; is free to arrange his own work and decide what proportion of his time to devote to the interests of the firm which he agrees to represent; whom that firm may not prevent from representing at the same time as other firms competing in the same sector; and who simply transmits orders to the parent undertaking without being involved in either their terms or their execution, does not have the character of a branch, agency or other establishment within the meaning of art 5(5) of the Convention (see *Blanckaert & Willems v Trost,* above).

For the purposes of company law, a 'branch', is distinguished from a 'place of business' and must be registered if it has the following features:

(a) the appearance of permanency,

(b) the presence of managers on the branch premises, and

(c) the ostensible capacity of branch personnel to conduct business with third parties on behalf of the company.

A place of business has the characteristic that the business carried on there is ancillary to, or incidental to, the overseas company's business. It is unlikely that a sole representative will be considered to have the requisite powers if he works from the company's place of business, and a place of business would not satisfy the requirements of the paragraph.

Acquiring and holding property in Great Britain for investment purposes does not on its own establish a branch (or even a place of business) for the purposes of company law (*Re Oriel Ltd* [1985] 3 All ER 216), and does not amount to the establishment of a business for the purposes of immigration law (see *Jain* (12203)). However, a company established a place of business where it stored works of art at premises in the UK. Art could be viewed at those premises and there were extensive deliveries on the company's account from them. There was also substantial insurance against the risk of loss or damage to the art works at the premises. These factors prevailed, although the company had no sign on the premises advertising its existence, and it also stored on the premises artwork which did not belong to it (*Cleveland Museum of Art v Capricorn Art International SA & Anor* [1990] 2 Lloyd's Rep 166).

An overseas company is unlikely to establish a branch (or place of business) in Great Britain by carrying on business through an agent who has offices in Great Britain (*Lord Advocate v Huron and Erie Loan and Savings Co* (1911) SC 612), as the phrase 'establishes a place of business' means something other than 'carrying on business' and signifies the requirement of a 'local habitation' for the company (see *Re Oriel* [1985] 3 All ER 216 at 220, *Re Tovarishestvo Manufactur Liudvig-Rabenek* [1944] Ch 404 and *Cleveland Museum of Art v Capricorn Art International SA* (above)). For the purposes of the immigration rules the company must have a representative, and the proposed representative must be the *sole* representative. Such an agent would not be a sole representative for the purposes of the immigration rules. The agency would have to be terminated before the application was made.

Subsidiaries The sole representative must be seeking entry to establish one of two forms of representative body:

(a) a registered branch; or

(b) a wholly-owned subsidiary

of the overseas firm.

The requirement of the immigration rules is that the wholly owned subsidiary should be operated by the sole representative. The overseas firm will be unlikely to be held to be operating a subsidiary in the UK if it cannot prove that it has established a place of business in Great Britain. For the purposes of company law it will not be regarded as having established a place of business unless it can prove various factors. Thus in *Deverall v*

Grant Advertising Inc [1954] 3 All ER 389, the factors indicated that there was no place of business being operated in the UK. The court concluded that the place of business in question was in fact that of the subsidiary, which was carrying on its own, and not the oversea company's, business. The regional director's functions were those of consultant and adviser. He did not carry on any trading or business activities, or enter into contracts on behalf of the oversea company with the subsidiary as the place of business in the UK. Such a director would not be viewed as a sole representative.

Registration   The overseas firm is obliged, under Part XXIII of the Companies Act 1985, to register the establishment of a branch in Great Britain, within one month of establishing it. Registration is required by s 690A of and Sched 21A to the Companies Act 1985. For the purposes of the immigration rules, the company or branch must be registered before any application for an extension of leave is made. The company or branch must in any event deliver a return on Form BR1 to the Registrar of Companies giving particulars about the oversea company and about the branch. It must disclose, *inter alia*:

(*a*) the corporate name of the company;

(*b*) its legal form;

(*c*) if it is registered in the country of its incorporation, the identity of the register in which it is registered and the number with which it is so registered;

(*d*) a list of its directors and secretary, giving their details;

(*e*) the extent of the powers of the directors to represent the company in dealings with third parties and in legal proceedings, together with a statement as to whether they may act alone or must act jointly and, if jointly, the name of any other person concerned.

In the case of a company which is not incorporated in a member state, the particulars also include, *inter alia*:

(*a*) the address of its principal place of business in its country of incorporation;

(*b*) its objects; and

(*c*) the amount of its issued share capital.

If the director is an individual, the particulars must contain:

(*a*) his name;

(*b*) any former name;

(*c*) his usual residential address;

(*d*) his nationality:

(*e*) his business occupation (if any);

(*f*) particulars of any directorships held by him; and

(*g*) his date of birth.

In the case of a corporation or Scottish firm, its corporate or firm name and registered or principal office, must be given.

In the case of a company secretary, the particulars must contain:

(*a*) if an individual, his name, any former name and his usual residential address;

(*b*) if a corporation or Scottish firm, its corporate or firm name and registered or principal office.

The overseas firm must provide particulars of:

(*a*) the address of the branch;

(*b*) the date on which it was opened;

(*c*) the business carried on at it;

(*d*) if different from the name of the company, the name in which that business is carried on;

(*e*) a list of the names and addresses of all persons resident in Great Britain authorised to accept on the company's behalf service of process in respect of the business of the branch and of any notices required to be served on the company in respect of the business of the branch;

(*f*) a list of the names and usual residential addresses of all persons authorised to represent the company as permanent representatives of the company for the business of the branch;

(*g*) the extent of the authority of any person falling within paragraph (*f*) above, including whether that person is authorised to act alone or jointly; and

(*h*) if a person falling within paragraph (*f*) above is not authorised to act alone, the name of any person with whom he is authorised to act

(see CA 1985, Sched 21A, para 3).

The return must state where any other branch in the UK is registered, and, if so, its registered number.

An oversea company which has registered a branch is obliged to notify any change of person authorised to accept service or to represent the branch of the company, or of any change in their particulars, on Form BR6.

Extensions

Requirements for an extension of stay as a sole representative

147. The requirements for an extension of stay as a sole representative are that the applicant:

(i) entered the United Kingdom with a valid United Kingdom entry clearance as a sole representative of an overseas firm; and

(ii) can show that the overseas firm still has its headquarters and principal place of business outside the United Kingdom; and

(iii) is employed full-time as a representative of that overseas firm and has established and is in charge of its registered branch or wholly-owned subsidiary; and

(iv) is still required for the employment in question, as certified by his employer; and

(v) meets the requirements of paragraph 114(iii)–(vi).

Extension of stay as a sole representative

148. An extension of stay not exceeding 3 years as a sole representative may be granted provided the Secretary of State is satisfied that each of the requirements of paragraph 147 is met.

Refusal of extension of stay as a sole representative

149. An extension of stay as a sole representative is to be refused if the Secretary of State is not satisfied that each of the requirements of paragraph 147 is met.

Indefinite leave to remain for a sole representative

150. Indefinite leave to remain may be granted, on application, to a sole representative provided:

(i) he has spent a continuous period of 4 years in the United Kingdom in this capacity; and

(ii) he has met the requirements of paragraph 147 throughout the 4 year period; and

(iii) he is still required for the employment in question, as certified by his employer.

Refusal of indefinite leave to remain for a sole representative

151. Indefinite leave to remain in the United Kingdom for a sole representative is to be refused if the Secretary of State is not satisfied that each of the requirements of paragraph 150 is met.

COMMENTARY

Where a person establishes a branch or subsidiary or other representation in the UK, an extension will be granted if he can show that at the time of the application he is in charge of that branch etc, and his employer confirms he wishes to continue to employ him. He must satisfy the requirements of para 144(iii)–(vi). Thus he must intend to be employed full-time as a representative of that overseas firm and must not be a majority shareholder in it. He must not intend to take employment except as a sole representative of that overseas firm in the UK. He must be able to maintain himself and any dependants adequately without recourse to public funds, and he must have had a valid entry clearance for entry as a sole representative.

The applicant will have to show that he acts as the sole representative of a trading concern whose activities remain centred overseas (*Lokko v S of S* [1990] Imm AR 111). He will still need to satisfy the requirements on entry, and the S of S will need information as to:

(*a*) the time and effort he puts into the business;

(*b*) what he has achieved;

(*c*) what he is expected to achieve; and

(*d*) the role his activities play in the overall commercial activities of the firm he represents (*Kongar* (6601)).

He must still satisfy the definition of 'sole representative'. Although a representative need not, in the light of modern communications, have considerable plenipotentiary powers, the affairs of the company must continue to occupy a considerable part of his time and effort (*Baydur* (5442)). The representative's authority must be more than that of a distributor or sales agent (see *Blanckaert & Willems v Trost*, above, and *Hope* (832)). He must be a senior employee with the authority to take operational decisions on behalf of the overseas firm for the purpose of representing it in the UK by establishing a branch or wholly owned subsidiary of that firm (para 144(ii)). By the time an extension is sought, the UK branch of the overseas firm must have been registered.

Indefinite leave is granted after a continuous period of four years spent in the UK as a sole representative. The rule stresses that throughout that period the applicant must have satisfied the requirements of para 147, which require that the applicant had an entry clearance as a sole representative. He must have been able to show that the overseas firm has its headquarters and principal place of business outside the UK. He must show that he was, throughout that time, in charge of the UK branch, and that his services were required throughout that period, as certified by his employer. The employer must certify that he is still required for the employment.

5   Private servants in diplomatic households

Requirements for leave to enter as a private servant in a diplomatic household

152. The requirements to be met by a person seeking leave to enter the United Kingdom as a private servant in a diplomatic household are that he:
(i)   is aged 18 or over; and
(ii)   is employed as a private servant in the household of a member of staff of a diplomatic or consular mission who enjoys diplomatic privileges and immunity within the meaning of the Vienna Convention on Diplomatic and Consular Relations or a member of the family forming part of the household of such a person; and
(iii) intends to work full-time as a private servant within the terms of this paragraph; and
(iv)   does not intend to take employment except within the terms of this paragraph; and
(v)   can maintain and accommodate himself and any dependants adequately without recourse to public funds; and
(vi)   holds a valid United Kingdom entry clearance for entry in this capacity.

Leave to enter as a private servant in a diplomatic household

153. A person seeking leave to enter the United Kingdom as a private servant in a diplomatic household may be given leave to enter for a period not exceeding 12 months provided he is able to produce to the Immigration Officer, on arrival, a valid United Kingdom entry clearance for entry in this capacity.

Refusal of leave to enter as a private servant in a diplomatic household

154. Leave to enter as a private servant in a diplomatic household is to be refused if a valid United Kingdom entry clearance for entry in this capacity is not produced to the Immigration Officer on arrival.

COMMENTARY

HC 395 introduced a requirement that the private servant must be 18 or over, as a result of EC legislation relating to the employment of young workers. To satisfy the requirement of full-time work it is insufficient that the person works two mornings per week (*Guinaban* (3475)).

Requirements for an extension of stay as a private servant in a diplomatic household

155. The requirements for an extension of stay as a private servant in a diplomatic household are that the applicant:

(i)   entered the United Kingdom with a valid United Kingdom entry clearance as a private servant in a diplomatic household; and

(ii) is still engaged in the employment for which his entry clearance was granted; and

(iii) is still required for the employment in question, as certified by the employer; and

(iv) meets the requirements of paragraph 152(iii)–(v).

Extension of stay as a private servant in a diplomatic household

156. An extension of stay as a private servant in a diplomatic household may be granted for a period not exceeding 12 months provided the Secretary of State is satisfied that each of the requirements of paragraph 155 is met.

Refusal of extension of stay as a private servant in a diplomatic household

157. An extension of stay as a private servant in a diplomatic household is to be refused if the Secretary of State is not satisfied that each of the requirements of paragraph 155 is met.

Indefinite leave to remain for a servant in a diplomatic household

158. Indefinite leave to remain may be granted, on application, to a private servant in a diplomatic household provided:

(i)   he has spent a continuous period of 4 years in the United Kingdom in this capacity; and

(ii) he has met the requirements of paragraph 155 throughout the 4 year period; and

(iii) he is still required for the employment in question, as certified by his employer.

Refusal of indefinite leave to remain for a servant in a diplomatic household

159. Indefinite leave to remain in the United Kingdom for a private servant in a diplomatic household is to be refused if the Secretary of State is not satisfied that each of the requirements of paragraph 158 is met.

COMMENTARY

HC 395 makes provision for a private servant to apply for indefinite leave to remain. Throughout a period of four years he must continually have satisfied the requirements of para 155. Thus, he must have entered the UK with a valid UK entry clearance as a private servant in a diplomatic household. He must remain in the employment for which that entry clearance was granted. His employer must require him for that employment throughout the period, and must provide a certificate to that effect. Additionally, for the whole of the period of four years, the applicant must intend to work full-time as a private servant within the terms of para 152. He must not intend to take employment except as a private servant in the household of a member of staff of a diplomatic or consular mission. He must be able to maintain and accommodate himself and any dependants without recourse to public funds throughout the period. If any of these requirements is not satisfied, indefinite leave to remain must be refused.

6   Overseas government employees

Requirements for leave to enter as an overseas government employee

160. For the purposes of these Rules an overseas government employee means a person coming for employment by an overseas government or employed by the United Nations Organisation or other international organisation of which the United Kingdom is a member.

161. The requirements to be met by a person seeking leave to enter the United Kingdom as an overseas government employee are that he:

(i)   is able to produce either a valid United Kingdom entry clearance for entry in this capacity or satisfactory documentary evidence of his status as an overseas government employee; and

(ii) intends to work full time for the government or organisation concerned; and

(iii) does not intend to take employment except within the terms of this paragraph; and

(iv) can maintain and accommodate himself and any dependants adequately without recourse to public funds.

Leave to enter as an overseas government employee

162. A person seeking leave to enter the United Kingdom as an overseas government employee may be given leave to enter for a period not exceeding 12 months, provided he is able, on arrival, to produce to the Immigration Officer a valid United Kingdom entry clearance for entry in this capacity or satisfy the Immigration Officer that each of the requirements of paragraph 161 is met.

Refusal of leave to enter as an overseas government employee

163. Leave to enter as an overseas government employee is to be refused if a valid United Kingdom entry clearance for entry in this capacity is not produced to the Immigration Officer on arrival or if the Immigration Officer is not satisfied that each of the requirements of paragraph 161 is met.

Requirements for an extension of stay as an overseas government employee

164. The requirements to be met by a person seeking an extension of stay as an overseas government employee are that the applicant:

(i)   was given leave to enter the United Kingdom under paragraph 162 as an overseas government employee; and

(ii) is still engaged in the employment in question; and

(iii) is still required for the employment in question, as certified by the employer; and

(iv) meets the requirements of paragraph 161(ii)–(iv).

Extension of stay as an overseas government employee

165. An extension of stay as an overseas government employee may be granted for a period not exceeding 3 years provided the Secretary of State is satisfied that each of the requirements of paragraph 164 is met.

Refusal of extension of stay as an overseas government employee

166. An extension of stay as an overseas government employee is to be refused if the Secretary of State is not satisfied that each of the requirements of paragraph 164 is met.

Indefinite leave to remain for an overseas government employee

167. Indefinite leave to remain may be granted, on application, to an overseas government employee provided:

(i) he has spent a continuous period of 4 years in the United Kingdom in this capacity; and

(ii) he has met the requirements of paragraph 164 throughout the 4 year period; and

(iii) he is still required for the employment in question, as certified by his employer.

Refusal of indefinite leave to remain for an overseas government employee

168. Indefinite leave to remain in the United Kingdom for an overseas government employee is to be refused if the Secretary of State is not satisfied that each of the requirements of paragraph 167 is met.

7 Ministers of religion, missionaries and members of religious orders

169. For the purposes of these Rules:

(i) a minister of religion means a religious functionary whose main regular duties comprise the leading of a congregation in performing the rites and rituals of the faith and in preaching the essentials of the creed;

(ii) a missionary means a person who is directly engaged in spreading a religious doctrine and whose work is not in essence administrative or clerical;

(iii) a member of a religious order means a person who is coming to live in a community run by that order.

Requirements for leave to enter as a minister of religion, missionary or member of a religious order

170. The requirements to be met by a person seeking leave to enter the United Kingdom as a minister of religion, missionary or member of a religious order are that he:

(i) (a) if seeking leave to enter as a minister of religion has either been working for at least one year as a minister of religion or, where ordination is prescribed by a religious faith as the sole means of entering the ministry, has been ordained as a minister of religion following at least one year's full-time or two years' part-time training for the ministry; or

(b) if seeking leave to enter as a missionary has been trained as a missionary or has worked as a missionary and is being sent to the United Kingdom by an overseas organisation; or

(c) if seeking leave to enter as a member of a religious order is coming to live in a community maintained by the religious order of which he is a member and, if intending to teach, does not intend to do so save at an establishment maintained by his order; and

(ii) intends to work full-time as a minister of religion, missionary or for the religious order of which he is a member; and

(iii) does not intend to take employment except within the terms of this paragraph; and

(iv) can maintain and accommodate himself and any dependants adequately without recourse to public funds; and

(v) holds a valid United Kingdom entry clearance for entry in this capacity.

Leave to enter as a minister of religion, missionary or member of a religious order

171. A person seeking leave to enter the United Kingdom as a minister of religion, missionary or member of a religious order may be admitted for a period not exceeding 12 months provided he is able to produce to the Immigration Officer, on arrival, a valid United Kingdom entry clearance for entry in this capacity.

Refusal of leave to enter as a minister of religion, missionary or member of a religious order

172. Leave to enter as a minister of religion, missionary or member of a religious order is to be refused if a valid United Kingdom entry clearance for entry in this capacity is not produced to the Immigration Officer on arrival.

COMMENTARY

HC 395 introduced definitions of 'minister of religion', 'missionary' and 'member of a religious order'. An ordained minister is now expected to have followed a period of one year's full-time study or two years' part-time study before ordination. Ministers of religion and members of religious orders do not require work permits if they are coming to work full-time as such (*Piara Singh v ECO New Delhi* [1977] Imm AR 1). Entry clearance is in practice issued only after due enquiry as to the need for such an appointment and other matters has been made in the UK (*Memi v S of S* [1976] Imm AR 129). Applicants must be able to maintain and accommodate themselves and their dependants without recourse to public funds.

Members of religious orders engaged in teaching at establishments maintained by their own order do not require work permits, but if they teach at outside institutions they will require work permits. The phrase 'religious orders' means monastic orders (*Abdul Hamid v ECO Dhaka* [1986] Imm AR 469), although para 169 defines a member of a religious order as a person who is coming to live in a community run by the order. The IAT, in *Mobley* (5368), considered that the phrases 'ministers of religion' and 'missionaries' included those who organised the propagation of a faith as well as those who actually propagate that faith. It is necessary to ascertain the person's purpose in seeking to do the work for which he seeks entry. He must be undertaking the work in order to spread doctrine; the rule requires that he should be directly engaged in spreading a religious doctrine, and that the work is not essentially administrative or clerical. Thus a person whose work is essentially administrative will not be a missionary, but it is likely that if the main purpose of his role included administrative tasks and the writing and dissemination of materials designed to spread a religious doctrine, he would still meet this requirement. The extent to which his experience or qualifications make him a minister of religion is a question of fact, to be interpreted in the light of the customs of the faith in question. A minister of religion is someone whose main regular duties comprise the leading of a congregation in performing the rites and rituals of the faith and in preaching the essentials of the creed. Thus a person who officiates and leads in matters of religion will be a minister of religion (*Kalsoom Begum v Visa Officer Islamabad* [1988] Imm AR 325). A full-time Imam will be a minister of religion (*Abdul Hamid* (above)).

Extensions

Requirements for an extension of stay as a minister of religion, missionary or member of a religious order

173. The requirements for an extension of stay as a minister of religion, missionary or member of a religious order are that the applicant:
(i) entered the United Kingdom with a valid United Kingdom entry clearance as a minister of religion, missionary or member of a religious order; and
(ii) is still engaged in the employment for which his entry clearance was granted; and
(iii) is still required for the employment in question as certified by the leadership of his congregation, his employer or the head of his religious order; and
(iv) meets the requirements of paragraph 170(ii)–(iv).

Extension of stay as a minister of religion, missionary or member of a religious order

174. An extension of stay as a minister of religion, missionary or member of a religious order may be granted for a period not exceeding 3 years provided the Secretary of State is satisfied that each of the requirements of paragraph 173 is met.

Refusal of extension of stay as a minister of religion, missionary or member of a religious order

175. An extension of stay as a minister of religion, missionary or member of a religious order is to be refused if the Secretary of State is not satisfied that each of the requirements of paragraph 173 is met.

Indefinite leave to remain for a minister of religion, missionary or member of a religious order

176. Indefinite leave to remain may be granted, on application, to a person admitted as a minister of religion, missionary or member of a religious order provided:
(i) he has spent a continuous period of 4 years in the United Kingdom in this capacity; and
(ii) he has met the requirements of paragraph 173 throughout the 4 year period; and
(iii) he is still required for the employment in question as certified by the leadership of his congregation, his employer or the head of the religious order to which he belongs.

Refusal of indefinite leave to remain for a minister of religion, missionary or member of a religious order

177. Indefinite leave to remain in the United Kingdom for a minister of religion, missionary or member of a religious order is to be refused if the Secretary of State is not satisfied that each of the requirements of paragraph 176 is met.

COMMENTARY

A person seeking an extension under this head must have had an entry clearance for this purpose on entry. He must still be engaged in the employment for which the visa was granted. His employer or the head of the religious order of which he is a member must certify that he is still required for the employment in question. He must also show that he intends to work full-time as a minister of religion or missionary, or for the religious order of which he is a member, and that he does not intend to take any other employment. He must maintain and accommodate himself without recourse to public funds.

A person who enters in another capacity may not, under the rules, change his status to that of minister of religion. The earlier practice that a person entering in another capacity might be permitted to remain in a religious position has been discontinued (for the old practice see *Dawood Patel v S of S* [1990] Imm AR 478; the letter of 1 June 1982 at 481 ff and ministerial letter dated 31 March 1987). An application from a visitor to remain as a minister of religion will be refused unless 'a *bona fide* minister of religion had been granted a visa or leave to enter as a visitor specifically to attend an interview for a job in the UK as a minister and was offered the job; or ... specifically for a preaching tour of the UK, was asked to fill a vacant post as a minister in this country, the job offer appeared to be genuinely unexpected at the time the applicant entered the UK and there were good community relations reasons for allowing him to stay' (see *Hansard*, 20 June 1995).

8   Airport-based operational ground staff of overseas-owned airlines

Requirements for leave to enter the United Kingdom as a member of the operational ground staff of an overseas-owned airline

178. The requirements to be met by a person seeking leave to enter the United Kingdom as a member of the operational ground staff of an overseas-owned airline are that he:
(i)   has been transferred to the United Kingdom by an overseas-owned airline operating services to and from the United Kingdom to take up duty at an international airport as station manager, security manager or technical manager; and
(ii) intends to work full-time for the airline concerned; and
(iii) does not intend to take employment except within the terms of this paragraph; and
(iv) can maintain and accommodate himself and any dependants without recourse to public funds; and
(v)   holds a valid United Kingdom entry clearance for entry in this capacity.

Leave to enter as a member of the operational ground staff of an overseas-owned airline

179. A person seeking leave to enter the United Kingdom as a member of the operational ground staff of an overseas-owned airline may be given leave to enter for a period not exceeding 12 months, provided he is able to produce to the Immigration Officer, on arrival, a valid United Kingdom entry clearance for entry in this capacity.

Refusal of leave to enter as a member of the operational ground staff of an overseas-owned airline

180. Leave to enter as a member of the operational ground staff of an overseas-owned airline is to be refused if a valid United Kingdom entry clearance for entry in this capacity is not produced to the Immigration Officer on arrival.

Requirements for an extension of stay as a member of the operational ground staff of an overseas-owned airline

181. The requirements to be met by a person seeking an extension of stay as a member of the operational ground staff of an overseas-owned airline are that the applicant:

(i) entered the United Kingdom with a valid United Kingdom entry clearance as a member of the operational ground staff of an overseas-owned airline; and

(ii) is still engaged in the employment for which entry was granted; and

(iii) is still required for the employment in question, as certified by the employer; and

(iv) meets the requirements of paragraph 178(ii)–(iv).

Extension of stay as a member of the operational ground staff of an overseas-owned airline

182. An extension of stay as a member of the operational ground staff of an overseas-owned airline may be granted for a period not exceeding 3 years, provided the Secretary of State is satisfied that each of the requirements of paragraph 181 is met.

Refusal of extension of stay as a member of the operational ground staff of an overseas-owned airline

183. An extension of stay as a member of the operational ground staff of an overseas-owned airline is to be refused if the Secretary of State is not satisfied that each of the requirements of paragraph 181 is met.

Indefinite leave to remain for a member of the operational ground staff of an overseas-owned airline

184. Indefinite leave to remain may be granted, on application, to a member of the operational ground staff of an overseas-owned airline provided:

(i) he has spent a continuous period of 4 years in the United Kingdom in this capacity; and

(ii) he has met the requirements of paragraph 181 throughout the 4 year period; and

(iii) he is still required for the employment in question, as certified by the employer.

Refusal of indefinite leave to remain for a member of the operational ground staff of an overseas-owned airline

185. Indefinite leave to remain in the United Kingdom for a member of the operational ground staff of an overseas-owned airline is to be refused if the Secretary of State is not satisfied that each of the requirements of paragraph 184 is met.

COMMENTARY

Paragraphs 178–185 limit the posts which qualify airport-based operational ground staff for permit-free employment to station managers, security managers and technical managers.

9   Persons with UK ancestry

Requirements for leave to enter on the grounds of United Kingdom ancestry

186. The requirements to be met by a person seeking leave to enter the United Kingdom on the grounds of his United Kingdom ancestry are that he:

(i)   is a Commonwealth citizen; and

(ii)   is aged 17 or over; and

(iii) is able to provide proof that one of his grandparents was born in the United Kingdom and Islands; and

(iv)   is able to work and intends to take or seek employment in the United Kingdom; and

(v)   will be able to maintain and accommodate himself and any dependants adequately without recourse to public funds; and

(vi)   holds a valid United Kingdom entry clearance for entry in this capacity.

Leave to enter the United Kingdom on the grounds of United Kingdom ancestry

187. A person seeking leave to enter the United Kingdom on the grounds of his United Kingdom ancestry may be given leave to enter for a period not exceeding 4 years provided he is able to produce to the Immigration Officer, on arrival, a valid United Kingdom entry clearance for entry in this capacity.

Refusal of leave to enter on the grounds of United Kingdom ancestry

188. Leave to enter the United Kingdom on the grounds of United Kingdom ancestry is to be refused if a valid United Kingdom entry clearance for entry in this capacity is not produced to the Immigration Officer on arrival.

Requirements for an extension of stay on the grounds of United Kingdom ancestry

189. The requirements to be met by a person seeking an extension of stay on the grounds of United Kingdom ancestry are that he is able to meet each of the requirements of paragraph 186(i)–(v).

Extension of stay on the grounds of United Kingdom ancestry

190. An extension of stay on the grounds of United Kingdom ancestry may be granted for a period not exceeding 4 years provided the Secretary of State is satisfied that each of the requirements of paragraph 186(i)–(v) is met.

Refusal of extension of stay on the grounds of United Kingdom ancestry

191. An extension of stay on the grounds of United Kingdom ancestry is to be refused if the Secretary of State is not satisfied that each of the requirements of paragraph 186(i)–(v) is met.

Indefinite leave to remain on the grounds of United Kingdom ancestry

192. Indefinite leave to remain may be granted, on application, to a Commonwealth citizen with a United Kingdom born grandparent provided:

(i)   he meets the requirements of paragraph 186(i)–(v); and

(ii)   he has spent a continuous period of 4 years in the United Kingdom in this capacity.

Refusal of indefinite leave to remain on the grounds of United Kingdom ancestry

193. Indefinite leave to remain in the United Kingdom on the grounds of a United Kingdom born grandparent is to be refused if the Secretary of State is not satisfied that each of the requirements of paragraph 192 is met.

COMMENTARY

Proof of descent is the main requirement of the rule. The entrant will need the following documents:

(a) the grandparent's birth certificate;

(b) the grandparents' marriage certificate;

(c) the birth certificate of the parent of the applicant who is descended from the relevant grandparents;

(d) the parents' marriage certificate; and

(e) the applicant's birth certificate.

The term 'grandparents' does not include the paternal grandparents of an illegitimate child (*C (an infant) v ECO Hong Kong* [1976] Imm AR 165). However, in a letter dated 14 March 1991, the Home Office stated that it is the S of S's practice to accept legitimate and illegitimate lines of descent, and adoptive lines, as qualifying an applicant for entry clearance as a person who does not need a work permit on the grounds of UK ancestry.

In *Leahy* (7981), the IAT held that where the applicant is employable and proposes to take employment if that becomes necessary, he satisfies the requirement of this paragraph that he wishes to take or seek employment. The intention to find work must be a genuine intention, even if it is unrealistic. Indeed it does not matter that the person has an undisclosed further intention, such as to secure the admission of relatives (*Thelma Smith* (8642)).

The main requirements of the rules relating to permit-free employment based on UK ancestry are that the applicant must be at least 17 years old; he must be able to work, and not likely to become a charge on public funds. The rules permit a person to change to this category from another category.

An applicant for indefinite leave to remain under this head must prove that he has spent a continuous period of four years in the UK in this capacity. He must also show that he has found work, and that the employer wishes to continue to employ him. If these conditions are not satisfied refusal is mandatory. This represents a significant tightening of the provisions relating to UK ancestry compared with the position before the current immigration rules came into force.

Where the claim is based on permit-free employment, the applicant must have been 'on call' for the employer during a period for it to count towards the period (*Marwah* (7422)).

10 Spouses

Requirements for leave to enter or remain as the spouse of a person with limited leave to enter or remain in the United Kingdom under paragraphs 128–193

194. The requirements to be met by a person seeking leave to enter or remain in the United Kingdom as the spouse of a person with limited leave to enter or remain in the United Kingdom under paragraphs 128–193 are that:

(i) the applicant is married to a person with limited leave to enter or remain in the United Kingdom under paragraphs 128–193; and

(ii) each of the parties intends to live with the other as his or her spouse during the applicant's stay and the marriage is subsisting; and

(iii) there will be adequate accommodation for the parties and any dependants without recourse to public funds in accommodation which they own or occupy exclusively; and

(iv) the parties will be able to maintain themselves and any dependants adequately without recourse to public funds; and

(v) the applicant does not intend to stay in the United Kingdom beyond any period of leave granted to his spouse; and

(vi) if seeking leave to enter, the applicant holds a valid United Kingdom entry clearance for entry in this capacity or, if seeking leave to remain, was admitted with a valid United Kingdom entry clearance for entry in this capacity.

Leave to enter or remain as the spouse of a person with limited leave to enter or remain in the United Kingdom under paragraphs 128–193

195. A person seeking leave to enter or remain in the United Kingdom as the spouse of a person with limited leave to enter or remain in the United Kingdom under paragraphs 128–193 may be given leave to enter or remain in the United Kingdom for a period of leave not in excess of that granted to the person with limited leave to enter or remain under paragraphs 128–193 provided that, in relation to an application for leave to enter, he is able, on arrival, to produce to the Immigration Officer a valid United Kingdom entry clearance for entry in this capacity or, in the case of an application for limited leave to remain, he was admitted with a valid United Kingdom entry clearance for entry in this capacity and is able to satisfy the Secretary of State that each of the requirements of paragraph 194(i)–(v) is met. An application for indefinite leave to remain in this category may be granted provided the applicant was admitted with a valid United Kingdom entry clearance for entry in this capacity and is able to satisfy the Secretary of State that each of the requirements of paragraph 194(i)–(v) is met and provided indefinite leave to remain is, at the same time, being granted to the person with limited leave to enter or remain under paragraphs 128–193.

Refusal of leave to enter or remain as the spouse of a person with limited leave to enter or remain in the United Kingdom under paragraphs 128–193

196. Leave to enter or remain in the United Kingdom as the spouse of a person with limited leave to enter or remain in the United Kingdom under paragraphs 128–193 is to be refused if, in relation to an application for leave to enter, a valid United Kingdom entry clearance for entry in this capacity is not produced to the Immigration Officer on arrival or, in the case of an application for limited leave to remain, if the applicant was not admitted with a valid United Kingdom entry clearance for entry in this capacity or is unable to satisfy the Secretary of State that each of the requirements of paragraph 194(i)–(v) is met. An application for indefinite leave to remain in this category is to be refused if the applicant was

not admitted with a valid United Kingdom entry clearance for entry in this capacity or is unable to satisfy the Secretary of State that each of the requirements of paragraph 194(i)–(v) is met or if indefinite leave to remain is not, at the same time, being granted to the person with limited leave to enter or remain under paragraphs 128–193.

COMMENTARY

The spouses of the following persons are subject to these paragraphs:
- (a) persons with work permits;
- (b) representatives of overseas newspapers, news agencies and broadcasting organisations;
- (c) representatives of overseas firms which have no branch, subsidiary or other representative in the UK (sole representatives);
- (d) private servants in diplomatic households;
- (e) overseas government employees;
- (f) ministers of religion, missionaries and members of religious orders;
- (g) airport-based operational ground staff of overseas-owned airlines; and
- (h) persons with UK ancestry.

Such persons must show that each of the parties to the marriage intends to live with the other as his or her spouse during the applicant's stay in the UK. The spouse must show that there will be adequate accommodation for the parties and any dependants without recourse to public funds in accommodation which they own or occupy exclusively (see p 207). The parties must be able to maintain themselves and any dependants adequately without recourse to public funds. The spouse must have a valid entry clearance for the purpose.

11 Children

Requirements for leave to enter or remain as the child of a person with limited leave to enter or remain in the United Kingdom under paragraphs 128–193

197. The requirements to be met by a person seeking leave to enter or remain in the United Kingdom as a child of a person with limited leave to enter or remain in the United Kingdom under paragraphs 128–193 are that:
- (i) he is the child of a parent with limited leave to enter or remain in the United Kingdom under paragraphs 128–193; and
- (ii) he is under the age of 18 or has current leave to enter or remain in this capacity; and
- (iii) he is unmarried, has not formed an independent family unit and is not leading an independent life; and
- (iv) he can and will be maintained and accommodated adequately without recourse to public funds in accommodation which his parent(s) own or occupy exclusively; and
- (v) he will not stay in the United Kingdom beyond any period of leave granted to his parent(s); and

(vi)   both parents are being or have been admitted to or allowed to remain in the United Kingdom save where:

    (*a*)   the parent he is accompanying or joining is his sole surviving parent;

    (*b*)   the parent he is accompanying or joining has had sole responsibility for his upbringing; or

    (*c*)   there are serious and compelling family or other considerations which make exclusion from the United Kingdom undesirable and suitable arrangements have been made for his care; and

(vii)   if seeking leave to enter, he holds a valid United Kingdom entry clearance for entry in this capacity or, if seeking leave to remain, was admitted with a valid United Kingdom entry clearance for entry in this capacity.

Leave to enter or remain as the child of a person with limited leave to enter or remain in the United Kingdom under paragraphs 128–193

198. A person seeking leave to enter or remain in the United Kingdom as the child of a person with limited leave to enter or remain in the United Kingdom under paragraphs 128–193 may be given leave to enter or remain in the United Kingdom for a period of leave not in excess of that granted to the person with limited leave to enter or remain under paragraphs 128–193 provided that, in relation to an application for leave to enter, he is able to produce to the Immigration Officer, on arrival, a valid United Kingdom entry clearance for entry in this capacity or, in the case of an application for limited leave to remain, he was admitted with a valid United Kingdom entry clearance for entry in this capacity and is able to satisfy the Secretary of State that each of the requirements of paragraph 197(i)–(vi) is met. An application for indefinite leave to remain in this category may be granted provided the applicant was admitted with a valid United Kingdom entry clearance for entry in this capacity and is able to satisfy the Secretary of State that each of the requirements of paragraph 197(i)–(vi) is met and provided indefinite leave to remain is, at the same time, being granted to the person with limited leave to enter or remain under paragraphs 128–193.

Refusal of leave to enter or remain as the child of a person with limited leave to enter or remain in the United Kingdom under paragraphs 128–193

199. Leave to enter or remain in the United Kingdom as the child of a person with limited leave to enter or remain in the United Kingdom under paragraphs 128–193 is to be refused if, in relation to an application for leave to enter, a valid United Kingdom entry clearance for entry in this capacity is not produced to the Immigration Officer on arrival or, in the case of an application for limited leave to remain, if the applicant was not admitted with a valid United Kingdom entry clearance for entry in this capacity or is unable to satisfy the Secretary of State that each of the requirements of paragraph 197(i)–(vi) is met. An application for indefinite leave to remain in this category is to be refused if the applicant was not admitted with a valid United Kingdom entry clearance for entry in this capacity or is unable to satisfy the Secretary of State that each of the requirements of paragraph 197(i)–(vi) is met or if indefinite leave to remain is not, at the same time, being granted to the person with limited leave to enter or remain under paragraphs 128–193.

COMMENTARY

These provisions apply to the child of a person who falls within the categories on p 161.

The person seeking to bring a child to the UK must show that:

(*a*) there will be adequate accommodation for the person admitted for work and the child(ren), without recourse to public funds; and

(*b*) they will be able to maintain themselves adequately without recourse to public funds. Children will not be admitted under these rules to join or accompany a parent if the spouse of that parent is not admitted under this rule, save as set out above.

The freedom of the spouse and children to take employment is not restricted.

The child must be under 18 or have current leave to enter the UK. He must not be married, and must not have formed an independent family unit. He must not be leading an independent life. He must be accommodated and maintained adequately without recourse to public funds in accommodation which his parent(s) own or occupy exclusively.

Chapter 11

Parts 6 and 7: Businessmen, Self-employed Persons, Investors, Creative Artists and Others

Part 6 of HC 395 concerns persons seeking to enter or remain in the UK as businessmen, self-employed persons, investors or creative artists. Part 7 deals with persons exercising rights of access to a child resident in the UK, holders of special vouchers and retired persons of independent means.

1 Business entry

Requirements for leave to enter the United Kingdom as a person intending to establish himself in business

200. For the purpose of paragraphs 201–210 a business means an enterprise as:
— a sole trader; or
— a partnership; or
— a company registered in the United Kingdom.

　201. The requirements to be met by a person seeking leave to enter the United Kingdom to establish himself in business are:

(i)　　that he satisfies the requirements of either paragraph 202 or paragraph 203; and

(ii)　　that he has not less than £200,000 of his own money under his control and disposable in the United Kingdom which is held in his own name and not by a trust or other investment vehicle and which he will be investing in the business in the United Kingdom; and

(iii)　　that until his business provides him with an income he will have sufficient additional funds to maintain and accommodate himself and any dependants without recourse to employment (other than his work for the business) or to public funds; and

(iv)　　that he will be actively involved full-time in trading or providing services on his own account or in partnership, or in the promotion and management of the company as a director; and

(v)　　that his level of financial investment will be proportional to his interest in the business; and

(vi)　　that he will have either a controlling or equal interest in the business and that any partnership or directorship does not amount to disguised employment; and

(vii)　　that he will be able to bear his share of liabilities; and

(viii)　　that there is a genuine need for his investment and services in the United Kingdom; and

165

(ix) that his share of the profits of the business will be sufficient to maintain and accommodate himself and any dependants without recourse to employment (other than his work for the business) or to public funds; and

(x) that he does not intend to supplement his business activities by taking or seeking employment in the United Kingdom other than his work for the business; and

(xi) that he holds a valid United Kingdom entry clearance for entry in this capacity.

202. Where a person intends to take over or join as a partner or director an existing business in the United Kingdom he will need, in addition to meeting the requirements at paragraph 201, to produce:

(i) a written statement of the terms on which he is to take over or join the business; and

(ii) audited accounts for the business for previous years; and

(iii) evidence that his services and investment will result in a net increase in the employment provided by the business to persons settled here to the extent of creating at least 2 new full-time jobs.

203. Where a person intends to establish a new business in the United Kingdom he will need, in addition to meeting the requirements at paragraph 201 above, to produce evidence:

(i) that he will be bringing into the country sufficient funds of his own to establish a business; and

(ii) that the business will create full-time paid employment for at least 2 persons already settled in the United Kingdom.

Leave to enter the United Kingdom as a person seeking to establish himself in business

204. A person seeking leave to enter the United Kingdom to establish himself in business may be admitted for a period not exceeding 12 months with a condition restricting his freedom to take employment provided he is able to produce to the Immigration Officer, on arrival, a valid United Kingdom entry clearance for entry in this capacity.

Refusal of leave to enter the United Kingdom as a person seeking to establish himself in business

205. Leave to enter the United Kingdom as a person seeking to establish himself in business is to be refused if a valid United Kingdom entry clearance for entry in this capacity is not produced to the Immigration Officer on arrival.

COMMENTARY

HC 395 provides a definition of 'a business'. It is an enterprise as a sole trader, or a partnership or a company registered in the UK. A passenger seeking admission for the purpose of establishing himself in the UK in business or in self-employment, whether on his own account or in partnership, must hold a current entry clearance for that purpose. An application on Form IM2A and IM2C may be made to a British Consulate, embassy or High Commission.

The wording of the rule must be observed, and if one requirement is not fulfilled, it is not possible to claim that the overall purpose is satisfied and so gain admission (*R v IAT, ex p Mohammed Rahman* [1987] Imm AR 313

(CA)). Thus if the applicant does not have entry clearance, then no matter how much money he may be proposing to invest in the UK, he will not be granted leave to enter as a business person (*Falah Al-Hasani* (4670)). It is not, however, necessary to identify in detail the exact nature of the business which it is intended to operate if leave is granted (*R v IAT, ex p Mawji* [1982] Imm AR 97). Of course in practice it will be difficult, if not impossible, to obtain leave unless fairly specific proposals are put forward (*Patel v ECO, Nairobi* [1987] Imm AR 116).

A passenger who has obtained entry clearance should be admitted provided there are no general grounds for refusing entry (*Parekh v S of S* [1976] Imm AR 84). Admission will be for 12 months or less with a condition restricting his freedom to take employment. The applicant must show that he will be occupied full-time running the business. This requirement may be satisfied if the applicant will be occupied full-time running two businesses; it is a matter of degree. He must also show that there is a genuine need for his services and investment. The ECO should consider the criterion of likely commercial survival on a competitive basis as an important factor, but also should consider the national benefit to trade and social need and the impact the business will have on existing businesses (*Otani* (3224)). It will be helpful if the applicant has undertaken market research; indeed it may be difficult for the applicant to convince the ECO that there is a genuine need for his services and investment in a business without it (*Jivanlal Patel* (4895)). However, it is not essential, as the Home Office has taken the view that the way the test is applied depends on the nature of the business. The main concern is whether the business is likely to be successful and whether it will make a profit (see *Business and Self-Employment: an Analysis of the Immigration Rules—Part 1*, by David Webb in INL&P vol 7, no 1 (1993) p 12).

(a) 'His own money'
The applicant must show that he will be bringing money of his own to put into the business, and in no case should the amount to be invested be less than £200,000. The rules require that the money should be under the applicant's control and disposable in the UK. The money must be held in his own name, and not by a trust or other investment vehicle. It must be invested in the business in the UK. Evidence that this amount or more is under his control and disposable in the UK must be produced. The phrase 'money of his own' includes monies freely given to him by his wife for their mutual benefit over which he has unfettered control (*S of S v Ally* [1972] Imm AR 258). The rules require the investment of 'monies' which are immediately available at the time of the decision. The monies do not have to be lodged in a UK financial institution, but must be freely transferable to the UK, and not, for example, subject to exchange controls which prevent this. Whether or not the money is the applicant's own has to be looked at 'in the round' (*R v IAT, ex p Joseph* [1977] Imm AR 70). The intention of the rules is that the applicant should be the controller of the business; that he shall not 'front' for

someone else; and that he shall have a stake in the business so that he has an incentive to make the business viable (*R v IAT, ex p Peikazadi* [1979–80] Imm AR 191 at 193).

If the applicant holds family monies it is important to consider the basis on which he holds those monies: whether as a free gift and therefore in his unfettered control and disposition, or as a loan, in which case the term of the loan would have to be considered (*Peikazadi's* case). Where a long-term loan is made by a family, the rule will be satisfied (*R v IAT, ex p Kwok on Tong* [1981] Imm AR 214). The rules do not contemplate that an entrant should be allowed to set up in business on borrowed money over which he has no control or where he may be unable to service the loan (*Haji v S of S* [1978] Imm AR 26). The rules will not be satisfied if the applicant simply inherits a business worth in excess of £200,000 which is already established in the UK (*R v IAT, ex p Mohammed Rahman* (above)), nor will it be satisfied by money invested in a freehold property which may be difficult to sell or may be used for some other purpose. The money must be immediately available for investment at the time of the decision by the ECO (*ECO Rome v Hussain Rahman* [1991] Imm AR 102). The Home Office will normally expect the monies to be invested in the business within 12 months of admission (see *Business and Self-Employment: an Analysis of the Immigration Rules—Part 1*, by David Webb in INL&P vol 7, no 1 (1993)). The Home Office accepts investment by way of share capital. It is not necessary for shares to be purchased. Investment may be by way of loan capital if the loan is fully unsecured and subordinated to third party creditors (see Bernard Adonian, *The new Immigration Rules and business migrants*, INL&P vol 9, no 1 (1995) at p 16). The monies must be invested in the business and the rule will not be satisfied if part of the monies is in fact invested for living expenses (*Devshi Patel* (above)).

(b) Maintenance and accommodation

The applicant must show that until the business provides him with an income he will have sufficient additional funds to maintain and accommodate himself and any dependants without recourse to public funds or employment other than work for the business. He must also show that once the business is established, his share of the profits will be sufficient to maintain and accommodate himself and any dependants without recourse to public funds or employment other than his work for the business. He must also show that he does not intend to supplement his business activities by taking or seeking employment in the UK other than his work for the business. He must show that he can obtain a livelihood without having to supplement his business activities by employment of any kind (*R v IAT, ex p Martin* [1972] Imm AR 275).

(c) Disguised employment

The proposed partnership or directorship must not amount to 'disguised employment'. On the facts in *Pritpal Singh v S of S* [1972] Imm AR 154, the

IAT concluded that the appellant was in reality a paid employee. He was a director and secretary of a private limited company trading in sports equipment on a salary of £1,200 per annum. He loaned money to the company and held 15 £1 shares out of the company's share capital of £100. He received no share of the profits and there was no agreement in writing as to the future of the company. He could be removed from the board and from his secretarial duties at any time by the majority shareholders.

(d) Meeting liabilities
It is only his share of those liabilities of a business which are reasonably foreseeable that the applicant must be able to meet (*R v IAT, ex p Hirani* (2 July 1981, unreported, DC)). It is not necessary for an applicant who intends to join a partnership to show that he can meet all its liabilities, but he must be able to show that he could bear his proportionate share of the liabilities. Where the business is to be conducted through investment in a company, the Home Office has stated that, ideally, what is sought is an investment of £200,000 by way of share capital (see INL&P, vol 7, no 1 (1993), p 10).

(e) Taking over or joining an existing business
In addition to the requirements under para 201, a person who wishes to take over or join as a partner or director an existing business in the UK will need to produce the terms of the takeover, audited accounts for the business for previous years and evidence that his services and investment will result in a net increase in the employment provided by the business to persons settled in the UK. He must produce evidence of the likely creation of at least two new jobs.

It is a mandatory requirement of the paragraph that the applicant provide accounts and evidence that they have been audited. If it is not satisfied, entry will be refused (*Seyed v S of S* [1987] Imm AR 303). There must be some evidence that the presence of the applicant will require the employment of persons who are settled in the UK (*Singh* (4620)). The creation of self-employment will not satisfy the rule (*Seyed* (above)). There must be evidence that normally the structure of the business is such that there will be in post those persons whose employment under a contract of service or apprenticeship has come about because of the establishment of the new business (*Jamnadas* (6597)).

The Home Office has stated that where a person is joining an existing partnership or company, if this does not result in the creation of new employment, but only the maintenance of existing employment, the rule is not satisfied. Earlier practice was that each case was examined in the light of all its circumstances, particularly the number of jobs involved, and leave could be granted (see INL&P (above), p 13). Such leave was exceptional and outside the immigration rules. It is not clear that this practice will continue under HC 395 para 202(iii). Thus, an overseas business person would not be able to obtain leave under the rules to enter the UK to ensure that a business and its attendant jobs continue to exist if he could not show that there would also be a net increase in employment.

(f) Establishing a new business

A person who intends to establish a new business in the UK must satisfy the requirements of para 201, and produce evidence that he will be bringing into the country sufficient funds of his own to establish a business. He must also show that the business will create full-time paid employment for at least two persons already settled in the UK.

(g) Concession relating to lawyers

The Home Office, in a letter of 21 March 1991 to a legal publisher, stated that solicitors, barristers and consultants in overseas law coming to the UK to work, generally will not need to invest £200,000 as required by these rules. If they are coming as employees, they will need permits, but if they are entering as partners or to set up practice, they are admitted on a concessionary basis outside the immigration rules. An applicant must have:

(a) entry clearance before travelling;

(b) the ability to maintain and accommodate himself without recourse to public funds or taking other work;

(c) evidence from The Law Society, Bar Council or chambers of his eligibility to practise in the UK;

(d) evidence that he has permission from the Bar Council to practise from home if he is a barrister intending to do so;

(e) evidence of his qualifications, and a letter from the appropriate Law Society confirming that there is no objection to his application (in the case of consultants in foreign law);

(f) evidence of his financial means if he is intending to establish a new practice in the UK.

Such a concession may give rise to a legitimate expectation that its terms will be observed, and may in certain circumstances give rise to judicial review of the decision to refuse entry.

(h) Extensions

Requirements for an extension of stay in order to remain in business

206. The requirements for an extension of stay in order to remain in business in the United Kingdom are that the applicant can show:

(i)   that he entered the United Kingdom with a valid United Kingdom entry clearance as a businessman; and

(ii) audited accounts which show the precise financial position of the business and which confirm that he has invested not less than £200,000 of his own money directly into the business in the United Kingdom; and

(iii) that he is actively involved on a full-time basis in trading or providing services on his own account or in partnership or in the promotion and management of the company as a director; and

(iv) that his level of financial investment is proportional to his interest in the business; and

(v)   that he has either a controlling or equal interest in the business and that any partnership or directorship does not amount to disguised employment; and

(vi)   that he is able to bear his share of any liability the business may incur; and

(vii)   that there is a genuine need for his investment and services in the United Kingdom; and

(viii) (a)   that where he has established a new business, new full-time paid employment has been created in the business for at least 2 persons settled in the United Kingdom; or

        (b)   that where he has taken over or joined an existing business, his services and investment have resulted in a net increase in the employment provided by the business to persons settled here to the extent of creating at least 2 new full-time jobs; and

(ix)   that his share of the profits of the business is sufficient to maintain and accommodate him and any dependants without recourse to employment (other than his work for the business) or to public funds; and

(x)   that he does not and will not have to supplement his business activities by taking or seeking employment in the United Kingdom other than his work for the business.

Extension of stay in order to remain in business
207. An extension of stay in order to remain in business with a condition restricting his freedom to take employment may be granted for a period not exceeding 3 years provided the Secretary of State is satisfied that each of the requirements of paragraph 206 is met.

Refusal of extension of stay in order to remain in business
208. An extension of stay in order to remain in business is to be refused if the Secretary of State is not satisfied that each of the requirements of paragraph 206 is met.

Indefinite leave to remain for a person established in business
209. Indefinite leave to remain may be granted, on application, to a person established in business provided he:

(i)   has spent a continuous period of 4 years in the United Kingdom in this capacity and is still engaged in the business in question; and

(ii)   has met the requirements of paragraph 206 throughout the 4 year period; and

(iii)   submits audited accounts for the first 3 years of trading and management accounts for the 4th year.

Refusal of indefinite leave to remain for a person established in business
210. Indefinite leave to remain in the United Kingdom for a person established in business is to be refused if the Secretary of State is not satisfied that each of the requirements of paragraph 209 is met.

COMMENTARY

The minimum amount of capital must have been invested in the business by this stage, and there must be evidence of employees engaged and working (*Jamnadas* (6597)). The requirement is for employment to have been created for more than one person. The employment of the same person at different times did not satisfy the rule (*Fanous v S of S* [1993] Imm AR 200).

Persons given limited leave to enter or remain in some other capacity have no claim to establish themselves in the UK for the purpose of setting up in business whether on their own account or as partners in a new or existing business, or to be self-employed. Their applications for extension of stay or leave to remain for these purposes are to be refused (*Al-Hasani v S of S* [1986] Imm AR 363).

If the requirements set out above are met then the applicant's stay may be extended for a further period on a condition restricting his freedom to take employment, provided that the aggregate of the extension in the capacity of businessman or self-employed person does not exceed three years. After four years' residence, the person may apply for permanent settlement.

2   Persons intending to establish themselves in business under EC Association Agreements

Requirements for leave to enter the United Kingdom as a person intending to establish himself in business under the provisions of an EC Association Agreement

211. For the purpose of paragraphs 212–223 a business means an enterprise as:
— a sole trader; or
— a partnership; or
— a company registered in the United Kingdom.

212. The requirements to be met by a person seeking leave to enter the United Kingdom to establish himself in business are that:

(i) he satisfies the requirements of either paragraph 213 or paragraph 214; and
(ii) the money he is putting into the business is under his control and sufficient to establish himself in business in the United Kingdom; and
(iii) until his business provides him with an income he will have sufficient additional funds to maintain and accommodate himself and any dependants without recourse to employment (other than his work for the business) or to public funds; and
(iv) his share of the profits of the business will be sufficient to maintain and accommodate himself and any dependants without recourse to employment (other than his work for the business) or to public funds; and
(v) he does not intend to supplement his business activities by taking or seeking employment in the United Kingdom other than his work for the business; and
(vi) he holds a valid United Kingdom entry clearance for entry in this capacity.

213. Where a person intends to establish himself in a company in the United Kingdom which he effectively controls he will need, in addition to meeting the requirements at paragraph 212, to show:

(i) that he is a national of Bulgaria, the Czech Republic, Hungary, Poland, Romania, Slovakia; and
(ii) that he will have a controlling interest in the company; and
(iii) that he will be actively involved in the promotion and management of the company; and
(iv) that the company will be registered in the United Kingdom and be trading or providing services in the United Kingdom; and

(v) that the company will be the owner of the assets of the business; and

(vi) where he is taking over an existing company, a written statement of the terms on which he is to take over the business and audited accounts for the business for previous years.

214. Where a person intends to establish himself in self-employment or in partnership in the United Kingdom he will need, in addition to meeting the requirements at 212 above, to show:

(i) that he is a national of Bulgaria, the Czech Republic, Poland, Romania or Slovakia; and

(ii) that he will be actively involved in trading or providing services on his own account or in partnership in the United Kingdom; and

(iii) that he, or he together with his partners, will be the owner of the assets of the business; and

(iv) in the case of a partnership, that his part in the business will not amount to disguised employment; and

(v) where he is taking over or joining an existing business a written statement of the terms on which he is to take over or join the business and audited accounts for the business for previous years.

Leave to enter the United Kingdom as a person seeking to establish himself in business under the provisions of an EC Association Agreement

215. A person seeking leave to enter the United Kingdom to establish himself in business may be admitted for a period not exceeding 12 months with a condition restricting his freedom to take employment provided he is able to produce to the Immigration Officer, on arrival, a valid United Kingdom entry clearance for entry in this capacity.

Refusal of leave to enter the United Kingdom as a person seeking to establish himself in business under the provisions of an EC Association Agreement

216. Leave to enter the United Kingdom as a person seeking to establish himself in business is to be refused if a valid United Kingdom entry clearance for entry in this capacity is not produced to the Immigration Officer on arrival.

COMMENTARY

This section (which had no predecessor in HC 251) provides for persons intending to establish themselves in pursuance of the EC Association Agreements. Nationals of Bulgaria, the Czech Republic, Hungary, Poland, Romania and Slovakia are affected at present. They do not have to show that they are investing a minimum of £200,000 in the UK when entering as persons intending to establish themselves in companies in which they have controlling interests (para 213). The provisions of para 214 apply to nationals of the specified countries who intend to establish themselves in self-employment or a partnership. A national of Hungary who intends to establish himself in self-employment or partnership must satisfy the requirements of paras 200 *ff* as a foreign national. These provisions apply to Bulgarian, Czech, Romanian and Slovak citizens who wish to establish themselves in business under the EC Association Agreements with their countries. Cm 3365 substituted Slovakia for Slovenia in para 213, which had been introduced by HC 329 in error.

(a) A national of an Association Agreement country establishing himself in a company

The agreements between EC states and Hungary and Poland are declared to be Community Treaties for the purposes of s 1(2) of the European Communities Act 1972 (The European Communities (Definition of Treaties) (European Agreement establishing an Association between the European Communities and their Member States and the Republic of Hungary) Order 1992 (SI 1992 No 2871), and the equivalent Order in respect of Poland (SI 1992 No 2872)). There are two types of Association Agreement. The aims of a treaty such as that with Hungary are:

    (*a*) to provide a framework for political dialogue;

    (*b*) a free trade area;

    (*c*) the promotion of economic, financial and cultural co-operation; and

    (*d*) supporting efforts to become a market economy.

See also SI 1994 No 760 for Romania and SI 1994 No 759 for the Czech Republic.

By contrast, Association Agreements may be a precursor to integration into the EU. One such is the agreement between EC states and Poland which is declared to be a Community Treaty for the purposes of s 1(2) of the European Communities Act 1972 (The European Communities (Definition of Treaties) (European Agreement establishing an Association between the European Communities and their Member States and the Republic of Poland Order 1992 (SI 1992 No 2872)). The aims of a treaty such as that with Poland are:

    (*a*) to provide a framework for political dialogue;

    (*b*) the promotion of cultural, trade and economic relations;

    (*c*) the provision of financial and technical assistance; and

    (*d*) the creation of an appropriate framework for Poland's gradual integration into the EC.

See also SI 1994 No 758 for Bulgaria and SI 1994 No 761 for the Slovak Republic.

As a result of both types of agreement, a national of one of these states does not have to show that he will be investing at least £200,000 of his own money in the company, or that he will be occupied full-time in running the company. He does have to show that he will be actively involved in the promotion and management of the company (para 213(iv)) and that he does not intend to supplement his business activities by taking or seeking employment in the UK other than his work for the business (para 212(v)). He does not need to show that his services and investment are needed and will create paid full-time employment in the company for persons already settled in the UK. Where taking over or joining as a partner an existing company he does not need to show evidence that the creation of full-time employment will result in a corresponding increase in the numbers of employees of the company.

Section 2 of the European Communities Act 1972 provides that all such rights, powers, liabilities, obligations and restrictions from time to time created or arising by or under the treaties and all such remedies and procedures from time to time provided for under the treaties as in accordance with the treaties are, without further enactment, to be given legal effect or used in the UK. They are to be recognised and available in the UK and enforced as enforceable Community rights. Quite apart from their introduction by domestic legislation, the rights created under the agreements may have direct effect where they are clear and precise enough. One of the requirements of HC 395 is that a person relying on the rule must show that he is a national of the relevant country. As a result of the Association Agreements' status as part of the EC legal framework, the question of a person's nationality is a matter of law, but is to be determined by the national law of the relevant country. Thus a person claiming to be Polish could rely on provisions of Polish nationality law to prove his nationality. Further, an error by the S of S regarding a person's nationality would be an error of law.

Nationals of countries with Association Agreements similar to that with Poland who are self-employed must comply with the provisions of para 214. Such a national is not required to show that he will invest at least £200,000 of his own money in the business. He does not need to show that he will be occupied full-time in running the business, nor that his services and investment are needed and will create new paid full-time employment in the business for persons already settled in the UK.

(b) Extensions and indefinite leave

Requirements for an extension of stay in order to remain in business under the provisions of an EC Association Agreement

217. The requirements for an extension of stay in order to remain in business in the United Kingdom are that the applicant can show that:
(i)   he has established himself in business in the United Kingdom; and
(ii) his share of the profits of the business is sufficient to maintain and accommodate himself and any dependants without recourse to employment (other than his work for the business) or to public funds; and
(iii) he does not and will not supplement his business activities by taking or seeking employment in the United Kingdom other than his work for the business; and
(iv) in addition he satisfies the requirements of either paragraph 218 or paragraph 219.

   218. Where a person has established himself in a company in the United Kingdom which he effectively controls he will need, in addition to meeting the requirements at paragraph 217 above, to show:
(i)   that he is a national of Bulgaria, the Czech Republic, Hungary, Poland, Romania or Slovakia; and
(ii) that he is actively involved in the promotion and management of the company; and
(iii) that he has a controlling interest in the company; and
(iv) that the company is registered in the United Kingdom and trading or providing services in the United Kingdom; and
(v)   that the company is the owner of the assets of the business; and
(vi) the current financial position in the form of audited accounts for the company.

219. Where a person has established himself as a sole trader or in partnership in the United Kingdom he will need, in addition to meeting the requirements at 217 above, to show:

(i)   that he is a national of Bulgaria, the Czech Republic, Poland, Romania or Slovakia; and

(ii) that he is actively involved in trading or providing services on his own account or in partnership in the United Kingdom; and

(iii) that he, or he together with his partners, is the owner of the assets of the business; and

(iv) in the case of a partnership, that his part in the business does not amount to disguised employment; and

(v)   the current financial position in the form of audited accounts for the business.

Extension of stay in order to remain in business under the provisions of an EC Association Agreement
220. An extension of stay in order to remain in business with a condition restricting his freedom to take employment may be granted for a period not exceeding 3 years provided the Secretary of State is satisfied that each of the requirements of paragraphs 217 and 218 or 219 is met.

Refusal of extension of stay in order to remain in business under the provisions of an EC Association Agreement
221. An extension of stay in order to remain in business is to be refused if the Secretary of State is not satisfied that each of the requirements of paragraphs 217 and 218 or 219 is met.

Indefinite leave to remain for a person established in business under the provisions of an EC Association Agreement
222. Indefinite leave to remain may be granted, on application, to a person established in business provided he:

(i)   has spent a continuous period of 4 years in the United Kingdom in this capacity and is still so engaged; and

(ii) has met the requirements of paragraphs 217 and 218 or 219 throughout the 4 years; and

(iii) submits audited accounts for the first 3 years of trading and management accounts for the 4th year.

Refusal of indefinite leave to remain for a person established in business under the provisions of an EC Association Agreement
223. Indefinite leave to remain in the United Kingdom for a person established in business is to be refused if the Secretary of State is not satisfied that each of the requirements of paragraph 222 is met.

COMMENTARY

The above provisions were also applied administratively to Bulgarian, Czech, Romanian, and Slovakian citizens before HC 395 was amended by HC 329 (letter from the IND to Baileys Shaw & Gillett, 6 December 1995). A person who has obtained leave to enter may also obtain an extension of stay to remain in business under the terms of an EC Association Agreement. A national of an Association Agreement country must show that he has established himself in business in the UK. He must also show that his share of the profits is sufficient to maintain and accommodate him and his dependants without recourse to public funds or employment other than his work for the business. He must show that he does not supplement his business activities by seeking or taking employment in the UK. When seeking an extension of leave in this capacity he does not need to show that he entered the UK with an entry clearance as a business person, nor satisfy the investment criterion or the employment creation criteria. He does not need to show that he will be occupied full-time in running the company.

The Association Agreements require separate provision to be made under the immigration rules for nationals of Agreement countries. A national of a country with an Association Agreement similar to that with Hungary (above) needs to satisfy the capital investment rule if he is seeking entry or an extension to be self-employed. If he effectively controls a company which he has established in the UK he will not need to satisfy the capital investment rule. It appears that nationals of any Association Agreement country entering in some other capacity can apply for an extension of their leave to establish themselves in business. The rules do not require an applicant to show that he entered with an entry clearance for the purpose of establishing himself in business. Such a person has to show that he has established a business.

When seeking an extension, a person benefiting from an Association Agreement of the kind with Poland does not need to have invested at least £200,000 of his own money in the business. He does not need to show that he will be occupied full-time in running the business, nor that his services and investment are needed and will create new paid full-time employment in the business for persons already settled in the UK. He does not have to produce evidence that his creation of new full-time employment will result in a corresponding increase in the numbers of employees of the business.

An applicant for indefinite leave to remain must have spent a continuous period of four years in the UK and be established in business under an EC Association Agreement. For the whole of the four years he must have satisfied the requirements of the rules. He must also submit audited accounts for the first three years of trading and management accounts for the fourth year.

3 Investors

Requirements for leave to enter the United Kingdom as an investor
224. The requirements to be met by a person seeking leave to enter the United Kingdom as an investor are that he:
(i) has money of his own under his control and disposable in the United Kingdom amounting to no less than £1 million; and
(ii) intends to invest not less than £750,000 of his capital in the United Kingdom by way of United Kingdom Government bonds, share capital or loan capital in active and trading United Kingdom registered companies (other than those principally engaged in property investment and excluding investment by the applicant by way of deposits with a bank, building

society or other enterprise whose normal course of business includes the acceptance of deposits); and

(iii) intends to make the United Kingdom his main home; and

(iv) is able to maintain and accommodate himself and any dependants without taking employment (other than self-employment or business) or recourse to public funds; and

(v) holds a valid United Kingdom entry clearance for entry in this capacity.

Leave to enter as an investor

225. A person seeking leave to enter the United Kingdom as an investor may be admitted for a period not exceeding 12 months with a restriction on his right to take employment, provided he is able to produce to the Immigration Officer, on arrival, a valid United Kingdom entry clearance for entry in this capacity.

Refusal of leave to enter as an investor

226. Leave to enter as an investor is to be refused if a valid United Kingdom entry clearance for entry in this capacity is not produced to the Immigration Officer on arrival.

Requirements for an extension of stay as an investor

227. The requirements for an extension of stay as an investor are that the applicant:

(i) entered the United Kingdom with a valid United Kingdom entry clearance as an investor; and

(ii) has no less than £1 million of his own money under his control in the United Kingdom; and

(iii) has invested not less than £750,000 of his capital in the United Kingdom on the terms set out in paragraph 224(ii) above and intends to maintain that investment on the terms set out in paragraph 224(ii); and

(iv) has made the United Kingdom his main home; and

(v) is able to maintain and accommodate himself and any dependants without taking employment (other than his self-employment or business) or re-course to public funds.

Extension of stay as an investor

228. An extension of stay as an investor, with a restriction on the taking of employment, may be granted for a maximum period of 3 years, provided the Secretary of State is satisfied that each of the requirements of paragraph 227 is met.

Refusal of extension of stay as an investor

229. An extension of stay as an investor is to be refused if the Secretary of State is not satisfied that each of the requirements of paragraph 227 is met.

Indefinite leave to remain for an investor

230. Indefinite leave to remain may be granted, on application, to a person admitted as an investor provided he:

(i) has spent a continuous period of 4 years in the United Kingdom in this capacity; and

(ii) has met the requirements of paragraph 227 throughout the 4 year period including the requirement as to the investment of £750,000 and continues to do so.

Refusal of indefinite leave to remain for an investor

231. Indefinite leave to remain in the United Kingdom for an investor is to be refused if the Secretary of State is not satisfied that each of the requirements of paragraph 230 is met.

COMMENTARY

HC 395 introduced a new category of investor to enable persons who wish to invest substantial amounts in the UK to engage in business. Unfortunately, the sums involved are so large that the rules will benefit only a very few people and may act as a disincentive to investment in the UK.

There is no requirement that the investor have a close connection with the UK. He must have £1 million or more under his control and disposal in the UK. He must have the intention to invest not less than £750,000 of his capital in the UK by way of UK government bonds, share capital or loan capital in active and trading UK registered companies. He must intend to make the UK his home. He must have an entry clearance for the purpose for which he seeks entry.

It is insufficient for the purposes of the requirement that the investor should have 'money of his own under his control' but which is not his in the sense of his having a right which can be enforced in law against anyone. Thus access to a father's wealth will not meet the requirements (*R v IAT, ex p Chiew* [1981] Imm AR 102). Income from a guaranteed pension may be taken into account (*S of S v Raval* [1975] Imm AR 72), as may income from a separation agreement, enforceable abroad (*S of S v Rohr* [1983] Imm AR 95).

For the purpose of the requirements on maintenance, the provision of accommodation (whether free or subsidised) and keep by relatives of the applicant should be disregarded (*S of S v Evgeniou* [1978] Imm AR 89). The financial position must be assessed on its own without taking into account any assistance provided by the applicant's family (*Randhawa v S of S* [1972] Imm AR 158; *ECO Canberra v Ward* [1975] Imm AR 129).

In order to obtain settlement the investor must, for a period of four years, have £750,000 invested in the UK in government bonds, or share or loan capital in UK companies. In a letter dated 26 April 1996 to Simmons & Simmons, the IND confirmed that, while to qualify as an investor para 224(i) above requires only that the applicant makes the UK his main home, to be eligible for indefinite leave to remain he must have spent at least 75 per cent of the four-year period in the UK. This is so despite the statement in para 230(iii) that residence for the four-year period must be continuous. Even if the investor does not meet the lesser requirement, but meets all the other requirements of the rule, further leave to remain will usually be granted.

4   Writers, composers and artists

Requirements for leave to enter the United Kingdom as a writer, composer or artist

232. The requirements to be met by a person seeking leave to enter the United Kingdom as a writer, composer or artist are that he:

(i)   has established himself outside the United Kingdom as a writer, composer or artist primarily engaged in producing original work which has been published (other than exclusively in newspapers or magazines), performed or exhibited for its literary, musical or artistic merit; and

(ii) does not intend to work except as related to his self-employment as a writer, composer or artist; and

(iii) has for the preceding year been able to maintain and accommodate himself and any dependants from his own resources without working except as a writer, composer or artist; and

(iv) will be able to maintain and accommodate himself and any dependants from his own resources without working except as a writer, composer or artist and without recourse to public funds; and

(v)   holds a valid United Kingdom entry clearance for entry in this capacity.

Leave to enter as a writer, composer or artist

233. A person seeking leave to enter the United Kingdom as a writer, composer or artist may be admitted for a period not exceeding 12 months, subject to a condition restricting his freedom to take employment, provided he is able to produce to the Immigration Officer, on arrival, a valid United Kingdom entry clearance for entry in this capacity.

Refusal of leave to enter as a writer, composer or artist

234. Leave to enter as a writer, composer or artist is to be refused if a valid United Kingdom entry clearance for entry in this capacity is not produced to the Immigration Officer on arrival.

Requirements for an extension of stay as a writer, composer or artist

235. The requirements for an extension of stay as a writer, composer or artist are that the applicant:

(i)   entered the United Kingdom with a valid United Kingdom entry clearance as a writer, composer or artist; and

(ii) meets the requirements of paragraph 232(ii)–(iv).

Extension of stay as a writer, composer or artist

236. An extension of stay as a writer, composer or artist must be granted for a period not exceeding 3 years with a restriction on his freedom to take employment, provided the Secretary of State is satisfied that each of the requirements of paragraph 235 is met.

Refusal of extension of stay as a writer, composer or artist

237. An extension of stay as a writer, composer or artist is to be refused if the Secretary of State is not satisfied that each of the requirements of paragraph 235 is met.

Indefinite leave to remain for a writer, composer or artist

238. Indefinite leave to remain may be granted, on application, to a person admitted as a writer, composer or artist provided he:

(i)   has spent a continuous period of 4 years in the United Kingdom in this capacity; and

(ii) has met the requirements of paragraph 235 throughout the 4 year period.

Refusal of indefinite leave to remain for a writer, composer or artist

239. Indefinite leave to remain for a writer, composer or artist is to be refused if the Secretary of State is not satisfied that each of the requirements of paragraph 238 is met.

COMMENTARY

HC 395 introduced the sub-category of 'composer' to this category. HC 395 requires the person seeking entry or leave to remain to show that he has established himself abroad before applying. The applicant will be admitted as a writer, composer or artist only if he can show, on the balance of probabilities, that he will be able to generate income from his work. He must show that for the year preceding entry he has been able to maintain and accommodate himself and any dependants from his own resources without working except as a writer, composer or artist. It is not, however, necessary to show that his work has been profitable (*Boehm-Bradley v Visa Officer, Washington* [1986] Imm AR 305). It will not be enough if he can show only that he will receive support from his family (*S of S v Jones* [1978] Imm AR 161). He must be able to show that he will be able to maintain and accommodate himself and any dependants from his own resources without working save as a writer, composer or artist. In some cases it will be difficult to draw the line between a self-employed journalist who writes mainly promotional articles, and a self-employed writer who is engaged on small literary works. If the writer is living off the proceeds of his own composition he will be classified as a writer (*Shevey v S of S* [1987] Imm AR 453). He must, however, show that he has established himself outside the UK as a writer engaged in producing original work which has been published (other than exclusively in newspapers or magazines).

The word 'artist' includes all those who cultivate or practise one of the fine arts, but excludes entertainers or performers, the distinguishing criterion being creativity: see *Raynor-Brown v S of S* [1994] Imm AR 565, criticising a more restrictive interpretation given in *S of S v Stillwaggon* [1975] Imm AR 132. Entertainers and performers who cannot show the necessary degree of creativity must apply for work permits.

The following evidence should be provided in support of an application for leave to enter or remain as a writer, composer or artist:

  (a) the applicant's curriculum vitae;
  (b) bank statements;
  (c) other evidence of his resources;
  (d) invoices from past sales;
  (e) examples of past work;
  (f) evidence relating to present and future commissions, stating the number per annum, and the approximate fee per work; and
  (g) letters of recommendation by past tutors or recipients of work.

(For a fuller discussion, see INL&P April 1990 p 73, *Practical Problems for Businessmen: Writers and Artists* by P Trott.)

The effect of the rule in practice will be that only established artists will be able to qualify for entry.

5 Spouses

Requirements for leave to enter or remain as the spouse of a person with limited leave to enter or remain under paragraphs 200–239

240. The requirements to be met by a person seeking leave to enter or remain in the United Kingdom as the spouse of a person with limited leave to enter or remain in the United Kingdom under paragraphs 200–239 are that:

(i) the applicant is married to a person with limited leave to enter or remain in the United Kingdom under paragraphs 200–239; and

(ii) each of the parties intends to live with the other as his or her spouse during the applicant's stay and the marriage is subsisting; and

(iii) there will be adequate accommodation for the parties and any dependants without recourse to public funds in accommodation which they own or occupy exclusively; and

(iv) the parties will be able to maintain themselves and any dependants adequately without recourse to public funds; and

(v) the applicant does not intend to stay in the United Kingdom beyond any period of leave granted to his spouse; and

(vi) if seeking leave to enter, the applicant holds a valid United Kingdom entry clearance for entry in this capacity or, if seeking leave to remain, was admitted with a valid United Kingdom entry clearance for entry in this capacity.

Leave to enter or remain as the spouse of a person with limited leave to enter or remain in the United Kingdom under paragraphs 200–239

241. A person seeking leave to enter or remain in the United Kingdom as the spouse of a person with limited leave to enter or remain in the United Kingdom under paragraphs 200–239 may be given leave to enter or remain in the United Kingdom for a period of leave not in excess of that granted to the person with limited leave to enter or remain under paragraphs 200–239 provided that, in relation to an application for leave to enter, he is able, on arrival, to produce to the Immigration Officer a valid United Kingdom entry clearance for entry in this capacity or, in the case of an application for limited leave to remain, he was admitted with a valid United Kingdom entry clearance for entry in this capacity and is able to satisfy the Secretary of State that each of the requirements of paragraph 240(i)–(v) is met. An application for indefinite leave to remain in this category may be granted provided the applicant was admitted with a valid United Kingdom entry clearance for entry in this capacity and is able to satisfy the Secretary of State that each of the requirements of paragraph 240(i)–(v) is met and provided indefinite leave to remain is, at the same time, being granted to the person with limited leave to remain under paragraphs 200–239.

Refusal of leave to enter or remain as the spouse of a person with limited leave to enter or remain in the United Kingdom under paragraphs 200–239

242. Leave to enter or remain in the United Kingdom as the spouse of a person with limited leave to enter or remain in the United Kingdom under paragraphs 200–239 is to be refused if, in relation to an application for leave to enter, a valid United Kingdom entry clearance for entry in this capacity is not produced to the Immigration Officer on arrival or, in the case of an application for limited leave to remain, if the applicant was not admitted with a valid United Kingdom entry

clearance for entry in this capacity or is unable to satisfy the Secretary of State that each of the requirements of paragraph 240(i)–(v) is met. An application for indefinite leave to remain in this category is to be refused if the applicant was not admitted with a valid United Kingdom entry clearance for entry in this capacity or is unable to satisfy the Secretary of State that each of the requirements of paragraph 240(i)–(v) is met or if indefinite leave to remain is not, at the same time, being granted to the person with limited leave to remain under paragraphs 200–239.

COMMENTARY

Spouses of the following are affected by these rules:
- (a) persons intending to establish themselves in business;
- (b) persons intending to establish themselves in business under provisions of EC Association Agreements;
- (c) investors;
- (d) writers, composers and artists.

A person entering as the spouse of a person in one of these categories must show that each of the parties intends to live with the other as his spouse during the applicant's stay and that the marriage is subsisting. For accommodation and maintenance requirements, see p 207. He must have an entry clearance for this purpose.

6 Children

Requirements for leave to enter or remain as the child of a person with limited leave to enter or remain in the United Kingdom under paragraphs 200–239

243. The requirements to be met by a person seeking leave to enter or remain in the United Kingdom as a child of a person with limited leave to enter or remain in the United Kingdom under paragraphs 200–239 are that:
- (i)   he is the child of a parent who has leave to enter or remain in the United Kingdom under paragraphs 200–239; and
- (ii)   he is under the age of 18 or has current leave to enter or remain in this capacity; and
- (iii) he is unmarried, has not formed an independent family unit and is not leading an independent life; and
- (iv)   he can and will be maintained and accommodated adequately without recourse to public funds in accommodation which his parent(s) own or occupy exclusively; and
- (v)   he will not stay in the United Kingdom beyond any period of leave granted to his parent(s); and
- (vi)   both parents are being or have been admitted to or allowed to remain in the United Kingdom save where:
  - (a) the parent he is accompanying or joining is his sole surviving parent; or
  - (b) the parent he is accompanying or joining has had sole responsibility for his upbringing; or

(c) there are serious and compelling family or other considerations which make exclusion from the United Kingdom undesirable and suitable arrangements have been made for his care; and

(vii) if seeking leave to enter, he holds a valid United Kingdom entry clearance for entry in this capacity or, if seeking leave to remain, was admitted with a valid United Kingdom entry clearance for entry in this capacity.

Leave to enter or remain as the child of a person with limited leave to enter or remain in the United Kingdom under paragraphs 200–239

244. A person seeking leave to enter or remain in the United Kingdom as the child of a person with limited leave to enter or remain in the United Kingdom under paragraphs 200–239 may be admitted to or allowed to remain in the United Kingdom for the same period of leave as that granted to the person given limited leave to enter or remain under paragraphs 200–239 provided that, in relation to an application for leave to enter, he is able to produce to the Immigration Officer, on arrival, a valid United Kingdom entry clearance for entry in this capacity or, in the case of an application for limited leave to remain, he was admitted with a valid United Kingdom entry clearance for entry in this capacity and is able to satisfy the Secretary of State that each of the requirements of paragraph 243(i)–(vi) is met. An application for indefinite leave to remain in this category may be granted provided the applicant was admitted with a valid United Kingdom entry clearance for entry in this capacity and is able to satisfy the Secretary of State that each of the requirements of paragraph 243(i)–(vi) is met and provided indefinite leave to remain is, at the same time, being granted to the person with limited leave to remain under paragraphs 200–239.

Refusal of leave to enter or remain as the child of a person with limited leave to enter or remain in the United Kingdom under paragraphs 200–239

245. Leave to enter or remain in the United Kingdom as the child of a person with limited leave to enter or remain in the United Kingdom under paragraphs 200–239 is to be refused if, in relation to an application for leave to enter, a valid United Kingdom entry clearance for entry in this capacity is not produced to the Immigration Officer on arrival or, in the case of an application for limited leave to remain, if the applicant was not admitted with a valid United Kingdom entry clearance for entry in this capacity or is unable to satisfy the Secretary of State that each of the requirements of paragraph 243(i)–(vi) is met. An application for indefinite leave to remain in this capacity is to be refused if the applicant was not admitted with a valid United Kingdom entry clearance for entry in this capacity or is unable to satisfy the Secretary of State that each of the requirements of paragraph 243(i)–(vi) is met or if indefinite leave to remain is not, at the same time, being granted to the person with limited leave to remain under paragraphs 200–239.

COMMENTARY

The children of the following are provided for by these paragraphs:

(a) persons intending to establish themselves in business;

(b) persons intending to establish themselves in business under provisions of EC Association Agreements;

(d) investors;

(c) writers, composers and artists.

The accommodation which must be provided for the child must be accommodation which his parents either own exclusively or occupy exclusively. For 'sole responsibility', see p 221. For 'serious and compelling family or other considerations', see p 222. The child must have an entry clearance for this purpose.

7   Persons exercising rights of access to a child resident in the UK

Requirements for leave to enter the United Kingdom as a person exercising rights of access to a child resident in the United Kingdom

246. The requirements to be met by a person seeking leave to enter the United Kingdom to exercise access rights to a child resident in the United Kingdom are that he:

(i)   produces evidence that a court in the United Kingdom has granted him access rights to his child; and

(ii)   is seeking leave to enter for the purpose of exercising access rights to his child; and

(iii)   is either divorced or legally separated from the other parent of the child; and

(iv)   intends to leave the United Kingdom at the expiry of his leave to enter; and

(v)   does not intend to take employment in the United Kingdom; and

(vi)   does not intend to produce goods or provide services within the United Kingdom, including the selling of goods or services direct to members of the public; and

(vii)   will maintain and accommodate himself and any dependants adequately out of resources available to him without recourse to public funds or taking employment; or will, with any dependants, be maintained and accommodated adequately by relatives or friends; and

(viii) can meet the cost of the onward or return journey; and

(ix)   holds a valid United Kingdom entry clearance for entry in this capacity.

Leave to enter as a person exercising rights of access to a child resident in the United Kingdom

247. A person seeking leave to enter the United Kingdom to exercise rights of access to a child resident in the United Kingdom may be granted leave to enter for a period which will enable him to exercise his access rights but in any case for no longer than 12 months provided he is able to produce to the Immigration Officer, on arrival, a valid United Kingdom entry clearance for entry in this capacity. Leave to enter is to be subject to a condition prohibiting employment.

Refusal of leave to enter as a person exercising rights of access to a child resident in the United Kingdom

248. Leave to enter as a person exercising rights of access to a child resident in the United Kingdom is to be refused if a valid United Kingdom entry clearance for entry in this capacity is not produced to the Immigration Officer on arrival.

COMMENTARY

HC 395 introduced this category in order that the UK should comply with the obligation to respect family life in arts 8 and 13 of the European

Convention on Human Rights: *Berrehab v Netherlands* (1988) 11 EHRR 322 and *Yousef* (App No 14830/89 unreported). HC 395 provides for a parent who is either divorced or legally separated to come to the UK for up to 12 months for the purpose of exercising access rights granted by a court in the UK to a child resident in the UK.

Immigration enforcement often takes place in the context of family breakdown or itself results in family breakdown, and it is difficult to see any practical benefit in this provision for any but the most wealthy families. In reality, the exercise of art 8 rights will continue to depend on the discretionary forbearance to deport under Home Office guidance contained in DP/3/96, DP/4/96 and DP/5/96 (see Chapters 5 and 14); and it seems that the art 13 right (the right to redress) is still unprotected by the rules. In *Ex p Meftah Zighem* [1996] Imm AR 194, Latham J held that para 246 applies only to cases where the parents are divorced or legally separated. In other cases the question of whether the S of S has considered art 8 of the Convention will properly arise. Where the S of S asserts, that he has taken account of art 8, and that there is no breach of it, it is open to the court to examine whether the S of S has considered whether there has been interference with family life in the terms of the article, or whether he has considered that there is a justified interference with family life within the terms of art 8(2) (*Zighem* (above)). It is also arguable that where the S of S states that he has taken art 8 into account, consideration must be given to the interpretation if that article by the European Court of Human Rights in order to determine whether the S of S has taken account of art 8 or something else.

8   Holders of special vouchers

Requirements for indefinite leave to enter as the holder of a special voucher
249. The requirements for indefinite leave to enter as the holder of a special voucher are that the person concerned:
(i)   is a British Overseas citizen; and
(ii)   is in possession of a special voucher issued to him by a British Government representative overseas or a valid United Kingdom entry clearance for settlement in the United Kingdom in this capacity.

Indefinite leave to enter as the holder of a special voucher
250. A British Overseas citizen may be granted indefinite leave to enter the United Kingdom provided he is able to produce to the Immigration Officer, on arrival, either a special voucher issued to him by a British Government representative or a valid United Kingdom entry clearance for settlement in this capacity.

Refusal of indefinite leave to enter as the holder of a special voucher
251. Indefinite leave to enter as the holder of a special voucher is to be refused if neither a special voucher issued by a British Government representative nor a valid United Kingdom entry clearance for settlement in this capacity is produced to the Immigration Officer on arrival.

Requirements for indefinite leave to enter as the spouse or child of a special voucher holder

252. The requirements for indefinite leave to enter the United Kingdom as the spouse or child of a special voucher holder are that the person concerned:

(i) is in possession of a valid United Kingdom entry clearance for settlement in the United Kingdom in this capacity; and

(ii) can and will be maintained and accommodated adequately by the special voucher holder without recourse to public funds.

Indefinite leave to enter as the spouse or child of a special voucher holder

253. Indefinite leave to enter as the spouse or child of a special voucher holder may be granted provided a valid United Kingdom entry clearance for settlement is produced to the Immigration Officer on arrival.

Refusal of indefinite leave to enter as the spouse or child of a special voucher holder

254. Indefinite leave to enter as the spouse or child of a special voucher holder is to be refused if a valid United Kingdom entry clearance for settlement is not produced to the Immigration Officer on arrival.

COMMENTARY

There is no claim as of right to a voucher, nor any right to appeal against the refusal to issue one, as it is not an entry clearance for the purposes of s 33(1) of the 1971 Act (*R v ECO Bombay, ex p Amin* [1983] 2 AC 818).

The following conditions must be fulfilled before a special voucher is issued:

(a) a male applicant must be over 18 to qualify as a 'head of household';

(b) a female must be over 18; and

    (i) single or widowed or divorced; or

    (ii) married to a man who, for medical reasons, is not able to act as the 'head of household';

(c) the applicant must have no other citizenship;

(d) the applicant must have a connection with East Africa;

(e) the applicant must be 'under pressure' to leave his country of residence;

(f) the applicant must have no other country to which he could go save the UK;

(g) the applicant must have an intention to settle in the UK.

If the applicant or his parents were born in Kenya, Tanzania, Uganda, Malawi, Zambia, Zimbabwe or Aden, or have been settled at any time in one of those countries, he will be deemed (a) to have a connection with East Africa; and (b) to be under pressure to emigrate if he normally resides in Kenya, Tanzania, Malawi, Zambia or India.

A refusal to issue a special voucher is amenable to judicial review in certain circumstances. A guidance leaflet (Form OF2, available from the Home Office), defining the conditions on which special vouchers will be issued, has been published. It gives rise to a legitimate expectation that its terms will be observed. Moreover, failure to follow its own guidance will lay the decision-maker open to the criticism that he acted inconsistently.

The term 'dependant' is to be construed by reference to the various classes of other relatives and dependants defined in the immigration rules (*Shah* (4618)). These are spouses, children, children over 18, parents, grandparents and other relatives. Unmarried children under 25 will also be admitted under the terms of the guidance if they are fully dependent on the BOC at the time the voucher is offered. Vouchers are issued by British representatives overseas. The scheme is administered by the Foreign and Commonwealth Office, not the Home Office. Vouchers cannot be issued in the UK (*Shah v S of S* [1972] Imm AR 56).

9 EEA nationals and their families

The paragraphs (255–262) relating to EEA nationals and their families are set out in Chapter 16, together with a detailed discussion of the applicable EU law. HC 395 sets out the criteria in national law to be met by EEA nationals and their family members seeking an EEA family permit and settlement. These provisions supplement the provisions of the Immigration (European Economic Area) Order 1994.

10 Retired persons of independent means

Requirements for leave to enter the United Kingdom as a retired person of independent means

263. The requirements to be met by a person seeking leave to enter the United Kingdom as a retired person of independent means are that he:
(i) is at least 60 years old; and
(ii) has under his control and disposable in the United Kingdom an income of his own of not less than £25,000 per annum; and
(iii) is able and willing to maintain and accommodate himself and any dependants indefinitely in the United Kingdom from his own resources with no assistance from any other person and without taking employment or having recourse to public funds; and
(iv) can demonstrate a close connection with the United Kingdom; and
(v) intends to make the United Kingdom his main home; and
(vi) holds a valid United Kingdom entry clearance for entry in this capacity.

Leave to enter as a retired person of independent means

264. A person seeking leave to enter the United Kingdom as a retired person of independent means may be admitted subject to a condition prohibiting employment for a period not exceeding 4 years, provided he is able to produce to the Immigration Officer, on arrival, a valid United Kingdom entry clearance for entry in this capacity.

Refusal of leave to enter as a retired person of independent means

265. Leave to enter as a retired person of independent means is to be refused if a valid United Kingdom entry clearance for entry in this capacity is not produced to the Immigration Officer on arrival.

Requirements for an extension of stay as a retired person of independent means

266. The requirements for an extension of stay as a retired person of independent means are that the applicant:

(i)   entered the United Kingdom with a valid United Kingdom entry clearance as a retired person of independent means; and

(ii) meets the requirements of paragraph 263(ii)–(iv); and

(iii) has made the United Kingdom his main home.

Extension of stay as a retired person of independent means

267. An extension of stay as a retired person of independent means, with a prohibition on the taking of employment, may be granted so as to bring the person's stay in this category up to a maximum of 4 years in aggregate, provided the Secretary of State is satisfied that each of the requirements of paragraph 266 is met.

Refusal of extension of stay as a retired person of independent means

268. An extension of stay as a retired person of independent means is to be refused if the Secretary of State is not satisfied that each of the requirements of paragraph 266 is met.

Indefinite leave to remain for a retired person of independent means

269. Indefinite leave to remain may be granted, on application, to a person admitted as a retired person of independent means provided he:

(i)   has spent a continuous period of 4 years in the United Kingdom in this capacity; and

(ii) has met the requirements of paragraph 266 throughout the 4 year period and continues to do so.

Refusal of indefinite leave to remain for a retired person of independent means

270. Indefinite leave to remain in the United Kingdom for a retired person of independent means is to be refused if the Secretary of State is not satisfied that each of the requirements of paragraph 269 is met.

COMMENTARY

HC 395 limits the 'persons of independent means' category to retired persons, who must be at least 60 years old. The applicant must have an income of not less than £25,000 per year.

In addition to satisfying the immigration officer of the maintenance and accommodation requirements, the applicant must show that he has a 'close connection' with the UK. A very long period of residence in the UK may in itself amount to a close connection (*R v IAT, ex p Zandfani* [1984] Imm AR 213). Whether or not the applicant has formed a strong sense of belonging and community as a result of his residence in the UK will, in most cases, be relevant. However, possessions or business connections, or having previously held British nationality, may be sufficient (see, for example, *S of S v Rohr* [1983] Imm AR 156).

11   Spouses of retired persons of independent means

Requirements for leave to enter or remain as the spouse of a person with limited leave to enter or remain in the United Kingdom as a retired person of independent means

271. The requirements to be met by a person seeking leave to enter or remain in the United Kingdom as the spouse of a person with limited leave to enter or remain in the United Kingdom as a retired person of independent means are that:

(i)   the applicant is married to a person with limited leave to enter or remain in the United Kingdom as a retired person of independent means; and

(ii)   each of the parties intends to live with the other as his or her spouse during the applicant's stay and the marriage is subsisting; and

(iii) there will be adequate accommodation for the parties and any dependants without recourse to public funds in accommodation which they own or occupy exclusively; and

(iv)   the parties will be able to maintain themselves and any dependants adequately without recourse to public funds; and

(v)   the applicant does not intend to stay in the United Kingdom beyond any period of leave granted to his spouse; and

(vi)   if seeking leave to enter, the applicant holds a valid United Kingdom entry clearance for entry in this capacity or, if seeking leave to remain, was admitted with a valid United Kingdom entry clearance for entry in this capacity.

Leave to enter or remain as the spouse of a person with limited leave to enter or remain in the United Kingdom as a retired person of independent means

272. A person seeking leave to enter or remain in the United Kingdom as the spouse of a person with limited leave to enter or remain in the United Kingdom as a retired person of independent means may be given leave to enter or remain in the United Kingdom for a period not in excess of that granted to the person given limited leave to enter or remain as a retired person of independent means provided that, in relation to an application for leave to enter, he is able to produce to the Immigration Officer, on arrival, a valid United Kingdom entry clearance for entry in this capacity, or, in the case of an application for limited leave to remain, he was admitted with a valid United Kingdom entry clearance for entry in this capacity and is able to satisfy the Secretary of State that each of the requirements of paragraph 271(i)–(v) is met. An application for indefinite leave to remain in this category may be granted provided the applicant was admitted with a valid United Kingdom entry clearance for entry in this capacity and is able to satisfy the Secretary of State that each of the requirements of paragraph 271(i)–(v) is met and provided indefinite leave to remain is, at the same time, being granted to the person with limited leave to enter or remain as a retired person of independent means. Leave to enter or remain is to be subject to a condition prohibiting employment except in relation to the grant of indefinite leave to remain.

Refusal of leave to enter or remain as the spouse of a person with limited leave to enter or remain in the United Kingdom as a retired person of independent means

273. Leave to enter or remain in the United Kingdom as the spouse of a person with limited leave to enter or remain in the United Kingdom as a retired person of independent means is to be refused if, in relation to an application for leave to enter, a valid United Kingdom entry clearance for entry in this capacity is not

produced to the Immigration Officer on arrival or, in the case of an application for limited leave to remain, if the applicant was not admitted with a valid United Kingdom entry clearance for entry in this capacity or is unable to satisfy the Secretary of State that each of the requirements of paragraph 271(i)–(v) is met. An application for indefinite leave to remain in this category is to be refused if the applicant was not admitted with a valid United Kingdom entry clearance for entry in this capacity or is unable to satisfy the Secretary of State that each of the requirements of paragraph 271(i)–(v) is met or if indefinite leave to remain is not, at the same time, being granted to the person with limited leave to enter or remain as a retired person of independent means.

COMMENTARY

The requirements placed on a person seeking leave to enter or remain in the UK as the spouse of a person with limited leave to enter as a retired person of independent means are that he is married to that person; that each intends to live with the other as the other's spouse; and that the marriage is subsisting. He must show that there will be adequate accommodation for them and their dependants without recourse to public funds in accommodation which they own or occupy exclusively (see p 207). He must have a valid entry clearance, and must intend to leave at the end of the period granted to his spouse. Indefinite leave in this category can be obtained only if, at the same time, the principal applicant is being granted indefinite leave to remain.

12   Children of retired persons of independent means

Requirements for leave to enter or remain as the child of a person with limited leave to enter or remain in the United Kingdom as a retired person of independent means

274. The requirements to be met by a person seeking leave to enter or remain in the United Kingdom as the child of a person with limited leave to enter or remain in the United Kingdom as a retired person of independent means are that:

(i)   he is the child of a parent who has been admitted to or allowed to remain in the United Kingdom as a retired person of independent means; and

(ii)   he is under the age of 18 or has current leave to enter or remain in this capacity; and

(iii) he is unmarried, has not formed an independent family unit and is not leading an independent life; and

(iv) he can, and will, be maintained and accommodated adequately without recourse to public funds in accommodation which his parent(s) own or occupy exclusively; and

(v)   he will not stay in the United Kingdom beyond any period of leave granted to his parent(s); and

(vi) both parents are being or have been admitted to or allowed to remain in the United Kingdom save where:

    (*a*) the parent he is accompanying or joining is his sole surviving parent; or

    (*b*) the parent he is accompanying or joining has had sole responsibility for his upbringing; or (*c*) there are serious and compelling family or other considerations which make exclusion from the United Kingdom undesirable and suitable arrangements have been made for his care; and

(vii) if seeking leave to enter, he holds a valid United Kingdom entry clearance for entry in this capacity or, if seeking leave to remain, was admitted with a valid United Kingdom entry clearance for entry in this capacity.

Leave to enter or remain as the child of a person with limited leave to enter or remain in the United Kingdom as a retired person of independent means

275. A person seeking leave to enter or remain in the United Kingdom as the child of a person with limited leave to enter or remain in the United Kingdom as a retired person of independent means may be given leave to enter or remain in the United Kingdom for a period of leave not in excess of that granted to the person with limited leave to enter or remain as a retired person of independent means provided that, in relation to an application for leave to enter, he is able to produce to the Immigration Officer, on arrival, a valid United Kingdom entry clearance for entry in this capacity or, in the case of an application for limited leave to remain, he was admitted with a valid United Kingdom entry clearance for entry in this capacity and is able to satisfy the Secretary of State that each of the requirements of paragraph 274(i)–(vi) is met. An application for indefinite leave to remain in this category may be granted provided the applicant was admitted to the United Kingdom with a valid United Kingdom entry clearance for entry in this capacity and is able to satisfy the Secretary of State that each of the requirements of paragraph 274(i)–(vi) is met and provided indefinite leave to remain is, at the same time, being granted to the person with limited leave to enter or remain as a retired person of independent means. Leave to enter or remain is to be subject to a condition prohibiting employment except in relation to the grant of indefinite leave to remain.

Refusal of leave to enter or remain as the child of a person with limited leave to enter or remain in the United Kingdom as a retired person of independent means

276. Leave to enter or remain in the United Kingdom as the child of a person with limited leave to enter or remain in the United Kingdom as a retired person of independent means is to be refused if, in relation to an application for leave to enter, a valid United Kingdom entry clearance for entry in this capacity is not produced to the Immigration Officer on arrival, or in the case of an application for limited leave to remain, if the applicant was not admitted with a valid United Kingdom entry clearance for entry in this capacity or is unable to satisfy the Secretary of State that each of the requirements of paragraph 274(i)–(vi) is met. An application for indefinite leave to remain in this category is to be refused if the applicant was not admitted with a valid United Kingdom entry clearance for entry in this capacity or is unable to satisfy the Secretary of State that each of the requirements of paragraph 274(i)–(vi) is met or if indefinite leave to remain is not, at the same time, being granted to the person with limited leave to enter or remain as a retired person of independent means.

COMMENTARY

For 'own or occupy exclusively', see p 207. For 'public funds', see p 60. For 'sole responsibility', see p 221. For 'serious and compelling family or other considerations', see p 222.

'Control' is defined as a right which can be enforced in law against anyone who might wish to interfere. Mere permission to use and spend is not enough, *per* Ralph Gibson J in *Chiew*; see p 179. The facts of *Chiew* were that the applicant was a Malaysian from the Chinese community. He had paid frequent visits to the UK over the years for various purposes. The evidence of an expert on Chinese customary law was accepted as proving that family assets always vest in the head of a family, but that they are regarded as a common fund on which the sons had a right to call. The judge held that the context of the phrase 'means under his control' signified that the paragraph was not concerned with the mere presence of a regular supply of funds, nor with the probability of the continuance of those supplies. It was concerned with the means necessary for supporting the applicant and his dependants in the foreseeable future. Those means should be under the applicant's own control. The question will be whether the applicant has the right to draw on the fund. The Home Office complained that the adjudicator, once he had found that the father in that case had ultimate control over the family funds, and could curtail the applicant's means if he wished, found that the applicant had control over the funds. The IAT had overruled the adjudicator's decision on the basis that if the phrase had not been intended to imply that such control is to the exclusion of everyone or everything else, some reference would have been made in the rules to proof of establishing the availability of funds for *bona fide* family members. But the purpose of the rule is to provide for the settlement of people of independent means, not the settlement of people relying on remittances, however large and however apparently never-ending. The ultimate control of these remittances lay with the appellant's father.

The Home Office submission that the phrase must be taken to mean a legal and enforceable right, and that a probability of continuance is not enough, was rejected. This case also echoes *ECO Canberra v Ward* (see p 179) that benefits in kind from relatives are to be ignored in calculating adequacy of means.

Chapter 12

Part 8: Family Members

1 Spouses

(a) Introduction

Marriage to a British citizen does not result in a right under s 1(1) of the 1971 Act for a wife or husband to join his or her spouse in the UK (*Ex p Rofathullah* [1988] 3 WLR 591). In *Abdulaziz, Cabales and Balkandali v UK* [1985] 11 EHRR 459, the European Court of Human Rights held that the provisions of HC 169 which made it more difficult for a husband to join his wife settled here than for a wife to join her husband, discriminated on the grounds of sex and contravened arts 8, 13 and 14 of the European Convention on Human Rights. In response to this decision, the rules were amended by HC 503. There is now no differentiation between the rules for husbands and for wives: it is more difficult for both to join their spouses than formerly. A more recent set of rules has been challenged as *ultra vires* the 1971 Act, but the challenge failed in the CA on the basis that the present rules are not so unreasonable, uncertain or unfair in their application that Parliament could not have intended them (*Rajput v IAT* [1989] Imm AR 350).

A member state of the European Union must permit to enter and reside in its territory the spouse, whether an EU national or not, of a national of that state who has travelled to another member state to exercise a Community right in that other state and who returns to exercise a Community right in the state of which he is a national (*R v IAT and Surinder Singh, ex p S of S* [1992] Imm AR 565). It is necessary to show that there is a factor linking the circumstances with any of the situations governed by EU law. Therefore if a UK national marries a non-EEA national, it is necessary for the couple to exercise a right, for example, of establishment in France, before they return to the UK to exercise a Community right in the UK. Other EEA nationals will, of course, be able to enter with their spouses to exercise a Community right. However, the marriage must be of substance and not a fraud (*Kwong* (10661), and *Kam Yu Kau* (10859)). In *Pinto* (12578), the IAT held that the right of a non-EU spouse of a EU citizen is contingent on the EU spouse's maintaining the exercise of a Treaty right (see p 298). Polygamous marriages, if valid in the EEA member state of origin of the EEA national, would not be subject to the restrictions to which such marriages are subject under domestic law (see below). In *Wong* (12602), the IAT considered that non-EEA nationals married to EEA nationals could appeal against a refusal of a residence permit under the EEA Order 1994 (see p 324), even where it is alleged that there is no right of appeal as the marriage is a sham (see p 327 and art 2(2), EEA Order).

The provisions of Part 8 of HC 395, on spouses are as follows:

277. Nothing in these Rules shall be construed as permitting a person to be granted entry clearance, leave to enter, leave to remain or variation of leave as a spouse of another if either party to the marriage will be aged under 16 on the date of arrival in the United Kingdom or (as the case may be) on the date on which the leave to remain or variation of leave would be granted.

278. Nothing in these Rules shall be construed as allowing a woman to be granted entry clearance, leave to enter, leave to remain or variation of leave as the wife of a man ('the husband') if:

(i)   her marriage to the husband is polygamous; and
(ii) there is another woman living who is the wife of the husband and who:
    (a) is, or at any time since her marriage to the husband has been, in the United Kingdom; or
    (b) has been granted a certificate of entitlement in respect of the right of abode mentioned in Section 2(1)(a) of the Immigration Act 1988 or an entry clearance to enter the United Kingdom as the wife of the husband.

For the purpose of this paragraph a marriage may be polygamous although at its inception neither party had any other spouse.

279. Paragraph 278 does not apply to any woman who seeks entry clearance, leave to enter, leave to remain or variation of leave where:

(i)   she has been in the United Kingdom before 1 August 1988 having been admitted for the purpose of settlement as the wife of the husband; or
(ii) she has, since her marriage to the husband, been in the United Kingdom at any time when there was no such other woman living as is mentioned in paragraph 278(ii),

but where a woman claims that paragraph 278 does not apply to her because she has been in the United Kingdom in circumstances which cause her to fall within sub-paragraphs (i) or (ii) of that paragraph it shall be for her to prove that fact.

280. For the purposes of paragraphs 278 and 279 the presence of any wife in the United Kingdom in any of the following circumstances shall be disregarded:

(i)   as a visitor; or
(ii) an illegal entrant; or
(iii) in circumstances whereby a person is deemed by Section 11(1) of the Immigration Act 1971 not to have entered the United Kingdom.

COMMENTARY

Section 11 of the 1971 Act provides that a person is deemed not to have entered the UK where he remains in a disembarkation approved area; while he is detained; while he is on temporary admission, and while released but liable to detention under Sched 2 to the 1971 Act.

Under 16   A spouse will not be admitted to the UK where either of the parties to the marriage is under 16. Therefore, although a valid marriage may have been contracted abroad, which is valid for the purposes of UK law, until the under-age party becomes of age, the spouse will be unable to enter. Further, s 3 of the Domicile and Matrimonial Proceedings Act 1973 has the effect that a child under 16 has the domicile of its father, so that a marriage before that age may be valid for the purposes of UK law by virtue of the child's domicile before the marriage. The paragraph prevents the spouse's entry until she becomes of age.

Polygamy   To be recognised as a valid marriage for the purposes of the immigration rules, a polygamous marriage must be:

   (a) in a form valid in the country in which it is celebrated; and
   (b) valid according to the law of the country in which each party is domiciled

(*Mohammed v Knott* [1968] 2 All ER 563). The validity of a marriage is often tested by reference to the law of the country with which it has the most real and substantial connection (*R v IAT, ex p Rafika Bibi* [1989] Imm AR 1). However, this test will be used only where it upholds the validity of the marriage.

A polygamous marriage or a potentially polygamous marriage is void in UK law if it was entered into outside the UK at a time when either party was domiciled in the UK (see Matrimonial Causes Act 1973, s 11*(d)*). Where the marriage is legal, and the father is a British citizen, the children of a polygamous marriage will have the father's nationality.

The 1988 Act made it impossible for a wife in a polygamous marriage, whose husband has already brought another wife into the UK as his wife, to enter on that footing (s 2, 1988 Act). She has a right of abode in the UK, but is prevented from exercising it if the other wife has already done so, or if there is another wife of the marriage who is, or any time since her marriage to the husband has been, in the UK. The *vires* of what is now the rule on polygamous marriage was tested in *R v IAT ex p Hasna Begum* [1995] Imm AR 249, and it was found not to be *ultra vires* s 2(3) of the 1988 Act, which Tucker J stated had the effect of simply making it clear that, during the period for which the polygamous wife was excluded from entry, if she wants to come to the UK, she must not be treated as coming as a bride, but subject to controls. The subsection does not confer a right of entry (see at p 251).

A marriage may be polygamous, even though at its inception neither party has any spouse additional to the other. On the other hand, not every marriage which takes place where polygamy is legal is potentially polygamous. In *Hussain (Aliya) v Hussain (Shahid)* [1983] Fam 26, the CA held that a marriage is potentially polygamous only if at least one party has the capacity to marry a second spouse while the marriage subsists. In that case the husband could not contract a second marriage because he was domiciled in the UK, and his wife was not able to contract a second marriage under Islamic law. Therefore the marriage was not potentially polygamous and was not invalid by virtue of s 11*(d)* of the Matrimonial Causes Act 1973.

(b) Preconditions for entry

Requirements for leave to enter the United Kingdom with a view to settlement as the spouse of a person present and settled in the United Kingdom or being admitted on the same occasion for settlement

281. The requirements to be met by a person seeking leave to enter the United Kingdom with a view to settlement as the spouse of a person present and settled in the United Kingdom or who is on the same occasion being admitted for settlement are that:

(i)   the applicant is married to a person present and settled in the United Kingdom or who is on the same occasion being admitted for settlement; and

(ii) the marriage was not entered into primarily to obtain admission to the United Kingdom; and

(iii) the parties to the marriage have met; and

(iv) each of the parties intends to live permanently with the other as his or her spouse and the marriage is subsisting; and

(v)   there will be adequate accommodation for the parties and any dependants without recourse to public funds in accommodation which they own or occupy exclusively; and

(vi) the parties will be able to maintain themselves and any dependants adequately without recourse to public funds; and

(vii) the applicant holds a valid United Kingdom entry clearance for entry in this capacity.

For the purposes of this paragraph, a member of HM Forces based in the United Kingdom but serving overseas is to be regarded as present and settled in the United Kingdom.

Leave to enter as the spouse of a person present and settled in the United Kingdom or being admitted for settlement on the same occasion

282. A person seeking leave to enter the United Kingdom as the spouse of a person present and settled in the United Kingdom or who is on the same occasion being admitted for settlement may be admitted for an initial period not exceeding 12 months provided a valid United Kingdom entry clearance for entry in this capacity is produced to the Immigration Officer on arrival.

Refusal of leave to enter as the spouse of a person present and settled in the United Kingdom or being admitted on the same occasion for settlement

283. Leave to enter the United Kingdom as the spouse of a person present and settled in the United Kingdom or who is on the same occasion being admitted for settlement is to be refused if a valid United Kingdom entry clearance for entry in this capacity is not produced to the Immigration Officer on arrival.

COMMENTARY

A person who is on temporary admission does not have limited, or any, leave to remain in the UK. If he marries a settled person while on temporary admission he cannot rely on paras 281–284. He does not have entry clearance for the purpose, and he has not obtained limited leave (see *Dyfan v S of S* [1995] Imm AR 206).

The onus is on the applicant to satisfy the ECO, on the balance of probabilities, that a valid marriage has taken place (*Visa Officer Islamabad v*

Kalsoom Begum [1978] Imm AR 206). If there is any doubt, a full inves-tigation into family relationships and everyday family matters will be conducted. If substantial discrepancies in the accounts of the sponsor and the applicant are discovered, entry clearance may be refused. It is not necessary, however, to pinpoint the date of the marriage. If there is evidence to show that the applicant and sponsor are now married, they should obtain entry clearance despite having claimed falsely that they had married at an earlier time than they actually did (*Khanom v ECO Dacca* [1979–80] Imm AR 182).

Validity of the marriage The validity of the marriage is determined by the law of the place in which it is celebrated (*Berthiaume v Dastous* [1930] AC 79). Capacity to marry is determined by the law of each party's domicile immediately before the marriage (*R v IAT, ex p Rafika Bibi* [1989] Imm AR 1). Domicile is determined according to the following principles:

(1) A person has a domicile of origin, which is acquired at birth, and is that of the father or mother (the former if legitimate, the latter if illegitimate).

(2) There is a very strong presumption for the continuance of domicile of origin (*Plummer v Commissioners for the Inland Revenue* [1988] 1 WLR 292 and *Commissioners for the Inland Revenue v Bullock* [1975] 1 WLR 1436), and the burden of proving a change is on the person who asserts that the domicile has changed.

(3) A person may shed his domicile of origin and acquire a domicile of choice in another country if the following conditions are satisfied:

(*a*) physical presence in the new country, not casually or as a traveller but as an inhabitant of it (see *Re Newcomb* 192 NT 238); the new country must be the applicant's sole or chief place of residence (*Re Fuld* [1968] P 675),

(*b*) he has the necessary intention, which was defined by Lord Westbury in *Udny v Udny* (1869) LR 1 Sc and Div Apps 441: 'Domicile of choice is a conclusion or inference which the law derives from the fact of a man fixing voluntarily his sole or chief residence in a particular place, with an intention of continuing to reside there for an unlimited time.'

In *Re Fuld (deceased)* [1968] P 675, Scarman J said, at 684F:

... the law so far as relevant to my task may be stated as follows: (1) the domicile of origin adheres unless displaced by satisfactory evidence of the acquisition and continuance of a domicile of choice; (2) a domicile of choice is acquired only if it be affirmatively shown that the propositus is resident within a territory subject to a distinctive legal system with the intention, formed independently of external pressures, of residing there indefinitely.

The expression 'unlimited time' in *Udny* requires some further definition. In *Bullock*, the test was stated to be 'whether he intends to make his home in the new country until the end of his days unless and until something happens to make him change his mind'. Thus, in *Winans v Attorney-General* [1904] AC 287, at p 291, Lord Macnaghten, referring to Lord Cairns in *Bell v Kennedy*

LR (1868) 1 Sc & Div 307, at p 311, said that the question was whether the person whose domicile was in question had 'determined' to make, and had in fact made, the alleged domicile of choice 'his home with the intention of establishing himself and his family there and ending his days in that country.'

If a person who has made his home in a country other than his domicile of origin has expressed an intention to return to his domicile of origin, or to remove to some third country, upon an event or condition of an indefinite kind (for example, 'if I make a fortune' or 'when I've had enough of it'), it may be difficult, if not impossible, to conclude that he retained any real intention of so returning or removing. In *Aikman v Aikman* (1861) 3 Macq 854, the Lord Chancellor (at p 858) said that a mere intention to return to a man's native country on a doubtful contingency would not prevent residence in a foreign country putting an end to his domicile of origin.

In determining the true nature and quality of the person's intention, the court will take into account all relevant circumstances. Domicile is distinct from citizenship, although declarations of citizenship are a relevant consideration. A declaration of domicile contained in a will is also a matter to be taken into account, although the weight to be attributed to it must depend on the surrounding circumstances. The fact that a man establishes his matrimonial home in a new country is an important consideration in deciding whether he intends to make that country his permanent home (see, for example, *Forbes v Forbes* (1854) Kay 341; *Platt v Attorney-General of New South Wales* (1878) 3 App Cas 336 at p 343; and *Attorney-General v Yule* (1931) 145 LT 9 at p 14), but this is not a conclusive factor, and may be rebutted by stronger evidence (*Forbes*).

For abandonment of domicile of choice in favour of domicile of origin, see *Duchess of Portland's case* [1982] Ch 314. Schooling can make a person resident in a country without affecting his domicile: *Miesegaes v Commissioners of Inland Revenue* [1957] 37 TC 493. Nor did a return to the place of origin nullify a change of domicile once effected if the return was for a limited purpose only (see the US case, *White v Tennant* 31 W Va 790). The validity of a marriage in UK law may depend on the domicile of the parties. In *Kanchan Bibi Anwara Khatun and others* (12488), the second and third wives of a Bangladeshi national were validly married to him because he retained his domicile of origin in Bangladesh. The husband was a seafarer who registered as a British citizen in 1951 and was on the electoral roll in the UK (see *Plummer*, above). However he maintained his matrimonial home in Bangladesh (see *Bullock*, above), and his three wives lived there. When his third wife was refused entry clearance on a previous occasion, he spent a long period in Bangladesh, and at other times had spent shorter periods there. He had not, therefore abandoned his domicile of origin in Bangladesh for a domicile of choice in the UK.

If the marriage is invalid but the couple state that they would, if necessary, marry in the UK, the application should be treated as an application by a fiancé or fiancée (*Mohammed Ach-Ccharki v ECO, Rabat* [1991] Imm AR

162). Islamic law may be taken into account in determining the validity of a marriage, but it is not binding. Thus a marriage may be presumed from 'prolonged and continual cohabitation as husband and wife' according to s 268 in *Mulla's Principles of Muhammedan Law* (6th edn), provided that the cohabitation is proved (*Inayat Begum v Visa Officer, Islamabad* [1978] Imm AR 174). For marriage by proxy, see *Nazir Begum v ECO Islamabad* [1976] Imm AR 31. Thus a marriage by telephone or letter may be valid in form (*Nasreen Akhtar* (2166)). The tradition of *Rukhsati* is not necessary for a Muslim marriage's validity (*Basharat Hussain v Visa Officer, Islamabad* [1991] Imm AR 182). The evidence of independent witnesses that the applicant had, when previously in the UK, lived with the sponsor as his wife satisfied the IAT in one case that the relationship claimed was genuine, in view of the Muslim custom whereby such cohabitation would have been inconceivable if the applicant had not been the sponsor's wife (*Visa Officer, Islamabad v Channo Bi* [1978] Imm AR 182).

Where the applicant or spouse has been married before, consideration should be given to whether the first marriage has come to an end. A customary marriage will result in a valid marriage. If that marriage is not dissolved properly it may render bigamous, and therefore invalid, the marriage on the basis of which entry is sought. A customary divorce will be effective if that form of divorce is recognised in the country of the parties' domicile. In *R v IAT ex p Asfar Jan* [1995] Imm AR 440, Tucker J considered the validity of a *talaq* divorce pronounced in the UK. He considered that it was an overseas divorce obtained otherwise than by means of proceeding within the meaning of s 46(2) of the Family Law Act 1986. The divorce was not recognised in the UK because the husband had been habitually resident in the UK during the preceding year. A marriage contracted after that 'divorce' was not void because the applicant's second husband had been domiciled in Pakistan, so that s 11(d) of the Matrimonial Causes Act 1973 did not apply. The sponsor, her third husband, was domiciled in the UK at the time of their marriage. In those circumstances he had no capacity to marry her because she was already married and her divorce was not recognised for the purposes of English law.

The primary purpose test Where a person seeks leave to enter the UK with a view to settlement as the spouse of a person present and settled in the UK or of someone who is being admitted for settlement on the same occasion, the immigration authorities will need to be satisfied of the following:

(a) that the couple are married; and

(b) that the marriage was not entered into primarily to obtain admission to the UK; and

(c) that the parties to the marriage have met; and

(d) each of the parties intends to live permanently with the other as his or her spouse and the marriage is subsisting; and *(e)* that there will be adequate accommodation for the couple and their dependants in accommodation which either the couple own or occupy exclusively; and

(f) the couple and their dependants will be able to maintain themselves without recourse to public funds; and

(g) the applicant has a valid entry clearance for entry as the spouse of a person settled in the UK or being admitted for settlement in the UK.

Without an entry clearance the applicant will not have a right of appeal against a decision to refuse entry. The primary purpose of the marriage must not be to obtain admission to the UK. The burden is on the applicant to satisfy the ECO, on a balance of probabilities, that the marriage was not entered into primarily to obtain admission to the UK (*R v IAT, ex p Kumar* [1986] Imm AR 446). The factors listed are of equal importance and the burden in each case remains on the applicant (*ECO Islamabad v Mohamed Hussain* [1991] Imm AR 476 and *R v IAT, ex p Bhatia* [1985] Imm AR 50).

The leading case on primary purpose is *R v IAT ex p Hoque & Singh* [1988] Imm AR 216, which sets out the following guidance relating to the application of the test:

(a) the onus falls on the applicant to satisfy the ECO that it is not the primary purpose of the marriage to obtain admission to the UK, and that the other requirements of the rule are satisfied;

(b) in considering an application the ECO is not limited to such evidence as the applicant may put before him, but is entitled to make inquiries of his own and test such evidence as the applicant chooses to put forward;

(c) it is the intention on the part of the applicant which is the central consideration, but the intention of both parties will be relevant in assessing the purpose of the marriage. Where it is an arranged marriage the reasons of those who arranged the marriage will also be relevant;

(d) the mere fact that the parties prove an intention to live together does not by itself suffice to enable an applicant to show that the primary purpose of the marriage was not to obtain admission:

   (i) in the case of a prospective marriage the intention at the present time is the relevant consideration; but

   (ii) in the case of a concluded marriage the intention of the parties at the time of the celebration of the marriage is the relevant consideration;

(e) whether the parties intend to live together permanently as spouses, and whether they have previously met, 'spell out' matters relevant to whether the primary purpose of the marriage was admission to the UK; in the case of married couples, intervening devotion (see below) may make it easier to satisfy the ECO on the question of whether the primary purpose of the marriage was to gain admission;

(f) the fact that a marriage is an arranged marriage, although a circumstance to be taken into account, does not, where arranged

marriages are the norm, show that the purpose of the marriage was to obtain admission to the UK;

(g) the fact that the applicant is applying for an entry clearance under these paragraphs usually presupposes an intention to settle in the UK with the spouse: admissions on the applicant's part that he seeks to obtain admission to the UK should not be taken as evidence that this was the primary purpose of the marriage.

An ECO may make inquiries as to the circumstances in which the marriage was entered into, and may not shut his eyes to evidence which shows that the primary purpose of the marriage is to gain admission. On the other hand, he should not be over-zealous in seeking evidence that the marriage was entered into primarily for admission purposes. It is easy, but wrong, to treat the desire of the applicant to gain admission as evidence that this is the primary purpose of the marriage (*Kumar* (above), and *Hoque & Singh*). The fact that other parts of the rule are satisfied, so that there is an intention to live together permanently, will often cast a flood of light on the primary purpose of the marriage. A marriage can, however, be described as one 'of convenience', even where the parties intend to live together as husband and wife, if it would not have been entered into had it not provided a means of securing entry into the UK (*R v IAT ex p Salazaar* [1994] Imm AR 190). The ECO should act as a kind of jury assessing the evidence as a whole, without fine analysis, to ascertain the real purpose of the marriage. The adjudicator also should consider the evidence as a whole. In *Sheikh* (11949), the IAT allowed an appeal where the adjudicator found the appellant's credibility damaged because she had applied for a visitor's visa when she knew her wedding was imminent. She intended to marry while in the UK on the visit. This deception was said to be one of many factors. The other factors outbalanced it when the whole of the evidence was taken into account. Where an appeal against a refusal of entry clearance as a fiancé is successful, and the adjudicator makes no directions (see p 390), the ECO is entitled to take account of information which subsequently comes to light before the entry clearance is collected. However, cases in which there has been a successful appeal should not be re-opened except where, without further enquiry, evidence which creates a justifiable foundation for subsequent inquiry comes to light (*Gurnam Singh* (10072)). The ECO should not 'trawl' for information to enable the inquiry to be reopened.

The *Hoque & Singh* guidelines have been considered in a number of cases. A sponsor to a marriage may make it a condition that she will only marry someone who is prepared to live in the UK (*R v IAT, ex p Shameem Wali* [1989] Imm AR 86, *R v IAT, ex p Mohammed Khatab* [1989] Imm AR 313, *Dar* (9542) and *Shah* (12035)). Without more, such a condition would not show that the primary purpose of the marriage was to gain admission. Farquharson J, in *Wali*, observed that 'there is no reason why a British citizen, a woman, living in this country, should not wish to make it a condition of her marrying that she would only do so to somebody who, like herself, was going to live in the UK' (at p 91).

There is something inherently unlikely in the proposition that two people would, as Simon Brown J stated in *Matwinder Singh* (unreported, DC, 23 March 1987), 'bind and commit themselves together for life in a marriage with all that implies primarily in order to achieve the husband's settlement in the United Kingdom'. The Court of Session thought Simon Brown J's view to be a factor which an adjudicator could not ignore in assessing primary purpose cases (*Safta v S of S* [1992] Imm AR 1). See also McCullough J in *R v IAT ex p Kaur* [1991] Imm AR 107.

Such general improbability does not prevent the ECO from considering whether the marriage was entered into primarily for the purposes of gaining admission where appropriate. Where one party to the marriage intends to live permanently with the other only if the other is able to gain the necessary consent to enter the UK, he will not be regarded as having a proper intention to live with that other person at all (*Sumeina Masood v IAT* [1992] Imm AR 69). However, the IAT, in *Akbar* (8670), stated that *Masood* should not be read as equating a precondition of residence in the UK by the sponsor with a conclusion that the primary purpose of the marriage was admission. Limiting *Masood* to its own facts, the IAT held that it showed how, on particular facts, a condition of residence can lead to the conclusion that the marriage was primarily for admission. Such a conditional intention would become an intention to live together (as opposed to a mere wish) only if there was some reasonable prospect of its being fulfilled. Where no such prospect exists, an ECO will be justified in taking the view that if the husband's intention to live permanently with his wife is contingent on entry, the primary purpose of the marriage is to gain entry.

A fairly fine, but proper, distinction is drawn in some of the cases, between a marriage whose primary purpose is to gain entry to the UK, and a marriage motivated by an intention to escape from adverse conditions in the applicant's home country, and to do so through marriage to a person who could provide economic advantages: see, eg *Tohsamrit v ECO, Bangkok* (12107) and *Nu Phonson* (12392). In other words, it would seem that a marriage motivated by a general desire on the applicant's part to improve his circumstances may pass the primary purpose test provided only that the motivation is not a specific desire to gain entry to the UK. If one party to the marriage has an ulterior motive which is not primarily to gain admission, but for example, to protect the welfare of his children, the marriage is not being entered into primarily to gain admission for that reason (*Promsom* (11804)). In the context of an arranged marriage, it ought to be easier for a woman to satisfy the primary purpose test as, in some traditions, it is usual for the husband to tell his wife to join him (*Ushaben Prdipbhai Patel* (10121)).

Caution should be exercised over answers given in interviews with ECOs concerning the strength of an applicant's desire to gain admission. It is wrong to treat the fact that a person has lied about the strength of such a desire to gain admission as evidence that the desire to gain admission was the primary purpose of the marriage (*R v IAT, ex p Kaur* [1991] Imm AR 107). An adjudicator will, however, be entitled to take into account general factors, such as whether during the course of an interview the applicant and sponsor had lied and the taint of those earlier lies is not removed on his hearing the oral evidence (*R v IAT, ex p Gondalia* [1991] Imm AR 519 and *Mohamed Haleem* (10048)). A finding that the witnesses at the adjudicator's hearing are basically credible is an important conclusion in a primary purpose appeal. It should have a significant impact on the conclusion reached. Thus, in *Saeed Ahmed* (12137), the ECO had refused an entry clearance because, on a previous application to visit, the applicant had alleged that he could not settle outside his country because his mother was ill. The ECO questioned why the applicant was now, on a marriage application, willing to leave his mother and live in the UK. It was open to the adjudicator to reverse the ECO's decision based on his view of the overall credibility of the witnesses, including the sponsoring wife, and the appellant's father. Thus there was some evidence of the intention from the persons arranging the marriage. By contrast, the IAT in *Jit Kaur* (11951) did not consider that inconsistent answers in interview were cured by the evidence of the sponsor, despite a finding by the adjudicator that the sponsor was credible, because the adjudicator was not present during the interview, and therefore could not cure the defect. The approach in *Ahmed* is to be preferred as consistent with *Gondalia*.

Where the only dispute is whether the primary purpose of the marriage was to gain entry, satisfaction of the requirement that the parties intended to live together does not by itself settle that dispute (*Mohammed Choudhury v IAT* [1990] Imm AR 211).

The rules require an intention to settle, but they do not exclude those who are genuinely undecided about their long-term intentions. Where there is uncertainty as to the duration of the couple's stay, the application should be treated as an application as if ordinary settlement was contemplated (*R v IAT, ex p Najma Rafique* [1990] Imm AR 235).

There is no duty on an adjudicator to make specific findings in relation to the intention to live together, but it is usually desirable if he makes such findings, as they will make clear that he has taken into account the matters which he should take into account. He should indicate the reasoning on which his conclusion is based, so as to show which factors he balanced in determining the question of the parties' motivation (*Kandiya v IAT* [1990] Imm AR 377 and *R v IAT, ex p Iqbal* [1993] Imm AR 270).

Evidence of intervening devotion   Cases from the Indian subcontinent form the bulk of refused applications. Immigration officers tend to be suspicious above love matches in this context. In *R v IAT, ex p Kumar* [1986] Imm AR 446, the CA held that events which have happened since a marriage was entered into may be material to the evaluation of the purpose of the marriage. If the couple can show evidence of affectionate contact between them during any time they have been separated, it may be easier for them to satisfy the requirement that the primary purpose of the marriage was not to gain admission. Such evidence has become known as evidence of 'intervening devotion'. It includes communications since meeting, such as letters, telephone calls and other contact, and presents given or received. If the couple have lived together for a time, that will be taken as evidence of such devotion, but it is only one factor, and may be outweighed by other factors such as deceit over the primary purpose of the marriage (*Girishkumar Patel v S of S* [1989] Imm AR 246).

In assessing the credibility of the couple, and those arranging an arranged marriage, the adjudicator should take account of signs of intervening devotion. In *Najib Hussain* (11454) there were marked discrepancies between the two accounts given by the parties to the marriage. The husband said the match was a love match. The sponsoring wife said it was arranged shortly before. The father said it was arranged a long time before. The IAT noted that there had been intervening devotion, and gave that great weight. The sponsor described her husband as an 'uneducated, simple man'. The IAT accepted that this in large part explained his bad performance at interview. In *Kramer* (12455) 'about six hundred' letters constituted strong evidence of intervening devotion. Similarly, in *Aroon Singpilla* (12185), the IAT allowed an appeal where the adjudicator ignored 'two large albums of photographs ... the telephone calls, tapes and letters and the fact that the couple have lived together as man and wife even though for short periods when the sponsor visits'. Advisors should therefore ensure that if there is evidence of intervening devotion, it is placed before the adjudicator.

Deception by a third party to facilitate entry will now render the applicant an illegal entrant under s 33 of the 1971 Act as amended by the 1996 Act (see pp 14–15). Thus, false statements made by relatives interviewed by the ECO in primary purpose cases may render a spouse seeking entry to the UK an illegal entrant. It is not clear that such statements merely constitute a matter for the adjudicator to weigh against the other evidence (cf *Arshad Mahmood* (12194)). The false statement will result in the applicant's being an illegal entrant only if it is made in the context of the current application to enter. Thus in *Majri* (12406) the applicant told one significant lie. The adjudicator believed the rest of the evidence which was given by the parents and fiancée. The lie had been told when the applicant was applying for a visit visa and concerned when the relationship had started. The adjudicator could weigh it against the other evidence.

Devotion, in cases of fiancés and fiancées, may not be in keeping with the cultural traditions of the couple, or an arranged marriage. In those cases post-decision evidence of devotion since the engagement may be considered irrelevant (*Ex p Prajapati* [1990] Imm AR 513, a case of post-decision pregnancy).

In reply to a Parliamentary Question on 30 June 1992 (210 HC (Official Reports 6th Series) col 52, 524) the Home Office Minister stated that in principle an application from a spouse for an entry clearance or leave to remain should be allowed when it is accepted that the marriage is genuine and subsisting, and either the couple have been married for at least five years, or one or more children of the marriage has the right of abode in the UK. An application could be refused, however, if the applicant has a criminal record which would make exclusion conducive to the public good, or where the sponsor in the UK is unable to meet the maintenance and accommodation requirements of the immigration rules. It is likely that a couple who satisfied the requirements for this concession would in any event be able successfully to appeal against a decision against them, but it does indicate that the ECO's investigation in such cases should be less rigorous than the investigation in any ordinary case. By contrast, the terms of the concession must be fulfilled strictly. The S of S was held not to have acted unreasonably where he refused to consider an application by reference to the concession where the child was not yet born (*Ex p Abu Shahed* [1994] Imm AR 200).

Finances and accommodation The requirement that the applicant should maintain and accommodate himself may be made a condition of leave to enter, and, if so, will be stamped on the person's passport. If the condition is breached knowingly a criminal offence may be committed (s 24(1)(*b*) and s 3(1) of the 1971 Act as amended by Sched 2, para 1(1) to the 1996 Act, and see Chapter 27). The rules require that there must be adequate accommodation for the parties to the marriage and their dependants without recourse to public funds. The HC 395 rules do not require that the accommodation is 'accommodation of their own', a phrase which caused needless litigation under HC 251. HC 395 does, though, require that the couple have adequate accommodation for the parties and any dependants, in accommodation which they own or occupy exclusively.

The IAT, in *Saghir Ahmed* (8260), concluded that the correct test of adequacy was that recognised in UK law in relation to accommodation, ie the criterion of overcrowding. The IAT stated that all that was required by the rule was that the couple should be able to live at least part of their lives in accommodation which they exclusively occupy. The IAT construed this in turn in its minimal sense that there should be a room which the couple occupy. It could not see why an applicant should be refused entry because he would have to share a bathroom with, or live in a house with, another family. In *Mushtaq* (9343), the IAT held that the proper approach to assessing whether accommodation is adequate is to use the test of overcrowding under UK housing law. Thus, they referred to the room standard and space standard of s 326 of the Housing Act 1985. They recommended that evidence on these aspects should be provided. With the addition, in the current rules, of the requirement of exclusive ownership or occupation of the accommodation, there will now have to be some area which the couple occupy exclusively. The best interpretation is that this could comprise a room which the couple occupy exclusively (see, on HC 251, *Zia v S of S* [1993] Imm AR 404 at 412 *per* Lord Prosser, Ct of Session). The Home Office explanatory note in 1994 (paras 34–36) stated that there was no policy change in HC 395 (see also 'public funds' at p 60).

As HC 395 does not represent a change in policy in relation to spouses, the previous case law serves as a guide to future interpretation of the accommodation provisions. The sponsor must show that there will be adequate accommodation for the couple. The rule can be satisfied by proof of any form of ownership of the accommodation, but is also satisfied by proof that the sponsor occupies the accommodation (*Kasuji* (5956) and *Jabeen* (4925)).

The rules require that the applicant and sponsor can and will maintain and accommodate themselves without recourse to public funds (see p 207). It was held in *R v S of S, ex p Bibi & Begum* [1995] Imm AR 157 that 'recourse to public funds' included the case where, although no extra public funds would be required for the maintenance of the couple, the applicant spouse would be maintained out of public funds which were already provided for another person (in this case, the sponsor spouses). This has been qualified by Home Office policy (expressed in a letter of 2 October 1995 written to Max Madden MP; see [1996] IN L&P 26) to the effect that leave will be refused under this rule only where extra public funds would be needed for the maintenance of the applicant. Clearly, where the settlement of the applicant will reduce the sponsor's reliance on public funds there will be no recourse (see *Latif* (11630)). In *Iqbal* (12521), the IAT held that the ministerial letter was a mere comment on a set of facts and not a change or alteration in the rules (see also *Quiambo* (12416)). The letter does, however, indicate the Minister's approach, and was issued in the light of *Bibi & Begum*, the approach in which it disavowed. As the immigration rules are a formulation of policy, it is open to the Minister to issue interpretative guidance on them. The approach in *Bibi & Begum* clearly does not represent the policy underlying the immigration rules in respect of the issue of recourse to public funds, and may be distinguished by reference to the clear wording of the above letter.

The appellate authorities will look at the state of affairs at the time the decision was taken, whether or not presented to the ECO, which would suggest that within a foreseeable period (generally six months) of the applicant's arrival, adequate maintenance will be available (see, for example, *R v IAT, ex p Rehana Begum* [1993] Imm AR 1). In the case of spouses, it is a reasonable assumption that, barring unforeseen problems, a couple will establish themselves and become independent (*Annis Akhtar* (11658)). Where accommodation and maintenance without recourse to public funds would be available within six months, the couple's ability to maintain and accommodate themselves is foreseeable (see *Ali* (11568) and *Tazeem Kausar* (11550)). Thus in *Ali*, free accommodation became available after the application for settlement was refused. Had the refusal been anticipated, arrangements would have been made for it to be available sooner, as it was 'there for the asking'. In *Hussain* (11614) and *Roberts* (11600), the IAT was prepared to recommend that a visa be issued without an appellant's having to make a fresh application for one where the accommodation and maintenance requirements were met.

Clearly there will be a difference in the attitude to couples setting up home, where the above assumption can be made, and other cases where it may not be reasonable to make an assumption about the length of time a relative, for example, would take to become independent.

The parties must have met   There is no requirement that the parties should have met in the context of marriage or marriage arrangements, but merely that each should have an appreciation of the other in the sense of appearance or personality. The IAT, in *Mohd Meharban v ECO, Islamabad* [1989] Imm AR 57, accepted that the rule required that at the date of the decision each party could point to the other as a person known and identified by the other. Beyond that, there is no requirement that in an arranged marriage the bride should appreciate the groom. The parties arranging the marriage will consider the qualities that lead to a lasting union, and in such contexts the bride or groom may not know very much about each other. Not too much should be read into that fact (*Ushaben Pradipbhai Patel* (10121)).

Evidence in primary purpose cases   The general rule is that the adjudicator will consider the state of affairs at the time the ECO or Home Office considered the application. Evidence which is brought forward later may, however, shed light on the state of the marriage at the time of that decision. In *Daley* (12494), the appellant applied for settlement but did not provide responses to the standard inquiries from the Home Office. At the appeal she and her husband gave evidence, which was accepted, that they had a genuine and subsisting marriage and that they had a child. The Home Office appeal was rejected as the evidence showed the state of affairs at the time of the decision by the Home Office (and see p 383).

An adjudicator has to consider motive in marriage cases (*R v IAT, ex p Manjula Jethva* [1990] Imm AR 450). He is entitled to make an analysis of the parties' motives. In some cases there may be one simple factor which can be described as the motive for the marriage; in other cases there may be many motives for the marriage. Ignorance of cultural traditions has led to assumptions being made about applications, particularly those from the Indian subcontinent (*Bhatia v IAT* [1985] Imm AR 50). A helpful study of the social practices of the Indian subcontinent has been made by Mr Philip Powell, a sociologist (*Notes for UK Lawyers on Custom and Practice in the Indian Subcontinent*, available from 1 Horton Road, London E8; see also INL&P July 1990 vol 4 no 3 at p 107). This evidence can be used to rebut some of the more subjective assumptions of ECOs and immigration officers regarding traditions relating to marriage. The study contains digests of erroneous views expressed by ECOs regarding marriage traditions. In *Khizer ur Rehman* (11650), the IAT noted that many of the appellant's family were already in the UK, thus indicating a willingness to break with a (simplistically expressed) tradition that the bride is expected to join the husband's family, and stated that this was not very significant. Advisors should initially be sceptical about ECO claims that a practice represents a tradition, and should investigate the validity of such claims, using expert evidence where necessary.

Cohabitants   There is no provision in the rules for the admission of unmarried cohabitants. Until recently, the exercise of the discretion outside

the rules was guided by an instruction issued to immigration officers on 8
November 1985, which closely shadowed the formal provisions applicable to
the admission of spouses (see [1986] 1 INL&P 8, 90). On 22 February 1996,
in rejecting an amendment to make provision in the rules for same-sex
couples, the Home Office Minister went further, and announced that he
would no longer use discretion in heterosexual non-marital relationships,
saying:

> 'A foreign national who wishes to join or remain here with a person settled here
> must be married to that person, except for those who qualify under the
> immigration rules as fiancés or fiancées. Foreign nationals who apply to enter or
> remain on the basis of a common-law relationship can, with immediate effect,
> expect to have their applications refused.'

(See JCWI Bulletin (1996) vol 5 no 11.) In a letter to ILPA from the IND
dated 14 March 1996 it was stated that 'All applications to enter or remain
on the basis of a common law heterosexual relationship will be refused.' The
only remaining comfort for heterosexual cohabitants would seem to be in the
Home Office policy on deportation in cases involving families and children;
see Chapter 14. For same-sex couples, the discretion outside the rules will be
exercised only in the most compelling compassionate circumstances: see
JCWI Bulletin (1994) vol 5 no 6.

Carers   The position of carers is dealt with at p 99.

(c) Extensions

Requirements for an extension of stay as the spouse of a person present and settled in the United Kingdom

284. The requirements for an extension of stay as the spouse of a person present
and settled in the United Kingdom are that:
(i)   the applicant has limited leave to remain in the United Kingdom; and
(ii)   is married to a person present and settled in the United Kingdom; and
(iii)   the marriage was not entered into primarily to obtain settlement here; and
(iv)   the parties to the marriage have met; and
(v)   the applicant has not remained in breach of the immigration laws; and
(vi)   the marriage has not taken place after a decision has been made to deport
        the applicant or he has been recommended for deportation or been given
        notice under Section 6(2) of the Immigration Act 1971; and
(vii)   each of the parties intends to live permanently with the other as his or her
        spouse and the marriage is subsisting; and
(viii) there will be adequate accommodation for the parties and any dependants
        without recourse to public funds in accommodation which they own or
        occupy exclusively; and
(ix)   the parties will be able to maintain themselves and any dependants
        adequately without recourse to public funds.

Extension of stay as the spouse of a person present and settled in the United Kingdom

285. An extension of stay as the spouse of a person present and settled in the
United Kingdom may be granted for a period of 12 months in the first instance,

provided the Secretary of State is satisfied that each of the requirements of paragraph 284 is met.

Refusal of extension of stay as the spouse of a person present and settled in the United Kingdom
286. An extension of stay as the spouse of a person present and settled in the United Kingdom is to be refused if the Secretary of State is not satisfied that each of the requirements of paragraph 284 is met.

Requirements for indefinite leave to remain for the spouse of a person present and settled in the United Kingdom
287. The requirements for indefinite leave to remain for the spouse of a person present and settled in the United Kingdom are that:
(i) the applicant was admitted to the United Kingdom or given an extension of stay for a period of 12 months and has completed a period of 12 months as the spouse of a person present and settled here; and
(ii) the applicant is still the spouse of the person he or she was admitted or granted an extension of stay to join and the marriage is subsisting; and
(iii) each of the parties intends to live permanently with the other as his or her spouse; and
(iv) there will be adequate accommodation for the parties and any dependants without recourse to public funds in accommodation which they own or occupy exclusively; and
(v) the parties will be able to maintain themselves and any dependants adequately without recourse to public funds.

Indefinite leave to remain for the spouse of a person present and settled in the United Kingdom
288. Indefinite leave to remain for the spouse of a person present and settled in the United Kingdom may be granted provided the Secretary of State is satisfied that each of the requirements of paragraph 287 is met.

Refusal of indefinite leave to remain for the spouse of a person present and settled in the United Kingdom
289. Indefinite leave to remain for the spouse of a person present and settled in the United Kingdom is to be refused if the Secretary of State is not satisfied that each of the requirements of paragraph 287 is met.

COMMENTARY

Paragraph 284 provides that the applicant for an extension of leave to remain based on marriage to a person settled in the UK must not have remained in breach of the immigration laws. Thus a person who has overstayed cannot rely on this rule to obtain an extension of his leave. Similarly, para 284(vi) provides that the marriage must not have taken place after a decision to deport the applicant has been made, or a criminal court has made a recommendation for his deportation.

Where a person is refused entry but is granted temporary admission under para 21 of Sched 2 to the 1971 Act, he is not granted leave to enter in a temporary capacity. He cannot rely on para 284 to obtain an extension of a leave he does not possess. Further, he may be refused indefinite leave to remain in the UK upon marriage to a person settled in the UK (*Ex p Kaur*

[1987] Imm AR 278). The marriage must not have been entered into with the purpose of obtaining settlement (*R v IAT ex p Nathwani* [1979–80] Imm AR 9). Where the marriage is genuine and subsisting, leave to remain should be granted, having regard to the Ministerial statement of 30 June 1992 (see p 206); see also the Home Office guidelines on enforcement action (Chapter 14).

The spouse seeking indefinite leave must have completed a 12-month period as the spouse of the settled person. The grounds on which an extension may be refused generally, and must be refused if the S of S is not satisfied regarding them, are set out in Chapter 13.

2 Fiancé(e)s

Requirements for leave to enter the United Kingdom as a fiancé(e) (ie with a view to marriage and permanent settlement in the United Kingdom)

290. The requirements to be met by a person seeking leave to enter the United Kingdom as a fiancé(e) are that:

(i)   the applicant is seeking leave to enter the United Kingdom for marriage to a person present and settled in the United Kingdom or who is on the same occasion being admitted for settlement; and

(ii)   it is not the primary purpose of the intended marriage to obtain admission to the United Kingdom; and

(iii)   the parties to the proposed marriage have met; and

(iv)   each of the parties intends to live permanently with the other as his or her spouse after the marriage; and

(v)   adequate maintenance and accommodation without recourse to public funds will be available for the applicant until the date of the marriage; and

(vi)   there will, after the marriage, be adequate accommodation for the parties and any dependants without recourse to public funds in accommodation which they own or occupy exclusively; and

(vii)   the parties will be able after the marriage to maintain themselves and any dependants adequately without recourse to public funds; and

(viii)   the applicant holds a valid United Kingdom entry clearance for entry in this capacity.

Leave to enter as a fiancé(e)

291. A person seeking leave to enter the United Kingdom as a fiancé(e) may be admitted, with a prohibition on employment, for a period not exceeding 6 months to enable the marriage to take place provided a valid United Kingdom entry clearance for entry in this capacity is produced to the Immigration Officer on arrival.

Refusal of leave to enter as a fiancé(e)

292. Leave to enter the United Kingdom as a fiancé(e) is to be refused if a valid United Kingdom entry clearance for entry in this capacity is not produced to the Immigration Officer on arrival.

Requirements for an extension of stay as a fiancé(e)

293. The requirements for an extension of stay as a fiancé(e) are that:

(i)   the applicant was admitted to the United Kingdom with a valid United Kingdom entry clearance as a fiancé(e); and

(ii) good cause is shown why the marriage did not take place within the initial period of leave granted under paragraph 291; and

(iii) there is satisfactory evidence that the marriage will take place at an early date; and

(iv) the requirements of paragraph 290(ii)–(vii) are met.

Extension of stay as a fiancé(e)

294. An extension of stay as a fiancé(e) may be granted for an appropriate period with a prohibition on employment to enable the marriage to take place provided the Secretary of State is satisfied that each of the requirements of paragraph 293 is met.

Refusal of extension of stay as a fiancé(e)

295. An extension of stay is to be refused if the Secretary of State is not satisfied that each of the requirements of paragraph 293 is met.

COMMENTARY

For the general grounds for refusal of entry, see Chapter 13.

For a commentary on the primary purpose test, accommodation and maintenance requirements, see p 201 above. The burden is on the applicant to show that the primary purpose of the proposed marriage is not to gain admission, but the ECO should not delve too deeply for evidence upon which to base a refusal, and should consider the evidence for and against as a whole. A series of propositions was put forward in *Hoque & Singh* (above, pp 202 *et seq*) as to the proper approach to the question of primary purpose. A mere desire to live in the UK with the wife does not amount to an attempt to use the marriage to the wife as a vehicle for entry to the UK. If the applicant and sponsor live in a community in which arranged marriages are the norm, the fact that the marriage was arranged is not significant.

It is possible to obtain an extension of leave as a fiancé(e) if there was good cause why the marriage did not take place within the initial period of leave granted under the rules. There must also be evidence that the marriage will take place at an early date.

3 Children

296. Nothing in these Rules shall be construed as permitting a child to be granted entry clearance, leave to enter or remain, or variation of leave where his mother is party to a polygamous marriage and any application by her for admission or leave to remain for settlement or with a view to settlement would be refused pursuant to paragraph 278.

Requirements for indefinite leave to enter the United Kingdom as the child of a parent, parents or a relative present and settled or being admitted for settlement in the United Kingdom

297. The requirements to be met by a person seeking indefinite leave to enter the United Kingdom as the child of a parent, parents or a relative present and settled or being admitted for settlement in the United Kingdom are that he:

(i) is seeking leave to enter to accompany or join a parent, parents or a relative in one of the following circumstances:

    (a) both parents are present and settled in the United Kingdom; or

    (b) both parents are being admitted on the same occasion for settlement; or

    (c) one parent is present and settled in the United Kingdom and the other is being admitted on the same occasion for settlement; or

    (d) one parent is present and settled in the United Kingdom or being admitted on the same occasion for settlement and the other parent is dead; or

    (e) one parent is present and settled in the United Kingdom or being admitted on the same occasion for settlement and has had sole responsibility for the child's upbringing; or

    (f) one parent or a relative is present and settled in the United Kingdom or being admitted on the same occasion for settlement and there are serious and compelling family or other considerations which make exclusion of the child undesirable and suitable arrangements have been made for the child's care; and

(ii) is under the age of 18; and

(iii) is not leading an independent life, is unmarried, and has not formed an independent family unit; and

(iv) can, and will, be maintained and accommodated adequately without recourse to public funds in accommodation which the parent, parents or relative own or occupy exclusively; and

(v) holds a valid United Kingdom entry clearance for entry in this capacity.

Requirements for indefinite leave to remain in the United Kingdom as the child of a parent, parents or a relative present and settled or being admitted for settlement in the United Kingdom

298. The requirements to be met by a person seeking indefinite leave to remain in the United Kingdom as the child of a parent, parents or a relative present and settled in the United Kingdom are that he:

(i) is seeking to remain with a parent, parents or a relative in one of the following circumstances:

    (a) both parents are present and settled in the United Kingdom; or

    (b) one parent is present and settled in the United Kingdom and the other parent is dead; or

    (c) one parent is present and settled in the United Kingdom and has had sole responsibility for the child's upbringing; or

    (d) one parent or a relative is present and settled in the United Kingdom and there are serious and compelling family or other considerations which make exclusion of the child undesirable and suitable arrangements have been made for the child's care; and

(ii) has limited leave to enter or remain in the United Kingdom, and

    (a) is under the age of 18; or

    (b) was given leave to enter or remain with a view to settlement under paragraph 302; and

(iii) is not leading an independent life, is unmarried, and has not formed an independent family unit; and

(iv) can, and will, be maintained and accommodated adequately without recourse to public funds in accommodation which the parent, parents or relative own or occupy exclusively.

Indefinite leave to enter or remain in the United Kingdom as the child of a parent, parents or a relative present and settled or being admitted for settlement in the United Kingdom

299. Indefinite leave to enter the United Kingdom as the child of a parent, parents or a relative present and settled or being admitted for settlement in the United Kingdom may be granted provided a valid United Kingdom entry clearance for entry in this capacity is produced to the Immigration Officer on arrival. Indefinite leave to remain in the United Kingdom as the child of a parent, parents or a relative present and settled in the United Kingdom may be granted provided the Secretary of State is satisfied that each of the requirements of paragraph 298 is met.

Refusal of indefinite leave to enter or remain in the United Kingdom as the child of a parent, parents or a relative present and settled or being admitted for settlement in the United Kingdom

300. Indefinite leave to enter the United Kingdom as the child of a parent, parents or a relative present and settled or being admitted for settlement in the United Kingdom is to be refused if a valid United Kingdom entry clearance for entry in this capacity is not produced to the Immigration Officer on arrival. Indefinite leave to remain in the United Kingdom as the child of a parent, parents or a relative present and settled in the United Kingdom is to be refused if the Secretary of State is not satisfied that each of the requirements of paragraph 298 is met.

Requirements for limited leave to enter or remain in the United Kingdom with a view to settlement as the child of a parent or parents given limited leave to enter or remain in the United Kingdom with a view to settlement

301. The requirements to be met by a person seeking limited leave to enter or remain in the United Kingdom with a view to settlement as the child of a parent or parents given limited leave to enter or remain in the United Kingdom with a view to settlement are that he:

(i) is seeking leave to enter to accompany or join or remain with a parent or parents in one of the following circumstances:

   (a) one parent is present and settled in the United Kingdom or being admitted on the same occasion for settlement and the other parent is being or has been given limited leave to enter or remain in the United Kingdom with a view to settlement; or

   (b) one parent is being or has been given limited leave to enter or remain in the United Kingdom with a view to settlement and has had sole responsibility for the child's upbringing; or

   (c) one parent is being or has been given limited leave to enter or remain in the United Kingdom with a view to settlement and there are serious and compelling family or other considerations which make exclusion of the child undesirable and suitable arrangements have been made for the child's care; and

(ii) is under the age of 18; and

(iii) is not leading an independent life, is unmarried, and has not formed an independent family unit; and

(iv) can, and will, be maintained and accommodated adequately without recourse to public funds in accommodation which the parent or parents own or occupy exclusively; and

(v) (where an application is made for limited leave to remain with a view to settlement) has limited leave to enter or remain in the United Kingdom; and

(vi) if seeking leave to enter, holds a valid United Kingdom entry clearance for entry in this capacity or, if seeking leave to remain, was admitted with a valid United Kingdom entry clearance for entry in this capacity.

Limited leave to enter or remain in the United Kingdom with a view to settlement as the child of a parent or parents given limited leave to enter or remain in the United Kingdom with a view to settlement

302. A person seeking limited leave to enter the United Kingdom with a view to settlement as the child of a parent or parents given limited leave to enter or remain in the United Kingdom with a view to settlement may be admitted for a period not exceeding 12 months provided he is able, on arrival, to produce to the Immigration Officer a valid United Kingdom entry clearance for entry in this capacity. A person seeking limited leave to remain in the United Kingdom with a view to settlement as the child of a parent or parents given limited leave to enter or remain in the United Kingdom with a view to settlement may be given limited leave to remain for a period not exceeding 12 months provided the Secretary of State is satisfied that each of the requirements of paragraph 301(i)–(v) is met.

Refusal of limited leave to enter or remain in the United Kingdom with a view to settlement as the child of a parent or parents given limited leave to enter or remain in the United Kingdom with a view to settlement

303. Limited leave to enter the United Kingdom with a view to settlement as the child of a parent or parents given limited leave to enter or remain in the United Kingdom with a view to settlement is to be refused if a valid United Kingdom entry clearance for entry in this capacity is not produced to the Immigration Officer on arrival. Limited leave to remain in the United Kingdom with a view to settlement as the child of a parent or parents given limited leave to enter or remain in the United Kingdom with a view to settlement is to be refused if the Secretary of State is not satisfied that each of the requirements of paragraph 301(i)–(v) is met.

COMMENTARY

For 'maintained and accommodated adequately without recourse to public funds in accommodation ... own or occupy exclusively' see p 207.

For polygamous marriages, see p 197. The child of a polygamous marriage may not obtain leave to enter or remain, or indefinite leave to remain, under HC 395 (para 296). The rule as currently drafted would prevent the entry of a child who otherwise has good grounds to enter, for example, because he is a British citizen by descent, or because he qualifies for asylum. For these reasons, the rule can probably be challenged as a fetter on the discretion of the S of S.

(a) Definition of 'a parent'

Paragraph 6 (see p 59) defines 'a parent' as including the stepfather of a child whose father is dead, the stepmother of a child whose mother is dead, and the father as well as the mother of a child of an unmarried couple, where he is proved to be the father. It also includes an adoptive parent where a child was adopted in accordance with a decision taken either by a UK court, or by the competent administrative authority or court in a country whose adoption orders are recognised by the UK and which are listed in the Adoptions (Designation of Overseas Adoptions) Order 1973 (SI 1973 No 19). In the case of a child born in the UK who is not a British citizen, a person to whom there has been a genuine transfer of parental responsibility on the grounds of the original parents' inability to care for the child is also included in the definition of 'a parent'. A bare promise to look after a child does not amount to a genuine transfer of parental responsibility (*R v IAT, ex p Haque* [1994] Imm AR 39). A stepparent cannot therefore be taken into account where a dependent child's parents are both living (*Manzar Alam v ECO Lahore* [1973] Imm AR 79).

(b) Proving blood relationships

Where the parentage of the child is disputed it may be necessary for the applicant to establish it. For first time applicants for entry clearance there is a government scheme of DNA testing of relationships between parents and children applying to join them. The internal guidance of the Foreign and Commonwealth Office (Circular 181/94) is set out in INL&P vol 9 no 2, page 71). Tests under the government scheme will not be requested to prove that a child is the child of a marriage doubted on primary purpose grounds, but applicants may offer such DNA evidence if they pay privately.

The ECO is given the following guidance on interview practice:

(a) The should try to establish the *bona fides* of an application before offering a test, by assessing the documentary evidence and conducting a short interview;

(b) if, after 15 minutes, he considers that there is a substantial doubt about the *bona fides* of the applicant, he should seek more senior authority to offer the opportunity of taking a test;

(c) where he is satisfied that there is no genuine doubt as to the identify of a sibling, a test of that sibling's DNA should not be conducted;

(d) applicants should be told that they do not have take the test, but that it is an extremely accurate way of determining identity and parentage.

Reports should be received by the ECO within 42 days of the testing laboratory receiving the samples. In assessing the result of the test, the ECO is instructed (para 5.4 of the Circular) that the question to be addressed is whether all the available evidence establishes the relevant relationship on the balance of probabilities. Further:

(a) where DNA evidence is the only evidence available, any result which suggests the applicants are related as claimed by a higher percentage than any alternative relationship may be regarded as decisive;

(b) where other evidence is available the DNA test result will provide only half the evidence relevant to reaching a decision. Circumstantial evidence (for example from field trips or denunciations) may weigh heavily against even an apparently decisive (eg 98 per cent) result supporting the claimed relationship;

(c) where the test result suggests that the probability of the relationship being as claimed is higher than 98 per cent it is less likely to be counterbalanced by other evidence than those with lower percentage probabilities.

The policy was set out to the House of Commons in a Written Answer (see 154 HC Official Report (6th Series) Written Answers, cols 463–5 (14 June 1989)). The following points should be noted:

(a) DNA testing is recognised to be the most accurate method of determining parentage in immigration cases;

(b) the results of tests commissioned by an applicant and performed by a recognised tester will be accepted;

(c) ECOs will offer tests in cases where the relevant relationship cannot be proved easily by other means;

(d) refusal to take a test will not by itself be a ground for refusing entry clearance;

(e) fees are charged for the service, except where the family agrees to take the test and is applying for entry clearance for the first time on this ground.

ECOs have also been issued with instructions concerning the use of DNA results:

(a) if both parents have been tested, and the result shows the disputed relationship to be two to three times more likely than another relationship, the tests should be regarded as conclusive;

(b) the result of the test creates a presumption in its favour in any event, but if the likelihood of the relationship is less than two to three times more likely than another relationship, the immigration officer should look also at the surrounding circumstances;

(c) care should be taken over the identity of the donor of blood, and information as to the donor should be obtained direct from the independent expert rather than the applicant;

(d) where what is being tested is the applicant's relationship to one parent, the result should be more than 60 per cent accurate if it is to be relied upon. There should be good reason for testing only one of the parents;

(e) if a relationship to one parent alone is established, disclosure of the result to other members of the family should be treated with utmost caution.

The Home Office has awarded the contract for DNA testing under the government scheme to University Diagnostics, University College, London, Gower St, London WC1E 6BT. DNA tests may be helpful to those who are applying to enter for a second or subsequent time, and by those preparing for appeals. The Foreign and Commonwealth Office Circular 181/94 provides guidance as to the possible results of such tests. It should be noted that the context of this guidance is that the relationship is doubted to be as claimed. It is uncertain how such guidance is compatible with the new definition of 'illegal entrant' in s 33 of the 1971 Act (see p 15). However, the claimed relationship may be simply incorrect rather than the result of a deception on the part of the parties to it. If the child is unrelated to both alleged parents but has been brought up as a member of the family unit, the ECO should consider para 297 of the rules (p 214). If one alleged parent is in fact a second degree relative, consideration should be given to para 297(f) if there are serious and compelling family or other considerations which make exclusion undesirable. Where the child is not related to the alleged mother, the ECO should establish whether the child was born to another wife, and if so whether the child lives with the natural mother or the alleged mother; depending on the circumstances, paras 297(i)(d)–(f) should be considered (see p 214). If the natural mother does not seek entry, or does not qualify for admission, the sponsor would normally have to show that he has exercised sole responsibility for the child's upbringing (para 6.3 of the Guidance). In cases where a child is shown not to be the alleged father's, sensitivity is called for. First, the ECO should interview the mother to try to establish the truth of the family circumstances. If no information can be obtained from the mother, the ECO should contact the sponsor's representatives. However, if the child has been brought up as a child of the family, para 297(f) should be considered. The fact that the child has been brought up as a child of the family should outweigh the fact that he is not the child of the alleged father.

Policy on adults refused entry as children, whose relationship is later proved In the Written Answer referred to above (14 June 1989), the S of S set out a policy on adults whose applications as children were refused on the basis that they could not prove that they were related to the sponsor, as claimed, but who, in the light of a DNA test, have later been proved to be so related. Some such adults may have fulfilled all the other requirements for admission as children, but as adults no longer fulfil them. The S of S stated that the rules relating to admission as adults would not be waived in such cases, but that, in relation to outstanding and future reapplications, the requirements of the rules would be waived in certain circumstances. To qualify for such consideration, a person aged 18 or over who is reapplying has to show:

(a) that he was refused entry clearance as a child on the ground that he was not related as claimed to the sponsor;

(b) that DNA evidence establishes that he was after all related as claimed;

(c) that he is still wholly or mainly dependent on his sponsor in the UK; and

(d) that there are compassionate circumstances in his case; however, the mere fact of the childhood refusal and consequent inability to join the sponsor will not be regarded as a compassionate circumstance.

The S of S went on to state that all the circumstances of the case would be considered, including:

(a) the degree and nature of the dependency;

(b) the nature and extent of the compassionate circumstances;

(c) the reapplicant's present age and marital status;

(d) whether other close family members such as siblings are already settled in the UK;

(e) the lapse of time between the original application and the re-application.

Greater weight is attached to compassionate circumstances relating to the situation of the reapplicant abroad than to those relating to the sponsor.

In *Hassan Miah v S of S* [1991] Imm AR 437, the CA refused to interfere with this policy on the basis that the decision whether or not to refer a matter for adjudication was essentially a matter within the discretion of the S of S (*Ex p Noor Uddin* [1990] Imm AR 181). There is, however, no obligation on the S of S to refer such cases in this way (*Sunam Uddin v S of S* [1991] Imm AR 587), and the court will not compel a reference (*R v IAT, ex p Jaifor Ali* [1990] Imm AR 531).

(c) Indefinite leave to enter

A person seeking indefinite leave to enter the UK as the child of a parent(s) or relative present and settled in the UK or being admitted for settlement must be in the circumstances set out in para 297.

Both parents present and settled in the UK The intention of this provision is that the child would be coming to the UK to be united with both his parents. It is not sufficient that both parents reside in the UK if they are separated (*Pinnock v ECO Kingston Jamaica* [1974] Imm AR 22). In practice, however, the Home Office allows children to enter if both parents are settled in the UK but are separated.

'On the same occasion admitted for settlement' Either both parents must accompany the child and be admitted for settlement; or, if one parent is settled in the UK, the other must accompany the child and be admitted for settlement. The child will be unable to gain admission for settlement if the parent who is not settled does not accompany him (*Ex p Rukshanda Begum* [1990] Imm AR 1). The accompanying parent must intend to settle (*R v IAT, ex p Rashida Bibi* [1988] Imm AR 298). The purpose of the provisions is the reunification of families. Thus, where a child's mother accompanied him from Pakistan although she would not settle as the sponsor's wife, and the sponsor's intention was to return to Pakistan on arranging employment for his son with a view to his son's contributing to the support of himself and his wife in Pakistan, entry clearance was properly refused (*Ibrahim v Visa Officer, Islamabad* [1978] Imm AR 18). The phrase 'admitted for settlement' does not include a person who was entitled to settlement or had applied for it, and was clearly going to obtain it (*R v IAT, ex p S of S* [1993] Imm AR 298).

Sole responsibility A child may join a single parent when it is shown that the parent has had sole responsibility for the child's upbringing for a 'not insubstantial' period of time (*R v IAT ex p Sajid Mahmood* [1988] Imm AR 121). Further, the fact that others play a part in the day-to-day care of the child does not prevent the parent having sole responsibility for the purposes of this rule (*R v IAT, ex p Uddin* [1986] Imm AR 203). Where responsibility for the child's upbringing is shared between father and mother, entry clearance will not be granted (*Eugene v ECO Bridgetown Barbados* [1975] Imm AR 111). There is such sharing if the child ordinarily lives with the mother even if his sponsoring father always maintains him financially (*Williams v S of S* [1972] Imm AR 207). The assumption of financial responsibility is not by itself conclusive (*Ravat v ECO Bombay* [1974] Imm AR 79). There must also be cogent evidence of genuine interest in and affection for the child by the parent (*Rudolph v ECO Colombo* [1984] Imm AR 84). Similarly there is sharing of responsibility where the child does not actually live with the mother, but with the child's maternal grandmother, even if there is close and regular contact with the mother (*S of S v Pusey* [1972] Imm AR 240). However, the words 'sole responsibility' do not mean absolute responsibility. Some form of responsibility for practical matters must, in nearly all cases, be exercised by the relative with whom the child is living outside the UK. This does not of itself prevent the parent in the UK having sole responsibility (*Emmanuel v S of S* [1972] Imm AR 69; *Rudolph v ECO Colombo* (above)). The evidence, taken over all, must show that the sponsor remains ultimately in sole control of the child's upbringing (*R v IAT ex p Sajid Mahmood* above), but, it is important that a broad approach to the evidence be taken, and checklists should be avoided; it is unclear that asking whether a parent is ultimately in sole control of the child's upbringing adds anything to the approach of considering the evidence as a whole in accordance with the rule (*Ramos v IAT* [1989] Imm AR 148).

The decision in each case will depend on its own particular facts. Day- to - day care by others is not fatal to the assertion of sole responsibility. The decision calls for consideration of the sources and degree of financial support of the child, and whether there is coherent evidence of genuine interest in and affection for the child by the sponsoring parent in the UK, such as making decisions about the child's education and upbringing and discussing important matters concerning the child with the child (*Alagon* v ECO Manila [1993] Imm AR 336, and see *Emmanuel's* case (above); *Sloley v ECO Kingston* [1973] Imm AR 54; and *ECO Kingston v Martin* [1978] Imm AR 100). The issue of sole responsibility for the upbringing of a child is not, however, to be decided only as between one parent and the other parent. The position of every member of the family contributing to the child's upbringing must be taken into account when deciding whether or not the sponsoring parent has 'sole responsibility' for that upbringing (*Martin v S of S* [1972] Imm AR 71).

Concession relating to children under 12 The sole responsibility test will not be applied where the child is aged under 12, by virtue of a concession made by the Home Office. The concession applies where one only of the parents is settled in the UK, and the other is overseas. Children under 12 will be permitted without difficulty to join one parent if there is adequate accommodation and maintenance, and (if the parent is the father) that there is a female relative (in practice including a partner) who is resident in the household, and who is willing and able to look after the child (see Home Office leaflet RON2(D) and *Hansard*, 11 December 1979, col 220).

Serious and compelling family or other considerations   A child may join one parent or relative, even where that person has not had sole responsibility for the upbringing of the child, if there are 'serious and compelling family or other considerations which make exclusion undesirable'. The words 'serious and compelling' were added in the present rules. It is clear from the old rules that only the most serious and compelling considerations were accepted in practice. A teenage boy living in overcrowded conditions in Jamaica and moving from household to household because relatives were reluctant to accept responsibility for him, was refused entry clearance. Although he may have been bitterly disappointed at not being allowed to come to the UK, there was no evidence that he was particularly unhappy (*Rennie v ECO Kingston* [1979–80] Imm AR 117).

The conditions under which the child is living in the home country are not to be weighed against the conditions available for the child in the UK (*S of S v Campbell* [1972] Imm AR 115). In *Pinnock (ME) v ECO Kingston* [1977] Imm AR 4, for example, entry clearance was refused although it was not in dispute that the sponsor and his wife in this country had a comfortable and well-maintained home and would be able to look after the appellant child satisfactorily. In Jamaica, by contrast, she had to share a bed with an 11-year-old half-brother and a room with another half-brother. Similarly, the fact that a child might be better off in the UK, because he was unable to obtain employment in his home country, was not *per se* a relevant consideration (*Williams v S of S* [1972] Imm AR 207).

An example of domestic overcrowding which was held to be an important qualifying factor leading to the admission of an applicant to the UK can be found in the facts of *ECO Kingston v Holmes* [1975] Imm AR 20. A 12-year-old girl lived with her mother and her five younger half-brothers in a house in a depressed area in Jamaica. Her family occupied a single room in the house and the kitchen and sanitary facilities were shared by five other families who were also tenants. The small room was furnished with two beds, one double and one single, a vanity dresser and a china cabinet, all in dilapidated condition. The fact that there were far worse conditions elsewhere in Jamaica was not relevant, since bad conditions were not made better by the existence of even worse conditions (*ibid*, p 23).

When assessing 'family or other considerations' the authorities will take into account, *inter alia*, the accommodation available, the age and health of the relative with whom the child is residing and the general state of relations between that person and the child (*S of S v Campbell* [1972] Imm AR 115; *Needham v Entry Certificate Officer, Kingston, Jamaica* [1973] Imm AR

75). Where that relative is incapable of looking after the child, it is likely that the child will be admitted into the UK (*Rudolph v ECO Colombo* [1984] Imm AR 84). Once the relative's incapability is shown there must be strong countervailing factors to show that, despite the incapability, no serious and compelling considerations making the child's exclusion undesirable exist (*Awuku* (4220)). Serious and compelling family or other considerations may arise out of factors other than mental or physical incapacity. An example would be where a person was unable to look after the child due to being deserted (*Caballero* (4605)). Once it is found as a fact that the parent overseas is incapable of looking after the child, it is arguable that the case for the child's joining the parent in the UK is made out. However, by itself it may not be enough. If there is something else, such as the care of young children being left to very elderly grandparents, that may be sufficient (*Tiongson* (11467)).

(d) Indefinite leave to remain

A person seeking indefinite leave to remain as the child of a parent or relative present and settled in the UK must satisfy the requirements under para 298. He must either be under 18 years of age, or must have been given leave to enter or remain with a view to settlement under para 302. That paragraph provides for admission of such a person for a period not exceeding 12 months, if he can produce a valid entry clearance for entry in this capacity on arrival. He must also satisfy the requirements of para 301(i)–(v) (pp 215–16). For the implications of the acquisition of indefinite leave to remain for entitlement to housing and social benefits see p 62.

4   Children born in the United Kingdom who are not British citizens

304. This paragraph and paragraphs 305–309 apply only to unmarried dependent children under 18 years of age who were born in the United Kingdom on or after 1 January 1983 (when the British Nationality Act 1981 came into force) but who, because neither of their parents was a British citizen or settled in the United Kingdom at the time of their birth, are not British citizens and are therefore subject to immigration control. Such a child requires leave to enter where admission to the United Kingdom is sought, and leave to remain where permission is sought for the child to be allowed to stay in the United Kingdom. If he qualifies for entry clearance, leave to enter or leave to remain under any other part of these Rules, a child who was born in the United Kingdom but is not a British citizen may be granted entry clearance, leave to enter or leave to remain in accordance with the provisions of that other part.

Requirements for leave to enter or remain in the United Kingdom as the child of a parent or parents given leave to enter or remain in the United Kingdom

305. The requirements to be met by a child born in the United Kingdom who is not a British citizen who seeks leave to enter or remain in the United Kingdom as the child of a parent or parents given leave to enter or remain in the United Kingdom are that he:

(i)   *(a)* is accompanying or seeking to join or remain with a parent or parents who have, or are given, leave to enter or remain in the United Kingdom; or

      (b) is accompanying or seeking to join or remain with a parent or parents one of whom is a British citizen or has the right of abode in the United Kingdom; or

      (c) is a child in respect of whom the parental rights and duties are vested solely in a local authority; and

(ii) is under the age of 18; and

(iii) was born in the United Kingdom; and

(iv) is not leading an independent life, is unmarried, and has not formed an independent family unit; and

(v) (where an application is made for leave to enter) has not been away from the United Kingdom for more than 2 years.

Leave to enter or remain in the United Kingdom

306. A child born in the United Kingdom who is not a British citizen and who requires leave to enter or remain in the circumstances set out in paragraph 304 may be given leave to enter for the same period as his parent or parents where paragraph 305(i)(*a*) applies, provided the Immigration Officer is satisfied that each of the requirements of paragraph 305(ii)–(v) is met. Where leave to remain is sought, the child may be granted leave to remain for the same period as his parent or parents where paragraph 305(i)(*a*) applies, provided the Secretary of State is satisfied that each of the requirements of paragraph 305(ii)–(iv) is met. Where the parent or parents have or are given periods of leave of different duration, the child may be given leave to whichever period is longer except that if the parents are living apart the child should be given leave for the same period as the parent who has day to day responsibility for him.

307. If a child does not qualify for leave to enter or remain because neither of his parents has a current leave (and neither of them is a British citizen or has the right of abode), he will normally be refused leave to enter or remain, even if each of the requirements of paragraph 305(ii)–(v) has been satisfied. However, he may be granted leave to enter or remain for a period not exceeding 3 months if both of his parents are in the United Kingdom and it appears unlikely that they will be removed in the immediate future, and there is no other person outside the United Kingdom who could reasonably be expected to care for him.

308. A child born in the United Kingdom who is not a British citizen and who requires leave to enter or remain in the United Kingdom in the circumstances set out in paragraph 304 may be given indefinite leave to enter where paragraph 305(i)(*b*) or (i)(*c*) applies provided the Immigration Officer is satisfied that each of the requirements of paragraph 305(ii)–(v) is met. Where an application is for leave to remain, such a child may be granted indefinite leave to remain where paragraph 305(i)(*b*) or (i)(*c*) applies, provided the Secretary of State is satisfied that each of the requirements of paragraph 305(ii)–(iv) is met.

Refusal of leave to enter or remain in the United Kingdom

309. Leave to enter the United Kingdom where the circumstances set out in paragraph 304 apply is to be refused if the Immigration Officer is not satisfied that each of the requirements of paragraph 305 is met. Leave to remain for such a child is to be refused if the Secretary of State is not satisfied that each of the requirements of paragraph 305(i)–(iv) is met.

COMMENTARY

Children under the age of 18 born in the UK on or after 1 January 1983 who are not British citizens are subject to these paragraphs. The rule requires that such children must be unmarried (and see *Ahmed v S of S* [1994] Imm AR 14).

For the general grounds for refusal of leave to enter or remain, see Chapter 13.

The previous rules were to the effect that a child in this category should obtain leave to remain before travelling outside the common travel area. The child still had to obtain leave to enter on his return, but the fact of the previous leave to remain was of use in assessing the application. HC 395 also introduced a requirement that the child should not have been absent from the UK for more than two years; if he has, leave to enter must be refused. Given that the child's parents may be settled in the UK, it may be that this provision could be challenged by way of judicial review as unreasonable.

5 Adopted children

(a) Adoptive parents present and settled or being admitted for settlement

Requirements for indefinite leave to enter the United Kingdom as the adopted child of a parent or parents present and settled or being admitted for settlement in the United Kingdom

310. The requirements to be met in the case of a child seeking indefinite leave to enter the United Kingdom as the adopted child of a parent or parents present and settled or being admitted for settlement in the United Kingdom are that he:

(i)   is seeking leave to enter to accompany or join an adoptive parent or parents in one of the following circumstances:

   (a)   both parents are present and settled in the United Kingdom; or

   (b)   both parents are being admitted on the same occasion for settlement; or

   (c)   one parent is present and settled in the United Kingdom and the other is being admitted on the same occasion for settlement; or

   (d)   one parent is present and settled in the United Kingdom or being admitted on the same occasion for settlement and the other parent is dead; or

   (e)   one parent is present and settled in the United Kingdom or being admitted on the same occasion for settlement and has had sole responsibility for the child's upbringing; or

   (f)   one parent is present and settled in the United Kingdom or being admitted on the same occasion for settlement and there are serious and compelling family or other considerations which make exclusion of the child undesirable and suitable arrangements have been made for the child's care; and

(ii)   is under the age of 18; and

(iii)   is not leading an independent life, is unmarried, and has not formed an independent family unit; and

(iv)   can, and will, be maintained and accommodated adequately without recourse to public funds in accommodation which the adoptive parent or parents own or occupy exclusively; and

(v)   was adopted in accordance with a decision taken by the competent administrative authority or court in his country of origin or the country in which he is resident; and

(vi)   was adopted at a time when:

    (a) both adoptive parents were resident together abroad; or

    (b) either or both adoptive parents were settled in the United Kingdom; and

(vii)   has the same rights and obligations as any other child of the marriage; and

(viii) was adopted due to the inability of the original parent(s) or current carer(s) to care for him and there has been a genuine transfer of parental responsibility to the adoptive parents; and

(ix)   has lost or broken his ties with his family of origin; and

(x)   was adopted, but the adoption is not one of convenience arranged to facilitate his admission to or remaining in the United Kingdom; and

(xi)   holds a valid United Kingdom entry clearance for entry in this capacity.

Requirements for indefinite leave to remain in the United Kingdom as the adopted child of a parent or parents present and settled in the United Kingdom

311. The requirements to be met in the case of a child seeking indefinite leave to remain in the United Kingdom as the adopted child of a parent or parents present and settled in the United Kingdom are that he:

(i)   is seeking to remain with an adoptive parent or parents in one of the following circumstances:

    (a) both parents are present and settled in the United Kingdom; or

    (b) one parent is present and settled in the United Kingdom and the other parent is dead; or

    (c) one parent is present and settled in the United Kingdom and has had sole responsibility for the child's upbringing; or

    (d) one parent is present and settled in the United Kingdom and there are serious and compelling family or other considerations which make exclusion of the child undesirable and suitable arrangements have been made for the child's care; and

(ii)   has limited leave to enter or remain in the United Kingdom, and

    (a) is under the age of 18; or

    (b) was given leave to enter or remain with a view to settlement under paragraph 315; and

(iii)   is not leading an independent life, is unmarried, and has not formed an independent family unit; and

(iv)   can, and will, be maintained and accommodated adequately without recourse to public funds in accommodation which the adoptive parent or parents own or occupy exclusively; and

(v)   was adopted in accordance with a decision taken by the competent administrative authority or court in his country of origin or the country in which he is resident; and

(vi)   was adopted at a time when:

    (a) both adoptive parents were resident together abroad; or

    (b) either or both adoptive parents were settled in the United Kingdom; and

(vii)   has the same rights and obligations as any other child of the marriage; and

(viii) was adopted due to the inability of the original parent(s) or current carer(s) to care for him and there has been a genuine transfer of parental responsibility to the adoptive parents; and

(ix)   has lost or broken his ties with his family of origin; and
(x)   was adopted, but the adoption is not one of convenience arranged to facilitate his admission to or remaining in the United Kingdom.

Indefinite leave to enter or remain in the United Kingdom as the adopted child of a parent or parents present and settled or being admitted for settlement in the United Kingdom
312. Indefinite leave to enter the United Kingdom as the adopted child of a parent or parents present and settled or being admitted for settlement in the United Kingdom may be granted provided a valid United Kingdom entry clearance for entry in this capacity is produced to the Immigration Officer on arrival.
    Indefinite leave to remain in the United Kingdom as the adopted child of a parent or parents present and settled in the United Kingdom may be granted provided the Secretary of State is satisfied that each of the requirements of paragraph 311 is met.

Refusal of indefinite leave to enter or remain in the United Kingdom as the adopted child of a parent or parents present and settled or being admitted for settlement in the United Kingdom
313. Indefinite leave to enter the United Kingdom as the adopted child of a parent or parents present and settled or being admitted for settlement in the United Kingdom is to be refused if a valid United Kingdom entry clearance for entry in this capacity is not produced to the Immigration Officer on arrival. Indefinite leave to remain in the United Kingdom as the adopted child of a parent or parents present and settled in the United Kingdom is to be refused if the Secretary of State is not satisfied that each of the requirements of paragraph 311 is met.

COMMENTARY

For the position of adoptive children of EEA nationals, see p 338.

HC 395 contains a number of requirements introduced as a result of the Resolution on the Harmonisation of National Policies on Family Reunification agreed by EC Ministers in Copenhagen in June 1993. Broadly, the scheme is that overseas adoptions must be in accordance with a decision taken by the appropriate administrative authority or court in the child's country of origin or residence. Both adoptive parents must be resident together abroad, or one or both must be settled in the UK, at the time of the adoption. The adopted child must have the same rights as a child of the marriage, and must have lost or broken his ties with his family of origin (see *R v IAT, ex p Tohur Ali* [1988] Imm AR 237).

All the requirements in (i) to (xi) have to be satisfied. One of the circumstances specified in (i) must therefore apply.

Entry as an adopted child   A person seeking indefinite leave to enter as an adopted child must satisfy the immigration authorities that he is under the age of 18, and is unmarried, not having previously formed an independent family unit, and not leading an independent life.

He must be joining or accompanying the adoptive parent in one of the following circumstances:
    (a) both adoptive parents are settled in the UK; or

(b) both parents are being admitted on the same occasion for settlement; or

(c) one parent is settled in the UK, and the other is being admitted to the UK on the same occasion for settlement;

(d) one parent is dead and the other parent is settled in the UK or being admitted at the same time for settlement;

(e) the parent who has had sole responsibility for the child is settled in the UK or being admitted on the same occasion for settlement; or

(f) one parent or a relative other than the parent is settled in the UK or being admitted on the same occasion for settlement in the UK, and there are serious compelling family or other considerations in the child's own country which make exclusion of the child undesirable and suitable arrangements have been made for the child's care.

The person being admitted must show that he will be maintained and accommodated adequately without recourse to public funds in accommodation which the parent, parents or relative own or occupy exclusively.

The general grounds for exclusion (see Chapter 13) must not apply to the child.

The child must have an entry clearance for the purpose of entry as an adopted child. The adoption must have taken place in accordance with a decision taken by the competent administrative authority or court of his country of origin in which he is resident, and at a time when both parents were resident together in a third country.

The adoption must not be one of convenience arranged to facilitate the admission of the child (*ECO New Delhi v Balbir Singh* [1977] Imm AR 109; *Baljinder Singh v ECO New Delhi* [1975] Imm AR 34; and *Ex p Dhahan* [1988] Imm AR 257).

Adoption after entry   There is no express provision in the rules for a child to be brought into the UK for the purpose of adoption. The S of S occasionally exercises a discretion to permit entry for this purpose. When a person applies for leave to enter the UK to be adopted, the decision is made outside the rules. The S of S may grant entry clearance having taken advice from the Department of Health. The S of S will need to be satisfied that it is in the child's best interests to be adopted, and there should be no obvious reason why an adoption order should not be made in the UK. Detailed information is contained in Home Office leaflet RON 117. It is possible to apply for judicial review of a decision made under these guidelines if it runs counter to a legitimate expectation created by them (*Ex p Asif Khan* [1984] Imm AR 68). A challenge to the exercise of the discretion under the guidelines was brought in *S of S for Health, ex p Luff* [1991] Imm AR 382. However, it could not be shown that the exercise of the discretion was unreasonable because the Department of Health had not recommended the prospective adoptive parents, due to health problems which they had. In this context, the provisions of the *United Nations Declaration on Social and Legal Principles relating to the protection of Children with special reference to Foster Placement and Adoption Nationally and Internationally* 1986 (see [1991] Imm AR 448) are also considered.

(b) Adoptive parents having limited leave to enter or remain with a view to settlement

Requirements for limited leave to enter or remain in the United Kingdom with a view to settlement as the adopted child of a parent or parents given limited leave to enter or remain in the United Kingdom with a view to settlement

314. The requirements to be met in the case of a child seeking limited leave to enter or remain in the United Kingdom with a view to settlement as the adopted child of a parent or parents given limited leave to enter or remain in the United Kingdom with a view to settlement are that he:

(i)   is seeking leave to enter to accompany or join or remain with a parent or parents in one of the following circumstances:

    (a) one parent is present and settled in the United Kingdom or being admitted on the same occasion for settlement and the other parent is being or has been given limited leave to enter or remain in the United Kingdom with a view to settlement; or

    (b) one parent is being or has been given limited leave to enter or remain in the United Kingdom with a view to settlement and has had sole responsibility for the child's upbringing; or

    (c) one parent is being or has been given limited leave to enter or remain in the United Kingdom with a view to settlement and there are serious and compelling family or other considerations which make exclusion of the child undesirable and suitable arrangements have been made for the child's care; and

(ii)   is under the age of 18; and

(iii)   is not leading an independent life, is unmarried, and has not formed an independent family unit; and

(iv)   can, and will, be maintained and accommodated adequately without recourse to public funds in accommodation which the adoptive parent or parents own or occupy exclusively; and

(v)   was adopted in accordance with a decision taken by the competent administrative authority or court in his country of origin or the country in which he is resident; and

(vi)   was adopted at a time when:

    (a) both adoptive parents were resident together abroad; or

    (b) either or both adoptive parents were settled in the United Kingdom; and

(vii)   has the same rights and obligations as any other child of the marriage; and

(viii) was adopted due to the inability of the original parent(s) or current carer(s) to care for him and there has been a genuine transfer of parental responsibility to the adoptive parents; and

(ix)   has lost or broken his ties with his family of origin; and

(x)   was adopted, but the adoption is not one of convenience arranged to facilitate his admission to the United Kingdom; and

(xi)   (where an application is made for limited leave to remain with a view to settlement) has limited leave to enter or remain in the United Kingdom; and

(xii) if seeking leave to enter, holds a valid United Kingdom entry clearance for entry in this capacity.

Limited leave to enter or remain in the United Kingdom with a view to settlement as the adopted child of a parent or parents given limited leave to enter or remain in the United Kingdom with a view to settlement

315. A person seeking limited leave to enter the United Kingdom with a view to settlement as the adopted child of a parent or parents given limited leave to enter or remain in the United Kingdom with a view to settlement may be admitted for a period not exceeding 12 months provided he is able, on arrival, to produce to the Immigration Officer a valid United Kingdom entry clearance for entry in this capacity. A person seeking limited leave to remain in the United Kingdom with a view to settlement as the adopted child of a parent or parents given limited leave to enter or remain in the United Kingdom with a view to settlement may be granted limited leave for a period not exceeding 12 months provided the Secretary of State is satisfied that each of the requirements of paragraph 314(i)–(xi) is met.

Refusal of limited leave to enter or remain in the United Kingdom with a view to settlement as the adopted child of a parent or parents given limited leave to enter or remain in the United Kingdom with a view to settlement

316. Limited leave to enter the United Kingdom with a view to settlement as the adopted child of a parent or parents given limited leave to enter or remain in the United Kingdom with a view to settlement is to be refused if a valid United Kingdom entry clearance for entry in this capacity is not produced to the Immigration Officer on arrival. Limited leave to remain in the United Kingdom with a view to settlement as the adopted child of a parent or parents given limited leave to enter or remain in the United Kingdom with a view to settlement is to be refused if the Secretary of State is not satisfied that each of the requirements of paragraph 314(i)–(xi) is met.

COMMENTARY

The child seeking limited leave to enter or remain with a view to settlement as an adopted child of parents who have limited leave to enter or remain with a view to settlement must satisfy the requirements set out in para 314. He must be under 18, not leading an independent life, unmarried, and must not have formed an independent family unit. He must satisfy the accommodation and maintenance requirements (see p 207) and the adoption requirements. He must also have an entry clearance. If he does not, he will have no right of appeal against a decision not to give him leave to enter the UK. A child who has limited leave to enter or remain in the UK, for whatever reason, may apply for limited leave to remain with a view to settlement under para 314(xi). The maximum leave which can be granted under para 315 is 12 months. A person seeking limited leave to remain under that paragraph may obtain leave not exceeding 12 months, on satisfying the requirements of para 314.

6 Parents, grandparents and other dependent relatives of persons present and settled in the United Kingdom

Requirements for indefinite leave to enter or remain in the United Kingdom as the parent, grandparent or other dependent relative of a person present and settled in the United Kingdom

317. The requirements to be met by a person seeking indefinite leave to enter or remain in the United Kingdom as the parent, grandparent or other dependent relative of a person present and settled in the United Kingdom are that the person:

(i) is related to a person present and settled in the United Kingdom in one of the following ways:

    (a) mother or grandmother who is a widow aged 65 years or over; or

    (b) father or grandfather who is a widower aged 65 years or over; or

    (c) parent or grandparents travelling together of whom at least one is aged 65 or over; or

    (d) a parent or grandparent aged 65 or over who has remarried but cannot look to the spouse or children of the second marriage for financial support; and where the person settled in the United Kingdom is able and willing to maintain the parent or grandparent and any spouse or child of the second marriage who would be admissible as a dependant; or

    (e) a parent or grandparent under the age of 65 if living alone outside the United Kingdom in the most exceptional compassionate circumstances and mainly dependent financially on relatives settled in the United Kingdom; or

    (f) the son, daughter, sister, brother, uncle or aunt over the age of 18 if living alone outside the United Kingdom in the most exceptional compassionate circumstances and mainly dependent financially on relatives settled in the United Kingdom; and

(ii) is joining or accompanying a person who is present and settled in the United Kingdom or who is on the same occasion being admitted for settlement; and

(iii) is financially wholly or mainly dependent on the relative present and settled in the United Kingdom; and

(iv) can, and will, be maintained and accommodated adequately, together with any dependants, without recourse to public funds in accommodation which the sponsor owns or occupies exclusively; and

(v) has no other close relatives in his own country to whom he could turn for financial support; and

(vi) if seeking leave to enter, holds a valid United Kingdom entry clearance for entry in this capacity.

Indefinite leave to enter or remain as the parent, grandparent or other dependent relative of a person present and settled in the United Kingdom

318. Indefinite leave to enter the United Kingdom as the parent, grandparent or other dependent relative of a person present and settled in the United Kingdom may be granted provided a valid United Kingdom entry clearance for entry in this capacity is produced to the Immigration Officer on arrival. Indefinite leave to remain in the United Kingdom as the parent, grandparent or other dependent relative of a person present and settled in the United Kingdom may be granted provided the Secretary of State is satisfied that each of the requirements of paragraph 317(i)–(v) is met.

Refusal of indefinite leave to enter or remain in the United Kingdom as the parent, grandparent or other dependent relative of a person present and settled in the United Kingdom

319. Indefinite leave to enter the United Kingdom as the parent, grandparent or other dependent relative of a person settled in the United Kingdom is to be refused if a valid United Kingdom entry clearance for entry in this capacity is not produced to the Immigration Officer on arrival. Indefinite leave to remain in the United Kingdom as the parent, grandparent or other dependent relative of a person present and settled in the United Kingdom is to be refused if the Secretary of State is not satisfied that each of the requirements of paragraph 317(i)–(v) is met.

COMMENTARY

Ostensibly to avoid discriminating between family members on the grounds of sex, HC 395 restricted the admission of widowed parents and grandparents, both male and female, to those of 65 years of age or over.

EEA nationals Under the provisions of the EEA Agreement (see Chapter 16) and Regulation EEC/1612/68, EEA states are required to facilitate the admission of any relative of a worker, if that relative is dependent on the worker or living under his roof in the country whence he comes. Parents and children may also 'instal themselves' with the worker (see p 303). In *Centre Public d' Aide Social Courcelles v Lebon* [1987] ECR 2811, the ECJ stated that it is only the fact of dependency, and not the motive for dependency, that can be considered (see also *Moustafa* (11495)).

The relevant relationships Paragraph 317 defines the relationship which must exist between the applicant and a person present and settled in the UK (subpara (i)). The applicant may be the parent or grandparent of the settled person and must be 65 or older. The settled person's parents or grandparents travelling together, of whom only one is 65 or older, also satisfy the requirement of the rules. Where the settled person's parent or grandparent is 65 or older and has remarried, but cannot look to the spouse or children of his second marriage for financial support, the relationship requirement is satisfied, subject to an additional requirement imposed by para 317(i)(*d*). Under that subpara, the settled person must be able and willing to maintain both the applicant and any spouse or child of the second marriage who would be admissible as a dependant. Where the applicant is related to the settled person as his parent or grandparent under the age of 65, who is living alone outside the UK in the most exceptional compassionate circumstances, and who is mainly dependent financially on relatives settled in the UK, the relationship requirement of the paragraph is satisfied (para 317(i)(*e*)). Other dependent relatives are categorised as the son, daughter, sister, brother, uncle and aunt over the age of 18 if living alone outside the UK in the most exceptional compassionate circumstances and mainly dependent financially on relatives settled in the UK.

HC 395 provides for the admission for settlement of the dependants of a person who is:

(a) physically present in the UK (*Begum v S of S* [1990] Imm AR 1, and *R v IAT, ex p Manek* [1978] 3 All ER 641); and

(b) settled in the UK when the dependants applied for admission; or

(c) given leave to enter with a view to settlement on the same occasion.

A passenger seeking admission under the dependants rules must hold a current entry clearance granted to him for the purpose of settlement (*Ex p Akhtar* [1975] 1 WLR 1717). The applicant must be joining the settled person. He must be financially (wholly or mainly) dependent on the settled person. Normally the sponsor and the settled person will be the same person, but the rules seem to envisage that the sponsor and the settled person might be different people (para 317(iv)). Thus, although subpara (*e*) of para 317(i) requires the settled person to maintain the applicant, such maintenance need not extend to accommodation which could be provided by a third (sponsoring) party under subpara (iv). The applicant must have no other close relatives in his own country to whom he could turn for financial support.

Asylum seekers who have been granted exceptional leave to remain will not be regarded as settled, and therefore cannot rely on this provision to have their dependants admitted (*Somasundaram v ECO Bombay* [1990] Imm AR 16). An entry clearance will be refused unless the ECO is satisfied that all the requirements of para 317 are satisfied. The prohibition on recourse to 'public funds' in this context includes the use of savings out of income support (*R v IAT, ex p Chhinderpal Singh* [1989] Imm AR 69, and see p 60). If the person seeking admission as a dependant does not have to depend on the sponsor, but has chosen to be, he will not come within these rules (*Chavda v ECO Bombay* [1978] Imm AR 40).

The rules provide that the relative must be wholly or mainly dependent on the relative settled in the UK. The rule does not permit the person on whom the applicant is dependent to be different from the person settled in the UK (*Shabir v Visa Officer, Islamabad* [1989] Imm AR 185). The purpose of the rule is to enable widowed mothers and elderly parents (as defined in the rule) to join children settled in the UK who are supporting them because the resources of the parents are insufficient to meet their own needs. To make a successful application it must be shown that the parents are necessarily dependent on their children in the UK either wholly or mainly (*Mohammad Zaman v ECO Lahore* [1973] Imm AR 71). Thus where the sponsor's father had two farms in Pakistan, producing an income which he chose to distribute between the members of his family in that country, it was held that the payments he received from his sponsoring son had not been shown to be necessary to him and his wife (*Mohammad Zaman's* case). Similarly, where there was no evidence to suggest that two teenage sons were not able-bodied or were unable to work to supplement the earnings coming into their mother's home, it was held that there was no necessary dependence on the sponsor in the UK (*Bibi Hasan v ECO Bombay* [1976] Imm AR 28). Nor can dependency be created by voluntarily giving up work (*ECO Port Louis v Grenade* [1978] Imm AR 143). However, it has been held that a mother may not be in a position to compel her sons to work. In these circumstances she and her daughter were necessarily dependent on her sponsoring son in the UK; but her three sons, who stated that they had not sought employment because they could live on the money sent to her mother, were not (*Chavda v ECO Bombay* [1978] Imm AR 40). A widowed mother is entitled to look to her only son for support in preference to relatives on her side of the family. If, therefore, the only son settled in the UK voluntarily takes over the main support of his mother from her brother and father in India, the suggestion that her dependence upon him was not a 'necessary' dependence should not preclude her admission to the UK as the dependent widowed mother of this sponsoring only son (*ECO, New Delhi v Malhan* [1978] Imm AR 209).

HC 395 introduced the requirement that in certain categories of relationship under subpara (i), the applicant must be 'mainly dependent financially' on the settled person. Paragraph 317(iii) places a general requirement on all categories of dependent relative applicant. The person must be 'financially wholly or mainly dependent' on the settled person. Under HC 251 the requirement was that the applicant be 'dependent' on the settled person. A necessary emotional dependence (*R v IAT, ex p Bastiampillai* [1983] 2 All ER 844) will no longer satisfy the requirements of the rule by itself. The rule is, however, to be interpreted in a humanitarian manner (*R v IAT, ex p Swaran Singh* [1987] 1 WLR 1394), although dependency must be found as a fact (*Kartar Kaur* (11549)).

The sponsor must show that he has sufficient means at the time of application. There should not be speculation as to what the family's income in the future may be, if, for example, the sponsoring son's wife were to obtain a teaching post (*ECO New Delhi v Parkash Kaur* [1979–80] Imm AR 114, and *ECO Bombay v Seedat* [1975] Imm AR 121).

No other close relatives to turn to   The requirement that there be no close relatives to whom the applicant can turn for support outside the UK is very restrictive on its face. No doubt if the immigration restrictions of the country in which the other close relative lived prevented the applicant from going to the other close relative, the latter would not be a close relative who is able to support the applicant.

'Close relatives' includes brothers, sisters, aunts, uncles, nephews and brothers in law. It is not limited to blood relatives (*Amar Kaur* (2517)). The fact that under the Hindu social code sisters are not responsible for brothers does not prevent sisters being regarded as close relatives to whom the applicant can turn (*Tilak Ram v ECO New Delhi* [1978] Imm AR 123, but see below). The applicant must have no other relative who has the ability to provide some assistance so as to make it reasonable to expect the applicant to depend on that relative rather than the child in the UK (see *Bastiampillai* (above)). The relative must be:

(*a*) outside the UK;

(*b*) able and willing to provide him with support; and

(*c*) a person to whom the applicant could turn in time of need (see *Swaran Singh* (above)).

The phrase 'without other close relatives in their own country to turn to' contemplates a situation where a person is isolated from his or her close relatives and is therefore unable to turn to them for the support a person can normally seek from his family, such as companionship, affection, discussion of problems and courses of action, advice and physical help. In *Raymundo* (10000), the IAT held that an applicant would not be disqualified because there were other relatives physically present. They must be ready and willing to meet the realistic and financial needs of the applicant.

Dillon LJ, in *Swaran Singh* [1987] 1 WLR 1394 at 1398, referring to the above factors, said:

> while the factors listed—companionship, affection, discussion of problems etc— are relevant in the sense that an elderly parent who does not have even these available to him or her is indeed a person 'without other close relatives in his or her own country to turn to,' they do not, in my judgment, go far enough.
>
> I read the phrase in the rule 'without other close relatives in his or her country to turn to' as importing 'to turn to in case of need'—any sort of need which may afflict elderly parents living together, or a widowed mother or a father who is a widower aged 65 or over. What the need may be will depend on the facts of the particular case. But what has to be covered is not merely the need of loneliness and isolation, which the factors listed in *Said Mar Jan v Secretary of State for the Home Department* (unreported), add up to, and which is indeed often a burden to such elderly people. There may also, as in *Reg v Immigration Appeal Tribunal, ex p Bastiampillai* [1983] 2 All ER 844, be a need for a home and financial support. But there are many other circumstances in which elderly parents may need help and support from a child or other close relative. One obvious instance is the need for some close relative to turn to in the event of chronic illness. Another, more important in my personal view, is the need for a close relative to turn to, and who will be able and willing to cope, in the event of accident or sudden emergency to the elderly parent; it is difficult to imagine anything more worrying to a loving child settled here than the fear of an accident to a parent thousands of miles away with no one to cope. Another instance is the possibility of hostile and violent behaviour by neighbours towards the elderly parent who is not adequately protected.

'The most exceptional compassionate circumstances'   The provisions of the rule may be extended to more distant relatives relatives only where there are 'the most exceptional compassionate circumstances'. The purpose of the rule is to aid persons who, without the help of their families, are subject to isolation and stigma, and who cannot support themselves or be supported by other relatives (*Iqbal Begum* (5580)). The relative must be living alone. A person will be regarded as living alone when the person with whom the applicant lives is dependent on him (*Choong* (6162)). An earlier set of rules required that the applicant have a standard of living substantially below that of his own country. This provision was held to be so manifestly unjust as to be invalid: *R v IAT, ex p Manshoora Begum* [1986] Imm AR 385 (*obiter, per contra,* in *Muthiah* (11852), must be regarded as incorrect). It is necessary to show the most exceptional circumstances. The word 'most' is not mere surplusage, but shows that a very strict test is being applied (*R v IAT, ex p Joseph* [1988] Imm AR 329). In each case, whether the circumstances are the

most exceptional compassionate circumstances, will be a question of fact, and it is therefore essential that the fullest possible statement of the facts of the applicant's compassionate circumstances should be provided to the ECO. In *Siu Ling Wu* (12359) the 59-year-old applicant was financially dependent on her daughter who was settled in the UK. However, the adjudicator had failed to place sufficient weight on the very close relationship between the appellant and the granddaughter she accompanied to the UK after caring for her for four years in Hong Kong. The circumstances were exceptional compassionate circumstances sufficient to warrant admission of the grandmother even though she was under 65.

Applicants suffering from serious physical or mental disabilities with no one to look after them may normally be living in the most exceptional compassionate circumstances (*Visa Officer Islamabad v Sindhu* [1978] Imm AR 147; see also *ECO New Delhi v Sibal* [1973] Imm AR 50; and *ECO Bombay v Sacha* [1973] Imm AR 5). However, blindness by itself may not amount to the most exceptional compassionate circumstances (*Visa Officer Islamabad v Bashir* [1978] Imm AR 77). Payments from sponsors are not to be disregarded in assessing whether the applicant is living in the most exceptional compassionate circumstances (*Begum v IAT* [1994] Imm AR 381). Whether an applicant is 'living alone' is not determined solely with reference to whether, physically, he lives with any other person; he may qualify if he has sole responsibility for any dependants who live with him *(Khan v ECO, Dhaka* (12767)). He will not, though, be regarded as living alone if the exceptional compassionate circumstances are created by the person with whom he is living, for example a drug addict (*Ibraheem* (11788)).

If the relative is found to be dependent on the sponsor, it follows that there is no close relative who could meet the relative's financial needs (*Ex p Kara* [1989] Imm AR 120 and *Saya Khatun* [1989] Imm AR 482).

Children aged 18 or over at the date of application must qualify for settlement in their own right unless there are the most exceptional compassionate circumstances.

Further, in *R v Secretary of State ex p Islam Bibi* [1995] Imm AR 157, it was held that if a person was in fact maintained out of public funds which were paid to and intended for someone else, there was recourse to public funds, in the light of *Chhinderpal Singh*. The rules embrace indirect as well as direct reliance on public funds (but see p 60 *et seq*).

Chapter 13

Parts 9 and 10: General Grounds for Refusal of Leave; Registration with the Police

1 Part 9: Refusal of entry clearance or leave to enter

320. In addition to the grounds for refusal of entry clearance or leave to enter set out in Parts 2–8 of these Rules, and subject to paragraph 321 below, the following grounds for the refusal of entry clearance or leave to enter apply:

Grounds on which entry clearance or leave to enter the United Kingdom is to be refused

(1) the fact that entry is being sought for a purpose not covered by these Rules;

(2) the fact that the person seeking entry to the United Kingdom is currently the subject of a deportation order;

(3) failure by the person seeking entry to the United Kingdom to produce to the Immigration Officer a valid national passport or other document satisfactorily establishing his identity and nationality;

(4) failure to satisfy the Immigration Officer, in the case of a person arriving in the United Kingdom or seeking entry through the Channel Tunnel with the intention of entering any other part of the common travel area, that he is acceptable to the immigration authorities there;

(5) failure, in the case of a visa national, to produce to the Immigration Officer a passport or other identity document endorsed with a valid and current United Kingdom entry clearance issued for the purpose for which entry is sought;

(6) where the Secretary of State has personally directed that the exclusion of a person from the United Kingdom is conducive to the public good;

(7) save in relation to a person settled in the United Kingdom or where the Immigration Officer is satisfied that there are strong compassionate reasons justifying admission, confirmation from the medical inspector that, for medical reasons; it is undesirable to admit a person seeking leave to enter the United Kingdom.

Grounds on which entry clearance or leave to enter the United Kingdom should normally be refused

(8) failure by a person arriving in the United Kingdom to furnish the Immigration Officer with such information as may be required for the purpose of deciding whether he requires leave to enter and, if so, whether and on what terms leave should be given;

(9) failure by a person seeking leave to enter as a returning resident to satisfy the Immigration Officer that he meets the requirements of paragraph 18 of

these Rules or that he seeks leave to enter for the same purpose as that for which his ealier leave was granted;

(10) production by the person seeking leave to enter the United Kingdom of a national passport or travel document issued by a territorial entity or authority which is not recognised by Her Majesty's Government as a state or is not dealt with as a government by them, or which does not accept valid United Kingdom passports for the purpose of its own immigration control; or a passport or travel document which does not comply with international passport practice;

(11) failure to observe the time limit or conditions attached to any grant of leave to enter or remain in the United Kingdom;

(12) the obtaining of a previous leave to enter or remain by deception;

(13) failure, except by a person eligible for admission to the United Kingdom for settlement or a spouse eligible for admission under paragraph 282, to satisfy the Immigration Officer that he will be admitted to another country after a stay in the United Kingdom;

(14) refusal by a sponsor of a person seeking leave to enter the United Kingdom to give, if requested to do so, an undertaking in writing to be responsible for that person's maintenance and accommodation for the period of any leave granted;

(15) whether or not to the holder's knowledge, the making of false representations or the failure to disclose any material fact for the purpose of obtaining a work permit;

(16) failure, in the case of a child under the age of 18 years seeking leave to enter the United Kingdom otherwise than in conjunction with an application made by his parent(s) or legal guardian, to provide the Immigration Officer, if required to do so, with written consent to the application from his parent(s) or legal guardian; save that the requirement as to written consent does not apply in the case of a child seeking admission to the United Kingdom as an asylum seeker;

(17) save in relation to a person settled in the United Kingdom, refusal to undergo a medical examination when required to do so by the Immigration Officer;

(18) save where the Immigration Officer is satisfied that admission would be justified for strong compassionate reasons, conviction in any country including the United Kingdom of an offence which, if committed in the United Kingdom, is punishable with imprisonment for a term of 12 months or any greater punishment or, if committed outside the United Kingdom, would be so punishable if the conduct constituting the offence had occurred in the United Kingdom;

(19) where, from information available to the Immigration Officer, it seems right to refuse leave to enter on the ground that exclusion from the United Kingdom is conducive to the public good; if, for example, in the light of the character, conduct or associations of the person seeking leave to enter it is undesirable to give him leave to enter.

COMMENTARY

The general grounds for refusal of leave to enter or remain in the UK are set out in Part 9 of HC 395. They apply to all the categories of person under the rules. Grounds (1) to (7) are grounds on which entry clearance or leave to enter must be refused. Numbers (8)–(19) are grounds on which entry clearance or leave to enter should normally be refused. Thus (1)–(7) are mandatory grounds of refusal, and (8)–(19) are discretionary grounds of refusal. An immigration officer may examine the holder of an entry clearance to determine whether any of the above grounds apply to him. In determining that question he may rely on inferences reasonably drawn from the results of that examination, and any other information available to him.

Although the first seven grounds are referred to as mandatory, the immigration officer may retain a discretion to grant leave to enter outside the immigration rules (*R v IAT ex p S of S* [1992] Imm AR 554). Some consideration must be given to the grounds of an application for leave to enter outside the rules. Likewise, when an application for indefinite leave to remain is made on 'exceptional and most compelling grounds' proper reasons should be given for its refusal, showing that consideration has been given to it. The adjudicator can consider whether such a decision is 'in accordance with the law'. That exercise is not limited by s 19(2) of the 1971 Act (*Evon* (11392)). If the S of S has agreed to depart from the rules by stating a policy, s 19(2) cannot limit consideration of the exercise of discretion by the adjudicator, otherwise a request to depart from the rules will be governed by s 19(2) (*Evon* and see p385 *et seq*).

2 The mandatory grounds

(a) Currently the subject of a deportation order
Such a person becomes an illegal entrant on entry to the UK by entering in breach of the immigration laws (see p 15).

(b) Failure to produce documents
If a person fails to produce to the immigration officer a valid national passport or other document satisfactorily establishing his identity and nationality, leave to enter will be refused. EEA nationals may be required to show a valid EEA passport or identity card under the Immigration (European Economic Area) Order 1994. However, this requirement may breach the EU law relating to free movement. In relation to EU citizens the requirement of submission to a border control is likely to breach art 8a of the Treaty on European Union, which provides that every citizen of the Union shall have the right to move and reside freely within the territory of the Member States.

(c) Acceptability to common travel area immigration authorities
Section 1(3) of the 1971 Act makes provision for the common travel area (see para 15, (p 69)).

(d) Visa nationals
A visa national must have a visa for all purposes under Parts 2–8 of the rules. Without a visa he will have no right of appeal against a decision to refuse him entry or entry clearance.

(e) Exclusion conducive to the public good

Medical reasons   Where the medical officer confirms that it is undesirable for medical reasons to admit a person seeking leave to enter the UK, an immigration officer must refuse entry. The only exceptions to this rule are where the immigration officer is satisfied that there are strong compassionate reasons justifying admission, or where the person is settled in the UK. The medical officer must confirm that it is undesirable to admit the person (see, eg, *Sudharkaran* [1976] Imm AR 5). The medical officer's diagnosis cannot be challenged on appeal (*ibid*). Paragraph 26 requires that a person who intends to remain in the UK for more than six months should normally be referred for medical inspection. Paragraph 38 provides that a returning resident should not be refused entry on medical grounds. Immigration officers may refer EEA nationals (when they are seeking to exercise a right of free movement pursuant to the EEA) to a medical inspector only if they show 'obvious signs of mental or physical ill health'. Such persons may be refused only if the medical inspector certifies that they are suffering from one of the diseases listed in the annex to EC Directive 64/2. Home Office guidance (BD 3/95) spells out the fact that a person who is suffering from AIDS or is HIV positive is not grounds for refusing leave to enter or remain.

Compassionate grounds   Such grounds were found to exist to enable the admission of the holder of an entry clearance certificate as a fiancé notwithstanding that on arrival he was found to be suffering from tuberculosis in an active (but non-infectious) form. The IAT was clearly influenced by undertakings given by the appellant's uncles here (one of whom was the father of his fiancée) that they would pay the considerable expense of recommended private medical treatment, their ability to do so, and the feelings expressed by the appellant's fiancée after waiting more than two years for his arrival (*Parvez v Immigration Officer, London (Heathrow) Airport* [1979–80] Imm AR 84). However, it should not be thought that a fiancé arriving for marriage and found to be suffering from tuberculosis should *ipso facto* be found to be in strong compassionate circumstances (*Immigration Officer, London (Heathrow) Airport v Bhatti* TH/57482/80 (1719) unreported, referred to in [1979–80] Imm AR at p 86, n 4).

In *Entry Certificate Officer, Bombay v Sacha* [1973] Imm AR 5, the IAT affirmed the decision of an adjudicator that a severely mentally retarded applicant in need of care and attention should not be refused admission because strong compassionate reasons existed. Her cousin in India who looked after her did so reluctantly and she would receive very much better care and attention from her half brother who was brought up with her from her birth till he came to the UK, and whose affection for her was manifest.

Under HC 395 it should be possible to argue that strong compassionate circumstances exist in such cases and that therefore the immigration officer has a discretion that should have been exercised differently.

3   The non-mandatory grounds

(a) Failure to furnish information

An adverse inference may be drawn from any prevarication by the applicant. Thus an applicant failed to discharge the onus on him to bring himself within a rule when he was unable or unwilling to define his position in order to bring himself within one or another immigration rule. He could not successfully appeal an adverse decision by the ECO not to grant him entry clearance (*Abid Hussain v ECO Islamabad* [1989] Imm AR 46). The examination should not be carried further than is necessary for a decision to be made on the grant of entry clearance, or to decide whether leave to enter should be given for a limited period and subject to any conditions.

(b) Returning residents

A returning resident may be refused admission when he fails to satisfy the immigration officer that he had indefinite leave when he last left the UK; that he has not been away from the UK for more than two years; that he did not receive assistance from public funds towards the costs of leaving the UK; and that he now seeks admission for the purposes of settlement (see para 18, p 70). HC 31 adds the requirement, from 1 November 1996, that the purpose of the leave to enter sought be the same as the purpose of the applicant's earlier leave.

(c) Passport not recognised

Passports issued by states which are not recognised by the UK, and 'world citizen' passports, will not be accepted and may form the basis of a refusal of admission.

(d) Failure to observe the time limit or conditions

The S of S may rely on breaches of the rules which occurred in any earlier period of leave, unless he is estopped from doing so. In *Clifford Ofoajoku v S of S* [1991] Imm AR 68 the IAT considered that the S of S could take account of a breach of condition in an earlier period of leave. He is not estopped from relying on a breach merely because a period of further leave had intervened, where that latter period of leave was granted without knowledge of the breach. It would, however, be arguable that the S of S would be estopped where the latter period of leave was granted in the knowledge of the earlier breach (see *Ofoajoku* at p 79).

Furthermore, where the breach comes to light after the date of refusal to grant a variation of leave, it may be relied upon before the appellate authorities (*Rajendran v S of S* [1989] Imm AR 512).

(e) Obtaining previous leave by deception

Where a person obtains leave by deception, clearly he is an illegal entrant. This provision, however, permits the immigration officer to consider periods of leave obtained in the past, irrespective of the *bona fides* of the current application.

(f) Sponsor's refusal to give an undertaking

Paragraph 35 provides that a sponsor may be required to give an undertaking. If he refuses, the application for admission may be refused (see p 80).

(g) False representations or failure to disclose material facts

If the immigration officer refuses leave to enter because false representations were made, the representations must have been made by the applicant. Deception of an ECO suffices, despite the fact that they are not mentioned in the 1971 Act (*Ex p Kwadwo Saffu-Mensah* [1991] Imm AR 43). Conduct can of itself amount to a representation. Silent presentation of a passport which the applicant knows to contain false information amounts to a false representation (*Ex p Patel* [1986] Imm AR 515). The representation is made at the time the passport is presented (*Ex p Mohammed Salim* [1990] Imm AR 316). There is no requirement, however, that deceit or fraud should have been involved in the representation, just that it is false (*Eusebio* (4739)). In *Tahzeem Akhtar v IAT* [1991] Imm AR 326, the CA held, in relation to the precursor of this rule under HC 251, that there was no justification for reading the word 'material' into the phrase 'false representations'. The only questions are:

(*a*) whether representations which were false were made;

(*b*) whether those representations were used for the purpose of obtaining an entry clearance; and

(*c*) whether they actually played a part in obtaining the entry clearance.

(h) Material non-disclosure

Non-disclosure must play a part in obtaining entry clearance for it to be a 'material' non-disclosure (cf *Eusebio* above). In *Edusi* (6598) the IAT held that failure to answer a question on a visa application form about previous periods of leave amounted to non-disclosure of a material fact. In *Marquez* [1992] Imm AR 354, the IAT held that the immigration officer need only prove that the person failed to disclose facts which he knew, or ought reasonably to have known, were relevant to the decision (in that case whether to grant a visa).

Material non-disclosure was held to justify refusal of leave to enter where an applicant with an entry clearance marked 'visitor' failed to inform the immigration officer that he had previously applied for an entry certificate, had been refused and his appeal had been dismissed; this was so despite the fact that it was apparent from the passport that a previous application had been unsuccessful (*Mustun v S of S* [1972] Imm AR 97); likewise where a student applicant failed to disclose that he had two brothers in the UK (*Qurasha v Immigration Officer, London* [1978] Imm AR 158). In *R v IAT, ex p Suily Begum* [1990] Imm AR 226 (QBD), on the other hand, it was not regarded as a material non-disclosure that a minor daughter did not disclose that she had a number of prospective fiancés, one of whom she contemplated marrying at some stage in the future.

(i) Parents' consent

A child under 18 years of age who seeks admission will normally be refused leave to enter if he does not have the consent in writing of his parent(s). Paragraph 320(16) does not apply to child asylum seekers.

(j) Criminal convictions

A person who has been convicted in any country, including the UK, of certain offences may be refused leave to enter unless the immigration officer considers admission to be justified for strong compassionate reasons (for an earlier rule, see *Liberto v Immigration Officer, London (Heathrow) Airport* [1975] Imm AR 61). The offences are those which, if they had been committed in the UK, would be punishable by 12 months or longer in prison. Thus a conviction for a relatively minor offence may lead to exclusion, even though the offence was committed in the UK and the court did not recommend deportation. However, the Rehabilitation of Offenders Act 1974 applies to these offences.

EU nationals EU law suggests that previous criminal convictions may not *per se* justify exclusion (see ECU Treaty, art 48(3) and EC Directive 64/221). Past conduct may justify exclusion only if it constitutes a present threat, but some past offences are so serious that the burden is on the applicant to show that the risk of similar conduct in the future is negligible (see *Puttick v S of S* [1984] Imm AR 118. See also *R v Bouchereau* [1978] 2 WLR 250 and *Ex p Santillo* [1981] 2 All ER 897 on the power of a court to make a recommendation for deportation). In *R v Escauriaza* [1989] 3 CMLR 281, the ECJ held that the public policy exemption (that the deportee be a genuine and sufficient threat to the requirements of public policy) is satisfied where the presence of the deportee would be to the detriment of the UK.

(k) Discretionary exclusion conducive to the public good

Any person may be refused leave to enter on the ground that his exclusion is conducive to the public good.

It is not possible to enumerate or define the types of circumstance in which the power should be used. Paragraph 320(19) does not provide an exclusive list (*R v IAT, ex p Ajaib Singh* [1978] Imm AR 59). According to the IAT in *Scheele v Immigration Officer, Harwich* [1976] Imm AR 1, it appears designed to deal with 'undesirables' of all kinds. As such it is not intended to be used only in rare or unusual circumstances. Nevertheless, it should not be used lightly or in trivial circumstances. In *Scheele*, however, the exclusion of the appellant was justified when he was found in possession of cannabis, although the amount was small and for personal use and he was in transit to another country.

It is in the public interest that persons should not be readily admitted to this country in contravention of immigration rules (see *R v IAT, ex p Ajaib Singh* [1978] Imm AR 59). However, that in itself would not form the basis for a refusal under this rule (see *Olufosoye* below). It may be conducive to the public good to exclude a person on the basis of previous periods of leave to enter which were obtained by deception (*R v IAT, ex p Anilkumar Patel* [1988] AC 910, and *Sarwa* [1978] Imm AR 190), although this should now be dealt with under para 320(12) (see *Olufosoye* below and p 238). An acquittal on a criminal charge does not preclude the immigration officer from concluding, on the balance of probabilities, that the person committed the offence. In such circumstances he may, without making further inquiries, exclude him on the basis that his exclusion would be conducive to the public good (*Ex p Nkiti* [1989] Imm AR 182).

The power cannot lawfully be exercised in an arbitrary manner, and its use in trivial circumstances will render the decision amenable to either review or appeal. The S of S must justify the proposition that exclusion is conducive to the public good. Proof will be to a high standard, on the balance of probabilities, if an allegation of dishonesty is involved. Factors taken into account when considering whether deportation would be conducive to the public good (s 3(5)(*b*), 1971 Act) will be relevant. The grounds will have to be other than that the applicant obtained a previous leave to enter or remain by deception or that he had failed to observe a time limit or condition on any grant of leave to enter or remain, as these form specific grounds under para 320 (320(11) and (12), and see *Olufosoye* [1992] Imm AR 141).

4 Persons in possession of an entry clearance

Refusal of leave to enter in relation to a person in possession of an entry clearance

321. A person seeking leave to enter the United Kingdom who holds an entry clearance which was duly issued to him and is still current may be refused leave to enter only where the Immigration Officer is satisfied that:

(i)   whether or not to the holder's knowledge, false representations were employed or material facts were not disclosed, either in writing or orally, for the purpose of obtaining the entry clearance; or

(ii) a change of circumstances since it was issued has removed the basis of the holder's claim to admission, except where the change of circumstances amounts solely to the person becoming over age for entry in one of the categories contained in paragraphs 296–316 of these Rules since the issue of the entry clearance; or

(iii) refusal is justified on grounds of restricted returnability; on medical grounds; on grounds of criminal record; because the person seeking leave to enter is the subject of a deportation order or because exclusion would be conducive to the public good.

COMMENTARY

A person who holds an entry clearance which was duly issued to him (*S of S v Idowu* [1972] Imm AR 197), and which is still current (*Andronicou v Chief Immigration Officer, London (Heathrow) Airport* [1974] Imm AR 87) is not to be refused leave to enter unless the immigration officer is satisfied that one of the following grounds applies to him.

(a) False representations and non-disclosure
See p 16 et seq and p 242.

(b) Change of circumstance
A change of circumstance since the entry clearance was issued which removes the basis of the holder's claim to admission may result in refusal of leave to enter. If the holder of the entry clearance is a child entering under the paragraphs relating to the entry of relatives and the only change of circumstance is that the holder has become an adult in the interim, leave to enter should not be refused. Where the change occurs after arrival, but before leave to enter, the immigration officer may take it into account (*Teflisi* (3522)).

The question whether there has been a change of circumstance is a matter of fact and degree (*Hossain v Immigration Officer, Heathrow* [1990] Imm AR 520). Where two Pakistani children under 18 years of age were granted entry clearances to enable them to join their parents in the UK, leave to enter was properly refused because, between the time they were interviewed and the time when the entry clearances were granted, their mother had returned to Pakistan. Their admission depended on both parents being present and settled in the UK. The mother's return removed the basis of the claim to admission, and was a change of circumstances affecting what should have been a continuing state of affairs subsisting from the time the clearances were issued until the children's arrival at the port of entry (*Arshad v Immigration Officer, London (Heathrow) Airport* [1977] Imm AR 19). In *R v S of S, ex p Rukshanda Begum* [1990] Imm AR 1 a child, who was granted entry clearance to accompany his mother to the UK, arrived in the UK without her. A change in circumstances was held to have occurred because the mother could not fulfil the requirements of the rules that she should be admitted for settlement at the same time. On the other hand, where the length of a visit was all that had changed, no change of circumstance affecting the basis of the application occurred (*Immigration Officer, Heathrow v Salmak* [1991] Imm AR 191).

A change of circumstances which removes the basis of the claim to admission of a person who holds an entry clearance is a matter of fact and degree (see *Esin* (12178) and *Cui* (9694)).

(c) Restricted returnability etc
For the definition of 'restricted returnability' see paras 21 to 23. For medical grounds, see paras 36 to 39. For criminal convictions and exclusion conducive to the public good, see p 243.

5 Refusal of variation or curtailment of leave

322. In addition to the grounds for refusal of extension of stay set out in Parts 2–8 of these Rules, the following provisions apply in relation to the refusal of an

application for variation of leave to enter or remain or, where appropriate, the curtailment of leave:

Grounds on which an application to vary leave to enter or remain in the United Kingdom is to be refused

(1)   the fact that variation of leave to enter or remain is being sought for a purpose not covered by these Rules.

Grounds on which an application to vary leave to enter or remain in the United Kingdom should normally be refused

(2)   the making of false representations or the failure to disclose any material fact for the purpose of obtaining leave to enter or a previous variation of leave;

(3)   failure to comply with any conditions attached to the grant of leave to enter or remain;

(4)   failure by the person concerned to maintain or accommodate himself and any dependants without recourse to public funds;

(5)   the undesirability of permitting the person concerned to remain in the United Kingdom in the light of his character, conduct or associations or the fact that he represents a threat to national security;

(6)   refusal by a sponsor of the person concerned to give, if requested to do so, an undertaking in writing to be responsible for his maintenance and accommodation in the United Kingdom or failure to honour such an undertaking once given;

(7)   failure by the person concerned to honour any declaration or undertaking given orally or in writing as to the intended duration and/or purpose of his stay;

(8)   failure, except by a person who qualifies for settlement in the United Kingdom or by the spouse of a person settled in the United Kingdom, to satisfy the Secretary of State that he will be returnable to another country if allowed to remain in the United Kingdom for a further period;

(9)   failure by an applicant to produce within a reasonable time documents or other evidence required by the Secretary of State to establish his claim to remain under these Rules;

(10) failure, without providing a reasonable explanation, to comply with a request made on behalf of the Secretary of State to attend for interview;

(11) failure, in the case of a child under the age of 18 years seeking a variation of his leave to enter or remain in the United Kingdom otherwise than in conjunction with an application by his parent(s) or legal guardian, to provide the Secretary of State, if required to do so, with written consent to the application from his parent(s) or legal guardian; save that the requirement as to written consent does not apply in the case of a child who has been admitted to the United Kingdom as an asylum seeker.

Grounds on which leave to enter or remain may be curtailed

323. A person's leave to enter or remain may be curtailed:

(i)   on any of the grounds set out in paragraph 322(2)–(5) above; or

(ii)   if he ceases to meet the requirements of the Rules under which his leave to enter or remain was granted; or

(iii) if he is the dependant, or is seeking leave to remain as the dependant, of an asylum applicant whose claim has been refused and whose leave has been curtailed under section 7 of the 1993 Act, and he does not qualify for leave to remain in his own right.

Crew members

324. A person who has been given leave to enter to join a ship, aircraft, hovercraft, hydrofoil or international train service as a member of its crew, or a crew member who has been given leave to enter for hospital treatment, repatriation or transfer to another ship, aircraft, hovercraft, hydrofoil or international train service in the United Kingdom, is to be refused leave to remain unless an extension of stay is necessary to fulfil the purpose for which he was given leave to enter or unless he meets the requirements for an extension of stay as a spouse in paragraph 284.

COMMENTARY

The requirements in Parts 2–8 of HC 395 are supplemented by these general grounds for refusal. They are divided into one mandatory ground and ten discretionary grounds. An application for a variation of leave to enter or remain must be refused where the variation of leave to enter or remain is being sought for a purpose not covered by HC 395. Where leave is curtailed after an unsuccessful asylum application, pursuant to s 7 or 7A of the 1993 Act, the person has no right of appeal (1993 Act, s 7(2)), although he may appeal against any subsequent decision to deport him.

(a) Non-disclosure

A person who obtained leave for one period, intending to apply later for extension of that leave, was treated as having made false representations where that longer period was held to have been his intention throughout (*Ding* (3304)). An application to vary leave to enter as a visitor to leave to enter as a student was properly refused by the S of S where a person falsely represented herself as a holiday visitor when she applied for an entry certificate, but her intention was to pursue a course of study. The IAT commented that the purpose of the rules was not to allow persons whose real purpose in coming to the UK was to study, to enter on the false pretence that they came for no purpose other than for a short visit. Such persons could not reasonably expect that, having presented the Home Office with a *fait accompli* of compliance with the formal requirements for students, they have a right to stay in that capacity (*Owusu v S of S* [1976] Imm AR 101).

A person may be treated as an illegal entrant where facts are suppressed. Thus in *Ex p Ming* [1994] Imm AR, the applicant deliberately suppressed his history of employment in the construction industry. Laws J considered *Jayakody* [1981] Imm AR 205 and stated that the applicant could be treated as an illegal entrant where material facts had not been disclosed despite the fact that, had they been disclosed, the applicant might or might not have been granted entry. Following *Bugdaycay* [1987] 1 AC 514, an entrant who seeks and obtains leave through a misrepresentation, but might have been given leave on a different basis had he put forward the true facts, was an illegal entrant. *Durojaye* [1991] Imm AR 307 at p 313–14 is authority for the proposition that if the revelation of the true facts would have led to further inquiries, the false representations are material (and see p 18).

(b) Breaches of earlier conditions

The S of S may rely on breaches which occurred in an earlier period of leave, for example, working in breach of a condition during an earlier stay with leave (*Ex p Sadiq* [1990] Imm AR 364). In *Clifford Ofoajoku v S of S* [1991] Imm AR 68 the S of S took account of a breach of condition in an earlier period of leave. He was not estopped from relying on it because a period of further leave had intervened, where that latter period of leave was granted without knowledge of the breach. Where the breach comes to light after the date of the refusal to grant the variation of leave, it may be relied on before the appellate authorities (*Rajendran v S of S* [1989] Imm AR 512).

An application is considered in the light of the circumstances at the time of the decision, and not in the light of the facts at the time of the application (*S of S v Patel* [1988] Imm AR 75). The only exception to this is where a child who applies to join his parents becomes older than 18 by the time of the decision. In *Clifford Ofoajoku v S of S* [1991] Imm AR 68 the IAT rejected the S of S's argument that estoppel can never operate in immigration cases, but stated that simply granting leave after knowledge that the applicant had worked in breach would not by itself estop the S of S from relying on the breach, since there is a discretionary power to refuse an extension of leave because of prior breaches. Although estoppel can operate against the Crown in certain cases the doctrine is of very limited application to the exercise of immigration control (see *Paet v S of S* [1979–80] Imm AR 185; and *R v IAT, ex p Ahluwalia* [1979–80] Imm AR 1). So, for example, neither a delay of four years in instituting deportation proceedings, nor alleged assurances by the police that if the appellants co-operated in a prosecution they would not be deported, estopped the S of S from ultimately deciding to deport (*Deen v S of S* [1987] Imm AR 543). Again the S of S was not estopped from refusing an extension because he had granted the appellant a number of extensions to enable her to find a firm of solicitors willing to accept her as an articled clerk (*S of S v Wedad* [1979–80] Imm AR 27). The immigration rules do not provide for the condonation, in the sense of full forgiveness, of past immigration offences (*S of S v Sidique* [1976] Imm AR 69).

(c) Maintenance and accommodation

See p 207. For public funds see p 60. Note also that a requirement that the person must not have recourse to public funds can be made a condition of leave to enter. Thus knowingly breaching that condition can be a criminal offence (see p 525).

(d) Character, conduct and associations

See p 243. This is a broad power to deal with undesirables of all kinds. The list is not exclusive. For the provisions relating to EEA nationals see Chapter 16.

(e) Refusal of a sponsor to give an oral or written undertaking
The sponsor can be required to give an undertaking under para 35 to be responsible for the maintenance and accommodation of the applicant (see p 80). If he refuses to give such an undertaking or fails to honour it the application may be refused. The sponsor should be advised, separately, of the liability he is undertaking.

(f) Declarations as to duration of stay
An application may be refused even if the undertaking had originally been honestly given (*Amoah v S of S* [1987] Imm AR 236). 'Undertaking' is used here to mean a promise or statement by the applicant as well as a written declaration or undertaking.

(g) Restricted returnability
If a person does not qualify for settlement he must satisfy the S of S that he can be returned to another country at the end of the further period of leave he seeks. A person who qualifies for settlement (and his spouse) does not have to satisfy the S of S of this.

(h) Provision of documents and failure to attend an interview
The applicant must provide the evidence on which his application for an extension may be assessed. However, there are no guidelines on what constitutes an unreasonable time for providing evidence. The S of S may take into account the delay of a person's agents. These provisions mirror the rules relating to the determination of asylum claims in this respect.

(i) Written consent
Children under the age of 18 seeking leave to remain in the UK must have the written consent of their parent or guardian. Paragraph 322 applies only to the determination of applications under Parts 2–8 of HC 395. There is no need for the express disavowal of para 322(11) in relation to Part 9 applications for asylum.

(j) Curtailment
A new para 323 was inserted into HC 395 by Cm 3365, as from 1 September 1996, to reflect the amendments made to s 7 of the 1993 Act by the 1996 Act (see below). The applicant's leave to enter or remain may be curtailed by virtue of any of the discretionary grounds, or if at any time he ceases to satisfy the terms of the para of Parts 2–8 under which he was given leave to enter or remain. In *Akinsanya* (11991) 1996 JCWI B Vol 5 No 11 Spring 1996, p 14, the applicant entered as a visitor and applied for a variation of leave to leave as a working holidaymaker. Her leave was curtailed on the basis of misrepresentations made by her on arrival. However, there had been a genuine change of circumstances only after the application for variation

had been made, and therefore she could not have concealed facts concerning that change (she had not at that time met the future father of her child).

Section 7 of the 1993 Act provides for the curtailment of leave to enter or remain. Where a person who has limited leave to enter or remain in the UK claims refugee status before the expiry of his limited leave, the S of S may in writing curtail the duration of his limited leave when refusing the refugee application. There is no appeal against the curtailment of the limited leave, but there may be an appeal against the refusal of asylum. Where the person's leave has been curtailed in these circumstances and the S of S has decided to make a deportation order, the person may be detained pending the making of the deportation order. Section 7(1A) extends the curtailment provisions to the limited leave granted to any dependant of the person whose leave has been curtailed. Such persons have no right of appeal against curtailment and may be detained pending the making of deportation orders against them. Paragraph 323 of HC 395 makes clear that if a dependant of a person whose leave has been curtailed qualifies for leave to remain in his own right, his leave cannot be curtailed under the immigration rules.

The S of S has indicated that the power of curtailment is to be used more frequently, but not automatically or punitively (*Hansard*, Written Answer no 274 for Wednesday 15 February 1995). There is a general presumption that curtailment will be used where available, except where it would be inappropriate. Each case will be looked at on its individual merits. Curtailment might be inappropriate (*inter alia*) in cases in which it would be right to allow existing leave to run after the asylum decision has been taken. Thus where the applicant qualifies for leave to remain under another category of the rules (eg because he is married to a British citizen), or where there are compelling compassionate or other circumstances which would make it inappropriate to proceed with deportation action, it may be inappropriate to curtail leave. Where the power is used, a notice of intention to deport is normally served at the same time, and triggers the right of appeal against the refusal of asylum (see p 502 and INL&P, vol 9, no 2, 1995 at p 74).

6   Part 10: Registration with the police

325. A condition requiring registration with the police should normally be imposed on any foreign national aged 16 years or over who is given limited leave to enter the United Kingdom:
(i)   for employment for longer than 3 months unless he has been admitted for permit free employment as a private servant in a diplomatic household or as a minister of religion; or
(ii)   for longer than 6 months under the following categories of these Rules:
    (a)   students;
    (b)   'au pair';
    (c)   businessmen and self-employed persons;
    (d)   investors or persons of independent means;
    (e)   creative artists;

(f) family members of European Economic Area nationals who are not themselves European Economic Area nationals; or

(iii) as the spouse or child of a person required to register with the police; or

(iv) exceptionally, in any other case where the Immigration Officer considers it necessary to ensure that a foreign national complies with the terms of a limited leave to enter.

326. A condition requiring registration with the police should also be imposed when a foreign national on whom a registration requirement was not imposed on arrival is granted an extension of stay which has the effect of allowing him to remain in the United Kingdom for employment for longer than 3 months, or otherwise for longer than 6 months, reckoned from the date of his arrival, save where:

(i) the person concerned is under the age of 16; or

(ii) the extension of stay was granted as a minister of religion or private servant in a diplomatic household; or

(iii) the extension of stay was granted on the basis of marriage to a person settled in the United Kingdom.

COMMENTARY

When an alien aged 16 or over is given leave to enter for a limited period he may be required (under s 3(1)(c) of the 1971 Act) to register with the police if he falls into one of the above categories. Family members of EEA nationals who are not themselves EEA nationals may be required to register, although this rarely happens in practice.

Pursuant to s 4(3) and (4), the S of S made regulations regarding registration with the police and the provision of information for hotel records. The term 'alien' means a national of another country who is neither a Commonwealth citizen nor a BPP (1981 Act, s 50(1), and reg 2(1) of the Immigration (Registration with the Police) Regulations 1972 (as amended)). A stamp is placed in the person's passport stating 'The holder is also required to register at once with the police'.

The current regulations setting out the particulars to be kept in the register are the Immigration (Registration with the Police) Regulations 1972 (SI 1972 No 1758 as amended by SI 1982 No 1024, SI 1990 No 400, SI 1991 No 965 and SI 1995 No 2928, made pursuant to s 4(3) of the 1971 Act. Failure to register without reasonable excuse is a criminal offence under s 26(1)(f) of the 1971 Act.

Registration Within seven days of the regulations becoming applicable to him, the alien must attend at the offices of the chief police officer for either his area of residence (if he is resident) or in any other case the chief police officer for the area in which for the time being he happens to be. In London the relevant office is the Aliens Registration Office, at 10 Lamb's Conduit Street, London WC1 3MX; otherwise it is the local central police station. If he registers within seven days he is taken to have registered 'at once'. He must furnish such information as the officer may require, including his name, address, marital status, employment or occupation, and the name and address of his employer (Schedule to the regulations). He must produce a passport or other documentation establishing his identity or nationality. If he cannot do this, he must explain why he is unable to do so.

Any change in address must be notified to the officer within seven days (reg 7). Other changes in the particulars must be notified to the officer within eight days of their occurrence (reg 8). If an alien is absent from his UK residence for a period exceeding two months he must notify the officer of his address for the time being, and of his return. Any other changes of address within that time must be notified to the officer within eight days, provided that the alien intends to remain at that address for more than eight days (reg 7). The alien is provided with a certificate of registration for which he is charged a fee (reg 10) and which he may be required to produce to any constable or immigration officer. The alien is required to provide the officer, if required, with two copies of a photograph of himself (reg 5, 8(b), and 9). If he fails to provide a photograph the officer may cause him to be photographed (reg 9).

EEA nationals   EEA nationals exercising Community rights (see Chapter 16) are exempt from registration. Members of the EEA national's family, who are not themselves EEA nationals, are subject to registration (*R v Pieck* [1981] QB 571).

Part 11: Asylum

The rules relating to asylum form Part 11 of HC 395. They are discussed in Chapter 25, together with the separate appeal system applicable to asylum claims.

Part 12: Rights of appeal

The rules relating to rights of appeal form Part 12 of HC 395. Part 12, and a commentary on it, are set out in Chapter 18.

Chapter 14

Part 13: Deportation

1 Introduction

Deportation is one method of removing a person from the UK. Others include removal under directions given in respect of an illegal entrant; and supervised and voluntary departures. In relation to deportation orders there are normally three stages before removal is effected. First, the S of S notifies the person concerned that he intends to deport him. Second, if an appeal against that notice is not made or is unsuccessful, the S of S signs the deportation order. Third, the deportation order is implemented. It is important to keep the stages clear, and in particular to note that such rights of appeal as exist relate to the first part of the process. Where there is a possibility that a criminal court will make a recommendation for deportation, a slightly different system operates: the defendant must be given the opportunity to address the court on this aspect of his sentence, and may appeal against that aspect through the criminal appeals system (see paras 381–389, below).

The power to make a deportation order may be exercised by immigration officers of the rank of inspector. Following *Oladehinde v S of S* [1991] 1 AC 254, the Home Office stated that written records of the decision-making process must be kept and that cases in which a person has been in the UK for a long time, or where there are compassionate circumstances, must be referred from the immigration officer to the Home Office for a decision. It was stressed in *Oladehinde* that the person making the decision should not have been involved in the investigation of the case in any way. However, there is no impropriety in an immigration officer interviewing a person to ensure that there has been no change in circumstances and then immediately serving a deportation order on him (*Ex p Beecham* [1996] Imm AR 87). If an immigration officer, having interviewed a person, considers a deportation order appropriate, the officer sends a fax to an inspector for confirmation of the decision. There is no impropriety in a senior executive officer in the enforcement unit of the IND considering deportation (*Elizabeth Mensah* [1996] Imm AR 223).

Separate legislation governs the surrender from the UK of persons who have committed crimes in other countries. Extradition to the Republic of Ireland is covered by the Backing of Warrants (Republic of Ireland) Act 1965; to Commonwealth and foreign countries, by the Extradition Act 1989. These statutes apply to nationals as well as to aliens. See also the Suppression of Terrorism Act 1978 and the European Convention on the Suppression of Terrorism. The European Convention on Extradition 1957 and the European Convention on Extradition Order 1990 set procedures for extradition to, broadly, the EU countries, Israel, Turkey, Cyprus, and Norway (see the full list in *Re Farinha* [1992] Imm AR 174). The Repatriation of Prisoners Act 1984 makes provision for foreign prisoners serving sentences in the UK to be returned to their own countries to complete their terms of imprisonment. All parties—the prisoner, the foreign country, and the UK—must consent to the repatriation. The law of extradition, deportation, and the right of asylum are closely inter-linked (see *R v Governor of Brixton Prison, ex p Soblen* [1963] 2 QB 243).

Detention pending deportation is an administrative matter (see p 288). No action lies for false imprisonment even if the notice of intention to deport is withdrawn provided the conditions precedent for lawful detention under para 16 of Sched 2 to the 1971 Act are met (see p 288 and *Ullah v S of S* [1995] Imm AR 166). Similarly where a person recommended for deportation by a criminal court appeals against his sentence, it is lawful for him to be detained despite the fact that the parole unit has decided that he should be paroled and deported (*In Re Nwafor* [1994] Imm AR 91). A person subject to control pending deportation may be made subject to restrictions as to residence, employment, or occupation, and as to reporting to an immigration officer or the police as may from time to time be notified to him by the S of S (para 2(5) of Sched 3 to the 1971 Act (as amended by the 1996 Act)). Appeals against deportation are dealt with in Chapter 18, p 349.

2   Long residence policies

Before turning to a statement of the rules, it is convenient to consider the S of S's policies relating to long residence. Applications for indefinite leave to remain may be made on the basis of concessions arising out of long residence. Such applications will be outside the rules. In *Vimalan* (12052) (JCWI B, vol 5, no 11, Spring 1996, p 15) the IAT stated that the rules list the circumstances in which settlement may be granted, and long residence is not one of them. The IAT stated that the adjudicator's jurisdiction concerned whether the S of S had acted in accordance with the law, for example, whether long residence policy had been taken into account in the circumstances (see p 385). The policies remain primarily of use in considering deportation cases.

(a) Ten years
Except where the grant of leave would not be in the public interest, if a person has resided lawfully in the UK for more than ten years continuously, and makes an application based on that residence, it will be considered on its

merits within the terms of a statement by the Minister of State for the Home Department (see *Hansard*, 5 November 1987 (121 HC Official Report (6th Series), Written Answers, cols 833–4)). The Home Office will take into account, among other considerations:

(*a*) strength of ties with the UK or another country;

(*b*) the total length of continuous residence;

(*c*) the proportion of that residence which was lawful.

Each case is considered on its merits. Article 3(3) of the European Convention on Establishment provides that nationals of its contracting parties who have lawfully resided for ten years in the territory of another party can be expelled only for reasons of national security, or serious reasons of public order, public health or public morality. The Home Office states that it applies the principle of the article more widely, the question of the establishment of close ties being of greatest concern.

Indefinite leave to remain should normally be granted if the applicant has ten or more years of lawful continuous residence, and there are no strong countervailing factors, but there is no legitimate expectation that the policy will always prevail: *R v S of S, ex p Musah* [1994] IAR 395. It is a question of fact. In *Umujakporue* ((12448) JCWI B, vol 5, no 10, Autumn 1995 p 10), the appellant had been a student for over ten years, but had spent two of those years in Sligo, Republic of Ireland. During those two years, he had maintained his rented accommodation in London, frequently went back there for long weekends, and met his girlfriend in England. The IAT held that its jurisdiction was to 'review the merits of any discretion contained in a policy if the effect of the policy is to waive the rules in regard to a class of applicants'. The IAT held that the absence of the applicant in Ireland for studies did not destroy his residence in the UK, and stated 'there is no ground on which the Secretary of State could refuse the application for indefinite leave and maintain the policy which he has promulgated'.

Persons with limited leave need to be careful about making applications for indefinite leave under this concession if their leave to be in the UK is approaching a total of ten years. In *Egbulefu* ((11884) JCWI B, vol 5, no 9, Summer 1995) a student applied for indefinite leave to remain based on long residence, or alternatively for an extension of stay as a student. The Home Office conceded before the IAT that an application for an extension in a temporary capacity is not bound to fail when there is also an application for indefinite leave, but the IAT held that it was common sense that an application for indefinite leave under this concession will raise doubts as to the applicant's future intentions which will be displaced only by cogent and credible evidence.

(b) Fourteen years

Where an applicant for indefinite leave to remain has 14 years' or more continuous residence in the UK, whether legal or not in whole or in part, indefinite leave to remain will normally be granted. It may be refused, however, if there is an extant criminal record or a deliberate positive and blatant attempt to evade immigration control. Where an applicant's stay in the UK has exceeded 14 years because of his pursuit of appeals against deportation, there is no obligation on the S of S to have regard to the appeals period in deciding whether to give him the benefit of the concession (*R v S of S, ex p Ofori* [1995] Imm AR 34). In *Frederick* (11747), the Home Office argued before the IAT that the period of 14 years does not lead automatically to indefinite leave to remain, nor would it create any legitimate expectation that such residence should result in the grant of leave. However, the IAT took account of the factors specified in the rules and decided, on the facts of that case, that deportation would not be the proper course. The IAT confined *Musah* (above) to its own facts.

Long residence of less than either of the above periods is also taken into account when considering whether to deport a person. Where the period of residence is long, but does not fall into the above categories, the proportion of lawful residence in the UK and the length of residence will be the primary factors in determining whether to deport.

In *Domfeh Gyeabour* [1989] Imm AR 94, the IAT considered that an overstayer who overstayed nearly 11 years had a legitimate expectation that he would be allowed to remain on the basis of an earlier ministerial statement on the removal of illegal entrants after ten years' residence, (but cf *Musah*, above). Each case is determined on its own facts (*Frederick* (11747)). No legitimate expectation that the applicant would not be deported can be raised on the basis of the ministerial statement where the applicant has been aware that, for half his period of long residence, the S of S intended to deport him (*Mohammed Hussain v IAT* [1991] Imm AR 413). Further, where ten years' residence is relied upon, it must be lawful residence. The person must have had leave for that period, and it is not enough that for some of the time he was protected from removal by s 14(1) of the 1971 Act because he had an appeal pending against a deportation order (*Ex p Mesirionye* [1993] Imm AR 119). Further, the residence required for 14 years must be more than merely ordinary residence (*Ex p F Ali* [1992] Imm AR 316). There have been two ministerial statements on this subject and the S of S relies on the later of the two. He is entitled to change his policy (*Mohammed Miah v S of S* [1992] Imm AR 106).

Appeals against deportation orders are dealt with in Chapter 18.

3 Deportation orders

362. A deportation order requires the subject to leave the United Kingdom and authorises his detention until he is removed. It also prohibits him from re-entering the country for as long as it is in force and invalidates any leave to enter or remain in the United Kingdom given him before the order was made or while it is in force.

363. The circumstances in which a person is liable to deportation are set out in the Immigration Act 1971 and include:

(i) failure to comply with a condition attached to his leave to enter or remain or remaining beyond the time limited by the leave;

(ii) where the Secretary of State deems the person's deportation to be conducive to the public good;

(iii) where the person is the spouse or child under 18 of a person ordered to be
deported; and

(iv) where a court recommends deportation in the case of a person over the age
of 17 who has been convicted of an offence punishable with imprisonment.

COMMENTARY

Under ss 3(5)–(6) and 5(1)–(4) of the 1971 Act the S of S may, if he thinks
fit, make a deportation order requiring a person who does not have the right
of abode to leave and to remain out of the UK:

(a) if the person has failed to comply with a condition attached to his
leave to enter or remain beyond the authorised time (see s 3(5)(a));

(aa) if the person has obtained leave to remain in the UK by deception;

(b) if the S of S deems the person's deportation to be conducive to the
public good (see s 3(5)(b));

(c) if the person is the wife or the child under 18 of a person ordered to
be deported (see s 3(5)(c); and

(d) if the person, after reaching the age of 17, is convicted of an offence
for which he is punishable with imprisonment and the court recommends deportation (see s 3(6)).

The power to deport applies generally to all persons subject to control
under the 1971 Act, including persons who have been granted settlement.
However, it does not apply to any member of a mission (within the meaning
of the Diplomatic Privileges Act 1964); any person who is a member of the
family and forms part of the household of such a member (*Gupta v S of S*
[1979–80] Imm AR 52); or any other person entitled to the like immunity
from jurisdiction as is conferred by the 1964 Act on a diplomatic agent
(s 8(3) of the 1971 Act). Immunity applies only to a member of a mission
other than a diplomatic agent if he enters the UK:

(a) as a member of the mission; or

(b) in order to take up a post which was offered to him before he travelled (s 8(3A) of the 1971 Act; see also *Ex p Bagga* [1990] 3 WLR
1013).

A citizen of the Irish Republic or a Commonwealth citizen who was settled
and has been ordinarily resident in the UK continuously since 1 January
1973 is not liable to be deported on the ground that his deportation is
conducive to the public good. If such a person was settled and ordinarily
resident in the UK on 1 January 1973 and has been so resident for the last
five years (*Mehmet v S of S* [1977] Imm AR 68; and *Rehman v S of S* [1978]
Imm AR 80), he is not liable to deportation on any ground (s 1 of the 1971
Act). In *Ex p O'Shea* [1988] Imm AR 484, the CA held that a woman against
whom a deportation order had been made could not subsequently render
herself immune from deportation by marrying a British citizen, a position

which is now confirmed in para 284(vi) of HC 395 (see also *Ex p Husseyin* [1988] Imm AR 129).

When giving notice of intention to deport, the letter notifying the decision does not have to incorporate precisely the wording of the relevant provision in the 1971 Act. It cannot be argued that because a letter does not incorporate such wording the S of S has applied the wrong test. Something more would be needed (*Jahromi v S of S* [1996] Imm AR 20).

(a) Breach of conditions or unauthorised stay (s 3(5)(a) 1971 Act)

The rules mirror the 1971 Act in stating that the S of S may make a deportation order where a person has failed to comply with a condition attached to his leave to enter or remain. Full account is to be taken of all the relevant circumstances known to the S of S before a decision is reached. An adjudicator should not impose on the appellant some general burden of showing that the S of S had not acted correctly under the rules (*Ashiwaju v S of S* [1994] Imm AR 233). Where there had been persistent failure over a period of nearly five years to comply with the immigration rules, the S of S was held to have exercised his discretion properly in ordering deportation (*S of S v Aluko* [1974] Imm AR 90). In *Jordan v S of S* [1972] Imm AR 201, the IAT emphasised that the exercise of the power of deportation should be 'consistent and fair as between one person and another'. The IAT held that, were the appellants to be permitted to remain in the country, it could hardly be said that such action would be 'consistent and fair' as between them and the many persons overseas subject to UK immigration control whose circumstances and background were similar to those of the appellants.

A person's ignorance that he has overstayed is a compassionate circumstance to be taken into account (*Hanif v S of S* [1985] Imm AR 57). In *Adams* (11657) the IAT considered the health of one of the dependants of the appellants. The appellants had three children who had been born in the UK. One of them had an ear condition which could not be treated in the appellants' own country. The IAT also took account of the disruption to the children's education. This case illustrates the IAT's in effect taking account of factors which also appear in the concession relating to carers (see p 99), and of matters which also arise in the context of the European Convention on Human Rights. The S of S is not, however, obliged to take into account art 12 (right to marry and found a family) when considering making a deportation order (*Ex p Harry Payne* [1995] Imm AR 48).

Students who work in breach Before the 1996 Act there was a concession that genuine students do not normally merit deportation if they work in breach of their conditions. There had to be no doubt about the quality or quantity of the studies they undertook. Deportation was still appropriate if they had seriously broken a prohibition on employment. (See letter from Home Office to JCWI dated 18 July 1989 and *Ex p Amoa* [1992] Imm AR 218.) There had been a move away from this concession in practice, and it is thought that, in the harsher atmosphere following the 1996 Act, this concession is likely to be a dead letter.

(aa) Leave to remain obtained by deception.

The 1996 Act, Sched 2, para 1(2), amended s 3(5) of the 1971 Act, introducing a new category—those who obtain leave to remain by deception— liable to deportation. The S of S will have to prove, on a high standard of probabilities, that the person committed an act of deception. Persons who are to be deported under this provision have a restricted right of appeal under s 5 of the 1988 Act (see p 350). A restricted right of appeal means that the only basis for challenging the S of S's decision to deport is that there was no power in law to make the deportation order. The extent to which this encompasses questions of public law is discussed at p 385. The effect of this amendment is to give power to the S of S to deport a person who has obtained leave to remain by deception *before* the expiry of their limited leave.

The person will not in most cases be able to appeal against the merits of the deportation order. If this power is used, there would be no power in law to make the deportation order if the adjudicator took the view that the extension of leave was not obtained by means of the deception. On the face of the provision the adjudicator could consider whether it was operative in obtaining the leave to remain (however see page 247). The adjudicator would decide this on the weighted balance of probabilities. Before the 1996 amendment it was possible to make a deportation order if the Home Office considered that the deception rendered deportation conducive to the public good, so it is unclear why the new power was necessary (s 3(5)(*b*), 1971 Act and *Re Owusu Sekyere* and *R v IAT, ex p Cheema*, below).

(b) 'Conducive to the public good'

The S of S has the power to deport a person if he deems it conducive to the public good (1971 Act, s 3(5)(*b*)). However, nowhere is the phrase 'conducive to the public good' defined. In *Sharma* (11696) a decision to deport on this ground was taken when a person stabbed his brother in law and was 'sectioned' under the Mental Health Act 1983. His schizophrenia responded well to treatment. The IAT balanced the public interest against the compassionate circumstances of his case. The appellant's parents in India could not afford his treatment. The IAT relied on *Talmasani* [1987] Imm AR 32, stating that it would be inhumane to deport the appellant unless the S of S satisfied himself that adequate arrangements had been made for his reception in the receiving country (see also *Bassi* (10707)). Where a person, after entry, has exercised deception to obtain enlarged rights of entry, this may justify deportation on 'public good' grounds (see *Re Owusu Sekyere* [1987] Imm AR 425 and *R v IAT, ex p Cheema* [1982] Imm AR 124, where marriages of convenience were held to be against the public good) in addition to forming a ground for deportation under *(aa)* above. Further, a person may be deported under this head simply because he was guilty of deception on entry (*R v IAT, ex p Patel* [1988] AC 910). 'Conducive to the public good' does not require the S of S to identify some discernible public interest (other than deterrence of others) to justify deportation (*Goremsandu v S of S* [1996] Imm AR 250).

In *Patel* Lord Bridge reconsidered the view he had expressed in *Khawaja*, that deportation on 'conducive' grounds was never intended to be invoked as a means of deporting a perfectly respectable citizen on grounds arising out of the circumstances of his original entry. He said that view was mistaken: 'Reading the judgment of Lord Lane CJ in *Cheema* I find myself in complete agreement with his opinion that the exercise of the power is within both the literal meaning of s 3(5)(*b*) and the spirit of the Act. If this is correct, there can be no possible ground to distinguish between a fraud practised in order to obtain leave to enter, and a fraud practised after entry to obtain indefinite leave' (see also, eg, the CA in *R v IAT, ex p Sheikh* (1988) *The Times*, 17 March: original bribery to gain entry justified deportation under s 3(5)(*b*) despite a respectable life thereafter).

Each case is to be considered carefully in the light of the relevant circumstances known to the S of S, including the general considerations listed above. Usually, the S of S should give a person in respect of whom deportation on this ground is contemplated an opportunity to state his case (*Afful v S of S* [1986] Imm AR 230). Both legal entrants and persons who are 'not legally here' may be deported for reasons of public good (*Villone v S of S* [1979–80] Imm AR 23).

In *Butt v S of S* [1979–80] Imm AR 82, the S of S deemed that it would be 'conducive to the public good' to deport the appellant, an illegal entrant, who was convicted of offences of theft and criminal damage and was given a suspended sentence, although the court made no recommendation for his deportation and his conviction followed several years of residence.

In *R v IAT, ex p A-V* (1989) *The Times*, 22 August, Rose J stated that an IAT should consider the effects of the deportation order when considering compassionate circumstances. In that case the person was to be deported to a country in which he would face the death penalty for the crime of which he had been convicted. The IAT should take into account double jeopardy, and should compare like cases only for the purposes of achieving consistency and fairness.

A decision to deport frequently arises where a person has been convicted of a criminal offence but the court has not made a recommendation for deportation (see *Patel v S of S* [1986] Imm AR 457). In *Villone*'s case (see above) the IAT considered it to be 'perfectly plain' that it was 'conducive to the public good' to make a deportation order against him. He was sentenced to three years' imprisonment for offences under the Misuse of Drugs Act 1971 and the Customs and Excise Act 1952. In addition, the appellant had been charged in the USA on 14 separate occasions with drug offences, armed robbery, possessing an unlawful weapon, and being a fugitive from justice. He had been sentenced to terms totalling ten years' imprisonment. Furthermore, he was at the time wanted in the USA on charges of possessing stolen credit cards and a concealed weapon.

Some criminal offences are of so serious a nature as to justify deportation under this head even if there is no record of previous offences and no great likelihood that the individual will reoffend (*R v IAT, ex p Florent* [1985] Imm AR 141, where the CA gave as an example the supply of heroin).

To show that a decision to deport as conducive to the public good based purely on a criminal conviction is not justified, it is necessary to show that it is either wrong in law or administratively unreasonable. The principles relating to the exercise by a court of its power to recommend deportation do not affect the S of S's power to make a deportation order on 'conducive' grounds (*Hukan Said v IAT* [1989] Imm AR 372 and *Al-Sabah v S of S* [1992] Imm AR 223).

Because of the general nature of this power it is often used in situations where a material fact has been omitted to deceive the S of S as to the effect and implication of what has been said (*R v IAT, ex p A R Patel* [1988] Imm AR 434, but now see *(aa)* above). A deportation order may be made on this ground notwithstanding that the deportee has made an application for variation of leave to remain which has not been determined (*Ex p Manvinder Kaur* [1991] Imm AR 426).

(c) Recommendation by a criminal court

By s 3(6) of the 1971 Act any person without the right of abode (save those listed on p 257), aged 17 and over, who has been convicted of a criminal offence punishable by imprisonment, may be recommended for deportation by the criminal court which sentences him for the offence as part of his sentence.

Before a criminal court makes a recommendation, the defendant must be given the opportunity to address it on the question (*R v Antypas* (1973) 57 Cr App R 207), and the criminal court should give full reasons for its decision to make a recommendation (*R v Compassi* (1987) 9 Cr App R(S) 270). In *R v Nazari* [1980] 3 All ER 880, the CA set out the following guidelines as to the matters that a criminal court considering recommending deportation should take into account (see also *R v Caird* (1970) 54 Cr App R 499):

(1) The court must consider whether the defendant's continued presence in the UK is to its detriment. A minor offence such as shoplifting would not normally merit recommendation of deportation.

(2) The courts are not concerned with the political systems which operate in other countries. That is a matter for the Home Secretary to take into account when deciding whether to act on the recommendation (however, in *R v Walters* (1977) *Thomas's Encyclopedia of Current Sentencing Practice* K 1.5(b), special hardship to the defendant was taken into account).

(3) The court must take into account the effect which an order recommending deportation will have on others who are not before the court and who are innocent persons. For example, will the order put an innocent spouse in the difficult position of having to choose between going abroad or remaining in the UK without the deported spouse in the interests of the children?

It may be appropriate to make a recommendation of deportation following a conviction even where the person concerned no longer has any ties to his country of origin (*R v Kanapathipillai* (1988) *The Times*, 26 March). If the defendant is an overstayer, that by itself is not a ground for a recommendation for deportation (*Miller v Lenton* (1981) Cr App R(S) 171). The court should give proper reasons for its recommendation. If it fails to do so, but the recommendation is nevertheless justified, the CA may supply reasons (see *R v Ozen* (1996) *The Times*, 15 August, *R v Belaifa* (1996) *The Times*, 27 February).

The 'detriment' must be to the community. Where a person was convicted of a single serious offence of wounding but otherwise was exemplary, a recommendation was not appropriate (*R v Idriss* (1977) *Thomas's Encyclopedia of Current Sentencing Practice* K1.5(a)). In *R v Ariquat* (1981) Cr App R(S) 83, the 19-year-old defendant was convicted of indecent assault for having had intercourse with a 15-year-old believing her to be over 16. A recommendation was quashed on appeal. Where the defendant was convicted of a serious offence of arson, the emotional stress under which he was acting was properly to be taken into account in deciding whether or not to make a recommendation (*R v Tshuma* (1981) 3 Cr App R(S) 97).

If the defendant is reliant on social security, that is not to the detriment of the community and should not be taken into consideration in deciding whether or not to make a recommendation (*R v Serry* (1980) 3 Cr App R(S) 336).

Where the court has not recommended deportation there may nevertheless be grounds, in the light of all the relevant information and subject to the right of appeal, for deportation, curtailment of stay or refusal to extend stay, followed, after supervised departure, by a prohibition on re-entry. A recommendation, or the failure to make a recommendation, by a criminal court, does not in any way limit the discretionary powers of the S of S under s 3(5)(*b*). In particular, it is not *res judicata* (*Martin v S of S* [1993] Imm AR 161). The recommendation may be appealed against via the criminal appeal system.

The European Convention on Human Rights In *R v IAT, ex p Chundawadra* [1987] Imm AR 227 the CA rejected the argument that the UK's signing of the European Convention on Human Rights created a legitimate expectation that the S of S would abide by its obligations under art 8 (right to family life) and art 13 (right to an effective remedy). The CA held that the S of S is duly obliged to take account of what was expressly or impliedly authorised by the 1971 Act and the immigration rules. However in *Beldjoudi v France* (1992) *The Times*, 10 April, the European Court of Human Rights held that a French deportation order against a man who had married was in breach of art 8. The court held that it was not justified by a pressing social need, nor proportionate to the legitimate aim of immigration control pursued by France. In *Chundawadra*, the CA stated that the European Court of Human Rights may give different answers to the questions 'Is the deportation conducive to the public good?' and 'Is it necessary for the protection of the public?'. It may be that a deportation order may be challenged before the European Court of Human Rights on the basis of a breach of art 8 if it breaks up a family, for example, or prevents a person having access to a child or *vice versa*. The deportation order would also have to be necessary for the public good or for the prevention of crime. In *Berrehab v Netherlands* (1988) 11 EHRR 322, the expulsion of a father on the basis of public order was successfully challenged on the ground that it was not so necessary as to outweigh his daughter's (and his) rights to family life. Moreover, in the course of the committee debates in the House of Commons on the Asylum and Immigration Appeals Act 1993, the Minister stated that exceptional leave to remain would be granted in genuine humanitarian cases in which the UK's international obligations would otherwise be broken. It is arguable therefore that if a deportation order is made which would have the effect of violating a child's right to family life, the S of S should grant the parent exceptional leave to remain as the only way of securing the child's right. Refusal to do so could be challenged by way of judicial review of the S of S's decision (see *Hansard,* Standing Committee A, 12 November 1992, col 52). It may further be argued that in any event a deportation order which would interfere with a family unit would be in breach of the S of S's own guidelines (set out on p 264 *et seq*) on enforcement of deportation action where marriage or children are involved.

4 Considerations to be taken into account

364. In considering whether deportation is the right course on the merits, the public interest will be balanced against any compassionate circumstances of the case. While each case will be considered in the light of the particular circumstances, the aim is an exercise of the power of deportation which is consistent and fair as between one person and another, although one case will rarely be identical with another in all material respects. Deportation will normally be the proper course where a person has failed to comply with or has contravened a condition or has remained without authority. Before a decision to deport is reached the Secretary of State will take into account all relevant factors known to him including:

(i) age;
(ii) length of residence in the United Kingdom;
(iii) strength of connections with the United Kingdom;
(iv) personal history, including character, conduct and employment record;
(v) domestic circumstances;
(vi) previous criminal record and the nature of any offence of which the person has been convicted;
(vii) compassionate circumstances;
(viii) any representations received on the person's behalf.

COMMENTARY

(a) The public interest

In considering whether deportation is the right course on the merits the public interest is balanced against any compassionate circumstances of the case. One case will rarely be identical with another in all material aspects. So, for example, a non-EU national cannot rely on the rules applicable to EU nationals in this area (see *R v IAT ex p Al-Sabah* [1992] Imm AR 223).

The only duty on the S of S is to take account of every relevant factor known to him at the time of the decision. There is no duty on the S of S to investigate any of the matters listed above. The list is not exhaustive. Thus the fact of a person's increasing age, and the fact that he did not 'go to ground' may outweigh the presumption in favour of deportation (*Sultan* (11885) and JCWI B, vol 5, no 9, Summer 1995, p 11). Likewise the effect on third parties, other than his family and persons immediately connected with him, of deporting a particular individual may well be a factor which is relevant to the discretionary decision whether he should or should not be deported. In *R v IAT, ex p Bakhtaur Singh* [1986] Imm AR 352, the HL held that it was relevant to take into account the loss to the Sikh community of a priest and musician with a rare talent. Likewise, account could be taken of the effect of deporting a successful businessman on the business concerned, or the effect of the loss of a scientist on important research. It is not appropriate to take into account improper pressure, such as the threat of industrial action, if a person is deported.

A person who has been deported may not return to the UK while the deportation order is in force. Where a person returns to the UK notwithstanding that a deportation order is in force against him, he may lawfully be detained as an illegal entrant and deported under the original order or removed as an illegal entrant.

(b) Policy guidance

In *R v IAT, ex p Chundawadra* [1987] Imm AR 227, Taylor J held that the European Convention on Human Rights, and specifically art 8, which requires that family life be respected, was not required to be taken into account in a decision whether or not to deport. However, since January 1993 immigration officers have been provided with guidance on cases involving marriage and children, which take into account the effect of the European Convention on Human Rights. The most recent guidance (superseding DP 2/93) is contained in Home Office policy guidance notices DP 3/96 (marriage policy), DP 4/96 (children), and DP 5/96 (children with long residence). See 1996 INL&P vol 10, no 2, p 71 for a discussion of these policies; for the full text see INL&P 1996 vol 10, no 3. A flow chart attached to DP 3/96 appears at the end of this chapter (see p 280).

The S of S should have regard to the policy in deciding whether to deport, and he may act irrationally if he fails to do so (*Ex p Amankwah* [1994] Imm AR 240). In *Plummer* (12167) the appellant against deportation argued that the S of S had not taken into account the marriage guidelines (then DP 2/93), and had therefore not considered all the relevant circumstances. European cases have shown that, however unmeritorious the applicant's immigration history, the European Court of Human Rights is disposed to find a breach of art 8 where the effect of an immigration decision is to separate an applicant from his spouse or child. In *Ex p Hastrup* (1996) *The Times* 15 August, the CA held that nothing in DP 2/93 fettered the S of S's discretion, although it did give him guidance, and in particular his discretion was not fettered by policy guidance that in such cases immigration history was rarely relevant. The policy did not say that immigration history was never significant and it was therefore not unlawful for him to deport a man with a bad record of immigration offences even though he was married to a British citizen and they had a British child.

The guidelines DP 2/93, 3/96, 4/96 and 5/96 contain limitations. In *Ex p Sekhon* [1995] Imm AR (QBD) 338 and (CA) 507, it was argued that DP 2/93 was in breach of art 8 of the European Convention on Human Rights, Longmore J stated that this was unarguable because art 8.1 of the ECHR makes clear that the duty to respect family life does not extend to a general duty to respect the choice by married couples of their matrimonial residence and to accept non-national spouses for settlement in that country (see paras 67 and 68 of *Abdul Aziz v UK* [1985] 7 EHRR 471). In *Ex p Bina Patel* [1995] Imm AR 223, Brooke J referred to *R v S of S ex p Brind* [1991] AC 696 at 748 to 749 (and see pp 404 below) and accepted the argument that when the court considers whether a reasonable S of S, on the material before him, could judge whether competing public interests justify an infringement of a Convention right, what it is not doing is standing in the shoes of the European Court of Human Rights and judging whether there has been a breach of the Convention. It is looking at the approach of the S of S and asking: could any rational S of S, reasonably reminding himself of the provisions of the ECHR by which the UK is bound, have reasonably formed the view that the S of S did when he took the administrative decision in this matter (see *Bina Patel*, p 229). The S of S is required to pay attention to an aspect of a case which would indicate a breach of art 8. In Scotland, the Court of Session, in *Irfan Ahmed* [1995] Imm AR 210, stated that the obvious humanitarian principle that respect should be had for family life should not be ignored by the S of S.

The marriage guidelines apply only to deportation and illegal entry cases. They do not apply to cases concerning entry to the UK (*Ex p Comfort Henry* [1995] Imm AR 42, and *Shahed v S of S* [1995] Imm AR 303). Similarly, the marriage has to be subsisting, so the guidelines will not apply where the marriage had broken down (*Dyfan v S of S* [1995] Imm AR 206).

(c) DP 3/96: Marriage policy

Under DP 3/96, marriage is a factor in the decision-making process relating to deportation under para 364 of HC 395 (see p 263). Enforcement action may be halted where there is a genuine and subsisting marriage to a person settled in the UK. A judgement needs to be made about the weight to be attached to the marriage as a compassionate factor. The Home Office will consider the factors relating to marriage in para 284 of HC 395 (see p 210). This sets out the requirements for an extension of stay as a spouse. A person who has overstayed or who has no limited leave does not satisfy the conditions in para 284.

As a general rule, in the absence of a criminal conviction, enforcement action should not normally be initiated if the following conditions are satisfied:

(a) the subject has a genuine and subsisting marriage with someone settled in the UK and the couple have lived together continuously since their marriage for at least two years before the commencement of enforcement action (see *Mirza v S of S* [1996] Imm AR 314); and

(b) it is unreasonable to expect the settled spouse to accompany his spouse on removal.

When the Home Office considers whether it would be unreasonable for the settled person to accompany the subject of the enforcement action, the onus is on the settled person to make out a case, with supporting evidence as to why it is unreasonable for him to live outside the UK (note (ii), DP 3/96). 'Settled' refers to a British citizen who lives in the UK and other nationals who have indefinite leave to enter or remain (note (i), DP 3/96).

The factors the Home Office takes into account, and which should therefore be investigated by advisors so that any evidence concerning them can be put before the case worker, include whether the settled spouse:

(a) has very strong and close family ties in the UK such as older children from a previous relationship that form part of the family unit; or

(b) has been settled and living in the UK for at least the preceding ten years; or

(c) suffers from ill-health and medical evidence conclusively shows that his life would be significantly impaired or endangered if he were to accompany his spouse on removal.

Advisors should therefore ensure that any representations made on behalf of a person who may be subject to enforcement action should cover the above points thoroughly. It may assist if an independent source produces a report on the family circumstances of the settled spouse. Other factors may also be taken into account, and representations should not be limited to the above points.

Under the superseded DP 2/93, the requirement was that the marriage should pre-date the enforcement action. This was held not to have been satisfied in *R v S of S, ex p Jonah* [1995] Imm AR 231, where the marriage preceded signature of the deportation order, but not the court's recommendation for deportation; and see *Ex p Ekewuba* [1995] Imm AR 89. The position under DP 3/96 is clear. The marriage must have existed for two years before commencement of enforcement action, and not just two years before the date on which consideration is given to deportation (see note (iv)). Time which elapses after the commencement of enforcement action while the subject is appealing, making representations, or applying for judicial review cannot be taken into account for the purpose of determining the length of the relationship. Enforcement action, for the purposes of DP 3/96, commences when:

(a) a specific instruction to leave is given, with a warning of liability to deportation if the subject fails to do so; or

(b) a notice of intention to deport, or a set of illegal entry papers is served (this will include cases where illegal entry papers were served during a previous stay in the UK, and the subject has returned illegally); or

(c) there is a recommendation by a criminal court that a person should be deported following a conviction (see p 261).

Each case should be considered on its own merits. A particularly poor immigration history may warrant the subject's enforced departure despite the fact that he satisfies the conditions under the guidance (see note (v), DP 3/96).

The provisions in respect of marriage are set out in the form of a flow chart on p 280.

Criminal convictions In cases where a person liable to immigration control has family ties in the UK which would be taken into account under the guidance for non-criminal cases (above), but has criminal convictions, the severity of the offence(s) should be balanced against the strength of the family ties. The guidance states that in the case of a serious crime which is punishable by imprisonment, or a series of lesser crimes which show a propensity to re-offend, the family ties would normally be outweighed (para 6, DP 3/96). Similarly, a very poor immigration record can be taken into account. The guidance requires case workers to use their judgement to decide what is reasonable in any individual case. Such a subjective reference will not necessarily render the guidance immune from judicial review. The judgement must itself be exercised reasonably.

Children Paragraph 7 of DP 3/96 relates to children. The presence of children with the right of abode in the UK is a factor to be taken into account. Children have this right usually as a result of having been born in the UK to a parent settled in the UK. An illegitimate child has the nationality of his mother, and the father's is irrelevant (see p 27 and note (i) to para 7, DP 3/96). Where the child has the right of abode, the central question is whether it is reasonable for the child to accompany his parents abroad. Paragraph 7 suggests the following as factors which are to be considered, among others:

(a) the age of the child. It states that in most cases a child of ten or younger could reasonably be expected to adapt to life abroad; or

(b) serious ill health for which treatment is not available in the country to which the family is going.

Advisors should ensure that the circumstances of the child are thoroughly covered, by an independent report if possible.

Marriage after enforcement commences Where a person marries after enforcement action commences, the normal course is to continue with enforcement action (see also para 284 at p 210). Marriage in these circumstances does not constitute a sufficiently compassionate circumstance to militate against removal. The Home Office instructs its staff not to make detailed inquiries to ascertain whether the marriage is genuine and subsisting. The onus is on the subject to put forward factors. The instruction is therefore that it is only in the most exceptional circumstances that removal action should be stopped.

For cases involving marriage to EEA nationals, no matter when contracted, see p 327. The internal guidelines will not apply. Where a foreign national has married an EU national who is exercising Community rights in the UK, he may be removed only where there are exceptionally strong grounds for suspicion that the marriage is one of convenience. The guidance refers to the exception to the right of a non-EU national who is a member of an EU national's family to free movement that was envisaged by the ECJ in *Surinder Singh* (see p 328) in cases of fraudulent marriage. The S of S is entitled to deport the husband of a EEA national exercising rights as a worker if he concludes that the marriage is a sham (*Ex p Wai Cheung* [1995] Imm AR 104).

(d) DP 4/96: Children

Divorced and separated parents   DP 4/96 instructs case workers that deportation or illegal entry action should not necessarily be conceded where a person liable to deportation or removal as an illegal entrant (whose marriage has broken down) has access to a child who is entitled to remain in the UK. If he has access rights to the child, the case worker will advise that he should make an application for access visits under paras 246–248 (see pp 185) of the rules. This application must be made from abroad, and entry clearance is required. The Home Office takes the view that because there is a right of appeal against the refusal of such an application, such cases are unlikely to breach art 8 of the European Convention on Human Rights (as family life has broken down) or art 13 (paras 6–8, DP). However, this has yet to be tested. If the person fails to leave after this advice, enforcement action is to be taken. The person should be told that before he can return for an access visit he will have to apply from abroad for revocation of the deportation order. Only in the most exceptional circumstances will the enforcement be conceded to enable a parent to continue access visits. The guidance points out that the immigration rules concerning access visits apply only where the parents are married (para 8). Case workers are instructed that where the parent is already the subject of a deportation order, it may be unreasonable to expect him to return from abroad to apply for entry clearance. In the ordinary case he would be debarred from re-entry for three years (see p 278). In such cases the quality and regularity of the access to the child should be weighed as a compassionate factor.

In respect of marriages which came to the notice of the Home Office before 13 March 1996, the previous (and more liberal) internal guidance (DP 2/93) still applies (see *Amankwah* (above) and DP 3/96 para 10). Under DP 2/93 where one of the divorced or separated parents is settled in the UK, and the removal of the other parent would result in the deprivation of frequent and regular access currently enjoyed by either parent, deportation or removal action will be abandoned by the S of S under the terms of the guidance note. The S of S cannot rely on the argument that the settled parent can travel abroad to continue access, in the light of *Berrehab v Netherlands* (1988) 11 EHRR 322. Where the person to be removed or deported has custody of a child (by a previous partner who is no longer in contact with the child) with the right of abode in the UK the guidance suggests that the factors to be considered are:

(a) the age of the child;

(b) the strength of the child's ties with the UK, including other UK resident family members;

(c) any medical conditions which would be better treated in the UK;

(d) the standard of living (including educational facilities) in the country to which the parent is to be removed.

The guidance assumes that a child of pre-school age can be expected to go to the foreign country. Article 2 of the First Protocol to the European Convention on Human Rights provides for the right to access to education.

Unaccompanied children DP 4/96 also deals with unaccompanied children who are liable to be removed as illegal entrants or deported. The guidance also considers the position of parents with children present in the UK. Enforcement action against children and young persons under the age of 16 who are on their own in the UK should be contemplated only when voluntary departure cannot be arranged. Removal must not be enforced unless the Home Office is satisfied that the child will be met on arrival in his home country and that arrangements for the child's care thereafter are in place. Where there is evidence that the care arrangements are seriously below the standard normally provided in the country concerned, or that they are so inadequate that the child would face a serious risk of harm if returned, consideration should be given to abandoning the enforcement action. In any event, consideration should be given to whether an escort is necessary on the journey (para 3).

Parents In relation to the parents of a child in the UK, the presence of the child in the UK is a factor which is to be balanced against the other factors (see above). In all cases, the longer the child has been in the UK the greater will be the weight to be attached to his existence as a compassionate factor. The general presumption will be that a child who has spent less than ten years in the UK would be able to adapt to life abroad (para 5, DP 4/96). Where the child has been in the UK for more than ten years, the guidance under DP 5/96 applies. As this is a general presumption it may be rebutted by contrary evidence, so advisors should ensure that any independent report dealing with the position of the child should, if possible, deal with the child's perception of a future in his parents' country and, where possible, his likely adaptability. Thus a child who has many friends in the UK may find difficulty adapting to life abroad. A report should also deal with any special medical aspects of a case which might suggest that it would be difficult for the child to adapt to life abroad (eg, a child who suffers from asthma might find it difficult to adapt to a highly polluted environment).

Court proceedings Under the old DP 2/93, where court proceedings for adoption, custodianship, wardship, or a residence order were taken to enable either the parent or child to evade immigration control, the Home Office could intervene in the proceedings only if there was strong evidence (not merely a suspicion) that there has been a serious attempt to circumvent immigration control. The Home Office would then seek to argue that the family proceedings were an abuse of process. The S of S is entitled to remove or deport a person even if a wardship order or residence order under the Children Act 1987 has been made in respect of the person. He does not commit a contempt of court in so doing (*Re T* [1994] Imm AR 368). Under DP 4/96, where there is reason to believe that the purpose of adoption or wardship, custodianship or residence order proceedings is to frustrate enforcement action, and there is evidence to that effect (as in DP 2/93), the Home Office may intervene in the proceedings, and may be joined as a respondent (paras 9–11, DP 4/96). The case worker is instructed that the making of an order under the Children Act 1989 (ie, not wardship) does not by itself deprive the S of S of his power to remove or deport, although it may be something to which he should have regard when deciding whether to exercise his powers.

In *In Re H (a Minor) (Adoption application)* (1996) *The Times*, 9 May, the CA considered the proper approach to intervention by the S of S. The S of S argued that an adoption order should be refused on the basis of *dicta* in *In Re H* [1982] Fam 121, *In Re W* [1986] Fam 54 and *In Re K* [1995] Fam 38. In *In Re H*, Hollings J stated (p 133):

> If the court considers on the evidence and information before it that the true motive of the application is based upon the desire to achieve nationality and the right of abode rather than the general welfare of the minor then an adoption order should not be made ... In every case it is a matter of balancing welfare against public policy, and the wider the implications of the public policy aspect the less weight may be attached to the aspect of the welfare of the particular individual.

The argument that the court should balance the motive to achieve nationality against the motive to promote the welfare of the child was rejected. The S of S argued that a breach of immigration law could be outweighed only by the promotion of the welfare of the child and not by any other consideration. There, the couple were trying to resolve their infertility problems, but the court held that in the ordinary adoption case, the child would have been abandoned by its parents or its parents would be disqualified by disability or conduct from providing adequate parenting themselves. In those circumstances it was natural that the court should pose the question in the form that it had been posed, namely, was the aim of the application to achieve nationality or promote welfare?

Those two are not the only aims that the court might have to consider. While the court has to be on guard against the possibility of abuse, it should investigate whether the arrangement culminating in the adoption application was a device to circumvent immigration regulations and controls.

In Re H does not represent a two-stage test (see *In Re W*). The Family Division judge must dispose of the adoption application by reference principally to s 6 of the Adoption Act 1976, under which he has to have regard to all the circumstances. The first, but not the paramount, consideration is the child's welfare. In that context it is an important consideration that immigration regulations and policy should be upheld. The CA stressed that a misuse of the right to apply for adoption as a device to circumvent immigration controls would always be fatal to an adoption application.

(e) DP 5/96: Children with more than ten years' residence in the UK

The position of children with long residence in the UK who (or whose parents) are subject to enforcement action is addressed in DP 5/96. This defines more clearly the criteria case workers are to apply in considering whether enforcement action should be proceeded with or initiated against parents who have children who were either born in the UK and are aged ten years or over, or where, having come to the UK at an early age, the child has accumulated ten or more years of continuous residence.

Each case is considered on its merits. However the following factors may be relevant:

(a) the length of the parents' residence in the UK without leave;

(b) whether removal has been delayed through protracted (and often repetitive) representations or the parties 'going to ground';

(c) the age of the children;

(d) whether the children were conceived at a time when either of the parents had leave to remain;

(e) whether return to the parents' country of origin would cause extreme hardship for the children or put their health seriously at risk;

(f) whether either of the parents has a history of criminal behaviour or deception.

(para 2, DP 5/96).

Case workers are instructed that, when notifying a decision either to concede or proceed with enforcement action, it is important that full reasons should be given, making it clear that each case is considered on its individual merits.

5 Family members

365. Section 5 of the Immigration Act 1971 gives the Secretary of State power in certain circumstances to make a deportation order against the spouse or child of a person against whom a deportation order has been made. The Secretary of State will not normally decide to deport the spouse of a deportee where:

(i)   he has qualified for settlement in his own right; or

(ii) he has been living apart from the deportee.

366. The Secretary of State will not normally decide to deport the child of a deportee where:

(i)   he and his mother or father are living apart from the deportee; or

(ii) he has left home and has established himself on an independent basis; or

(iii) he married before deportation came into prospect.

367. In considering whether to require a spouse or child to leave with the deportee the Secretary of State will take account of the factors listed in paragraph 364 as well as the following:

(i) the ability of the spouse to maintain himself and any children in the United Kingdom, or to be maintained by relatives or friends without charge to public funds, not merely for a short period but for the foreseeable future; and

(ii) in the case of a child of school age, the effect of removal on his education; and

(iii) the practicability of any plans for a child's care and maintenance in this country if one or both of his parents were deported; and

(iv) any representations made by or on behalf of the spouse or child.

368. Where the Secretary of State decides that it would be appropriate to deport a member of a family as such, the decision, and the right of appeal, will be notified and it will at the same time be explained that it is open to the member of the family to leave the country voluntarily if he does not wish to appeal or if he appeals and his appeal is dismissed.

COMMENTARY

Under the 1971 Act, for the purposes of deportation, X was regarded as a member of Y's family, if Y was a woman, and X was her child under the age of 18 (s 5(4)(b)). If Y was a man, X was regarded as belonging to Y's family if X was either Y's wife, or his child under 18. Schedule 2, para 2, to the 1996 Act replaced this provision with the simpler formulation that, for the purposes of deportation, X is regarded as a member of Y's family, if Y is a woman and X is her husband, or her husband's or her child under the age of 18. Thus, under s 5 of the 1971 Act as amended by the 1996 Act, there is now a power to make a deportation order against the husband or wife or child(ren) under 18 of a person ordered to be deported (this includes an adopted child: *R v IAT, ex p Tohur Ali* [1988] Imm AR 237). It does not matter whether the deportation is following a conviction, breach of a condition, unauthorised stay or on 'conducive' grounds, unless more than eight weeks have elapsed since the deportee left the country under the order (s 5(3)). If the deportation order against the principal deportee ceases to have effect, then the spouse or children under 18 of such a person cannot be deported under this rule (*R v IAT, ex p Ekrem Mehmet* [1977] 1 WLR 795). The amendment under the 1996 Act removes the discrepancy between the sexes under the previous provision.

The S of S can make an order to deport the family members before he makes the order to deport the principal deportee, provided he has already made the decision to deport the principal deportee (*R v IAT, ex p Ibrahim* [1989] Imm AR 111). This is based on the view that in immigration control the family is to be treated as a unit, and that in s 3(5)(c), the words 'is or has been ordered to be' are to be interpreted encompassing the following situations:

(a) where the principal deportee is deported;

(b) where he is ordered to be deported; and

(c) where he is to be deported.

Where the S of S decides that it would be appropriate to deport a member of a family as such, the decision, and the right to appeal, will be notified, and it will at the same time be explained that it is open to the member of the family to leave the country voluntarily if he does not wish to appeal or if he appeals and his appeal is dismissed.

In considering whether to require a wife and children to leave with the 'head of the family' the S of S will take into account all relevant factors known to him, including those listed in para 364 and the following (which is probably not an exclusive list *R v IAT, ex p Bakhtaur Singh* [1986] Imm AR 352):

(a) the ability of the wife to maintain herself and any children in the UK or to be maintained by relatives or friends without charge to public funds, not merely for a short period, but for the foreseeable future;

(b) in the case of a school age child, the effect of removal on his education;

(c) the practicability of a child's care and maintenance in this country if one or both of his parents were deported;

(d) any representations made by or on behalf of the wife or child.

Consideration of the effect on the child's education of removal of a school-age child is designed to address the right of the child to access to education under the First Protocol to the European Convention on Human Rights.

The S of S must give separate consideration to each person considered for deportation (*Yan Yak Wah and Another v Home Office* [1982] Imm AR 16).

Where an appellant obtained entry to this country by deception, remained unlawfully for some four years, and took employment in breach of her conditions of admission, the IAT held that the public interest far outweighed the matters advanced on her behalf, inasmuch as if her conduct was to be condoned it was considered that immigration control would be rendered nugatory (*Anand v S of S* [1978] Imm AR 36).

Where a wife has qualified for settlement in the UK in her own right, for example following four years in approved employment, she has a valid claim to remain notwithstanding the expulsion of her husband, and her deportation will not normally be contemplated. Where the wife has been living apart from the principal deportee it will not normally be right to include her, or any children living with her, in the deportation order.

Paragraph 389 of HC 395 provides that family members may be able to seek readmission to the UK after they cease to be members of the family. This rule reflects the 1971 Act, s 5(3) and (4). A wife ceases to be a family member when the marriage comes to an end. Children cease to be 'members of the family' as defined in the 1971 Act on reaching the age of 18, and their deportation will not normally be contemplated if they have spent some years in the UK and are near that age. Deportation will not normally be appropriate if the child left the family home on taking employment and has established himself on an independent basis, or if he married before deportation came into prospect. In the case of children of school age it is also right to take into account, on the one hand, the disruptive effect of removal on their education and, on the other, whether plans for the care and maintenance in this country are realistic and are likely to be effective if one or both parents were deported. A person who, at the time a deportation order was made against him, was over the age of 18, but near that age, may still be deported despite this view (*Panayiotis Karantoni v S of S* [1987] Imm AR 518).

The IAT will not readily accept that children should be permitted to remain in the UK if this results in their being separated from their parents. In *Ozter and Others v S of S* [1978] Imm AR 137, the IAT held that the disruptive effect on the children's lives, should they be sent back to Cyprus, had been grossly overstated, and to maintain the family unit the children should be with their parents. Thus the S of S, in all the circumstances, was justified in the decision, following the deportation orders against their parents, to deport the appellants (see also *Mustafa and Others v S of S* [1979–80] Imm AR 32).

6 Appeals

Right of appeal against destination
369. In all cases of deportation the person in respect of whom the order has been or is to be made has a right of appeal against the removal directions on the ground that he ought to be removed (if at all) to a country or territory specified by him, other than the one named in the direction (Section 17 of the 1971 Act).

Restricted right of appeal against deportation in cases of breach of limited leave
370. By virtue of Section 5(1) of the Immigration Act 1988, a person who was last given leave to enter the United Kingdom less than 7 years before the date of the decision to make a deportation order against him:
(i)   by virtue of Section 3(5)(*a*) of the Immigration Act 1971 (breach of limited leave); or
(ii) by virtue of Section 3(5)(*aa*) of that Act (leave to remain obtained by deception);
(iii) by virtue of Section 3(5)(*c*) of that Act (as belonging to the family of a person who is or has been ordered to be deported by virtue of Section 3(5)(*a*))
shall not be entitled to appeal under Section 15 of the 1971 Act against that decision except on the ground that on the facts of his case there is in law no power to make the deportation order for the reasons stated in the notice of the decision.

Exemption to the restricted right of appeal
371. This restriction on the right of appeal does not apply to a person who is exempt by virtue of an order made under Section 5(2) of the 1988 Act. The Immigration (Restricted Right of Appeal against Deportation) (Exemption) Order 1993 provides that a person is exempt if he would last have been given leave to enter 7 years or more before the date of the decision to deport but for his having obtained a subsequent leave after an absence from the United Kingdom within the period limited for the duration of the earlier leave.

372. The Order also provides that a person is exempt if his limited leave has been curtailed by the Secretary of State under Section 7(1) or Section 7(1A) of the 1993 Act.

A deportation order made on the recommendation of a Court
373. There is no appeal within the immigration appeal system against the making of a deportation order on the recommendation of a court; but there is a

right of appeal to a higher court against the recommendation itself. An order may not be made while it is still open to the person to appeal against the relevant conviction, sentence or recommendation, or while an appeal is pending.

Where deportation is deemed to be conducive to the public good

374. There is no right of appeal except as to the country of destination (see paragraph 369) where a deportation order is made on the ground that the Secretary of State deems the person's deportation to be conducive to the public good as being in the interests of national security or of the relations between the United Kingdom and any other country or for other reasons of a political nature. Such cases are subject to a non-statutory advisory procedure and the person proposed to be deported on that ground will be informed, so far as possible, of the nature of the allegations against him and will be given the opportunity to appear before the advisers, and to make representations to them, before they tender advice to the Secretary of State.

[Paragraph 375 was deleted by Cm 3365.]

Hearing of appeals

[Paragraph 376 was deleted by Cm 3365.]

377. An appeal against a decision to make a deportation order will be heard by the Tribunal when:
(i) the ground of the decision was that the deportation of the applicant is conducive to the public good, on other than security or political grounds;
(ii) it is an appeal against a decision to make a deportation order against a person as belonging to the family of another person, or an appeal against a refusal to revoke such an order;
(iii) there is a pending appeal under (ii) and the appellant is that other person and the appeal is not under section 8 of the 1993 Act.

378. An order may not be made while it is still open to the person to appeal against the Secretary of State's decision, or while an appeal is pending.

Persons who have claimed asylum

379. In addition to the rights of appeal mentioned above, a person who has claimed asylum may, unless paragraph 379A below applies, also appeal under Section 8 of the 1993 Act against:
(i) a decision to make a deportation order against him by virtue of Section 3(5) of the 1971 Act; or
(ii) a refusal to revoke a deportation order made against him by virtue of Section 3(5) or (6) of the 1971 Act; or
(iii) directions for his removal from the United Kingdom given under Section 16(1)(a) or (b) of the 1971 Act. In such circumstances the appeal will be before a special adjudicator who will also consider any appeal under Part II of the 1971 Act.

379A. A person who has claimed asylum may not appeal under Section 8 of the 1993 Act if:
(i) a deportation order has been made against him on the ground that it is conducive to the public good; or
(ii) the Secretary of State has issued a third country certificate under Section 2(1) of the 1996 Act in respect of his application for asylum, and that certificate has not been set aside upon appeal.

380. A deportation order will not be made against any person if his removal in pursuance of the order would be contrary to the United Kingdom's obligations under the Convention and Protocol relating to the Status of Refugees.

COMMENTARY

For rights of appeal, see Chapter 18. For appeals in asylum cases see Chapter 26. For 'no power in law' see p 351. For the Immigration (Restricted Right of Appeal against Deportation) (Exemption) Order 1993 see p 350. For appeals against destination see p 353. Note that a British Overseas Citizen may be deported on 'conducive' grounds. However, there is a long standing policy that BOCs will not be deported if they are not admissible to any other country. The S of S may have reason to believe that a person will be admitted to another country even where that country states that it is not sure about its decision and that it normally would not admit a person with the criminal convictions of the proposed deportee (see *Kinnare* (11879); see also *R v IAT ex p Sunsara* [1995] Imm AR 15). Appeal against a recommendation of the criminal court is made within the criminal appellate system, as it forms part of the sentence of the court (see p 261).

Paragraph 374 refers to deportations deemed to be conducive for reasons of national security, relations between the UK and any other country, or for other reasons of a political nature. In *Jahromi v S of S* (above), the CA held that the S of S was under no obligation to expand on a statement that the deportation was conducive to the public good on the grounds of national security. There, the reason given was 'the likelihood of your involvement in terrorist activity'. The Court accepted that the S of S is bound to give such reasons as he can. However, expanded reasons for the assertion that a deportation is being made for reasons of national security will not be ordered unless there is evidence that the assertion is being made in bad faith. Where a person has engaged in terrorist activities, whether in the UK or elsewhere, national security could ground a deportation order (*Ex p Raghbir Singh* [1995] Imm AR 446).

There is no right of appeal in such cases, but a panel of advisors (before whom there is no right to be represented) reviews the decision, and the subject of the order is to be informed as far as possible of the nature of the allegations against him. For this procedure see p 360. Where national security etc is not an issue, there is a right of appeal to the IAT against a decision that deportation is conducive to the public good.

The obligation on a state not to expel or return a refugee to the frontiers of a country where his life or freedom would be threatened for a Convention reason does not apply to a refugee if there are reasonable grounds for regarding him as a danger to the security of the country in which he is recognised, or who, having been convicted by a final judgment of a particularly serious crime, constitutes a danger to the community (art 33(2), 1951 Convention; see Chapter 25). In such cases the status of refugee does not avail the person. However, in the context of deportation, the possibility of ill-treatment in the country to which he is to be returned is a factor to be taken into account (*Raziastaraie v S of S* [1995] Imm AR 459).

7 Procedure

381. When a decision to make a deportation order has been taken (otherwise than on the recommendation of a court) a notice will be given to the person concerned informing him of the decision and of his right of appeal, or facility to make representations in the case of the security and political cases subject to the advisory procedure.

382. Following the issue of such a notice the Secretary of State may make a detention order, or any order restricting a person as to residence, employment or occupation and requiring him to report to the police, pending the making of a deportation order.

383. Where a person is detained pending an appeal, he may apply to an adjudicator for release on bail.

384. If a notice of appeal is given within the period allowed, a summary of the facts of the case on the basis of which the decision was taken will be sent to the appellate authorities, who will notify the appellant of the arrangements for the appeal to be heard.

Arrangements for removal

385. A person against whom a deportation order has been made will normally be removed from the United Kingdom. The power is to be exercised so as to secure the person's return to the country of which he is a national, or which has most recently provided him with a travel document, unless he can show that another country will receive him. In considering any departure from the normal arrangements, regard will be had to the public interest generally, and to any additional expense that may fall on public funds.

386. The person will not be removed as the subject of a deportation order while an appeal may be brought against the removal directions or such an appeal is pending.

Supervised departure

387. A person liable to deportation may, in certain circumstances, leave the United Kingdom by means of supervised departure without having a deportation order made against him.

Returned deportees

388. Where a person returns to this country when a deportation order is in force against him, he may be deported under the original order. The Secretary of State will consider every such case in the light of all the relevant circumstances before deciding whether to enforce the order.

Returned family members

389. Persons deported in the circumstances set out in paragraphs 365–368 above (deportation of family members) may be able to seek re-admission to the United Kingdom under the Immigration Rules where:
(i) a child reaches 18 (when he ceases to be subject to the deportation order); or
(ii) in the case of a wife, the marriage comes to an end.

COMMENTARY

The rules do not clearly distinguish the stages of enforcement by deportation. First, the decision to make a deportation order is made. In the normal case, the subject of the order is informed of his right to appeal (para 381). For rights to apply for bail, see p 373. Where there is no appeal against that decision, or the appeal fails, the S of S then signs a deportation order, and at that stage in practice there is usually an opportunity to make further representations. There is no right of appeal against the signing of the deportation order. For time limits on appeals, see Chapter 18.

The deportee may renounce his right to appeal against the decision to deport him and leave voluntarily. His passport is endorsed to reflect the fact that he was served with the decision to deport. The three-year exclusion period does not apply to him. He is not automatically an illegal entrant if he attempts to return within the three-year period. He pays his own fare if the departure is voluntary.

A person who is liable to deportation may in certain circumstances leave the UK by means of a supervised departure instead of a deportation order being made against him. After his departure the S of S may direct that he should be refused leave to enter or entry clearance, to prevent his return to the UK. Again, his passport is endorsed to reflect that he was served with a notice of intention to deport. The S of S pays his air fare. Obviously, the endorsements will be taken into account on any attempted return.

There is no limitation on the period of the prohibition, nor is there a right of appeal if the person is refused entry or entry clearance on the grounds that he is prohibited (1971 Act, s 13(5)). In those circumstances his only potential remedy is judicial review.

8   Revocation

390. An application for revocation of a deportation order will be considered in the light of all the circumstances including the following:
(i)   the grounds on which the order was made;
(ii)   any representations made in support of revocation;
(iii) the interests of the community, including the maintenance of an effective immigration control;
(iv)   the interests of the applicant, including any compassionate circumstances.

391. In the case of an applicant with a serious criminal record continued exclusion for a long term of years will normally be the proper course. In other cases revocation of the order will not normally be authorised unless the situation has been materially altered, either by a change of circumstances since the order was made, or by fresh information coming to light which was not before the court which made the recommendation or the appellate authorities or the Secretary of State. The passage of time since the person was deported may also in itself amount to such a change of circumstances as to warrant revocation of the order. However, save in the most exceptional circumstances, the Secretary of State will not revoke the order unless the person has been absent from the United Kingdom for a period of at least 3 years since it was made.

392. Revocation of a deportation order does not entitle the person concerned to re-enter the United Kingdom; it renders him eligible to apply for admission under the Immigration Rules. Application for revocation of the order may be made to the Entry Clearance Officer or direct to the Home Office.

Rights of appeal in relation to a decision not to revoke a deportation order

393. Where an application for revocation is refused there is a right of appeal, in the first instance to an adjudicator, unless the order was made against a person as belonging to the family of another person in which case it lies to the Tribunal.

394. No appeal lies while the person is in the United Kingdom or where the Secretary of State personally decides that continued exclusion from the United Kingdom is conducive to the public good.

395. Where an appeal does lie the right of appeal will be notified at the same time as the decision to refuse to revoke the order.

COMMENTARY

An application for revocation of a deportation order may be made to an ECO or direct to the Home Office. Once the order is revoked, the applicant for entry must satisfy the entry conditions afresh. The grant of entry clearance by an ECO who is not aware that there is a deportation order extant against the applicant cannot amount to an implied revocation of the deportation order (*Watson v Immigration Officer, Gatwick Airport* [1986] Imm AR 75).

Applications for revocation are considered in the light of all the circumstances, including the grounds on which the order was made and the community's interests, including the interest in maintaining effective immigration control. Where the deportee was convicted of a serious criminal offence, it is unlikely that the order will be revoked until the offence is spent under the Rehabilitation of Offenders Act 1974, and para 391 makes it clear that exclusion for a long term of years will normally be appropriate. Otherwise the order probably will not be revoked unless the applicant can point to a change in circumstances, or to fresh information which was not available to the authorities who made or approved the original order. Marriage after the order has been signed may be taken into account (*Ex p Yesufu* [1987] Imm AR 366, but see *R v IAT ex p Palomeno* [1987] Imm AR 42). It was not unreasonable for the S of S to refuse to revoke a deportation order where the order had been 'served on the file' of the subject of it. This practice was acknowledged to be unfair, but in *Ex p Makhan Singh* (14 December 1976) noted at [1995] Imm AR 299), Bridge LJ stated that the regulation which in effect permitted service on the file where the whereabouts of the person cannot be ascertained, was *intra vires* (see *Ex p Yurteri* [1995] Imm AR 296). For the practice of service of the notice of deportation at the last known address of the person see p 365 and *Tongo v S of S* [1995] Imm AR 109.

Passage of time itself may amount to a change in circumstances, but unless 'the most exceptional circumstances' are shown to exist, an order will not be revoked before the subject of the deportation order has been absent from the UK for a period of at least three years since it was made.

There is a right of appeal to the adjudicator where the application for revocation is refused. A family member may appeal to the IAT. There is no right of appeal against a decision that continued exclusion is conducive to the public good.

9   Deportation of EEA nationals

This topic is dealt with in Chapter 16. A EEA national may be deported under the terms of EC Directive 64/221, only if for example, the person demonstrates a propensity to commit crimes (*Beierlein* (11352) and JCWI B, vol 5 no 7, Winter 1994; see by way of contrast *Maio* (11881) and p 304). In *Ex p Radiom* (Lexis, 3 February 1995) Jowitt J referred questions of the proper interpretation of arts 8 and 9 of Directive 64/221, relating to removal of EU citizens, to the ECJ (see p 304).

Flow chart from DP 3/96: marriage policy

This flow chart should be used as a guide only. Occasionally cases fall outside the guidelines.

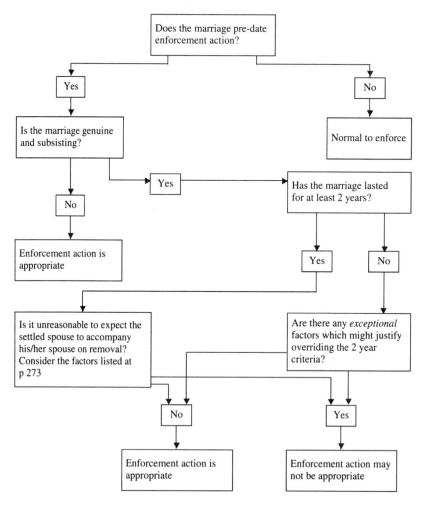

Part III

Procedure

Chapter 15

Examination, Detention and Release

1 Examination by the immigration authorities

(a) Powers to examine

Under the 1971 Act, Sched 2, immigration officers have extensive powers of examination and detention. These must be exercised without regard to the race, colour or religion of prospective entrants (HC 395, Introduction, para 2).

In order to carry out an examination, an immigration officer may board and search any ship, aircraft or vehicle entering via the Channel Tunnel system. He may examine any person on board a ship or aircraft which has landed in the UK, or in a vehicle entering through the Channel Tunnel system, whether or not the person intends to enter the UK. An immigration officer may board a train entering via the Channel Tunnel system and exercise powers of examination in relation to its passengers (Channel Tunnel Act 1987, s 12).

The purpose of the examination is:

  (a) to discover whether or not any passenger is a British citizen;
  (b) if not, whether or not he may enter the UK without leave; and
  (c) if not, whether he should be given leave, and if so for what period and subject to what conditions.

Immigration officers may also examine persons seeking to leave the UK.

Schedule 2 provides for two types of examination by an immigration officer. First, the immigration officer may question an entrant in a wide-ranging way and may draw adverse inferences from a refusal to answer questions (*Immigration Officer Birmingham v Mohammad Sadiq* [1978] Imm AR 115). An entrant is not subject to any duty of candour amounting to a requirement of utmost good faith to disclose all material facts if he has not been specifically asked a question regarding them (*R v S of S, ex p Khawaja* [1984] AC 74). If a person has had a stamp placed in his passport before or during his journey to the UK by an immigration officer, which states that he may enter the UK for either an indefinite period or a limited period, he shall be deemed to have been given the leave on his arrival, and may be examined at the port of entry by an immigration officer only for the purposes of ascertaining whether he is such a person. He is not subject to examination under the powers conferred on the immigration officer under the 1971 Act for any other purpose (Immigration Act 1988, s 8). Such a person may have his deemed leave to enter cancelled within 24 hours of his arrival at the port at which he sought entry, or within 24 hours of his examination as to his identity. Such cancellation must be notified to the person in writing (1988 Act, s 8(5)).

The second type of examination pursuant to Sched 2 is a medical examination. This is done to establish whether there are medical reasons for refusing entry. If an immigration officer gives a person leave to enter, but considers that a further medical examination may be desirable in the interests of public health, he may require the entrant, by notice in writing, to submit to one. The procedure for further examination is that the entrant is required to report his arrival to a medical officer of health, and thereafter, if that officer considers it necessary, to undergo a further examination.

(b) Documents

A document of particular importance which may be demanded by the immigration officer is a valid passport with a photograph, or some other means of establishing identity and nationality. The immigration officer is entitled to detain the passport until either leave to enter is given, or the applicant is about to depart, having been refused entry (1971 Act, Sched 2, para 4(2A) as amended by the 1988 Act).

A person who is being examined by an immigration officer must, if required by the officer, declare whether or not he is carrying or conveying, or has carried or conveyed, documents which appear to the officer to be relevant for the purpose of the examination. The person must produce any documents of the description specified by the officer which he is carrying or conveying (Sched 2, para 4(2)(b), 1971 Act as amended by Sched 2, para 5(1), 1996 Act). By para 4(3), after he has made a declaration, he and any baggage belonging to him or under his control may be searched with a view to ascertaining whether he is carrying such documents. By para 5(3), Sched 2, 1971 Act (as amended by para 5(2), Sched 2, 1996 Act), the power of the immigration officer, or person acting under his directions, to search baggage is extended, first, for the purpose of ascertaining whether the person *has been* carrying or conveying documents. Second, the places which may be searched are extended to:

(a) any baggage or vehicle belonging to him or under his control;
(b) any ship, aircraft or vehicle in which he arrived in the UK.

Third, the purpose of the search is broadened to include checking to see whether the person has carried or conveyed the documents.

In addition, an immigration officer may ask to see documents of 'any description appearing to an immigration officer to be relevant for the purposes of carrying out the examination'. By necessary implication, such documents must be genuine (*Chan v S of S* [1992] Imm AR 233). In order to see if a person is carrying (or has carried) relevant documents the immigration officer may search that person's luggage. If any documents are found the person may be detained for up to seven days by the immigration officer. If it seems likely that any such document may be required for an appeal under the Act, the officer may keep it until it appears no longer to be necessary. Finally, under the Immigration (Landing and Embarkation Cards) Order 1975 (SI 1975 No 65), passengers who:

(a) are over 16;

(b) are leaving and entering the UK;

(c) do not have the right of abode;

(d) are not travelling within the common travel area

may be required to produce embarkation and landing cards to the immigration authorities. This provision does not apply to EC nationals.

(c) PACE

Guidelines have been issued to immigration officers requiring them to follow the Police and Criminal Evidence Act 1984 (PACE) Codes of Practice when conducting examinations pursuant to their power under the 1971 Act. However, a person does not have a right to have a legal representative present at an interview. The immigration officer's discretion to permit legal representation at an interview must be exercised on proper and relevant grounds (*Ex p Vera Lawson* [1994] Imm AR 58). The CA, in *Agbenowossi-Koffi* [1995] Imm AR, 524, held that an immigration officer is not under an obligation to administer a caution before questioning a person seeking leave to enter the UK. This was an unreserved decision on a renewed application for leave to apply for judicial review (see Chapter 22). In many cases the immigration officer may be interested in establishing whether or not the person he is interviewing is an illegal entrant. He will be bound by the PACE Codes where he is investigating offences. Moreover, he is bound by the administrative guidelines referred to above when he is not conducting investigations into offences. A variety of views have been expressed. In *Ex p Ogunlande* [1992] COD 46, it was doubted whether the Codes applied. However, in *Ex p Okusanya* [1993] Imm AR 13, Macpherson J acknowledged that the S of S has decided that immigration officers will apply the relevant aspects of the Codes in investigations. In *Ex p Eid Mohammed Ibrahim* [1993] Imm AR 125 he proposed a solution to the apparent difficulty that in any interview a charge of illegal entry may potentially be brought:

> the fact is that the immigration officers were considering immigration questions but they were also investigating an offence because, to come into this country by deception and to be an illegal entrant, does constitute a criminal offence for which a charge can be levelled. So that the Code and [PACE] plainly, in my judgment applied to the interview.

Evidence obtained as a result of a breach of the PACE Codes may be excluded. The test is whether the particular investigations relate to a matter in respect of which 'a charge can be levelled', not whether there is an intention on the part of the immigration officers to level such a charge. No cases were brought to the attention of the CA in *Agbenowossi-Koffi* (above). The correct position is probably that where the immigration officer is concerned with whether the person is an illegal entrant, PACE applies; but where the immigration officer is simply questioning an entrant to determine whether leave to enter should be granted, no caution is necessary.

(d) Notice of leave or refusal

A person is to be told the outcome of an examination within 24 hours of the end of the examination. However, an examination may continue for a long period, and in *R v Chief Immigration Officer, Manchester Airport, ex p Insah Begum* [1973] 1 All ER 594, the CA held that it was not concluded until all the necessary information has been gathered (see also *Perera v Immigration Officer, London (Heathrow) Airport* [1979–80] Imm AR 58). An examination is ended when the immigration officer concludes that a second interview is not necessary (*Ex p V* [1988] Imm AR 561).

If no notice refusing leave to enter is given within 24 hours of the conclusion of the examination, the entrant is deemed to have been granted six months' leave to enter subject to a condition prohibiting employment (1971 Act, Sched 2, para 6(1), as amended by the Immigration Act 1988, Sched, para 8). Indefinite leave to remain is obtained if the stamp was made before 1 August 1988, when para 6(1) was amended. There must be an examination of the person for the benefit of para 6(1) to be claimed (*Ex p Balwinder Kumar* [1990] Imm AR 265). Such leave is not obtained where an entrant is mistakenly waived through without inspection, even where the person behaves with no impropriety personally and where the immigration officer had no knowledge or thought of the need for a decision to be made on the person's entry (*Ex p Rehal* [1989] Imm AR 576). Clearly a person who absconds from detention before enquiries were completed could not subsequently claim that he had secured leave to enter because his 'examination' had not been completed in accordance with Sched 2 to the 1971 Act (*Ex p Awais Butt* [1994] Imm AR 11 and see para 21(3) of Sched 2 to the 1971 Act). Where the immigration officer concludes that the person does not need leave to enter, whether or not that conclusion is the result of a mistake, negligence or deception, the person entering is an illegal entrant and cannot claim the benefit of Sched 2, para 6(1) (*Ex p Bagga* [1990] 3 WLR 1013). Further, the examination must have been concluded for the paragraph to apply (*S of S v Sittampalam Thirukumar* [1989] Imm AR 402). If a notice is withdrawn as procedurally incorrect, the examination to which the 1971 Act refers is deemed to continue from the moment the notice loses its effect until a further decision is taken. Thus the person does not obtain six months' leave to enter from the moment the first notice is withdrawn (*Ex p Siddique* [1992] Imm AR 127). Schedule 2, para 21(3) disapplies para 6(1) in the case of absconders (see p 289).

Illegible stamps Where an entry stamp is ambiguous because it is illegible, the stamp does not constitute effective notice in writing for the purposes of the 1971 Act, s 4(1) (*Ex p Betancourt* [1988] Imm AR 78).

Accordingly, a person was deemed by virtue of para 6(1) to have been given six months' leave to enter, 24 hours after the illegible stamp was made (see also *IAT v Lakhani* [1988] Imm AR 474 and *Ex p Minton* [1990] Imm AR 199). If the illegible stamp was made before 1 August 1988 its effect is to grant the entrant indefinite leave to remain 12 hours after the stamp was made. The notice may be defective for other reasons, and where no statement of appeal rights appears on a notice, the applicant may rely on para 6(1) (*Ex p Lateef* [1991] Imm AR 334). Where a stamp contains two dates, either of which may be that from which a period of leave runs, any ambiguity is resolved in favour of the applicant (*S of S v Behrooz* [1991] Imm AR 82).

(e) Removal of illegal entrants and persons refused leave

Immigration officers are empowered to make arrangements for the removal of illegal entrants and persons who are refused leave to enter. This they may do by giving directions to the captain of the ship or aircraft on which the passenger arrived, or to the owners or agents of any such ship or aircraft (*R v Immigration Officer, ex p Shah* [1982] 1 WLR 544), or to the concessionaires of the Channel Tunnel. Paragraph 9(1) provides that the power to remove arises where the person is an illegal entrant and is not given leave to enter. Paragraph 9(2) provides that any leave to enter the UK which is obtained by deception is disregarded for the purposes of considering whether the illegal entrant was given leave to enter (para 9(2) inserted by para 6, Sched 2, 1996 Act).

The power therefore arises where the person is an illegal entrant, is known to be such, and is not subsequently given leave to enter. Leave to enter, given at a time when it is not known whether a person is a legal or illegal entrant, is irrelevant for the purposes of the exercise of the removal power (*Ex p Lapinid* [1984] 3 All ER 257, and para 9(2), Sched 2, 1971 Act). The power to remove arises where a person has entered unlawfully and is not thereafter given leave to remain (*Ex p Razak* [1986] Imm AR 44).

Directions for removal, when issued by an immigration officer, must be issued within two months of the date on which leave was refused; after that time they are ineffective *(Ex p Singh (Parshottam)* [1989] Imm AR 469). In any case in which the S of S considers it to be impracticable for directions to be given by an immigration officer, he may give directions himself. The same applies if such directions, if given, would be ineffective. He *must* give the directions himself if two months have expired since the entrant was refused leave. These directions must specify the country to which the entrant is to be removed (paras 10(1) and 8(1)(c)). In the normal case, the entrant will be removed to his country of citizenship. The S of S pays the costs of complying with a removal direction which he issues. Before removal from the UK a person should be given an opportunity to contact friends and relations in the UK, or his High Commission or consul.

Asylum seekers Asylum seekers are protected from removal while their applications are being considered and in certain cases during the period in which they either appeal or may appeal (1993 Act, s 6 and Sched 2, paras 7 and 8; and see the ministerial statements referred to in Chapter 26). However, the provisions of Sched 2 to the 1971 Act apply to asylum seekers, and pending the giving of a direction for their removal they could be detained while the appeal process is exhausted. During that time no deportation order could be signed, but para 16(2) of Sched 2 to the 1971 Act applies to a person in respect of whom removal directions *could* be given, and authorises detention (*S of S v Rehmat Khan* [1995] Imm AR 348).

2 Detention of persons liable to examination or removal

The 1971 Act, Sched 2, para 16 gives wide powers of detention to immigration officers in two circumstances. The first is that if a person is liable to examination, he may be detained under the authority of an immigration officer until he is examined and the result of the examination is notified. The second is that any person in respect of whom directions for removal may be made may be detained until those directions are given and, once they are given, until he is removed pursuant to them. A person may be removed from a ship or aircraft in order to be detained under para 16. At the same time, an entrant may be ordered by an immigration officer to be detained on board a ship or aircraft if he has been refused leave to enter.

Any person who is thus liable to detention may be arrested without a warrant by an immigration officer or police constable (para 17, Sched 2, 1971 Act). Justices of the peace have wide powers to issue warrants authorising a police constable to enter into and search premises where such persons are thought likely to be, and to arrest them.

While detained, a detainee may be photographed and measured by an immigration officer, constable or prison officer and any other steps necessary to establish his identity may be taken in relation to him. Such a person may be conveyed in the custody of a constable or immigration officer from place to place in order to establish his nationality. Under the 1993 Act an asylum seeker may be fingerprinted irrespective of whether he is in detention, and may be detained if he fails to attend to be fingerprinted (see p 479).

Under Sched 2, para 19, the owners or agents of the ship or aircraft on which the person arrives may be liable, if he is refused leave to enter and directions for his removal are given, to pay to the S of S on demand any expenses incurred in detaining that person in the UK for a period not exceeding 14 days. There is no such liability if the detainee was the holder of a certificate of entitlement, current entry clearance, or work permit, unless these are patent forgeries or where he is an illegal entrant who obtained leave to enter by deception where his leave has not been cancelled under para 6(2) of Sched 2 (Sched 2, para 20(1A), 1971 Act). Detention is an instrument of last resort. In the debates on the 1993 Act in the HL, Earl Ferrers stated the government's policy in relation to the detention. He said in relation to an amendment:

> The amendment would provide that a person could only be detained if there were reasonable grounds for believing that he would not comply with the

requirement to report to an immigration officer. That is essentially what happens already. It is our practice when considering detention in all immigration cases. The specific power to detain in Clause 7 of the Bill will only be exercised if we do not believe that the person would in fact keep in touch with the immigration authorities, and that unless he were detained, it would be impossible to enforce that departure. That is what happens.

I can assure noble Lords that there is no intention whatever to exercise the powers of detention when there is a practical alternative. Apart from the obvious effect on the detainee, detention is costly. The Home Office has no wish to tie up limited detention accommodation unnecessarily (see HL Debs Vol 543 No 104, 2 March 1993, col 631).

3 Temporary admission and release

(a) Temporary admission

A person who is liable to detention or who is in fact detained may never-theless be temporarily admitted to the UK. An immigration officer may authorise this in writing. The person will then be released from detention. The immigration officer may make temporary admission subject to con-ditions such as reporting and as to residence, or prohibiting employment or occupation (1971 Act, Sched 2, para 21 as amended by the 1988 Act, Sched, para 10). A person may be released on temporary admission, subject to a restriction as to reporting to an immigration officer, with a view to the conclusion of his examination (Sched 2, para 21(3), 1971 Act as inserted by Sched 1, para 10, 1996 Act). If such a person fails at any time to comply with the restriction on reporting to the immigration officer, the immigration officer may direct that his examination is treated as concluded at that time. In such circumstances, the notice of the decision giving or refusing the person leave (which would otherwise be required by Sched 2, para 6) does not have to be given to him within 24 hours (Sched 2, para 21(4), 1971 Act as amended by the 1996 Act).

(b) Bail for examination detainees

The following may be released on bail under para 22, Sched 2, 1971 Act as amended by the 1996 Act:

(a) a person who has been detained pending examination and pending a decision either to give or refuse him leave to enter (under para 16(1)); and

(b) a person detained pending the giving of directions and pending his removal pursuant to those directions (under para 16(2).

A chief (or senior) immigration officer, or an adjudicator, may release a person detained under these two provisions on his entering into a recog-nizance or bail bond which has a condition attached to it that the person should appear before an immigration officer at a time and place named in that recognizance/bail bond. The recognizance may specify that some other time or place may be notified to him in writing in the meantime (para 22(1A), Sched 2, 1971 Act, as amended by 1996 Act). However, the power to release on bail a person who has been detained pending examination and pending a decision either to give or refuse him leave to enter (under para 16(1)) arises only where seven days have elapsed since the date of the person's arrival in the UK. The recognizance may be subject to any conditions which seem likely to the adjudicator or immigration officer to result in the appearance of the person, and may be subject to sureties (para 22(2) as amended). The adjudicator or immigration officer may, instead of taking the surety himself, specify its amount and conditions so that it can be taken by another person, such as a police officer, specified by the officer or adjudicator (para 22(3) as amended). The same principles apply to bail for asylum seekers who are appealing against a decision to remove or exclude them from the UK under the 1993 Act, s 10. There is no tariff for the amount of a surety (see below and *Ex p Shamamba* [1994] Imm AR 502).

(c) Bail pending removal

Before the 1996 Act, where temporary admission was refused in the case of a person pending removal, the decision could be challenged only in judicial review proceedings (*Vilvarajah v S of S* [1990] Imm AR 457). A person who is temporarily admitted has not entered the UK (1971 Act, s 11(1)), and if he absconds he becomes an illegal entrant.

Schedule 2, para 12 of the 1996 Act adds para 34 to Sched 2 to the 1971 Act. This provides that the provisions applicable to persons detained for examination pending a decision on leave to enter, also apply to persons who are detained pending the giving of directions for removal under para 16(2) of the schedule. Thus an application for bail may be made by a person:

(a) in relation to whom directions for removal are currently in force; and

(b) who is detained under the provisions of Part I, Sched 2, 1971 Act.

The provisions apply to:

(a) persons refused leave to enter or illegal entrants including those subsequently refused leave to enter (paras 8 and 9);

(b) seamen and aircrews (para 12);

(c) persons liable to examination (para 2).

The provisions of paras 23–25 of Sched 2 to the 1971 Act apply to the detention of such subjects of removal directions (para 34(2)). Thus an immigration officer or an adjudicator may grant bail subject to recognizances and sureties (see above). The effect of this amendment is that a person seeking release will not have to apply for temporary admission and will be able to challenge a decision not to grant him bail by an application to the adjudicator. This is a welcome development, as the applicant for bail will no longer have to show that a decision not to grant temporary admission was unreasonable or unlawful.

(d) Sureties

In a circular (reproduced in (1991) 5 INL&P 123) the Chief Adjudicator indicated that it would be rare for an adjudicator to release an applicant without sureties of at least £1,000 each being available, and that frequently the total value of the sureties will be £5,000. In any event a recognizance will be demanded of an applicant in a nominal sum (eg £5).

If a recognizance is forfeited by reason of the failure of the person to appear, the adjudicator may order the persons bound by the recognizance to pay the sums they are bound to pay under it, or part of those sums. The order must specify a magistrates' court which will deal with the collection, enforcement and remission of the sums as if it had forfeited the sums in question.

Immigration officers and police constables have wide powers of arrest in relation to a person thus temporarily released or bailed. They may arrest him without a warrant if they believe on reasonable grounds that such a person is likely to break, is breaking, or will break a condition of his recognizance by failing to appear or otherwise. They may also arrest him without a warrant if they are notified in writing by a surety that he believes that the person bailed is unlikely to appear and that the surety wishes to be relieved of his obligations as surety (Sched 2, para 24(1)).

A person who is thus arrested should be brought before an adjudicator within 24 hours, or if this is not practicable, he should be brought before a magistrate within 24 hours. He may instead be brought before an immigration officer within 24 hours if it was a condition of the recognizance under which he was originally released that he appear before an immigration officer within that time limit.

When a person is brought before an adjudicator or magistrate under these provisions, they may adopt one of three courses. If they are of the opinion that no breach has occurred, and is not likely, they must release the person under his original recognizance. If, however, they take the view that there has been a breach, they may release him on a new recognizance, or order his detention under the authority of the person by whom he was arrested (Sched 2, para 24(2) and (3)).

4 Detention and release of persons subject to a recommendation for deportation by a court

Where a recommendation for deportation made by a court is in force in respect of a person who is neither detained in pursuance of the sentence or order of any court, nor bailed by a court, he is to be detained unless the S of S directs him to be released pending further consideration of his case (para 2(1), Sched 3, 1971 Act). However, the court recommending deportation may direct that he is not to be detained pending the making of an order for deportation. If a court makes a recommendation for deportation and the person successfully appeals against the sentence, the appeal court may order that he be released without setting aside the recommendation (para 2(1A)).

Where notice of the intention to make a deportation order has been given (see p 253), and the person is neither detained pursuant to a sentence or order of the court, nor on bail, he may be detained under the S of S's authority pending the making of the deportation order (para 2(2)). Pending removal, a person against whom there is a current deportation order may be detained (para 2(3)). Such persons may be arrested without warrant and photographed, measured and otherwise identified (see above and para 2(4)).

A person subject to control pending deportation may be made subject to such restrictions as to residence, employment, or occupation, and as to reporting to an immigration officer or the police as may from time to time be notified to him by the S of S (para 2(5), Sched 3, 1971 Act (as amended by the 1996 Act)).

5 Bail pending appeal

When an appeal is pending, an appellant may be released on bail by a chief immigration officer, a police inspector, an adjudicator, or the IAT. The appellant may be released on his entering into a recognizance subject to conditions, one of which is that he will appear before an adjudicator or the IAT at a stated time and place. An adjudicator or the IAT must grant bail to a person who has filed a notice of appeal from the adjudicator's decision in certain circumstances (see below). There must be an appeal pending for the power to arise. Where, for example, an appeal against removal directions was made but no alternative destination was referred to, the appeal was not properly constituted and was therefore not pending, so that the adjudicator had no power to grant bail (*R v An adjudicator, ex p Umeloh* [1991] Imm AR 602).

(a) Restrictions on the power to grant bail pending appeal

The consent of the S of S to the granting of bail is required if directions for removal have been made in respect of the appellant, or there is a power to make such directions. In fact, however, where an appeal is pending, any directions for removal have no effect, and so the S of S's consent will not be required (*R v IAT, ex p Alghali* [1984] Imm AR 106).

The power of the IAT or adjudicator to release on bail a person who has lodged an appeal against the adjudicator's decision is limited to where:

- *(a)* no leave to appeal to the IAT is required; or
- *(b)* the person has been granted leave to appeal to the IAT; and in either case;
- *(c)* the appellant has entered into proper recognizances; and
- *(d)* if required, the sureties are sufficient;
- *(e)* none of the following applies:
  - (i) the appellant has failed to comply with previous bail;
  - (ii) he is likely to commit offences if released on bail;
  - (iii) he is likely to cause a danger to public health;
  - (iv) he suffers from a mental disorder and continued detention is in his own interests or for the protection of any other person;
  - (v) he is under 17 and arrangements ought to be made for his care in the event of release, and no satisfactory arrangements can be made (1971 Act, Sched 2, para 30(2)(*a*)–(*e*)).

The IAT may release on bail a person to whom it has granted leave where the above conditions are observed.

Adjudicators and the IAT have powers of forfeiture in relation to recognizances when they release a person on bail under Sched 2, para 22. Immigration officers and constables have powers of arrest in relation to persons released pending an appeal, as they do in relation to persons released under para 22.

(b) Habeas corpus

The writ of *habeas corpus* is another route to release from detention under the Act. *Habeas corpus* can be considered, in particular, where the length of a person's detention is unreasonable (see Chapter 23).

Part IV

Free Movement in the EEA

Chapter 16

The Impact of European Law

1   The sources and nature of European law

The United Kingdom is a signatory to the Treaty of Rome which established the European Economic Communities. European Community law is part of domestic law and it is a well-established principle that it takes precedence over domestic law where the two are in conflict (s 2, European Communities Act 1972 and *Van Duyn v Home Office (No 2)* [1975] 3 All ER 190). The importance of EC law has increased since the Treaty of Economic Union (TEU), signed at Maastricht, which widened the scope of the Community and created the European Union which is concerned with social as well as economic matters. Indeed, the move towards co-operation in the fields of justice and home affairs, which includes immigration policy, is one of the three 'pillars' of the TEU.

The treaties have the status of primary legislation throughout the EC. They therefore represent the highest form of law for member states (*Costa v ENEL* [1963] ECR 1). Various other sources of law which emanate from the organs of the EC are considered in brief below.

Regulations are binding in their entirety on member states and take precedence over all domestic law. They are issued by the Council or Commission and are directly applicable, thereby enabling an individual to rely on them in domestic courts.

Directives, which are also issued by the Council or Commission, have a similar level of binding force but are expressed in terms of policy aims, and leave each member state with a discretion as to how the objective is to be implemented in domestic law. Nevertheless, where a directive is unambiguous, an individual can rely on it in a domestic court, and, in appropriate cases, obtain damages against a member state for failure to implement its provisions.

Decisions, which are again promulgated by the Council or Commission, are also fully binding but deal with specific legal entities, either individuals or corporations, as well as member states.

The case law of the European Court of Justice (ECJ) is obviously of great importance. As with treaty provisions, regulations and directives, decisions of the ECJ take precedence over domestic law and can be used as an aid in construing EC legislation. The effect of Maastricht was to amend the various treaties signed by member states in the past and create the European Union (EU). However, very little legislation relevant to the discussion which follows was promulgated by the EU as a distinct legal entity. Therefore, while it is correct to talk of EU nationals and EU member states, the legislation which is germane for present purposes is that made under the Treaty of Rome, otherwise known as the EC Treaty.

The EEA Agreement

In 1992 the EC entered into the European Economic Area (EEA) Agreement with the member states of the European Free Trade Area (EFTA), which at that time consisted of Austria, Finland, Iceland, Norway, Sweden and Liechtenstein. Austria, Finland and Sweden are now members of the EU, which consists also of Belgium, Denmark, France, Germany, Greece, Ireland, Italy, Luxembourg, the Netherlands, Portugal, Spain and the UK. The effect of the agreement is that the EC provisions relating to freedom of movement apply to those parties who remain outside the EU but are signatories to the EEA. The EEA Agreement is part of domestic law by virtue of The European Economic Area Act 1993. Provision as to permits is made under the Immigration (European Economic Area Agreement) Order 1994 (SI No 1895); the latter came into force on 20 July 1994. EEA nationals who are not also EU nationals were entitled to exercise their rights of free movement with effect from 1 January 1994 when the EEA Agreement itself came into force. As a matter of national law the European Economic Area Act 1993 amended s 1(2) of the European Communities Act 1972 to include the EEA Agreement in the list of Community Treaties. It modifies all earlier relevant legislation that was limited in scope to the EC to include the EEA, and modifies all earlier provisions to take account of the EEA Agreement.

The aim of the Agreement is to promote the strengthening of trade and economic relations and to create a homogeneous European Economic Area. To achieve this goal the Agreement provides for the free movement of persons (art 2(b)). Article 4 provides that any discrimination on the grounds of nationality shall be prohibited within the scope of the application of the Agreement.

The effect of the EEA Agreement is that, broadly speaking, the rights given to EU nationals in respect of freedom of movement, freedom of establishment, freedom to provide services and rights of residence apply equally to nationals of EFTA member states. There is a small number of differences between the two classes of national, but these are of limited application. It is therefore proposed to discuss the relevant provisions by reference to EC law.

2 Freedom of movement under EC law

EC law gives citizens of member states three fundamental rights in relation to freedom of movement. These are: the right to take or seek employment (art 48); the right to set up in business or become self-employed (art 52); and the right to provide or receive services (art 59). By virtue of art 6, these Treaty rights are to be accorded to all individuals without discrimination on the grounds of nationality.

Article 8a of the TEU provides that 'every citizen of the Union shall have the right to move freely within the territory of the Member States, subject to the limitations and conditions laid down in the Treaty and by the measures adopted to give it effect.' On the other hand, art 7a of the EC Treaty, inserted by the Single European Act 1986, simply guarantees the free movement of goods, persons, services and capital within an internal market which has internal frontiers. However, in this country at least, it would appear that there is still a wide discretion invested in the S of S as far as border controls are concerned. In *Ex p Flynn* [1995] Imm AR 594, the CA held that, although the date for the completion of the internal market was 31 December 1992, this was an aim, rather than an obligation on member states. Therefore, there was no duty on member states to abolish all border controls. Further, it was held that the wording of art 7(a) was not specific and clear enough to enable an individual to rely on it in a domestic court. In *Ex p Vitale* [1996] Imm AR 275, the CA held that art 8a does not confer an unqualified right of residence on nationals of member states and must be read subject to the derogations contained in art 48 (discussed below) and other EC legislation qualifying the right of free movement. Thus the right of free movement within the EU is still subject to many restrictions, and the UK courts seem to consider that the abolition of these restrictions can be attained only by clear words which expressly amend the Treaty of Rome in its present form.

3   Rights of free movement for workers

The rights of free movement for workers are set out in art 48 of the Treaty of Rome in the following terms:
  (a) to accept offers of employment actually made;
  (b) to move freely within the territory of member states for this purpose;
  (c) to stay in the territory of a member state for the purpose of employment in accordance with the provisions governing the employment of nationals of that state laid down by law, regulation or administrative action;
  (d) to remain in the territory of a member state after having been employed there.

Limitations on the freedom of movement of workers can be justified only on the grounds of public policy, public security or public health. There is, further, an exception from the free movement provisions in respect of those employed in the public service (art 48(4)).

(a) Meaning of 'worker'

A 'worker' is a person who provides services for and under the direction of another in return for remuneration (*Lawrie Blum v Land Baden-Wurttemberg* [1986] ECR 2121, [1987] 3 CMLR 389, [1987] ICR 483 (ECJ)). A person coming to the UK in search of work is a 'worker', provided he seriously wishes to work (*Hoth v S of S* [1985] Imm AR 20), as is a person who is involuntarily unemployed (*Giangregorio v Home Secretary* [1983] Imm AR 104).

In *R v IAT, ex p Antonissen* [1991] ECR I-745, [1991] 2 CMLR 373, the ECJ held that the UK time limit of six months on those seeking work was not contrary to Regulation 1612/68. An EU national who, after six months, cannot produce evidence that he is continuing to look for work, or that he has a genuine (or 'good', 'real', or 'more than illusory') chance of being engaged, can be required to leave the UK. The burden of proving that the unemployment is involuntary, or that there is a genuine prospect of obtaining work, is on the EU national.

In *Levin v S of S for Justice* [1982] ECR 1035, [1982] 2 CMLR 454 the ECJ held that a person was a 'worker' even where her job was part-time and she could not hope to survive on the proceeds of the employment alone. Indeed, this applies even where the worker needs to supplement his or her income from public funds (*Kempf v Staatssecrestaris van Justitie* [1986] ECR 1741, [1987] 1 CMLR 764). All that is necessary is that the employment is an effective and genuine economic activity.

A person seeking work is also entitled to rely on art 48 (*The State v Royer* [1976] ECR 497, although he is not entitled to all the social rights accorded to workers (*Centre Public d'Aide Social, Courcelles v Lebon* [1987] ECR 2811, [1989] 1 CMLR 337).

(b) Derogation in respect of public service

The public service derogation in art 48(4) has not yet been satisfactorily defined by the ECJ, partly due to the wide differences in the concept of public service between member states. However, a narrow construction has been favoured, with the exception apparently applying only to those posts which involve direct or indirect participation in those powers and activities designed to safeguard the interests of the state or other public authorities (*EC Commission v Belgium* [1980] ECR 3881, [1981] 2 CMLR 413).

(c) Regulation EEC No 1612/68 and Directive 68/360

The rights of workers under these provisions are complemented by Regulation EEC No 1612/68 of 15 October 1968 on freedom of movement for workers within the Community (OJ 19 October 1968 L 257/2), which is directly enforceable by individuals in the national courts. This provides an EU national with the right to take up employment in another member state with the same priority as, and subject to the laws governing, nationals of that state. The Regulation applies to any national of a member state falling within art 1 (see below) or his family. Article 10 deals with the position of family members and provides that the following have the right to instal themselves (irrespective of their nationality) with the worker who is employed in the territory of another member state:

(a) the spouse of the worker and their descendants who are under the age of 21, or are dependants; and,

(b) dependent relatives in the ascending line of the worker and spouse.

The host state must facilitate the admission of a dependant who does not fall within those definitions, such as a cohabitee of the worker in his own country, provided that the person actually lived with the worker in his own country, was dependent, and the worker can provide accommodation for him or her (art 10 of the Regulation).

Article 1 of the Regulation states that any national of a member state shall, irrespective of his place of residence, have the following rights:

(a) to take up an activity as an employed person;

(b) to pursue an activity as an employed person;

(c) to take up available employment in the territory of another member state in accordance with the provisions governing the employment of nationals of the host state.

There must be no discrimination between EC workers and the nationals of the host state in relation to contracting and performing contracts (art 2). If immigration rules or practices:

(a) limit applications for and offers of employment or the right of foreign nationals to take up and pursue employment;

(b) impose conditions on their so doing which are not applied to nationals of the member state concerned;

(c) impose conditions which have the aim or effect of keeping nationals of other member states away from employment offered;

(d) prescribe a special recruitment procedure for foreign nationals;

(e) limit the advertising of vacancies; or

(f) subject eligibility to a condition of registration with employment offices,

they are of no effect on EC nationals (art 3).

Where restrictive quotas apply to foreign nationals in a particular type of employment, nationals of other member states are not to be counted in them (art 4). The same facilities are to be offered to nationals of other member states as are offered to nationals of the host state, and no discriminatory medical, vocational, or other criteria may be applied, save vocational tests which the prospective employer requires to be taken when making the offer of employment. Remuneration, terms and conditions of employment and trade union rights are protected by arts 7 and 8, and housing by art 9.

Cohabitees are not spouses under art 10(1), although it may be possible for such persons to obtain admission if the member state operates a principle of non-discrimination (*Netherlands v Reed* [1986] ECR 1283, [1987] 2 CMLR 448).

By art 7(2) of the Regulation, a worker or a member of a worker's family enjoys the same social advantages, such as the right to claim state benefits, as national workers. By art 12 the children of the national are to receive the same educational and training facilities as nationals of the host state.

Directive 68/360/EEC of 15 October 1968 (OJ 19 October 1968 L257/13) deals with a number of formalities in respect of the abolition of restrictions on freedom of movement and residence within the Community for workers of member states and their families. It has the same scope as Regulation 1612/68 in that it confers the right to leave and enter a member state's territory on production of a passport or valid entry card. An entry visa may be required only of a member of a non-EC national's family. Member states must allow nationals of member states to enter their territory on the production of a valid identity card or passport if they are exercising their right to take or pursue employment in that host state, and no entry visa may be demanded save from members of the family of the EC national who are not themselves EC nationals (art 3). Family members must prove their relationship to the worker by a document issued by the original member state, and those covered by art 10 of Regulation 1612/68 need proof (issued by the original member state) of their dependency or that they lived under the same roof as the worker. The Directive states that 'a relationship is proved by a document issued by a competent authority'. Thus it is not possible to look behind that document, for example, to claim that a marriage does not exist where such a document is produced. However in *R v IAT and Surinder Singh, ex p S of S* [1992] Imm AR 565, the ECJ envisaged that free movement rights based on marriage to an EC national would not accrue to a non-EC national if the marriage was fraudulent. The marriage must be of substance and not a fraud (*Kwong* (10661), and *Kam Yu Kau* (10859)). In *Pinto* (12578) the IAT held that the right of a non-EU spouse of an EU citizen is contingent on the EU spouse maintaining the exercise of a treaty right. Polygamous marriages, if valid in the EEA member state of origin of the EEA national, would not be subject to the restrictions placed on such marriages under domestic law. Non-EEA nationals married to EEA nationals can appeal against refusal of a residence permit under the EEA Order 1994, even where it is alleged that there is no right of appeal because the marriage was a sham marriage (*Wong* (12602) and art 2(2), EEA Order; see p 327).

(d) Right of residence following employment
Regulation (EEC) No 1251/70 of 29 June 1970 (OJ 30 June 1970 L 142/24) deals with the right of residence of workers after the end of their employment through retirement or incapacity. As far as the retired are concerned, the right to residence arises when they reach the age at which they are entitled to a retirement pension under the member state's domestic law, provided that they have been employed in that state for the preceding 12 months and have resided there continuously for more than three years (art 2(1)(*a*)). Those who are permanently incapacitated acquire the right if they have resided continuously in the territory of the member state for two years (art 2(1)(*b*)). In both cases, the right is to permanent residence. Further, there

is no minimum period of qualifying residence where any incapacity is a result of an accident at work. A worker who has had three years' continuous employment and residence in a member state and then works in another member state, while retaining and returning to his place of residence at least once a week, also has the right of permanent residence (art 2(1)(c)).

The Regulation allows a worker to exercise the right of residence within two years of the entitlement arising, even though he may have left the territory of the member state (art 5). Further, temporary absences which do not exceed a total of three months a year do not affect the continuity of residence required to qualify (art 4).

Article 3 of the Regulation gives the members of the worker's family the right of residence in the relevant member state. This right subsists if the worker dies before acquiring rights of residence under the Regulation, provided that the worker had resided in the member state for two years or more; the death resulted from an accident at work or an occupational disease; and the surviving spouse is either a national of the member state or lost the nationality of his or her 'home' state by marriage to the worker.

Workers, former workers and their families are entitled to residence permits in order to prove the right of residence. A worker is to be issued with a permit on production of the document with which he entered the territory, and confirmation of employment by the employer (art 4 of Directive 68/360). The permit is to be issued for a minimum of five years unless the duration of the employment is expected to be less than 12 months, in which case the permit is to be limited to that period (art 6). Family members are entitled to a permit on production of the entry document; a document proving the relationship claimed; and, in dependency or co-habitation cases, a document proving the dependency or the fact that the person previously lived under the same roof as the worker (art 4). The last two documents are issued by the member state of origin or the state from which the person came.

The permit is simply evidence of the worker's right of residence. No charge may be made for its issue or renewal unless there is a charge for identity cards issued to nationals, in which case payment of an amount not exceeding that charged to nationals may be made. Breaks in residence of up to six months do not affect its validity (art 6(2)). A valid residence permit may not be withdrawn on the sole basis that the worker is involuntarily unemployed (either through illness or accident or otherwise). The Department for Education and Employment is the UK national authority competent to confirm whether or not unemployment is voluntary (art 7). It is sufficient, however, if the S of S puts the worker to proof that his unemployment was involuntary for immigration purposes (*Giangregorio v Home Secretary* [1983] Imm AR 104).

Former workers and their family members who are entitled to rely on Regulation 1251/70 are also entitled to a residence permit (art 6). Again, this must be issued for at least five years, and issued and renewed free of charge unless an amount is payable for an identity card by nationals.

(e) Derogations and expulsion

Derogations from the freedom of movement provisions are provided for in:

> *(a)* art 48(3), Treaty of Rome;
>
> *(b)* Directive 64/221/EEC of 25 February 1964 on the coordination of special measures concerning the movement and residence of foreign nationals which are justified on grounds of public policy, public security or public health (OJ 4 April 1964 56/850);
>
> *(c)* Directive 72/194/EEC of 18 May 1972 extending to workers exercising the right to remain in the territory of a member state after having been employed in that state the scope of Directive 64/221/EEC (OJ 26 May 1972 L 121/32);
>
> *(d)* Directive 75/35/EEC of 17 December 1974 extending the scope of Directive 64/221/EEC (OJ 20 January 1975 L 14/14).

These derogations cannot be used simply for economic purposes (art 2(2) of Directive 64/221) and so expulsion cannot be justified on the basis that a genuine holder of a Community right has had resort to public funds. The refusal of entry or the expulsion of a person may be based only on the personal conduct of the individual against whom the action is taken (art 3(1)). Previous criminal convictions do not in themselves constitute grounds for taking such action, nor does the expiry of an identity card or passport (art 3(2)). EU nationals who are refused admission may not be removed until they have had the opportunity of making representations: art 9(2) of Directive 64/221 (*Pecastaing v Belgian State* [1980] ECR 691, [1980] 3 CMLR 685).

To justify expulsion on the ground of criminal convictions, there must be a present threat to public policy or security (*Van Duyn* [1975] Ch 358, [1974] ECR 1337, [1975] 1 CMLR 1), which must be sufficiently serious to the requirements of public policy affecting the fundamental interests of society. Past conduct alone may constitute a threat to the requirements of public policy or security where criminal convictions imply a propensity on the part of the individual concerned to act in the same way in the future (*R v Bouchereau* [1978] QB 732 (ECJ)). Some past offences are so serious that the burden is on the applicant to show that the risk of similar conduct in the future is negligible (*Puttick v S of S* [1984] Imm AR 118). However, in *Puttick*, the IAT rejected the submission that public outrage at the past conduct of a person could of itself amount to a present threat to public policy or security. Further, in *Bonsignore* [1975] ECR 297, [1975] 1 CMLR 472, the ECJ stressed that exclusion could not be justified on the basis of deterrence.

A recommendation for deportation made by a criminal court is to be judged by the Directive, and in *R v Spura* (1988) 10 Cr App R(S) 376, the CA held that the Directive, and principles of natural justice, require that before a recommendation is made, there should be a full enquiry into the circumstances of the case. The recommending court should also give its reasons for the recommendation. The relevant test is whether the detriment to the country justifies the recommendation in accordance with the Directive (cf the position of non-EC nationals, *Al-Sabah v IAT* [1992] Imm AR 223). Exclusion on the grounds of public policy requires a genuine threat and one which affects the fundamental interests of the host society. In *R v Escauriaza* (1988) 87 Cr App R 344, however, it was held that this requirement meant nothing more than that the continued presence of the EC national in the UK would be to its detriment.

By art 6 of Directive 64/221, the person to be expelled must be informed of the grounds of public policy, security, or health on which the decision of the S of S is based, unless it is contrary to the interests of state security. It follows that no court should make an order recommending deportation without a full enquiry into the circumstances. The court should give reasons for the recommendation, indicating the extent to which the current previous criminal convictions of the accused have been taken into account, and the light which such convictions throw on the likely nature of the accused's personal conduct in future (*Ex p Santillo* [1981] 2 WLR 362).

In *Ex p Gallagher*, the CA referred to the ECJ questions relating to the correct construction of art 9 of Directive 64/221 and its compatibility with s 7 of the Prevention of Terrorism (Temporary Provisions) Act 1989 ((1994) *The Times*, 16 February). Under art 9, a person is entitled to the opinion of a competent authority before an exclusion order is made. The competent authority in such cases, argued the S of S, was the advisor appointed by him to hear objections to the exclusion order pursuant to Sched 2 to the 1989 Act.

The ECJ held ([1995] ECR I-4253) that the competent authority can be appointed by the S of S provided that the competent authority can perform its duties in absolute independence and is not subject to any control by the authority empowered to take the measures provided for in the Directive. As a consequence, the UK legislation had to be amended to provide for a totally independent right of appeal.

As far as public health is concerned, the immigration rules concerning refusal of entry on medical grounds draw no distinction between EU and non-EU nationals. However, it would appear that immigration officers are to refer EU nationals to a medical inspector only if they show 'obvious signs of mental or physical ill-health'. They may be refused leave to enter only if the medical inspector certifies that they are suffering from one of the diseases listed in the Annex to Directive 64/221. The same rules apply to members of the EU national's family who are not themselves EU nationals.

4   The right of establishment

The effect of the right of establishment created by arts 52–59 of the EC Treaty is to confer a right of free movement on EU nationals wishing to enter a member state to set up or manage a business or to become self-employed. Article 52 provides that freedom of establishment includes the rights to take up and pursue activities as self-employed persons, and to set up and manage undertakings.

These rights are substantiated by various Directives. Directive 73/148/EEC of 21 May 1973, on the abolition of restrictions on movement and residence within the Community for nationals of member states with regard to establishment and the provision of services (OJ 28 June 1973 L 172/14), provides for the right of free movement for those exercising the right of establishment. It requires the abolition of restrictions on movement and residence of nationals of a member state who are established or wish to be established in another member state as self-employed. This also applies in respect of the spouse and children aged under 21 of such nationals and dependent relatives in the ascending or descending line of such nationals and their spouses, irrespective of nationality. Further, member states are required to favour the admission of any other members of the family of the national.

The provisions of Regulation 1251/70, discussed above, which concern the right of workers to remain in member states, apply to the self-employed by virtue of Directive 75/34. Derogations similar to those in relation to freedom of movement also apply to the right of establishment (arts 55 and 56).

The above Directives also contain provisions for the issue and renewal of residence permits for the self-employed, the former self-employed and their families. By virtue of arts 4, 6 and 7 of Directive 73/148, a self-employed person or a member of his or her family entitled to residence under the Directive is entitled to a residence permit valid for at least five years. The applicant need produce only the identity card and passport with which he entered the member state and proof that he has a right of residence. As far as the former self-employed are concerned, the relevant provision is art 6 of Directive 75/34, which governs the issue of permits in terms similar to those in Directive 73/1148.

5   Freedom to provide services

Articles 59–66 of the Treaty give a right of free movement to persons wishing to provide services. Article 60 defines 'services' as those activities which are normally provided for remuneration, (in so far) as they are not governed by the provisions relating to freedom of movement for goods, capital and persons. Article 60 further states that 'services' includes, in particular, activities of an industrial and commercial character, activities of craftsmen and activities of the professions. Further substantiation of these rights is contained in Directives 73/148 and 75/34 which are discussed above, and the usual derogations again apply (see p 304).

The rights extend to persons who wish to travel to receive services. In *Luisi and Carbone v Ministero del Tesoro* [1984] ECR 377, [1985] 3 CMLR 52, the ECJ held that tourists, persons travelling for business or educational purposes, and persons seeking medical treatment were recipients of services. Services must be 'normally provided for remuneration'. Private students would therefore benefit from these rights. An example of how such individuals may rely directly on EC rights is the case of *Cowan v Le Tresor Public*

[1990] 2 CMLR 613. Here, it was held that the right to the same social advantages as nationals of the host state required the state to award compensation to a victim of an assault who was an EC national on the same basis as it would be awarded to a French national.

The requirements in respect of the issue of residence permits for the providers and recipients of services are identical to those discussed above in respect of the self-employed, the former self-employed and their families (see p 305).

6 Students

Directive 93/96 (OJ 18 December 1993 L 317/59) provides for the right of residence for students who are taking part in a vocational training course. The right subsists for the duration of the course of studies provided that the student can declare that he has sufficient private resources to avoid becoming a burden on the member state's social security system and is covered by sickness insurance. The usual derogations and Directive 64/221 apply (art 2(2); see p 304).

The right of residence for students is evidenced by a residence permit, the validity of which may be limited to the duration of the course, or one year if the course lasts longer. If the course does last longer, the permit is renewable annually. The permit is issued on the student's providing proof that he fulfils the conditions giving rise to the right of residence. If a member of the student's family is not an EU national he must be issued with a residence document of the same validity as that issued to the national upon whom he depends.

7 Other rights of residence

To harmonise provisions on the rights of EC nationals to reside in a member state other than their own, Directive 90/364/EEC of 28 June 1990 on the right of residence (OJ 13 July 1990 L 180/26) confers the right of residence on all EU nationals who have sufficient resources to avoid becoming a burden on the social security system of the member state in which they wish to reside, and who are covered by sickness insurance. The dependent ascendant and descendant family members of the holder of the right and his spouse are also entitled to instal themselves with the holder of the right irrespective of their nationality, as long as sufficient subsistence provision is made for them and they are covered by sickness insurance. The usual derogations apply to this Directive (see p 304).

Directive 90/365/EEC of 28 June 1990, on the right of residence for employees and self-employed persons who have ceased their occupational activity (OJ 13 July 1990 L 180/28), confers the right of residence on EU nationals who have previously pursued activities as employed or self-employed persons; are in receipt of a sufficient amount of invalidity, retirement or industrial accident pension to avoid becoming a burden on the social security system of the member state; and are covered by sickness insurance. The remainder of the provisions are identical to those of Directive 90/364 above.

A permit which is valid for five years must be issued to those who are exercising residence rights under the above two Directives where the applicant presents a valid identity card or passport and proves his or her right of residence. The member state may, where it is thought necessary, require that the permit be re-validated after the first two years. Such a requirement may be imposed only where it is necessary for the purposes, set out in the preamble to the Directive, of achieving an internal market without internal frontiers, and without residents becoming a burden on the host state's public finances. The requirement cannot be justified on grounds which are not necessary to achieving the purpose of the Community legislation (see *Jones v Chief Adjudication Officer* [1990] IRLR 533 and *Allue v Universita degli Studi di Venezia* [1989] ECR 1591, [1991] 1 CMLR 283).

8 Appeals

The rights of appeal available to EU nationals in immigration matters are, in practice, similar to those of other persons. So, for example, there is an in-country right of appeal against refusal of entry under s 13(1) of the 1971 Act, and against a decision to deport under s 15(1) of the Act. Where an EU national or a member of his family, of whatever nationality, wishes to appeal against a decision to require him to leave the UK or to curtail his residence, s 14(1) grants a right of appeal against refusal to vary leave only where a person has limited leave to enter. Despite the fact that limited leave operates as a condition on leave on entry, and is therefore incompatible with EU law (*R v Pieck*, above), the IAT held that the grant of the initial six months' residence is the grant of limited leave for the purposes of s 14(1) and so may be the subject of an appeal to the adjudicator (*Lubberson v S of S* [1984] Imm AR 56). Where a person's right of residence is (under UK law) withdrawn, the S of S's practice has been to permit a direct appeal to the IAT.

Directive 64/221 (above, p 304) provides, in art 8, that the person to be expelled shall have the same legal remedies in respect of any decision concerning entry, or refusing the issue or renewal of a residence permit, or ordering expulsion, as are available to nationals of the member state in respect of administrative acts. Article 9 provides that if there is no right of appeal on the law and the facts of a case to a court of law, or if such an appeal does not suspend any administrative action to be taken, a decision refusing a residence permit or one expelling the holder of a residence permit from the member state may not be taken (save in cases of urgency) until an opinion has been obtained from a competent authority of the host member state. The person to be expelled must be accorded rights of defence, legal representation and assistance before this authority as provided for by domestic law. The requirements of the Directive are not satisfied where the authority reviewing the decision is the same body as that which made the decision. The effect of this provision is that a decision to deport a person, which the S of S then refers to the IAT, must be void and subject to judicial review even if the IAT upholds the decision, as the S of S has no power to make a decision until the opining authority has been consulted. (See *Ex p Gallagher* [1995] ECR I-4253 and *Pecastaing v Belgian State* [1980] ECR 691, [1980] 3 CMLR 685, discussed above, p 304.)

9   Nationals of a member state relying on EC provisions

The courts have held that, to found an EC legal right, the facts of the case must have some link with the kind of situation intended to be covered by EC law (*Morson and Jhanjan v Netherlands* [1982] ECR 3723, [1983] 2 CMLR 221). Where, therefore, a woman became the wife of a British citizen one month *after* the signing of a deportation order against her, she could not claim the benefit of Directive 64/221, which deals with the rights of spouses of an EU national on deportation (*S of S v Tombofa* [1988] Imm AR 400). In *R v IAT, ex p Aradi* [1987] Imm AR 359 it was held that there is no such linking factor where the right to move within the EU has not been exercised. In *Knoors v S of S for Economic Affairs* [1979] ECR 399, the ECJ held that the wording in art 52, namely, 'nationals of one Member State in the territory of another', applies so as to permit nationals of the 'home' state to rely on the provisions of art 52 of the Treaty against their own state. It is necessary to show that the person's situation had been assimilated to that of any other person enjoying rights under the Treaty. The Commission argued that an individual employed in a member state of which he is not a national can assert a right in his own state to go back to his member state, and can assert a right under EC law for his spouse to be installed there with him. The Advocate General at that time was Sir Gordon Slynn (now Lord Slynn), who thought that it was neither necessary nor desirable to comment on the argument.

However, the argument re-emerged in *R v IAT and Surinder Singh, ex p S of S* [1992] Imm AR 565, where an Indian national married a British national, and they worked in the EC outside the UK. They returned to the UK to set up a business. The husband was granted limited leave to remain, during which time the marriage broke down. Before the decree absolute, the S of S decided to initiate deportation proceedings against the husband. The ECJ held that a member state must grant leave to enter and reside in its territory to the spouse, regardless of nationality, of a national of that state who has gone to another member state to work there as an employed person and returns to establish himself in the 'home' state.

The spouse must be granted the same rights as would be granted to the national under Community law if the spouse had entered and resided in another member state. It is clear that the same principle would hold good for persons exercising other EC rights; in particular, the provisions of the immigration rules relating to the primary purpose of the marriage could not be applied to a couple who, having exercised a right to use services in another member state, then return to seek employment. The ECJ, in *Saunders* [1980] QB 72, [1979] ECR 1129, stated, however, that nothing in EC law prevented the introduction of provisions to ensure the effective implementation of domestic criminal law.

Section 7 of the Immigration Act 1988
A person does not require leave to enter or remain under the 1971 Act where he is entitled to enter or remain by virtue of an enforceable EC right or any provision made under s 2(2) of the European Communities Act 1972. Section 3 of the European Economic Area Act 1993 provides that where the EEA Agreement requires modification of a provision, which can be ascertained from the Agreement, the provision has effect subject to those modifications. Section 7 of the 1988 Act must therefore be viewed as modified by s 3 of the European Economic Area Act 1993 so as to declare that EEA nationals do not require leave to enter or remain in the UK where they are exercising enforceable rights under the EEA Agreement. An alternative analysis, with the same result, is that, since the EEA Agreement is binding on member states with the force of EC law, any domestic provision which is incompatible with the EEA Agreement is of no effect.

10   Third country agreements

The member states of the EU may enter into agreements with other countries under art 238 of the EC Treaty, the EEA Agreement being an example. Section 2 of the European Communities Act 1972 provides that all such rights, powers, liabilities, obligations and restrictions from time to time created or arising by or under the Treaties and all such remedies and procedures from time to time provided for under the Treaties as in accordance with the Treaties are without further enactment to be given legal effect or used in the UK, and shall be recognised and available in the UK and shall be enforced as enforceable Community rights. As with other provisions of Community law, the rights created under these agreements may have direct effect where they are clear and sufficiently precise.

(a) The agreement with Turkey
An Association Agreement was signed between the EC and Turkey in 1963. It provides that the parties should be guided by arts 48 to 50 of the Treaty of Rome in securing the free movement of workers between them (Agreement establishing an Association between the European Economic Community and Turkey, Ankara, OJ 1963 C 113/2). The aim was to secure freedom of movement by the end of 1993, the principles governing this right to be determined by the Council of Association established under the Association Agreement. Those principles can be found in the Council of Association Decisions 2/78, 1/80 and 3/80.

A worker from Turkey who is registered as being in the member state's work-force is entitled to the renewal of his work permit in respect of the same employer after a year of legal employment with him. After three such years he may change jobs to other registered employment, and after four years of legal employment he may have free access to any job of his choice which is available. His family may join him and are entitled to take work which they are offered after three years' residence; after five years' residence they too may have free access to any paid employment. The derogations in Directive 64/221 in respect of public policy, public security and public health apply to Turkish workers by virtue of art 14(1) of Decision 1/80.

In *Demirel v Stadt Schwäbisch Gmünd* [1987] ECR 3719, [1989] 1 CMLR 421 the ECJ held that an Association Agreement creates special privileged links with the non-member country, which must to a certain extent take part in the Community system. Rights of workers under the Association Agreement between a particular state and a non-member state fall to be considered under the Community part of the Agreement, rather than the national part of the mixed treaty. Where a provision in such an agreement concluded by the Community is clear and sufficiently precise, having regard to the wording and nature of the agreement, it is directly applicable. However, the court ruled that the provisions of the Agreement between Turkey and the EC were not clear and precise enough to give rise to rules of Community law which are directly applicable in the internal legal order of the member states. In *Unal Narin v S of S* [1990] Imm AR 403, the CA held that the obligations laid out in the Agreement were not sufficiently clear, and emphasised that the Agreement merely provided that the member state and Turkey would be guided by art 48 of the Treaty of Rome.

During the implementation period, the Council of Association had power to make such decisions as it thought fit in relation to the Agreement, and its decisions are regarded as directly associated with the Agreement and an integral part of the Community legal system (*Demirel*, above). These decisions are also directly applicable where, having regard to their wording and the purpose and nature of the agreement in question, they contain clear and precise obligations which are not subject in their implementation or effects to the adoption of any subsequent measure. However, the fact that a state may have to take administrative measures to implement such decisions does not prevent them from being directly applicable. In *Sevince v Staatssecretariat van Justitie*, Case 192/89 [1990] ECR I-3473, the ECJ held that art 2(1)(*b*) of Decision 2/76, providing that a Turkish worker who has been in legal employment for five years in a member state is to enjoy free access in that member state to any paid employment of his choice in that state, and art 6(1) of Decision 1/80, providing that a Turkish worker who is duly registered as belonging to the labour force is to enjoy free access to any paid employment of his choice after four years' legal employment, were directly applicable. It is not possible for a member state to make the rights granted by the Association Agreement conditional, or to restrict the application of the precise and unconditional right which the decisions grant to Turkish workers. The ECJ held also that the right conferred on the Turkish worker to take work of his choice after a specified period of legal employment necessarily carried with it a right of residence.

For the purposes of acquiring rights under a member state's law it is irrelevant how the worker entered the member state, as long as the entry was lawful. If the Turkish worker has a stable position in the labour force and has been in continuing employment for one year, he can use the directly applicable member state's law to gain an extension of leave to continue in the same employment. Article 6 of Decision 1/80 of the Association Council provides that after one year's legal employment the Turkish national is entitled to renewal of his permit to work for the same employer if the job is available. In *Kus v Landeshauptstadt Wiesbaden* [1992] ECR I-6781, [1993] 2 CMLR 887, the Turkish national originally entered the state for the purpose of marriage to a national of that member state, but remained to work; he was able to rely on art 6. Further, the court indicated that the provisions relating to deportation of Turkish workers protected by a member state's law may be interpreted in the same way as Directive 64/221.

In most respects the rights granted to workers and their families are much narrower than the equivalent rights under EC provisions. In *Bayer v ECO (Istanbul)* [1995] Imm AR 365, the appellant claimed that the ECO's refusal to grant entry clearance so that he could join his father in the UK was contrary to the anti-discrimination provisions in the Ankara Agreement. The IAT held that the right to free access to employment conferred by the agreement could not be construed as including or implying a right of entry for the family of a Turkish worker and so there was no discrimination. Likewise, the IAT, in *Harman* (12360), held that the Agreement did not result in the right of a wife to settle in the UK, at a time (1980) when the immigration rules gave that right immediately. It was not a restriction on the conditions of access to employment. Further, in *Bozkurt v Staatssecretaris van Justitie* [1995] ECR I-1475, the ECJ held that it was for the national court of the member state to determine whether or not a Turkish worker belongs to a legitimate labour force for the purposes of art 6(1) of Decision 1/80. It was said that, although the Agreement does not explicitly grant the right of residence, the fact that a worker is in employment implies the grant of a right of residence. However, art 6(2) of Decision 1/80 does not confer on such a Turkish national the right to remain in the territory of a state following an accident at work which renders him permanently incapacitated for work.

(b) Co-operation agreements with Algeria, Morocco and Tunisia
Provision is made for the treatment of workers from the Maghreb countries under the Co-operation Agreements with Algeria (Regulation 2210/78), Morocco (Regulation 2211/78) and Tunisia (Regulation 2212/78) (OJ 27 September 1978 L 263, L 264 and L 265 respectively). Each Agreement provides that the treatment accorded by the member state to workers from those countries employed in its territory shall be free from any discrimi-

nation based on nationality, as regards working conditions or remuneration in relation to its own nationals. Thus, they prohibit discrimination on the ground of nationality in relation to the requirement of leave to remain after limited leave has expired, the renewal of a work permit, and expulsion. The terms of the Agreements with Morocco, Tunisia, and Algeria are clear and precise in so far as they prohibit discrimination (reference could be made to the almost identical provision in Directive 76/207/EEC of 9 February 1976 (OJ 14 February 1976 L 39/40) regarding sex discrimination). The effect of this, as far as it relates to the UK, is that workers from Morocco, Tunisia and Algeria must not be in a worse position than UK nationals who do not require work permits to continue to work in the UK. Further, the Agreements provide that workers from those countries and any family members living with them must be accorded non-discriminatory treatment in so far as social security benefits are concerned. The relevant benefits are set out in Regulation (EEC) No 1408/71 of 14 June 1971 on the application of social security schemes to employed persons and their families moving within the Community (OJ 5 July 1971 L 149/2). They include maternity and illness benefits, occupational accidents and disease benefits and unemployment benefit. Since the Agreements prohibit discrimination in relation to the provision of benefits, the prohibition would apply to a person taking part-time work to enable a particular level of benefit to be claimed.

In *Office National de l'Emploi v Kziber* [1991] ECR I-999, the ECJ held that the provisions concerning social security and employment have direct effect. So, if a worker from one of the Agreement countries is unable to make contributions to the national insurance scheme in the UK, he suffers direct discrimination in relation to the nationals of the UK. Similarly, if the worker cannot make those contributions from whatever resources he may have, he suffers discrimination. Thus a worker from the countries covered by the Agreements cannot be prohibited from changing jobs because of his or her immigration status. Similarly, because certain benefits are available only if purely voluntary contributions have been made, and because the right to unemployment benefit accrues only if national insurance contributions have been made, a person seeking work in one of the Agreement countries cannot be prevented from claiming such a benefit even if he enters the UK in some other capacity, such as that of visitor.

In *Kziber*, the Advocate General considered the nature and purpose of the Moroccan Agreement. He stated, and the ECJ held, that an Agreement does not have to be directed towards the integration of a Maghreb country for its provisions to have direct effect in member states' law. The Moroccan Agreement (and the other Maghreb Agreements) was reached with the purpose of harmonising provisions and measures in the field, *inter alia*, of labour. The Advocate General noted that the Maghreb Agreements do not have the programmatic nature which was the basis on which the provisions of the Agreement with Turkey were held not to have direct effect. He further remarked that the provisions relating to equality in the field of labour not infrequently contain rules which are plainly designed to govern the legal situation of individuals. He concluded that the nature and purpose of the Agreement did not prevent it from being directly enforceable. He considered whether the provisions relating to discrimination in relation to working conditions or remuneration were sufficiently clear and precise to be directly enforceable and concluded that they were. The provisions of the Agreement prohibiting discrimination on the grounds of nationality between workers of the Agreement state and those of the member state, and their families, he concluded, were sufficiently precise to be of direct application. Finally, he took the view that the word 'worker' must be interpreted to include a person who is, or who has been, pursuing an occupation in the territory of a member state. It would exclude, however, someone who was registered for a certain time with the employment agencies of a member state but without ever having been engaged in a genuine and effective occupation within the framework of an employment relationship.

The court was concerned only with the article of that Agreement dealing with social security discrimination. However, it is clear that the provisions dealing with discrimination in relation to working conditions would also be found to be directly applicable since it was held that the concept of 'worker' encompasses both an active worker and one who has left the labour market in circumstances giving rise to an entitlement under the social security system, or upon reaching pensionable age.

11   Third-country nationals employed in EEA undertakings

Nationals of non-EU countries who are working for undertakings established in member states are entitled to exercise freedom of movement for the purposes of the undertaking for which they are employed while it is carrying out a project in another member state. In *Rush Portuguesa LDA v Office National d'Immigration* [1990] ECR I-1417, [1991] 2 CMLR 818, a Portuguese building and public works undertaking entered into a contract to carry out works on a French railway line. The Portuguese company wished to bring a work-force, including third country nationals, from Portugal to France. The effect of arts 59 and 60 of the EC Treaty was that the French authorities were not entitled to require the company to obtain work permits for its employees. The imposition of such a condition on a company from another member state providing services constituted discrimination with regard to its competitors established in the host member state, which were able freely to use their own employees. The condition would also affect the ability of the provider of services to provide its services. Further, foreign nationals working for an undertaking in another member state cannot be required to qualify both under the immigration conditions of the member state in which the employing undertaking is established, and under the immigration requirements of the member state in which their employer requires them to work in order to provide a service (and see *Raymond Vander Elst v OMI*, Case C-43/93 [1994] ECR I-3803; [1995] CMLR 513, ECJ).

12   Agreement on the external frontiers of the member states

The Treaty on European Union signed at Maastricht on 7 February 1992 states, at Title VI, art K1, that matters such as asylum policy, the rules governing the crossing of member states' external borders, conditions of entry and movement and immigration policies regarding nationals of non-member states are to be matters of common interest. They are, however, to be dealt with in compliance with the European Convention for the Protection of Human Rights and Fundamental Freedoms and the 1951 Geneva Convention on Refugees (art K2). Thus, member states are required to comply with both Conventions, and if art K2 of the TEU gives rise to individual rights, asylum and immigration law must conform to all the obligations under those Conventions. The member states agreed to inform and consult one another within the Council of Ministers with a view to coordinating their actions. The Maastricht Treaty also provides that wherever reference is made to nationals of the member states, the question whether an individual possesses the nationality of a particular member state shall be settled solely by reference to the national law of the member state concerned. Member states may declare who are to be considered their nationals for Community purposes by way of a declaration lodged with the Presidency, and may amend that declaration when necessary.

In the light of the provisions of the Treaty, consideration is being given to the establishment of a common European border. The draft Convention on the External Frontiers of the EC is being considered for signature by the member states. The draft Convention calls for external frontiers to have established border posts, patrols, and procedures enabling the member states to establish the authenticity of the documents carried by entrants. Carriers will be required to make enquiries of entrants as to their visa status and eligibility. Provisions similar to those under the Immigration (Carriers' Liability) Act 1987, whereby the carrier becomes liable for the costs of removal of an entrant who was not entitled to enter, are likely to be implemented. The proposals would require that nationals of non-member states who are illegally present in a member state should, in normal circumstances, leave at once. The draft Convention makes no provision for the ECJ's intervention, but has been seen by the Commission as part of the programme to be undertaken by the Community to achieve the objective set out in art 8a of the EC Treaty of an internal market without internal borders (see Commission Communication (Abolition of Border Controls), SEC/92/877 final, Brussels, 8 May 1992).

The draft Convention proposes the use of a common visa and a common transit visa. The common visa would be valid for one or more member states, for not more than three months in any six-month period. The common transit visa would permit a non-member state national to travel to a non-member state, spending not more than four days in transit in any member state. Visas valid for more than three months would thereafter be valid only at a domestic level, and other member states would be obliged to permit the holder to pass in transit to the issuing state only. The common visa would be issued when the following conditions are fulfilled:

    (a) the non-member state national holds a valid travel document for crossing frontiers and, if needed, a visa for the state through which he enters;

    (b) the non-member state national:

        (i)   presents documentary evidence proving the purpose of the intended stay and any conditions attached to that stay;

        (ii) has sufficient means of subsistence for the period of the proposed stay and his return or onward journey to a non-member state, or can obtain those means;

    (c) the non-member state national must not be a threat to domestic public policy or security, nor may his name appear on a joint list of persons whose presence the member states considers to be a threat to the security or public policy of particular member states.

The draft Convention envisages that persons who are not eligible in any of the above ways, or whose names appear on the prohibitive list, may be admitted to a particular member state on the grounds of the international commitments of that state, the national interests of the state or humanitarian reasons.

The ECJ has held that principles of international obligations, to which the member states are signatories, are to be taken into account when considering questions of a member state's law (*Johnston v Chief Constable of RUC* [1987] QB 129, [1986] ECR 1651, [1986] 1 CMLR 8; *Wachauf v the State,* Case 5/88 [1989] ECR 2609, [1991] CMLR 328; and *Hoechst v EC Commission* [1989] ECR 2859, [1991] 4 CMLR 410). Further, a member state's power to deport or exclude a national of a member state under arts 66 and 56 of the Treaty of Rome must be read in the light of the general principle of freedom of expression embodied in art 10 of the ECHR (*ERTAE v Pliroforissis & Kouvelas* [1991] ECR I-2925). The ECJ held that the fundamental principles in the ECHR form an integral part of the general principles of law which the court enforces. Measures which are incompatible with these principles are not to be permitted in Community law, and so national courts interpreting Community law must have regard to them.

Most recently, the Commission has proposed a new draft directive (OJ 1995 C 289/16) which, if adopted, would have to be implemented by 31 December 1996. It provides for the elimination of frontier controls and formalities when all persons, whatever their nationality, are crossing the frontiers of member states. However, a member state would be entitled to reinstate controls for a period of not more than 30 days where there is a serious threat to public policy or public security and for renewable periods of 30 days thereafter after consultation with other member states and the Commission. The controls which may be imposed in such a situation may not exceed that which is strictly necessary to respond to the threat.

13 The application and enforcement of EC law in member states

(a) Treaty provisions

By art 5 of the Treaty of Rome, the UK has an obligation to take all appropriate measures to ensure fulfilment of its obligations arising out of the Treaty or resulting from actions taken by institutions of the EC. The UK must also abstain from any measure which could jeopardise the attainment of the objectives of the Treaty. Thus, the provisions of the Treaty and the directly applicable measures of the institutions render automatically inapplicable any conflicting measure of current national law. They also preclude the adoption of national legislative measures to the extent that they are incompatible with Community provisions (*Amministrazione delle Finanze dello Stato v Simmenthal SpA* [1978] ECR 629, [1978] 3 CMLR 263). UK courts and tribunals have an obligation to apply the provisions of Community law by virtue of the European Communities Act 1972. Section 2(1) provides for the enforcement of directly effective provisions of EC law as contained in the Treaty or arising under it. By s 2(2), EC law is given further effect by the duty to enact subordinate legislation in order to implement binding provisions of EC law. Finally, statutory enactments are to be interpreted so as to give effect to the mandatory requirements of EC law (s 2(4)).

The EEA Agreement is a Treaty for the purposes of the EEC Treaty. Article 6 of the EEA Agreement states that the provisions of the Agreement, in so far as they are identical in substance to corresponding rules of the EEC Treaty, or to Acts adopted in application of that Treaty, shall in their implementation and application be interpreted in conformity with the relevant rulings of the ECJ given before 2 May 1992 (the date of the signing of the EEA Agreement). Any act corresponding to an EC Regulation or Directive is made part of the internal legal order of the EEA states in the same way as Regulations and Directives of the EC are made part of a member state's legal order. For the purposes of a claim in any of the member states of the EU, matters of legal interpretation of the Agreement are to be dealt with in the same way as matters of interpretation of the EC Treaty. In the EFTA states, an EFTA court will determine the interpretation of the Agreement, although provision is made for the resolution of conflicting judgments of the EFTA court and the ECJ.

Any question as to the effect of the Treaties, or as to the meaning or effect of any Community instrument, is to be treated as a question of law and determined as such in accordance with the principles laid down by the ECJ if the question is not referred to the ECJ for determination by a national court (s 3(1)).

Article 169 of the EC Treaty provides for the enforcement of EC obligations against member states by the EC Commission through infringement proceedings.

(b) Direct effect

A provision has direct effect, and may be relied on by an individual, where:

(a) the provision does not by its nature indicate that it concerns the member states only in their relations *inter se* (*Costa v ENEL* [1964] ECR 585);

(b) the provision is clear and precise;

(c) the provision is unconditional and unqualified and not subject to any further measures on the part of the member states of the community (but see below);

(d) the provision is not one which leaves any or any substantial latitude to member states (*Salgoil v Italian Ministry for Foreign Trade* [1968] ECR 453);

It is irrelevant that the Commission or other member states have alternative remedies for breach of the provision in question (*Van Gend en Loos v Nederlandse Administratie der Belastingen* [1963] ECR 1).

The requirement that the provision must be unconditional and unqualified must be read in the light of a number of cases which indicate that an obligation which is originally conditional or qualified may become unconditional or unqualified by lapse of time or on the happening of an event (see, for example, *SACE v Italian Ministry for Finance* [1970] ECR 1213, *Eunomia di Parro v Ministry of Education* [1971] ECR 811 and *Ianelli v Meroni* [1977] ECR 557). Where a member state has failed to comply with its obligations under a Treaty provision which is conditional before the end of the implementation period, that provision may become directly effective from the end of that transitional period. Where a member state has failed to implement a Directive, then providing the terms of the Directive are clear and precise, the state cannot rely on its own failure to prevent an individual relying on the terms of the Directive against the state (*Pubblico Ministero v Ratti* [1979] ECR 1629).

(c) Relationship between EC and UK provisions

The provisions of the 1971 Act and the immigration rules may be overridden by provisions of European law to the extent that they are contrary to it (*Van Duyn v Home Office (No 2)* [1975] 3 All ER 190). Further, all national legislation, whether or not it was passed to implement EC obligations, is to be construed so as to be consistent with EC obligations (*Marleasing SA v La Commercial Internacional de Allimentacion SA* [1992] 1 CMLR 305). Special provision is made in the immigration rules for EC nationals (see Chapter 17). In addition, any Association and Co-operation Agreements, some of which were discussed above, extend the scope of Community rights to certain non-EC nationals. They form part of Community law, so that rights created by them are actionable in the ECJ (see below). Further, it is possible to obtain interim relief, such as injunctive remedies against the Crown, where a question of European law is involved, and it may be possible to obtain damages for a breach by the S of S of certain provisions of European law relating to immigration control.

By s 7 of the Immigration Act 1988 a person does not require leave to enter or remain in the UK if he is entitled to enter or remain by virtue of an enforceable Community right or by virtue of any provision made under s 2(2) of the ECA 1972. Section 7(2) provides that the S of S may make statutory instruments to grant leave to enter for a limited period to any class of persons, who although EU nationals, are not entitled to enter by virtue of a Community right. If the S of S acts in breach of the provisions of Community law upon which an individual may rely, he may become liable for breach of statutory duty. However, a mere breach of Community law may also render a member state liable in damages for the purposes of national law, and it is possible that the S of S could be liable in damages for misfeasance in public office (*Bourgoin SA v Ministry of Agriculture Fisheries and Food* [1985] 3 All ER 585). Relying on another principle of Community law, an individual may be entitled to damages, regardless of the position in national law, where a member state has not implemented a piece of Community legislation which is designed to protect the monetary interests of the individual and that individual has suffered financial loss by reason of that failure (*Francovich v Italian Republic* [1992] IRLR 84, [1991] ECR I-5357, [1993] 2 CMLR 66, *R v HM Treasury ex p British Telecommunications* [1996] QB 615 and *R v Ministry of Agriculture, Fisheries and Food ex p Hedley Lomas* (1996) *The Times*, 6 June). In *Brasserie du Pêcheur SA v Federal Republic of Germany* [1996] 2 WLR 506, the ECJ further clarified the circumstances in which such reparation will be made, laying down three conditions which have to be satisfied;

(*a*) the rule of Community law breached was one which conferred rights on individuals;

(*b*) the breach of Community law was sufficiently serious, and where the national legislature has a wide discretion, the institution alleged to have committed the breach must have manifestly and gravely disregarded the limits on the exercise of its powers;

(*c*) there must be a direct causal link between the breach and the damage sustained.

The court further stated that reparation was not limited to damage to specific individual interests, such as property, but could also cover loss of profit. This would certainly appear to establish the possibility of claims in the immigration law context where persons are prevented from exercising the right to establishment or to provide services. Further, the ECJ explicitly stated that any condition in UK law which made state liability dependent on proof of misfeasance in public office would be of no effect since this would make it impossible or extremely difficult for individual Community rights to be adequately protected. (See also *Dillonkofer v Federal Republic of Germany* (1996) *The Times*, 14 October.)

Where a person asserts a right of Community law against the S of S, it will be possible to obtain injunctive relief to prevent, for example, the removal of a person from the jurisdiction, or to prevent a person (eg a non-EC member of an EC national's family) being returned to his country of origin (*R v S of S for Transport, ex p Factortame (No 2)* [1991] 1 AC 603). The claim for injunctive relief should be granted by a national court where it finds the following factors:

- *(a)* the case concerns a point of European law;
- *(b)* the sole bar preventing it from granting interim relief is a rule of national law;
- *(c)* damages are an insufficient remedy;
- *(d)* if damages are not a sufficient remedy, where the balance of convenience lies (the court will consider the circumstances of the case, and the duty owed by the S of S to the public).

The grant of such an injunction will be an exceptional course, but it is not necessary to show a *prima facie* case that the UK law is incorrect. In addition, since the case of *M v Home Office* [1994] 1 AC 377, there is no reason why courts cannot grant injunctive relief against the Crown in purely domestic law situations.

(d) Preliminary rulings

Where a question concerning the interpretation of a provision of EC law arises before a national court, the court or tribunal may request the ECJ to give a ruling on the question if it is necessary for that tribunal's decision (art 177, EC Treaty). If there is no reasonable scope for doubt as to the way in which the question of EC law is to be answered, no reference should be made, but the national court should apply the EC law provision, or interpret the national provision so as to be consistent with the EC provision. Where there is no appeal from a decision of a court or tribunal, the court must refer to the ECJ a question of EC law necessary for its decision. Thus, the HL, or the CA when leave to appeal to the HL is refused (*Haegen v Fratelli & Moretti SNC* [1980] 3 CMLR 253 and *Generics (UK) Ltd v Smith Kline & French Laboratories Ltd* [1990] 1 CMLR 416), or upon refusal of leave to move for judicial review, is obliged to refer a question of European law to the ECJ.

The procedure for obtaining a preliminary reference is governed by RSC, Ord 114. Rule 2 provides that a reference may be made at any stage of the proceedings, whether before hearing evidence or having heard it. A reference cannot be made after the court has delivered judgment, and so the application must be made during or before the hearing (r 2(2)). The reference should contain a brief summary of the facts; the order sought by the applicant; an outline of the respondent's defence; and a summary of the arguments for both parties on the issue under reference. The court will include in its order the reason for making the reference, a statement of the relevant national law and the questions for reference.

Chapter 17

The UK Provisions on Free Movement

1 Introduction

Paragraph 5 of HC 395 provides that, save where expressly indicated, the rules do not apply to a national of the European Economic Area (EEA) or the family member of such a national who is entitled to enter or remain in the UK by virtue of the provisions of the Immigration (European Economic Area) Order 1994 ('the EEA Order'). But an EEA national or his family member who is not entitled to rely on the provisions of that order is covered by the rules. Specific provisions are made in para 7 and paras 255–62, set out below, p 322. The immigration rules purport to make entitlement to enter or remain conditional on satisfaction of the EEA order or the rules. However, in *R v Pieck* [1981] 3 All ER 46, the ECJ held that any formality, beyond mere production of a valid identity card or passport at the frontier, on granting leave to a national of a member state to enter another member state, whenever or wherever it was imposed, fell within the prohibition of entry visas or equivalent documents by art 3(2) of Council Directive 68/360/EEC (see p 304). The ECJ was clear that the special residence permit to which a national of a member state was entitled under art 4 of that Directive was merely a declaration of the right of the person to reside in another member state. It therefore differed from a general residence permit granted to persons from countries other than member states. The ECJ held that a member state could not require a person enjoying the protection of Community law to possess a general residence permit (see also *Sagulo, Brenca and Bakhouche*, Case 8/77 [1977] ECR 1495). The Advocate General stated that the right of Community workers to enter the territory of a member state, conferred by Community law, may not be made subject to the issue of a clearance to this effect by the authorities of that member state (see para 8 of the Opinion). He went on to state, in para 9:

> Admittedly the right of entry for the workers in question is not unlimited. Nevertheless the only restriction which article 48 of the Treaty lays down concerning freedom of movement in the territory of member states is that of limitations justified on grounds of public policy, public security or public health. This restriction must be regarded not as a condition precedent to the acquisition of the right of entry and residence but as providing the possibility, in individual cases where there is sufficient justification, of imposing restrictions on the

exercise of a right derived directly from the Treaty. It does not therefore justify administrative measures requiring in a general way formalities at the frontier other than simply the production of a valid identity card or passport.

In *URBSSA v Bosman* [1996] 1 All ER 97 (EC), the ECJ pointed out that art 48 operates to render unlawful not merely discriminatory provisions in relation to free movement, but also any obstacles to free movement, whether or not they can be termed 'discriminatory'. Thus it rendered unlawful provisions which were likely to restrict the free movement of footballers wishing to pursue their activities in another member state by preventing or deterring them from leaving the clubs to which they belonged. Further, art 6 of the EC Treaty forbids not only overt discrimination on the grounds of nationality, but also covert discrimination which, by the application of other criteria of differentiation, lead in fact to the same result (*Sotgiu v Deutsches Bundesposte* [1974] ECR 153 at 164 (para 11); and Case C-279/93 *Finanzamt Koeln-Altstadt v Schumacker* [1995] All ER 319 (EC) (para 26)). The provisions of art 48 of the Treaty prohibit any discrimination between nationals of member states, whether overt or covert. If the effect of the provisions of the immigration rules, or the EEA Order, is to render the terms on which free movement is exercised by nationals of other member states less favourable than the terms on which British citizens may move in and out of the UK, and reside there, those provisions may be disregarded in favour of the person's entitlement under the relevant EU provision. It is arguable that the provisions of the immigration rules and the EEA Order 1994 discussed below are unlawful to the extent that satisfaction of the requirements of the EEA Order 1994 is treated as a precondition of lawful entry or residence (including settlement), and to the extent that the provisions of the EEA Order 1994 fail properly to implement EU law. The European Economic Area Act 1993 amended s 1(2) of the European Communities Act 1972 (see p 298 above). The EEA Order 1994 purports to implement the free movement aspects of the EEA. It is limited in scope, however, and should be seen in the light of the proper interpretation of the EEA and EU provisions on free movement.

2 Paragraphs 255–62, HC 395: Settlement

255. An EEA national (other than a student) and the family member of such a person, who has been issued with a residence permit or residence document valid for 5 years, and who has remained in the United Kingdom in accordance with the provisions of the 1994 EEA Order for 4 years and continues to do so may, on application, have his residence permit or residence document (as the case may be) endorsed to show permission to remain in the United Kingdom indefinitely.

256. A self-employed EEA national who has a right to reside in the United Kingdom by virtue of having ceased such activity in the United Kingdom within the meaning of the 1994 EEA Order, and the family member of such a person, will be permitted to remain in the United Kingdom indefinitely.

257. In addition, the following persons will be permitted to remain in the United Kingdom indefinitely:

(i) an EEA national who has been continuously resident in the United Kingdom for at least 3 years, has been in employment in the United Kingdom or any other Member State of the EEA for the preceding 12 months, and has reached the age of entitlement to a state retirement pension;

(ii) an EEA national who has ceased to be employed owing to a permanent incapacity for work arising out of an accident at work or an occupational disease entitling him to a state disability pension;

(iii) an EEA national who has been continuously resident in the United Kingdom for at least 2 years, and who has ceased to be employed owing to a permanent incapacity for work;

(iv) a member of the family of an EEA national (as defined in the 1994 EEA Order) to whom (i), (ii) or (iii) above applies;

(v) a member of the family of an EEA national (as defined in the 1994 EEA Order) who dies during his working life after having resided continuously in the United Kingdom for at least 2 years, or whose death results from an accident at work or an occupational disease.

Paragraph 255 of HC 395 deals with settlement conditions for EEA nationals other than students. Under EU law a person is entitled to move and reside freely as long as he is exercising a Community right. Once a person has obtained settlement under para 255 it is irrelevant that he subsequently ceases to exercise a Community right.

Paragraph 255 requires the EEA national and his dependants to have remained for the requisite time in accordance with the provisions of the EEA Order. The definition of 'EEA national' excludes British citizens (see p 326).

Paragraph 255 also makes provision for the endorsement of the residence documents or permits of the family members of EEA nationals. Each must have been issued with a residence permit or residence document valid for five years. He must have remained in the UK for four years. The EEA Order 1994 is intended to ensure that the EC directives on free movement and residence apply to nationals of all EEA states across the whole of the EEA. It provides that a person must have been resident in the UK for four years before he qualifies for settlement in the UK. Settlement may be obtained only if the residence document of the person claiming settlement is valid for five years. The EEA national's residence document or permit is then endorsed to show permission to remain in the UK indefinitely.

Those exercising the rights of self-employed EEA nationals with a right to reside in the UK by virtue of having ceased such activity in the UK within the meaning of the 1994 Order (see p 330) will be permitted to remain in the UK, along with their family members, indefinitely (para 256). EEA nationals of pensionable age, who have been continuously resident in the UK for at least three years and have been in employment in the EEA for the preceding 12 months will receive permission to remain indefinitely. Those who have been incapacitated at work or due to an occupational disease also have the right of permanent residence (para 257(ii)). Permission to remain indefinitely will also be granted to EEA nationals who have been continuously resident in the UK for at least two years and who have ceased to be employed because of a permanent incapacity to work. The members of the families of persons in these categories also obtain the right to permission to remain indefinitely. The members of the family of a EEA national who dies during his working life after having resided continuously in the UK for at least two years, or whose death results from an accident at work or occupational disease, are permitted to remain indefinitely.

3 Paragraphs 258 and 259, HC 395: The EEA family permit

258. An 'EEA family permit' means an entry clearance issued, free of charge, to a family member (as defined in the 1994 EEA Order) who is not an EEA national and who is a visa national or a person who wishes to install himself in the United Kingdom with an EEA national who is a qualified person in the terms of the 1994 EEA Order.

Requirements for the issue of an EEA family permit

259. The requirements for the issue of an EEA family permit are that:
(i) the applicant is the family member (as defined in the 1994 EEA Order) of an EEA national who is a qualified person in the terms of the 1994 EEA Order; and
(ii) the applicant is coming to the United Kingdom for a purpose provided for in the 1984 EEA Order; and
(iii) the applicant is not a person who falls to be excluded on grounds of public policy, public security or public health.

Issue of an EEA family permit

260. An application for an EEA family permit shall be granted provided the Entry Clearance Officer is satisfied that each of the requirements of paragraph 259 is met.

Refusal of an application for an EEA family permit

261. An application for an EEA family permit is to be refused if the Entry Clearance Officer is not satisfied that each of the requirements of paragraph 259 is met.

Registration with the police for family members of EEA nationals

262. The requirements relating to registration with the police are set out in Part 10.

The family permit is an entry clearance which is issued to a family member who is not an EEA national, and who is a visa national (see p 541 for list). A person who wishes to install himself in the UK with an EEA national and who is a 'qualified person' within the terms of the 1994 Order also requires a family permit. For the definition of 'qualified person' see p 325. For the definition of 'family member' see p 327. The original draft of the 1994 Order was debated (and withdrawn) in the House of Lords on 29 April 1994 (see House of Lords Official Report Vol 554 No 79, cols 974–984).

Paragraph 259(iii) deals with the exclusion of an EEA national on grounds of public policy, public security or public health. It is an attempt to implement the EEA Agreement relating to free movement. Grounds of exclusion and removal will be interpreted according to the provisions of Directive 64/221/EEC (see p 304).

Family members of EEA nationals may be required to register with the police according to the terms of Part 10 of HC 395 (para 262).

4 The Immigration (European Economic Area) Order 1994

The Agreement on the European Economic Area, signed at Oporto on 2 May 1992 and adjusted by the Protocol signed at Brussels on 17 March 1993, forms part of the ECJ legal order. The EEA Order 1994 implements freedom of movement and residence, for EC nationals and nationals of EFTA countries save Liechtenstein, under nine Directives.

The Directives in question are:

(a) 64/221/EEC on grounds for exclusion or removal of an EC national (OJ 4 April 1964 056/850);

(b) 68/360/EEC on free movement for workers (OJ 19 October 1968 L 257/13);

(c) 72/194/EEC on residence rights for workers (OJ 26 May 1972 L 121/32);

(d) 73/148/EEC on the right of establishment (OJ 28 June 1973 L 172/14);

(e) 73/34/EEC on residence rights for the self employed (OJ 20 January 1975 L014/10);

(f) 75/35/EEC on the application of the grounds for removal or exclusion to the self-employed (OJ 20 January 1975 L 014/14);

(g) 90/364/EEC on residence rights (OJ 13 July 1990 L 180/26);

(h) 90/365/EEC on residence rights for the retired self-employed (OJ 13 July 1990 L180/28);

(i) 93/96/EEC on the right of residence for students (OJ 18 December 1993 L 317/59).

Where there is a conflict, the EEA Agreement and Directives prevail (see p 297). Article 21 of the EEA Order provides that s 8 of the 1993 Act, dealing with appeals to a special adjudicator, extends to persons to whom the 1994 Order applies, as it does in relation to a person who requires leave to enter or remain in the UK. Appeals by asylum seekers are thus subject to the same regulatory regime regardless of their status under the EEA Order (see Chapter 25).

Under the Order, on arrival in the UK, an EEA national must produce a valid EEA passport or national identity card. The EEA national is processed in a separate EEA immigration channel at most airports. His passport is inspected to confirm his identity and nationality, but no stamp or endorsement is placed in it. Once he enters he may work in employment or self-employment. He may study and he may retire or reside in the UK.

(a) Personal scope of the 1994 Order

Under art 2 of the Order 'EEA national' is defined as a national of a state which is a contracting party to the EEA, save nationals of Liechtenstein which has not yet brought the Agreement into force. An 'EEA family permit' is an entry clearance, issued free of charge, to a family member who wishes to locate himself in the UK with a person known as a 'qualified person'.

A 'qualified person' is an EEA national undertaking the activities set out below in the UK. It does not include a UK national (art 6). Under EU law the question whether a person is a national of a member state is to be determined by that state's domestic law. Annexed to the Treaty of Rome was a definition of 'United Kingdom national', which the government has sought to revise by means of a further unilateral declaration, *On the Meaning of a UK National* (Cmnd 9062 of 1983 (TS No 67)). This indicates that where the term 'national' and cognates are used in Treaty provisions as regards the UK, it means:

(a) British citizens;

(b) British subjects by virtue of Part IV of the 1981 Act who have a right of abode;

(c) British Dependent Territories citizens who acquire their citizenship from a connection with Gibraltar.

The relationship between the exclusion of UK nationals in the EEA Order and the definition annexed to the Treaty is unclear. However, the effect of the exclusion of UK nationals is to prevent the provisions of the Order applying to a British citizen who has exercised a right of free movement in one of the other EEA states and is bringing his non-EU spouse to reside with him in the UK where he seeks to establish himself. Such a person is entitled, however, to rely on the ECJ decision in *Surinder Singh* (see p 302) to do precisely this, and the provisions of the Order could not lawfully be relied on to prevent him.

A detailed discussion of the nationality provisions of the other member states is beyond the scope of this book, but the definition of the member states in art 227 of the Treaty of Rome refers to certain overseas territories of individual member states. Further, domestic definitions of 'national' may not always be coterminous with 'origin within the borders' of the country or its ex-colonies. Thus, persons of German ethnic origins from certain parts of Poland (eg Silesia and East Prussia) may be within the German definition of 'national' in Germany's Basic Law. A further illustration of how the nationality provisions can affect a decision is to be found in *Kaeffer and Proacci v France* (1991) *The Times*, 25 February, Cases C-100/1/89. A holder of a Swiss passport claimed to be of Italian nationality and became an overstayer in Polynesia after a visit. He worked. He was able to claim the EC right of establishment.

Article 6 of the EEA order is intended to implement the rights of free movement on which EEA nationals may rely. The activities to which it relates are those of:

(a) a worker as covered by art 48 of the Treaty of Rome;

(b) a self-employed person, including a person intending to pursue such an activity;

(c) a provider of services, including a person who seeks to provide services within art 60 of the EC Treaty;

(d) a recipient of services, including a person who seeks to receive services within the meaning of art 60 of the EC Treaty;

(e) a self-employed person who has ceased economic activity in the UK;

(f) a self-sufficient person;

(g) a retired person;

(h) a student.

(b) Family members
Under the 1994 Order 'family member', in relation to an EEA national, means:
  (a) that national's spouse;
  (b) a descendant of that national or his spouse who is under 21 years of age or is their dependant;
  (c) a dependent relative in the ascending line of the EEA national or his spouse. A residence permit and residence document is a permit or document issued by the S of S as proof of the holder's right of residence in the UK.
'Family member' includes adopted children (see p 338).

(c) Spouses
The term 'spouse' include's all persons validly married to one another (see below). Article 2(2) of the 1994 Order states that the term 'spouse' (in art 2(1) of the Order) does not include a party to a marriage of convenience. No definition of the term 'marriage of convenience' is offered. 'Marriage of convenience' is a popular, not a legal, description. A marriage may be valid for the purposes of domestic law even if it lacks 'all the purposes and intentions of a genuine and generally accepted union, namely, mutual love, support and comfort; cohabitation in the matrimonial home as husband and wife; a union for life and the production of children' (*Puttick v A-G* [1979] 3 WLR 542 at 549). That is immaterial to the validity of the marriage (*Silver (orse. Kraft) v Silver* [1955] 1 WLR 728).
  The term was considered in *R v IAT ex p Cheema* [1982] Imm AR 124 and *R v IAT ex p Mahmud Khan* [1983] 2 WLR 759, where it was said that there were two ingredients of a marriage of convenience:
  (a) the marriage is entered into for the primary purpose of evading the immigration law and rules, and
  (b) there must be no intention, or there must be a lack of intention, to live together permanently as man and wife.
It is, however, clear from Ministerial statements on the concept as used in the 1994 Order, that something more must be proved before a marriage can be said to be one of convenience for the purposes of EEA marriages.
  In a letter to the S of S dated 30 March 1994, the Clerk to the Joint Committee on Statutory Instruments questioned the *vires* of the Order. Community instruments relating to free movement confer rights on the spouses of EEA nationals. None of these instruments contains a definition of 'spouse'. It is questionable whether the Order is *intra vires* the various Directives and Regulations it purports to implement. The S of S replied to that letter by a Memorandum of 12 April 1994 in which he stated:

> the word spouse in these Community provisions cannot include those who have merely entered into the formalities of a marriage. In particular it cannot include a person who is a party to a marriage contracted for the sole purpose of acquiring a right of residence conferred by Community law. Otherwise the purpose of Community law (namely facilitating the free movement of persons by conferring rights of residence on family members) would be defeated.

The memorandum goes on to say that the 'primary purpose' test will not be applied to the spouses of EEA nationals relying on Community law, but that 'a ground of disqualification can be the fact that the marriage is a ''paper marriage'' designed solely to acquire Community rights to which the party to the marriage would not otherwise be entitled'. On 12 July 1994 Earl Ferrers wrote to Lord MacIntosh, the Opposition spokesman on Home Affairs, expressing the intention behind the term 'marriage of convenience'. He said that the S of S will not regard as a marriage of convenience the case of a couple who are living apart for work reasons, or where there has been a breakdown leading to separation in a genuine marriage. He went on:

> Furthermore, although it is an important principle that parties to a marriage of convenience should not benefit from Community law, *we would make further enquiries into a marriage application only when there were reasonable grounds for suspecting that the marriage is a sham—for example a marriage involving a non-European Area national who was on the point of deportation and where there was no evidence of any relationship prior to the marriage.*

When the motion to approve the draft Order came before the House of Lords on 18 July 1994, Earl Ferrers repeated the part of the above statement italicised. He also stated 'I would like to make it quite clear that the provision (Article 2(2)) has been included to deal with marriages which are entirely bogus, the purpose of which is simply to circumvent immigration control' (HL Debs vol 557, no 120, col 116). He also confirmed that the primary purpose test was not to be applied to EEA marriage cases (col 123).

Considering these ministerial statements, it is suggested that the S of S must prove that the sole intention of the couple was to circumvent the immigration rules. A much higher test is envisaged than that used in primary purpose cases. The position adopted by Earl Ferrers was not that contemplated by earlier formulations of the S of S's position, which referred to marriages of convenience in terms of a 'settled and genuine relationship'.

The interpretation adopted by the minister also appears to be at odds with EU law. For the purposes of EU law, it is the existence of the marriage that renders a person a member of the family of a person exercising EU rights of free movement, so as to give rise to the right of the spouse to install himself with that person. Thus in *Diatta v Land Berlin* [1985] ECR 567, the Advocate General stated that for the purposes of EU law it is not required that the member of the family must live permanently with a worker in order to obtain the right to install himself with the worker. He added that the marital relationship cannot be regarded as dissolved until it has been terminated by the competent authority. The only exception to this principle was that envisaged in *R v IAT and Surinder Singh, ex p S of S* [1992] Imm AR 565, that the marriage was fraudulent (and see *Kwong* (10661), and *Kam Yu Kau* (10859)). The proper approach to the standard of proof in such cases would therefore be that the S of S has to prove that the marriage was contracted fraudulently. The civil standard of proof, by a preponderance of probability, will suffice, although the court should not be satisfied with anything less than probability of a high degree (*Ex p Khawaja* [1984] AC 74, at 124, *per* Lord Bridge of Harwich). (See, eg, *R v IAT ex p Cheung* [1995] Imm AR 104.)

Members of an EEA national's family entitled to admission, whether accompanying him or joining him later, are to be admitted on the same terms, whether or not they themselves are EEA nationals. Whether a person is a dependant is an issue of fact (*Centre Public d'Aide Social, Courcelles v Lebon* [1987] ECR 2811, [1989] 1 CMLR 337). The dependency must pre-date entry to the UK (*Ex p Yennin* [1995] Imm AR 93). Family members who are not EEA nationals themselves and who are coming for settlement must hold a current entry clearance granted for that purpose. When the EEA national leaves the UK, any dependants who are not themselves EEA nationals lose the right to residence and so their residence permits will not be renewed (*Ex p Sandhu* [1983] 3 CMLR 131). If the non-EEA national is deported, then the right to residence is lost from the date the deportation order takes effect (*Ex p Botta* [1987] Imm AR 80). Where all parties remain in the UK, however, there is no requirement that they live together under one roof. In particular, in the case of marriages, there is no requirement that the marriage continue to be a genuine and subsisting relationship (*Diatta v Land Berlin* [1986] 2 CMLR 164).

(d) Carriers' liability

The Immigration (Carriers' Liability) Act 1987 applies to a visa national who is required to hold a family permit as it applies to a person required to hold a visa under the 1971 Act. It is likely that such a person will be checked by the carrier before arrival in the UK (see Chapter 4).

(e) Entry

Articles 3 and 4 of the EEA Order set out the principal rights of EEA nationals. By art 3, an EEA national must be admitted to the UK if he produces, on arrival, a valid national identity card or passport issued by another EEA state. A family member of an EEA national must also be admitted to the UK if he produces, on arrival, a valid national identity card issued by an EEA state or a valid passport. He may also be required to produce proof that he is a member of the EEA national's family. If he is not an EEA national himself, and is a visa national, he must also have an EEA family permit (art 3). The rights in art 3 apply to all EEA nationals and their family members. In particular, it is not necessary for the EEA national to be a 'qualified person'.

(f) Residence

The right to residence may be enjoyed by a qualified person and members of his family (art 4). The right is conferred on the qualified person as long as he remains a qualified person, and on the family members of a qualified person for as long as they remain members of his family. Qualified persons, and members of their families, may reside and pursue an economic activity in the UK. They may do this whether or not any application for a residence permit or residence document that the Order requires them to make has been determined by the S of S (art 4(3)). (For a discussion of residence rights under the applicable EU law see Chapter 16.)

(g) Workers and unemployment

Article 48 grants rights of entry and residence to work seekers for as long as they are engaged in genuine and effective activities (*R v IAT ex p Antonissen* [1991] ECR 745). Such persons should therefore be entitled to residence permits under the 1994 Order. The residence permit to be granted to a worker takes the form set out in Directive 68/360/EEC. By that Directive, as proof of the right of residence, the national must be given a document entitled 'Residence permit for a National of a Member State of the EEC'. The document must include a statement in the following form:

> This permit is issued pursuant to Regulation (EEC) No 1612/68 of the Council of the European Communities of 15 October 1968 and to the measures taken in implementation of the Council Directive of 15 October 1968. In accordance with the provisions of the above mentioned Regulation, the holder of this permit has the right to take up and pursue an activity as an employed person in [UK] territory under the same conditions as [UK] workers (art 11(1)).

A person who has obtained work does not cease to be a qualified person on the ground of unemployment, if he is either temporarily incapable of work as a result of illness or accident, or he is involuntarily unemployed. In the latter case, the fact of his involuntary unemployment must be recorded by the relevant employment office (art 7(1)). In other words, the person must sign on, and must be involuntarily unemployed for the purpose of unemployment law. The conditions for disqualification from receiving jobseeker's allowance are set out in s 19 of the Jobseekers Act 1995. A claimant may be disqualified from receiving jobseeker's allowance if he is not actively seeking work; see also The Jobseekers Allowance Regulations 1996 (SI No 207).

On the first renewal of a residence permit, however, the validity of the permit may be limited to one year if the worker has been involuntarily unemployed in the UK for more than one year (art 13(2), 1994 Order). Again the issue of whether the person is exercising a Treaty right is distinct from whether he is entitled to a residence permit. Further, art 7(2) of Directive 68/380 states that before the residence permit may be limited to one year, the period of involuntary unemployment must be 12 consecutive months. The 1994 Order will have to be interpreted consistently with this provision.

(h) Self-employed person who has ceased economic activity in the UK

A self-employed person who has ceased economic activity in the UK is defined as a person who satisfies one of the following set of conditions:

   (1) On terminating his economic activity in a self-employed capacity, he has reached the age at which he is entitled to a state pension. He must also satisfy the following requirements:

      (i) he must have pursued an activity in a self-employed capacity in the UK for at least 12 months before ceasing his self-employed activity;

      (ii) he must have resided in the UK for more than two years.

(2) (i) he has resided in the UK for more than two years, and

      (ii) he has terminated his activity in a self-employed capacity as a result of a permanent incapacity to work.

(3) (i) he has been continuously resident and continuously active in a self-employed capacity in the UK for three years, and

      (ii) he is active in a self-employed capacity in the territory of another EEA state, but resides in the UK and returns to his residence at least once a week.

When calculating length of residence in the UK, or length of time a self-employed activity has been pursued, periods of absence from the UK not exceeding three months in any year, or any period of absence from the UK due to military service, are not taken into account. Periods of inactivity caused by circumstances outside the control of the self-employed person, or by illness or accident, are taken into account, and are treated as periods of activity in a self-employed capacity (art 6(3)). A self-employed person does not cease to be a qualified person if he is temporarily incapable of work as a result of illness or accident (art 7(2)). Persons seeking to establish themselves in self-employment remain entitled to reside and enter as long as they are engaged in genuine and effective economic activity which is more than merely marginal. These are questions of fact.

A family member of a self-employed person (who has ceased economic activity) is a qualified person. If the self-employed person dies, the family member continues to be a qualified person if the following conditions are satisfied: the family member must have resided with the self-employed person before the latter's death; alternatively if the death took place before the retirement of the self-employed person, the self-employed person must have resided continually in the UK for at least two years. Further, a family member of a self-employed person whose death was the result of an accident at work or occupational disease will continue to be a qualified person for the purposes of the Order (art 8).

(i) Self-sufficient persons

A 'self-sufficient person' is defined in art 6 as one who does not enjoy a right of residence under any provision of EC law other than Directive 90/364, which provides for the admission and residence of persons who have sufficient means to avoid becoming a burden on the social security system. Such a person must, for the purpose of the Order, have sufficient resources to avoid becoming a burden on the social assistance system of the UK. The term 'social assistance' is nowhere defined, but for these purposes a person's resources or income are regarded as sufficient if they exceed the level in respect of which the recipient of those resources or income would qualify for social assistance (art 6(4)). The calculation will require the immigration officer to consider the applicant's capital and income, so as to be able to calculate whether the person's requirements exceeded his resources for the purposes of being able to claim any of the types of social assistance available in the UK.

(j) Retired persons

A 'retired person' is defined as a person who has pursued an activity as an employed or self-employed person, who is covered by sickness insurance in respect of all risks in the UK. He must also be in receipt of one of the following benefits:

    (a)   an invalidity or early retirement pension;

    (b)   old age benefits;

    (c)   survivor's benefits;

    (d)   a pension in respect of an industrial accident or disease.

The amount payable under any of these benefits is paid to the applicant and must be sufficient to avoid his becoming a burden on the social security system of the UK (art 6(2)(g)). In contrast to the provisions relating to 'social assistance' referred to in the definition of self-sufficient persons, the retired person need only avoid becoming a burden on the social security system of the UK.

(k) Students

A 'student' is defined as a person who is enrolled at a recognised educational establishment in the UK for the principal purpose of following a vocational training course. He must have sufficient resources to prevent his becoming a burden on the social assistance system of the UK, and he must be covered by sickness insurance for all risks in the UK (art 6(2)(h)). The only persons who are treated as the family members of a student are his spouse and dependent children (art 9).

The Joint Committee of both Houses of Parliament appointed to scrutinise delegated legislation, in its fifteenth report, drew special attention to the EEA Order on the ground that there is doubt whether it is *intra vires*. The doubt concerns art 6(2)(h). Article 1 of Council Directive 93/96/EEC requires only that the student 'assures the relevant national authority by means of a declaration or by such alternative means as the student may choose that are at least equivalent, that he has sufficient resources to avoid becoming a burden on the social assistance system of the host member state'. The Committee suggested that the requirement of the Order may be more oner-ous than the Directive intended. To satisfy the requirement, it should be sufficient for a student to produce a declaration giving details of his resources which on the face of it are not clearly inadequate. Also, he may, under the Directive, produce a letter from his funding body confirming his financial position. The S of S sought to reply by means of a Memorandum dated 12 April 1994, stating that the Order 'does not specify by what means the student is to prove that he has sufficient resources: indeed it does not place any burden of proof on him. It is submitted that the question whether his resources are sufficient is one of fact'. The Memorandum went on to state that art 1 of the Directive requires the assurance of the national authority that the student has sufficient resources, and that a mere statement would be insufficient. The S of S stated:

> It cannot, for example, be the case that a student who misrepresents the sufficiency of his resources in a declaration thereby automatically becomes entitled to a right of residence under the Directive (and possibly a burden on public funds) without the risk of removal from the United Kingdom. Resources must in fact be sufficient and this is provided for in the Order.

Arguably, the Government's view is at variance with the clear wording of the Directive. Having seen the Memorandum, the Committee concluded '... but the Committee believes that it is doubtful whether the Order does in this respect implement the Directive. There is therefore doubt whether the Order is *intra vires*.' Earl Ferrers stated in the debate on the Order of 18 July 1994:

> We will only require applicants for student residence permits to show reasonable evidence of funds, such as bank statements. A declaration, consisting of a letter indicating financial support from parents or other sponsors would generally be regarded as sufficient. Our clear view remains that it cannot be right that a student should be able to acquire a right of residence—possibly also thereby becoming a burden on public funds—by misrepresenting the adequacy of his resources through a false declaration (HL Debs, vol 557, no 120, 18 July 1994, col 118).

The Directive, however makes a requirement merely about *how* the student may be required to assure the national authority. The *vires* of the Order therefore remains in question.

(l) Residence permits
Grant of residence permits   The S of S must grant a residence permit to a qualified person who applies for a residence permit, and:
   (a) produces a valid identity card or passport issued by an EEA state; and
   (b) proves that he is a qualified person (art 5(1)).
If he is a worker, he may prove only that he is a qualified person by means of confirmation of his engagement from his employer or a certificate of employment (art 5(3)). If a member of the qualified person's family applies, the S of S must grant him a residence permit or residence document, provided that he produces:
   (a) a valid identity card issued by an EEA state or a valid passport; and
   (b) proof that he is a family member of a qualified person.
If the person applying for the residence permit or residence document is not an EEA national and requires a family permit for admission to the UK, he must, instead of satisfying the requirement that he produce proof that he is a family member of a qualified person, produce the permit (art 5(2)). A residence document issued to a family member who is not an EEA national may take the form of a stamp in his passport (art 11(2)).

The S of S is not obliged to issue a residence permit in certain circumstances, regardless of whether a person satisfies the above requirements. Thus, the S of S is not obliged to grant a residence permit to a person other than a qualified person. Nor is he obliged to issue a residence permit to the following persons (art 10):

  (a) a worker whose employment in the UK is limited to three months and who either holds a document from his employer certifying that his employment is limited to three months, or who is a person whose employment is within the scope of the Directive of 25 February 1964 on the freedom to provide services as an intermediary in commerce, industry and small craft industries, or the provisions of Directive 68/360;

  (b) a worker who is employed in the UK, but who resides in another EEA state, returning to that residence at least once a week;

  (c) a seasonal worker whose contract of employment has been approved by the Department of Education and Employment;

  (d) a person who provides or receives services if the services are to be provided for no more than three months.

The S of S may also refuse to grant a residence permit or document to a qualified person or a member of his family if the refusal is justified on grounds of public policy, public security or public health (art 16).

Duration   A residence permit is valid for at least five years (art 12), although there are exceptions to this rule. In all cases the validity of the residence permit is not affected by the absence of the holder from the UK for no more than six consecutive months, or absence of whatever length for military service (art 12(7)). The S of S is obliged to renew a residence permit on application, save that certain limitations apply in the cases of workers and students (art 13(1)).

The permit may be limited to the duration of the employment of:

  (a) a worker who is to be employed in the UK for less than 12, but more than three, months (art 12(2));

  (b) a seasonal worker who is to be employed for more than three months. The duration of the employment must be indicated in the document confirming the worker's engagement or certificate of employment.

In the case of a provider or recipient of services, the residence permit may be limited to the period for which services are to be provided (art 12(4)). In the case of a student the residence permit may be limited in the following ways:

  (a) to the duration of the course;

  (b) to one year if the course lasts longer than a year (art 12(5)), in which case, renewal of the permit may be for periods limited to one year.

The residence permit may be limited to two years in the case of a self-sufficient person or a retired person. The initial period of two years may be extended for a further three years (art 12(6)).

A family member of an EEA national is entitled to a residence permit or residence document of the same duration as the residence permit granted to the qualified person of whose family he is a member. The permit or document is subject to the same terms as to renewal as apply to the EEA national's permit (art 14).

Appeals   An EEA national or the family member of an EEA national who is refused a residence permit or residence document, or has it withdrawn by the S or S, may appeal against the refusal or withdrawal. He is treated as a person who has limited leave under the 1971 Act who is appealing against refusal to vary that leave. The refusal or withdrawal shall not take effect while an appeal is pending, nor shall a person be required to leave the UK during that time. His right to appeal is subject to art 20 of the Order which applies the following provisions of the 1971 Act (the effect of which is considered below):

(a) s 5 (procedure for deportation);
(b) s 13(5) (exclusion conducive to the public good);
(c) s 14(3) (departure conducive to the public good);
(d) s 15(3) (deportation conducive to the public good);
(e) Sched 2 (examination).

(m) Exclusion and removal of an EEA national from the UK
The provisions of the Order relating to exclusion and removal are designed to implement the provisions of Directive 64/221/EEC.

Exclusion   Under art 15 of the 1994 Order a person is not entitled to be admitted to the UK by virtue of art 3 if his exclusion is justified on grounds of public policy, public security or public health. A person who is excluded may appeal against the refusal of admission as if he had been refused leave to enter and was entitled to appeal by virtue of s 13(1) of the 1971 Act. Under this provision the appellant may not appeal while he is in the UK. It may be that this requirement is at odds with EU law. Where directly applicable Community rights are sought to be enforced in the national courts, it is for the national legal order to specify the competent national courts and applicable procedural rules. The rules must not, however, be less favourable than those governing the same or similar rights of action under national law and must not make it impossible or virtually impossible in practice to exercise rights which the national courts have a duty to protect under Community law (*Amministrazione delle Finanze dello Stato v SpA San Giorgio,* Case 199/82 [1983] ECR 3595). It may be that the requirement that a person refused admission may appeal only from abroad renders it virtually impossible for the appellant to exercise his right of free movement.

The right to appeal conferred by art 15 is subject to art 20(2) of the Order. This states that the procedure for deportation under s 5 of the 1971 Act shall apply. Further, the appellant will be treated as if he is not entitled to appeal if the S of S has certified that directions have been given by him personally (and not a person acting under his authority) for the appellant not to be given entry. The direction must be given on the basis that his exclusion is conducive to the public good (1971 Act, s 13(5)). Such a person is also subject to Sched 2 to the 1971 Act which makes provision for the administration of control on entry. In the Order, the scope of Sched 2 is summarised as relating to examination. However, Sched 2 includes provisions relating to removal of illegal entrants (para 8), detention of persons liable to examination (para 16), the effects of appeals, and bail pending appeal (Part II).

Removal   An EEA national and a member of his family may be removed from the UK under the 1994 Order when the EEA national ceases to be a qualified person. A family member may also be removed if he ceases to be a member of the qualified person's family. The EEA national, or the member of his family, may also be removed if removal is justified on the grounds of public policy, public security or public health (art 15(2)).

A right of appeal against removal is also conferred by art 15(2). A person who ceases to be a qualified person or the member of the family of a qualified person is deemed to be a person in respect of whom the S of S has decided to make a deportation order and who is entitled to appeal by virtue of s 15(1)(*a*) of the 1971 Act. This provides for a right of appeal by a person whom the S of S intends to deport under s 3(5) of the 1971 Act:

(*a*) for having breached a condition of his limited leave or overstaying; or

(*b*) because the S of S deems his deportation to be conducive to the public good; or

(*c*) because another person to whose family he belongs is or has been ordered to be deported.

A person who is to be removed because he has ceased to be a member of an EEA national's family is treated as if he is entitled to appeal under the 1971 Act (art 15(2)(ii)). There are, however, further requirements and procedures to be satisfied or followed in such a case. The person is subject to the procedures for deportation under s 5 of the 1971 Act. In addition, he is not entitled to appeal against a variation of his leave which reduces its duration; or against any refusal to enlarge or remove the limit on its duration where the S of S certifies that the appellant's departure from the UK would be conducive to the public good, as being in the interests of national security or of the relations between the UK and any other country or for other reasons for a political nature. He will not be able to appeal against a decision which was taken on one of those grounds by the S of S personally, and not by a person acting under his authority (art 20(2) applying the 1971 Act, s 14(3)). There is no appeal against a decision to make the removal order if the ground of the decision is that his deportation is conducive to the public good as in the interests of national security or of relations between the UK and any other country or for other reasons of a political nature (art 20(2), applying the 1971 Act, s 15(3)). Article 15(2)(ii) also applies s 15(7). Thus a person who has ceased to be a member of an EEA national's family is entitled to appeal to the IAT in the first instance if a deportation order has been made and the ground for making that order was either:

(*a*) that deportation is conducive to the public good; or

(*b*) the ground of the deportation order is that he belongs to the family of another person.

He must also appeal to the IAT if there is a pending related appeal.

The scheme is, to say the least, confused. First, the appeal is against a decision to remove a person in respect of whom removal is justified on the grounds of public policy, public security or public health. These terms have a specific meaning under EC law and refer to the grounds in EC Directive 64/221. However, the circumstances in which there is or is not a right of appeal refer to grounds 'conducive to public good'. Such considerations limit the right of appeal to which a person is entitled under the Directive, and may breach EC law (see above). Second, the requirement that the person be out of the UK at the time of appeal also acts, in practice, as an (albeit temporary) exclusion, and to that extent may be in breach of EC law. (See *Ex p Gallagher*, p 305 above.)

Public policy, public security and public health   Article 17 of the Order attempts to set out the principles on which decisions on the grounds of public policy, public security and public health are to be taken. They are as follows:

(a) the relevant grounds shall not be invoked to secure economic ends;

(b) a decision taken on one or more of the relevant grounds shall be based exclusively on the personal conduct of the individual in respect of whom the decision is taken;

(c) a person's previous criminal convictions shall not, in themselves, justify a decision on grounds of public policy or public security;

(d) a decision to refuse admission to the UK or to refuse to grant the first residence permit to a person on the grounds that he has a disease or disability shall be justified only if the disease or disability is of a type specified in council Directive 64/221/EEC;

(e) a disease or disability contracted after a person has been granted a first residence permit shall not justify a decision to refuse to renew his residence permit or a decision to remove him;

(f) a person shall be informed of the grounds of public policy, public security or public health on which the decision taken in his case is based unless it would be contrary to the interests of national security to do so.

Treatment of persons ceasing to be qualified persons or members of a qualified person's family   Upon ceasing to be a qualified person, an EEA national who is in the UK and the family member of an EEA national in the UK are both to be treated as if they were persons who require leave to enter or remain in the UK under the 1971 Act. It is only when the person has actually ceased to have a right of free movement or residence pursuant to EU law that he can be so treated. It is suggested that the deeming words 'as if', used in the 1994 Order, make no difference to the legality of such treatment.

(For a useful discussion of the 1994 Order, see *The Immigration (European Economic Area) Order 1994* by Sofia Gondal, INL&P vol 9, no 1, 1995, p 21.)

(n) Adoptive children of EEA nationals

In a letter dated 5 February 1996 to Bindman and Partners, the IND set out its position on the rules governing the adoptive children of EEA nationals. 'Family member' under the EEA Order is taken to include adoptive children, but the IND takes the view that the adoption must have taken place in a country whose adoption orders are recognised by UK law (see the Adoption (Designation of Overseas Adoptions) Order 1973). However, it is suggested that if the adoption is recognised by the EEA national's country, that would suffice for the purpose of EEA Agreement law.

Where the child is not adopted in accordance with the 1973 Order, an application for entry clearance for the child to come to the UK for adoption through the courts is considered under the following concession:

> The immigration requirements which would have to be met are that the child:
>
> (i)   will be adopted by persons at least one of whom must be an EEA national exercising Treaty rights in the United Kingdom;
>
> (ii)   is under 18;
>
> (iii) is not leading an independent life, is unmarried and has not formed an independent family unit;
>
> (iv) can, and will, be accommodated adequately without recourse to public funds in accommodation which the prospective adoptive parents own or occupy exclusively;
>
> (v)   has the same rights and obligations as any other child of the marriage;
>
> (vi) was available for adoption due to the inability of the natural parents or current carers to care for him and there has been a genuine transfer of parental responsibility to the prospective adoptive parents;
>
> (vii) has lost or broken his ties with his natural family;
>
> (viii) will be adopted through the United Kingdom courts but the adoption is not one of convenience arranged to facilitate his admission to the United Kingdom.

Local social services carry out a home study on the prospective adoptive parents and this must be endorsed by the territorial health authority. Provided such endorsement is forthcoming and the above conditions are met, entry clearance may be granted.

On arrival, the potential adoptee is normally granted 12 months' leave to enter. After adoption, an EEA residence document may be applied for, and is normally co-terminous with the EEA adoptive parents' residence permit.

De facto adoption   Children who lived for a considerable time with the adoptive parents are considered on a discretionary basis. However, in addition to (i) and (viii) above, the *de facto* adoption must have occurred when both adoptive parents resided together abroad. By contrast with legal adoptions, there is no requirement for adoption through the UK courts or to involve the social services before admission.

On arrival, no conditions are attached to the child's stay and he may apply for a residence document as a family member under the EEA Order.

Part V

Remedies

Chapter 18

Rights of Appeal

Part 12 (paras 353–61) of HC 395 provides the procedures relating to rights of appeal. New Asylum Appeals (Procedure) Rules have now been made under the Asylum and Immigration Act 1996 ('the 1996 Act'), and came into force on 1 September 1996. Asylum appeals are discussed in Chapter 26. This part of this work, deals primarily with non-asylum appeals, although much of what is said about general procedure also applies to asylum appeals.

1 Introduction

Part 12, HC 395 provides as follows:

Notice of refusal of leave to enter
353. Where refusal of leave to enter is confirmed, the person concerned should be served with a notice informing him of the decision and of the reasons for refusal. This notice will also inform him whether he has a right of appeal under Section 13 of the 1971 Act and, if so, how the right of appeal might be exercised.

Rights of appeal in relation to a person claiming to have the right of abode
354. A person who claims to have the right of abode is not entitled to appeal against a decision that he requires leave to enter unless he holds either a United Kingdom passport describing him as a British citizen or as a citizen of the United Kingdom and Colonies having the right of abode in the United Kingdom, or a certificate of entitlement duly issued to him by or on behalf of the Government of the United Kingdom certifying that he has such a right of abode.

Rights of appeal in relation to a person who holds an entry clearance or work permit
355. Subject to Section 13(5) of the Immigration Act 1971 and Section 2(1) of the 1996 Act, a person in possession of a valid United Kingdom entry clearance or work permit who is entitled to appeal against refusal of leave to enter the United Kingdom may exercise his right of appeal before removal from the United Kingdom. If such a person sought entry through the Channel Tunnel he may, upon giving notice of appeal, be brought through the tunnel to enable him to pursue his appeal.

Rights of appeal exercisable from abroad

356. A person who is entitled to appeal against refusal of leave to enter may exercise that right only after he has left the United Kingdom, irrespective of his national status, unless:

(i)   the person has applied for asylum; or

(ii) the circumstances described in paragraph 354 or 355 above apply,

and the Secretary of State has not issued a certificate under section 2(1) of the 1996 Act.

Rights of appeal against a time limit or condition

357. A person aggrieved by the imposition on entry of a time limit or condition may apply to the Home Office for variation of his leave. Subject to paragraph 358 below, he will have a right of appeal if variation is refused.

Rights of appeal against variation of leave to enter or refusal to vary it

358. A person may appeal against any variation of his leave to enter or any refusal to vary it except:

(i)   when a refusal is on one of the grounds specified in Section 14(2ZA) or Section 14(2A) of the 1971 Act; or

(ii) if the case comes within Section 14(3) of the 1971 Act following a decision taken personally by the Secretary of State and not by a person acting under his authority; or

(iii) when a variation of leave is made by statutory instrument; or

(iv) if leave is curtailed under Section 7(1) or Section 7(1A) of the Asylum and Immigration Appeals Act 1993.

Notice of appeal rights

359. Where an application for variation of leave to enter is refused; or a variation is made otherwise than on the application of the person concerned, or is less favourable than that for which he applied, notice of the decision and, if an appeal lies, of his right of appeal, will normally be handed to the person concerned or sent to his last known address. Applicants should therefore keep the Secretary of State informed of any change of address. The notice may alternatively be given or sent to a person who has either made the application on behalf of another, or has subsequently been appointed to act on another's behalf in connection with an application.

Explanatory statement

360. If notice of appeal is given within the period allowed, an explanatory statement summarising the facts of the case on the basis of which the decision was taken will normally be prepared and be sent to the independent appellate authorities, who will notify the appellant of the arrangements for any appeal to be heard.

Rights of appeal in asylum cases

361. Rights of appeal in asylum cases are covered in paragraph 348 above [see p 498].

Cm 3365 amended paras 353, 355, 356, 358 and 359. Sections 13–17 of the 1971 Act and s 10 of the 1993 Act set out the circumstances in which there is or is not a right of appeal in non-asylum cases. Paragraph 353 states that the applicant should, on refusal, be handed a notice informing him of the decision and of the reasons for it. The notice also tells him whether or not he has a right of appeal. Such a notice cannot give or deprive a person of a right of appeal. Since rights of appeal are purely statutory, the Acts are a comprehensive statement of those rights. The first step is to ascertain if there is a right of appeal.

An appeal can be launched if there is a dispute as to whether the appellant is entitled to appeal. Under the Immigration Appeals (Procedure) Rules 1984 (SI No 2041, 'the 1984 Appeals Rules'), the existence of a right to appeal will be taken as a preliminary point by the respondent, and at the hearing of the appeal it will be determined as a preliminary issue (see rr 8 and 11). In asylum cases, however, such a preliminary point is not a final determination for the purposes of the 1993 Act, and there is no right of appeal to the CA against a decision on a preliminary point (see p 399 and *S of S v Dahir and Abdi* [1995] Imm AR 570).

Where the appellant is entitled to be notified of a decision subject to a right of appeal, the decision is deemed to have been taken on the date the notification is posted to, or served on, the appellant (see 4 below). Unless otherwise stated, the appeal lies in the first instance to the adjudicator. Leave to appeal is not required for any appeal to an adjudicator or to the IAT if the IAT is sitting at first instance. There is an appeal pending for the purposes of the 1971 Act when a notice of appeal has been duly given (s 33(4)).

The grounds for refusal of an application can normally be varied or amplified by amendment up to the start of the hearing of an appeal. The S of S may not, however, amend the reasons given in a notice of intention to make a deportation order when the appeal concerns only whether there is a power in law to make the decision to deport under s 5(1) of the 1988 Act. In *Egbale* (11563) the IAT considered a case in which the original notice of intention to deport stated that the appellant had remained without authority. She was married to a Commonwealth citizen, and had settled in the UK before repeal of the provision of the 1971 Act that Commonwealth citizens and their wives should not be any less free to come to and go from the UK (s 1(5), 1971 Act, before amendment by 1988 Act). The S of S purported to amend the ground of refusal at the hearing to an allegation that the appellant had remained 'without leave'. However, she could rely on the unrepealed s 1(5) of the 1971 Act, thus the amendment raised a wholly different set of considerations. If she was an overstayer that was irrelevant to whether she had remained without authority because of the unamended s 1(5). The S of S could not therefore amend the grounds for refusal in such a radical way.

As already noted, whether there is a right to appeal may be determined as a preliminary issue at the hearing. This is not a question which the S of S has power to determine even if a notice of appeal has to be lodged with him. The S of S may not declare that a person has no right of appeal, or has forfeited that right (*Ex p Ken'aan* [1990] Imm AR 544). However, the kind of leave granted to the applicant may determine whether he has a right of appeal. Thus in *Ishaq v S of S* [1996] Imm AR 80 the CA held that there was no right of appeal in the case of a returning resident who was refused entry in that capacity, but was granted leave to enter as a visitor. He had not made an application for variation of leave. He therefore had no right of appeal from abroad in respect of the refusal of leave to enter as a returning resident.

A person may appeal against refusal of entry while in the UK only if:

(a) he is an asylum seeker whose claim has not been certified under s 2(1) of the 1996 Act (see p 461); or

(b) he was refused leave at the port of entry, and held a current entry clearance or was named in a current work permit, is not claiming asylum or has not had his claim certified under s 2(1) of the 1996 Act (para 355 and s 13(3), 1971 Act).

Under HC 395 the right of appeal is to be exercised only after the person has left the UK, except in the following cases:

(a) asylum cases (para 348 and p 498, but see *(d)*);

(b) where the person claims to have the right of abode and he has either a UK passport describing him as a British citizen or as a CUKC having the right of abode, or a certificate of entitlement (para 354);

(c) where the person is in possession of a valid entry clearance or is named in a current work permit; save that a person may not appeal if the S of S certifies that directions have been given by him personally for the appellant not to be given entry to the UK on the ground that his exclusion is conducive to the public good (para 355).

(d) where a person has made a claim for asylum which is certified under s 2 of the 1996 Act (see p 461), unless and until such a certificate is set aside on appeal (s 3, 1996 Act). If removal is to a member state of the EU, no appeal may be brought while the applicant is in the UK (s 3(2)).

For the purposes of s 13, a stamp relating to an earlier grant of leave does not constitute a current entry clearance (*Ex p Oyo* [1995] Imm AR 553). A person who is refused entry to the UK may make further applications for leave to enter before his removal from the UK. However, a refusal of that application (in some other capacity) will attract a right of appeal under s 13 of the 1971 Act which will be exercisable only from outside the UK. The exception is an appeal under s 8 of the 1993 Act on asylum grounds which has not been certified under s 2 of the 1996 Act. If a second application is made after a first application has been refused there is no entry clearance conferring a right to appeal on the applicant while he is in the UK. The second appeal can be made only from abroad. However, if the second application is made before the decision on the first application has been made, both decisions attract an in-country right of appeal (*Ashraf v IAT* [1989] Imm AR 234 and *Moussavi* [1986] Imm AR 39).

There is no right of appeal against refusal of entry clearance or leave to enter if the refusal is based on the failure of the applicant to have a relevant document or to satisfy a requirement of the immigration rules as to age or nationality or citizenship, or if the person seeks entry for a period exceeding that permitted under the immigration rules (1971 Act, s 13(3B) as inserted by 1993 Act). A person who seeks entry to the UK as a visitor, or to follow a course of study of not more than six months' duration for which he has been accepted, or who has the intention of studying but has not been accepted on a course, or who is a dependant of a person in one of these categories, may not appeal against a refusal of entry clearance. He may appeal only against refusal of leave to enter if he has a current entry clearance (s 13(3A), 1971 Act).

2   Rights of appeal under s 13, 1971 Act

Under s 13 of the 1971 Act, there are rights of appeal in the following circumstances:

(1) A person is refused leave to enter the UK.

(2) A person is refused an entry clearance or certificate of entitlement to the right of abode.

(3) It has been decided that a person requires leave to enter.

(4) A person is refused entry and holds a passport stating that he has a right of abode in the UK, or is a British citizen, or bears a certificate of entitlement to the right of abode in the UK. Such a person may appeal on the grounds that he has a right of abode in the UK.

(5) A person who holds a current entry clearance or is named in a current work permit is refused leave to enter. If he is refused entry while trying to enter through the Channel Tunnel system, he may (on giving notice of appeal) be brought through the tunnel to enable him to pursue his appeal (HC 395, para 355). However, where a claim for asylum has been certified under s 2 of the 1996 Act, there is no in-country right of appeal (see p 461).

(a) Destination

There is a right of appeal where directions are given under the 1971 Act for a person's removal from the UK either:

(a) on his being refused leave to enter; or

(b) on a deportation order being made against him; or

(c) on his having entered the UK in breach of a deportation order.

Such a person may appeal to an adjudicator against the directions on the ground that he ought, if at all, to be removed to a different country or territory specified by him (s 17(1)) (see p 353).

If a person is refused leave to enter, and, before he appeals against refusal, directions are given for his removal from the UK to any other country, or the S of S or an immigration officer serves on him a notice stating that any directions which may be given for his removal will be for his removal to a country specified in the notice, he may appeal both against the refusal of leave to enter and against the destination in the same proceedings (s 17(2) of the 1971 Act). In all cases, if the adjudicator is satisfied either that the appellant was an illegal entrant at the time he was refused entry, or there was a deportation order in force against the appellant at the time he was refused entry, the adjudicator must refuse the appeal.

(b) Asylum claimants

A person who makes a claim for asylum may appeal, in the same proceedings, against both the refusal of the claim and against any refusal of leave to enter. He appeals to the special adjudicator. He may appeal to the special adjudicator at any time on asylum grounds. In particular, where he arrived in the UK and applied for leave to enter on a non-asylum ground but was refused, he is entitled to make a further application on an asylum ground while still in the UK. Such an application is a valid application for leave to enter and will now attract an in-country right of appeal (cf *R v IAT, ex p S of S* [1990] Imm AR 652 (see Chapter 26)).

(c) Time limits

Rule 4 of the 1984 Appeals Rules imposes the following time limits on s 13 appeals:

(1) Where the appeal is against refusal of leave to enter or the decision that leave to enter is required, then the time limit is 28 days after the person departs from the UK if the refusal was not at the port of entry, or the person refused did not carry a current entry clearance.

(2) If the appeal does not have to be made from outside the UK, it can be made at any time before or after departure from the UK, but must be made before 28 days from the date of departure at latest.

(3) If the appeal is against the refusal of a certificate of entitlement to the right of abode, and the application for the certificate was made to the ECO, the appeal may be lodged up to three months after the decision.

(4) If the appeal against the refusal of the certificate of entitlement arises from an application to the S of S, the appeal must be lodged within 14 days from the date of the decision.

(5) If the appeal is against the refusal of entry clearance the time limit is three months from the date of the decision.

(See further, on time limits, pp 348–9 and 502.)

The effect of these provisions is that where the application is refused while the person is still abroad, there is generally a three-month period in which to appeal, whereas if the decision is made after the person has come to the UK, the shorter time of 14 or 28 days applies.

3 Rights of appeal under s 14, 1971 Act

Where a person has limited leave to enter the UK, he may appeal to the adjudicator against a variation of his leave, or against refusal to vary his leave. He may appeal whether the variation relates to the conditions of his leave or the length of his leave. Thus where an applicant applied for indefinite leave to remain and was granted limited leave, he could appeal under s 14 for the removal of the limitation (*S of S v Behrooz* [1991] Imm AR 82 (IAT)). The appeal must be made while the appellant has limited leave. Under the Immigration (Variation of Leave) Order 1976 (SI No 1572) as amended by SI 1993 No 1657, if a person has limited leave to enter and applies before the expiry of that leave for a variation of leave, the duration of his leave is extended to the date of the decision on the application for variation. Thus if an appeal is lodged in the course of the 28 days allowed under the order, it attracts the s 14 right of appeal; but if the appeal is made 29 days or later after the decision refusing the variation, there is no right of appeal (see *Ex p Selo Wa-Selo* [1990] Imm AR 76, and *Akhtar* [1991] Imm AR 232).

While an appeal under s 14 is pending, the *status quo* is maintained, and the variation which it is sought to impose does not take effect. The appellant is not to be required to leave the UK during that time merely because his leave expires (s 14(1)). If, however, a deportation order is made against a person whose appeal is pending, then his appeal lapses (s 14(5)). Where a person who is appealing under s 14 leaves the country, he has no right to re-enter (*R v Immigration Officer, ex p Nikhat Ali* [1982] Imm AR 1). Under s 8, certain categories of person are exempt from the provisions of the 1971 Act; members of diplomatic missions are also exempt. Where a person ceases to have this immunity, or ceases to be a British citizen, and is given limited leave to remain, he may appeal to the adjudicator against any provision which limits his leave, and likewise is protected from removal.

Paragraph 358 of HC 395 provides that a person may appeal against any variation of leave to enter or refusal to vary it except where:

   (a) the refusal is on the ground that:
      (i) a relevant document required by the immigration rules has not been issued;
      (ii) the person does not satisfy a requirement of the immigration rules as to age, nationality or citizenship;
      (iii) the variation would result in the duration of the person's leave exceeding that permitted by the immigration rules; or
      (iv) any fee required by or under any enactment has not been paid (s 14(2A), 1971 Act as inserted by the 1993 Act);
   (b) the S of S certifies that the departure of the person is conducive to the public good, or in the interests of national security, or relations of the UK to another country;
   (c) a variation of leave results from a statutory instrument;
   (d) the leave is curtailed under s 7(1) or 7(1A), Asylum and Immigration Appeals Act 1993;
   (e) the appeal would be against a variation of his leave which adds a condition requiring the applicant to maintain and accommodate himself and any dependants of his without recourse to public funds (s 3(1)(*c*)(ii), 1971 Act as amended by the 1996 Act), or against a refusal to vary his leave by revoking such a condition.

(a) Leave exceeding permitted maximum

In *R v IAT ex p Sam* [1996] Imm AR 272, May J held that where leave had exceeded the maximum period permitted by the immigration rules, refusal to extend leave beyond that necessarily resulted in leave exceeding that which is permitted by the rules, so that there was no right of appeal (s 14(2A), 1971 Act). In *Wong v S of S* [1995] Imm AR 451 the appellant originally obtained six months' leave as a visitor. Before that expired, he obtained leave to remain as a working holidaymaker. At the end of that leave, he applied for a further three months' leave as a visitor. If granted, this further leave would have brought the total leave as a visitor over the six months' maximum. The appellant had not, though, been in the UK for a full six months as a visitor. Because the S of S should have considered granting leave for the unexpired portion of the six months, the appellant retained his right of appeal against the decision to refuse to vary his leave. In *Low* [1995] Imm AR 435 it was not clear whether the appellant had been granted leave to enter as a transit passenger, with a maximum period of leave of 48 hours, or in some other capacity. The IAT held that she was therefore a visitor, and so had not lost her right of appeal as a result of s 14(2A) when she applied for a variation of leave.

(b) Relevant documents

An entry clearance issued for one purpose will not be regarded as a relevant document if it is sought to appeal against a decision refusing to vary a person's leave to remain for another purpose. Thus in *Ex p Ahmed v S of S* [1995] Imm AR 590 the applicant came to the UK as the dependant of his father (a work permit holder) and had entry clearance for that purpose. He was refused a variation to permit him to remain as a student. He was not barred from bringing an application for judicial review against the decision to refuse that variation because, without a relevant document, s 14(2A) deprived him of a right of appeal, so that there was no alternative remedy to judicial review (and see *Ex p Ashfaque Ahmed* [1995] Imm AR 590). Schedule 2, para 3 to the 1996 Act substituted s 14(2B)(c) so that 'relevant documents' include work permits or equivalent documents issued after entry. Such documents would include work approvals.

(c) Curtailment

A person's leave may be curtailed if an application for asylum made by him is refused (see p 249). A dependant of a person whose leave is curtailed, who also has leave, may have his leave curtailed at the same time (see p 250).

Section 14(2A) removes the right of appeal only where the relevant immigration rule requires a document to be issued. Thus where an application was made for a variation of leave to remain on an extended work permit, and that work permit extension was refused by the Department of Education and Employment, the applicant retained his right of appeal because the relevant immigration rule (para 122 of HC 251) did not require any document to be issued (*Pang v S of S* [1995] Imm AR 470 (IAT)).

(d) Time Limits

Under r 4 of the 1984 Appeals Rules, the time limit under s 14 is 14 days from:

(a) the variation of leave or refusal to vary (s 14(1)); or

(b) the grant of limited leave after the cessation of exempt status (s 14(2)).

Rule 5 of the 1984 Appeals Rules provides that an immigration officer, ECO or the appellate authorities may treat a notice as if it has been given in accordance with r 4. This cannot be invoked to override s 14 of the 1971 Act and extend time during which a late appeal can be admitted (*Ex p Lai* [1995] Imm AR 613 (a leave application)). By contrast, the terms of the rule are clear and the various bodies have the power to extend time, although an argument that they are obliged to do so would be doomed to failure, save possibly where the body has been perverse in refusing.

4 Rights of appeal under s 15, 1971 Act (deportation)

Section 3(5) of the 1971 Act permits a deportation order to be made in the following circumstances:

(a) where the person has limited leave to enter or remain, and does not observe a condition (eg a prohibition on work) attached to the leave, and remains beyond the time limited by the leave;

(b) where the S of S deems that the person's deportation is conducive to the public good; or

(c) where there is another member of the person's family who is or has been ordered to be deported.

Section 15 confers a right to appeal against either a decision to make a deportation order, or a decision to refuse to revoke a deportation order. There is a distinction between a decision to deport and the signing of a deportation order (see p 253). The order itself cannot be made so long as an appeal may be brought against the decision to make the deportation order. Likewise, where an appeal has been duly brought and lodged in proper form, no order may be signed while the appeal is pending (s 15(2)). Where the decision to deport or the refusal to revoke the deportation order is made on the grounds that deportation would be conducive to the public good there is no right of appeal to the adjudicator, but there is a right of appeal to the IAT at first instance, save where the appellant has also lodged an appeal against a refusal of asylum (*Raziastaraie v S of S* [1994] Imm AR 330). Where, however, the decision to deport or the refusal to revoke is made on the grounds that it is in the national interest, for political reasons, or for national security reasons, there is no right of appeal. The refusal to revoke for these reasons may be taken only by the S of S, and not by a person acting under his authority (s 15(3)). Where a decision of this nature is made on these special grounds, there is merely an opportunity for the person to state, before the advisors, that he disagrees with the decision, under the special procedure which the Home Office has adopted in these cases (see p 359).

There is no right of appeal against a refusal to revoke a deportation order while the person is still in the UK, or where he has entered the UK while the deportation order is in force.

If the decision to deport (or refusal to revoke) is made on the grounds that another member of the person's family is or has been ordered to be deported, the appellant is barred from disputing statements made with a view to obtaining leave to enter or remain, for the purpose of showing that he does not or did not belong to the family of the principal deportee. He may, however, dispute such a statement if he can show that it was not made by him or anyone acting with his authority for the purposes of gaining leave to enter or remain. He must also show that when he took the benefit of the leave he did not know that any such statement had been made. Where a child under 18 years of age knows that a statement was made on his behalf to obtain entry or leave to remain, he may still dispute the statement, and appeal on the basis that he is not a member of the principal deportee's family. Certain decisions to deport attract a right of appeal direct to the IAT.

(a) Limits on the right to argue merits

Section 5 of the Immigration Act 1988 severely reduced the right of appeal to the adjudicator. Any person who was last given leave to enter the UK less than seven years before the date of the decision to deport is not entitled to appeal against the merits of a decision to make a deportation order against him if the decision is based on either:

(a) a breach of limited leave (under s 3(5)(a) of the 1971 Act); or

(b) the fact that the person is a member of the family of a person who is or has been ordered to be deported (under s 3(5)(c));

(c) the fact that he obtained leave to remain by deception (under s 3(5)(aa) of the 1971 Act).

It is presumed that an appellant was last given leave to enter less than seven years before the decision to deport was made unless the appellant can prove on the balance of probabilities that he was last given leave to enter more than seven years before the decision (1988 Act, s 5(4)). A person may still appeal against the decision to deport, even if falling within (a) or (b) above, if, on the facts of his case, there is no power in law to make the deportation order for the reasons stated in the notice of the decision to make the deportation order.

Under the Immigration (Restricted Right of Appeal against Deportation) (Exemption) Order 1993 (SI No 1656) as amended by SI 1996 No 2145, there are two further categories of person who may argue the merits of their cases:

(a) any person whose limited leave to enter or remain in the UK has been curtailed by the S of S under s 7(1) or 7(1A) of the 1993 Act; and

(b) any person who would have last been given leave to enter the UK seven years or more before the date of the decision to make a deportation order against him, but for his having obtained a subsequent leave after any absence from the UK within the period limited for the duration of the earlier leave.

On return within the period of an earlier leave, leave is normally for the remainder of the earlier leave. Where a person argues that he is a refugee, he may argue the merits of that point, or that there is no power to make the decision to deport for the reasons set out in the decision to deport, but may not argue other merits of the claim. Otherwise there is a full right of appeal under s 15 of the 1971 Act for those who returned within the period of an earlier leave, with the benefit of s 3(3)(b), and those whose last leave to enter was more than seven years before the decision to deport.

(b) Facts to be taken into account by the adjudicator

In considering an appeal under s 15 the adjudicator may take account of facts which were not known to the S of S but which existed at the time of the decision to make a deportation order (*R v IAT, ex p El Hassanin* [1986] 1 WLR 1448 (CA)). In a case not falling within the exceptions above, however, the adjudicator is confined to considering whether the S of S had power in law to make the decision to deport. The appellate authorities may not examine whether the decision is invalid because of the invalidity of the decision-making process leading up to it (*Ex p Mahli* [1990] 1 WLR 932, *R v IAT, Ex p S of S* [1992] Imm AR 554, *Sasiharan v S of S* [1993] Imm AR 253, and *Aujla* (6459)). Such excluded matters relate to the exercise of power, and not to the existence of the power to make the decision, and are properly the subject of judicial review (*Oladehinde and Alexander* [1990] 3 All ER 393). There is no power to make a decision to deport where the appellant remains in the UK with authority. Such authority may exist where the appellant is subject to the order of one of the organs of state (eg a prisoner) and cannot therefore leave the country (*Makinde v S of S* [1991] Imm AR 469). A 'period of grace' to enable a person to make a voluntary departure is not a period of leave and a deportation order made during it is therefore unlawful (*Ex p Smith* [1996] Imm AR 337).

Section 5 has effect at the time the decision is made, and it does not matter that the period of overstaying started before the 1988 Act came into force (*Ex p Panchan* (1991) *The Times*, 7 May), or that the period of overstaying commenced at a time when the person appealing would have had rights under the now repealed s 1(5) of the 1971 Act (*Ex p Ouakkouche* [1991] Imm AR 5). It is sufficient if the written notice of the decision to deport was given after the Act was in force (*Mundowa v S of S* [1992] Imm AR 80). The adjudicator in other immigration cases will have jurisdiction to investigate procedural matters relating to the claim (*Ex p Bakhtaur Singh* [1986] Imm AR 352).

(c) The IAT as a first-instance tribunal

In certain deportation cases, the IAT sits as a tribunal of first instance and the adjudicator has no jurisdiction. These cases are:

(a) the ground of the deportation decision was that it was conducive to the public good (s 15(7)(a));

(b) the appeal is against a decision to make a deportation order against a person as a family member;

(c) the appeal is against refusal to revoke a deportation order on the grounds of family membership (s 15(7)(*b*));

(d) 'pending related appeal' cases (s 15(7)(*c*)).

Pending related appeals (s 15(8) and (9))   There is a pending appeal, for the purposes of the 1971 Act, when a notice of appeal has been duly given (s 33(4)). A related appeal is one against a deportation order made on family membership grounds against another member of the family of the person whose appeal is pending. Where:

(a) an appeal by X to the adjudicator is pending; but

(b) the adjudicator has not begun to hear it; and

(c) an appeal is brought by Y, a member of X's family, against a decision to deport him on the basis of membership of X's family,

the appeal lies in the first instance to the IAT and the adjudicator has no jurisdiction to hear X's appeal, or that of his family (s 15(8)). If the decision to deport the family member was made on other grounds, that would not affect his right to appeal to the adjudicator.

(d) Recommendations for deportation made by criminal courts

The recommendation of a criminal court for deportation is part of the sentence of the court, and is subject to appeal in the same way as any other part of the sentence, within the time limits applicable to the forum in which sentence was passed (s 6(5)(*a*) of the 1971 Act and s 50 of the Criminal Appeals Act 1968). Where there is pending an appeal (or further appeal) through the criminal appeals system, no deportation order may be made.

(e) Time Limits

The time limit for an appeal against the S of S's decision to make a deportation order is 14 days from the date of the decision (1984 Appeals Rules, r 4(7)). The time limit for appealing against refusal to revoke a deportation order is 28 days from the refusal (1984 Appeals Rules, r 4(8)). The time limit for appealing against a refusal of asylum, in a case which the S of S has certified as without foundation, is two working days (see Chapter 26); and the time limit for appealing against any other refusal of asylum is ten working days.

Appeals out of time   Difficulties may arise where notice of the decision to order deportation is not communicated to the person concerned within the time limits set out under r 4 of the 1984 Appeals Rules. This may occur because the Home Office does not know the person's whereabouts. If the person is missing, the Home Office usually dates the decision to deport from the date he is traced, but it is not unreasonable for the S of S to serve the notice of deportation on the person's last known address, even where it is apparent that the person no longer lives there (*Pargan Singh v S of S* [1992] 1 WLR 1052).

If the S of S alleges that an appeal is out of time, the point must be taken as a preliminary point. The adjudicator has power to allow the appeal to be heard out of time if there are special circumstances (1984 Appeals Rules, r 11(4)). In *R v IAT, ex p Ekrem Mehmet* [1977] 2 All ER 602 it was held that 'special circumstances' should be liberally construed and may include the merits of a case as well as an explanation for the delay. Thus in *Sonoiki* (12424) the person responsible for preparing the appellant's appeal (which was prepared within the time for appeal) had travelled out of the country. His failure to send off the notice of appeal came to light only when the appellant contacted his representatives. The adjudicator and the IAT held that the appeal, which was received two days out of time, should proceed. Separate considerations apply in asylum cases which are dealt with in Chapter 26.

5 Rights of appeal under s 16, 1971 Act (directions for removal)

Under paras 8–10 of Sched 2 to the 1971 Act immigration officers and the S of S have powers to give directions for the removal from the UK of persons refused leave to enter and of illegal entrants refused leave to enter. In addition there are special powers of removal in relation to crew members of ships and aircraft, contained in paras 12–15 of the same schedule. Removal is normally to the country where the person boarded the vessel (aircraft, hydrofoil or train) which brought him to the UK (see also *Mustafa v S of S* [1979–80] Imm AR 32 and *Kelzani v S of S* [1978] Imm AR 193).

There is a right of appeal in both kinds of case. The appeal is limited to a challenge of the validity of the directions. Under s 16 the appellant can appeal only on the basis that there is no power in his case to make directions for removal. The appeal cannot normally be made in the UK, but there is one exception. If the directions for removal are based on entry in breach of a deportation order and the appellant claims he is not the person named in the deportation order, then he may appeal while still in the UK. On any appeal under this section, the appellant is precluded from challenging the validity of any deportation order on which the directions for removal are based. If the appellant appeals successfully against directions made against him as a member of the crew of a ship or aircraft, his appeal is nevertheless to be dismissed by the adjudicator if the adjudicator is satisfied that there was power to give further directions for removal based on the fact that the appellant was, in any event, an illegal entrant.

Time limits If the appellant is not entitled to appeal while still in the UK, his appeal must be lodged not later than 28 days after his departure from the UK. In any other case, the appeal must be lodged not later than 28 days after the appellant's departure, but may be made at any stage before his departure (1984 Appeals Rules, r 4(9), above).

6 Rights of appeal under s 17, 1971 Act (destination)

When directions are made for the removal of an entrant he may in certain circumstances appeal on the ground that he objects to the destination named in them. If such directions are made on refusal of leave to enter, or on making a deportation order, or when the entrant enters the UK in breach of a deportation order, the entrant may appeal on the basis that the directions (if they arc to be made at all) should name a different country specified by the appellant.

On an appeal against refusal of entry under s 13(1), if, before the appeal against refusal is launched, directions for removal are given, or if at any stage the S of S or an immigration officer notifies the appellant that if directions are made, they will specify one or more particular countries, the appellant may, in the course of the appeal against refusal of leave to enter, object to the country or countries specified. Similarly, if a person appeals under s 15 against the decision to make a deportation order against him and he is at any stage notified by the S of S of the country or countries to which he will be removed by direction, he may on that appeal object to the destination(s) notified.

The consequence of those two provisions is that if an objection to the destination for removal is challenged on an appeal under s 13 or 15, and the appeal fails, or if no appeal is mounted in respect of destination, the question of destination cannot be reopened on a further appeal if the directions are ultimately made and specify the same destination.

The right to object to the destination for removal on refusal of leave to enter is limited. Such an appeal can be made only in two circumstances: first, where the appellant is appealing against the decision that he requires leave to enter at all; second, where the appellant, though holding a current entry clearance or work permit, was refused leave at a port of entry. Most people who are refused leave to enter may not therefore object to the destination chosen for them.

Whenever an appeal is made, whether under this section, or under s 13(1) or 15, in which objection is taken to the destination specified in the directions for removal, the appellant must, with his notice of appeal, serve a supplementary statement. This must be in writing and must support his objection to the destination specified and his claim to be removed to an alternative destination (see *Kroohs v S of S* [1978] Imm AR 75 and *S of S v Croning* [1972] Imm AR 51 for some relevant considerations). In the normal case, a person is removed to his country of citizenship. Where the alternative destination is not set out in the notice of appeal, the appeal is a nullity (*R v An adjudicator, ex p Chuks Umeloh* [1991] Imm AR 602, *Ex p Omishore* [1990] Imm AR 582 and *Ex p Durali Tuglaci* [1993] Imm AR 47).

Where directions have been given on refusal of leave to enter, the appeal may be made at any stage before the appellant's departure, but not thereafter. In any other case the appeal must be made before the appellant's departure, and not later than 14 days after the directions are given (1984 Appeals Rules, r 4(10)).

7   Circumstances in which there is no right of appeal

(a) Exclusion from the UK (s 13)

There is no right of appeal against refusal of entry if the entrant does not hold a passport describing him as a British citizen or CUKC with the right of abode in the UK, or a certificate of entitlement. However, there is a right of appeal if the entrant claims to have the right of abode and is able to produce a UK passport describing him either as a British citizen or as a CUKC with the right of abode in the UK, or produces a certificate of entitlement.

Equally, a woman in this situation may appeal if she claims to be a British citizen by virtue of her Commonwealth citizenship and her marriage to a British citizen who holds or held that citizenship by virtue of birth, adoption, naturalisation or registration in the UK, or by virtue of descent from a parent who so held that citizenship. Such a woman must show that, immediately before the commencement of the 1981 Act, she was a CUKC and had the right of abode in the UK by virtue of her marriage as described above.

There is no right of appeal against refusal of an entry clearance or of entry if it is certified by the S of S that the appellant should not be given entry to the UK on the ground that the exclusion of the appellant is conducive to the public good and that directions to that effect have been given by the S of S himself, and not by someone acting on his behalf. Nor is there any right of appeal if leave to enter or entry clearance is refused pursuant to such directions.

Visitors, short-term and prospective students and their dependants A person who seeks entry to the UK or entry clearance to travel to the UK on the following grounds:

(a) as a visitor (see paras 40–56, p 83 *et seq* above);

(b) to follow a course of study of not more than six months' duration for which he has been accepted (paras 57–62, p 101 *et seq* above);

(c) with the intention of studying but without having been accepted for any course (paras 82–87, p 116 *et seq* above); or

(d) as a dependant of a person in *(b)–(c)* (paras 79–81 and p 115),

is not entitled to appeal against refusal of leave to enter unless he holds a current entry clearance. He is not entitled to appeal against refusal of an entry clearance (1971 Act, s 13(3A) inserted by 1993 Act, s 12). Further, a person may not appeal against refusal of entry or of entry clearance if the refusal is based on any of the following grounds:

(a) he does not hold a relevant document (see p 356 below);

(b) he does not satisfy a requirement of the immigration rules as to age or nationality or citizenship; or

(c) he seeks entry for a period exceeding that permitted by the immigration rules (1971 Act, s 13(3B) as inserted by 1993 Act, s 13).

The effect of these provisions is draconian, and is discussed below at p 357.

(b) Conditions of leave (s 14)

A person has no right of appeal against a variation of leave which reduces its time limit, or against a refusal to enlarge or remove that limit, if the S of S makes the requisite declaration in relation to the appellant. The S of S must certify, first, that the appellant's removal from the UK would be conducive to the public good; and second, that the grounds are the interests of national security or the relations between the UK and any other country, or other reasons of a political nature. Similarly, there is no appeal if the S of S certifies that the decision appealed from was taken by himself (and not by a functionary) on those grounds. There is no appeal against any variation in the conditions attached to a person's leave to enter and remain if that variation is effected by any statutory instrument. By the same token, there is no appeal under s 13 against the refusal of the S of S to make a statutory instrument.

If a deportation order is made against a person, any appeal against refusal to vary or extend leave which is pending at that time lapses (1971 Act, s 14(5)).

There is no right of appeal against refusal to vary leave to enter or remain if the refusal is based on any of the following grounds:

 (a) a relevant document required by the immigration rules has not been issued; or

 (b) the person, or a person whose dependant he is, does not satisfy a requirement of the immigration rules as to age or nationality or citizenship; or

 (c) the variation would result in the duration of the person's leave exceeding that permitted under the immigration rules; or

 (d) any fee required by or under any enactment has not been paid (1971 Act, s 14(2A));

 (e) because the variation adds a condition that the person maintain and accommodate himself and his dependants (see 1971 Act, s 14(2ZA)).

If a person with limited leave seeks asylum and the S of S has considered the claim and given the person notice in writing of rejection of that claim, the S of S may, by notice given at the same time as the notice of rejection of the asylum claim, curtail his limited leave to remain (1993 Act, s 9(1)). In such circumstances the person may not appeal against the curtailment of leave under s 14 of the 1971 Act, or under s 10(2) of the 1993 Act which deals with asylum appeals and mixed appeals. Although the person may appeal against refusal to grant him refugee status under s 10(2), he may not appeal against the decision to curtail his leave. His remedy will be to bring proceedings for judicial review if the decision to curtail is one to which no reasonable decision-maker could come, or which is procedurally flawed (for example, because the person has not been given an opportunity to make representations as to whether the S of S should exercise his discretion to curtail), or is based on an error of law of some sort.

(c) Refusals which are mandatory under the immigration rules

Relevant documents   A person who has been refused leave to enter or entry clearance, and a person who has had an application for variation of leave refused on the grounds that he does not possess relevant documents, may not appeal under the 1971 Act. For these purposes 'relevant documents' means:

 (a) entry clearances;

 (b) passports or other identity documents; and

 (c) work permits or equivalent issued after entry (1971 Act, ss 13(3C) and 14(2B)).

The obvious remedy of a person refused a variation or leave to enter is to apply for judicial review. In that context it is important to note the scheme introduced by the S of S for the consideration of applications for entry clearances. Those refused visas now receive a more detailed refusal notice than under the old system. It sets out the reason for the refusal of the visa. The applicant should be told by the notice:

(a) the reason for the refusal; and

(b) what points of information are lacking;

(c) that a previous refusal will not prejudice any subsequent application; and

(d) that there is no right of appeal.

The notice is to be provided to the person seeking entry clearance, on the day the interview takes place, wherever that is possible (Charles Wardle, Official Report of Standing Committee A, 8 December 1992, col 667).

The mandatory grounds for refusal, against which no appeal lies, relate to refusals of entry clearance or of leave to enter, and to applications for variation of leave by persons already in the UK.

Thus a visa national who arrives at a port without a visa may not appeal against refusal of entry; nor may a person who arrived seeking entry for a purpose for which a prior entry clearance is required, such as marriage, or establishment in business, or settling as a dependent relative. However, not all documents required by the immigration rules are included in the definition of 'relevant documents'. Thus a person applying for leave to remain as a businessman will have a right of appeal if the reason for refusal is that he did not produce audited accounts.

Those who are already in the UK in one capacity, for example as students, and who then apply for leave to remain in another capacity for which they should, under the rules, have obtained an entry clearance before coming to the UK (such as setting up in business), are not able to appeal against a refusal of that variation application. The position is similar to that relating to the refusal of approval of work by the Department of Education and Employment. Such refusal may be amenable to judicial review (see *Ex p Barry Allan* [1991] Imm AR 336). However, the effect of the wording of the section is that the genuineness of such documents is now properly a matter for judicial review. This is because failure to possess the relevant documents is a precedent fact which must be established before the S of S is able to treat the person as a person who does not have a right of appeal, and as a person who, in particular, does not have a pending appeal under s 33(4) of the 1971 Act. If a person has a pending appeal, removal directions and deportation proceedings against him are generally suspended. Thus a person who is accused of possessing false documents may in certain circumstances be entitled to seek judicial review of any attempt to treat him as a person without appeal rights, and without the protection of a pending appeal.

A person who marries a person settled in the UK, after entering in another capacity, remains entitled to appeal, as does a person who entered in one capacity, but seeks to remain as a dependent relative of a person settled in the UK. Such applications, if refused, are refused not on the basis of the absence of an entry clearance on entry, but because the application fails in substance.

Age nationality or citizenship   The second circumstance giving rise to mandatory refusal under the current immigration rules, and in which a person will not have a right of appeal, is where a person does not meet a requirement as to age or nationality or citizenship under the rules. Thus, au pairs and working holidaymakers must be between the ages of 17 and 27 (paras 89(ii) and 95(ii)). Similarly, under paras 186 (exception to the work permit rule on the grounds of UK ancestry) and 95 (working holidaymakers), there is a requirement that the applicant should be a Commonwealth citizen. Anyone failing to fulfil those criteria will not have a right of appeal. Powers of removal may be challenged by way of judicial review if there is a factual dispute about age or nationality in these circumstances. If, as a result of those proceedings, it is established that the person did have the right of appeal, he would then be able to challenge the refusal through the appeals system.

Total period of leave exceeding that permitted   The third ground of mandatory refusal is that a person seeks entry, or a variation of stay, which would result in his being in the UK for, a period in excess of that permitted by the immigration rules. Thus a visitor may not seek entry for a period of more than six months, and an au pair or working holidaymaker may not stay for more than two years.

Non-payment of fees   Finally if any fee required by or under any enactment has not been paid, no appeal against a refusal to vary leave to enter or remain is possible. Under s 9 of the 1988 Act indefinite leave to remain is not granted if a fee in connection with the grant has not been paid. Regulations under s 9 for the charging of fees have not been made, although at the time of writing it is the government's intention to introduce fees for indefinite leave to remain. It is clear, however, that the power is broader by virtue of the way in which it is worded, and would seem to permit immigration officials to refuse a variation of leave to remain on the basis that any fee required under any Act has not been paid, without that decision being challenged by way of appeal.

Internal review   When promoting the 1993 Act in the House of Lords, Earl Ferrers set forth the safeguards against low standards of decision-making by ECOs (HL Debs 16 February 1993, vol 542, no 96, cols 1041–2):

(1)   The leaflets to be made available to visitors and their sponsors are to be amplified and added to, in order to show what can be done to facilitate initial applications; such forms will be available from the IND.

(2)   Where a person is refused he will receive a more detailed notice setting out the reasons for the decision (see above).

(3)   The notice will make clear that the refusal will not prejudice a further claim.

(4)   If any exceptional compassionate circumstances, illogicalities or procedural errors are raised with the FCO in the UK, they will ask the diplomatic post concerned to review the decision.

(5)   Wherever possible the review will be carried out by a more senior officer.

(6) If further information is put forward in that application, it will be considered wherever possible by a different ECO.

(7) In larger posts where entry clearance work is overseen by entry clearance managers, those managers will conduct a daily review of all refusal decisions. Where the senior officer reverses the decision of the ECO, the applicant will be contacted and the visa will be issued. It will occur in every case (in a larger post) which has been reviewed.

It is quite clear that this internal review system does not constitute an alternative appeal mechanism, so that time for the purposes of judicial review will run from the date of the original decision. Lord Ackner, speaking from the cross benches in the House of Lords, said of the above safeguards:

> As I understand it, the decision will have been made initially by a junior official on the issue of credibility. I do not see how an office manager, when the applicant has gone home, can confirm an issue on credibility, having never seen the party. If that is not rubber stamping, I do not know what is. (HL Debs, 16 February 1993, col 1045).

The purpose of the internal review system is in some way to make applications for judicial review more difficult, in that it is thought to be more difficult to obtain judicial review if the applicant has already gone through two suits before applying for judicial review. The proposed system is clearly procedurally flawed, in that the applicant will not be given a right to make representations to the reviewing officer in those places at which such reviews are to take place. Further, the system of review will not be treated as an alternative appeal which would prevent an applicant from reviewing the initial decision. Such powers of review are already common in areas such as social security law, and do not have that effect. (See JCWI B, vol 5, no 8, Spring 1995.)

The S of S has appointed a person to monitor refusals of entry clearance where there is no right of appeal by reason of s 13(3A) of the 1971 Act. She conducts an audit of ECOs' decisions, and makes an annual report on the discharge of his functions to the S of S, who lays it before each House of Parliament (1971 Act, s 13(3AA)). Thus the S of S seeks to put a quality control on the decisions of ECOs. It is unlikely that such a review will provide any adequate remedy for the individual. Lady Anson produced her second report in December 1995.

(d) Deportation orders (s 15)
If a decision is made to deport a person on the basis that deportation would be conducive to the public good, on the limited grounds of the interests of national security or relations between the UK and another country, or for other reasons of a political nature, there is no right of appeal or review whatsoever, so long as the decision has been reached following the correct procedure (*Ex p H* [1988] Imm AR 389). There is a non-statutory advisory procedure only. This was considered by the CA in *Ex p Hosenball* [1977] 3 All ER 452 and *Ex p Cheblak* [1991] 2 All ER 319. The court, quite apart from the advisory procedure, is necessarily restricted by the nature of the

subject matter (see also *Ex p B* (1991) *The Independent,* 29 January). Such supervision as the court allows itself is very limited indeed.

The procedure was set up as a result of an undertaking given by the S of S to the House of Commons during the passage of the 1971 Act. The deportee is permitted to call witnesses before, and make representations to, three advisors appointed by the S of S. He is not entitled to legal representation, but may, at the advisors' discretion, be represented by a friend. Mr Hosenball attempted to quash a deportation order made after the advisory procedure had been invoked, on the ground of breaches of the rules of natural justice in that he had not been given sufficient particulars of the allegations against him. The CA declined to intervene, in essence because it took the view that the interests of national security took precedence over the individual's interest in natural justice. However, Lord Denning MR and Cumming-Bruce LJ did indicate that the court retained a vestigial supervisory jurisdiction over the advisory procedure.

Such supervisory jurisdiction was considered in *Ex p Chahal* [1995] 1 All ER 658, [1995] 1 WLR 526. The S of S must consider the Geneva Convention on Refugees, the European Convention on Human Rights and the Convention against Torture when considering deportation on these grounds, and must balance the rights of the individual against the threat to national security.

Similarly, there is no right of appeal from a refusal to revoke a deportation order if the S of S certifies that the appellant's exclusion from the UK is conducive to the public good. If the S of S personally refused to revoke the order on that ground, there is no right of appeal either.

(e) Decisions outside the statutory appeals machinery
Some types of decision are outside the statutory appeals machinery. One such type concerns the issue of special vouchers in East Africa. A further example of a decision against which there is no right of appeal is a refusal to depart from the immigration rules. In *Tosir Khan v ECO Dacca* [1974] Imm AR 55, the appellant sought to question a refusal of an entry certificate on the basis, *inter alia*, that other applicants in his position had been granted certificates on a discretionary basis because of the civil disturbances in Bangladesh. The IAT held that it was precluded from allowing an appeal on that basis because it amounted to a request for the S of S to depart from the rules. The language of s 19(2) of the 1971 Act therefore precludes such an appeal, provided the discretion exercised by the S of S does not actually conflict with the immigration rules. The same is true of a discretionary amnesty (*Purwal v ECO New Delhi* [1977] Imm AR 93). Equally, refusal to issue a work permit carries no right of appeal under the 1971 Act (*Pearson v IAT* [1978] Imm AR 212; see also *Latiff v S of S* [1972] Imm AR 76 in relation to training schemes operated by the Department of Education and Employment).

Where, however, there is no applicable rule and a discretion is exercised outside the rules there is power to hear an appeal relating to the exercise of that discretion (*Jinnah Rahman v S of S* [1989] Imm AR 325). Where there is a request to depart from the rules the appellate authorities have jurisdiction to decide whether or not the decision of the S of S was in accordance with the law under s 19 (*Saemian v Immigration Officer, Heathrow* [1991] Imm AR 489). This jurisdiction includes the whole of UK and EC law, and in particular may include points of public law in cases which are not governed by s 5(1) of the 1988 Act (deportation); see *Andereh* (91331).

Chapter 19

Appeals to the Adjudicator

1 Notification of rights of appeal

(a) Requirement to give notice

Section 18 of the 1971 Act empowers the S of S to provide, by regulations, for a potential appellant to be notified in writing of his rights of appeal. This power was exercised by the Immigration Appeals (Notices) Regulations 1984 (SI 1984 No 2040) ('the 1984 Notices Regs'). The regulations follow the requirements stipulated in s 18. Notice of any decision or action which is appealable is to be given to the appellant 'as soon as practicable' (1984 Notices Regs, reg 3). The phrase 'decision ... which is appealable' connotes a decision in respect of which there is a right of appeal that is not bound by operation of law to fail (*Al-Zagha v S of S* [1994] Imm AR 20). Where the decision is to give limited leave to enter, or to refuse leave to enter, it is 'practicable' to give notice of rights of appeal at the same time as the notice of the decision itself. Under para 6 of Sched 2 to the 1971 Act, the notice is to be given within 24 hours of the making of the decision, and if it is not, the entrant is deemed to have received six months leave to enter, with a condition prohibiting employment.

Where a notice is given under para 6 of Sched 2, the notice is to be treated as satisfying the regulations. In every case the notice should inform the person of the decision, the reasons for the refusal, and whether he has a right of appeal under s 13 of the 1971 Act. If he does have a right of appeal the notice should explain how that right may be exercised. The notice should be explained to the person if he appears not to understand it (para 352). The right for a person to communicate with friends, relations, a legal advisor, his consul or High Commission if he wishes, to assist him in deciding whether to appeal, which was conferred by para 91 of HC 251, does not appear in HC 395.

The notice issued under these regulations is conclusive both of the identity of the person who made the decision, and of the grounds on which that decision was made (s 18(2) of the 1971 Act). The result is that such a notice is the authorities' last word on the identity of the decision-maker and the grounds on which the decision is made. Thus, for instance, if the notice records that the S of S has certified that directions have been given by the S of S for the appellant to be refused entry to the UK on the ground that his exclusion is conducive to the public good, then that is the end of the matter. The appellant has no right of appeal in that situation (1971 Act, s 13(5)) and the notice cannot be challenged as it could be, for example, if some one other than the S of S had so certified. There may, however, be grounds for an application for judicial review.

It is open to the respondent to an appeal before the adjudicator to rely on a ground for his decision which is different from that given in the notice, provided the appellant is given proper notice of the case he has to meet on appeal, and provided that the adjudicator does not seek to go behind a finding of fact of the S of S which is favourable to the applicant (*R v IAT, ex p Hubbard* [1985] Imm AR 111, especially at 118–19, approved in *Nadeem Tahir v IAT* [1989] Imm AR 98), *Dagdalen v S of S* [1988] Imm AR 425, and *Parsayian v Visa Officer Karachi* [1986] Imm AR 155, but see *Swati v S of S* [1986] Imm AR 88, *per* Sir John Donaldson MR at 93–4).

Notice complying with the regulations need not be given in two circumstances. The first is when the officer or authority concerned has no knowledge of the whereabouts or address of the potential appellant. There is then no requirement to give a notice at all. This rule was considered in *R v IAT, ex p Mehmet* [1977] Imm AR 56 and *Rhemtulla v IAT* [1970–80] Imm AR 168. It was argued that the rule was *ultra vires* s 18(1)(*a*) of the 1971 Act. The argument was rejected in both cases. The second situation in which notice is not required is where the decision relates to an application for variation of leave and the outcome is favourable to the appellant. In that case, the notice need inform the appellant only of the outcome and need not give reasons, or information as to rights of appeal and their method of exercise.

(b) Methods of service

Notices may be served either personally, or, under reg 6 of the 1984 Notices Regs, by post. In the latter case, registered post or recorded delivery must be used. There is no *requirement* of personal service: postal service by one of the above two methods, to the appellant's last known or usual address, or to the address given by him for the service of notice, suffices. If a person makes an application to the authorities on behalf of another person, the former, and not the latter, may be notified of the result of the application (1984 Notices ,Regs, reg 3(3)). A typical example of this is where solicitors act for an applicant. A notice addressed to the solicitors rather than the applicant would be sufficient. In *R v Chief Immigration Officer of Manchester Airport, ex p Insah Begum* [1973] 1 All ER 594, the CA held that service on an illiterate entrant's solicitor was sufficient in circumstances where it could be presumed he had authority to act for her.

Where a person subject to immigration control fails to advise the Home Office of a change of address, the Home Office can effect good service of notices by sending them to the individual's last known address (*Ex p Yeboah* [1987] 1 WLR 1586), even where the knowledge of that address came to the S of S's attention via a third party (*Ex p Kamara* [1991] Imm AR 423). Further, if a notice of hearing is sent to the address on a notice of appeal, the adjudicator is entitled to proceed in the absence of the appellant. The fact that the appellant's representative failed to inform the appellate authorities of a change of the appellant's address is irrelevant. The appellate authorities are under no obligation to check that the notice of hearing is sent to the latest address (*Hassan v S of S* [1994] Imm AR 482). Likewise, where the notice of hearing was sent to the representatives in the ordinary post, and not returned by the Post Office, it was deemed to have been properly served and a determination could be made in the absence of the representative or appellant (*Kayanja v S of S* [1995] Imm AR 123 (CA)).

(c) Effect of serving notice

The effect of service of a notice under the regulations is that, for the purposes of the time limits for appealing, the decision which is the subject of the notice is deemed to have been made on the date of sending or service of the notice (1984 Appeals Rules, r 4(11)). The document is sent at the time it is despatched in the post, and not at the time it is received (*Ex p Yeboah* [1987] 1 WLR 1586). Time starts to run from that point. In *Ex P Yeboah*, Sir Nicolas Browne-Wilkinson VC regretted the consequence that 'an immigrant who in fact never receives notice of a decision is deprived of his right of appeal' (at p 1594). The question of the date of the S of S's decision to deport a person is a question of fact. It cannot be inferred as a matter of law from the requirement that notice be served 'as soon as practicable' after the decision, that the date of the decision is the date of the notice (*Rehman v S of S* [1978] Imm AR 80).

If the immigration officer does not know the person's whereabouts, he need not serve notice on him (1984 Notices Regs, reg 3(4)). Nor does the S of S need to ensure that he serves a notice while he knows of the person's whereabouts (*Al-Anbari v S of S* [1988] Imm AR 567). The 1984 Notices Regs apply at the date the S of S's decision is taken, so that if at that time the whereabouts of the person is not known, the S of S may rely on reg 3(4).

(d) Contents of notice

Regulation 4 of the 1984 Notices Regs requires that a notice must contain certain information. If it does not, it is invalid. This can be important, because in many cases time for appealing runs from the service of the notice. If an invalid notice is served, time arguably should not run. The information which must appear in the notice is:

(a) a statement of the reasons for the decision or action notified;
(b) if the decision is to remove a person from the UK, a statement of the country to which he is to be removed;
(c) a statement of the rights of appeal (if any) under the 1971 Act;

(d) how the rights are to be exercised;

(e) the address to which the appeal should be sent;

(f) the time limit for appealing; and

(g) the facilities available for advice and assistance in connection with appeals.

If the notice does not contain a statement of the reasons for the decision or action to which it relates, it is invalid. The potential appellant is not, however, entitled to a written statement of the facts relating to the decision or action in question. He is entitled to such a statement only on giving notice of appeal. The notice need give only sufficient information for the applicant to be able to decide whether or not to appeal (*Swati v S of S* [1986] 1 All ER 717). There is no obligation to give reasons for the reasons in the notice (*Ex p Khushi Mohammed and Khawaja* [1990] Imm AR 439), and the notice need contain only the conclusions of the decision-maker which led to the decision.

A notice which is invalid because it does not comply with the 1984 Notices Regs sometimes invalidates the decision to which it relates, but not always. The appellant will be left without a remedy if he has suffered no prejudice by an irregularity in the notice (*Labiche v S of S* [1991] Imm AR 263, where a notice of a refusal was not accompanied by a statement of the right of appeal but was held to be valid). However, it is possible for the invalidity of a notice to be cured by waiver, including waiver by conduct (*Mawji v S of S* [1986] Imm AR 290).

The notice need not be very specific as to the type of decision of which it informs the potential appellant. In *R v IAT, ex p Ahluwalia* [1979–80] Imm AR 1, the wife of a Commonwealth citizen was served with a notice of intended deportation which referred to s 3(5) of the 1971 Act, without specifying which sub-paragraph was relied on. Lord Widgery CJ said that, provided the facts of the case fell within two or more of the sub-paragraphs, the S of S need not rely on one exclusively. Furthermore, it has been held that the appellate authorities have jurisdiction to permit amendments to the notice of refusal (see p 369 below).

A notice should give the legal basis for the decision. It should identify the basis of the S of S's authority, and indicate the reason why he proposes to exercise it (*R v IAT, ex p Dukobu* [1990] Imm AR 390). Thus where a notice relates to a person who has overstayed his leave, the notice should give details of the date of the original leave, its length, and the extent to which the person has overstayed it. Where the notice relates to a deportation under s 3(5)(*b*) it should state why the deportation is conducive to the public good, and should recite the offence or conduct of which complaint is made (*R v IAT, ex p Razaque* [1989] Imm AR 451).

A notice must be served even if, on the facts of his particular case, a person does not have a right of appeal.

2 Launching an appeal

(a) Written notice

Generally, an appeal is launched (or 'given' in the words of the 1984 Appeals Rules) by serving a notice of appeal containing the particulars described in the rules:

(*a*) name, address, date of birth and nationality of the appellant;

(*b*) particulars of the decision or action to which the appeal relates; and

(*c*) the grounds of appeal on which the appellant intends to rely

(1984 Appeals Rules, r 6(3)(*c*)).

The terms of r 6(3) are mandatory only in so far as they require the appellant and the case to be identified (*Jarvis v ECO Manilla* [1994] Imm AR 102). The notice must be signed by the appellant or his duly authorised representative. However, where the notice of appeal gave only the representative's address and not that of the appellant, it was a valid notice (*Sogunle v S of S* [1994] Imm AR 554). Further, even if it is unsigned by the appellant or his representative, but contains the mandatory particulars, these defects do not render it a nullity (*Harminder Dhesi* (11453)).

The notice must be served on the appropriate officer. If the action or decision appealed against is that of an immigration officer, he is the appropriate officer. If the decision is a refusal to grant an entry clearance or a certificate of entitlement, the notice of appeal should be served on the ECO who made it. In the case of any other decision, the notice should be served on the S of S (1984 Appeals Rules, r 6(2)). In the case of an appeal against the first two types of decision, the S of S may, if he is satisfied that, because of special circumstances, it is impossible or impracticable for the appropriate officer to be served, designate another appropriate officer instead, or may designate himself. An obvious instance where this substitution would be necessary would be if the immigration officer who had refused the appellant entry had died after the refusal and before notice of appeal could be served. Where the appellant sent the notice of appeal to the wrong address, and the notice could not be traced, the appeal was not valid (*Ex p Samuel Adeniyi* [1995] Imm AR 101).

Time limits should be borne in mind. A notice of appeal must be *received* within the relevant time limit; its mere posting is insufficient (*R v IAT, ex p Rocha* [1982] Imm AR 12), and if the notice of appeal is sent by ordinary post it will not be deemed to have been received by the appellate authorities (*Ex p Debney* [1995] Imm AR 361 (QBD)). Recorded delivery is therefore advisable.

The regulations make clear that the notice of appeal need not set out the grounds of appeal in a detailed, final form. The grounds may be varied or amplified at any stage during the course of the appeal. In addition, the appellate authorities have powers to require either party to the appeal to furnish any particulars which seem necessary to the determination of the appeal. This is just as well, since the time limits for appealing do not give appellants the opportunity to formulate lengthy and sophisticated grounds of appeal. The possibility of amendment during the progress of the proceedings and the powers to require particulars mean that advisors should in the first instance concentrate on complying with the time limits rather than on elaborating grounds of appeal. Thus, short grounds of appeal may be submitted. However, the contention that the decision appealed against is either not in accordance with the law or with any applicable immigration rule, or, if it is a decision involving the exercise of a discretion by the S of S or an officer, that the discretion should have been exercised differently, should at least be included. Where short grounds are submitted, they should be supplemented by further grounds submitted shortly after by way of amendment. If the appellant has submitted short grounds, which are sufficient to constitute a notice of appeal, together with a statement that further grounds are to follow, the appellate authorities may act unfairly if they do not wait for these grounds, or at least indicate that they should be submitted by a certain date (*R v IAT, ex p Pollicino* [1989] Imm AR 531, dealing with appeals to the IAT).

(b) Oral notice

In certain circumstances an appeal may be launched without service of a written notice of appeal. If the appellant wishes to appeal against refusal of leave to enter, or against a decision that he requires leave to enter (s 13 of the 1971 Act), he may do so simply by telling an immigration officer that he desires to appeal. The immigration officer need not be the officer who made the decision. This right may be exercised either by the appellant or by someone duly authorised to act on his behalf (for example, a relative or a solicitor). This right may be exercised only if the appellant is in the UK. Furthermore, this right cannot be exercised by a person who is not entitled to appeal while he is still in the UK (s 13(3) of the 1971 Act).

3 Interlocutory matters

(a) Respondent's explanatory statement

As soon as practicable after a notice of appeal is given, the respondent to the appeal (whether an immigration officer, ECO or the S of S) must prepare a written statement (1984 Appeals Rules, r 8). This must:

(a) deal with the facts on which the decision appealed from is based;

(b) give reasons for that decision; and,

(c) if the appellant is illiterate, take account of his illiteracy (*Ex p Dinesh* [1987] Imm AR 131).

The statement should be referred to the adjudicator (or IAT, as the case may be). A copy should be sent to the appellant, although there is no absolute requirement that this be done. If the immigration officer concerned considers it impracticable to do so, in view of the lack of time before the appeal is due to be heard, he may instead notify the authority and the appellant that the statement will be given orally at the hearing of the appeal (r 8(2)). Similarly, if the respondent intends to take a preliminary point, his statement need only contain an indication to that effect.

The respondent may, in any event, amplify the written statement at the hearing. In *Bhagat v S of S* [1972] Imm AR 189, the IAT emphasised that it was not permissible for the immigration authorities to rely on and argue on appeal any ground which, though contained in the explanatory statement, was not in the notice of the decision.

However, *Bhagat's* case was distinguished in *Immigration Officer, Ramsgate v Cooray* [1974] Imm AR 38. In that case the IAT held that the adjudicator had jurisdiction to give leave to amend the notice of refusal so that it corresponded with the explanatory statement, in order to arrive at the real issue between the parties. The appellate authority is to consider the immigration authority's decision in the round, and not just in the light of the reasons given for it at the time. *Bhagat's* case is therefore likely to be treated as confined to its own facts. (See *R v IAT, ex p Hubbard* [1985] Imm AR 111, 151.)

An explanatory statement can be prepared by the Home Office in concert with the immigration officer concerned, even if the Home Office is not a respondent to the appeal (*Akhtar Jan v ECO, Islamabad* [1977] Imm AR 107). The adjudicator may hear an appeal once the notice of appeal is lodged, even if no explanatory statement is lodged (*Lokko v S of S* [1990] Imm AR 111). However, both parties should be given an opportunity to be heard (*ECO Islamabad v Mohammad Ishfaq* [1992] Imm AR 289).

(b) Amendment, particulars and directions
The 1984 Appeals Rules expressly permit the amplification or variation of the grounds of appeal at any time during the course of the appeal. The IAT held, in *Francis v S of S* [1972] Imm AR 162, that amendments are permissible if they 'vary slightly' the grounds of appeal, but not if they are 'a material alteration'. A material alteration should form the basis of a fresh application. A similar conclusion was reached by the IAT in *Muthulakshmi v S of S* [1972] Imm AR 23. An amendment, however drastic, may be made at any stage, if it is simply a change in the legal basis on which the appeal is to be argued. If, on the other hand, an amendment fundamentally alters the factual basis of the initial application, then it would fall within the principles enunciated in *Francis* and *Muthulakshmi*.

There is no equivalent express facility for the respondent: he may simply amplify his written statement at the hearing. However, in *Tambimuttu v S of S* [1979–80] Imm AR 91, the IAT held that the respondent could amend the notice of refusal, providing the amendment did not change 'the legal basis' of the refusal. The IAT was reluctant to lay down a 'hard and fast rule applicable to every case' (see also *R v IAT, ex p Ekrem Mehmet* [1978] Imm AR 56). If the amendment is only 'an amplification, correction or clarification of the original notice', it should be allowed. It should not be allowed where it changes the whole basis of the case. The appellant must be notified; if need be, an adjournment should be granted.

Under r 25 of the 1984 Appeals Rules, the appellate authority may at any time require any party to an appeal to supply particulars, and if such particulars appear necessary, they should be requested prior to appeal; if the other party does not comply, the appellate authority should be requested to give directions on the matter. The appellate authority may at any stage give directions relating to the appeal to any party who requests them (r 37(b)). The power to give directions can be exercised only by the appellate authority which is seised of the appeal. Thus the IAT has no jurisdiction to give directions in a matter which is part-heard before the adjudicator (*Hussain v S of S* [1972] Imm AR 264). The power to order particulars does not permit an adjudicator to order documents (*R v An Adjudicator, ex p S of S* [1989] Imm AR 423).

(c) Discovery and inspection of documents

Rule 10 of the 1984 Appeals Rules provides that the appellate authority is responsible for ensuring that copies of all notices and other documents required for an appeal are supplied to every party to an appeal. By virtue of r 30, the appellate authority is required, when it takes into consideration any documentary evidence, to give every party to the appeal an opportunity of inspecting that evidence and taking copies of it. There is an exception to this general rule in the case of an appeal in which it is alleged that the appellant relies on a forged travel document, if it would be against the public interest for the method of detection of the forgery to be disclosed, and supplying the document would involve such disclosure (r 30(2)). There is no provision in the rules for automatic discovery, for parties to request discovery, or for the appellate authorities to order discovery of their own motion (*R v An Adjudicator, ex p S of S* [1989] Imm AR 423). If the appellate authority has not complied with r 30 well in advance of the hearing, and disclosure takes place only at the hearing, no doubt an application by the appellant for an adjournment, if time is needed to consider the documents, would be sympathetically received. Further, it is open to the adjudicator to order a witness to attend with documents in his custody or under his control which may relate to any matter in question in the appeal (Appeals Rules 1984, r 27 and see *R v An Adjudicator, ex p S of S* (above)).

(d) Service of documents

Under the 1984 Notices Regs, service may be effected by registered or recorded delivery letter, directed to a person's last known or usual place of abode (reg 6). Thus in *Ex p Abassi* [1992] Imm AR 349, the notice was delivered to the ship on which the appellant worked, as his last known address. Personal service is also clearly contemplated by the regulations.

Under the 1984 Appeals Rules, service may be effected in the same ways (r 44). Documents intended for the IAT may be served on the Secretary to the IAT; for the adjudicator, on his clerk; for the S of S, on the IND (Appeals Section) of the Home Office; for the immigration officer or ECO, on him at the address specified in the notice of refusal. The HL, in *Pargan Singh v S of S* [1992] 1 WLR 1052, held that r 3(4), which has the effect of dispensing with the need for service where the appellate authorities do not know the whereabouts of the appellant, was *intra vires* the 1971 Act. So if an appellant in these circumstances does not receive notice of refusal, that does not prevent time from running against him for the purposes of appealing.

(e) Adjournments
Applications for adjournments should be dealt with in the light of the following principles which are set out in Buckley J's decision in *R v Kingston upon Thames Justices ex p Martin* [1994] Imm AR 48:

(a) the importance of the proceedings and their likely adverse consequences for the party seeking the adjournment;

(b) the risk of a party being prejudiced in the conduct of proceedings or other disadvantage to each party if the adjournment was granted or refused;

(c) the convenience of the court;

(d) the interests of justice generally in the efficient dispatch of court business;

(e) the desirability of not delaying future litigants by adjourning early and thus leaving the court empty;

(f) the extent to which the party applying for the adjournment had been responsible for creating the difficulty which had led to the application.

Where the applicant does not attend, but submits a medical certificate and requests an adjournment, the adjudicator can determine the application in his absence if the medical certificate does not show that he cannot attend (*R v IAT, ex p Baira* [1994] Imm AR 487). The appellate authorities are attempting to cut down the number of adjournments, and frequently require the parties to attend to make an application orally on the day proposed for the hearing. Where it is likely that an adjournment will be needed, advisors should make the application in good time, so that the appellate authorities can list other matters instead of the aborted hearing. Applications for adjournments on the grounds of sickness should be supported by some form of medical evidence. Further, if the adjudicator is not provided with reasons for the non-attendance of the appellant, he may determine the case in the absence of both the representative and the appellant (*Ex p Yeboah* [1995] Imm AR 392). Leave to appeal to the IAT will be refused unless reasons for the absence are offered to the IAT in the application for leave to appeal (*Ex p Mubiru* [1994] Imm AR 516).

4 Preliminary points and further opportunity to appeal

(a) Preliminary points
Rules 8 and 11 of the 1984 Appeals Rules provide that the respondent to an appeal may take a preliminary point in four situations:

(a) it is alleged that the appellant has no statutory right of appeal (for example, where no destination is specified in a destination appeal (*Ex p Omishore* [1990] Imm AR 582));

(b) he relies on a travel document which is a forgery;

(c) the appellant has not signed the notice of appeal; or

(d) the appellant has submitted his notice of appeal outside the limit prescribed by r 4.

If a preliminary point is taken, the respondent's statement need only advert to that point. The appellate authority is obliged to determine the point as a preliminary issue only if the respondent insists. There is no obligation to hold a hearing. If the preliminary issue is determined in the appellant's favour, the appellate authority then gives directions for the preparation of a full written statement by the respondent.

Time limits   If the preliminary point is that the application is out of time, the question (if raised by the respondent) must be taken before considering the substantive issues of the case (*Ogunde v S of S* [1990] Imm AR 257). It is not an interlocutory application, and an appeal to the IAT is available (*S of S v Ibrahim* [1994] Imm AR 1). The appellate authority has a discretion whether to allow the appeal to proceed: it may allow it if 'it is of the opinion that by reason of special circumstances it is just and right to do so' (rr 8(3) and 11). There is no such discretion if there is a deportation order currently in force against the appellant.

The Home Office does not normally take the limitation point if a person who has applied for a variation of leave and has been refused lodges the appeal within his 'packing up' time. The time limit for such an appeal is 14 days, but the S of S may in his discretion not take a limitation point if the application is lodged within 28 days of the decision.

Extending time   The 'special circumstances' rule has been considered in many cases. In *Rhemtulla*'s case (above), the CA refused to interfere with the appellate authorities' exercise of their discretion. The facts were that the appellant had not been served with notice of refusal because he had changed his address and had not notified the authorities. This was not a 'special circumstance' case. *Rhemtulla*'s case underlines that appellants must keep the authorities informed of changes of address. That case is to be contrasted with another decision of the CA in *Cheema (MA) v IAT* [1982] Imm AR 46, in which it was held that a mistake on the part of the appellant's legal advisors was capable of constituting 'special circumstances'. The court also indicated that the substantive merits of the appeal were a factor which the appellate authority could take into account in deciding whether or not there were 'special circumstances'. The discretion to allow an appeal out of time should be used liberally (*R v IAT, ex p Mehta (VM)* [1976] Imm AR 174). 'Special circumstances' may include the merits of the case as well as an explanation for the delay in appealing (*R v IAT, ex p Ekrem Mehmet* [1977] Imm AR 56). No special circumstances will be found where the appellant receives notice of refusal after the expiry of his leave because he did not advise the Home Office of his change of address (*Ex p Selo Wa Selo* [1990] Imm AR 76), nor where the original application for variation was out of time, due to the fault of the advisor. There the applicant has no right of appeal.

(b) Further opportunity to appeal

Rule 5 of the 1984 Appeals Rules provides an alternative course for an appellant if his appeal is submitted out of time. This is the procedure of petitioning the appropriate officer in writing for a further opportunity to appeal. The petition is referred to the appellate authorities, who may give a further opportunity to appeal if they are 'of opinion that by reason of special circumstances it is just and right to do so'. This procedure is not available to persons in respect of whom there is a deportation order in force.

There is no advantage in following this procedure rather than submitting the appeal out of time and waiting for the respondent to take a preliminary point. The reason is that the petition procedure is a cul-de-sac. In *Ex p Bahadur Singh* [1976] Imm AR 143, the DC decided that if a petition is made and considered by the adjudicator with a result that is adverse to the appellant, there is no further right of appeal to the IAT.

5 Other interlocutory matters

(a) Bail

Rule 23 makes provision for the grant of bail while persons are detained under Sched 2 to the 1971 Act and while appeals are pending. Under Sched 2 to the 1971 Act the authorities have wide powers to detain persons who are liable to examination or removal. They may detain a person for examination under para 16(1), and they may detain a person pending removal under para 16(2). Under paras 22, 29 and 34 of that schedule, adjudicators and immigration officers are empowered to release on bail persons who are being detained (see p 401).

If an appellant is granted leave to appeal to the IAT (or does not require leave and has appealed) he must, if he requests, be released on bail (see Sched 2, para 29(4)).

Applications for bail to chief immigration officers or police officers of the rank of inspector or above may be made orally; applications to the appellate authorities may be made orally or in writing. The appellant must enter into a recognizance. The authorities may require sureties to be taken. Once those having custody of the appellant are satisfied that all required recognizances have been taken, they are to release the appellant (see Sched 2, para 29(6)).

At some hearing centres, bail applications and applications for extensions of bail go into a 'floating list'. They are listed early and can go to any available adjudicator. Written requests for bail hearings are being dispensed with in favour of telephone requests. On receipt of a telephone request for a bail hearing, the clerk will take down particulars of the applicant, particulars of the sureties, and particulars of the sums offered by way of recognizances. These details may then be faxed to the Home Office so that checks can be made. (Full details of the procedure appear in a letter from the Chief Adjudicator to ILPA, the text of which appears in (1991) 5 INL&P 122.) The speed of the process requires early preparation of the application for bail.

The whole process should take between three and five working days once full information is received by the appellate authority.

(b) Procedure at an adjudicator's bail hearing

The adjudicator first confirms that jurisdiction for a bail application exists (see p 401). The adjudicator then checks whether there are any objections to bail from the Home Office. If there are not, he will grant bail subject to satisfactory sureties. If there are objections, the Home Office Presenting Officer will be invited to oppose bail, and the applicant will have an opportunity to reply.

When considering whether or not to grant bail, in opposed applications, the adjudicator considers the following factors:

- (a) whether the applicant will answer bail;
- (b) whether he has previously failed to comply with bail conditions;
- (c) whether he is likely to commit offences if released on bail;
- (d) whether his release will be likely to cause danger to public health;
- (e) the period of time he has been and is likely to remain in custody pending a decision or appeal;
- (f) whether he is suffering from a mental disorder necessitating his detention in his own interests or the protection of the public;
- (g) whether he is younger than 17 and whether arrangements have been made for his care on release if he is

(1971 Act, Sched 2, para 30).

If the adjudicator is minded to grant bail, he next considers sureties. The Home Office is invited to examine or check the sureties offered if it has not already done so. If the Presenting Officer can state that the sureties are fit and proper persons to stand, that the sums offered are adequate in all the circumstances, and that the sureties are good for the recognizances offered, the adjudicator will generally accept them. The sums assured do not have to be readily available (*R v Special Adjudicator, ex p Shamamba* [1994] Imm AR 502). The amount of the recognizance is entirely a matter for the discretion of the adjudicator, and the Presenting Officer is merely invited to express a view. There is no tariff for sureties whereby requirements imposed by one adjudicator can be compared with those imposed by another. Such discrepancies are not errors of law or signs of perversity in themselves (see *Shamamba* (above)).

Where the Presenting Officer is not satisfied as to the factors listed above, the adjudicator hears his objections and the applicant has the opportunity to reply. If bail is granted, the Presenting Officer may request the imposition of conditions in addition to the two that appear in Form APP 6, namely the sum of the recognizances and the date and place of the next hearing. The adjudicator may then impose those conditions. The adjudicator may direct that the recognizance be taken by the police or the governor of the detention centre at which the applicant is held. Finally, he stresses to the sureties the personal nature of the liabilities attaching to the offer of surety.

(c) Summoning witnesses

Under r 27 of the 1984 Appeal Rules, the appellate authorities have power to summon witnesses to attend the hearing of the appeal to give evidence and produce documents in their custody or control. It is clear from r 27 that a summons may be issued at the request of any party to the appeal. A witness is not obliged to attend if it involves travelling more than 16 kilometres and his expenses are not paid, or offered to him, by the party at whose request the summons issues. If a person disobeys a witness summons, without reasonable excuse, he is guilty of an offence and liable on summary conviction to a maximum fine of £200 (1971 Act, s 22(6)).

(d) Transfer and consolidation of proceedings

Transfer of proceedings   Rule 33 of the 1984 Appeals Rules provides that the chief adjudicator may transfer proceedings between adjudicators; before the proceedings have been determined. This could be necessary, for example, if one adjudicator is taken ill in the course of proceedings; it would not then be 'practicable' for the proceedings to be completed by the first adjudicator 'without undue delay'. There is no power to transfer where the proceedings may be dealt with without undue delay (*ECO Dhaka v Rayful Bibi* [1993] Imm AR 63). The adjudicator can himself transfer an appeal to another adjudicator if there are better facilities elsewhere for medical examination, or the adjudicator has a personal connection with, or interest in, the appeal.

Consolidation of proceedings   If two or more appeals raise common issues of law or fact, or relate to members of the same family or it is for some other reason desirable that they be consolidated, the appellate authority may decide to hear them together (r 36). The consent of the parties is necessary.

(e) Notification of hearing

Under r 24 of the 1984 Appeals Rules the appellate authority is to notify the parties in writing of the time and place of hearing as soon as is practicable after the notice of appeal is served. If the appellant is detained under para 16 of Sched 2 the authorities may instead orally inform an immigration officer, who is to ensure the parties are present. Similarly, notice of adjournment hearings must be given to the parties unless a party has been absent throughout the proceedings, or it is impracticable to notify him.

(f) Withdrawal of appeal

The 1984 Appeals Rules, r 6(6)(*a*), provide that after notice of appeal has been given to the appropriate officer, it may be withdrawn by a written notice of withdrawal addressed to that officer. In *Saleh v S of S* [1975] Imm AR 154, the IAT held that an appellant has an inherent right to withdraw his appeal notwithstanding that r 6(6)(*a*) is not complied with. It was decided in that case that the adjudicator was not entitled to refuse an oral application to withdraw an appeal made at the start of the hearing before the adjudicator. The IAT did not say at what stage the right to withdraw would be lost, although it noted Lord Goddard's remarks in *R v Hampstead and St Pancras Rent Tribunal, ex p Goodman* [1951] 1 All ER 170 at p 172, that an appeal could be withdrawn at any time before a tribunal gives its decision. Thus it may be withdrawn during the course of a hearing (*Rahman v IAT* [1995] Imm AR 372).

It appears that counsel can withdraw a case on behalf of an absent client (*Fauzia Khan v S of S* [1987] Imm AR 543 (CA)). Where solicitors withdraw an appeal without instructions they have no authority to do so, and the IAT will review the case (*Nachtar Singh v S of S* [1991] Imm AR 195). Where someone who does not have the right of audience before the appellate authorities, but who does have the authority of the appellant, withdraws the appellant's appeal, the withdrawal is effective (*Tamakloe v S of S* [1991] Imm AR 611).

Once an appeal has been withdrawn it cannot be reinstated or resuscitated. If an appeal has been withdrawn from the adjudicator, the IAT has no jurisdiction to entertain a further appeal or application for leave (*Ancharaz v Immigration Officer, London (Heathrow) Airport* [1976] Imm AR 49).

(g) Costs

There are no powers under the rules to award costs. If a case is adjourned, for example, because an interpreter has not been provided by the appellate authority, despite a request by the appellant, or because the Presenting Officer does not have the file because the appellate authority's staff failed to notify the hearing date to the Home Office, or because documents required for the hearing have not been verified, the Lord Chancellor's department will authorise payment of costs thrown away due to the fault of the appellate authority. It will not make such payments where the Home Office has asked for an adjournment in advance and has been granted it, and the appellate authority bears no responsibility for the circumstances leading to the request. This is an informal concession, and has limited application. However, if the adjudicator indicates that the fault necessitating the adjournment lies with the appellate authority, such costs thrown away may be recovered on an application in writing either to the Chief Adjudicator or to the senior civil servant in the appellate authority.

(h) Appeals on interlocutory matters

Finally, there is no right of appeal against a decision on an interlocutory (as opposed to a preliminary) point: *R v IAT, ex p Lila* [1978] Imm AR 50. In that case the appellant attempted to appeal against an adjudicator's refusal to admit certain documentary evidence. The DC held that there was no right of appeal on an interlocutory point since it was not a 'determination' on an appeal by an adjudicator. The court observed that if the decision on the interlocutory point affected the outcome of the substantive appeal, then it could, of course, be challenged as part of a substantive appeal. Decisions relating to jurisdiction which can be taken as preliminary issues are amenable to appeal, and the IAT does have power to rule on them (*Lokko v S of S* [1990] Imm AR 111).

6 Determination without a hearing or in the absence of a party

(a) Without a hearing

The appellate authority at first instance has a discretion, under r 12 of the 1984 Appeals Rules, to determine an appeal without a hearing. Only those cases falling within the restricted category under r 12 may be determined in this way (*ECO Islamabad v Mohammed Ishfaq* [1992] Imm AR 289). Thus, a case may be determined without a hearing:

- (a) if neither party has asked for an oral hearing, having been given the opportunity to do so (*ECO Islamabad v Thakurdas* [1990] Imm AR 288);
- (b) if the authority decides to allow the appeal on written representations. If the case turns on documentary evidence, the parties must have sight of it and the opportunity to comment on it (*Immigration Officer, Heathrow v Ekinci* [1989] Imm AR 346);
- (c) if the appellant is outside the UK, or cannot be contracted and has authorised no representative to act in his stead (*R v Diggines, ex p Rahmani* [1986] AC 475);
- (d) if the only issue on appeal is an objection to destination for removal, and the matters put forward in support of the appeal do not, in the opinion of the authority, warrant a hearing;
- (e) if the appeal involves a preliminary issue and the appellant has either failed to put forward a written rebuttal of the respondent's allegation under r 8(3), or that rebuttal does not appear to warrant a hearing.

If the appellant is abroad and wishes to attend the hearing, he may seek entry clearance to visit for that purpose. Provided there are no other reasons for refusing, such entry should be granted. In particular, a visit for that purpose should not be treated as a visit for an unascertainable period (*Chhaganbhai Patal v Visa Officer, Bombay* [1991] Imm AR 97 and *Aiyub Patel v ECO Bombay* [1991] Imm AR 273).

The IAT may dispense with the hearing of an appeal from an adjudicator (r 20). It can do so if neither side has requested a hearing; or if the appellant is outside the UK or cannot be contacted and has not authorised a representative to act for him. Where a person has an automatic right to appeal to the IAT because he is appealing against a refusal of leave to enter when he arrived with entry clearance, and the IAT is of the opinion, after giving the appellant an opportunity of responding to any evidence submitted in writing by the respondent, that the matters put forward in support of the appeal do not warrant a hearing, it may refuse a hearing (r 20(c)). Such a decision is appropriate only in cases where it is plain that no advantage could be gained by a hearing (*R v IAT, ex p Ross Wayne Jones* [1986] Imm AR 496 affd [1987] Imm AR 210).

(b) Summary disposal

Under r 35, the appellate authority may dispose of an appeal summarily, without a hearing, if certain conditions are met. The issues raised by the appeal must have been previously decided by an appellate authority co-ordinate or superior in jurisdiction to that before which the appeal has been presented. The appellant must have been a party to that determination. The facts must not have been materially different from those on which the instant appeal is based. It is inappropriate for the adjudicator to apply r 35 to a husband appeal on the basis of an earlier fiancé appeal. The evidence, and the applicable rule, differ. The adjudicator should not take into account the possibility that he might arrive at the same conclusion as another adjudicator. This is an irrelevant consideration. The issues in such a case have not been determined already (*Bagdadi v ECO Bombay* [1994] Imm AR 431).

Before an appeal is determined in this way, an opportunity must be given to the parties to make representations to the contrary. If an appeal is determined, the parties must be notified in writing. The notice must specify what issues were raised in the appeal and in what previous proceedings they had been determined.

In *Ramzan v Visa Officer, Islamabad* [1978] Imm AR 111, the respondent to the appeal invoked the summary procedure at the outset of the hearing before the adjudicator. The adjudicator assented and determined the case summarily. It was argued before the IAT on appeal that the procedure could not be used after the case had been listed for a full hearing. The IAT concluded that it could be invoked at any stage. Rule 35 does not envisage only a pre-hearing written procedure. Two previous IAT decisions, *Ahmed v ECO Islamabad* and *Taj Bibi v ECO Islamabad* [1977] Imm AR 25 were followed. (See also *Sae-Heng v Visa Officer, Bangkok* [1979–80] Imm AR 69.)

(c) Hearing in absence

Last, the appellate authorities may hear an appeal in the absence of the appellant. They may do so if the appellant is not in the UK, or is suffering from a communicable disease or mental disorder, or is unable through illness or accident to attend the hearing; or the authority is satisfied that it is impracticable to give him notice of the hearing and no person is authorised to represent him at the hearing. Furthermore, the hearing may take place in the absence of any party who has been notified of its time and place. However, if that party has explained his absence, the hearing should proceed without him only if it appears proper in the circumstances of the case. Notice of a pre-hearing review may be given. Such a hearing is an intermediate step before hearing. An appeal should not be dismissed if the applicant fails to attend (*Singh and Kaur v S of S* [1993] Imm AR 382). Notice of hearing is deemed to have been given if it has been posted not later than seven days before the date of the hearing.

In one situation the hearing *must* take place in the absence of the appellant. Under s 22(4) of the 1971 Act, if it is alleged that the appellant relies on forged documents and disclosure of the method of detection would be against the public interest, the appellant and his representatives must be absent while that allegation is investigated.

7 The hearing

(a) Procedure at oral hearings

At the hearing, the parties may address the appellate authority, give evidence, call witnesses and question persons giving evidence before the authority. The parties may, at the conclusion of the evidence, make representations on the effect of the evidence. In most other respects the appellate authority determines its own procedure. However, it is obliged by rr 8(4) and 11(3) of the 1984 Appeals Rules to give the respondent an opportunity to amplify the explanatory statement (see r 28). This procedure does not apply in asylum or mixed appeals.

The appellate authority is not entitled to adopt a procedure which results in a denial of natural justice. Such a decision is outside the IAT's jurisdiction, and therefore amenable to the supervisory jurisdiction of the High Court to quash proceedings. However, where the applicant is denied an opportunity to have a fair hearing, not because of the fault of the adjudicator, but because of the fault of his advisors, the decision of the adjudicator is not amenable to judicial review (*Ex p Al-Mehdawi* [1990] Imm AR 140). Thus, where an IAT sitting at first instance was not told of the existence of another (ultimately successful) appeal on the same facts, that fault cannot result in the decision of the IAT being quashed (*S of S v Yasin* [1995] Imm AR 118). In such circumstances the applicant could ask the S of S to exercise his powers under s 21 of the 1971 Act to refer back to the adjudicator any matter which was not put before the adjudicator.

In *Oberoi v S of S* [1979–80] Imm AR 175, the adjudicator decided an appeal on a basis that had not been relied on by the Home Office either in its notice or at the hearing. The adjudicator had not indicated that he saw it as important, with the result that the appellant had no chance to address him on it. The IAT allowed the appeal. It held that, although the adjudicator could have decided the case on a ground not put forward by the Home Office, he should have given the appellant the opportunity to address him on it, if necessary by granting an adjournment. In *Wadia v S of S* [1977] Imm AR 92, the appellate authority's discretion to regulate procedure was also considered. It was held that the adjudicator was entitled to exclude witnesses from the room in which the hearing was being held while evidence was being given, until the time came for them to give evidence, although there is no rule of law that witnesses must be excluded (*R v IAT, ex p Jebunisha Patel* [1996] Imm AR 161).

There is no inherent power to control procedure in the interests of fairness (see *R v An Adjudicator, ex p S of S* [1989] Imm AR 423; the adjudicator's

powers are limited to those vested in him by statute and subordinate legislation). The public may be excluded from a hearing under r 32, although the
general rule is that hearings are to be held in public. If the appellant is
excluded under s 22(4) of the 1971 Act, the public must also be excluded. A
member of the public may also be excluded at the request of a party, or
because he is behaving disruptively, or because evidence is being given
which, in the interests of a party, should not be heard in public. Any member
of the Council on Tribunals may attend a hearing at any time.

Representation   A party may be represented (1971 Act, s 22(3) and 1984
Appeals Rules, r 26). The appellant may appear in person or may, as of right,
be represented by counsel, a solicitor, a consular official (or equivalent), or a
person appointed by a voluntary organisation receiving a grant from the S of
S under s 23 of the 1971 Act. With leave, he may be represented by anyone
else, such as a member of the Free Representation Unit. While such leave is
discretionary and may be refused, reasons for refusing it should be given; the
representative and the appellant should be given the opportunity to appear
before the adjudicator to argue why the representative should be permitted to
appear and to state the consequences of a refusal of representation (*Iqbal v
ECO Islamabad* [1992] Imm AR 255 (IAT)). The S of S (or other officer)
may be represented by counsel, a solicitor or any Home Office official.

Records   The appellate authority is obliged, by r 40 of the 1984 Appeal
Rules, to ensure that there is a record of the proceedings. This may be
a manuscript summary or a record kept by way of shorthand notes or
mechanical methods. In *S of S v Sidique* [1976] Imm AR 69 it was emphasised that the parties' submissions should be summarised in the adjudicator's notes. Further, it is desirable that adjudicators record their
impressions of witnesses (*Asfaw* (5339) and *R v IAT, ex p Iram Iqbal* [1993]
Imm AR 270). It is, though, proper for an adjudicator to be cautious in
recording his findings as to credibility where he knows that the witness is
involved in other immigration appeals (see *Ex p Toko Makombo* [1995] Imm
AR 548).

Where an appellate authority does not reserve its decision, the 1984
Appeals Rules, r 39, provides that it shall pronounce the determination and
reasons for the decision at the conclusion of the hearing, and then send to the
parties a record of that determination.

If the appellate authority does reserve its determination, the rule provides
that it shall, as soon as is practicable, notify every party to the appeal of its
determination and send them a copy of the document recording it. Thus an
indication by an adjudicator, made at the end of a hearing, that he was
intending to allow an appeal but that the written determination would follow,
does not constitute a determination (*R v IAT, ex p Rasiah Kandiah* [1991]
Imm AR 431). Inordinate delay in promulgating a determination may form
the basis for a successful appeal to the IAT to have the case remitted for
rehearing (*Amanor* (11664), four months; *Jeyanathan* (11975) five months;
Begum (11709), six months; and see JCWI B, vol 5, no 9, p 8).

Reasons for the adjudicator's decision A determination should set out:

 (a) the legal principles, and the burden and standard of proof;
 (b) the factual points at issue;
 (c) the adjudicator's evaluation of *(b)*;
 (d) his findings as to credibility;
 (e) his conclusion, making clear what evidence is accepted or rejected.

(see *Ex p Dhaliwal* [1994] Imm AR 387). Reasons are to be given to enable the appellant to understand the grounds on which the appeal was decided (*Morgan* (11935)). An adjudicator should therefore indicate with clarity (although not necessarily at length):

 (a) what evidence he accepts;
 (b) what evidence he rejects;
 (c) where there is any evidence on which he cannot make up his mind, whether he accepts it or not;
 (d) what, if any, evidence he regards as irrelevant

(*R v IAT ex p Amin* [1992] Imm AR 367 at 374; see also *ECO Islamabad v Ajaib Khan* [1993] Imm AR 68 and *Raja Zia v S of S* [1993] Imm AR 404). The appellant should be able to see why he was not believed, if that is the reason for the failure of the appeal (*Jagtar Saini v S of S* [1993] Imm AR 96). It is enough, however, for the adjudicator to have referred to the discrepancies and inconsistencies in the applicant's evidence. He does not have to give further reasons regarding credibility (*Ex p Makombo* [1995] Imm AR 548; *Ex p Yogeswaran* [1995] Imm AR 293). It would also appear that he does not need to put to the appellant such discrepancies, or invite the appellant's explanation (*R v IAT, ex p Joseph Williams* [1995] Imm AR 518). Further, the CA held, in *Sahota v IAT* [1995] Imm AR 500, that the adjudicator has no duty to question an appellant further about a matter which is central to his case and which was raised in the course of proceedings but had not been investigated by the S of S.

There may be a duty on an adjudicator to give reasons for reaching a conclusion different from that of another adjudicator on similar facts. In the asylum claim *Gnanavarathan v A Special Adjudicator* [1995] Imm AR 64 the CA held that if an adjudicator comes to a conclusion different from that of his colleagues on the basis of like facts, he must give reasons for that conclusion. When the adjudicator is contemplating this, he should inform the representatives of cases on which he would rely, but he is not obliged to search files for like cases. Representatives may wish to draw the adjudicator's attention to like facts in other determinations.

Irregularities Irregularities in proceedings before the appellate authorities, which occur before a decision has been reached, and arise from a failure to comply with the rules, do not by themselves render the proceedings void. The authorities have a wide discretion to cure irregularities, for example by the amendment of documents (1984 Appeals Rules, r 38).

(b) Burden of proof

The burden of proof is on the appellant. The 1984 Appeals Rules, r 31, provides that if, on appeal, the appellant asserts that a decision under the 1971 Act should not have been taken against him because he is not a person to whom the provisions apply, he must prove that assertion. Equally, if on appeal a fact is put forward, the existence of which it would have been for the appellant to satisfy the immigration authorities in the first instance, the appellant must prove that fact.

The stringency of this rule is shown by the facts of *Visa Officer, Islamabad v Channo Bi* [1978] Imm AR 182. In that case the IAT said that a previous successful application for entry to the UK did not raise an estoppel against the immigration authorities. On a second application, the applicant has to prove all the facts again. However, the IAT did indicate that although the burden of proof was unaffected by the previous application, the fact of that application was an important part of the evidence in the applicant's favour on the second application. The S of S cannot be estopped by representations made by officials (*Deen v S of S* [1987] Imm AR 543, *Paet v S of S* [1979–80] Imm AR 185), nor by a long delay before initiating proceedings (*Deen*, above).

There is no reference in the 1984 Appeals Rules to standard of proof, but it is assumed throughout the reported cases that it is the civil standard: that is to say, proof on the balance of probabilities. In *R v IAT, ex p Mehra* [1983] Imm AR 156, an IAT decision was quashed because the IAT had applied a higher standard of proof (see also *Nadeem Tahir v IAT* [1989] Imm AR 98). (For the burden of proof in political asylum cases, see Chapter 26.)

(c) Evidence

By virtue of rule 29 of the 1984 Appeals Rules, the appellate authority is entitled to admit any evidence in whatever form, whether or not it would be admissible in an ordinary court, so long as it is evidence of any fact which appears to be relevant to the appeal. Notes of an interview are admissible without the need for them to be produced by the immigration officer who made them (*Giri Poudel v S of S* [1991] Imm AR 567). The authorities have a judicial discretion to exclude irrelevant evidence (*R v IAT, ex p Lila* [1978] Imm AR 50 (documentary evidence) and *Wadia v S of S* [1977] Imm AR 92 (oral evidence)). Oral evidence may be given on oath or affirmation. The authority's powers to compel persons to give evidence or produce documents are narrower than those of the civil courts. So an appellate authority cannot compel a witness to give an answer which is self-incriminatory, or to produce a document which is privileged (for example, a communication between solicitor and client relating to the appeal). However, evidence derived from a search of baggage conducted in a manner of which the adjudicator does not approve cannot be excluded on that basis if it is relevant (*Immigration Officer Heathrow v Neil Mirani* [1990] Imm AR 132). It is arguable that evidence which is derived from a search conducted in breach of the PACE codes, which the S of S has instructed immigration officers to observe, could be excluded by an adjudicator exercising his judicial discretion.

Fresh evidence   The question of admissibility of evidence frequently arises in the course of appeals. A significant point is what evidence of facts, not before the immigration authorities, the appellate authorities should receive. In *R v IAT, ex p Hassanin Kandemir and Farooq* [1986] Imm AR 502, the CA held that on any appeal where the question is whether a discretion of the S of S or an officer should have been exercised differently, evidence of any facts which existed at the time the relevant decision was made is admissible, even though those facts were not known to the decision-maker at the time. The credibility of the evidence and weight to be attached to it are different matters.

In *Visa Officer, Cairo v Ashraf* [1979–80] Imm AR 45, the IAT held that evidence of events occurring after the decision of a visa officer to refuse an application for an entry clearance as a visitor was properly admissible. In that case the ground of refusal was that the applicant's *bona fides* was suspected. The evidence admitted by the adjudicator was that after the visa officer's decision the appellant had embarked on a course of study in Egypt, and the applicant's father had emigrated to the USA. This evidence strongly supported the applicant's contentions as initially declared to the visa officer, and so was rightly admitted by the adjudicator. This should be contrasted with the IAT's decision in *Yosef v S of S* [1979–80] Imm AR 72.

The IAT in *Yosef* referred to the principles set out in *Visa Officer, Karachi v Hassan Mohammed* [1978] Imm AR 168. These are that fresh evidence should always be received on appeal provided it is relevant evidence of facts already in existence at the time of the decision under appeal. If the evidence is documentary, it matters not that it bears a date later than the decision, provided it concerns facts existing at the date of the decision. So where the applicant for an entry clearance as a visitor tendered at the appeal documentary evidence, which was not available to the visa officer, that he owned land in Pakistan, this was held to be admissible. This followed the approach of the DC in *R v IAT, ex p Abdul Rashid* [1978] Imm AR 71. In *Mohammed*'s case, the IAT observed that evidence of facts occurring after the decision should normally form the basis of a fresh application, not an appeal. If this seems likely to lead to injustice, it is open to the adjudicator dealing with the appeal so to indicate to the S of S.

The adjudicator cannot admit evidence concerning facts that came into existence subsequent to the decision of the authority (*R v IAT, ex p Weerasuriya* [1982] Imm AR 23). A similar conclusion was reached in *R v IAT, ex p Kotecha* [1982] Imm AR 88, and the guidelines laid down in *Hassan Mohammed*'s case (above) were approved. However, in *R v IAT, ex p Amirbeaggi* (1982) *The Times*, 25 May, these cases were explained as not laying down any rigid rule that fresh evidence which is relevant to the issue before the authority will not be admitted. *Amirbeaggi* itself was explained by the CA in *Mohammed Ashraf v IAT* [1988] Imm AR 101. Where the relevant decision of the immigration authority is based on a view of a state of affairs in existence at the time the decision was made, fresh evidence should not, on the whole, be admitted. Where, however, the authority had based its decision on a forecast, for example as to the future prospects of a business, the admission of fresh evidence as to the performance of the business is appropriate. Evidence of funding may be admitted where there is a question of whether funding will be available to a couple (*ECO Islamabad v Bashir Ahmed* [1991] Imm AR 130). However, evidence of a subsequent pregnancy was considered irrelevant in *Ex p Prajapati* [1990] Imm AR 513. The IAT is not bound to grant leave to appeal on the basis that there is fresh evidence to support evidence which the adjudicator rejected (*Ex p Jasmine Miah* [1991] Imm AR 184).

Hearsay evidence   An interesting case on the admissibility of hearsay evidence is *Visa Officer, Islamabad v Moh'd Altaf* [1979–80] Imm AR 141. In that case the respondent applied for settlement as a dependant of his sponsor. The application was refused, partly on the basis of information gathered by an ECO on a field visit to the respondent's village in Pakistan. The officer showed photographs of the applicant and his relations to the villagers and as a result was satisfied that the applicant was not who he claimed to be. The IAT, following an unreported CA decision, *Mod'd Ejaz v S of S* (21 December 1978), held that the adjudicator had not attributed sufficient weight to this evidence and had, accordingly, wrongly allowed the appeal. The CA decision is itself authority that the S of S is entitled to take into account hearsay evidence from informers in reaching a determination. It may be dangerous, however, to rely on hearsay alone (*R v IAT, ex p Lulu Miah* [1987] Imm AR 143).

Oral evidence   In *Kassam v S of S* [1976] Imm AR 20 the IAT considered what attitude an adjudicator should adopt towards oral evidence by appellants. The IAT observed that even if there are inherent implausibilities in that evidence, it should not properly be discounted unless it has been challenged in cross-examination before the adjudicator and rebutting evidence, even if only by way of affidavit, has been tendered. It was perhaps significant to the IAT's approach in that case that the Home Office had advance notice of the nature of the evidence to be given by the appellants. Although the immigration officer, if he is the respondent to the appeal, is not obliged to attend and give evidence, this is clearly desirable in the light of the observations in *Kassam*. Indeed, in *Padmore v S of S* [1972] Imm AR 1, the IAT emphasised that the officer should attend, if it is practicable, so that he can be questioned both by the appellant and by the adjudicator. On an appeal from a decision of an ECO, where the adjudicator does not see or hear the applicant, and the ECO has had that advantage, the IAT has recommended that adjudicators should not usually interfere with the ECO's findings of fact concerning the applicant (*ECO Karachi v Zafar Ahmed* [1989] Imm AR 254). In such cases further evidence should be made available. Conversely, where an appeal has been remitted from the IAT to a different adjudicator, it is an error of law to fail to consider the evidence afresh while taking note of the previous adjudicator's hearing and the hearing in the IAT. The adjudicator is not entitled to accept the earlier adjudicator's assessment of the credibility of the witnesses without proper consideration of the evidence (*ECO Bombay v Vali Patel* [1991] Imm AR 147).

It is clear from the cases on evidence and the rules as to burden of proof, that an appeal is very much a re-hearing of the facts and matters on which the decision of the S of S or the immigration official was based. It is not a re-hearing on the documents, but closer to a re-trial, since evidence may be called of all facts which are relevant to the grounds of the decision, even if those facts were not before the immigration authorities. This should be borne in mind when appeals are being prepared.

If the adjudicator can consider the merits of an appeal against deportation, he should consider all the compassionate circumstances that could be put and were put before him. These include any that have been considered in relation to another earlier appeal (*Anima Umarji v S of S* [1989] Imm AR 285). It is also open to the adjudicator, in considering whether or not the discretion of the S of S has been exercised properly, to reach findings of fact which are at variance with those of the S of S, without allowing the appeal for that reason (*R v IAT, ex p Kalsoom Razaque* [1989] Imm AR 451). In considering marriage a compassionate circumstance in a deportation appeal, the question of the primary purpose of the marriage should be approached in accordance with the *Hoque* guidelines (see p 202). If it is found that the primary purpose of the marriage was not to obtain settlement that might lessen the weight to be given to any overstaying that has taken place (*Ex p Rakesh Arora* [1990] Imm AR 89).

8   Duties and powers of adjudicator

(a) Section 19, 1971 Act
The primary source of an adjudicator's duties on appeal is s 19 of the 1971 Act. This provides that an adjudicator must allow an appeal in two cases. First, if he considers that the decision questioned was not in accordance with the law or any applicable immigration rule; and second, in relation to a decision which involves the exercise of discretion, if he considers that the S of S or the officer involved should have exercised his discretion differently.

'*Not in accordance with the law*' *R v IAT, ex p S of S* [1992] Imm AR 554 (the case of *Mumin*) gave rise to a debate concerning the scope of the jurisdiction of the adjudicator. Can an adjudicator review the exercise of the S of S's discretion under an extra-statutory concession on the grounds that it is not in accordance with the law? The better view is that expressed in a line of IAT cases, such as *S of S v Abdi* (CA, 30 October 1995) [1996] Imm AR 148, where Peter Gibson LJ stated:

> To my mind the only substantial point taken on behalf of the Respondents was that the decision of the Secretary of State was 'not in accordance with the law' within the meaning of s 19(1)(*a*)(i) in that the Adjudicator and the Tribunal

found that he had ignored or acted in contravention of the Somali family reunion policy in reaching that decision. In *R v Immigration Appeal Tribunal, ex parte Bakhtaur Singh* [1986] 2 All ER 721, [1986] Imm AR 352 Lord Bridge (with whose speech Lord Brandon, Lord Brightman, Lord Mackay and Lord Goff agreed) said at p 360 of the latter report:

'Mr. Laws' argument encounters its final and, to my mind, insurmountable hurdle, in a consideration derived from the general law. On classic *Wednesbury* principles (*Associated Provincial Picture Houses Ltd v Wednesbury Corporation* [1948] 1 KB 223), in exercising his discretion whether to implement a court recommendation for deportation or whether to decide to make a deportation order against an overstayer, the Secretary of State is bound to take account of all relevant considerations. If, therefore, some interest of third parties which is known to the Secretary of State and which would be adversely affected by deportation is in truth relevant to the proper exercise of the discretion, a decision made without taking it into account would in any event be open to challenge by judicial review and consequently would be open, in the case of an overstayer, to appeal under section 19(1) as being 'not in accordance with law' quite apart from the immigration rules. It follows that to construe the rules in the sense for which the appeal tribunal contends would not only conflict with the general law but would also be ineffective to restrict the relevant matters which the appellate authorities may, and indeed must, take into consideration.'

These remarks are only *obiter dicta* and it is not obvious that Parliament by s 19(1)(*a*)(i) intended adjudicators to have the power to examine the validity of the Home Secretary's decision by reference to all the matters that would be relevant for a judicial review of the decision. But Mr Singh did not suggest that Lord Bridge's remarks were wrong and they are supported by similar comments by Mustill LJ in *R v Secretary of State for the Home Department, ex parte Malhi* [1991] 1 QB 194, [1990] Imm AR 275 at p 283 of the latter report. I shall therefore proceed on the footing that if it can be shown that the Home Secretary failed to act in accordance with established principles of administrative or common law, for example if he did not take account of or give effect to his own published policy, that was not 'in accordance with the law'.

Thus a decision made outside the rules may be challenged on appeal by reference to s 19(1)(*a*)(i). Decisions such as *Agirbas* [1993] Imm AR 452 and *George* (11886) (see JCWI B, vol 5, no 9, Summer 1995) in which the IAT stated that the way in which the S of S chooses to exercise his extra-statutory discretion is not a matter for the appellate authorities, and believed that the IAT should be guided by the (*obiter*) comments in the *Mumin* case [1992] Imm AR 554 that issues of public law should be left to the Divisional Court, are not to be followed.

The only other express statutory fetters on the adjudicator's discretion have already been noted. The IAT has identical powers and duties when it sits as the court of first instance. Thus in a deportation case where the appellant was unrepresented, the IAT was under an obligation to put the details contained in the explanatory statement (see the Court of Session, *Johangir Ahmed v S of S* [1994] Imm AR 457).

Section 19 makes clear that the adjudicator is entitled to investigate the factual basis of the immigration authority's decision. (See also *Ex p Malhi* [1991] 1 QB 194 and *R v IAT, ex p Khan (SGH)* [1975] Imm AR 26.) It also provides that a decision made in accordance with the immigration rules is not to be treated as a decision involving the exercise of a discretion if the S of S has been invited to depart from the rules and has refused. It is important to distinguish between the exercise of a discretion outside the immigration rules to refuse some immigration status to a person by criteria set out in a policy, and a refusal, having been requested to do so, to depart from the immigration rules. The appellate authorities cannot review the factual merits of a refusal to depart from an applicable immigration rule (*Somasundaram v ECO Colombo* [1990] Imm AR 16 and see *Evon* (11392) JCWI B, vol 5, no 7, p 9). Thus in *Abdi* (30 October 1995, above), by reason of s 19(2), the S of S's exercise of discretion was not reviewable by the adjudicator under s 19(1)(*a*)(ii). His decision to refuse entry was in accordance with the immigration rules (paras 52 and 78 of HC 251). He had impliedly been requested to depart from the immigration rules and had refused to do so. However, the adjudicator may look to see whether the decision is in accordance with the law in general, whether or not it involves a request to depart from the immigration rules, as *Abdi* impliedly did. The adjudicator is not confined to the rules and the various Immigration Acts. If an adverse decision is based on the rules, it is treated as a refusal to depart from the rules, but the decision may still be scrutinised to see if it is in accordance with the law (*Dawood Patel v S of S* [1990] Imm AR 478). A refusal to depart from the rules may not be in accordance with principles of natural justice, or may be perverse on the particular facts of the case.

Certain cases suggest that principles of the law on children, such as that the interests of the child are paramount, may not apply to immigration cases (*R v IAT, ex p Girishkumar Patel* [1990] Imm AR 153 and *In Re A (a minor)* [1991] Imm AR 606, where an attempt to make a child, whose father was an illegal entrant, a ward of court was struck out as an abuse of process). Clearly where a child's welfare is involved, the S of S must take it into account in deciding whether or not to take or continue enforcement action. It is arguable that where one of the extra-statutory policies concerning children is being considered the welfare principle is to be taken into account as part of the informing principles of those policies.

(b) The applicable rule

In *S of S v Purushothaman* [1972] Imm AR 176, the IAT held that the adjudicator's task on appeal is to take the immigration authority's decision as the starting point. In deciding whether the decision conforms with the law and immigration rules, the adjudicator is to take into consideration all the evidence, including further evidence, and review any conclusions of fact on which the decision was based. The appellate authority has a duty to consider the applicability of all relevant parts of a rule under consideration in a case, even if a particular part of a rule has not been drawn to its attention by either party (*R v IAT, ex p Tohur Ali* [1988] Imm AR 237), or in situations where the rule could be relied on by the applicant in two different ways but is relied on in only one (*Hawa Uddin v IAT* [1991] Imm AR 134). It is the duty of the applicant to present to the ECO the factual basis on which he relies, and the ECO should then apply all the relevant rules to the facts before him. If he does not, the appellate authority may consider rules not applied by the ECO (*Shabir Hussain v ECO Islamabad* [1991] Imm AR 483). Where there is a close connection between two rules, and the factual basis put forward by the applicant could fall under either, the appellate authorities can apply either rule (*Ach-Charki v ECO Rabat* [1991] Imm AR 162). However, an adjudicator cannot review an application made on a particular ground, on another ground which is inconsistent with it (see *Tahid* [1992] Imm AR 157 and *Shabir Hussain* (above)).

Where an appellant does not challenge an allegation of fact, there is no duty or obligation on the appellate authority to make an enquiry into that allegation of its own volition (*R v IAT, ex p Martinez-Tobon* [1987] Imm AR 536). Where an adjudicator considers that an appeal should be determined on an issue not argued before him, he should afford the parties an opportunity to make submissions to him on that issue (*Moussavi v S of S* [1986] Imm AR 39. See also *R v IAT, ex p Hubbard* [1985] Imm AR 111 and *Tahir* (above)). There is no requirement for the case to be remitted to the S of S for reconsideration in those circumstances, if the adjudicator takes a view of the basis of the decision which differs from that of the S of S on the facts (see *Tahird* above).

In *R v Peterkin (Adjudicator), ex p Soni* [1972] Imm AR 253, the DC emphasised that the adjudicator's task is to exercise his own discretion on the facts. The adjudicator is not confined to intervening only in cases where it can be shown that the immigration authority's exercise of a discretion is plainly wrong or perverse. (See also *R v IAT, ex p Desai* [1987] Imm AR 18.) Furthermore, the adjudicator is not restricted to considering the case under the rules applied to it by the immigration authorities as evidenced by the notice of refusal (*R v IAT, ex p Kwok on Tong* [1981] Imm AR 214). However, if the adjudicator does decide the case under a rule not relied on by the immigration authorities, and under that rule the immigration authorities have a discretion, the adjudicator has no jurisdiction to exercise that discretion in their stead. The case must, in effect, be remitted to the statutory authorities for them to decide it (*R v IAT, ex p Malik* (1981) *The Times*, 16 November (overturned on its facts at [1985] Imm AR 92, although the CA expressly declined to address this issue)). Thus the application is not to be determined by the adjudicator's considering how the S of S would have exercised his discretion, but should be remitted (*Yau Yak Wah* [1985] Imm AR 16).

The adjudicator must decide the case under the rules and not under his own concept of natural justice (*S of S v Glean* [1972] Imm AR 84), nor under his own amalgam of rules (*R v IAT, ex p Martin* [1972] Imm AR 275). The adjudicator is limited to the rules applicable to the case before him. He cannot therefore deal with an application to enter as a wife on the basis that it is an application (outside the rules) to enter as a cohabitee, which has been refused (*Hawa Uddin v IAT* [1991] Imm AR 134). In considering rules other than those taken into account by the S of S the appellate authorities are required to do only what is reasonable, and not to construct ingenious arguments. The adjudicator should not embark upon 'any roving expedition among the rules to see if there is anything which might be of assistance to one side or another' (*Hawa Uddin, per* McCowan LJ at p 144).

(c) Findings on evidence

The adjudicator is obliged to make findings on the evidence, but it is not possible to infer from the fact that he has not referred to certain specific matters that he had not taken them into account (*R v IAT, ex p Gondalia* [1991] Imm AR 519). The adjudicator's determination should deal with every issue which has been identified by the deciding officer as leading to the refusal of the application (*ECO Islamabad v Mohammed Hussain* [1991] Imm AR 476). The adjudicator must also take care to avoid language which would suggest that the wrong standard was being used to assess the S of S's decision. Thus the adjudicator should not suggest that he is considering the S of S's decision purely on the basis of administrative law principles instead of considering the case on its merits (*Clifford Ofoajoku v S of S* [1991] Imm AR 68); or use language which suggests that a non-civil standard is being used, such as that some evidence is 'unconvincing' or that he was 'satisfied certainly' (*Abdul Azid v ECO Dhaka* [1991] Imm AR 578). An adjudicator is entitled to make adverse findings on a person's credibility even if that person's evidence was not challenged before him (*R v IAT, ex p Jasmine Miah* [1991] Imm AR 184). Conversely, the adjudicator is not obliged to refer to matters contained in notes of interview if they are not raised by the parties before him (*R v IAT, ex p Sumeina Masood* [1991] Imm AR 283).

The adjudicator's determination should make clear what approach he adopts to the consideration of the relevant factors. Thus where the merits of a decision to deport are considered, the adjudicator should start from the proposition that deportation will normally be the proper course where a person has failed to comply with a condition of his leave, or remained without authority, and then take account of all the relevant factors listed in para 364, balancing those factors. It is merely desirable, not essential, that the adjudicator should refer to the relevant rule explicitly (*Adaah v S of S* [1993] Imm AR 197).

(d) Interpreters

The Home Office and appellate authorities have recognised that difficulties are caused by interpreters who are not of the highest quality or trained in the appropriate dialects. During the course of the passage of the 1993 Act, the S of S rejected the idea that interpreters should be approved by the Institute of Linguists.

At a hearing, the interview interpreter's qualifications should nevertheless be put before the adjudicator if there is an issue of mistranslation of replies in interview. Where the allegation against the interpreter is incompetence rather than bias, it has to be shown that the S of S knew that the interpreter was incompetent to conduct the interview. The court cannot simply judge the competence of the interpreter (*R v Mayor and Burgesses of the London Borough of Tower Hamlets, ex p Jalika Begum* [1991] Imm AR 86). Where an allegation of bias is made against an interpreter used at an interview, the suspicion of bias raised by the applicant may be dispelled by something less than persuasive evidence that the allegation is untrue. A reasonable suspicion of bias however, if not disproved, is a ground on which a decision based on the translated answers may be quashed (*Saichon Chomsuk* [1991] Imm AR 29). The fact that the interviewer fails to translate the caution correctly does not mean that the evidence obtained at the interview cannot be admitted in the context of judicial review proceedings (*Ex p Yasin* [1996] Imm AR 62). The appellate authorities issue guidance on working with interpreters which advisers should request and observe.

If there appears to be a problem with a quality of interpretation at the hearing, this should be put before the adjudicator immediately. Problems arise when interpreters attempt to summarise what the applicant is saying to them, instead of translating literally. In some cases this can be significant as the credibility of the applicant can be affected by the way in which his evidence comes across. The adjudicator should, if the objections appear to be founded, make a direction to the interpreter that he should interprete literally what is being said to him by the representative and by the applicant. If the problem persists, it may be that proceedings will have to be adjourned for a different interpreter to be obtained.

(e) Power to give directions

If the adjudicator allows the appeal, he is empowered to give such directions for giving effect to that determination as he thinks proper at any stage, including after the promulgation of the determination. Such directions should, however, be given only if a party requests them (*Mohammed Yousuf v ECO Karachi* [1990] Imm AR 191). The adjudicator may also make recommendations with respect to any other action which he considers should be taken in the case under the Act. He may hear evidence on an application for directions (*Yousuf* (above)). An adjudicator may not give directions where the merits of the application on which the directions are to be based have not been considered by the S of S (*S of S v Razaq Abdel* [1992] Imm AR 152). The authorities are obliged to implement directions, although they need not do so while an appeal may be brought against the adjudicator's decision, and, if such an appeal is brought, for so long as it is pending. In *Visa Officer, Aden v Thabet* [1977] Imm AR 75, the IAT examined the adjudicator's powers to give directions and concluded that they were narrow; thus, the adjudicator had no power to impose stringent conditions on the successful appellant's entry clearance, such as conditions as to place of residence and length of stay, and a condition prohibiting a subsequent application for a variation of status. The adjudicator was entitled only to give a direction that the appellant be granted a visitor's entry clearance. Conditions were for the immigration authorities alone. The adjudicator is not obliged to give directions, and if it becomes apparent that there has been a significant change in circumstances since the decision under appeal, so that the applicant would no longer satisfy the rule, a direction would be inappropriate (*Rahman v IAT* [1995] Imm AR 372).

This power should not be confused with the power to give procedural directions in the course of an appeal under r 33 of the 1984 Appeals Rules (*S of S v Fardy* [1972] Imm AR 192).

If, after directions have been given, the ECO attempts to prevent entry by pursuing further enquiries seeking to circumvent the adjudicator's decision, his decision would be amenable to judicial review (*Ex p Mohammed Yousuf* [1989] Imm AR 554). However, where no directions are given, the ECO has a duty to make further enquiries, and is not limited to a right of appeal against the adjudicator's decision if he finds that there has been a change of circumstances (*Mohammed Yousuf* (above)).

When an appeal is dismissed there is no statutory duty to make recommendations so that the adjudicator is not under a duty to consider making one if the applicant does not request one (*Ex p Kumar* [1993] Imm AR 401). Further, the recommendation or refusal to make one does not form part of the adjudicator's determination (*IAT ex p Chavrimootoo* [1995] Imm AR 267). The adjudicator occasionally makes comments which the S of S may take or ignore. They do not raise a legitimate expectation that they will be carried out by the S of S (*Fozlu Miah v S of S* [1991] Imm AR 581). Also, there is no basis for an appeal against failure to make a recommendation when the adjudicator dismisses an appeal, nor can an adjudicator who comes to reconsider the decision of the first adjudicator be obliged to make a recommendation merely because the first one did (see *Gillegao (Grenda) v S of S* [1989] Imm AR 174). The adjudicator has no duty to record that he has refused to make a recommendation or to give reasons for his decision (*Ex p Kanagaratnam* [1995] Imm AR 253). In *Visa Officer, Islamabad v Hussain* [1987] Imm AR 39, the IAT stated that in most cases it was inadvisable for an adjudicator to dictate his determination at the end of the hearing, since errors could easily creep in.

In a letter dated 21 October 1996 from the IND to Richard McKee of the IAS, the IND confirmed that the S of S's policy is not to follow an adjudicator's recommendation that exceptional leave to remain be granted unless fresh information is brought up at the hearing, as exceptional leave to remain will have been considered as part of the asylum determination process. The written determination must disclose clear exceptional compassionate circumstances which have not previously been considered by the S of S and which merit the exercise of discretion outside the immigration rules. In cases of refused entry clearance, if maintenance and accommodation will not be adequate by the date of the hearing, a recommendation will not result in an entry clearance being issued without a fresh application being made.

Chapter 20

Appeals to the Immigration Appeal Tribunal and the Court of Appeal

1 Appeals to the IAT

The 1971 Act, s 20 provides that any party to an appeal to an adjudicator may appeal to the IAT if dissatisfied with the outcome. Thus the immigration authorities as well as appellants are entitled to appeal from the adjudicator. Appeals to the adjudicator consisting of, or containing, an issue of asylum are dealt with in Chapter 26. The IAT's jurisdiction is fixed by statute, and may not be extended by agreement (*O v Immigration Officer, Heathrow* [1992] Imm AR 584). The IAT may confirm the adjudicator's conclusion or reach any other decision which could have been reached by him. In reaching its decision the IAT duly notes matters of principle laid down in previous IAT decisions, but more emphasis is placed on the facts of the case before it (*Entry Certificate Officer, New Delhi v Bhambra* [1973] Imm AR 14). The IAT may alter or add to any recommendations made by the adjudicator, or replace them altogether. It may also remit a case to the adjudicator for him to determine it in accordance with the IAT's directions, or for him to take further evidence with a view to a determination by the IAT (1971 Act, s 22(2)(*a*); and r 21, 1984 Appeals Rules).

Where a case is referred to an adjudicator for a hearing *de novo*, he is fully entitled to have regard to the record of the evidence given in previous proceedings. He should then apply his mind afresh to the issues, the law and the evidence, without regard to the previous adjudicator's determination (*Mohammed Karim v Visa Officer, Islamabad* [1986] Imm AR 224). He should make his own assessment of the credibility of the witnesses, and not rely on the assessment made by the previous adjudicator (*ECO Bombay v Vali Patel* [1991] Imm AR 147). The second adjudicator is, however, entitled to conclude that the appellant is not credible even though the first adjudicator heard oral evidence and the second did not but determined the matter on the papers (see *R v IAT, ex p Nalokweza* [1996] Imm AR 230 and *Owalabi* [1995] Imm AR 399).

There is an indication in s 20(1) that the 1971 Act contemplates that leave to appeal may be necessary. However, the Act does not lay down the circumstances in which leave to appeal is required. These requirements are contained in the 1984 Appeals Rules, r 14 which states that an appeal in all cases will lie only with the leave of the adjudicator or of the IAT. The IAT has no power to determine whether an appeal against a decision of the S of S is out of time (*ECO Antananviro v Hansa Popat* [1990] Imm AR 598).

(a) Criteria to be satisfied before leave will be granted
Under r 14(2) of the 1984 Appeals Rules there are various circumstances in which leave to appeal must be granted. First, there are cases under the 1971 Act, s 22(5):

> *(a)* where there is an appeal against a decision that the appellant required leave to enter the UK and the appellate authority is satisfied that the appellant held a current entry clearance or certificate of entitlement; and
>
> *(b)* where the appeal is against refusal of leave to enter and the appellate authorities are satisfied that at the time of the refusal the appellant held an entry clearance (and that dismissal of the appeal is not required because the appellant was an illegal entrant).

Second, there are those cases set out in the 1984 Appeals Rules, r 14. These were considered by Simon Brown J in *R v IAT, ex p Rashida Bi* [1990] Imm AR 348. Leave is required in all cases and involves an element of discretion. If one of the grounds submitted is that the adjudicator misdirected himself in law, the IAT has to reach a preliminary view as to that ground. If that ground is arguable, the IAT must decide whether, without error of law, the adjudicator could properly have come to the conclusion he arrived at. If he could, there is no requirement to grant leave. In such a case the IAT should look at the case and exercise its discretion as to whether, considering the facts, it would itself have come to the same conclusion (in which case leave should be refused), otherwise leave should be granted.

By the Asylum Appeals (Procedure) Rules 1996, r 13, in an asylum appeal, or an appeal containing an asylum element, leave to appeal from the special adjudicator is required (see Chapter 26). Under the law before the 1993 Act, the IAT was required to grant leave where the applicant had a well-founded fear of persecution, but was entitled to see if the fear was well-founded before granting leave. There is no obligation to hear the applicant for leave before making a decision (*R v IAT, ex p Bouchtaoui* [1992] Imm AR 433).

The requirement that there should be an 'arguable point of law' is fairly strict. In many cases leave to appeal will be refused because, although there may be two views on the facts, the view taken by the adjudicator does not give rise to an 'arguable point of law'. A clear example of a case in which leave was refused under the rule is *Harmail Singh v IAT* [1978] Imm AR 140. In that case the point was whether the applicant's 'whole family' was being admitted for settlement when an elder brother was staying in India. In essence it was a question of fact, not law, whether or not the elder brother was still a member of the family unit. Leave was therefore refused. This is a harsh result, but within the rules. However, if the adjudicator reaches what is apparently a determination of fact on the evidence before him, but the determination is entirely unsupported by that evidence, or he apparently directs himself correctly in law but reaches a conclusion which offends common sense, then it is submitted that this would give rise to an arguable point of law. In that situation, the appellant would be entitled to leave to appeal. Both types of error are errors of law (see *Edwards v Bairstow* [1956] AC 14, *per* Viscount Simmonds at p 29 and *per* Lord Radcliffe at p 36). In *R v IAT, ex p Khan* [1975] Imm AR 26 the DC applied such a test to determine whether the applicant should have been granted leave to appeal. In *R v IAT, ex p Kirimetiyane* (1982) *The Times*, 17 June, the DC suggested that the *Wednesbury* test (*Associated Provincial Picture Houses v Wednesbury Corporation* [1948] 1 KB 223) was appropriate for determining whether there was an arguable point of law entitling the appellant to leave to appeal. (See also *R v IAT, ex p Ahmud Khan* [1982] Imm AR 134 on the need for the appellate authority to give reasons for its decision.)

The statute and rules provide, in addition, that there are two circumstances in which leave to appeal must be granted. They involve exclusions from the UK. First, if an entrant appeals against a decision that he requires leave to enter the UK and the appellate authority is satisfied that he held a certificate of entitlement at the time of the decision, he must be given leave to appeal. This is so even if the appellant freely admits that his entry certificate was obtained by a false representation (*Williams v Immigration Officer, Heathrow* [1986] Imm AR 186). Second, if the appellant was excluded from the UK at a time when he held an entry clearance, he must be given leave unless he was either an illegal entrant at the time of the exclusion, or there was a deportation order in force against him at the time of the exclusion.

There is a curious disparity between the criteria governing the grant of leave to appeal and the nature of the IAT's appellate jurisdiction. As we have seen, with a few exceptions, leave will be granted only if it is shown that the appeal turns on an arguable point of law. However, the IAT can intervene and overturn an adjudicator's decision on a pure question of fact. It seems, at the least, unfair, that a more difficult hurdle has to be overcome in obtaining leave than in appealing successfully.

This point emerges very clearly from *Alam Bi v IAT* [1979–80] Imm AR 146. In that case the CA held that the IAT did not err in law in rejecting the adjudicator's assessment of the credibility of a witness whom he had seen and the IAT had not, and preferring the entry clearance officer's assessment instead. The CA noted that the officer, who had conducted an interview in a non-judicial atmosphere, was probably in a better position to assess the credibility of a witness than the adjudicator. The CA was anxious to stress that this was an unusual case, but the principle seems plain enough. The IAT is entitled to overturn adjudicators' decisions on what are essentially questions of fact: but most appeals cannot reach the IAT unless they turn on an arguable point of law. The IAT will generally be wary of interfering with the adjudicator's assessment of the credibility of witnesses and the findings of fact reached by him, and there is no obligation on the IAT to review the adjudicator's findings (see *R v IAT, ex p Mahendra Singh* [1984] Imm AR 1 and *R v IAT, ex p Dauda (No 2)* [1995] Imm AR 600). However, they may reverse the adjudicator's findings without hearing evidence (*R v IAT, ex p Hussain* [1989] Imm AR 382 and see *Assah v IAT* [1994] Imm AR 519).

(b) Application for leave to appeal

The first step in appealing to the IAT is to obtain leave if it is a case in which leave is required. There are three ways of obtaining leave:

  (a) by applying to the adjudicator orally (usually at the hearing of the appeal);
  (b) by applying to the adjudicator in writing;
  (c) by applying to the IAT itself.

If application is made to the adjudicator, it must be made 'forthwith' after his determination. Time runs from the pronouncement of the decision if it is announced orally, or the date it is posted to or served on the appellant if the decision is reserved. Where the decision is given orally, then the application for leave must be made at the end of the hearing; where the decision is reserved, the application must be made immediately on receipt of the written decision. If application is made to the IAT, it must be made within 14 days of the adjudicator's determination, except that where the appellant is not in the common travel area the time limit is 42 days. This time limit goes to the jurisdiction of the IAT (*R v IAT, ex p Samaraweera* [1974] 2 All ER 171; *R v IAT, ex p Armstrong* [1977] Imm AR 80). If an application for leave has already been made to the adjudicator and has been refused, it is submitted that time ought to run from that refusal, and not from the initial decision of the adjudicator to dismiss the appeal. However, the DC, in *Samaraweera*'s case, thought otherwise.

If the adjudicator allows an oral application, notice of appeal must be served on the adjudicator 'as soon as practicable' after that decision. In *Samaraweera*'s case these words were held to mean that notice of appeal should be served within the time limit applying to service (seven days under the rules then in force: 14 days now) and 'as soon as practicable'.

This limit should therefore be borne in mind in submitting notices of appeal when leave has been granted orally by the adjudicator. If the adjudicator allows a written application, notice of appeal must be served on the IAT within 14 days. If the IAT allows an application for leave to appeal, the written application is treated as a notice of appeal. In any case where leave is not required, notice of appeal must be served on the IAT within 14 days of the adjudicator's decision. Time runs from the time the appellant or his representatives first learned or ought to have learned of the adjudicator's decision (*R v IAT, ex p Suleman* [1976] Imm AR 147). The IAT has no power to extend the time limit for serving an application for leave to appeal (*R v IAT, ex p Flores* [1995] Imm AR 85). It is irrelevant that an appellant seeks, but fails, to serve the application in time (*R v IAT and An Adjudicator, ex p S of S* [1990] Imm AR 166).

An application for leave to appeal to the adjudicator or the IAT is normally dealt with on the documents, but the appellate authority may hold a hearing if 'special circumstances render such a hearing desirable'. In *Mehta (BKD) v IAT* [1979–80] Imm AR 16 the CA emphasised that if a hearing is desired, it is up to the appellant to request it. The CA also said that in such a case the appellant must indicate in his grounds of appeal the 'special circumstances', which must be relevant to the grounds of appeal, rendering a hearing desirable.

Applications for leave to the IAT may be, and usually are, dealt with by the President or a chairman alone. A notice of appeal or a notice of application for leave must contain:

   (a) the full name, address, date of birth, nationality or citizenship of the appellant;
   (b) particulars of the relevant determination of the adjudicator; and
   (c) the grounds on which the appellant intends to rely. The grounds may be amplified or varied at the hearing.

(c) Refusal of leave to appeal
There is no right of appeal from a refusal of leave to appeal to the IAT. A refusal may be amenable to judicial review if, for example, the IAT has failed to give proper reasons for the refusal. Decision-making bodies are normally obliged to give proper and adequate reasons for their decisions (*R v Criminal Injuries Compensation Board, ex p Cummins* (1992) *The Times*, 21 January; *R v IAT, ex p Khan* [1983] Imm AR 134). The IAT's decisions on leave may accordingly be brief, but should give reasons which are sufficient to show the applicant why he failed. There is nothing improper in the IAT using a standard formula in refusing leave to appeal (see *Sahota v IAT* [1995] Imm AR 500 (CA), *Ex p Rajendra Kumar* [1995] Imm AR 386, *Ex p Beyazit* [1995] Imm AR 534, *Ex p Yaziki* [1995] Imm AR 98, *Ex p Rashid* [1995] Imm AR 194 (both Auld J); see also *Legal Action*, November 1995 at p 25). Even where the grounds of appeal are themselves brief, the IAT should be careful to see whether there is an obvious point of law in the decision, regardless of whether it is raised (*Ex p Chugtai* [1995] Imm AR 559 at 566, but cf *Akkulak v IAT* [1995] Imm AR 114).

The IAT is entitled to refuse leave to appeal if there is an issue on which the whole appeal must fail, without considering the merits of another ground raised in the application for leave (see *R v IAT, ex p Khan (Majid)*, [1995] Imm AR 19 and *IAT, ex p Asfar Jan* [1995] Imm AR 440 (both Tucker J)).

(d) Grounds of appeal
Where an application for leave has been sent to the IAT, consideration should be given to the grounds of appeal before the leave application is determined. If short grounds were put in to preserve the appellant's right of appeal, there is an opportunity to put in full grounds when the IAT notifies the parties that the leave application is to be determined by a particular date. Plainly the IAT's reasons for refusing leave will be considered to be more or less adequate on a review depending on whether the grounds of appeal were more or less full. The full grounds should therefore be submitted before the

date on which the IAT have notified that the determination of leave will take place. The IAT can reconsider the refusal of leave if additional grounds in support of the appeal are brought to their attention, which were not before them when the application for leave was first made. However, they will do so only where an administrative error on the IAT's part had prevented all the grounds submitted in support being considered earlier (*ECO Bombay v Khalid Patel* [1991] Imm AR 553). There is no obligation on the IAT to wait for further evidence before determining an application for leave to appeal. This is particularly so in relation to applications for leave to appeal in asylum cases, where there is a five-day period during which leave must be determined (*Ex p Sherif Seidu* [1994] Imm AR 577 (Schiemann J)), but for the view that time could be extended under the 1993 Appeals Rules see *Ex p Kiyingi* [1994] Imm AR 580 (Judge J). For the position under the 1996 Appeals Rules see p 513).

(e) Evidence and documents

The basic evidence which the IAT is obliged to consider on appeal is the evidence received by the adjudicator as contained in the record of proceedings before the adjudicator (1984 Appeals Rules, r 18). If a party wishes to adduce further evidence before the IAT, he must notify the IAT in writing. This notice must be served either with the notice of appeal, or as soon as is practicable thereafter. If it is the respondent who wishes to rely on further evidence, he must notify the IAT as soon as is practicable after he has been notified of the appeal. The notice must indicate the nature of the further evidence.

If the notice is not served, it would seem, on the wording of r 18, that the IAT has no discretion to admit further evidence at the request of a party. If the notice requirement is complied with, the IAT may admit the evidence in its discretion. In addition, the IAT may of its own motion request further evidence to be furnished to enable it to arrive at a proper determination of the appeal. If the IAT decides to admit further evidence, it may either direct it to be given orally, before it or before an adjudicator, or direct that it be submitted in writing.

Except in a case which involves forgery of documents, it is for the IAT to ensure that all notices and other documents required for an appeal, other than those already supplied to the parties, are supplied to the parties. It is therefore the IAT's responsibility to ensure that the parties receive, in particular, copies of the adjudicator's record of proceedings, since this is pre-eminently a document required for an appeal.

2   Reference to the S of S for further consideration

There is a final avenue of 'appeal' provided for in the statute. The 1971 Act, s 21 gives the S of S power to refer any case to the appellate authorities for further consideration. If an adjudicator has dismissed an appeal and leave to appeal to the IAT has been refused, or there has been no further appeal, or if the IAT has affirmed the adjudicator's dismissal of an appeal, or reversed an adjudicator's decision to allow an appeal, the S of S may at any stage refer the case either to the adjudicator or the IAT. This is a procedure expressly designed to bring to the appellate authority's attention an aspect of the case which was not previously before it. The authority is then required to report its opinion of the case to the S of S. This procedure is not available as of right to parties to the appeal, although there is nothing to prevent an unsuccessful appellant from requesting the S of S to invoke the procedure. However, whether or not the S of S invokes it is wholly within his discretion. If the S of S refuses to use the procedure, there can be no appeal from that decision (*R v IAT, ex p Nathwani* [1979–80] Imm AR 9; and see *Ex p Uddin* [1990] Imm AR 181, and *R v IAT, ex p Ali* [1990] Imm AR 531). There may be circumstances in which it would be appropriate for the S of S to make such a reference. In *Ex p Bello* [1995] Imm AR 537, Judge J declined to give general guidance, but quashed the refusal of the S of S to refer under s 21 on the basis that there was fresh evidence obtained after an appeal had been dismissed which could affect the findings as to credibility made by the adjudicator. This power has been discussed in the context of proving blood relationships (see p 217).

3 Appeals to the Court of Appeal

The 1993 Act introduced a right in all immigration cases, whether or not involving an asylum element, to appeal, with leave, to the CA. Where the IAT has made a final determination of an appeal any party to the appeal may bring a further appeal to the CA (or the Court of Session in Scotland) on any question of law material to that determination (1993 Act, s 9). A question of law includes matters of public law and in particular will include irrationality or perversity in the decision (see *Edwards v Bairstow* (above) and p 395). Thus where the adjudicator misdirected himself in law or misunderstood the law, or where there was no evidence to support a finding of fact or conclusion, or where the decision was perverse, there is an error of law. Further, failure to give reasons is an error of law, as is the exercise of a discretion on wrong principles. There was debate in the House of Lords over whether the words 'any question of law material to that determination' restricted consideration to matters of immigration law. Earl Ferrers stated that this was not the intention behind the words:

> The court can look at any issue of law which is involved in the tribunal decision, including any other kind of law such as European Community law. Any part of the law in which the tribunal decision was made can be included. Therefore it does not only refer to immigration law. (HL Debs, 2 March 1993, vol 543, no 105, cols 649–50).

Further, he stated, in response to a request for an assurance that any part of the law relating to the basis on which the original decision was made included issues relating to administrative law, that administrative law is covered if that was a matter which the IAT considered (col 650). An appeal can be brought only in respect of a final determination of the IAT, and a refusal of leave to appeal to the IAT is not such a determination (*El-Assall v S of S* (22 February 1995), unreported, CA).

A decision by the IAT to remit a case to the adjudicator is not a final determination for these purposes. There is no right of appeal to the CA against the decision to remit, and the only potential method of challenge is by judicial review (*R v IAT, ex p Jebunisha Patel* [1996] Imm AR 161 and *Kara v S of S* [1995] Imm AR 584 (CA)).

(a) Leave to appeal

An appeal may be brought only with the leave of the IAT, or where such leave has been refused, with leave of the CA (1993 Act, s 9(2)). Within 28 days from the date on which the IAT refuses leave to appeal an application for leave may be made to the CA (RSC Ord 59, r 24(2)). The application is by notice of *ex parte* application together with a draft notice of appeal, containing the draft grounds of appeal, and requesting allocation to the Immigration Appeal Tribunal (Final) List. The decision of the IAT refusing leave and the application for leave should be lodged (in triplicate), with the appropriate fee, in the Civil Appeals Office. Where the application for leave to appeal is brought out of time an affidavit explaining why it is out of time should be sworn and lodged. The application is initially considered by a single judge, and a bundle, consisting of any determinations and decisions of the IAT and adjudicator on the appellant's appeal, should be supplied for his use (RSC Ord 59, r 24(4) and see Jim Gillespie's useful article: *Appeals from the IAT to the CA: a short guide for the practitioner* INL&P vol 9, no 3, 1995, p 92). Applications are usually determined without an oral hearing.

Asylum or mixed cases   In asylum or mixed cases an application for leave to appeal to the CA must be made not later than ten working days after the receipt of the written notice or the determination. The President or a chairman of the IAT determines the application and must notify the parties to the proceedings of the determination and the reasons therefor not later than ten working days after the IAT has received the application (Asylum Appeals (Procedure) Rules 1996, r 21(5)). Where the application is refused, and an application to the CA has failed, the refusal may be amenable to judicial review.

Non-asylum cases   Where there is no question of asylum involved in the appeal, the appellant must rely on the rules in Part IIIA of the 1984 Rules, as inserted by the Immigration Appeals (Procedure) (Amendment) Rules 1993 (SI 1993 No 1662). An application to the IAT for leave must be made not later than 14 days after the party seeking to appeal has received notice of the determination (1984 Appeals Rules, r 21B). The application for leave is made by serving on the IAT a notice of the application for leave to appeal prescribed in the rules (1984 Appeals Rules, Sched, Form 4), and may be determined by the President or Chairman acting alone, and without a hearing, unless the IAT considers that there are special circumstances making a hearing necessary or desirable.

(b) Notice of appeal

If leave is granted, the notice of appeal must be served on the Treasury Solicitor and on the Chairman of the IAT within seven days of the order granting leave (RSC Ord 59, r 4(3)). Within seven further days, the appeal must be set down by lodging in the Civil Appeals Office two copies of the notice of appeal together with proper endorsements under Ord 59, r 5(1) (fee and certificate of the date of service). When the appeal appears in the List of Forthcoming Appeals, the appellant's solicitors must, within 14 days, lodge at the Civil Appeals Office three copies of a bundle conforming to RSC Ord 59, rr 9(1) and 24 (Note also the Practice Statement at 59/9/14 of the *Supreme Court Practice*).

(c) Bail pending appeal

Where an appellant has pending an appeal to the CA under the 1971 Act and is detained, he may be released on bail (s 9A, 1993 Act, inserted by the 1996 Act). A chief immigration officer or higher, a police inspector, or an adjudicator may release the appellant on his entering into a recognizance (or in Scotland, a bail bond) which has as a condition that he appear before the CA (or Court of Session in Scotland) at a time and place named in the recognizance or bail bond (s 9A(2), 1993 Act). The IAT must, if he requests it, release the appellant on bail where an appeal has been brought by the S of S or he has sought leave to appeal to the CA or the appellant has sought and been granted leave to appeal (s 9A(3)). The provisions of para 29 of Sched 2 to the 1971 Act (see p 373) relating to bail pending appeal apply (s 9A(4)). The restrictions on the grant of bail under para 30 of Sched 2 to the 1971 Act (see p 374) apply to the grant of bail under this provision. Likewise the provisions relating to forfeiture of recognizances and arrest of appellants released on bail apply to bail granted under s 9A (s 9A(4) and (5)).

Chapter 21

The European Convention on Human Rights

1 Introduction

The UK ratified the European Convention for the Protection of Human Rights and Fundamental Freedoms (ECHR) in 1951 and it came into force in 1953 (Cmnd 8969 of 1953). In 1966 the UK recognised the compulsory jurisdiction of the European Court of Human Rights (ECtHR) and accepted the right of an individual to petition the court. The UK's obligations under the Convention are treaty obligations in international law but since the Convention has not been expressly incorporated into national law by statute, its provisions cannot be directly relied on in the domestic courts. Nevertheless, there are two principal ways in which the Convention affects the law and practice of immigration. First, British courts may have regard to the Convention in their interpretation of domestic legislation and second, an individual who is aggrieved by the operation of the immigration legislation may petition the ECtHR for redress.

A number of articles of the Convention are of relevance in the immigration context. The most important of these are art 3 (the right not to be subjected to inhuman or degrading treatment or punishment); art 5 (the right to liberty); art 8 (the right to respect for family life); art 12 (the right to marry); art 13 (the right to an effective remedy before a national authority); and art 14 (the right to enjoy the freedoms set out in the Convention without discrimination).

2 The Convention as an interpretative guide

Perhaps the clearest exposition of the role of the Convention in statutory interpretation is to be found in *Waddington v Miah* [1974] 1 WLR 683 where Lord Reid, referring to art 1 of the Convention (which proscribes the retrospective creation of criminal offences), said, 'it is hardly credible that any government department would promote or that Parliament would pass retrospective criminal legislation'. In *R v Chief Immigration Officer, London (Heathrow) Airport, ex p Salamat Bibi* [1976] 3 All ER 843, the CA emphasised that the Convention is not part of UK domestic law and disapproved *dicta* in earlier cases which supported the view that immigration officers were bound to have regard to the provisions of the Convention. The limited application of the Convention in domestic law was stressed again by Taylor J in *R v IAT, ex p Chundawadra* [1987] Imm AR 227 (and see *R v IAT, ex p Patel* [1990] Imm AR 153 and *Ex p Jibril* [1993] Imm AR 308).

More recent cases, however, would appear to leave the way open for a more flexible judicial attitude to the applicability of the Convention by the domestic courts. In *Ex p Brind* [1991] 1 AC 696, Lord Templeman appeared prepared to accept its applicability in cases involving interference with human rights (at 751), although the majority of the HL was clear that the doctrine of proportionality did not form part of domestic law in general. The CA went further in *Derbyshire County Council v Times Newspapers Ltd* [1992] QB 770 where the Convention was expressly relied on to justify the conclusion that a local authority could not sue for defamation. Most recently, in *Ex p McQuillan* [1995] 4 All ER 400, Sedley J commented that it would be 'unreal and potentially unjust' to develop English public law without reference to the principles and standards of the Convention.

The principles of the ECHR may be invoked, in conjunction with policy statements made by the government when promoting the 1993 Act, as giving rise to a legitimate expectation that they will be honoured. For example, Charles Wardle stated (Official Report, Standing Committee A, 12 November 1992, cols 52–3):

> A number of Hon Members have referred to exceptional leave to remain. This is, by definition, outside the immigration rules. The essence of exceptional leave to remain is flexibility, and it provides the ability to respond to individual circumstances. It cannot be spelt out in legislation. As I have said we use exceptional leave to remain to respond to cases that are outside the 1951 Convention but within the terms of our other obligations, including the European Convention on Human Rights and the UN Convention on Torture. That will remain the case under the Bill. We have no intention of removing exceptional leave to remain in genuine humanitarian cases.

These remarks were made in the context of a proposed amendment, the purpose of which was to include the ECHR, the UN Convention Against Torture, and the UN Convention on the Rights of the Child, in the definition of 'Convention' in the 1993 Act. It would seem to be a clear statement of policy, and to support the grant of exceptional leave to remain to the parent of a child who is to be deported, as the only way in which the right of the child to family life (under art 8) may be preserved, while at the same time preserving the child's right to education (art 2). There is clear authority that the ECHR will be interpreted as imposing an obligation on the UK to preserve the child's rights in these circumstances (*Berrehab v The Netherlands* (1988) 11 EHRR 322; *Moustaquim v Belgium* (1991) 13 EHRR 802). Thus in such circumstances it should be possible to challenge removal directions or a deportation order by means of judicial review of the S of S's refusal to grant the parent exceptional leave to remain (see also IND guidelines, Chapter 14).

A person may be granted entry to exercise rights of access to a child (see p 185). This occurred most recently in *Ex p Zighem* [1996] Imm AR 194. The applicant was an illegal entrant who had a daughter in the UK following a relationship with a British national. He argued that in deciding to remove him to Algeria, the S of S had failed properly to take into account whether or not there would be an interference with family life and whether or not such an interference was justified. The High Court accepted without question that art 8 applied and held that it was impossible to see the basis for the decision letter which had been sent to the applicant. The decision to remove was therefore quashed.

3 The Convention as a remedy

Since 1966 an individual aggrieved by an action of the UK has been able to petition the ECtHR for redress. The procedure is lengthy and complicated, but it may be a valuable course when all other appeals fail. As detailed below, a new structure is planned, although it is not yet in force. It will therefore be necessary to deal with both procedures and the transitional provisions.

The first stage in the present procedure is that the individual petitions the European Commission for Human Rights. This body investigates the complaint and issues a report. The Commission must first decide if a *prima facie* case of violation of the Convention has been made out: in other words, if the case is admissible. The petitioner must have exhausted all domestic remedies and have brought the petition within six months of the last effective domestic decision.

In *Kamal v UK* (1982) 4 EHRR 244, the Commission adopted a liberal attitude in respect of the exhaustion criterion. The applicant had not pursued judicial review after his appeal was dismissed by the IAT, but it was held that he had exhausted his domestic remedies since his complaint related to a dispute of fact with the immigration authorities for which judicial review would afford no remedy. However, in *Caprino v UK* (1982) 4 EHRR 97, the applicant, whose complaint related to deportation, was held not to have exhausted his domestic remedies. He had not applied for a writ of *habeas corpus*. On the facts of the case the Commission held that it could not find a violation unless the applicant had invoked the remedy (and failed), or could show why it did not apply to him.

In *Soering v UK* (1988) 11 EHRR 439, the ECtHR dealt with the question of whether judicial review is an effective remedy under art 13, holding that the 'death row' phenomenon was a breach of art 3 which was relevant to the question of whether or not to deport, and would render a decision to extradite unreasonable. The applicants accepted that where the facts of the case are not in dispute, judicial review is an effective remedy. However, in *Vilvarajah v UK* (1991) 14 EHRR 248, the applicants argued that where the facts of a case are in dispute, judicial review, which examines only the reasoning process, is not an effective remedy. The court did not consider that there was a material difference between *Vilvarajah*'s case and *Soering*'s case. They based their decision on the fact that it was not disputed that in asylum cases the courts in the UK can review refusal to grant entry. The court recognised that there are limitations on the powers of the national court, but took the view that judicial review provided an effective degree of control over the decisions of the administrative authorities in asylum cases.

Most recently, in *Chahal v UK* (1995) 20 EHRR CD19, the Commission considered the effectiveness of judicial review of a decision to deport on the grounds of national security. It was pointed out that even in a case where some facts may be made available to the court, the process of judicial review merely empowers the court to consider whether or not there is evidence that the S of S balanced national security considerations against all the circumstances of the case. In such a case, the court has no choice but to accept the evidence and therefore allow the deportation order to stand. The Commission therefore held that judicial review is not an effective remedy in such circumstances. At the time of writing, the case was due to be considered by the ECtHR.

If the complaint is found to be admissible it is fully investigated by the Commission, which then attempts to achieve a friendly settlement between the parties. If no settlement is reached, the case is referred to the Committee of Ministers. They may deal with it themselves, or it may be referred to the ECtHR within three months by the Commission or by the state concerned. The court may award just reparation to the individual, including damages. Few cases actually reach the stage of a determination by the court.

The most celebrated case relating to immigration pursued under the Convention is that of the 31 East African Asians who claimed that their exclusion from the UK under the Commonwealth Immigrants Act 1968 was a violation of the Convention, arts 3, 8 and 14. The Commission reported to the Committee of Ministers on 14 December 1973 that art 3 had been violated in relation to the 25 Asians who were citizens of the UK and Colonies, but not in relation to the six who were British Protected Persons; and that arts 8 and 14 had been violated in relation to three of the applicants. The Committee of Ministers finally issued a resolution on 21 October 1977 (reported at (1981) 3 EHRR 76) to take no further action, since by then all 31 claims had been settled by administrative action.

In *Berrehab v The Netherlands* (1988) 11 EHRR 322 the deportation of a father was challenged by the father and his minor daughter. The father and mother had been separated and the child had lived with the mother. The father, however, saw his daughter regularly. The deportation was held to threaten the father's and the child's rights to respect for their family life. Although travel was possible between the father's country of origin and that of the child, the possibility of maintaining family relationships was theoretical in a situation in which regular contacts were essential in view of the very young age of the child.

The derogations in art 8(2) (in favour of public policy) are less likely to apply in the case of a proposed deportation of one who has lived in a country lawfully for several years, and against whom the government has no complaint. Thus the deportation of an innocent overstayer with a family in the UK could be challenged on this ground. Even where the government does have a complaint against the proposed deportee, the deportation can be challenged if it represents a disproportionate means to achieve the legitimate aim pursued under the derogation. The ECtHR will make allowance for a margin of discretion left to the state (*W v UK* (1988) 10 EHRR 29).

The best example of the effect which the ECHR has had on the state of immigration law in this country comes from the case of *Abdulaziz, Cabales and Balkandali v UK* [1987] EHRR 471. In that case, the ECtHR held that the old rules discriminated against women because they made it easier for a husband settled in the UK to be joined by his wife than for a wife to be joined by her husband. This decision precipitated amendments to the immigration rules relating to fiancés and spouses, introduced by HC 503 in 1985 (see Chapter 12). Predictably, perhaps, the effect of the amendments was restrictive, making it as difficult for fiancées and wives to enter the UK as it had previously been for fiancés and husbands.

The Court, in *Beldjoundi v France* (1992) 14 EHRR 801, was asked to consider the applicability of art 8 where a deportation order had been made against a man with a number of serious convictions. Although the court accepted that deportation could be justified by a pressing social need, it found that since the effect of the order in this case would be to threaten the existence of a marriage (with no children), the means employed were disproportionate to such a aim. On the other hand, in *Gul v Switzerland* (1996) 22 EHRR 93, it was held that a failure by the state to allow the applicant's son, who was born and brought up in Turkey, to enter the country was not a breach of art 8. The court pointed out that the applicants had failed to show that there was an obstacle to the development of a family life in Turkey.

A matter which often causes concern is the imminent deportation or expulsion of an individual who may have a potential claim under the Convention. In *Uppal v Home Office* (1978) *The Times*, 20 October, which eventually gave rise to an application to the ECtHR, an application in the national court for a declaration that an order to deport Uppal should not be enforced pending the outcome of the case before the ECtHR, was refused. A petition to the ECtHR does not, as a matter of law, operate as a stay on further action by the Home Office. However, the Commission does have power to suggest to a state that it take no expulsion or other action pending the determination of a petition; such requests are nearly always complied with.

4 The Convention and EC law

The principles on which the ECHR is based should be taken into account in cases involving the application of EC law (*Johnston v Chief Constable of RUC* [1987] QB 129). The Convention forms an integral part of the principles of EC law. The European Court of Justice will not permit measures which are incompatible with the fundamental rights recognised and guaranteed by constitutions (*Hoechst v EC Commission* (Cases 46/87, 227/88) [1989] ECR 2859). The Convention, to which member states are parties, can also supply indications of the principles to be taken into account in EC law. Thus, derogations from EC rights may not infringe its provisions unless based on objective factors (*Nold v EC Commission* (Case 4/73) [1974] ECR 491 para 14, and *The State v Watson and Belmann* [1976] ECR 1185). The European Court of Justice will take the provisions of the Convention as the general principles stemming from the constitutional traditions of the member states. The public policy derogations from the freedom of movement articles must be construed strictly, and in the light of the provisions of the Convention, art 2, Protocol 4 (*Rutili v Minister of the Interior* [1975] ECR 1219 para 32; see also the Advocate General in *Henn and Darby v DPP* (C 34/79 [1979] ECR 3795) on ECHR art 10, and *ERTAE v Kouvelas* (C 260/89 [1991] ECR I-2925). The European Court of Justice has power to safeguard the protection of the Convention rights when acts of the EC authorities may have an effect upon them (*Procureur de la République v Waterkyn* (Case 314–6/81 [1982] ECR 4337).

The European Court of Justice cannot, however, examine the compatibility with the provisions of the Convention of national legislation outside the scope of EC law (*Demirel v Stadt Schwabisch Gmund* (Case 12/86) [1989] 1 CMLR 421). Where the national law is within the field of EC law, the member state must comply with the provisions of the Convention in complying with the provisions of EC law (*SPUC v Grogan* [1991] 3 CMLR 849). Most recently, the European Court of Justice has ruled that the European Community could not accede to the Convention except by amendment of the Treaty on European Union, since such accession would involve a fundamental constitutional change for which the treaty, in its present form, does not provide (Opinion No 2/94, *The Times*, 16 April 1996). It was, though, said that respect for human rights was a condition of the lawfulness of Community acts.

The third pillar of the Maastricht Treaty (Treaty of Economic Union, OJ 1993, C 224/1) provides that member states and/or the Council may take steps to further the interests of member states in respect of justice and home affairs. This includes immigration policy. In considering the implementation of such co-operation measures, the member states and institutions of the EC are bound to have regard to the provisions of the ECHR (art K 2(1)).

5 Procedure for applying to the ECHR Commission

The first step in the procedure for bringing a claim before the ECtHR is to make an application to the European Commission for Human Rights. An application should be made on a form available from the Commission for Human Rights, 67006 Strasbourg Cedex, France (tel 88 614961). The form is an Application under Article 25 of the European Convention on Human

Rights and Rules 37 and 38 of the Rules of Procedure of the Commission. When completed, it constitutes the petition under art 25, and is the basis for the Commission's examination of the case. A full statement of the case should therefore be enclosed with it. By the Commission's Rules of Procedure (CPR), r 37, the application must be in writing and signed by the applicant or his duly authorised representative, or, in multiple applications, by the person authorised to represent a group of persons.

The application must contain the name, age and occupation, if any, of the applicant, together with details of his representative including the basis of his authority. It must identify the contracting party against which the complaint is made. As far as possible, the purpose of the application and the provision of the Convention breached should be stated, together with a full statement of the facts and arguments (CPR, r 38). The documents in the case must be attached to the application, and if there is a judicial act or judgment involved in the case, a copy of it should be sent with the application. The application should contain sufficient information to show that the domestic remedies are exhausted, and that the final decision was made not more than six months before the date of the first communication from the applicant to the Commission in which the purpose of the application was set out, even in summary form.

If another appeal or domestic remedy was available, the applicant should state why he has not used it, giving full details. The article which is alleged to have been breached may contain derogations permitting interference with the rights conferred. These may be, for example, acts done in the interests of:

(a) national security;
(b) public safety;
(c) the economic well-being of the country;
(d) the prevention of crime; or
(e) the protection of public morals or the rights of others.

Where the applicant relies on such an article (for example, art 8) an explanation of why the derogation does not apply should be given.

Because a complaint may be rejected by the Commission on a preliminary examination, the importance of giving detailed information as soon as possible cannot be stressed too highly.

(a) The New Procedure under Protocol 11

The new procedure under Protocol 11 is due to enter into force one year after ratification by all the contracting states (art 4 of the Protocol). The Protocol also makes transitional provisions which are dealt with below.

The major change is the abolition of the Commission and its replacement by a single-tier court which will deal with a complaint in all its stages (new art 19 of the Convention). The new art 27 provides that the court will sit in Committees of three, Chambers of seven and a Grand Chamber of seventeen. The right of individual application is contained in art 34, and art 35 allows the court to deal with an application only after the exhaustion of all domestic remedies and within six months of the final decision. Article 35 further gives the court the power to reject any such application which is incompatible with the provisions of the Convention, manifestly ill-founded or an abuse of the right of application.

Article 28 gives a Committee of the Court power to declare inadmissible or strike out an individual application 'where such a decision can be taken without further examination'. This is the same as the present power of the Commission to screen cases at the preliminary stage, and the decision is final. Where a committee make no decision to declare inadmissible or to strike out, a Chamber is empowered to consider both admissibility and merits (art 29).

The Grand Chamber will deal with cases where a serious question in relation to the Convention has been raised; where the Chamber relinquishes jurisdiction; and where the parties do not object (art 30). In exceptional cases a party will be able to seek leave from a panel of the Grand Chamber to refer a case to the Grand Chamber within three months of the date of a Chamber's judgment. The panel of five judges will grant leave where the case raises a serious question relating to the interpretation or application of the Convention or a serious issue of general importance.

Article 5 of the Protocol sets out various transitional provisions pending the implementation of the new procedure. Unconsidered cases already before the Commission will be dealt with under the new procedure. The Commission will have a year to compile a report on those cases which have been declared admissible, and where a report is adopted within this period the case may be referred to the court or decided by the Committee of Ministers. Cases which are referred to the court may go before a Chamber or the Grand Chamber. If a report is not prepared within the year it will be dealt with under the new procedure. Any cases pending before the Committee of Ministers will be decided by that body, and the Grand Chamber will decide any cases pending before the court.

(b) Legal Aid
If the Commission finds the complaint admissible it may grant legal aid to cover the proceedings. If the ECtHR thinks fit, it may grant legal aid to cover representation before it, if the applicant has not obtained it from the Commission. In an appropriate case, and where legal aid is not available, it is permissible for legal representatives to act on a conditional fee basis in proceedings before the ECtHR.

Chapter 22

Judicial Review

1 Introduction

(a) The relevance of judicial review

As detailed in previous chapters, there are various statutory appeal procedures available to individuals aggrieved by decisions of the adjudicator or the IAT. However, there remains a significant number of cases where the statutory procedure may not be available or an appeal cannot be pursued because leave to appeal is not granted. In such cases, judicial review may be the only means by which the decision can be challenged.

Although the courts have stated on a number of occasions that judicial review is not available where other means of challenge are available, exceptions have been made. The possibility of judicial review is therefore important since the special facts of a particular case may render it appropriate.

(b) The nature of judicial review

Judicial review is a supervisory jurisdiction, exercised by the Queen's Bench Division of the High Court and regulated by s 31 of the Supreme Court Act 1981 and Ord 53 of the Rules of the Supreme Court ('RSC'). Its purpose is to regulate the public law functions of public bodies. The fundamental principle is that judicial review does not address the merits of a decision, but the nature of the decision-making process. In theory, this means that the court will not substitute its own view for that of the decision-maker. This reflects in nature the remedies which commonly direct that the decision in question be quashed (*certiorari*) and that the decision-maker reconsider in accordance with the court's ruling on the law (*mandamus*).

An issue which receives much attention is the distinction between errors of law and errors of fact. In theory, a court exercising supervisory jurisdiction can interfere only where the decision-maker has made an error of law. However, in many contexts, the exercise of a legal power is predicated on the finding of particular facts. Immigration law contains many such cases; for example, an illegal entrant may be detained and removed from the UK only if he is in fact an illegal entrant, and the power to detain and remove is dependent on the finding of this precedent fact. The question of precedent fact is one on which the court will adjudicate (*Ex p Khawaja* [1984] AC 74, but cf *Ex p Onibiyo* [1996] Imm AR 370).

2   The grounds of challenge

As discussed above, the purpose of judicial review is to examine the decision-making process. In *CCSU v Minister for the Civil Service* [1985] AC 374, Lord Diplock identified three distinct grounds of challenge: illegality, irrationality and procedural impropriety. In addition, he recognised the growing importance of proportionality in European jurisprudence, but did not feel that in itself it could yet stand as an independent ground of challenge in domestic law.

(a) Illegality

'Illegality' refers to the decision-maker's acting in a manner inconsistent with its powers (*Ex p World Development Movement* [1995] 1 All ER 611). So where, for example, the S of S purports to deport a person under a provision of the immigration rules, and the court decides that in fact the rules confer no such power, the S of S will have acted beyond the powers conferred on him. Acting *ultra vires* can manifest itself in other ways. The courts have consistently held that when exercising powers, the decision-maker must address all relevant considerations and ignore irrelevant matters (*Padfield v Minister of Agriculture, Fisheries and Food* [1968] AC 997). Failure to do so will render the decision unlawful. Other aspects of acting *ultra vires* include fettering discretion (*BOC Ltd v Minister of Technology* [1971] AC 610), frustration of the legislative purpose (*Padfield*) and improper delegation of power (*Carltona Ltd v Works Commissioners* [1943] 2 All ER 560).

(b) Irrationality

In Lord Diplock's view, the notion of irrationality is equivalent to the well-known *Wednesbury* test (*Associated Provincial Picture Houses v Wednesbury Corporation* [1948] 1 KB 223). It can be invoked where an applicant for judicial review claims that the decision reached is one which no reasonable person could have made (*Ex p Norney* [1995] 7 Admin LR 861). At first sight, this would appear to have a wide ambit, but the courts have restricted its application to cases where, to paraphrase Lord Diplock, the decision-maker has acted in such defiance of natural logic that it would offend common sense to allow the decision to stand. The courts have interpreted this test restrictively so that it is only in a few cases that a decision will be successfully challenged on this ground alone.

(c) Procedural impropriety

Procedural impropriety encompasses a wide range of matters and offers the greatest scope for review. As well as principles of natural justice, such as the right to representation and the right to a fair hearing, the courts have developed concepts such as the duty to give reasons for decisions (*Ex p*

Moon (1995) *The Times*, 8 December; *Bolton Metropolitan Borough Council v S of S for the Environment* (1995) *The Times*, 25 May), and legitimate expectation (*Ex p Baker* [1995] 1 All ER 73 at 88–9), which are dealt with below. The essence of these bases of challenge is that the decision will be treated as unlawful if there was an identifiable flaw in procedure which renders the decision questionable.

Over the last few years, many, including leading members of the judiciary, have called for the adoption of proportionality as a distinct ground of challenge. The doctrine states that where the method used to accomplish a particular aim is excessive, having regard to the nature of the aim to be achieved and the other methods available, then the decision may be struck down as unlawful. In *Ex p Brind* [1991] 1 AC 696, the HL refused to recognise this as a separate head on the basis that it would involve an investigation of the merits of the decision-making process. However, the concept is now a well-established part of European Union law with the consequence that domestic tribunals have to take it into account when considering such legislation (*Thomas v Chief Adjudication Officer* [1991] 2 QB 164). In this context, the action proposed by a decision-maker must be necessary for the achievement of an accepted goal in EC law, and bear a reasonable relationship to that objective.

3 The applicability of judicial review to immigration decisions

When considering the application of these principles in the immigration law context, it is important to bear in mind the appeals structure as set out in the 1971 and 1993 Acts. In particular, the 1993 Act, by introducing a statutory route of appeal to the CA from the final determination of an appeal by the IAT on 'any question of law material to that determination' (s 9), restricts the applicability of judical review to some extent. On the other hand, since the 1993 Act also removed the right of appeal in a large number of cases, most notably from visitors seeking to enter the country (s 13(3A(*a*)) of the 1971 Act), the potential for judicial review has been widened in some cases.

(a) Illegality
Immigration officers have certain discretionary powers. The exercise or purported exercise of these powers may therefore be subject to challenge in the following circumstances:

- *(a)* where the discretion of the immigration officer to take decisions has been fettered (*Ex p Tarrant* [1985] QB 251);
- *(b)* where the decision-maker has taken account of irrelevant matters or failed to take into account relevant matters (*R v IAT, ex p Bakhtaur Singh* [1986] 1 WLR 910);
- *(c)* where there has been an unlawful sub-delegation of decision-making powers.

Judicial review is often the only mechanism by which a practice or policy of the S of S may be challenged. However, since the powers conferred on the

S of S under the 1971 Act are broad, it will be difficult to argue that a policy or rule fetters the discretion of immigration officers, or that there has been an improper delegation of his decision-making power. An example of this is *Ex p Samya Ounejma* [1989] Imm AR 75, where the applicant challenged the S of S's direction that immigration officers must refuse entry to certain persons who have not obtained entry clearance in advance, on the basis that this fettered the discretion vested in the immigration officer under the 1971 Act. The CA held that the 1971 Act permitted the S of S to impose such a fetter, but left open the question whether an immigration officer was free to exercise a discretion in exceptional cases.

The width of the S of S's powers can be seen from the HL decision in *Oladehinde v IAT* [1990] 3 All ER 393. It was held that since immigration officers were not holders of a statutory office, but civil servants within the Home Office, the S of S was entitled to delegate the exercise of his statutory powers in accordance with normal administrative law principles. The 1971 Act did not expressly or impliedly limit his powers of delegation in relation to deportation decisions.

There is greater scope for challenge on the basis of a decision-maker's failure to consider relevant matters and/or his having taken into account irrelevant matters. In *Mowla* [1991] Imm AR 210, for example. Ralph Gibson LJ stated (at p 86H) that a decision could be open to challenge if it could be shown to have been made in disregard of the facts known to the immigration officer concerning the applicant's conduct or history while in the UK for the purposes of consideration under para 60 of the rules. Similarly, in a deportation case it is possible to argue that known unacceptable consequences of a deportation order should be taken into account when considering compassionate circumstances. Thus in *Ex p Alavi Veighohe* (1989) *The Times*, 22 August, the availability of the death penalty for drug smuggling in the proposed country of return should have been taken into account in considering compassionate circumstances. Further, in *Re Musisi* [1987] AC 514, the HL held that in an asylum case the S of S should consider a third country's policy of repatriation if the facts require him to do so.

These principles apply equally to oral decisions of a decision-maker where there is a discernible error of law in the reasons for the decision (*R v Crown Court at Knightsbridge, ex p International Sporting Club (London) Ltd* [1982] QB 304). Thus a reasoned oral decision of an immigration officer should be fully noted, since it may be amenable to review.

(b) Irrationality

The court needs to be persuaded that it would not merely be substituting its own discretion for that of the decision-maker before it will grant relief on the basis of irrationality (*Swati v S of S* [1986] 1 WLR 477 and *Hukan Said v IAT* [1989] Imm AR 372). Whether the decision was unreasonable will be weighed against the needs of good administration. The courts are particularly reluctant to interfere with questions of the weight given to evidence (*Mohammed Jaifrey v S of S* [1990] Imm AR 6; *Ex p Mohammed Davda* (No 2) [1995] Imm AR 600).

Where the S of S is challenged on the basis of failure to adhere to a policy statement, it will be necessary to show that the facts of the case satisfied the terms of that policy before the applicant can show that the decision not to observe it was inconsistent and so unreasonable that it should be quashed (*Ex p Steve Ken Amoa* [1992] Imm AR 218). An assertion of irrationality will have to be weighed against the needs of good administration, and the court will weigh the assertion of the decision-maker that he took into account all relevant circumstances when considering whether a reasonable decision-maker, properly aware of his duties and powers, could have reached the same decision. Thus in *Ex p Nzamba-Liloneo* [1993] Imm AR 225, where leave to move for judicial review had been granted, the S of S withdrew the decision under review. He gave the same reasons for a second refusal as for the first, but the court refused to find that this automatically resulted in an unreasonable decision on the second occasion.

(c) Procedural impropriety

This ground of challenge is available where there is a flaw in the procedure followed during the decision-making process. The court will look to the effect of that non-compliance and, unless the procedural impropriety made no difference to the result, is likely to impugn the decision (*Ali Celik v S of S* [1991] Imm AR 8). Breaches of procedure are regarded seriously where the consequences are weighty for the applicant, as where there is a threat to life or liberty.

Fairness The fundamental principles of natural justice or fairness should be observed in immigration matters as in other administrative decisions. However, as Lord Denning said in *Ex p Santillo* [1981] QB 778 at 795; 'the rules of natural justice are not cut and dried. They vary infinitely'. What they demand depends on the character of the decision-maker and the kind of decision being made in the statutory framework of the 1971, 1993 or 1996 Acts. Therefore, in the immigration context, regard is to be had to the immigration rules and the Appeal Rules, together with the requirements of the Acts and the consequences of the decision, before deciding what the requirements of fairness are in the particular case.

Fairness includes the right to a fair hearing (*Ridge v Baldwin* [1964] AC 40), which is of universal application (*per* Lord Reid, p 69). This requirement will be implied into a procedure under a statute where it is clear that the statutory procedure alone is insufficient to achieve justice and that to require additional steps would not frustrate the apparent purpose of the legislation (*Wiseman v Borneman* [1971] AC 297, *per* Lord Reid at p 308). For example under s 13(3AA) of the 1993 Act. provision is made for auditing an ECO's refusals of applications for leave to enter. The statute clearly aims to provide a review of the ECO's decision. The provisions of the 1993 Act do not, in relation to any individual case, provide a procedure sufficient to achieve justice in any particular case. The courts will be likely to infer that the rules of fairness are to be observed in relation to any review of the ECO's decision on a particular application and so the applicant should have the right to be heard (see in particular the non-statutory scheme of review under the 1993 Act, p 358). A court will be reluctant to hold that the requirements of fairness are not to be applied unless the legislation clearly states that they are not, as is the case for special procedure asylum appeals under the 1996 Asylum Appeal Rules, which state that hearings are not required.

Fairness further requires that a person should know the case against him and should have a fair opportunity of answering it (*Kanda v Government of Malaya* [1962] AC 322 at 337, *Fairmount Investments Ltd v S of S for the Environment* [1976] 1 WLR 1255 and *Afful v S of S* [1983] Imm AR 236). This entails that the person should have notice of the allegations sufficiently far in advance of a decision being made so that he has the opportunity of making representations on them. If the decision-maker is minded to proceed on the basis of a matter which has not been aired with the applicant, the applicant should be alerted to the possibility of the decision-maker's taking the point into account so that he may have the opportunity to put forward any argument which might be persuasive (*R v Mental Health Review Tribunal, ex p Clatworthy* [1985] 3 All ER 699). If he does not receive such notice due to the default of his solicitors or representatives there is no breach of natural justice by the decision-maker (*S of S v Al-Mehdawi* [1990] 1 AC 876). The applicant should have the opportunity of dealing with the real basis of a refusal (*Ex p Awuku* [1988] Imm AR 606).

In relation to most immigration decisions, the burden is on the applicant to present the relevant information to the immigration officer, but the latter must act with fairness, and give the applicant a real opportunity of satisfying him on any point about which he is suspicious (*Ex p Mughal* [1974] QB 313). Decisions which are taken on the basis of inadequate information given by the applicant will generally not be reviewable on this ground, even if the true facts are more favourable to the applicant and come to light later. There is an exception to the rule that judicial review of a decision will take into account only the information available to the decision-maker at the time of making the decision (*Ex p Syed Kazim* [1994] Imm AR 94). This exception applies in cases where it is necessary to establish a fact before the decision-maker has power to act (*Ex p Muse* [1992] Imm AR 282). Where there has been a significant change in the applicant's circumstances between the time of making a decision to deport and the upholding of that decision, the S of S may review the original decision in the light of any additional material put before him. He is not, in those circumstances, restricted to considering matters as they stood at the time of the original decision (*S of S, ex p Ul-Haq* [1993] Imm AR 144).

Reasons In recent years the courts have extended the ambit of procedural impropriety in two significant respects. First, there is more willingness to impose a duty to give reasons for a decision even where the decision-maker is not obliged to give reasons by a statutory scheme (*R v IAT, ex p Khan* [1982] Imm AR 134, *R v Civil Service Appeal Board, ex p Cunningham* [1991] 4 All ER 310, *R v S of S ex p Doody* [1994] 1 AC 531, HL). However, after being notified of a challenge by way of judicial review, the S of S may then supply full reasons for the decision. On that basis, in *Ex p Ul-Haq* [1993] Imm AR 144, Hutchison J refused to restrict consideration of the S of S's reasons to those given at the date of the original decision where new material had been placed before the S of S after that time. Even where there is no duty to give reasons, as when the S of S refuses an application for citizenship (see 1981 Act, s 44), fairness may require him to inform the applicant *before* any decision is taken why he is minded to refuse (*Ex p Al Fayed* (1996) *The Times*, 14 November, CA).

On the other hand, the courts have been unwilling to impose a duty to give reasons in respect of certain decisions. The notorious case of *Ex p Cheblak* [1991] 1 WLR 890 illustrated the principle that the S of S is not required to give reasons for a decision to deport where it is asserted that the presence of an individual in the country is not conducive to the public good. This case has been followed on a number of occasions with the courts holding that the S of S has satisfied the requirements of fairness by swearing an affidavit deposing that he has evidence to suggest, for example, that the deportee is involved in terrorist activity (*Ex p Jahromi* (1995) *The Times*, 6 July). On the other hand, it may be possible to challenge the failure to give reasons in such a deportation case under EC law (*Ex p McQuillan* [1995] 4 All ER 400).

Legitimate expectation The second major modern development has been the doctrine of legitimate expectation. The courts will, in appropriate circumstances, protect the expectation of an individual who has been led to believe that he will obtain or retain a benefit, or will be given a hearing before a decision is taken (*CCSU v Minister for Civil Service* [1985] 1 AC 374). The expectation must be created or induced by the decision-maker by an express promise or representation, or an implied representation based on the established policy of the decision-maker. It must be clear and unambiguous.

A legitimate expectation of entry was raised where a foreign child for adoption satisfied four criteria set out in the relevant Home Office circular, and where the prospective adoptive parents had followed the procedures set out in the circular. A new policy could be adopted against the recipient of the circular only after considering whether the overriding public interest demanded it. As a result, the S of S was permitted to refuse entry only if he offered interested persons a hearing (*Khan (Asif) v IAT* [1984] Imm AR 68).

Home Office customary practices and procedures will not, however, give rise to a legitimate expectation in every case (*Ex p Yusufa* [1987] Imm AR 366). The courts are, in general, sensitive to the notion that the needs of good administration require giving latitude to the decision-maker in so far as changes of policy are concerned (*R v S of S for Health ex p United States Tobacco International Inc* [1992] 1 QB 353). In *R v IAT, ex p Anilkumar Patel* [1988] AC 910, the CA held that the mere fact that a person held a re-entry visa did not give rise to a legitimate expectation (see also *Ex p Bolanle Balogun* [1989] Imm AR 603). Ministerial statements may give rise to a legitimate expectation that the policy they set forth will be honoured. In *Domfeh Gyeabou* [1989] Imm AR 94, an overstayer acquired a legitimate expectation that he would not be deported following a statement in Parliament by the Home Secretary that ten years' residence would *prima facie* be a reason to permit a person to remain. On the other hand, in *R v S of S ex p Sakala* [1994] Imm AR 143, a statement by a minister in Parliament that the S of S would 'almost invariably' accept the recommendation of a special adjudicator did not give rise to a legitimate expectation that such a recommendation would be followed in a particular case (see also *Ex p Katoorah* [1996] Imm AR 482).

Where the Home Office changes its policy and the terms of the new policy have been communicated to immigrants' advisory services, an applicant can have no legitimate expectation that the old policy will be followed (*Dawood Patel v S of S* [1990] Imm AR 478). A legitimate expectation was said to arise in the GCHQ case ([1985] AC 374), above, where a specific representation has been made to the applicant. Likewise, where a specific course of conduct has been followed it may give rise to a legitimate expectation that a particular course is to be followed (*Singh (Madanjit) v S of S* [1990] Imm AR 124, CA).

A number of cases concern whether stamps in passports can create a legitimate expectation that there will be a right to enter or re-enter the UK. In *Oloniluyi v S of S* [1989] Imm AR 135 the applicant held a passport which, prior to the expiry of her leave to remain, was endorsed with further leave, a s 3(3)(*b*) stamp, and a visa exempt stamp. She also received oral assurances from an official at Lunar House that she could return without any difficulties prior to the expiry of her earlier leave. The CA held that she had a legitimate expectation that she would be given leave to enter on her return, although the extension of leave in itself did not give rise to such an expectation. In *Ex p Mowla* [1992] 1 WLR 70, the CA considered a number of cases relating to the stamps themselves, and held that such stamps either singly or together do not give rise to a legitimate expectation. The CA held that oral assurances given on the basis of full knowledge of the immigrant's situation had founded the legitimate expectation in *Oloniluyi*'s case, and considered that the only legitimate expectation is that the applicant will be permitted to re-enter if the full facts are known and if there is no change of circumstances in the meanwhile (see also *Ex p Fida Bhatti* [1989] Imm AR 189).

There is no need for the applicant to have relied on the representation for the court to protect the legitimate expectation (*AG of Hong Kong v Ng Yuen Shiu* [1983] AC 629, but cf *R v S of S ex p Akyol* [1990] Imm AR 571). In accordance with the normal rules relating to fairness, the court will, though, refuse relief if no injustice has resulted from the non-fulfilment of the expectation (*Nkiti v Immigration Officer, Gatwick* [1989] Imm AR 585).

4 Remedies

(a) Certiorari

An application for *certiorari* brings a decision of an inferior court, tribunal or authority before the High Court for review with a view to its being quashed because the inferior body exceeded its powers or acted contrary to law. The grounds of the application are to be considered at the date of the judgment, order, or other proceedings complained of (RSC Ord 53, r 4(2)). If leave is granted, it operates as a stay on the proceedings to which the application relates until disposal or further order (RSC Ord 53, r 3(10)(*a*)). Such a stay is binding on the minister concerned (*R v S of S for Education, ex p Avon County Council* [1991] 2 WLR 702 and see *Ex p Muboyayi* [1992] 1 QB 244).

(b) Mandamus
Mandamus is an order of the court requiring a public duty to be performed; powers of enforcement are attached to it under RSC Ord 45, r 5 and Ord 52, r 1. Such an order would be appropriate, for example, to challenge a policy statement refusing to consider some category of person following the quashing of a policy by *certiorari*.

(c) Prohibition
Where the act complained of is continuing or prospective and is unlawful, prohibition is the appropriate remedy, preventing the carrying out of the action. The grant of leave operates as a stay of the proceedings complained of.

(d) Injunction
An injunction will be granted if it is just and convenient to do so, having regard to the respondent, the nature of the matters in respect of which relief can be granted by a prerogative order, and the other circumstances of the case (Supreme Court Act 1981, s 31(2)). The grounds for an injunction are the same as those for the substantive remedies under the judicial review procedure (ie, *certiorari*, prohibition, and *mandamus*). Most importantly, in *M v Home Office* [1994] 1 AC 377, the HL held that injunctions could be granted in judicial review proceedings against ministers and other officers of the Crown.

(e) Declaration
A declaration is often sought, as an alternative to *certiorari*, as a means of vindicating an applicant's rights. In the immigration context, it is most likely to be used where interest groups bring applications for declarations that particular government policy is unlawful.

(f) Damages
Two requirements must be satisfied before an award of damages is made on an application for judicial review. First, the applicant must have joined a claim for damages with the application for judicial review, such a claim relating to the subject matter of the application. Second, the court must be satisfied that if the claim for damages had been made by way of ordinary action, the applicant would have been awarded damages. Such claims are rare, but may arise in the immigration context where, for example, an

individual from another member state of the EU is prevented from taking up employment in the UK through detention which the court rules is contrary to EC law (and see *Brasserie du Pêcheur v Federal Republic of Germany* [1996] 2 WLR 506).

5 Barriers

(a) Standing

A potential applicant for judicial review must have a sufficient interest in the decision which it is sought to review before a challenge is permitted (RSC Ord 53, r 3(7)). Although early cases on the interpretation of 'sufficient interest' were restrictive, more recent decisions exhibit a flexible approach so that, for example, an organisation concerned with the promotion of fair trading in developing countries was considered to have standing to challenge a decision to spend certain monies on the Pergau Dam (*R v S of S for Foreign Affairs ex p World Development Movement* [1995] 1 WLR 386). Similarly, the Equal Opportunities Commission had sufficient interest to challenge the legality of UK employment law in relation to part-time workers, even though it was incapable of being directly affected by discriminatory treatment (*R v S of S for Employment, ex p Equal Opportunities Commission* [1995] 1 AC 1).

Standing does not normally raise a difficulty in immigration cases. The applicant is inevitably the individual who is the subject of the decision, who clearly has sufficient standing, as may others who will be affected by the outcome of the case. For example, a wife has sufficient interest to bring a judicial review of the IAT's decision to refuse her husband leave to appeal (*R v IAT, ex p Sumeina Masood* [1991] Imm AR 283), as has the sponsor of a visitor who is refused entry clearance or leave to enter. It is arguable that, in the light of recent cases, an interest group which would be affected by a decision (eg the congregation of a place of worship in relation to a religious leader) would have sufficient standing.

The question of standing can arise both at the leave stage and at a full hearing. Leave may be granted on the basis of a *prima facie* view of the applicant's standing, but at the full hearing regard is to be had to the whole of the complaint. It is necessary to consider the powers and duties in law of those against whom relief is sought, and the position of the applicant in relation to them (*Inland Revenue Commission v National Federation of Self-Employed and Small Businesses Ltd* [1982] AC 617).

(b) Time limits

RSC Ord 53, r 4(1) states that an application for judicial review must be made promptly and in any event within three months from the date when grounds for the application first arose, although the court has discretion to extend the period where there is good reason. Section 31(6) of the Supreme Court Act 1981 further directs that the court may refuse leave or relief if it considers that there has been undue delay and that the application or relief sought would be likely to cause substantial hardship to, or substantially prejudice the rights of, any person or would be detrimental to the interests of good administration. It follows that there may be undue delay even where the application has been made within three months, if it was not prompt (see, for example, *R v Independent Television Commission ex p TV NI Ltd* (1991), *The Times*, 30 December).

In *R v Dairy Produce Quotas Tribunal, ex p Caswell* [1990] 2 AC 738, the HL gave guidance as to time limits in judicial review applications. Lord Goff pointed out that delay and its repercussions may be considered at three stages of the judicial review procedure, namely, the *ex parte* leave application, the renewed leave application and the substantive application. Further, even though the court may extend the period for the application, it may still refuse leave or substantive relief if it considers that the provisions on hardship, prejudice or detriment to good administration in s 31(6) apply. Lord Goff went on to say that it would normally be right, where there had been delay but the court was minded to extend the time, to leave the issues under s 31(6) to the substantive application, where they could be fully canvassed.

In a number of situations the court may be prepared to extend the time for applying. The most relevant of these for immigration law purposes is attempts to obtain legal aid, where the courts have generally been sympathetic to delays (*R v Stratford on Avon DC, ex p Jackson* [1985] 1 WLR 1319 and *In re Wilson* [1985] AC 750). In addition, an applicant is unlikely to be prejudiced if the delay is due to an attempt to pursue an alternative statutory remedy (*R v S of S ex p Oladehinde* [1991] 1 AC 254, cf *Ex p Mande Ssenyonjo* [1994] Imm AR 310. See also *Ex p Bina Patel* [1995] Imm AR 223 for situations where leave is granted but there is substantial delay.).

It would appear that the time limit cannot be side-stepped by seeking a review of a decision by the Home Office, when in reality review by the court is sought, and, upon refusal of review by the Home Office, taking the matter to the court promptly (*Ex p Hindjou* [1989] Imm AR 24).

(c) Alternative remedies

The courts have generally been unwilling to entertain a claim for judicial review where the applicant has other remedies open to him or her (*R v Chief Constable of Merseyside, ex p Calveley* [1986] 2 WLR 144; *Ex p Ssenyonjo*, above and *Gurnam Singh* [1995] Imm AR 616). Indeed, in many cases, it will be advantageous to use a statutory route of challenge since this will allow a true appeal and not simply a consideration of the decision-making process. There are, however, circumstances in which a court will make an exception to the general rule (*Attivor v S of S* [1988] Imm AR 109), although the criteria applied are not always clear.

The test of whether an appeal machinery is an alternative remedy, such as to provide a basis for refusal of relief, was considered in *Johny Suarez v S of S* [1991] Imm AR 54. Here, on a renewed application for leave before the CA, the applicant argued that the proper test was whether judicial review was the most convenient and effective of two alternative remedies. In dismissing the application, the court said, *obiter*, that there was no distinction proved between that test and the one set out in *Swati v S of S* [1986] Imm AR 88, namely that the jurisdiction of judicial review would not be exercised where there was an alternative remedy by way of appeal, save in exceptional circumstances.

In *Soon Ok Ryoo v S of S* [1992] Imm AR 59, the CA held that it need not be shown that the alternative remedy was as effective or as convenient as judicial review where the case turns on the credibility of the applicant. Russell LJ stated that judicial review is not geared to the exercise of assessing the credibility of the applicant. In *Ex p Hindjou* [1989] Imm AR 24, Schiemann J held that the proper test was whether the decision-maker misapplied the criteria applicable to the decision to be made. Where all relevant information is contained in the documents and such an error is found, the court will consider the existence of an alternative appeals procedure as a factor in deciding whether or not to quash the decision. Generally, where a tribunal has misunderstood its functions and therefore not exercised them in the correct manner, judicial review is the correct avenue (see, eg, *R v Windsor Licensing Justices, ex p Hodes* [1983] 1 WLR 685). However, in *Doorga v S of S* [1990] Imm AR 98, the CA, without expressly overruling *Hindjou*, indicated that the alternative appeal argument should prevail save in exceptional circumstances. These circumstances are very tightly drawn.

In considering whether exceptional circumstances exist, regard should be had to the following factors, although they are not exhaustive (*R v Hallstrom, ex p Waldron* [1986] 1 QB 824, *per* Glidewell LJ):

   (a) whether the alternative statutory remedy would resolve the question at issue fully and directly;
   (b) whether the statutory remedy would be quicker or slower than review; and
   (c) whether the case depends upon some particular or technical knowledge which was more readily available to the appellate body.

The CA has indicated that to take a case outside the general rule in *Swati*, the circumstances must be germane to the decision whether or not the applicant ought to follow the normal rule and make an appeal (*Jorge Grazales v S of S* [1990] Imm AR 505; *Hassan Khan* [1991] Imm AR 174). Applicants must therefore show that some feature of the case distinguishes it from one in which an appeal is appropriate.

There may, for example, be particular circumstances in which a right of appeal from abroad will be worthless. This was the case in *R v Chief Immigration Officer, Gatwick Airport, ex p Kharrazi* [1980] 1 WLR 1396, where an Iranian would have been obliged to exercise his right of appeal from that country, which had imposed a ban on any children of his age leaving. Thus, where, even if successful, the appeal would not result in the applicant's being able to enter the country, it is arguable that there are exceptional circumstances which make judicial review the appropriate remedy.

The courts have not been consistent in their approach to the question of exhausting alternative appeal rights before embarking on an application for judicial review. In *Ex p Hindjou* [1989] Imm AR 24, Schiemann J held that *Swati* did not require the applicant to show that there is no appeal procedure available to him, but he had to show that the decision-maker misapplied the criteria for granting leave to enter. In *Doorga* [1990] Imm AR 98, however, this case was confined to its own facts. Some guidance can perhaps be found in *R v IRC ex p Preston* [1985] AC 835, in which Lord Scarman indicated, in relation to a taxpayer, that it would be unfair in certain circumstances to require him to initiate appeal procedures. Those circumstances were that the conduct of the Commissioners in commencing action against him was such that, had they not been a public authority, it would have amounted to either breach of contract or breach of representation giving rise to an estoppel (at p 852F–H). More recently, in *Harley Developments v CIR* [1996] 1 WLR 727, the Privy Council held that where there is a comprehensive system of appeals, a court is likely to entertain judicial review proceedings where there has been an abuse of power, this being an exceptional situation.

The specific guidance that can be obtained from the cases is rather more negative than positive. Thus the threat of imminent removal from the UK is not *per se* a special circumstance (*Ex p Su-san Chong* [1990] Imm AR 59); the fact of having to exercise the appeal from abroad when that would be inconvenient to the applicant is not an exceptional circumstance (*Grazales* and *Soon Ok Ryoo* (above); *Ex p Pulgarin* [1992] Imm AR 96); nor is the length of time a person spends in custody (*Re Balasingham* (1987) *The Times*, 22 July). There were no exceptional circumstances where there was no practical obstacle and no danger to a person returning to his own country and appealing the decision from there, despite the fact that he would be put to domestic and professional inconvenience (*Ex p Salamat* [1993] Imm AR 239). The trend of recent decisions has been to refuse to allow judicial review where there is an alternative remedy by way of appeal which has not been exhausted (*Ex p Sakda* [1994] Imm AR 227). Further, where, on advice, a person abandons an appeal in favour of judicial review, he will be permitted to apply for leave only in exceptional circumstances (*Attivor v S of S* [1988] Imm AR 109) Imm AR 227) and his application for leave may be rejected in the court's discretion (*Ex p Allegret* [1989] Imm AR 211).

(d) Discretion

The remedies available in judicial review are discretionary. Relief may therefore be refused on the basis of the undeserving conduct of the applicant (*Ex p Ketowoglo* [1992] Imm AR 268, and see *Ex p Pushpaben Patel* [1993] Imm AR 392, where the applicant had stated that she would not apply for a visa which she could have obtained). In *Ketowoglo*, the CA expressed concern at the length of time a case may take to come to a full hearing, and stated that any failure to make full disclosure at the *ex parte* stage may be such misconduct on the part of the applicant as to affect the exercise of its discretion, unless there was a good explanation for the lack of full disclosure.

6 Procedure and appeals

(a) The leave stage

Judicial review is a two-stage process. Before a court will consider in full the substantive merits of an application, leave to apply must be obtained. The purpose of this preliminary stage is to exclude from a full hearing those cases which are weak and without merit. Advisors should note the importance of a comprehensive letter before action, where practicable, before the commencement of judicial review proceedings. Failure to place the proposed respondent on notice in this way may well lead the court to refuse leave (*R v Horsham District Council ex p Wenman* (1992) *The Times*, 21 October 1993), and possibly lead to a wasted costs order.

The application for leave is made by lodging a Form 86A with the Crown Office. This must set out the grounds on which review is sought and the relief sought. An affidavit, usually sworn by the applicant, deposing to the facts which form the basis of the application, must also be filed. These documents are usually considered by a single judge without an oral hearing, although such a hearing may take place if the issues are complex or if a hearing is requested.

Judicial criticism of vague grounds in applications has been expressed. Submissions which do not define the issues but which are so broad as to cover any ground, eg the decision is against the immigration laws and rules and against natural justice (*Ex p Fauzia Bagga Khan* [1987] Imm AR 543), should be avoided. Despite the fact that many of these applications have to be made with utmost speed, a well-structured and full application will ensure that the case is more likely to be taken seriously. It is important to explain the reasons for any delay in making the application. *Practice Direction* [1979] 2 All ER 880 set out special forms for use in immigration cases; they are available from the Chief Clerk of the Crown Office.

The applicant's representatives have an obligation to lodge the application for judicial review expeditiously and to place before the court at the earliest opportunity all material documents, including any that have come into existence since the application for leave was lodged with the court (*Ex p Nwosu* [1993] Imm AR 206). Since the application is *ex parte*, there is a duty of full and frank disclosure to the court, and any failure to observe this duty will be viewed with utmost seriousness. Indeed, the court may refuse an application on this ground alone (*Ex p Anjorin* [1994] Imm AR 276), or subsequently set aside leave on the ground that it was obtained in breach of the duty.

On learning that an application for judicial review is being made the Home Office frequently sends the applicant a letter containing an outline of its case. The letter normally ends with a request to the recipient to place it before the court; failure to refer to such a letter or to put it before the court will generally result in the legal advisor responsible paying the costs of the application, and the application being dismissed (*Ex p William Berko* [1991] Imm AR 127, *per* Popplewell J applying RSC Ord 62, r 11). Counsel who fail to exhibit such a letter or to ensure that the court sees it, while knowing of its existence and contents, may find that they or their instructing solicitors are ordered to pay the costs (*Sushma Lal v S of S* [1992] Imm AR 303), and may face disciplinary action. However, if the applicant is distanced from his advisor's fault and there is any risk that the applicant will be prejudiced, it is unlikely that the court will refuse to exercise its discretion. Where the evidence before the court shows that the grounds for the application were misleading, this will be drawn to the attention of the taxing master or the legal aid authority. Where the conduct of the case falls below proper standards, the bills of the defaulting party are likely to be disallowed (*Ex p Guiled* [1993] Imm AR 236). Conduct such as the late withdrawal of a case without informing the Crown Office or the S of S will in certain circumstances result in costs being awarded against the representative (*Ex p Mudzengi* [1993] Imm AR 320). If the applicant's case is hopeless, he may have costs awarded against him (*Ex p Atrvinder Singh* [1993] Imm AR 450; see *Ifzal Ali v S of S* [1994] Imm AR 69; *Ex p Kyasanku* [1994] Imm AR 547).

At the leave stage the applicant must show that he has an arguable case and, in general, that there is no alternative remedy available (see, eg, *Tadimi v S of S* [1993] Imm AR 90). Normally the judge will quickly peruse the available material to see if it discloses an arguable case under the heads of challenge, without investigating the matter in any depth (*Inland Revenue Commissioners v National Federation of Self-Employed Businesses* [1982] AC 617). If, on such perusal, the court considers that the material discloses what might on further consideration turn out to be an arguable case, it ought to give leave.

In immigration cases a trend in favour of *inter partes* leave applications has developed. If the court is not sure whether or not an arguable point of law has been disclosed, because, for example, the facts are not clear, the respondent may be invited to attend and make representations (*Ex p Angur Begum and Rukshanda Begum* [1990] Imm AR 1). In *Doorga v S of S* [1990] Imm AR 98 at p 101, Lord Donaldson MR set out the principles to be followed on these applications:

(1) Where there are *prima facie* reasons for granting judicial review, leave should be granted.
(2) Where the application is wholly unarguable, leave should be refused;
(3) Where the judge is left with an uneasy feeling as to whether on a weak case leave should be refused, or on a stronger looking case, that there might be a quick and easy answer to the points raised so that leave should in fact be refused, then the proper course is to adjourn for the leave application to be heard *inter partes*. At the *inter partes* leave hearing the respondent does not have to put forward his full argument, but if he can produce some sufficiently strong point which makes it clear that there is no basis for the application at all, then leave will be refused.

More recently, the CA in *Mehmet Oral v S of S* [1991] Imm AR 208 held that where, on consideration of an *ex parte* application, it was apparent that there might be a dispute on evidence, it would be desirable for the S of S to have the opportunity to put in evidence, which could be done by directing that the matter of leave be heard *inter partes*. Where the court has directed that an *inter partes* leave application should take place, although there is no formal statement of the duties of the applicant, he should serve the respondent with the papers in the case. A refusal to do so on request by the respondent will result in an order being made, possibly incurring a penalty in costs (*Ex p Dyfan* [1993] Imm AR 180).

At the leave stage, issues of fact may be determined on the basis of the affidavits, and there is no necessity for leave to be granted merely because issues of fact are raised on the affidavits (*Fawehimi v S of S* [1990] Imm AR 1). The requirement to have an arguable case is not affected by the burden on the Home Office to prove that the applicant is in fact an illegal entrant, or the requirement to scrutinise precedent facts with care in illegal entry cases where liberty is at issue. *Khawaja* does not oblige the court to grant leave in every case concerning illegal entry by deception, including a concealed intention (*Ubakanwa Uche v S of S* [1991] Imm AR 252), nor to permit strong identification evidence to be tested at a full hearing (*Irawo-Osan v S of S* [1992] Imm AR 337).

The normal rule is that only the evidence which was before the decision-maker at the time of the decision will be admitted, as it forms the pool of information on the basis of which the decision was or ought to have been made. There are exceptions to this rule, such as where the jurisdiction of the decision-maker depends on the existence of a precedent fact or where there is a dispute over the procedure observed, or misconduct of the proceedings by the decision-maker, such as bias (see *Ex p Muse* [1992] Imm AR 282).

The documents comprising the application for leave should be bundled. Where the documents exceed ten pages they must be paginated and supplied with an index. In addition, the court should be provided with a list of essential reading (*Practice Note* [1994] 1 All ER 671).

Where counsel has advised that there is no merit in a claim, the client is legally aided and the legal aid certificate is still operative when the application for leave is dismissed, the applicant has 14 days to persuade the area director that his case has merit. In such circumstances the order of the court will not be drawn up for 28 days (*Ex p Olokodana* [1992] Imm AR 499).

Where the applicant is likely to be removed from the jurisdiction of the court, and it is not possible to obtain an undertaking from the Home Office that he will not be removed until the outcome of the application for leave is known, an application for an interlocutory injunction to prevent the removal of the individual from the jurisdiction should be considered (*M v Home Office* [1994] 1 AC 377).

The Home Office stated their practice in relation to judicial review proceedings where removal is planned in the course of *Ex p Muboyayi* [1992] 1 QB 244, as follows:

(1) Where leave to move is granted they will not remove until the case is disposed of in the High Court.

(2) If removal takes place notwithstanding the grant of leave either because the application is made extremely late or because of a mistake, the S of S will do his best to return the applicant to the jurisdiction.

(3) In all cases removal directions are made in advance of removal and the person is given notice. In cases where applications for leave to the High Court or CA are pending, adequate notice will be given to enable the appropriate application to be made (see *Muboyayi* [1992] 1 QB 244).

(b) Renewal of application for leave

If the judge refuses the paper application or grants it on terms, the applicant may renew the application for leave before a single judge sitting in open court, or a Divisional Court if so directed by the court, lodging notice of intention to renew with the Crown Office within ten days on Form 86B (RSC Ord 53, r 3(5)). An oral application can be the first stage in the process.

An applicant refused leave by the single judge in open court may, on an *ex parte* application on notice, renew the application before the CA. The renewed application must be made within seven days of the single judge's refusal. When leave has been refused after an *inter partes* hearing of an application, it is inappropriate for the court to grant leave to appeal, renewal being the proper channel (*Soon Ok Ryoo v S of S* [1992] Imm AR 59).

In addition to the increase in judicial review applications, there has been an increase in renewals, and several points have now been established in relation to them. First, the CA regards itself as bound by its previous reasoned judgments in *ex parte* renewal applications (*David Thevarajah v S of S* [1991] Imm AR 371). Second, a point which was not raised below cannot be taken on the renewal (*Fozlu Miah v S of S* [1991] Imm AR 581). Third, if the CA refuses leave to apply for judicial review there is no appeal to the HL (*Re Poh* [1983] 1 WLR 2). Finally, where the application for leave has been refused by the High Court, a renewal should not be made to the CA where the S of S has written clarifying his reasons for the decision and demonstrated that the initial application was meritless (*Mahtab Ahmed v S of S* [1992] Imm AR 538).

The CA has a system for identifying renewed applications in immigration cases and if there is any urgency it is generally possible to have a case renewed within a matter of days.

(c) Setting aside leave

Once leave has been granted *ex parte*, the respondent may apply for it to be set aside under RSC Ord 32, r 6. The respondent should apply promptly, and cannot leave it to the full hearing. Leave should be set aside only in very special circumstances, such as where the proceedings were fundamentally misconceived, either in law or fact, or where there has been fraud on the part of the applicant or non-disclosure of material facts. On an application for leave to be set aside, the court should go through a process similar to that on the application for leave (*Ex p Begum* [1989] Imm AR 302).

In *Ex p Sholola* [1992] Imm AR 135 the court considered the circumstances in which the grant of leave should be set aside when leave was granted *ex parte*. It was said that the power should be exercised only in an extremely plain case. It is not enough to show that the application for judicial review is very likely to fail, nor that the judge hearing the application would not himself have granted the application for leave if it had been made before him. It is therefore necessary to show that there is something almost amounting to a quasi-jurisdictional bar to review, such as the plain existence of an alternative appeal mechanism which should be used. If some bald point of statutory construction on which the applicant's case was founded is manifestly unarguable, or if leave was granted in ignorance of some leading authority, the application for leave to be set aside will be granted. Similarly, if the application was based on factual premises which can shortly be shown not to exist, leave will be set aside. Finally, if there has been serious non-disclosure, leave will be set aside. See also *Ex p Beecham* [1996] Imm AR 87.

Where leave has been granted, it is possible to obtain a stay of the action complained of if prohibition or *certiorari* has been applied for by Ord 53, r (10)(a). In cases of urgency an expedited hearing should be requested (ie that the case be included in Part D of the Crown Office List). If granted, a further application should be made that time for service of the respondent's affidavit be abridged in accordance with *Practice Note (QBD) (Judicial Review: Affidavit in Reply)* [1989] 1 WLR 358. It may be necessary at this stage, or upon receipt of the respondent's affidavit, to make amendments to the Form 86A (RSC Ord 53, r 3(6)) to add new grounds or seek new relief.

(d) Interlocutory applications and bail

Order 53, r 8 deals with interlocutory applications, which include an application for leave to cross-examine the deponent on an affidavit, discovery and inspection. The court, may on granting leave, direct that deponents attend to be cross-examined (*Fawehimi v S of S* [1990] Imm AR 1). In *Re H* (1990) *The Guardian*, 17 May, Roch J stated that discovery would not be ordered except as necessary for disposing fairly of the case or saving costs. There could be no discovery on a contingent basis in the hope that it will show the contents of affidavits to be untrue or inaccurate, but where there is some matter which suggests that the affidavits are not accurate, discovery of documents which will clarify the position will be permitted. In relation to discovery of interview notes in particular, it is necessary to depose to what the applicant remembers was said at the interview. It is only if the applicant's memory of the interview is different from that of the immigration officer that discovery of the notes may be possible (*Yadvinder Singh v S of S* [1988] Imm AR 480). The standard to be applied when deciding whether discovery should be made is no higher than that applied when considering whether or not to grant leave (*R v Governor of Pentonville Prison, ex p Herbage (No 2)*

(1986) *The Times*, 29 May). Discovery will be limited to the issues arising out of the affidavits, but should not be ordered unless reasonable grounds on the merits are disclosed (*Inland Revenue Commissioners v National Federation of Self-employed and Small Businesses Ltd* [1982] AC 617).

The court has an inherent jurisdiction to grant bail. The principles on which that jurisdiction will operate in immigration cases were considered in *Ex p Turkoglu* [1987] Imm AR 484. The court held that it has power to grant bail when an application for leave to apply for judicial review has been made but not disposed of, and where leave was granted but the full hearing has not occurred; but there is no jurisdiction where leave to move has been refused. Where the applicant is refused admission and is in custody pending removal, the court will grant bail only when it considers that the S of S has committed an error of law in failing to grant temporary admission pending the outcome of the judicial review, or that his decision was unreasonable on *Wednesbury* principles (*Re Vilvarajah* [1990] Imm AR 457). The same approach has been adopted by the Court of Session in Scotland (*Jaswant Singh v S of S* [1993] Imm AR 4). However, in illegal entrant cases, a bail application to the adjudicator is possible.

(e) The substantive hearing

Once leave has been granted, the notice of motion in Form 86, a copy of Form 86A and a copy of the affidavit in support must be served on any person directly affected by the proceedings (RSC Ord 53, rr 5(1), 6(1)). An affidavit of service which accords with Ord 53, r 5(6) must be filed before the motion is entered for hearing. The motion for judicial review must be entered for hearing by filing a copy of the notice of motion in the Crown Office within 14 days of leave being granted, but after filing the affidavit of service (RSC Ord 53, r 5(5)).

The respondent has 56 days after the service of the notice in which to file an affidavit in reply, unless time has been abridged (Ord 53, r 6(4)). The time limit is strict, and extensions will be granted only in wholly exceptional circumstances. Notice of intention to use a further affidavit must be given to the respondent by an applicant (Ord 53, r 6(3)).

Prior to the hearing, the advocate for the applicant should ensure that a skeleton argument is lodged with the court at least five working days before the warned or fixed date. The skeleton argument should give the time estimate, a list of issues, a list of propositions of law to be used, a chronology of events, a list of essential advance reading and a list of *dramatis personae* where appropriate. The applicant's solicitors are responsible for the provision of a paginated, indexed bundle (*Practice Direction (Crown Office List: Preparation for Hearings)* [1994] 1 WLR 1551).

At the full hearing legal argument is heard only on the basis of Form 86A, including any amendments, and the evidence on affidavit (and, when ordered, evidence arising from cross-examination on the affidavit). As a rule, the court will not permit fresh evidence which was not in existence at the time of the decision, but will admit fresh evidence to determine a precedent fact, or as to whether there was a procedural breach (see *Marchano Singa v S of S* [1992] Imm AR 160).

(f) Interlocutory appeals

An interlocutory appeal is to the Divisional Court, but otherwise follows Ord 58, and is treated as an appeal from a Queen's Bench judge in chambers. The appeal is by way of a rehearing of the interlocutory application, at which fresh evidence may be adduced as of right. A further appeal on interlocutory matters lies to the CA, with leave either of the Divisional Court or of the CA. On appeal to the CA, no fresh evidence may be adduced save at the discretion of the CA.

(g) Appeals from full hearings

Appeals are governed by the Supreme Court Act 1981, s 16(1), and are initially to the CA, whose powers are governed by RSC Ord 59. There is a time limit of four weeks from the date of judgment. By Ord 59, r 10, the CA has the same powers and duties as the High Court. There is a discretion, which is wider than in other civil matters, to admit fresh evidence on such an appeal. In *Ex p Momin Ali* [1984] 1 WLR 663, the majority of the CA observed that public law required finality in litigation save in the interests of justice. Therefore, while the specific rules in *Ladd v Marshall* [1954] 3 All ER 745 do not apply in full, the presumption against admitting fresh evidence remains.

(h) Legal aid

Many of the preliminary steps in an immigration case may be covered by the Green Form scheme. Where judicial review is contemplated, assistance may be obtained to cover preliminary steps, such as obtaining counsel's opinion on the merits of the claim, and legal aid thereafter if so advised. Where an application for leave has been made and refused, it is possible to renew the application to the CA. However, if the case is legally aided, counsel should not sign an opinion supporting an application for an extension of legal aid to cover the renewed application unless he expresses that opinion on full information and believes that there is a reasonable chance of success (*Marchano Singa v S of S* [1992] Imm AR 160).

Chapter 23

Habeas Corpus

It may be possible to challenge the lawfulness of a person's detention by applying for a writ of *habeas corpus* in accordance with the procedures set out in RSC Ord 54. An *ex parte* application is made, usually to a High Court judge, although it may be directed to be made to a Divisional Court of the Queen's Bench Division. The application must be supported by an affidavit sworn by the person detained, which states that he instigated the application and describes the nature of the detention. If the detainee is unable to make the affidavit it may be made by his representative. The respondent to the application is usually the person who has custody of the detainee.

On an *ex parte* application the court may issue the writ immediately or make directions for an *inter partes* hearing. The court may direct the writ to issue in the meantime, or adjourn the application for the writ. If the writ is issued, the return (ie the reply) must set out the reasons for the applicant's detention. Otherwise, the respondent files an affidavit setting out the justification for detention. At the hearing there is an inquiry into the legality of the applicant's detention and if the applicant is successful, the court must order release, since *habeas corpus* is a writ of right.

The effectiveness of *habeas corpus* as a remedy for those detained under the 1971 Act has been rather less than impressive. The cases on applications for *habeas corpus* by detained immigrants have shown a pronounced executive-mindedness on the part of the courts (see *Ex p Choudhary* [1978] 3 All ER 790 (overruled by *Khawaja*); also *Ex p Phansopkar* [1975] 3 All ER 497, *per* Lord Denning MR, at p 508; *Ex p Zamir* [1980] AC 930; *Re Olusanya (Olugbenga)* [1988] Imm AR 117).

In *Ex p Khawaja* [1984] AC 74, however, the HL emphasised that on an application for judicial review or for a writ of *habeas corpus*, the facts on which the Home Office had reached a decision had to be carefully reviewed by the court. Lord Wilberforce (at p 340) stated the respective functions of the immigration authorities and of the courts as follows:

(1) The immigration authorities have the power and the duty to determine and to act upon the facts material to the detention as illegal entrants of persons prior to removal from the UK.

(2) Any person whom the S of S proposes to remove as an illegal entrant, and who is detained, may apply for a writ of *habeas corpus* or for judicial review.

Upon such an application the S of S or the immigration authorities, if they seek to support the detention or removal (the burden being on them), should depose to the grounds on which the decision to detain or remove was made, setting out essential factual evidence taken into account and exhibiting documents sufficiently fully to enable the courts to carry out their function of review (see also *Ex p Choudhary* (1981) *The Times,* 16 December).

(3) The court's investigation of the facts is of a supervisory character and not by way of appeal. It should appraise the quality of the evidence and decide whether it justifies, for example, a conclusion that the applicant obtained permission to enter by fraud or deceit. If the court is not satisfied with any part of the evidence it may remit the matter for reconsideration or itself receive further evidence. It should quash the detention order where the evidence was not such as the authorities should have relied on or where the evidence received does not justify the decision reached or, of course, for any serious procedural irregularity.

(4) Where the power of an immigration officer or the S of S to make a decision affecting a person's liberty is dependent on the existence of certain facts, the court has to be satisfied on a civil standard of proof to a high degree of probability that those facts did in fact exist at the time the power was exercised.

Further, in *Re Hardial Singh* [1983] Imm AR 198, Woolf J held that the power of the S of S to detain persons pending removal was limited to a period reasonably necessary for his purpose. If there was unreasonable delay before removal, the court would issue a writ of *habeas corpus.*

An application for *habeas corpus* is appropriate only where the facts justifying the detention are challenged. If the underlying decision which gives rise to the power to detain is challenged, the proper challenge is by way of judicial review (*Ex p Muboyayi* [1992] 1 QB 244, *Ex p Cheblak* [1991] 1 WLR 890). In *Muboyayi* the S of S advanced the argument that the practical effect of issuing a writ of *habeas corpus* would be to enjoin the Crown contrary to the principles in *R v S of S for Transport, ex p Factortame* [1990] 2 AC 85. The CA, disagreeing with this, stated that it was their duty to uphold the classic statement of the rule of law in Chapters 39 and 40 of Magna Carta which provide that no freeman shall be arrested or imprisoned or exiled except by lawful judgment of his peers and by the law of the land. The CA held that *Factortame* did not prevent *habeas corpus* issuing against the Crown for that reason. It was, though, accepted in *Ex p Muboyayi* (above) that the 1971 Act, Sched 2, para 18(4) does not have the object of ousting *habeas corpus* in favour of judicial review of detentions in immigration cases, but permits a person detained to be kept in detention at any place, not only in a lawful prison, even if no place is specified in the order for detention.

Chapter 24

Legal Aid and Best Practice

Specific rules apply to obtaining civil legal aid and legal advice and assistance (otherwise known as the 'green form' scheme) under the Legal Aid Act 1988 and reference should be made to the annual *Legal Aid Handbook 1996/7* (Sweet & Maxwell, 1996) for detailed guidance. This chapter provides pointers which should help avoid some common pitfalls in this area.

For most asylum and immigration advice and representation the only legal aid available is under the green form scheme. The green form scheme was never designed to deal with complex cases in which emergency situations frequently arise, but for simple 'one off' advice. Full civil legal aid is available for judicial review and *habeas corpus* applications in the HC and for appeals to the CA and HL.

1 The 'green form' scheme

(a) Availability

The 'green form' scheme is the common name for legal advice and assistance, one of the schemes to provide legal advice to those on low incomes. It is available for advice on any aspect of English law. Advice on matters of foreign law, including applications to the ECHR, is specifically excluded. It is, however, possible to use it to obtain opinions on international law if they will influence a decision based on English law.

Green form advice and assistance is not available for representation at appeals or for time spent briefing counsel. There is no legal aid for representation at immigration tribunals. Applicants must therefore:

- *(a)* pay privately
- *(b)* be referred to advice agencies who make no charge (eg the Refugee Legal Centre, law centres, the Free Representation Unit); or
- *(c)* find a barrister or solicitor who is prepared to act *pro bono*. The Free Representation Unit and the Bar Council *Pro Bono* Project are both able to help.

However, the preparation of appeals, apart from time spent briefing counsel (see Costs Appeals Committee decision LAA 6 of 30 January 1995 and paras 2–19 and 2–44 of the *Legal Aid Handbook*) is covered by the green form scheme.

Some solicitors have tried to deal with the non-availability of green form advice and assistance at IAT hearings by acting as 'McKenzie advisors' (*McKenzie v McKenzie* [1971] P 33; see also para 2–20 of the *Legal Aid Handbook*). The Legal Aid Board has been advised that the green form scheme may extend to a solicitor advising a client informally without actually representing that client in any proceedings. An extension to the green form limit may therefore be granted by the Legal Aid Board to cover work as a McKenzie advisor. In practice this is often cumbersome in that any aspect of 'representation' is outside the scope of the scheme and thus unpaid for. To justify a green form extension for a Mckenzie advisor the matter must be:

> *(a)* sufficiently difficult (for example, does the case turn on a point of law?); or
>
> *(b)* of importance to the client, applying the test of a privately paying client of moderate means; or
>
> *(c)* one where the client is unable to act on his own without legal help (for example, the *Legal Aid Handbook* specifically states that insufficient knowledge of English, material disability, or learning difficulties, will not be sufficient to justify a McKenzie advisor under the green form scheme),

so that it is necessary for the client to have the services of a solicitor acting as a McKenzie advisor. The client must be present at the hearing. The Legal Aid Board will not pay for a solicitor's agent or counsel acting as a McKenzie advisor.

(b) Signing a green form

Normally the person who approaches the solicitor for advice, or whose problem the case is, signs the green form. This permits the relative of someone who wants to bring a family member to the UK to sign it. However there are other options. Anyone who knows the personal details of the client and his finances can sign on his behalf if authorised by the client and if there is good reason why the client cannot attend in person (reg 10 of the Legal Advice and Assistance Regulations 1989, at p 252 of the *Legal Aid Handbook*). This is particularly useful in respect of detained persons. Some referral agencies may have special forms on which detainees give them all the required information and authority to sign. Recently, the Legal Aid Board decided that a detainee can telephone the solicitor's office and give details to an employee of the firm who could then be authorised to sign on his behalf in front of the solicitor (see para 2–48 of the *Legal Aid Handbook*).

A number of specific situations need consideration:

If there is no one in the UK, prior authority can be obtained from the Legal Aid Area Director for the client to sign a green form by post (reg 15 of the Legal Advice and Assistance Regulations 1989; p 255 of the *Legal Aid Handbook*).

Where the client is a child under school leaving age, the child's parent or guardian normally signs and his means are taken into account. However, advance authority can be obtained from the Area Director for a child to sign if the usual procedure is inappropriate for some reason (for example in the case of an unaccompanied minor asylum-seeker) (reg 14 of the Legal Advice and Assistance Regulations 1989; p 254 of the *Legal Aid Handbook*).

Where the client has earlier signed a green form with other solicitors, and the green form has been billed more than six months before the new solicitors became involved, no prior authority is needed. Where, on the other hand, the previous firm billed less than six months prior to the new firm's involvement, prior authority must be obtained (reg 16 of the Legal Advice and Assistance Regulations 1989; p 255 and para 2–12 of the *Legal Aid Handbook*).

The solicitor cannot post a green form to a client within the UK unless he has a franchise.

(c) Prior authority

Prior authority is obtained by completing and submitting form GF5 to the Legal Aid Board. The solicitor must submit a GF5 to confirm prior authority even when he obtains authority on the telephone in an emergency situation.

(d) Filling in the green form

It is essential to fill in all the boxes before signing the green form. The need for prior authority should always be checked; it can be obtained by telephone. It is important to complete and sign the green form immediately.

(e) Financial assessment

The 'key card' supplied by the Legal Aid Board should be used to make the financial assessment of the client's eligibility. A number of sections need to be completed:

Disposable capital (see reg 13 of, and Sched 2 to, the Legal Advice and Assistance Regulations 1988)   Capital refers to savings and money in the bank, but not belongings. Reference should be made to para 8 of Sched 2 to the Legal Advice and Assistance Regulations 1988 (see p 264 of the *Legal Aid Handbook*), when dealing with a client with a property worth over £100,000. Even those who are in receipt of income support, family credit or disability working allowance must complete this section.

Disposable income   The 'income' section is straightforward for those in receipt of social security benefits. If the client is not in receipt of income support, family credit or disability working allowance, all income for the last seven days must be aggregated. This includes wages, rent income, and child benefit. Various deductions must be made, and these are set out on the key card. Where maintenance is paid for a spouse and children abroad, or children in the UK, the actual amounts paid in the last seven days may be deducted (see paras 9, 9A and 10 of Sched 2 to the Legal Advice and Assistance Regulations 1988; *Legal Aid Handbook*, pp 264–5).

Once a green form is signed it is not affected by changes in the client's financial situation. He does not have to inform the solicitor or the Legal Aid Board of any changes. Further, if a client's income decreases he may become eligible, even if initially his income was in excess of the maximum for green form assistance. Solicitors should advise their clients about this if it is likely to be relevant, for example in cases involving relatives or those in low paid work.

(f) Extending the green form financial limit

See paras 9, 9A and 10 of Sched 2 to the Legal Advice and Assistance Regulations 1988; *Legal Aid Handbook*, pp 264–5.

The initial limit when a green form is signed is two hours' work. This entitles the solicitor to a specific limited amount. In 1996 it was set at £88 (outside London) and £93 (within London). Rates are reviewed, but not necessarily increased, every April. Key rates for 1996, with London rates in brackets, are as follows (see Sched 6 to the Legal Advice and Assistance Regulations 1989, as amended):

Preparation and attendance: £44.00 (£46.50);

Travelling and waiting: £24.50 (£24.50);

Letters and telephone calls: £3.40 (£3.55);

Interpreters: interpreting £15 an hour, travelling and waiting £12;

Interpreter's translation: £8.50 per double spaced page;

Travel expenses: either actual fares or petrol at 36p per mile.

The following disbursements are usually approved by the Legal Aid Board under the green form scheme:

Psychiatric report: £250–£300, or, if detained, £400–£500;

GP's report, up to £50;

Other expert, around £200.

Obviously there will be cases where larger amounts will be justified, but the solicitor will have to argue the case at length with the green form section of the local Legal Aid Board (see paras 2–15 to 2–18 of the *Legal Aid Handbook* for the guidelines on the assessment of applications for an extension of the legal aid limit).

Almost all immigration cases involve more than £93, and an application for an extension should be made as soon as possible on form GF3. When an extension is granted, a number is allocated to the client. The solicitor should quote this number on applications to extend the green form. In emergencies, extensions can be granted by telephone. The solicitor should complete the GF3 before telephoning and be prepared to give a breakdown of capital and income and expenses, together with reasons for the emergency. The solicitor should also telephone the green form section if a paper application does not reappear on time. The Legal Aid Board will then require written confirmation. The guidance for franchisees should be followed when applying for periods of time likely to be granted, and to ensure that the solicitor gives the necessary justification. Where more than is set out is required, the solicitor should be ready to justify the greater sum. The franchise guidance applies to non-franchised firms in so far as the Legal Aid Board has set out amounts it regards as reasonable for different situations.

Copies of all previous extensions granted should be attached to the application, otherwise the application will be returned to the solicitor. Given the number of applications received by the green form section, the solicitor should be as clear and neat as possible; it is unlikely that the green form section will expend a great deal of time and energy on a poor application.

There is no provision to back date authorities under the scheme. If, for instance, the solicitor is half way through an asylum interview and runs out of green form cover, he must telephone for an extension there and then. Amounts granted on an application for an extension are effectively only authority to apply to be paid for this work; there is no assurance that the Legal Aid Board will ultimately pay.

(g) Separate matters

See paras 2–13 and 2–14 of the *Legal Aid Handbook* and reg 17 of the Legal Advice and Assistance Regulations 1989.

The Legal Aid Board regards all immigration advice as the 'the same matter' (see para 2–14.2 (g) of the *Legal Aid Handbook*). This means that the solicitor will often not be paid if he signs a new green form rather than extending the existing one. The *Legal Aid Handbook* and the latest guidance to franchisees states that one green form is appropriate for all aspects of immigration advice including asylum applications, applications for work permits, visas and leave to enter. It also says that any appeal against refusal, both in the immigration appeal process and by way of any judicial review, should also be dealt with under the original green form. The only concession seems to be where the solicitor deals with two matters for different family members which do not depend on each other in any way.

(h) Billing

Billing is done on the back of the green form (or GF1). The solicitor simply completes all boxes as required. Green forms of different ages have different layouts and the solicitor may have to bill at the work at varying rates, depending on when the work was done.

Green form billing and obtaining extensions can be aided by good file-keeping techniques such as:

(a) keeping the green form and all extensions, copies and invoices in a separate green form folder;

(b) keeping the file orderly: front sheet, proper attendance notes with times and dates and travel expense, all correspondence on a treasury tag and all documents in a documents folder, or second file where this becomes necessary;

(c) making sure receipted invoices for disbursements are obtained. It may be wise to produce an invoice for community interpreters to use.

The solicitor may bill the file when it becomes dormant or the case is concluded. The solicitor should ensure that a copy of the billed green form, the GF3 extensions, invoices etc are kept in case they are mislaid by the Legal Aid Board. This practice also enables the solicitor to determine the green form status of any file. This is important in relation to future work; see below.

(i) After billing

The green form does not expire when submitted for payment in the way that a legal aid certificate does when notice of discharge is issued. It is therefore possible to bill belatedly a disbursement omitted from an original claim. If the matter is continuing, then the file should contain a note of the current green form situation following billing; either there will be some time left, and this may be used at any time (the green form continues until the limit is reached), or the green form is completely used up. In the latter case, where the solicitor needs to work on the green form within six months, it is then extended from the billed amount. Alternatively a new green form must be signed with the client.

(j) Franchising

It is outside the scope of this book to advise on how to obtain a franchise from the Legal Aid Board. However, the following will be seen as good practice in relation to green form matters should an application be made:

(1) The solicitor should first send a standard letter to the client, giving key information about the green form scheme, including an estimate of how much the solicitor will be billing the Legal Aid Board.

(2) The solicitor should keep on the file a running total of the amount of green form assistance remaining available. This may be done by completing the next GF3 'work done' section as the matter progresses, showing all attendances, travel, preparation. Disbursements, telephone calls and letters should also be recorded.

(3) Periodically, for example every three to six months, the solicitor should review the file and let the client know if the original estimate of how much the Legal Aid Board will be billed has changed.

Franchisees are paid more by the Legal Aid Board than non-franchisees and have greater flexibility. It may be prudent for all solicitors or organisations engaged in this work to consider applying for a franchise.

2 Civil legal aid

In immigration and asylum work, civil legal aid is available for judicial review and *habeas corpus* applications, and for appeals to the CA and HL. In emergency situations, where the client will be removed within the next 48 hours, civil legal aid is available by telephone application to the Area Office as well as by making a written application to the Legal Aid Board. Forms must be submitted following an emergency telephone grant. All judicial review and CA work justifies using the pink emergency legal aid form, even if the solicitor is making a paper application, due to the time limits. To be refused legal aid in emergency immigration and asylum cases presents considerable difficulties, as appeals from Legal Aid Board decisions are cumbersome and slow. It is therefore worth spending time on the legal aid application.

The following practical tips may help in making applications:

(1) The solicitor should type rather than hand write the statement of case for the form CLA4A.

(2) A chronology setting out important facts and a summary of the relevant law should be set out.

(3) An explanation should be given of why the case has legal merits and why the client would bring the action if he was privately paying and of moderate means.

(4) Many counsel are happy to be telephoned for preliminary advice; the solicitor is then able to state whether counsel believes there are good chances of succeeding. Of course, this is not necessary if the merits are immediately obvious.

(5) All relevant materials should be appended to the application (this will also help in assembling the brief to counsel. The solicitor can use the legal aid application and enclosures along with any subsequent material).

(6) It should be noted whether a bail application is to be made.

An extension of two hours may be obtained under the green form scheme for a legal aid application, according to the franchise guidance. Franchisees may grant their own emergency legal aid certificates.

Part VI

Asylum

Chapter 25

Applications for Asylum

1 Eligibility

(a) Introduction

The Asylum and Immigration Appeals Act 1993 provides for the treatment of asylum seekers and the determination of their claims. Section 1 provides that a person makes a claim for asylum where he claims that it would be contrary to the UK's obligations under the United Nations Convention and Protocol relating to the Status of Refugees 1951 (Cmnd 9171 and Cmnd 3906) ('the Convention and Protocol') for him to be removed from or required to leave the UK. Nothing in the immigration rules may lay down any practice which would be contrary to the Convention and Protocol (1993 Act, s 2). Part 11 of the rules provides for the consideration of asylum applications. The 1993 Act put into statutory form the UK's recognition of the primacy of the Convention (s 2) and its obligation of 'non-refoulement' under art 33 of the Convention. 'Refoulement' denotes return to a country or territory in which the life or liberty of the asylum seeker is threatened for a 'Convention reason' (see p 445). Before the 1993 Act, the Convention was recognised under the immigration rules only (see *per* Simon Brown LJ in *R v Secretary of State for Social Security, ex p B* 146 NLJ 985 (1996) *The Times*, 27 June; *The Independent* 26 June). The 1996 Asylum and Immigration Act extended the special appeals procedures set up under the 1993 Act (see p 506), and made provision for the removal of applicants in 'certified' asylum claims to safe third countries (see p 459). It also made provision for appeals against the certification of safe third country claims (see p 511); and amended the 1993 Act in respect of curtailment of leave, appeals to the special adjudicator, and bail pending appeals to the CA from the IAT (see p 401). Finally, the immigration rules (HC 395) have been amended by Cm 3365 to reflect the new regime for asylum applicants.

Possibly the most controversial aspect of the 1996 Act is the provision in Sched 1 reversing the decision in *Ex p B* (above) in relation to the availability of income-related benefits to asylum seekers. These provisions are dealt with in Appendix B to this book. Asylum seekers are not eligible for income-related social benefits after their claims have been determined. In practical terms it is difficult to see how an impoverished asylum seeker can be expected to remain in the UK to pursue his appeal. The CA in *Ex p B*, stated:

Parliament cannot have intended a significant number of genuine asylum seekers to be impaled on the horns of so intolerable a dilemma: the need either to abandon their claims to refugee status or alternatively to maintain them as best they can but in a state of utter destitution. Primary legislation alone could in my judgment achieve that sorry state of affairs.

That is, however, the precise effect of Sched 1 to the 1996 Act (see p 489 below). For an excellent collection of the *Hansard* material relating to the 1996 Act, see *The Asylum and Immigration Act 1996: A Compilation of Ministerial Statements*, compiled by Katie Ghose, 1996, available from ILPA at Lindsey House, 40–42 Charterhouse Street, London EC1M 6JH, by written request only; and The Law Society library and the Inns of Court libraries.

Paragraphs 327–35 of the immigration rules HC 395, as amended, provide as follows:

Definition of asylum applicant

327. Under these Rules an asylum applicant is a person who claims that it would be contrary to the United Kingdom's obligations under the United Nations Convention and Protocol relating to the Status of Refugees for him to be removed from or required to leave the United Kingdom. All such cases are referred to in these Rules as asylum applications.

Applications for asylum

328. All asylum applications will be determined by the Secretary of State in accordance with the United Kingdom's obligations under the United Nations Convention and Protocol relating to the Status of Refugees. Every asylum application made by a person at a port or airport in the United Kingdom will be referred by the Immigration Officer for determination by the Secretary of State in accordance with these Rules.

329. Until an asylum application has been determined by the Secretary of State, or the Secretary of State has issued a certificate under section 2(1)(a) of the 1996 Act, no action will be taken to require the departure of the asylum applicant or his dependants from the United Kingdom.

330. If the Secretary of State decides to grant asylum and the person has not yet been given leave to enter, the Immigration Officer will grant limited leave to enter.

331. If a person seeking leave to enter is refused asylum, the Immigration Officer will then resume his examination to determine whether or not to grant him leave to enter under any other provision of these Rules. If the person fails at any time to comply with a requirement to report to an Immigration Officer for examination, the Immigration Officer may direct that the person's examination shall be treated as concluded at that time. The Immigration Officer will then consider any outstanding applications for entry on the basis of any evidence before him.

332. If a person who has been refused leave to enter applies for asylum and that application is refused, leave to enter will again be refused unless the applicant qualifies for admission under any other provision of these Rules.

333. A person who is refused leave to enter following the refusal of an asylum application will be provided with a notice informing him of the decision and of the reasons for refusal. The notice of refusal will also explain any rights of appeal available to the applicant and will inform him of the means by which he may exercise those rights. Subject to paragraph 356(ii) below, the applicant will not be removed from the United Kingdom so long as any appeal which he may bring or pursue in the United Kingdom is pending.

Grant of asylum

334. An asylum applicant will be granted asylum in the United Kingdom if the Secretary of State is satisfied that:

(i) he is in the United Kingdom or has arrived at a port of entry in the United Kingdom; and

(ii) he is a refugee, as defined by the Convention and Protocol; and

(iii) refusing his application would result in his being required to go (whether immediately or after the time limited by an existing leave to enter or remain) in breach of the Convention and Protocol, to a country in which his life or freedom would be threatened on account of his race, religion, nationality, political opinion or membership of a particular social group.

335. If the Secretary of State decides to grant asylum to a person who has been given leave to enter (whether or not the leave has expired) or to a person who has entered without leave, the Secretary of State will vary the existing leave or grant limited leave to remain.

COMMENTARY

(b) Definition of asylum applicant

The rules define an asylum applicant in para 327 as a person who claims that it would be contrary to the UK's obligations under the Convention and Protocol for him to be removed from or required to leave the UK. For the purposes of the rules a person may become an asylum applicant only when he is in the UK. Nothing in the Convention and Protocol prevents the S of S refusing to consider the application of a person who has not yet arrived in the UK (*Ex p Sritharan* [1993] Imm AR 184). Old case law suggests that a claim for asylum will not generally be accepted at a British Embassy (see *Tekle v Visa Officer Prague* [1986] Imm AR 71). This is, however, contrary to what is frequently stated in press releases when new visa restrictions are introduced, that 'refugee visas' can be obtained from Embassies outside the rules. Some such visas have been issued, but they are very few in number and, given that they are outside the rules, it is hard to advise clients on whether or not to apply. Visa fees will probably be payable. The criteria stated by Ann Widdecombe MP were: the merits of the case and 'ties with the UK and reasons for preferring it to other countries', with the proviso that neither merits nor ties with the UK would suffice on their own (HC Consideration of Lords Amendments, 15 July 1996, col 824).

(c) The UK's obligations under the Convention and Protocol

The rules are primarily concerned with the obligations arising under art 33 of the Convention. This provides:

> No Contracting State shall expel or return ('refouler') a refugee in any manner whatsoever to the frontiers of territories where his life or freedom would be threatened on account of his race, religion, nationality, membership of a particular social group or political opinion.

The UK courts have consistently maintained that the Convention obligations arise only when a person is recognised as satisfying the definition in art 1A(2). By art 1A, a refugee is anyone who:

owing to a well founded fear of being persecuted for reasons of race, religion, nationality, membership of a particular social group, or political opinion, is outside his country of nationality and is unable or owing to such fear is unwilling to avail himself of the protection of that country; or who not having a nationality and being outside the country of his former habitual residence is unable or owing to such fear is unwilling to return to it.

This definition is discussed below. In the UK, the 1993 and 1996 Acts, together with the immigration rules, regulate the recognition of refugees.

The UK may not impose a penalty on the refugee on account of his illegal entry if he comes directly from a country in which his life or liberty is threatened, provided that he presents himself to the authorities without delay and shows good cause for his illegal entry or presence (art 31). The prohibition on penalties applies only if the illegal entrant comes directly from a country in which his life or liberty is threatened. This does not protect asylum seekers who come to the UK via a third country in which there is no threat to their life or liberty. There is nothing to prevent charges of obtaining services by deception and possession with intent to use false instruments (carrying a sentence of two to six months' imprisonment) being brought against such persons if they travel on false documents. However, if they are shown to be refugees, no penalties may be imposed for the illegal entry.

The UK may not restrict the movements of refugees save as may be necessary, and such restrictions shall be applied only until either their status in the country is regularised, or they obtain admission into another country (art 31.2). Article 32 imposes a negative obligation on the S of S not to expel a refugee lawfully in the UK save on grounds of national security or public order (*Ex p Chahal* [1994] Imm AR 107).

(d) Construing the Convention

In interpreting the Convention regard should be had to any practice in the application of the Convention which establishes the agreement of the parties regarding its interpretation (see the international law principles now embodied in the Convention on the Law of Treaties, Vienna, 1969, art 31(3)(b) (Cmnd 7964)). Such practice is set out in the *Handbook on Procedures and Criteria for Determining Refugee Status*, which is a product of the representatives of signatory states sitting on the Executive Committee of the United Nations High Commission on Refugees ('UNHCR'). The Handbook was published in 1988, and is available from the UNHCR office in London.

In *Bugdaycay v S of S* [1987] AC 514; Imm AR 250, the HL held that the 1979 version of the Handbook had no binding force in municipal or international law, and its recommendations could not override the express terms of the 1971 Act. In *Ex p Sivakumaran* [1988] 2 WLR 92, the Handbook was said to amount to a statement of the points of view espoused by the High Commissioner for Refugees. The Handbook is an aid to the construction of the Convention, but should there be a conflict between the Handbook and the rules, the rules prevail. In *Viraj Mendis v IAT and S of S*

[1989] Imm AR 6 it was said that although the provisions of the Handbook have no legal status, it has been cited with approval in some cases, and deserves proper consideration. In *Ex p Hidir Gunes* [1991] Imm AR 278 it was held, applying *Mendis*, that the Handbook provided helpful guidance as to the content and application of the Convention. In *Ex p Aouiche* (1991) *The Times*, 4 June, the CA held that the relevant part of the Handbook could provide guidance to the proper approach to applications for refugee status by deserters from military service. The Handbook may be taken into account by special adjudicators as a 'best practice' guide to issues such as credibility in asylum cases. In *Birungi v S of S* [1995] Imm AR 331 the CA stressed that the Handbook is no more than guidance, and that the adjudicator is to evaluate the evidence put to him. Thus the adjudicator is obliged to give the benefit of the doubt to the applicant in accordance with para 204 of the Handbook only if satisfied as to the applicant's general credibility (see p 482).

Advisors should verify any assertion by the Home Office as to the content of the Handbook. For example, the Home Office often alleges that the 1951 Convention does not cover punishment or prosecution for draft evasion. This is not the case; para 171 of the Handbook clearly states that if military action is condemned by the international community as contrary to the basic rules of human conduct, punishment for desertion or draft-evasion in connection with such action could, in the light of all other requirements of the definition, in itself be regarded as persecution.

Persecution by non-governmental groups and persecution in the context (*inter alia*) of the total break-down of government is stated in the Handbook to be within the definition of persecution (para 65 and see *Ex p Jeyakumaran*: see note at [1994] Imm AR 45 and see Baroness Blatch, HL Report, 20 June 1996, cols 531–2). However, the Justice and Home Affairs Council of the EU has attempted to redefine 'refugee' so as to exclude persons subject to such persecution. At the time of writing, no EU legislation has emerged, and the issue for advisors will therefore be whether such an attempt at redefinition constitutes a new international practice.

Advisors should, in such circumstances, have particular regard to cases from common law jurisdictions such as Canada and Australia. The interpretation placed on the Convention in such jurisdictions is highly persuasive as demonstrating the international practice relating to the Convention definition. Australian cases are available on the Internet either via the Electronic Immigration Network (http//www.poptel.org.UK/ein), or via the Australian Legal Information Institute (http//www.austLii.edu.au).

The document *Conclusions on the International Protection of Refugees of the Executive Committee of the Office of the UNHCR* 30th session, 1979, has been held to have no binding force in UK law (*R v IAT, ex p Alsawaf* [1988] Imm AR 410), nor to give rise to any legitimate expectation that it will be followed (*Ex p Akyol* [1990] Imm AR 571).

(e) Applications for asylum

HC 251, the earlier version of the immigration rules, made separate provision for applications at the port of entry and applications after entry. The current HC 395 does not have separate rules for each category, although the procedures differ quite significantly. An immigration officer at a port of entry receiving an application for asylum must refer it for determination to the S of S. Paragraph 328 provides that all asylum applications will be determined by the S of S in accordance with the UK's obligations under the Convention and Protocol. By para 329, until that is done, no action is to be taken to remove the applicant or his dependants from the UK, unless:

(a) the S of S has issued a certificate under s 2(1) of the 1996 Act that in his opinion certain conditions are fulfilled; and

(b) the certificate has not been set aside on appeal (if brought in time) under s 3 of the 1996 Act (see p 511).

The conditions are:

(a) the person is not a national or citizen of the country/territory to which he is to be sent;

(b) his life and liberty would not be threatened there for a Convention reason; and

(c) the government of that country/territory would not send the applicant to another country/territory otherwise than in accordance with the Convention (s 2(2), 1996 Act).

If a person is refused asylum, the immigration officer must then consider whether or not to grant him leave to enter under any other provision of HC 395. If the person fails to comply with any requirements relating to examination of his claim that may be made under para 331, the immigration officer may direct that the examination is concluded at that time and make a decision on the basis of the existing evidence. Moreover, a person may apply for leave to enter, and be refused. He may then apply for asylum and be refused, although this is one of the factors indicated in the rules as undermining credibility (see p 481). Paragraph 331 states that the immigration officer must then consider whether he qualifies under any other rule. A person who is refused leave to enter following the refusal of an asylum application is provided with a notice informing him of the decision and the reasons for refusal. The notice of refusal also explains any rights of appeal available to the applicant and the means by which he may exercise those rights. The applicant will not be removed from the UK as long as any appeal which he may bring or pursue in the UK is pending (para 333 as amended by Cm 3365). This right is subject to para 356(ii) which provides, broadly, that appeals in certificated asylum cases may be brought from outside the UK only (see p 512).

(f) Grant of asylum

A person will be granted asylum in the UK if the S of S is satisfied that:

(a) he is in the UK or has arrived at a port of entry in the UK; and

(b) he is a refugee as defined by the Convention and Protocol; and

(c) refusing his application would result in his being required to go (whether immediately or after the time limited by an expiring leave to enter or remain) in breach of the Convention and Protocol, to a country in which his life or freedom would be threatened on account of his race, religion, nationality, membership of a particular social group or political opinion (para 334).

If the S of S decides to grant asylum to a person who has been given leave to enter (whether or not the leave has expired) or to a person who has entered without leave, the S of S will vary the existing leave, or grant limited leave to remain (para 335).

'a refugee ... as defined by the Convention and Protocol' A person becomes a refugee when he satisfies the definition set out in art 1A of the Convention and Protocol.

The Convention and Protocol are given primacy in UK law as a result of the Asylum and Immigration Appeals Act 1993 (s 2). The 1993 Act makes provisions for the determination of a claim by a person (whether before or after the Act came into force) that it would be contrary to the UK's obligations under the Convention either for him to be removed from the UK or for him to be required to leave the UK. The 1993 Act gives asylum seekers a right of appeal: it ensures a right of appeal wherever an asylum seeker would, on refusal of refugee status, be required to leave the country. In the past, many of the cases in which UK asylum law had been considered were judicial review applications. The scope of an appeal is clearly broader than that of judicial review, and earlier cases need therefore to be approached with care.

The asylum seeker must satisfy the immigration authorities that he is within the definition of 'refugee' in art 1 of the Convention and Protocol. The material date for assessing whether the person satisfies the Convention definition is the date of the decision, and not that of the application, as the appellate structure is regarded as an extension of the decision-making process (*Ravichandran v S of S* [1996] Imm AR 97). Thus if the circumstances alter, so that the applicant's fear can no longer be said to be well-founded, the application will fail (*Samuel Musisi v S of S* [1992] Imm AR 520).

'owing to a well-founded fear' According to the case law, the applicant must actually have the fear described in the Convention (*Ex p Gurmeet Singh* [1987] Imm AR 489), and he must be outside his country owing to the fear (or inability to return; see *Ivanov* (125836)). The standard interpretation of the Convention states that there must be both a subjective fear and an objective basis for that fear. In practice the Home Office does not refuse asylum because of the applicant's lack of subjective fear where there is substantial evidence that he should fear. The need for this element has also been questioned by Hathaway in *The Law of Refugee Status* (1993, Butterworths Canada). The fear may arise after the applicant has left the country, producing the *refugee sur place*. He is required to prove the causal link between the fear and his remaining outside the country at the time of the decision.

The applicant must also show that the fear is well-founded, and for this purpose an objective test is used (*Naqui* (13243)). There is no obligation on the S of S to confine himself to the facts known to the applicant. The S of S may objectively determine the facts and ask whether there is a real and substantial risk of persecution for 'Convention reasons' (as to the standard of probability properly to be applied, see *Sivakumaran*, below). His duty is to consider the application, and use his experience of similar applications and his knowledge of conditions in the country to determine whether the fear is well-founded. In doing so, he is entitled to rely on information regarding those conditions supplied by the Foreign and Commonwealth Office.

There is no duty on the S of S to make enquiries in the country of persecution (*Akdag v S of S* [1993] Imm AR 172). Both the Home Office and adjudicators have *Amnesty International* reports and UNHCR material available to them, although little reference is made to such materials. In addition, the US State Department produces country reports, some of which are available on the Internet. Advisors should verify both past persecution and the risk of future persecution, using general human rights reports, specific expert opinions, medical reports verifying ill-treatment and the client's own documentation, such as court documents and membership papers, wherever possible. It may be valuable to produce a report from an academic or other expert with knowledge of the country concerned, specifically commenting on the circumstances of the individual applicant. The report should set out the credentials of the expert in sufficient detail to establish the expertise claimed. Asylum applications made without detailed supporting materials generally have negligible prospects of success.

There must be 'a reasonable chance', 'substantial grounds for thinking', or 'a serious possibility' that the fear of persecution is well-founded. The phrase 'real and substantial risk' has been said to equate to these expressions of the test. ('It is satisfied by a probability well below the civil standard of proof of persecution on the balance of probabilities and could be satisfied by a one in 10 chance of persecution' (*Ex p Sivakumaran* [1988] AC 958, [1988] 2 WLR 92, citing the American case *INS v Cardoza-Fonseca* [1987] 420 US 421).) The burden of proof is on the asylum seeker. Although there is dispute among different divisions of the IAT, the current law is as laid down in *Koyazia Kaja* [1995] Imm AR 1. The lower standard of proof applies both to past events and to the risk of future persecution (cf *Ex p Bahiba* [1995] Imm AR 173 (QBD)).

The fear may be well-founded on the basis of past events, if they suggest that there is a risk of future ill-treatment. Indeed a case without a previous history of persecution would be hard to establish, save in certain cases where the events giving rise to the fear occurred after the person had left the country of persecution. The S of S should consider the history of the case, and relate past events to the likely interest of the persecutor in the asylum seeker in the future (*Ex p P* 23 January 1992 QBD CO 702/90; and *R v S of S, ex p Halil Direk* [1992] Imm AR 330).

Children A different approach is adopted to applications by children. The rules indicate, at para 351 of HC 395, that more weight should be attached to the objective situation than to the child's subjective understanding of the risks (see also *Jakitay* (12658)). The matter should be dealt with without an interview if possible. This accords with the guidance given in the UNHCR Handbook, paras 213–19. The Refugee Council provides special advocates to co-ordinate the various services on the child's behalf. Note that under DP 5/96 (see p 271), the S of S will not deport children if there is no adequate child care in the country of origin. This, combined with the Children Act 1989, which makes the welfare of the child the paramount consideration, means that there may be material to put together a secondary claim for exceptional leave to remain on the child's behalf.

'Persecution for reasons of race, religion' etc To come within the Convention, an asylum seeker must show that the treatment feared would amount to *persecution*; also, that the persecution would be 'because of race, religion, nationality, membership of a particular social group or political opinion' (or, in the shorthand commonly adopted by practitioners, that the persecution would be 'for a Convention reason').

The dictionary definition of 'persecution' as 'to pursue with malignancy or injurious action, especially to oppress for holding a heretical belief' was used in *R v IAT, ex p Jonah* [1985] Imm AR 7. Persecution requires a degree of persistence by the persecutor. Evidence of past ill treatment should be related to the likelihood that the persecutor would be interested in the asylum seeker in the future (*Ex p P* 23 January 1992 QBD CO 702/90). Professor James Hathaway, in his book *The Law of Refugee Status* (1991, Butterworths Canada) argues for an analysis of persecution based on the violation of what he terms first, second, third and fourth order human rights. 'First category' rights are those from which no derogation (such as for reasons of national security) can ever be permitted. These are rights such as freedom from arbitrary deprivation of life, and protection against cruel, inhuman or degrading punishment or treatment. 'Second category' rights are those such as freedom from arbitrary arrest or detention, free movement, opinion, association, or privacy from which only a short-term emergency derogation of a non-discriminatory nature is permissible. For third and fourth order rights, see Hathaway, *op cit*, pp 105–12.

This approach has been adopted in Canada in *Canada v Ward* [1993] 2 RCS 689, and was referred to in *Sandralingham & Ravichandran* [1996] Imm AR 97. There, the CA stated that the issues of whether the definition in art 1 is satisfied, and whether the applicant's life or liberty would be threatened if he were returned to the country of alleged persecution (ie art 33), raise a single composite question. Simon Brown LJ stated that it was unhelpful and potentially misleading to try to reach separate conclusions as to whether conduct amounts to persecution, and as to what reasons underlie it. Having said that, the court went on to adopt an analysis of the facts relating to persecution in that case which accords with Hathaway's model. It is suggested that in practice Hathaway's analysis of what amounts to persecution requires consideration of:

(a) the nature of the right which is interfered with;

(b) whether such interference can be justified in theory;

(c) if it is possible to justify interference with the right in theory, the degree of the interference in the particular case;

(d) whether the degree of actual interference is permitted.

In *Sandralingham & Ravichandran v S of S* [1996] Imm AR 97, mass arrests of young Tamils were held not to amount to persecution because the arrests were justifiable rather than arbitrary and unlawful. The CA stated that whether a person is at risk of persecution should be looked at in the round, and all the relevant circumstances should be brought into account. (see also *Naqui* (13243)).

It was legitimate in that case for the appellate authorities to look at the frequency of the mass arrests, and the length of the resulting detention. They also looked at the situation prevailing in Colombo and the Sri Lankan government's need to combat Tamil terrorism. It was also legitimate for them to consider the true purpose of the arrests and the efforts made by the authorities to arrest only the 'prime suspects'. The relevant Sri Lankan law permitted arrest without warrant of any person reasonably suspected of being concerned in any unlawful activity. However, the CA emphasised that the real purpose of the detrimental action should be considered. If the purpose is malignant, that would constitute persecution if it was sufficiently serious. Torture could not be justified so as not to constitute persecution on the basis that it was to discourage terrorism, rather than to oppress. Where the action of the state authority amounts to unlawful detention, but the loss of liberty involved is relatively limited, the action of the state may not amount to persecution if its purpose is not to oppress, but to maintain public order. It is the degree and nature of the activity by the authorities that characterises it as either persecution or something else. However, the court would not condone unlawful actions by a state authority, so that mass detentions involving more than merely temporary loss of liberty cannot be a justifiable interference with a person's rights unless they are lawful. In *Ravichandran* it was the fact that the loss of liberty was relatively limited and for the maintenance of public order that prevented it from amounting to persecution (see also *Veluff* (12988)—a round-up of suspects was not persecution).

Thus a series of relatively minor incidents sometimes may not give rise to a well-founded fear of persecution (*Ex p Onay* [1992] Imm AR 320). However, although it may not be unreasonable of the S of S to treat discrimination as not amounting to persecution (*Ex p Moezzi*, unreported, 6 October 1988, CA), a special adjudicator may take the view that discrimination, on the facts of a particular case, does amount to persecution within the ordinary meaning of that word (see *Chiver* (10758) and *Grahovac* (11761)). Likewise, the special adjudicator may take the view that a series of minor incidents amounted to persecution (see *Ex p Jeyakumaran* [1994] Imm AR 45; see para 55 of the UNHCR Handbook). At para 54, the Handbook states that discrimination which has serious consequences can amount to persecution.

Similarly, the passing of a law may amount to persecution, depending on the extent to which it prevents the activities of the individual applicant, as opposed to those of some members of a group of which he is a member (*Ahmad v S of S* [1990] Imm AR 61). The test is the effect of the legal instrument on individual members of the group, and the application will be considered against that background. Account will be taken of the evidence of the applicant that he will feel bound to break that law. The persecution may be based on a misapprehension by the persecutors that the individual holds a political belief or was likely to commit acts in support of a political cause. The asylum seeker does not in those circumstances have to hold the belief (*Asante v S of S* [1991] Imm AR 78). On the other hand, the risk of random violence in a civil war would not amount to persecution on this analysis (see *Adan* (12768)).

Two cases illustrate that low levels of persecution may nevertheless result in entitlement to recognition of refugee status. In *Dumitrescu* (12237) the applicant had been part of a demonstration which was broken up. He had been injured and shortly thereafter lost his job. After leaving Bucharest for safety he was followed by a car, from which he believed he was being spied upon, for two weeks. The adjudicator dismissed the claim, finding that he had not been singled out for persecution, and that the level of persecution he had faced was not sufficiently high. The IAT, however, accepted that there was evidence of a serious possibility of persecution for a Convention reason. In *Lucreteanu* (12126), the applicant was the secretary of a youth organisation and left Romania after a series of threatening telephone calls to her and her husband. After she left he was made to divorce her. The IAT held that the telephone calls themselves would amount to persecution under the Convention and that they were connected to her political activity.

Political opinion The Home Office may allege that an asylum seeker's experiences do not amount to past persecution or do not give rise to a likelihood of future persecution because he was involved only in low-level political activity. However, there is no requirement in the Convention or the Handbook that an asylum seeker should have been involved in political activity at any particular level. Indeed, the Convention talks of persecution based on political *opinion*, there being no requirement for activity at all. The assumption that those who are not political activists are unlikely to be of interest to the authorities in the country where they claim to fear persecution may be rebutted by evidence to the contrary. If the applicant's political involvement is comparatively low-level (for instance, he is a non-active member of an opposition political party), advisors should explore whether specific expert evidence can be obtained to the effect that someone with that level of involvement is nevertheless at risk of persecution. On perceived political opinion, see *Seya* (12842) and *Quijano* (10699). Making a claim for asylum may give rise to a perception, the claimant's political opinion leading in some cases to persecution *Mavangu* (12938)).

Social Group In *Otchere* [1988] Imm AR 21, the UNHCR suggested three factors as characteristic of a social group:

(a) the group must be distinct within the broader society and definable by characteristics shared by its members;

(b) such characteristics could be ethnic, cultural, linguistic or educational, and could include family background, economic activity, shared experiences or outlook, values or aspirations;

(c) the attitude of other members of society to the group should be considered.

For a valuable general analysis of the meaning of 'membership of a particular social group' see the article by Bamforth in [1995] *Public Law* 382. In the US Board of Immigration Appeals case of *Acosta* (Interim Decision 2986, 1 March, 1985), the Board stated that the term 'membership of a social group' is:

> aimed at an immutable characteristic: a characteristic that either is beyond the power of an individual to change or is so fundamental to individual identity or conscience that it ought not be required to be changed ... [and that persecution is] directed toward an individual who is a member of a group of persons all of whom share a common, immutable characteristic. The shared characteristic might be an innate one such as sex, color, or kinship ties, or in some circumstances it might be a shared past experience such as former military leadership or land ownership. The particular kind of group characteristic that will qualify under this construction remains to be determined on a case-by-case basis.

This approach was discussed in *S of S v Binbasi* [1989] Imm AR 595, and was applied by the IAT in *Vraciu v Home Secretary* (11559), where it was held that homosexuals could constitute a 'particular social group' for Convention purposes (see also *Goldin* (7623), *Jacques* (11580) and *Re G* [1995] 1 312/93 (NZ)).

In *S of S v Savchenkou* [1996] Imm AR 28, the IAT held that persons who refused to join the Russian mafia could constitute a particular social group (relying in part on the decision in *S of S v Otchere* [1988] Imm AR 21). The CA ([1996] Imm AR 28) allowed the S of S's appeal against the IAT decision, accepting that the other 'Convention reasons' (race, religion, nationality and political opinion) reflect a civil or political status, and so 'membership of a particular social group' should be interpreted *ejusdem generis* (ie in the same sense). The concept of a 'particular social group' must have been intended to apply to social groups which exist independently of persecution. Otherwise there would be a social group, and so a right to asylum, whenever a number of persons fear persecution for a reason common to them. The mere fact of persecution therefore could not of itself play any part in establishing the existence of a social group (see also *Ntando* [1994] Imm AR 511; *Mbanza* [1995] Imm AR 136).

In *Savchenkou*, the S of S submitted that the concept of membership of a particular social group covers persecution in three types of case:

(a) membership of a group defined by some innate or unchangeable characteristic of its members analogous to race, religion, nationality or political opinion, for example, their sex, linguistic background, tribe, family or class;

(b) membership of a cohesive, homogenous group whose members are in a close voluntary association for reasons which are fundamental to their rights, for example, a trade union activist (see *Canada v Ward* [1993] 2 RCS 689 (for reasons so fundamental to their human dignity) and *Morato v Minister for Immigration, Local Government and Ethnic Affairs* (1992) 106 ALR 367); and

(c) former membership of a group covered by *(b)*.

However, *S of S v Otchere* (above) indicates that former membership of a group (in that case, the Ghanaian Military Intelligence) other than those covered under *(b)* above can give rise to a social group (see also *Osorio-Bonillo* (11451) and *Morato*, above). It is suggested that the true scope of *(c)* above is that set out in *Canada v Ward*, namely 'groups associated by a former voluntary status, unalterable due to historical permanence'. On the family as a social group, see *Hernandez* (12773).

Applicants who can show a fear of persecution but cannot show they are within a social group (or within any of the other heads under the Convention) may obtain exceptional leave to remain in the UK (see *Savchenkov* (above) and *Zibrila-Alassini* [1991] Imm AR 367). In such cases a recommendation for exceptional leave to remain should be sought from the special adjudicator if he rejects the substantive appeal.

Although it is not necessary for a person to have been singled out for persecution for his claim for asylum to succeed, as there may be persecution of a community or social group of which he is a member, and he may have a well-founded fear of being caught up in that persecution in the future, the fact that he has not been persecuted personally is a factor which the S of S may reasonably take into account (*Ex p Gulbache* [1991] Imm AR 526). Claims other than those based on political opinion are badly catered for by the immigration service questionnaires used for certain port cases. Refusal letters often fail to address the claim as made out, instead referring to the political situation in the country in question. Representations should be made with any such claim, setting out why the asylum seeker is covered by the Convention, so that the basis of the claim is clear. The Court of Session, in *Ex p Gurnam Singh* [1995] Imm AR 616, held that if the claimant has been interviewed and the S of S decides that his account of the events was vague and unsubstantiated, the S of S has no duty to advise the claimant of this before refusing the application.

In *Ex p Mendis* [1989] Imm AR 6, the CA was divided as to whether future acts could found a claim for asylum on the basis that a person's views would inevitably clash with those who would then persecute him, when no events which would attract persecution have yet taken place. Balcombe LJ thought that in that case there could not be persecution for Convention reasons, but Neill LJ left open the question whether or not a person of settled political conviction could claim asylum because, should he be returned, it would be unrealistic to expect him to refrain from expressing his political views for ever. Staughton LJ stated that if a person has such strong convictions that he will inevitably speak out against the regime of the country and will inevitably suffer for it, he should be treated as a refugee (and see *Ahmad* (above)). On the other hand, where the asylum seeker engages in political activities against a regime only after applying for asylum in the UK, it is open to the S of S to conclude that he does not genuinely hold those political opinions (*Gilgham v IAT* [1995] Imm AR 129 (CA)).

The persecutor need not be the authorities of the country of persecution. Sections of the population who do not respect the standards established by the laws of the country may persecute. Where serious discriminatory or other offensive acts are committed by the local populace, they can be considered as persecution if they are knowingly tolerated by the authorities, or if the authorities refuse or prove unable to offer effective protection (*Ex p Jeyakumaran* [1994] Imm AR 45; *Manga Singh* (1175) and *Al-Asfoor*). Thus where a claimant comes from a territory in which Government has effectively broken down, he may claim asylum on the basis of persecution by members of another clan (*Hawa Nur Ali* (11544)). This is the position of the Handbook at para 65.

Draft evasion   A deserter from an army, who is not willing to take part in activity condemned by the international community, such as repressing his fellow countrymen, will be persecuted if punished at all for his refusal to do so (*Ex p Aouiche* (1991) *The Times*, 4 June). Paragraphs 167–74 of the Handbook deal with deserters and persons avoiding military service, and para 170 with those who have moral objections to conscription. Clearly if a person has a moral objection to taking part in activities which are condemned, in most contexts, he will have a political opinion for which he may be persecuted. Others will have religious objections, and thus fall within the Convention. However, evidence that refusal to perform military service would result in persecution is essential as a basis for a claim for asylum (*Petrovski v S of S* [1993] Imm AR 134). Cases on draft evasion suggest that persecution will arise where the punishment for evasion is excessive. However, in *Filtcher* (11899), the IAT held that an eight-year prison sentence for a Bulgarian draft evader was not excessive. Evidence in support from specialist groups such as War Resisters International should be obtained. When presenting claims based on draft evasion, care should be taken to specify in detail:

   (a) the conscientious objections involved, and whether they are political or religious or arise from the fact that the applicant belongs to a particular racial group (as in *Padhu* (12328));

   (b) the nature of the persecution arising from the punishment meted out to draft evaders, and why in the circumstances the punishment is excessive so as to amount to persecution

(see paras 56–60 Handbook; *Mir* (12267)). Advisors should ensure that the S of S has a thorough picture of the applicant's personality and background in order to establish that the objection is genuine. Relevant considerations include whether the applicant manifested his views before being called to arms, and whether he encountered difficulties with the authorities because of his convictions (para 174, Handbook).

(g) Cessation of status

By art 1C of the Convention, the Convention does not apply where a person falls into any of the following categories:

(1) He has voluntarily re-availed himself of the protection of the country of his nationality (eg by obtaining a passport).

(2) He lost his nationality, but has voluntarily taken it up again.

(3) He has acquired a new nationality, enjoying the protection of the country of his new nationality.

(4) He has re-established himself in the country from which he fled.

(5) He can no longer, because the circumstances in connection with which he has been recognised as a refugee have ceased to exist, continue to refuse to avail himself of the protection of his country of nationality; but he can still be recognised as a refugee if he can show compelling reasons arising out of previous persecution for refusing to avail himself of that protection.

(6) If he has no nationality, he is able to return to his country of former habitual residence because the circumstances causing him to be a refugee have ceased, unless he can show compelling reason for refusing to return to that country.

For the cessation provisions to be triggered, refugee status must have been given, and the person must then cease to be a refugee. Guidance to interpretation is set out in the UNHCR Handbook at paras 111–39. This provision is rarely used.

On occasions, very minor contact with Embassies, such as reporting the loss of a passport, has been interpreted in other jurisdictions as amounting to voluntarily receiving protection from the country of origin under art 1C(1). In relation to art 1C(4), the IAT held that a Jamaican asylum seeker persecuted by Yardie Gangs had voluntarily reavailed herself of the protection of the authorities by returning to Jamaica, although she had done this only because she had been detained in HMP Holloway with those accused of Yardie drug activity and suffered violence at their hands (*Immigration Officer, Gatwick v Nareeka Hutchinson* HX/71192/94). Article 1C(5) has seldom been used. Although a person granted exceptional leave to remain is not subject to the cessation clause, it might be inadvisable for him to reavail himself of the protection of his national authorities by, for instance, obtaining a passport, as this may be viewed as a relevant change of circumstance when the S of S considers an application for an extension of the status.

(h) Exclusion of status

By contrast to cessation, exclusion is considered before the grant of refugee status. A person is excluded from refugee status under arts 1D–F, which, in summary, provide that the Convention does not apply to persons who:

(a) are at present receiving protection or assistance from organs of the UNHCR (art 1D);

(b) are recognised by the authorities of the country in which they have taken residence as having the rights and obligations which are attached to its own nationals (art 1E);

(c) are considered, with serious reason:
(i) to have committed a crime against peace, a war crime, or a crime against humanity (as defined in the international instruments drawn up to make provision in respect of such crimes);
(ii) to have committed a serious non-political crime outside the country of refuge prior to his admission to that country as a refugee;
(iii) to have been guilty of acts contrary to the purposes and principles of the UN (art 1F).

The S of S will first determine whether or not the person satisfies the other requirements for refugee status, and then apply an exclusion clause if relevant (*Gurprit Singh* (10860)). The burden of proof of exclusion is on the S of S. The UNHCR Handbook provides guidance on the proper interpretation of these clauses at paras 140–63.

Article 1D applies only if the person is receiving protection or assistance at present. Mere availability of such protection would appear not to exclude refugee status.

By art 1E, where a person has taken up residence in a country in which he is recognised as having the full rights and obligations of a national of that country he ceases to be a refugee. The UNHCR took the view that ethnic Turks fleeing from Bulgaria to Turkey were covered by this provision despite the fact that, prior to naturalisation, they did not have full political rights.

Articles 1F(a) and (c) are rarely invoked, although those responsible for human rights abuses in deposed regimes could qualify to be excluded under these provisions.

A crime is a political crime for the purposes of art 1F(b) if it is committed for a political purpose and there is a sufficiently close and direct link between the crime and the alleged political purpose. The court will consider the means used to achieve the political end in determining whether such a link exists. In particular, the S of S should consider whether the crime was aimed at a military or government target, or a civilian target. In either event, the S of S will consider whether it was likely to involve the indiscriminate killing or injuring of members of the public (*T v S of S* [1996] 2 All ER 865). *T v S of S* concerned an Algerian fundamentalist who had been involved in the bombing of an airport. The HL held that it was clear that the organisation to which he belonged was a political organisation and that T's motive in becoming involved in the airport bombing was to overthrow the government. However, the crime was almost bound to involve the indiscriminate killing of civilians. Therefore the link between the crime and the political object which T was seeking to achieve was too remote (see *Re O* [1995] Imm AR 494). Article 1F(b) requires a finding of fact that a crime has been committed.

'Serious' implies significant violence against persons, such as murder, rape or armed robbery. The term 'political' has taken its interpretation from the Extradition Act 1870; the judgement to be made is not whether the act is to be approved of, but whether it was part of a power struggle.

The IAT has stressed the need to look at the individual circumstances of each case in deciding whether art 1F applies. Mere support for a terrorist organisation does not give rise to an exclusion (see *Nanthakumar* (11619)).

Persecution or prosecution Exclusion clauses apart, the S of S is entitled to distinguish between fear of persecution and fear of prosecution for a criminal offence; see paras 56–60 of the Handbook. Excessive punishment for an offence, for a Convention reason, would constitute persecution for these purposes (para 57, Handbook). The mere fact of prosecution does not end the matter, and the S of S should consider whether the applicant also has a fear of persecution for other reasons. In addition, if the laws of the country concerned do not conform to accepted human rights standards, prosecution under them may amount to persecution (if the applicant can show that it is for a Convention reason (para 59, Handbook)). Thus, even if it is accepted that the applicant would not receive a fair trial if returned, this may not ground a claim under the Convention if the unfairness is not for a Convention reason (*Elvis Ameyaw v S of S* [1992] Imm AR 206). Similarly, a person linked with a terrorist organisation who faces legitimate prosecution in his country cannot be regarded as a refugee as this is not persecution unless it is for a Convention reason (*Ex p Baljit Sijngh* [1994] Imm AR 42). However, in *Ozer* (12233) the IAT pointed out that there are two aspects to persecution to be considered in such cases:

(a) whether or not the accused person will be persecuted before he ever reaches trial; and

(b) whether the trial he will undergo will amount to persecution.

2 Refusal

Paragraphs 336–9 and 345–8 of HC 395 contain the following provisions on refusal of asylum:

336. An application which does not meet the criteria set out in paragraph 334 will be refused.

337. [deleted by para 11 of Cm 3365].

338. When a person in the United Kingdom is notified that asylum has been refused he may, if he is liable to removal as an illegal entrant or to deportation, at the same time be notified of removal directions, served with a notice of intention to make a deportation order, or served with a deportation order, as appropriate.

339. When a person's leave is curtailed under section 7(1) or 7(1A) of the Asylum and Immigration Appeals Act 1993, he may at the same time be served with a notice of the Secretary of State's intention to make a deportation order against him. Full account will be taken of all relevant circumstances known to the Secretary of State including those listed in paragraph 364.

[For paras 340–4, see p 472]

Third country cases

345. (1) In a case where the Secretary of State is satisfied that the conditions set out in section 2(2) of the 1996 Act are fulfilled, he will normally refuse the

asylum application and issue a certificate under section 2(1) of the 1996 Act without substantive consideration of the applicant's claim to refugee status. The conditions are:

    (i)   that the applicant is not a national of the country or territory to which he is to be sent;

   (ii)   that the applicant's life and liberty would not be threatened in that country by reason of his race, religion, nationality, membership of a particular social group, or political opinion; and

  (iii)   that the government of that country or territory would not send him to another country or territory otherwise than in accordance with the Convention.

(2) The Secretary of State shall not remove an asylum applicant without substantive consideration of his claim unless:

    (i)   the asylum applicant has not arrived in the United Kingdom directly from the country in which he claims to fear persecution and has had an opportunity at the border or within the third country or territory to make contact with the authorities of that third country or territory in order to seek their protection; or

   (ii)   there is other clear evidence of his admissibility to a third country or territory.

Provided that he is satisfied that a case meets these criteria, the Secretary of State is under no obligation to consult the authorities of the third country or territory before the removal of an asylum applicant to the country or territory.

Previously rejected applications

346. Where an asylum applicant has previously been refused asylum during his stay in the United Kingdom the Secretary of State will determine whether any further representations should be treated as a fresh application for asylum. The Secretary of State will treat representations as a fresh application for asylum if the claim advanced in the representations is sufficiently different from the earlier claim that there is a realistic prospect that the conditions set out in paragraph 334 will be satisfied. In considering whether to treat the representations as a fresh claim the Secretary of State will disregard any material which:

(i)   is not significant; or

(ii)   is not credible; or

(iii)   was available to the applicant at the time when the previous application was refused or when any appeal was determined.

    347. [deleted by Cm 3365, para 17].

Rights of appeal

348. Special provisions governing appeals in asylum cases are set out in the Asylum and Immigration Appeals Act 1993, the Asylum and Immigration Appeals Act 1996 and the Asylum Appeals (Procedure) Rules 1996. Where asylum is refused the applicant will be provided with a notice informing him of the decision and of the reasons for refusal. At the same time that asylum is refused the applicant may be notified of removal directions, or served with a notice of the Secretary of State's intention to deport, as appropriate. The notice of refusal of asylum will also explain any rights of appeal available to the applicant and will inform him of the means by which he may exercise those rights.

COMMENTARY

For rights of appeal, see Chapter 26.

(a) Rejection without consideration

The provisions of HC 395 were amended by Cm 3365 to reflect the provisions of the 1996 Act regarding removal of asylum applicants to safe third countries. Section 2(1) of the 1996 Act provides that the protection from removal conferred on asylum seekers under the 1993 Act does not apply in certain cases. First the S of S must have certified that the conditions set out in para 345(1)(i)–(iii) above are satisfied. These conditions also appear in s 2(2)(*a*)-(*c*) of the 1996 Act. Second, the certificate must not have been set aside on appeal under s 3 of the 1996 Act. This right of appeal is dealt with at p 511 below. Briefly, the ground of appeal is that any of the above conditions either was not fulfilled at the time the certificate was issued, or has since ceased to be fulfilled (s 3(1)(*a*), 1996 Act). Until the certificate is set aside, the applicant may not appeal under the 1971 Act or the 1993 Act while he remains in the UK. Third, the time for giving notice of a s 3 appeal has expired and no s 3 appeal is pending (s 2(1)(*c*), 1996 Act). This third requirement does not apply in the case of a person who is to be sent to a country or territory which is or forms part of a 'member state' or is designated by Order. Such a person is not entitled to bring or pursue an appeal under s 3 so long as he is in the UK, regardless of whether the time for appealing has expired (s 3(2)). No definition of 'member state' is offered, but presumably this is a reference to the member states of the EU. The subsection refers to territories which form part of a member state. Thus protection from removal may be excluded in relation to certain territories which, under the law of the member state concerned, form part of that member state (see p 512). A person who is to be sent to a non-designated country or to a country outside the member states may appeal under s 3 while in the UK. It is only the substantive appeal that may not be brought in the UK until the certificate is set aside. An appeal under s 3 is pending during the period beginning when the notice of appeal is duly given and ending when the appeal is finally determined or withdrawn.

Safe third country A safe country is one in which the life or liberty of the asylum seeker would not be threatened (within the meaning of art 33 of the Convention), and the government of which would not send the asylum seeker to another country or territory otherwise than in accordance with the Convention (and see s 2(2), 1996 Act).

The S of S must be satisfied that the life and liberty of the asylum seeker would not be threatened before issuing a certificate under s 2, 1996 Act. A serious violation of a liberty guaranteed by an international treaty may constitute persecution (para 51, UNCHR Handbook, *Ex p Jonah* [1985] Imm AR 7, and *Sandralingham* [1996] Imm AR 97; and see Hathaway, 1991, Butterworths, Canada at pp 108–112). On this analysis 'freedom' or 'liberty' includes freedom from interference with the right to life, protection from torture and slavery, freedom from prosecution for *ex post facto* offences, and the other Convention rights. 'Freedom' or 'liberty' would also be threatened if rights such as equal protection, fair and public hearings, protection of personal and family privacy or free movement were interfered with. Further, when issuing a certificate, the S of S has to be satisfied that the third country would not return the person to another country otherwise than in accordance with the Convention. The S of S would not have power to issue a certificate if there was evidence that the third country would return the person to a country in which his life or liberty would be threatened for a Convention reason.

It is not a requirement of the Convention that a refugee must claim at the first safe country in which he arrives, but this has become a general principle of refugee law by virtue of the fact that the principal obligation on contracting states under art 33 is simply not to return a person to a country in which his life or freedom would be threatened for a Convention reason, rather than a positive obligation to grant refugee status to someone who qualifies.

The S of S must prove that the country to which the asylum seeker is to be sent is safe on the balance of probabilities (*Ex p Turus* [1996] Imm AR 388). Any risk of return to a country in which his life or liberty would be threatened must be taken into account by the S of S (*Musisi* [1987] 2 WLR 606). However, the S of S has to consider only whether the safe third country will discharge its obligations under the Convention, and not whether any country to which the claimant might be returned by the country to which it is proposed to send him is safe (*Martinas v Special Adjudicator* [1995] Imm AR 190 (CA) and *Ex p Srikantharajah* [1996] Imm AR 326). The special adjudicator is not limited to checking whether the S of S had material on which he could issue a certificate, but must make an independent judgment and consider whether he is satisfied that the country is a safe country (see *Ex p Mehari* [1994] QB 474 at 490 and *per* Glidewell LJ in *Thavathevathasan v S of S* [1994] Imm AR 249 at 254). He must consider whether, on the material before the S of S, and on any other material placed before him, the S of S's conclusion is justified. The adjudicator must consider the issue on its merits in accordance with the highest standard of fairness (see *Bugdaycay v S of S* [1987] AC 514 at 531; *S of S v Thirukumar* [1989] Imm AR 402 at 414; and *Ex p Abdi & Gawe* [1996] 1 WLR 298 at 305). Thus if, on the balance of probabilities, there is a risk that the asylum seeker would be returned by the intermediate country to a country in which life or liberty would be threatened, the certificate should be set aside. The applicant must produce evidence that there is a risk of such return (or 'refoulement', *Ex p Rubanra* [1993] Imm AR 447). Although not a ground for judicial review (*Ex p Murali* [1993] Imm AR 311), the assertion by an applicant that a third country will not consider his application seriously, and return him to a country in which his life or liberty would be threatened, may be sufficient. It may be possible to argue that where an application has already been considered in a third country, but has not been considered rationally, or the decision contained procedural defects which would constitute a breach in UK courts, the third country would return the applicant to a country in which his life or liberty would be threatened so that s 2(2)(*c*) of the 1996 Act is not satisfied. (See *Ex p Tania Stefan* [1995] Imm AR 410 for the S of S's obligations under the now deleted para 347, HC 395.)

The S of S is entitled to take account of any assessment by the UNHCR of a country as safe, despite the hostility of non-governmental groups (see *Ex p Mangal Singh* [1992] Imm AR 376). The proposition that the S of S must establish by direct enquiry with the third country that proper consideration will be given to the applicant's application for asylum was rejected in *Ex p Thavathevathasan*, CA, 22 December 1993, FC3, 94/6744/D. Advisors should obtain evidence on the procedures in third countries so that the danger that the case will not be properly considered is argued before the special adjudicator. For the position where the applicant has had a hearing in another country see p 469.

Highly individualist standpoints on the safety of various countries have been reached by different adjudicators. Where an adjudicator's determination differs from those of other adjudicators of whose determinations he is aware, in relation to the same third country and to the same or similar facts, he is under a duty to give clear and cogent reasons for reaching any different conclusion (*Gnanavarathan v A Special Adjudicator* [1995] Imm AR 64; *Turus* (above); and see p 381). A special adjudicator is in principle entitled to hold that a third country is safe, even if others have previously held the opposite (*Kanapathypillai v A Special Adjudicator* [1996] Imm AR 116). There is great doubt about the safety of return to many of the EU states. However, if a certificate has been issued under s 2 of the 1996 Act and removal is to be to one of these countries, no appeal may be brought under s 3 of the 1996 Act while the asylum seeker is in the UK (s 3(2)).

Although the S of S may rely on an assessment made by the UNHCR that a country is safe (*Ex p Mangal Singh* [1992] Imm AR 376), the S of S will not be justified in refusing to consider a claim for asylum on its merits where a third country said to be safe is not a signatory to the Convention, and there is evidence of a risk of refoulement (*S of S v Razaq Abdel* [1992] Imm AR 152).

The S of S must be satisfied that the third country would consider the safety of any removal on to a fourth country (s 2(2), 1996 Act and *Mehari* (above)). If there is evidence that the third country will return the person to the place of threat to life or liberty a certificate cannot be issued under s 2(1) of the 1996 Act.

With the abolition of internal frontiers in Europe, a Convention on The Determination Of The Member State Responsible For Considering An Application For Asylum (the 'Dublin Convention') has been agreed but not ratified. It is, however, likely to come into force in the near future. Under the Dublin Convention, an asylum seeker has one opportunity to obtain refugee status in the EU. If one country rejects his application after a consideration of its merits, no other member state will consider it (for details see p 490).

'His life and liberty would not be threatened in that country'   In *Ex p Abdullah* [1992] Imm AR 438, the argument of the applicant that the third country was itself not a safe country because he feared persecution there from neo-Nazi groups, was rejected by the CA. Where it is suggested that a third country is not safe the Convention test should be applied. A s 2 certificate could not be issued in such a case, and under para 345 of HC 395

the application could not be rejected without substantive consideration, unless it is certified under Sched 2, para 5, 1993 Act. Otherwise the claim is a substantive one concerning the alleged safe third country. However, in *Ex p Murugendran* [1995] Imm AR 12, it was said that it would be very unlikely that an applicant could claim a fear of persecution in Germany.

Further, the evidence from the Foreign and Commonwealth Office which the S of S received in the judicial review of *Abdullah*, that there had been a decline in the number of attacks on foreigners following changes to German government policy, could now be scrutinised by the special adjudicator, subject to arguments on public interest immunity preventing disclosure of FCO reports (see also *Balbir Singh v S of S* [1992] Imm AR 426 and cf *Ex p Roj Singh* [1992] Imm AR 607).

Returnability   The applicant is returned to the country from which he embarked, unless that country is one in which his life or freedom would be threatened for a Convention reason or would return him to the country from which he fled (see also *Balbir Singh v S of S* [1992] Imm AR 426). He may be returned to that country whether or not he wishes to go there as opposed to somewhere else (*R v IAT, ex p Miller* [1988] Imm AR 358). The applicant can be returned to a country without substantive consideration where there is clear evidence of his admissibility to that country. Where a country has a rule about re-admitting persons who have been absent for more than a specified period, the S of S is entitled to take account of evidence which suggests that the country will admit persons after that time (see *R v A Special Adjudicator ex p Babatinca* [1995] Imm AR 484). Section 6 of the 1993 Act protects asylum seekers from removal under the 1971 Act while there is an appeal pending. Section 2 removes that protection in certified cases. Even where that protection is removed, the person cannot be returned to a country unless it is one of the countries to which he can be removed under para 8 of Sched 2 to the 1971 Act.

The countries to which a person can be removed are set out at para 8 of Sched 2 to the 1971 Act. They are:
   (a) his country of nationality;
   (b) the country in which he obtained his passport or identity document;
   (c) the country of embarkation to the UK; or
   (d) any other country to which there is a reason to believe he would be admitted.

In *Ex p Yassine* [1990] Imm AR 354, Schiemann J held that the S of S must believe that the applicant *will* be admitted to the country, not merely that he *should* be admitted. In the absence of such a belief there is no power under *(d)* above to remove the applicant to that country. For these purposes it is only necessary that the third country should admit the applicant temporarily, including for the purposes of considering an application for asylum. It is not necessary for the S of S to have reason to believe that the applicant will be admitted for the purposes of settlement (*Alsawaf v S of S* [1988] Imm AR 410 and *Ex p Delarvalho* [1996] Imm AR 435). There is now a growing number of readmission agreements with EU countries (for instance with

France and Spain). The UNHCR has expressed concern about whether or not these agreements will result in more than the person's admission to the country, rather than his admission to the asylum procedure.

The rules state there is no obligation to obtain the assurance of a third country that the applicant will be accepted (*Ex p Mehari* [1994] Imm AR 151, following *Bouzeid v S of S* [1991] Imm AR 204).

Evidence   Evidence that the asylum seeker will be 'bounced back' to the UK is relevant to the question whether the person will be admitted to the third country only if that evidence demonstrates that there is no reason to believe that the applicant will be admitted to the third country. Repeated 'bouncing back' would amount to inhuman and degrading treatment contrary to art 3 of the European Convention on Human Rights. On an applicant's return by the third country to the UK for the second time, the S of S would be obliged to consider any asylum claim, and would not be able to return the applicant to the third country without further enquiry (subject to the issue of whether para 346 applies to such claims, see p 469). The S of S is not obliged to provide evidence of admissibility to the third country, but evidence to the contrary should be considered.

An application by a person who is a national of a country in which he does not fear persecution may be treated as without foundation under Sched 2, para 5(4)(b) to the 1993 Act (as amended by the 1996 Act; see *R v A Special Adjudicator ex p Abudine* [1995] Imm AR 60; for the consequences of such a finding—that the claim may be certified under Sched 2, para 5, 1993 Act—see p 506). An asylum seeker should not be returned to a country if it will, in all probability, return him to the country of persecution (*Yassine*, above).

Opportunity   Under para 345(2) the asylum claim must be considered on its substantive merits if the applicant did not have an opportunity to make contact with the authorities of the safe third country, either at its borders or within it, in order to seek protection. Cases relating to the application of this aspect of the third country principle before HC 395 are relevant. In *Ex p Bokele* [1991] Imm AR 124, the applicant had been in Belgium for six weeks before entering the UK. The S of S referred to art 5 of the Dublin Convention (see p 490), which provides that the responsibility for determining an asylum application lies with the member state which issues an applicant with a residence permit, as Belgium had done. Much shorter periods of time can bring the principle of the third country into play. In *Ex p Akyol* [1990] Imm AR 571, Kennedy J held that the S of S's refusal to determine the applicants' applications for asylum in the UK because the applicants had spent 10–15 days in transit through other countries to the UK was not unreasonable. In *Kemal Karali v S of S* [1991] Imm AR 199 it was held that it was not unreasonable to apply this policy to applicants who had hidden for two days in the transit area of a Dutch airport, fleeing from Turkey (see also *Bouzeid v S of S* [1991] Imm AR 204, where the applicant spent one night in the airport transit lounge in Austria; and *David Thevarajah v S of S* [1991] Imm AR 371, where the applicants spent one night in France). It is not possible to argue that an English speaking applicant has no opportunity to claim asylum in a country where there are many English speakers (*Dursun v S of S* [1993] Imm AR 169). The Minister stated that an hour in Schipol airport would be long enough to trigger this rule, but emphasised that it is the opportunity to seek protection, and not the length of stay, which is important (Official Report, Standing Committee A, 3 December 1992, col 567). A person has the opportunity to apply for asylum in a third country if he knows that he is in a different country; is able to contact the authorities; and has no reason to believe that the authorities will not receive his application for asylum (*R v Special Adjudicator ex p Kandasamy* [1994] Imm AR 333 (QBD)).

Substantial links with the UK Where a person can be removed to a third country, his application for asylum can, exceptionally, be considered on the grounds of his having substantial links with the UK which make it reasonable for the claim to be considered in the UK. Under the terms of a concession, a person who has substantial links with the UK may present evidence of them, and the S of S may decide that it would be reasonable for the claim for asylum, as an exception to the general rule, to be considered in the UK (see *Hansard*, 25 July 1990, Written Answers, col 263). The terms of the substantial links required were set out in a letter to the Refugee Unit on 21 March 1991 (see *Conteh v S of S* [1992] Imm AR 594 at 602).

A third-country case will normally be considered substantively where the following conditions are fulfilled:

(*a*) the applicant's spouse is in the UK;

(*b*) the applicant is an unmarried minor and a parent is in the UK;

(*c*) the applicant has an unmarried minor child in the UK.

The relative must have either leave or temporary admission to remain in the UK as an asylum seeker. However, the S of S retains a discretion and these factors may be outweighed by other factors, such as the character of the asylum seeker (*Conteh*).

Discretion will need to be exercised according to the merits of the case where any of the following conditions are fulfilled:

(*a*) the minor is married but has a parent in the UK, or has an unmarried minor child in the UK as an asylum seeker (discretion will probably be exercised favourably where the minor has a parent in the UK, rather than when he has a child in the UK);

(*b*) the applicant is an elderly or otherwise dependent parent;

(*c*) the family link is one which will not normally be considered, but there is clear evidence that the applicant is wholly or mainly dependent on the relative in the UK and that there is no similar support elsewhere.

In these cases the factors which may influence the exercise of the discretion in the favour of the applicant are:

(*a*) language skills, eg the applicant is fluent in English, but not in the language of the third country;

(*b*) cultural links;

(*c*) the number of family members the applicant has in the UK as opposed to other countries.

Where a person claims family links which do not fall within *(a)–(c)* above, and do not display any of the features which will be considered in the exercise of the discretion (such as dependency), the application will not be considered, no matter how strong the links of language or culture. The phrase 'substantial links with the United Kingdom' in the ministerial statement of 1990 has the same meaning in substance, and is subject to the same restrictions, as the provisions of art 4 of the Dublin Convention (*Ex p TK* [1993] Imm AR 231). Earl Ferrers, promoting the 1993 Act, stated that it was the S of S's practice to waive the normal third country policy if a person arriving in the UK could show that he has close ties with the UK, and that immediate family members might constitute such a tie, particularly if there was a degree of dependency on such family members (HL Committee 9 February 1993, col 599). Timothy Kirkhope gave an assurance that the 'close ties' concession will continue to apply (*Hansard*, 23 January 1996, col 263). However, Baroness Blatch stated that in exceptional cases there may be circumstances where it would be entirely appropriate to remove an applicant to a safe third country, even though they may have close ties or connections with the UK. She gave the example of a non-EU national committing an offence in another member state and claiming asylum to avoid prosecution there (HL *Hansard*, 20 June 1996, col 546).

Cases certified under s 2 of the 1996 Act are not subject to the provisions on torture which negate a certificate under para 5 of Sched 2 to the 1996 Act (see pp 506 and 510).

Statement on refugees from the former Yugoslavia   In a letter to UNHCR dated 10 August 1992, the S of S stated that in the normal course of events the S of S would not make third country returns where an applicant has merely transited through other countries, staying less than a day or two in any one of them.

(b) Rejection on consideration of the merits

Where a person applies for asylum and is refused because he does not fall within the definition of 'refugee', or for some other reason, but his removal would be in breach of another of the UK's international obligations, he should be granted exceptional leave to remain. Earl Ferrers, promoting the 1993 Act, stated that when a person applies for asylum and his case is considered and it is found that he cannot be granted asylum, the immigration officer has a duty to consider the UK's obligations under the UN Convention on Torture and the European Convention on Human Rights ('ECHR'; see Chapter 21) to see whether, if the person is sent away from the UK, such action would contravene obligations under other international Conventions (HL Committee, 9 February 1993, cols 546, 548 and 551).

In *Chahal v UK* (Application No 22414/93, 27 June 1995) the European Commission of Human Rights found that Mr Chahal's proposed deportation to India on grounds of national security was a violation of arts 3, 5, 8 and 13 of the ECHR. By contrast to *Vilvarajah* (1992) 14 EHRR 248, Chahal had not been deported by the time of the application. The Commission considered whether there was a real risk of ill treatment, and stated that art 3 of the Convention (which protects against torture, inhuman and degrading treatment or punishment) does not permit any exception for proportionality (see Chapter 21), and in particular the risk of ill treatment cannot be outweighed by a threat to national security. The *Chahal* case will now go to the European Court of Human Rights for further consideration. Article 3 of the ECHR is wider than the protection against a well-founded fear of persecution conferred by the Convention and Protocol. Advisors should therefore cite the relevant articles of the ECHR when setting out an asylum claim, particularly given Home Office practice on considering a grant of exceptional leave to remain when refusing an asylum claim (see the comments in *Ex p Zibirila Alasini* [1991] Imm AR 367).

The Home Office states that exceptional leave to remain is considered before an application is refused outright. The Home Office is reluctant to grant exceptional leave to remain at any later point, even if it is recommended by a special adjudicator. According to the Home Office, in asylum cases, there is no presumption in favour of accepting an adjudicator's recommendation for exceptional leave since it will already have been considered by the S of S in the context of the asylum claim itself. Although, generally, a recommendation would not create a legitimate expectation (*Ex parte Sakala* [1994] Imm AR 143), *Ex p Alakesan* (1995) 11 April QBD (CO/3774/94) suggests that, on the basis of parliamentary comments in debate, such a legitimate expectation could exist in asylum cases.

Good practice must be to put all relevant matters before the S of S as soon as possible in the hope that the Home Office will grant exceptional leave to remain if refusing asylum. Where this has been done, it may later be necessary to consider seeking judicial review of any refusal of exceptional leave to remain on the basis that the S of S fettered his discretion or exercised it unreasonably.

In addition, the S of S occasionally makes a concession relating to persons who have leave to enter or remain in the UK in some capacity other than as a refugee, but who have expressed a fear of returning to the country to which they are returnable (see, eg, *Ex p Zib* [1993] Imm AR 350, Lebanon).

An application which does not meet the criteria in para 334 will be refused. An illegal entrant liable to removal, or a person liable to deportation, may be notified of removal directions or of the appropriate deportation enforcement action when his asylum claim is refused (see para 338). If a person has leave to enter or remain and makes an asylum claim, his leave may be curtailed under s 7(1) of the 1993 Act. That of his dependants may also be curtailed (s 7(1A), 1993 Act). He may at the same time be served with a notice of intention to make a deportation order. Full account is to be taken of all relevant circumstances known to the S of S, including those listed in para 364 (p 263 (para 339)). Section 7(1A) of the 1993 Act was inserted by the 1996 Act, and provides that where the leave of an asylum seeker is curtailed, the duration of the leave of any of his dependants may also be curtailed to the same extent by notice. The dependants may likewise be served with a notice of intention to deport at the same time. No appeal may be brought under s 14 of the 1971 Act, or under the appeal provisions permitting an appeal against the curtailment of the limited leave, by either the asylum seeker or his dependants (1993 Act, s 7(2)).

(c) Previously rejected applications

Paragraph 346 was amended by Cm 3365 in the light of *Ex p Onibiyo* ([1996] 2 WLR 490: and see *Kalunga v S of S* [1994] Imm AR 585; *Ex p Singh (Manvinder)* [1996] Imm AR 41; and *Ex p Kazmi* [1995] Imm AR 73). The amended rule appears to apply where more than one asylum application is made during the course of a person's stay in the UK. Whether it could apply to a person who is returned from a third country, having been removed from the UK without substantive consideration of his application, will no doubt be an issue. It is suggested that the wording of the first sentence of para 346 precludes its application in such circumstances, as it envisages that the applicant has been refused asylum earlier in his stay, and not during a previous stay.

Where further representations are made, the S of S will treat them as a fresh application if the claim advanced is sufficiently different from the earlier claim that there is a realistic prospect that the applicant will show that he is a refugee, and that if he were removed from the UK it would be to a place where his life or liberty would be threatened. Material will be disregarded if it falls into the categories in para 346(i)–(iii). A decision that further representations do not constitute a fresh application does not give rise to a right of appeal under s 8 of the 1993 Act: *Ex p Ravichandran (No 2)* [1996] Imm AR 418.

The principle that the applicant could be removed from the UK to a country in which he had made an unsuccessful application, and invited to raise any new circumstances with the authorities in that other country, was deleted by Cm 3365 which removed para 347 from HC 395 (see *Ozdemir* [1995] Imm AR 39 and *Ex p Zeynal Avci* [1994] Imm AR 35). Such cases will probably be treated as third country cases under s 2 of the 1996 Act (see p 506).

(d) Safe countries of origin

The 1996 Act introduces special procedures for dealing with safe countries of origin (so called 'white list' countries). Section 1 of the Act (amending para 5 of Sched 2 to the 1993 Act) provides that the S of S may by statutory instrument designate countries or territories in which there is in general no serious risk of persecution. In such cases, there are special provisions on rights of appeal, which are discussed in more detail in Chapter 26. In most such cases, the right to appeal to the IAT has been abolished. The designation of a country as a safe country of origin is important quite apart from its effect on rights of appeal. Obviously, the fact that an asylum seeker is from such a country makes it more likely that his application will be rejected by the S of S, and will make it difficult to succeed before the special adjudicator. Asylum applications in such circumstances will therefore call for especially careful preparation. Without supporting evidence of the applicant's case (including both general human rights reports, and expert evidence addressing the specific circumstances of the applicant's case), the prospects of success are likely to be low.

The criteria by which countries were designated The S of S makes a judgment as to whether the general level of risk to people living in a particular country is sufficiently low to warrant designation (Baroness Blatch, HL *Hansard*, 14 March 1996, col 1067). On 30 April 1996, she went on to state 'I have made clear that the words "in general no serious risk" do not mean that it would be lawful to designate a country where there was a serious level of persecution aimed at minorities' (see col 1541). In line with the factors considered in a joint report on a third country (see p 495), Ann Widdecombe (Minister of State, Home Office) stated that the factors to be considered are the stability of the country, the state's adherence to international human rights instruments, democratic institutions, elections and political pluralism, freedom of expression for individuals and the media, and the availability and effectiveness of legal avenues of protection and redress (see HC Official Report Committee 16 January 1996 at col 166). In addition, the Minister stated that there would be no question that, merely because a country is designated, an individual would not have his asylum claim thoroughly examined (HC Committee 21 February 1996, col 439). Baroness Blatch gave the following undertaking:

> Asylum seekers often base their claim at least partly on allegations of human rights abuses and persecution in their country. Wherever that is a significant issue in the claim, the letter giving reasons for refusal will respond by setting out the Secretary of State's views ... each case is considered on its individual merits taking account of the facts and the circumstances relating to the particular case. An applicant from a country with human rights defects may be at no risk of persecution and an applicant for a country with a good record may nevertheless have a well founded fear of persecution. In short the obligation on the Secretary of State should be to give reasons for refusing the application.

(see Baroness Blatch, HL *Hansard*, 30 April 1996, col 1613). Ann Widdecombe was clear that designation would not constitute a blanket ban on applications. It creates a rebuttable presumption against the application, but claims will still be considered on their merits (see HC Committee 16 January 1996, col 158). The Parliamentary Under-Secretary of State Timothy Kirkhope stated:

> When considering an applicant's case we shall take a high note of the subjectivity of the individual's circumstances. The proposed measures, including the nature of a country's designation will allow us to ensure that our consideration of an individual case remains both subjective and objective.

(See Official Report, HC Committee, 11 January 1996, col 64.)

During the debates on the 1996 Act, the Home Secretary (Michael Howard) gave the following indication as to the selection of countries for designation (HC, 11 December 1995, col 703: Second Reading):

> I intend to apply three criteria to the selection of countries for designation: that there is in general no serious risk of persecution; that they generate significant numbers of asylum claims in the United Kingdom; and that a very high proportion of claims prove to be unfounded ... designation will not amount to a declaration that we necessarily consider countries to be universally safe, or to have political and judicial institutions that function to western standards. We could not possibly accept an obligation to apply such standards, and no such obligation exists in international law. What we will be saying is that a country has functioning institutions, and stability and pluralism in sufficient measure to support an assessment that, in general, people living there are not at risk.

The Home Secretary evidently accepts that a safe country of origin may give rise to genuine claims. Note also the following statement by a Minister of State at the Home Office (Ann Widdecombe) in Committee (HC Committee, 11 January 1996, col 87):

> ... the designation of a country as safe would not necessarily rule out an individual being able to make a case for asylum. The individual concerned might belong to a minority that has suffered persecution, or he might have suffered as a result of problems that were confined to a specific geographical area. If that individual were able to present a case showing why he could not resolve those problems (for example, by moving within the country, which is not inconceivable) his case would be taken on its merits.

Before the passage of the 1996 Act, the Home Office had already introduced a system for expediting decision-making in asylum applications from particular countries (see [1996] *Public Law* 196). The Asylum (Designated Countries of Destination and Designated Third Countries) Order 1996 (SI 1996 No 2671) designated the following as countries in which it appears to the S of S that there is in general no serious risk of persecution: Bulgaria, Cyprus, Ghana, India, Pakistan, Poland and Romania. (For the shortened procedure applied in these cases, see p 506 below.)

Torture It is particularly important in 'safe country of origin' cases to establish whether there is evidence of a reasonable likelihood that the applicant has been tortured in the country or territory to which he is to be sent (Sched 2, para 5(5), 1993 Act, as amended by the 1996 Act). The S of S has to certify that the evidence adduced in support of the asylum claim does not establish a reasonable likelihood that the applicant has been tortured in that country (para 5(1)). The special appeal procedures under the 1996 Procedure Rules, and the exclusion of a right of appeal to the IAT, do not apply where the evidence adduced in support of the claim establishes such a reasonable likelihood (para 5(5) and (7)). The nature and extent of the evidence which will establish a reasonable likelihood of past torture in such a country is unclear. Although medical evidence would assist in proving the likelihood of past torture, it may not be the only means of proof.

3 Consideration of cases

Paragraphs 340–4 of HC 395 provide:

340. A failure, without reasonable explanation, to make a prompt and full disclosure of material facts, either orally or in writing, or otherwise to assist the Secretary of State in establishing the facts of the case may lead to refusal of an asylum application. This includes failure to comply with a notice issued by the Secretary of State or an immigration officer requiring the applicant to report to a designated place to be fingerprinted, or failure to complete an asylum questionnaire, or failure to comply with a request to attend an interview concerning the application, or failure to comply with a requirement to report to an immigration officer for examination.

341. In determining an asylum application the Secretary of State will have regard to matters which may damage an asylum applicant's credibility. Among such matters are:

(i)   that the applicant has failed without reasonable explanation to apply forthwith upon arrival in the United Kingdom, unless the application is founded on events which have taken place since his arrival in the United Kingdom;

(ii)   that the application is made after the applicant has been refused leave to enter under the 1971 Act, or has been recommended for deportation by a court empowered by the 1971 Act to do so, or has been notified of the Secretary of State's decision to make a deportation order against him or has been notified of his liability for removal;

(iii)   that the applicant has adduced manifestly false evidence in support of his application, or has otherwise made false representations, either orally or in writing;

(iv)   that on his arrival in the United Kingdom the applicant was required to produce a passport in accordance with paragraph 11(i) and either:
(a)   failed to do so without providing a reasonable explanation; or
(b)   produced a passport which was not in fact valid and failed to inform the immigration officer of that fact;

(v)   that the applicant has otherwise, without reasonable explanation, destroyed, damaged or disposed of any passport, other document or ticket relevant to his claim;

(vi)   that the applicant has undertaken any activities in the United Kingdom before or after lodging his application which are inconsistent with his previous beliefs and behaviour and calculated to create or substantially enhance his claim to refugee status;

(vii)   that the applicant has lodged concurrent applications for asylum in the United Kingdom or in another country.

If the Secretary of State concludes for these or any other reasons that an asylum applicant's account is not credible, the application will be refused.

342. The actions of anyone acting as an agent of the asylum applicant may also be taken into account in regard to the matters set out in paragraphs 340 and 341.

343. If there is a part of the country from which the applicant claims to be a refugee in which he would not have a well-founded fear of persecution, and to which it would be reasonable to expect him to go, the application may be refused.

344. Cases will normally be considered on an individual basis but if an applicant is part of a group whose claims are clearly not related to the criteria for refugee status in the Convention and Protocol he may be refused without examination of his individual claim. However, the Secretary of State will have regard to any evidence produced by an individual to show that his claim should be distinguished from those of the rest of the group.

COMMENTARY

(a) Preparation of asylum claims

Asylum claims call for speedy and careful preparation. An applicant's credibility can be affected by imprecise formulation of his claim. The comments set out below are based largely on *Best Practice Guide to the Preparation of Asylum Applications from Arrival to First Substantive Decision* (Fiona Lindsley, May 1994, Immigration Law Practitioners Association, London) which provides check lists with explanations for preparing an asylum claim at the initial stage.

Initial interviews The initial interview between the applicant and his advisor should be conducted privately, in a sympathetic manner, while emphasising the need for the client to tell the truth. The advisor should not attempt to obtain all the details of the claim at this interview, unless there is no other option. At the initial interview, it is important for the advisor to see how far the claim has progressed; explain the definition of a refugee and make it clear that the burden of proof lies with the applicant; explain the procedure by which the asylum seeker's claim will be examined; explain any requirements of temporary admission; sort out any immediate problems such as eligibility for income support or the need for medical treatment; explain how the advisor's work will be paid for; and undertake any necessary immediate work on the claim.

Copies of all notices served on the client, documents submitted in support of his claim, interview records and political asylum questionnaires should be obtained. The immigration status of the applicant should be established. If the applicant is highly literate, it may be appropriate for him or her to write a statement of claim, which can be discussed and amplified in a further interview.

An interpreter should be used if there are any language problems, but family and friends, and anyone who does not have proper experience as an interpreter, are to be avoided if possible. The interpreter should only interpret, and should not be allowed to conduct the interview. The applicant should be asked whether he is happy with the interpreter; applicants are sometimes intimidated by an unknown person acting as interpreter, or by someone who may speak in a way which indicates an adverse political affiliation.

Green form legal advice and assistance is available to solicitors for the preparation of claims. The Legal Aid Board issues guidance on the exercise of devolved powers which applies to all users of the green form scheme (see Chapter 24). Extensions will be granted to prepare the statement, attend interviews, prepare appeals, and for disbursements such as:

(a) expert reports on the political situation in the country of origin, including any relevant area of the country of origin;

(b) medical (physical or psychiatric) reports on the applicant (for example, from the Medical Foundation for the Care of Victims of Torture, 96–98 Grafton Road, London, NW5 3EJ);

(c) counsel's advice on the merits or evidence;

(d) interpreter's fees.

The asylum seeker's statement For both port and in-country cases, it is essential to prepare a statement setting out the background and the basis for the claim. In port cases and short procedure in-country cases, this sets out the facts that the asylum-seeker must spell out at his or her interview. In non-short procedure in-country cases, it forms part C of the political asylum questionnaire. The account must be accurate, detailed and truthful. The primary consideration is credibility. Earl Ferrers said in Parliament:

> Ideally one could wish for conclusive independent corroboration of everything which is claimed by an applicant. That would be of benefit both to the applicant and the assessor. However in reality that is rarely possible. As a result the asylum division staff must rely on a combination of factual information which is obtained from a variety of sources and an assessment of the individual who is making the claim. In other words the credibility of the asylum seeker is a key factor (HL Committee, 9 February 1993, col 594).

It should be stressed to the applicant that the Home Office has facilities to check facts and that inaccuracies and falsehoods can be uncovered. If a statement has already been submitted or significant inaccurate information has been given in interview, this should be corrected at the first possible opportunity.

The statement should commence with details of the applicant's social, economic, educational and work background. Any matters which indicate that it is implausible that the applicant is an economic migrant should be emphasised. The ethnic, religious and political family background should be set out, to put in context the claim that follows. The statement should then focus on the central issues and will usually deal with the following:

(a) the beliefs held by the applicant, how they were acquired, and when;

(b) affiliations: the party(ies) or organisations to which the applicant belonged; posts held or functions performed; and the names of persons the applicant worked with (but if the applicant is afraid to give them, this should be respected and an explanation of that fear should be obtained and noted);

(c) any activities the applicant had been involved in (demonstrations, for example) or non-compliant behaviour (avoiding conscription, for example, or refusing to be involved in the activities of another group);

(d) any detention, arrests, ill-treatment, torture, trials, and harassment such as restrictions on activities;

(e) any medical attention received;

(f) why it was not reasonable to escape to a safe area of the country;

(g) what would happen to the applicant if he were to return to the country of origin;

(h) what prompted the flight and details of the escape from the country of origin to the UK;

(i) any activities since coming to the UK revealing a continued involvement or affiliation.

Under Part 11 of HC 395 the whereabouts of documentation and an explanation of such documentation as is available is important. Undocumented claims are easily dismissed, and the client should be made aware that evidence to support any part of the claim is vital. Thus, an advisor should check for and obtain where possible:

(a) passports, travel documents or ID documents;

(b) details of plane tickets;

(c) documents which may support what the applicant asserts including:
  (i) membership cards for any organisation, or group;
  (ii) newspaper articles;
  (iii) photographs;
  (iv) letters from friends and family;
  (v) medical reports by doctors who have treated the applicant after torture or ill treatment
  (vi) lawyers' letters and court documents.

Anything not in English should be translated. The advisor must know what it means. The applicant should understand that any false document will destroy the claim. Nothing should be sent to the Home Office without understanding it or without the prior approval of the applicant.

Background materials The current situation of the country of origin should be studied in newspapers, *Amnesty International* reports, *Watch* reports and *Minority Rights Group* reports and Refworld's CD ROM, or the Worldwide Web. Additional information may be available from academics who studied the political situation in the country concerned; see the ILPA Directory of Experts for a compilation of academics prepared to write reports in asylum cases. The S of S is not obliged to provide parties with all the information on which he has relied in concluding that a country is a safe country (*S of S v Khalif Abdi* [1994] Imm AR 402 and [1996] Imm AR 288).

Advisors should consider obtaining a report from the Protection Officer of the UNHCR, who is able to provide information in appropriate cases. Referring the case to Amnesty International for comment may also be appropriate.

Medical Reports Medical reports from a reputable source greatly increase the chances that an applicant's complaint of torture or other physical or mental persecution will be accepted. Any medical report deserves careful and specific consideration. In particular there may be psychological consequences of ill-treatment which may affect the evidence given by the applicant. In *Mohammed* (12412), the IAT stated (*obiter*) that it is 'incumbent upon an adjudicator to indicate in the determination that careful attention has been given to each and every aspect of medical reports, particularly given that these are matters of expert evidence which cannot easily be dismissed out of hand'. A dismissive attitude to such reports in itself indicates an error of law, and an application will be remitted by the IAT to a different adjudicator in those circumstances (see, eg, *Gurgur* (12239)). However, there is no obligation on a special adjudicator to accept the medical evidence as proving the applicant's version of events to show a fear is well-founded where it relates to the consequences of a traumatic experience which may or may not amount to persecution, depending on the circumstances in which it occurred (see, eg, *Mageto v IAT* [1996] Imm AR 56 (CA); *Ex p Hassib Khanafer* [1996] Imm AR 212; *Ex p Thirugnanasampanther* [1995] Imm AR 425; and *O v IAT* [1995] Imm AR 494).

In-country cases   These cases include those of persons seeking to vary existing leave, overstayers and those who have entered clandestinely. An application may be made by post or by attending at the screening unit at the IND. Those making postal applications will receive a date to attend the screening unit at Lunar House, Croydon. On attending, the applicant will be finger printed and interviewed about his journey to the UK and his identity. If the applicant satisfies the Home Office on these matters, and has the requisite four passport photographs and evidence of address, he or she will be issued with a standard acknowledgement letter ('SAL'). A SAL does not give rise to a legitimate expectation that the asylum claim will be considered substantively (*Ex p Kyomya* [1993] Imm AR 331). The practice hitherto has been not to treat in-country applications under the procedures relating to safe third country cases, so the claims have been considered substantively. However, this may change following the 1996 Act, as all asylum claims may now be treated as subject to the special procedures under s 1 of the 1996 Act (see p 506).

(b) The short procedure

Most applicants are interviewed immediately (after being fingerprinted) under a new short procedure which has recently been extended to most applications, and will ultimately apply to all in-country applicants and to most applications at ports which have appropriate interviewing facilities. Instead of an interview to establish travel details and identity, the asylum applicant is interviewed as to the substance of his case. This takes place on the day of arrival, or as soon as possible thereafter in port cases, unless the person is not fit to be interviewed at that time. The asylum seeker may attend the interview with a legal representative, but there is no right for a legal representative to attend, and the Asylum Division will not postpone or delay interviews for this reason. In practice, however, an interpreter is quite often required, and the Asylum Division will delay interviews for this reason. The representative is treated as an observer.

The applicant or his representative has the right to submit written representations within a set timescale. Five working days are allowed for further representations where the applicant is detained, and 10 working days if not detained. At the end of that period the S of S may make a decision without waiting for further representations. Where an applicant was not represented at the interview the interviewing officer has a duty to explore the basis of the claim properly. It may be unreasonable for the S of S to draw an adverse inference on credibility from the applicant's failure to reveal in the interview events which he thereafter reveals and relies upon (*Ex p Murat Akdogan* [1995] Imm AR 176 and see *Ex p Khanafer* [1996] Imm AR 212). On the other hand, the adjudicator is entitled to take into account the record of interview even if it is not read over to the applicant or the applicant does not sign it (*Ex p Agbonmenio* [1996] Imm AR 69). If, for any reason, items of information or supporting documents cannot be provided within the timescale, applicants should provide whatever information is available. Further evidence can be submitted at any time; obviously, it is better to submit it before the Home Office considers the claim. The whole process is envisaged to take roughly three months. If a victim of torture needs to obtain medical evidence, the Home Office will normally extend these periods (Blatch, HL Report 20 June 1996, col 493).

The short procedure will present serious difficulties for asylum seekers. On arrival it is likely that the asylum seeker will not wholly trust the authorities, and may not be as forthcoming about his history as he would be if given a proper period of time in which to make the application. Representatives will find attendance at interviews logistically difficult. There is a danger that applicants will be refused the opportunity to consult a representative, as the notice informing entrants of the services of the Refugee Legal Centre is not given until the start of the interview. Taking a statement of the kind envisaged in the best practice discussion above (see p 473) will be difficult in such circumstances. Advisors should ensure that the definition in the Convention is explained to the applicant, and that he understands the importance of explaining in detail the whole of his claim, including each and every factor that may be relevant.

(c) Full procedure

Nationals of the following countries are not dealt with under the short procedure: Afghanistan, Bosnia, Croatia and the former Yugoslavia, Gulf States (except Kuwait), Iran, Iraq, Liberia, Palestine, Rwanda and Somalia. This list varies from time to time depending on political developments. Under the full procedure, the applicant is given a questionnaire to fill in. He has a *pro forma* interview, and is allowed four weeks in which to make written representations. Later, when the claim comes up for a decision, the applicant may be interviewed again. If there is a policy of granting exceptional leave to remain to asylum seekers from a certain country, an applicant from that country is not always interviewed before such leave is granted. However, if an application is made to vary exceptional leave to remain to full asylum status the applicant will probably be interviewed.

Port applications   In these cases the interview is of paramount importance. The first *pro forma* interview concerns the route to the UK, identity and the brief basis of the claim. Photographs and fingerprints are taken, and if identity is not in doubt a standard acknowledgement letter issued. Port applicants can use this document to claim income support and housing benefit if they have no funds. The client is then either temporarily admitted, or detained. A date for a second interview may then be fixed, at which fuller details of the asylum claim can be taken and recorded.

Once the asylum statement is prepared (see above), the advisor should explain the format of the interview and the questions the applicant is likely to face. He should discuss how the content of the particular claim will fit the questionnaire. Representatives should try to ensure that the applicant is accompanied to the interview by a competent representative and interpreter who will make sure that the interview is conducted in a reasonable fashion and that any interpreting is correct. The clerk should note everything that happens at the interview. The clerk and interpreter should ensure that complaints are immediately recorded, and that words are correctly interpreted. The interviewer's notes should be read thoroughly at the end, to ensure that everything is correct and to enable the applicant to check that he has mentioned all relevant information. Even if the clerk is only an observer, his notes may be produced at a later stage.

After the *pro forma* interview, the S of S may certify the application under Sched 2, para 5 to the 1993 Act (see p 506), or treat it as a substantive claim. Under the Asylum Appeals (Procedure) Rules 1996, r 5, notice of appeal must be given in a certified case within two days where the applicant is in custody and the decision was personally served on the applicant. Otherwise the appeal period is seven days (r 5(1)).

(d) Substantive claims

Substantive asylum applications are dealt with by the Asylum Division of the IND at the Home Office. The application may be (i) refused outright; (ii) granted; or (iii) refused, but the applicant may be granted exceptional leave to remain (ie, the applicant is not required to leave the UK because there are reasons why he should not be returned to his country, as where the UK has other obligations under international conventions or the applicant cannot practically be returned). If the application is refused, the applicant may appeal under the system described in Chapter 26. The applicant has seven working days in which to appeal. Unless his case falls to be determined under the special procedure for cases certified under Sched 2, para 5, to the 1993 Act (as amended by the 1996 Act), he may appeal to the IAT, with leave; and, with leave of the IAT or CA, he may appeal to the CA (see p 514). The applicant has the right to free legal representation from the Refugee Legal Centre at appeal hearings, or may instruct solicitors or agents to represent him. There is no form of legal aid to represent at asylum appeals, but green form legal advice and assistance is available for preparation (see Chapter 24). Free representation by a barrister or trainee barrister may be available through the Free Representation Unit.

(e) Refusal for lack of co-operation

Failure without reasonable explanation to make a prompt and full disclosure of material facts, either orally or in writing, whether by the applicant or his agent (para 342) or otherwise, to assist the S of S in establishing the facts of the case may lead to refusal of an asylum application (para 340). This includes:

(a) failure to comply with a notice issued by the S of S or an immigration officer requiring the applicant to report to a designated place to be fingerprinted; or

(b) failure to complete an asylum questionnaire; or

(c) failure to comply with a request to attend an interview concerning the application; or

(d) failure to comply with a requirement to report to an immigration officer for examination.

(f) Fingerprinting

Section 3 of the 1993 Act gives powers to prison officers, constables and immigration officers:

(a) to take reasonably necessary steps to take the fingerprints of the asylum seeker or any of his dependants;

(b) by notice in writing to require the asylum seeker or any of his dependants to attend at a place specified in the notice in order that fingerprints may be taken from them. The S of S may also authorise other categories of person to exercise these powers.

Asylum seekers are fingerprinted immediately before the interview (or *pro forma* interview). If the asylum seeker abandons his claim, or if the claim is determined, any notice ceases to have effect, and the powers to fingerprint the asylum seeker or his dependants may not be exercised. By s 3(4) the notice to attend for the taking of fingerprints must give the asylum seeker at least seven days within which he is to attend. The notice may require attendance at a particular time or between specified times of day. If a person fails to comply with a requirement to attend for fingerprinting, s 3(5) gives an immigration officer or constable power to arrest him without warrant. Having been arrested, he may be taken to a place where his fingerprints may conveniently be taken before he is released. Further, constables and immigration officers are entitled to take such steps as may be reasonably necessary for taking the person's fingerprints before he is released, whether or not he is also brought to a place where his fingerprints may conveniently be taken. However, the section does not give the Home Office powers to fingerprint someone who has been detained in another way, for example at a DSS office (Charles Wardle, HC Committee, 19 November 1992, col 195).

A person must be an asylum seeker for the Home Office to have the power to fingerprint him. There is no provision for the Home Office to fingerprint a person who is suspected of being an asylum seeker (Charles Wardle, HC Committee, 19 November 1992, col 195).

By s 3(6) and (7) the person's fingerprints, and any copies, must be destroyed either within one month of the day on which he is granted indefinite leave to remain in the UK, or within ten years from the date on which they were taken, whichever is the earlier. Any data relating to the fingerprints must be rendered inaccessible by the S of S as soon as is practicable after the fingerprints are destroyed. A person may require the S of S to sign and issue to him a certificate stating that such computer data as exists in relation to his fingerprints have been rendered inaccessible. The certificate must be issued to him not later than three months from the date on which he makes the request.

Powers under Sched 2 to the 1971 Act permit a person detained for examination or removal to be photographed and measured, and for other reasonable steps to be taken for the purposes of identifying him (see p288).

Children are not fingerprinted as a matter of course (Earl Ferrers, HL Committee, 9 February 1993, col 627). Lack of identity papers has led to very young children being fingerprinted on occasions (*Ex p Tabed* [1994] Imm AR 468). A police constable, immigration officer or prison officer may not take steps to take the fingerprints of an asylum seeker who is under the age of 16, except in the presence of the child's parent or guardian, or a person other than an immigration officer, constable or prison officer or civil servant, who for the time being takes responsibility for the child. Such persons must be over 18 (s 3(2)(*b*)).

(g) Credibility
Credibility is a key issue in all asylum claims, and is identified as such in the UNHCR Handbook at para 41. The overwhelming majority of asylum claims are refused due to the alleged lack of credibility of the applicant. Under the rules, the S of S must have regard to certain matters which, if no reasonable explanation is adduced, may damage an asylum applicant's credibility. Among these matters are that the applicant or his agent:

(*a*) has failed to apply forthwith upon arrival in the UK, unless the application is founded on events which have taken place since his arrival in the UK;

(*b*) has adduced manifestly false evidence in support of his application or has otherwise made false representations, either orally or in writing;

(*c*) has, without reasonable explanation, destroyed, damaged or disposed of any passport, other document or ticket relevant to his claim;

(*d*) has undertaken any activities in the UK before or after lodging an application which are inconsistent with his previous beliefs and behaviour and which are calculated to create or substantially to enhance his claim to refugee status (see *R v IAT, Ex p B* [1989] Imm AR 166, discussed in *Gilgham v IAT* [1995] Imm AR 129);

(e) has lodged concurrent applications for asylum in the UK and another country;

(f) has made an application after he has been refused leave to enter under the 1971 Act, or has been recommended for deportation by a court empowered by the 1971 Act to do so, or has been notified of the S of S's decision to make a deportation order against him or has been notified of his liability for removal;

(g) on his arrival in the UK, was required to produce a passport in accordance with paragraph 11(i) and either:

    (i) failed to do so without providing a reasonable explanation; or

    (ii) produced a passport which was not in fact valid and failed to inform the immigration officer of that fact.

If the S of S concludes, for these or any other reason, that the applicant's evidence is not credible, the application will be refused (para 341). The activities of the agent may be taken into account by the S of S (para 342). Credibility may be affected by failure to disclose on arrival that the passport which the person produces is not valid, if no reasonable explanation is offered.

As to the way in which these rules are to be interpreted, Mr Kenneth Clarke, when promoting the 1993 Act as Home Secretary, stated:

> We recognise that genuine refugees may be shocked by their experiences and may be forced to use irregular and difficult means to escape from their own countries. The draft rules make clear that wherever a reasonable explanation is provided for behaviour of this sort it will not go against the applicant. We must, however, take account of those cases where applicants have plainly been lying, behaving irregularly or deliberately destroying their own documents (HC *Hansard*, 2 November 1992, col 35).

Common reasons given for alleging the applicant lacks credibility are:

(a) the applicant failed to claim asylum in the first safe country to which he came. He cannot avoid that duty by shielding himself behind instructions given to him by his agent to keep silent until he has reached the UK (*Ex p Musa* [1993] Imm AR 210);

(b) false representations by an asylum seeker. These should be viewed in the light of their intention, and a person's credibility should not be affected because he is mistaken about a piece of information, but only when he is plainly lying. Untrue statements by themselves are not a reason for refusal, and according to the UNHCR it is the examiner's responsibility to evaluate such statements in the light of all the circumstances of the case (Handbook, para 199). Further, the Parliamentary Under S of S for the Home Department stated that the rules reflect that entirely genuine refugees may be reticent or at times actively misleading in the initial presentation of their cases, but that if there is a reasonable explanation those factors will not go against the applicant's credibility (HC Committee, 17 November 1992, col 141; see also *Agbonmenio* [1986] Imm AR 69);

(c) inconsistency in the answers given at successive interviews (*Ex p K* [1990] Imm AR 393; *Munongo* [1991] Imm AR 616; and *Bolat* [1991] Imm AR 417). This may include alleged inconsistencies between *pro forma* interviews and full asylum interviews;

(d) failure to make an application for asylum on arrival in the UK (*Ex p Alupo* [1991] Imm AR 538); and the delay of the applicant in making an application for asylum (*Bila v S of S* [1994] Imm AR 130). However, in *Bila*, the court stated that it was understandable that an illegal entrant might not ask for asylum at the first opportunity. It is suggested that fear of immediate return might constitute a reasonable explanation for not making such a claim forthwith.

In assessing the credibility of the applicant, the S of S and the adjudicator should ensure that their views of the credibility of one part of the evidence does not unduly influence their views of the truthfulness of other parts of the evidence (*Haji* (13046)). Thus in *Nomelagne* (12236), the issues were:

(a) how a passport was obtained by the applicant;

(b) how the applicant was released from detention; and

(c) whether he subsequently had difficulty in obtaining work.

The adjudicator did not accept the explanation concerning the passport, and permitted that fact to influence his view of the credibility of the applicant on the other points, thus falling into error. Clearly the S of S and the adjudicator must make a proper decision on the credibility of the applicant in respect of each factor that might go to prove that he has a well-founded fear of persecution. Where the adjudicator does not find the applicant credible on the whole of the material evidence, he does not necessarily have to give detailed reasons for rejecting every particular item of evidence (*IAT Ex p Singh (Sukh Jeevan)* [1994] Imm AR 513; *Kingori* [1994] Imm AR 539; *Kassa* [1995] Imm AR 246; and *Ramirez-Espana* [1996] Imm AR 329).

The terms of paras 199, 203 and 204 of the Handbook are of particular significance in the context of the short procedure. These deal with the duty of the examiner and of the claimant at the initial interview and when the claimant should be given the benefit of the doubt. Paragraph 199 states that while an initial interview may suffice to bring the applicant's story to light, it may be necessary for the examiner to clarify any apparent contradictions and inconsistencies in a further interview and to find an explanation for any misrepresentation or concealment of material facts. Where the claimant has made a genuine effort to substantiate his story but there is still a lack of evidence in respect of some of his statement, he should be given the benefit of the doubt (Handbook, para 203), but only when all available evidence has been obtained and checked and where the examiner is satisfied as to the applicant's general credibility (Handbook, para 204).

Internal flight   If there is a part of the country from which the applicant claims to be a refugee in which he would not have a well-founded fear of persecution and to which it would be reasonable to expect him to go, the application may be refused (para 343). This rule reflects the practice before the Asylum and Immigration Appeals Act 1993. In *Jonah* (above) it was held that a man who had been a trade union official for 30 years could not reasonably be expected to live in a remote part of the country, and so this principle did not apply to him. In *Ex p Yurekli* [1990] Imm AR 334, Otton J held that if it is possible for an applicant to live in another part of the country of origin without persecution, that was a factor which the S of S could reasonably take into account (and *Ex p Gunes* [1991] Imm AR 278; and *Ex p El-Tanoukhi* [1993] Imm AR 71). In refusal letters, the S of S frequently fails to take the reasonableness of the applicant's going to the other part of the country into consideration and to show that the place would actually be safe. Letters refusing asylum to mixed race Bosnians at the height of the civil war contained allegations that there was a safe place to go in Bosnia, but no suggestions as to where that might have been, or how the applicant could have known about the place or gone there. In such circumstances, expert evidence may be relevant to reply to the allegations.

The way in which the rule was to operate was commented on by Earl Ferrers promoting the 1993 Act in the Lords (HL Report, col 801):

> Refusal in those cases will not be automatic. A full assessment will be made in each case of all the circumstances of the case including any links which the asylum seeker may have here in this country; an assessment of the whole situation in the country of origin, including the extent of any alleged persecution; the ability of the national authorities to offer protection; the reasonableness of expecting the applicant to move to another part of that country and the practicalities of returning him to a safe part of his own country. Even if a person comes from a war torn part of the world in which the war is localised, it does not mean that he would necessarily be returned automatically.

The UNHCR Handbook starts from the perspective that fear of persecution need not extend to the whole of the applicant's country, and then qualifies this with the observation that if there is a safe area, and it would have been reasonable to expect the applicant to go there, then status could be denied (para 91; see also *Ashokanathan* (13294) and *Sulasan* (12543)).

In *Dupovac* (11846), the IAT stated that the applicant must show that there is a serious possibility of persecution in each and every part of the country of alleged persecution (and see *Baglan* (12620) and *Montiero-Fighererdo* (12785)). In *Ahmed* (13371), the IAT stated that the issue of whether it was reasonable to go to an allegedly safe part of the country of persecution was not within the jurisdiction of the special adjudicator. However, in *Ikhlaq* (13679), a different IAT held that *Ahmed* was decided *per incuriam* in this respect. The IAT also considered the practical difficulties of internal flight to a part of the country in which, *ex hypothesi*, there is not a well-founded fear of persecution. It considered *R v IAT, Ex p Anandanadarajah* (CA 6 March 1996), the Australian case *Randhawa* (1994) 124 ALR 265 (at paras 8 and 14) and *Canada v Ward* (1993) 103 DLR (4th) 1. Contrary to *Dupovac*, it concluded that the practical realities of internal flight must be carefully considered. The IAT accepted Hathaway's suggestion (Hathaway, *The Law of Refugee Status*, 1991 Butterworths, Canada) that there may be circumstances where financial, logistical or other barriers prevent the claimant from reaching internal safety. The IAT accepted as a correct statement of the law the following passage of Black CJ in *Randhawa*:

> If it is not reasonable in the circumstances to expect a person who has a well-founded fear of persecution in relation to the part of a country from which he or she has fled to relocate to another part of the country of nationality it may be said that, in the relevant sense, the person's fear of persecution in relation to that country as a whole is well-founded:

The IAT took that passage to refer to the barriers mentioned to by Hathaway.

In *R v IAT, Ex p Anandanadarajah* (CA 6 March 1996), the S of S accepted that in an appropriate case, the test is one of reasonableness. How far and how wide the concept of reasonableness goes remains unresolved under para 343 of HC 395 in the CA. It is suggested that the approach in *Ikhlaq* is correct (see also *Manivannan* (12876) and *Rasathurai* (12584)).

If the applicant does hide in his country and does not leave immediately it is often alleged that this is evidence that he did not leave out of fear of persecution, or that he is not really at risk of persecution because he subsequently escaped.

4 Dependants

Paragraphs 349–52 of HC 395 concern spouses and children, and provide:

> 349. A husband or wife or minor children accompanying a principal applicant may be included in an application for asylum. If the principal applicant is granted asylum any such dependants will be granted leave to enter or remain of the same duration. The case of any dependant who claims asylum in his own right and who would otherwise be refused leave to enter or remain will be considered individually in accordance with paragraph 334 above. If the dependant has a claim in his own right it should be made at the earliest opportunity. Any failure to do so will be taken into account and may damage credibility if no reasonable explanation for it is given. Where the principal applicant is refused asylum, and the dependant has previously been refused asylum in his own right, the dependant may be removed forthwith, notwithstanding any outstanding right of appeal that may be available to the principal applicant. At the same time that asylum is refused the applicant may be notified of removal directions or served with a notice of the Secretary of State's intention to deport him, as appropriate. The notice of refusal of asylum will also explain any rights of appeal available to the applicant and will inform him of the means by which he may exercise those rights. In this paragraph and paragraphs 350–352 a child means a person who is under 18 years of age or who, in the absence of documentary evidence, appears to be under that age.

> **Unaccompanied children**
> 350. Unaccompanied children may also apply for asylum and, in view of their potential vulnerability, particular priority and care is to be given to the handling of their cases.
>
> 351. A person of any age may qualify for refugee status under the Convention and the criteria in paragraph 334 apply to all cases. However, account should be taken of the applicant's maturity and in assessing the claim of a child more

weight should be given to objective indications of risk than to the child's state of mind and understanding of his situation. An asylum application made on behalf of a child should not be refused solely because the child is too young to understand his situation or to have formed a well-founded fear of persecution. Close attention should be given to the welfare of the child at all times.

352. A child will not be interviewed about the substance of his claim to refugee status if it is possible to obtain by written enquiries or from other sources sufficient information properly to determine the claim. When an interview is necessary it should be conducted in the presence of a parent, guardian, representative or another adult who for the time being takes responsibility for the child and is not an Immigration Officer, an officer of the Secretary of State or a police officer. The interviewer should have particular regard to the possibility that a child will feel inhibited or alarmed. The child should be allowed to express himself in his own way and at his own speed. If he appears tired or distressed, the interview should be stopped.

COMMENTARY

A person of any age may qualify for refugee status under the Convention and the criteria in para 334 apply to all cases. A child means a person who is under 18 years of age, or who, in the absence of documentary evidence, appears to be under that age (para 349). A dependant may be included in an application for asylum. If the principal applicant is granted asylum any such dependants will be granted leave to enter or remain of the same duration. If the dependant claims asylum in his own right and would otherwise be refused leave to enter or remain his claim is considered separately. Paragraph 349 was amended by Cm 3365. If the dependant fails to make his own claim at the earliest opportunity this may damage his credibility if he can give no reasonable explanation for the delay. Where the principal applicant is refused asylum, and the dependant has previously been refused asylum in his own right, the dependant may be removed forthwith, notwithstanding any outstanding right of appeal that may be available to the principal applicant. This may result in the anomaly that a dependant may have been removed by the time a successful appeal is brought by the principal applicant. It is doubtful that such a practice would be lawful under art 8, ECHR as there would appear to be nothing to prevent the applicant having two concurrent claims, one in his own right and one as the dependant of another person, provided they are based on different facts. There are frequent difficulties at the screening unit when minors attempt to claim asylum with guardians : there appears to be a practice of refusing the application unless social services approve of the guardian and unless the Refugee Council Children's Panel representative attends the initial screening interview; the Home Office cites obligations under the Children Act to justify this practice. The immigration rules contain provisions on considering applications by unaccompanied children, so it is not clear why a child whose guardian is not accepted by social services should be in a worse position.

A child will not be interviewed about the substance of his claim to refugee status if it is possible to obtain by written enquiries or from other sources sufficient information properly to determine his claim. When an interview is necessary it should be conducted in the presence of a parent, guardian, representative or another adult, who for the time being takes responsibility for the child, and is not an immigration officer, an officer of the S of S or a police officer. The interviewer should have particular regard to the possibility that a child will feel inhibited or alarmed. The child should be allowed to express himself in his own way and at his own speed. If he appears tired or distressed, the interview should be stopped (para 352). Care should be taken to ensure that the immigration service or Home Office does not arrange interviews with applicants under the age of 18 without considering whether or not these principles are observed.

An Unaccompanied minor child asylum seeker cannot necessarily be expected to give a comprehensive and reasoned account of why he is likely to be persecuted. It is necessary to look for information from other sources. The S of S's approach in such cases is to look at the objective likelihood of persecution. If he considers there to be a real threat, an application will not be dismissed simply because a child had not properly comprehended the risk or seemed insufficiently frightened or had inadequately articulated it (see HL *Hansard*, 2 March 1993, col 575). This is in accordance with the provisions in the UNHCR Handbook para 217. An unaccompanied child's claim for asylum is to be given particular priority and care in view of his potential vulnerability (para 350). Close attention should be given to the welfare of the child at all times (para 351); under the Children Act 1989, the welfare of the child is the paramount consideration.

The child of an asylum seeker does not lose his own claim to asylum under para 351 merely because the asylum claim of the person on whom he is dependent is refused. The child's claim under para 351 stands alone (*Ex p Fahmi* [1994] Imm AR 447). However, the change in para 351, introduced by Cm 3365, stresses the need for the child's claim to be made at an early stage.

The Refugee Council operates an extra-statutory panel which provides advocates for unaccompanied child asylum seekers. This person should co-ordinate services for the child and make sure that all the needs of child are met.

5 Exceptional leave to remain, settlement, housing and social security

(a) Exceptional leave to remain

Where a person is not granted full refugee status, but there are compelling humanitarian reasons why he should not be required to leave the UK, he may be granted leave to remain on an exceptional basis. Note the comments above about other international obligations guiding the award of exceptional leave, as well as practical considerations such as unreturnability due to civil war. Such leave, known as 'exceptional leave to remain', does not carry the same security as the grant of refugee status. When a person has applied for refugee status, but has been granted exceptional leave to remain, the S of S does not always give reasons for the refusal of refugee status. It may be possible to challenge such a refusal to give reasons by way of judicial review (*Ex p Muslu* [1993] Imm AR 151).

The policy on granting settlement to those granted exceptional leave to remain, and on the admission of members of their families, was set out in a Written Answer in Parliament (see *Hansard*, 28 July 1988, col 424; [1993] Imm AR 152). A person given exceptional leave to remain is normally granted settlement on making an application after seven years with exceptional leave to remain in the UK. Settlement may be withheld at that point, or granted earlier than that: absences from the UK are sometimes used as a reason not to grant indefinite leave to remain. Exceptional leave is initially granted for one year: the normal pattern is two further grants of three years. The dependants of a person granted exceptional leave to remain may apply to join him. Such applications from the spouse and minor children will usually be granted after four years and are subject to the general requirements of the immigration rules on the admission of spouses and dependants: principally, that there is sufficient accommodation and funds that they will not be reliant on public funds (see, eg, para 5 of the letter of 29 February 1996 from IND to ILPA on Somali family reunion applications). If there are compelling compassionate circumstances, an application for such a family reunion may be granted at an earlier stage. If the S of S refuses to depart from this policy, the decision can be challenged only by way of an application for judicial review (*Muslu* (above)).

Family reunion   There is no provision in the Convention or Protocol about family unity. However, in the resolution in the Final Act of the Conference that concluded the Convention there was a recommendation that governments take the necessary measures for the protection of the refugee's family especially with a view to:

> Ensuring that the unity of the refugee's family is maintained particularly in cases where the head of the family has fulfilled the necessary conditions for admission to a particular country ...

The Handbook, para 183, states that the Convention does not incorporate the principle of family unity in the definition of the term refugee. However, from time to time, the S of S chooses to adopt a policy on family reunion which permits admission of dependants: two recent examples are the Somali concession (see letters from IND to ILPA 17 May 1990 (First concession governing applications up to the date of the second concession); 20 May 1993 (Second concession), and 29 February 1996, where much wider family reunion was allowed and the requirements to show accommodation and support waived); and the practice of immediate family reunion in relation to the spouse and minor children of UNHCR programme Bosnian refugees given temporary refugee status, initially for six months. Temporary refuge was never defined and, although given for shorter periods, operates as exceptional leave.

If the sponsor has been recognised as a refugee, immediate admission may be agreed for the spouse and minor children if, immediately before the refugee's flight to the UK, they formed a family unit. Maintenance and accommodation requirements are waived in these circumstances (see, eg, the letter of 29 February 1996 above).

Where the S of S refuses to extend or vary exceptional leave to remain, the applicant may appeal to the adjudicator, although it has been argued that this practice is unlawful (*Muslu* (above)).

It is possible to apply to upgrade a client from exceptional leave to remain to full refugee status. Such a step must be considered carefully as it may lead the Home Office to decide that they should not have given even exceptional leave, or, if taken to an appeal, to an adjudicator making comments to that affect.

(b) Settlement

An asylum seeker who is recognised as a refugee has no right to settlement under the rules. Settlement is dealt with by way of extra-statutory discretion. The Home Office usually grants four years' leave to remain, after which the refugee is able to apply for indefinite leave to remain, which is normally granted. On occasions the Home Office requires a refugee to 'make up' time spent outside the UK before granting indefinite leave.

The refugee should not be expelled save on the grounds of national security, or public order, after due process of law (art 32 of the Convention). When considering the deportation of a person who seeks asylum, the S of S has an obligation to balance the interests of national security against those of the refugee. However, a crime may be political for the purposes of art 1F(b) of the Convention regardless of the adverse consequences for the fugitive (*T v S of S* [1996] 2 All ER 865; *Chahal v S of S* [1994] Imm AR 107).

If the refugee leaves his country of refuge, and enters another country subscribing to the European Agreement on the Transfer of Responsibility for Refugees (16 October 1980, Cmnd 8127), after two years' lawful residence there, responsibility is transferred to that country. However, residence for the purposes of study, medical treatment, training, or imprisonment does not count towards that two-year period.

In *Jinah Rahman v S of S* [1989] Imm AR 325, the IAT considered this Agreement as a relevant circumstance which the S of S should have taken into account when considering an application for transfer of refugee status from the Netherlands to the UK in his discretion outside the rules, which the IAT has power to review. They held that the principal purpose of the Agreement was to avoid difficulties for refugees who were factually resident in one state, but have their refugee status from another state (see also *Shrokh Shami* [1992] Imm AR 542). Asylum may be transferred in other circumstances where the S of S is convinced that there are compelling compassionate circumstances, or where the S of S cannot return a refugee, for instance where the refugee is serving a prison sentence in the UK and loses residence rights in his country of recognition. Consideration should be given to making a simultaneous claim for political asylum where there has been persecution, such as racial attacks, in the original country of refuge.

(c) Housing and social security
Section 4 of the 1993 Act concerns the housing of asylum seekers and their dependants. The local authority's powers are limited to providing temporary accommodation only while an application for asylum is pending. By s 5 of the 1993 Act, an asylum seeker, or his dependant, acquires and ceases to have that status for the purposes of housing provision when the S of S records that fact. Accommodation is not available for the applicant's occupation if it is not available both for the occupation of the applicant and those who might reasonably be expected to reside with him. Thus the accommodation would have to be available for his family or any cohabitee (s 5(8)). There is no duty to house an asylum seeker if he and any family have any accommodation available to them, however temporary.

With effect from 5 February 1996, the rights of asylum seekers to social security benefits were severely curtailed by the Social Security (Persons from Abroad) Miscellaneous Amendment Regulations 1996 (SI 1996 No 30), which removed all right to income-related benefits (including housing benefit and income support) from: (i) in-country asylum applicants; and (ii) port applicants whose applications had been rejected by the S of S. The provisions preserved the benefit rights of those already receiving benefit when the regulations came into force until the next negative decision on their claims.

The 1996 Regulations were declared to be *ultra vires* the Social Security (Contributions and Benefits) Act 1992 by the CA in *R v S of S for Social Security ex p JCWI* (*The Times*, 27 June 1996). The 1996 Act in its final form effectively reversed the *JCWI* case. Section 11 of the Act provided a statutory basis for the reintroduction of regulations, essentially in the same form as those declared *ultra vires* the 1992 Act by the CA. Schedule 1 to the 1996 Act effectively reinstates the regulations with effect from the date of passage of the 1996 Act, removing local authorities' duty to house asylum seekers (and see Appendix B).

Those asylum applicants who are entitled to benefit receive 90 per cent of income support and the full amounts of housing and child benefit (Income Support (General) Regulations 1987 (SI 1987 No 1971), reg 71(1)). Unless there are grave doubts about the applicant's identity, he or she should be issued with a standard acknowledgement letter which will assist the processing of the income support claim.

An asylum seeker who has been admitted on a temporary basis is normally prohibited from taking work. An application must be made for the prohibition to be varied to a restriction before employment is taken. This is not usually granted until the application has been outstanding for more than six months, except where the applicant has been offered a specific job before that time, or where there are exceptional reasons (Letter from Home Office to British Refugee Council, 28 January 1988). However, lack of entitlement to income support is not considered an exceptional reason, even where there is an offer of work and the applicant has no other funds.

6 EU law

Asylum law in the UK now has to be seen in the wider context of EU provisions on free movement and the internal market. The Treaty of Rome, as amended by the Single European Act 1986, provided that internal frontiers be abolished by the end of 1992. Controls on crossing an internal frontier were to be abolished after that time. The Dublin Convention (see below) is an intergovernmental Convention, which at present is not amenable to EU jurisdiction, but which has been agreed between the member states of the EU with a view to harmonising asylum policies in the light of art 8a of the Treaty of Rome. Article 8a provides that the European Union should consist of an internal market without frontiers. The Commission took the view that art 8a applies to all individuals within the internal market area, and is not restricted to nationals of member states. Since EC measures have not been adopted, it might be thought possible to rely on art 8a to prevent an asylum seeker being returned to a member state through which he has travelled. However, the CA has taken the view that the provisions of art 8a are compatible with the third-country practice of the S of S (*Ex p Colak* [1993] Imm AR 581 and *Ex p Ghebretatios* [1993] Imm AR 585). In the latter case, the court held that, as the Dublin Convention was negotiated with a view to the requirements of art 8a, that article permitted the practice of third country removals. Further, in *Ex p Flynn* (1995) *The Times*, 20 July it was held that in any event art 8a does not confer a general right of free movement without frontier controls on EU citizens (see Chapter 16).

(a) The Dublin Convention

As noted above, the UK is party to the Dublin Convention Determining the State Responsible for Examining Applications for Asylum Lodged in one of the Member States of the European Communities, which was signed by all EC member states by 26 June 1991 (a copy of the text is at [1990] Imm AR 604). It has the effect of permitting an asylum seeker one chance to achieve recognition as a refugee in the EC states. Its purpose is that the EC may achieve an area without internal frontiers. The main provisions are considered below. The Dublin Convention is not yet in force, but it has been referred to by the courts (see, eg, *Ex p Akyol* [1990] Imm AR 571 and *Kerali* (*Kemal v S of S* [1991] Imm AR 199). The law and practice relied upon in this area are the domestic provisions in the 1993 Asylum and Immigration Appeals Act in relation to third country cases and case law established under this recent legislation (see above). However, when the Convention comes into force it may be possible to argue that it forms part of EU law and may in certain cases confer directly enforceable rights on individual asylum seekers (see Chapter 16).

If the applicant is an adult and has a spouse or unmarried child under 18, either of whom has been recognised as a refugee legally resident in one member state, the responsibility for determining the asylum claim falls to that state (art 4). If the applicant does not consent to that state's determining the application, it may not do so. If the applicant is an unmarried child, the state will be responsible for the determination of the asylum application only if the father or mother has been recognised there as a refugee. If the applicant has a valid visa or residence permit, the state which issued it is responsible for examining his application (art 5). However, if another member state gave written authorisation for the visa, that other member state is responsible. If the applicant is in possession of a transit visa, and makes his application en route to another member state, where he is not subject to a visa requirement, the other member state is responsible for determining the application. Similarly, where no visas are required in the member state through which a person is travelling on a transit visa, and he makes his application in that member state, the member state to which he is travelling will be responsible if the transit state receives written confirmation from the member state to which the person is travelling that the applicant fulfils its entrance requirements.

The Convention also makes provision for an applicant who is in possession of a visa which permits him entry to more than one member state. The member state which has issued the longest visa, or that with the latest expiry date, will usually be responsible. Where the visas are transit visas issued on the presentation of a member state's entry visa, the state which issued the entry visa must determine the application. Where a person had visas permitting entry and residence in more than one member state, but which expired more than two years previously, the state in which he lodges the application is responsible for determining it. However, where he lodges the application in one state, and it has been less than two years since one or more of those visas expired, he is treated as if he is in possession of two current visas, and the state which issued the one that expires last or is longest is responsible.

Special provision is made in art 6 for persons who have entered the EC illegally from a third state. The state to which entry is made is responsible, unless it can be shown that the applicant had been living for the last six months in another member state. In all cases of entry, legal or otherwise, the first state to which the applicant comes is responsible for making the determination, unless in law the applicant has entered another member state where the requirement for him to have a visa has been waived.

Until there is agreement on the definition of 'external borders' of the Community, an applicant who does not leave the transit zone of an airport does not enter the member state for the purposes of having his application for asylum determined there. However, if he makes his application in the transit zone of the airport, that state is responsible for determining his claim (art 7). A definition of 'external borders' is to be reached as part of the work programme for the implementation of the internal market under art 8a of the Treaty of Rome. The Draft Convention on the Crossing of External Frontiers is currently awaiting agreement between Spain and the UK on the status of Gibraltar. This again will be an intergovernmental agreement which may not therefore be amenable to Community jurisdiction without being adopted by the Community.

If no member state is identified as responsible for determining the application by the above procedure, the member state in which the application is lodged is responsible (art 8). Article 9 permits a member state, at the request of another member state, to examine applications for which it is not responsible, for humanitarian reasons. These will often be based on family or cultural grounds. If the member state agrees, responsibility is transferred to it.

Where one member state considers that another is responsible, it may request that other member state to take responsibility as speedily as possible, within six months of the application being lodged. If the second state fails to take responsibility within that time, the first remains responsible. The requesting state must set out reasons why the second state is responsible under the criteria of the Convention. The second member state must reply within three months of receipt of the request. If it fails to do so, it becomes responsible for determining the application. When the second state becomes responsible it must take charge of the applicant, and must complete the examination of the application. The applicant must be transferred to the second member state within one month of acceptance of responsibility by that member state. The applicant may object to the transfer (arts 10 and 11).

Where the applicant lodges an application in a member state, having withdrawn it in another member state, he may be returned to the member state in which the application was withdrawn, with a view to having the determination completed. The following conditions must be fulfilled:

(1) The request by the second state for the first to take the applicant back contains indications enabling the first state to ascertain that it is obliged to take the applicant back, because it was determining the application or because the applicant is illegally in the state in which the new application was lodged, or because the applicant withdrew an application in the first state, or because the applicant is illegally in the second state having had his application rejected in the first state.

(2) The first state must give an answer to the request within eight days of the matter being referred to it. If it acknowledges responsibility it must take the applicant back within one month.

The state found responsible under the criteria set out above has the following duties under art 10. It must take charge of the applicant; complete the examination; and take the applicant back if he goes irregularly to another member state, or if he withdraws his application and lodges it with another member state, or if it rejects the application, and the applicant illegally enters another member state. These responsibilities pass to a member state which issues a residence permit for more than three months; and all duties except the duty to take back a rejected applicant who goes elsewhere in the EC illegally, cease to apply if the applicant leaves EC territory for a period of more than three months. There is no responsibility to take back an applicant who lodges an application in another EC state or one who, having been rejected, enters another EC state illegally, if the state responsible for examining following withdrawal or rejection, has taken measures to return the applicant to the country of origin or such country as he may lawfully enter (art 10).

Article 14 provides for the mutual exchange of information regarding legislation or practices on asylum, and statistics on arrivals and their nationalities. The states may also exchange information on trends in asylum, circumstances in countries of origin, or the provenance of applicants for asylum. The details which may be exchanged in relation to particular applications and the determination of responsibility are dealt with in art 15.

No express provision has been made under this Agreement for the applicant to raise particular grounds of objection, but the applicant will be able to object to a particular country's dealing with the application on the grounds that it is not a safe country (see *Abdullah* [1992] Imm AR 438).

(b) Other EU provisions

The position papers generated by the intergovernmental process, and in particular the *ad hoc* immigration group asylum subgroup, on matters such as fast track procedure, manifestly unfounded claims, and, most recently, the harmonisation of the definition of a refugee, will be of increasing significance for practitioners. These may be voluntarily adopted in domestic law by the member states to harmonise law and practice. Awareness of this procedure, for instance by reading *Migration Newsheet* (available from 172–174 rue Joseph II, B-1000 Brussels), is important for practitioners as indicating future developments and any potential reductions in the rights of asylum seekers. Finally, the third pillar of Maastricht provides for co-operation in the fields of justice and home affairs; is deemed to include asylum policy (art K1(1)); and establishes (art K4) a committee to provide opinions to the Council.

Council Decision 96/C 274/01 of 23 November 1995 lists the acts and other texts in the field of asylum and immigration which have been adopted to date by the Council since the entry into force of the Treaty on European Union.

(c) Asylum procedures

On 20 June 1995 the EU Council adopted, pursuant to art K1 of the TEU, a resolution on minimum guarantees for asylum procedures (OJ 19.9.96 C 274/13). This cites the common humanitarian tradition of the member states of guaranteeing adequate protection to refugees in need of such protection in accordance with the 1951 Convention and Protocol, the ECHR, and the principles of the Dublin Convention (see p 490). These require decisions on asylum applications to be taken on the basis of equivalent procedures in all member states and for common procedural guarantees to be adopted.

Examinations of asylum applications within the meaning of art 3 of the Dublin Convention must meet the guarantees set out in the resolution. The resolution sets out programmatic guarantees which the Executive Committee also sets out universal principles concerning fair and effective asylum procedures (Title II). Clearly, when the Dublin Convention comes into force, reference may be made to the resolution for the intention behind the Dublin Convention. Significantly Title II, art 1, requires the procedures to be applied in full compliance not merely with the 1951 Convention and Protocol, but also with other obligations under international law in respect of human rights and in respect of refugees. Thus, consideration may be given to whether a procedure breaches obligations under conventions relating to torture and civil and political rights (see Chapter 21). No definition of 'refugee', other than that used in the Convention and Protocol, may be adopted in the procedures of the member states. Title II, art 2 provides that no expulsion measure will be carried out as long as no decision has been taken on the asylum application.

Title III provides for guarantees concerning the examination of asylum applications. Article 3 provides that the regulations on access to the asylum procedure, the basic features of the procedure, and those responsible for examining the applications, are to be laid down by the member states individually. Article 5 provides that when examining an application for asylum the national authority must, of its own initiative, take into consideration and seek to establish all the relevant facts, and give the applicant the opportunity to present a substantial description of the circumstances of the case and to prove them. The applicant is obliged to present all the facts and circumstances known to him and to give access to all the available evidence. Recognition of refugee status cannot, however, be made dependent on the production of any formal evidence. Articles 18–22 deal with manifestly unfounded asylum applications, referring to resolutions adopted on 30 November 1992 and 1 December 1992 which provide procedures for the disposal of such claims. A curtailed procedure may be adopted in relation to such claims (see arts 21 and 22). In addition, the resolution makes special provisions for claims at the border of a territory. A state may refuse admission to a person whose application has been refused before admission, and the suspensive effect of an appeal (see art 17) need not apply (art 24). There are additional safeguards for unaccompanied minors. Article 26 requires representation of a minor asylum seeker by an adult specifically appointed for the task. The adult is to safeguard the minor's interests. Women should be interviewed by women where the nature of their experience makes it difficult for them to present their grounds for asylum. Female interpreters should also be used on these occasions (art 28).

(d) The means of proof in the framework of the Dublin Convention

On 20 June 1994 the Council adopted a text, *Means of proof in the framework of the Dublin Convention*, which puts in place the principles regarding the collection of evidence under that system. The principles are adopted to avoid delays which may result in 'refugees in orbit' (*sic*), ie asylum seekers whose applications would not be examined until the Dublin Convention procedure was completed. Responsibility for processing an

Convention procedure was completed. Responsibility for processing an asylum application should be determined on the basis of as few requirements of proof as possible. The text refers to a system of indicative evidence. A member state should be prepared to assume responsibility on the basis of that evidence once it emerges, from an overall examination of the asylum seeker's situation, that in all probability responsibility lies with the state in question. The text also refers to a system of probative and indicative evidence. Probative evidence conclusively proves responsibility under the Dublin Convention, save where rebutted by evidence to the contrary, such as evidence that the documents in question are not genuine. Indicative evidence comprises indications to be used to determine responsibility. This may be sufficient, depending on the weighing up of evidence in a particular case. The same factor may be probative in relation to one issue, yet indicative in relation to another. Thus fingerprints may prove presence in a state, but not that the asylum applicant entered at a particular external frontier. The means of proof are listed in relation to the points to be determined under the Dublin Convention, arts 3–10; see OJ 19.9.96 C274/37–41.

Member states must provide to one another examples of official documents issued by them. They will be considered to be the best evidence of matters to be proved under arts 4 and 5(1)–(4) of the Dublin Convention. The standard form for determining the state responsible for examining an application for asylum is set out at pp 44–48 of OJ 19.9.96 C 274.

Among the other developments surrounding the harmonisation of the analysis of asylum applications, embodied in the Dublin Convention and other instruments, guidelines for joint reports on third countries have been drawn up by the member states. The joint reports cover matters such as the general political situation in the third country, and in particular whether its regime conducts free elections, a multi-party system, and has religious freedom, freedom of assembly and opinion, and an independent judiciary. They should also cover security service activity and the situation of minorities. Such a report should also deal with the stability of the political situation, and whether there are any known political deadlines in prospect. The second heading of a report should deal with the country's general human rights situation, including the human rights instruments to which the country is party, and whether they are observed in practice. The actual practice of the country regarding human rights, and in particular whether people are exposed to acts contrary to human rights such as torture, the frequent use of the death penalty, and the conditions of imprisonment, arbitrary arrest and lack of free movement should be examined. The report should consider not only whether there is state persecution, but also whether there is indirect persecution in the form the state's unwillingness to give sufficient protection to members of a particular group who are seriously threatened by their fellow citizens. The report should also consider whether internal flight is an option, and the controls at the country's external frontiers, especially the formalities to be completed on exiting the country. The credibility to be given to documents held by nationals and issued by the national authorities, especially travel documents, including the availability of false official documents or certificates, should be covered. The attitude of the country towards returning nationals, and in particular those who have sought asylum abroad, should be dealt with.

It is not clear how widely available joint reports will be, but the guidelines for their contents suggest matters to which practitioners should pay particular regard in formulating appeals against asylum decisions in future.

Chapter 26

Appeals and Removal

1 Introduction

The main framework for an asylum seeker's rights of appeal is provided by the 1993 Act. The 1996 Act has amended and supplemented the 1993 Act, in particular in relation to what have previously been known as 'fast track' and 'third country' cases. The Asylum Appeals (Procedure) Rules 1996 (SI 1996 No 2070, 'the 1996 Appeal Rules') set out the procedure applicable to asylum appeals.

The basic scheme is as follows. The S of S decides whether or not to grant asylum status. There is an appeal against the decision of the S of S, which lies in the first instance to a special adjudicator, and thereafter to the IAT. An appeal to the IAT may be brought only with the leave of that tribunal. Thereafter there is a further appeal on a question of law to the CA, or, in Scotland, the Court of Session. Such a further appeal may be brought only with the leave of the IAT or of the Court of Appeal or Court of Session (as appropriate).

The Lord Chancellor appoints special adjudicators under the 1971 Act, designated to deal with claims involving asylum issues.

A more abbreviated procedure applies in what are referred to below as 'special procedure cases' (which include what have hitherto been known as 'fast track' cases and 'third country' cases). That procedure is discussed below; see p 506.

2 The immigration rules

The rules set out below are in HC 395, as amended by Cm 3365 to take account of the 1996 Act and the 1996 Rules:

> 333. A person who is refused leave to enter following the refusal of an asylum application will be provided with a notice informing him of the decision and of the reasons for refusal. The notice of refusal will also explain any rights of appeal available to the applicant and will inform him of the means by which he may exercise those rights. Subject to paragraph 356(ii) below, the applicant will not be removed from the United Kingdom so long as any appeal which he may bring or pursue in the United Kingdom is pending.

345.(1) In a case where the Secretary of State is satisfied that the conditions set out in section 2(2) of the 1996 Act are fulfilled, he will normally refuse the asylum application and issue a certificate under section 2(1) of the 1996 Act without substantive consideration of the applicant's claim to refugee status. The conditions are:

(i) that the applicant is not a national or citizen of the country or territory to which he is to be sent;

(ii) that the applicant's life and liberty would not be threatened in that country by reason of his race, religion, nationality, membership of a particular social group, or political opinion; and

(iii) that the government of that country or territory would not send him to another country or territory otherwise than in accordance with the Convention.

(2) The Secretary of State shall not remove an asylum applicant without substantive consideration of his claim unless:

(i) the asylum applicant has not arrived in the United Kingdom directly from the country in which he claims to fear persecution and has had an opportunity at the border or within the third country or territory to make contact with the authorities of that third country or territory in order to seek their protection; or

(ii) there is other clear evidence of his admissibility to a third country or territory.

Provided that he is satisfied that a case meets these criteria, the Secretary of State is under no obligation to consult the authorities of the third country or territory before the removal of an asylum applicant to that country or territory.

348. Special provisions governing appeals in asylum cases are set out in the Asylum and Immigration Appeals Act 1993, the Asylum and Immigration Act 1996 and the Asylum Appeals (Procedure) Rules 1996. Where asylum is refused the applicant will be provided with a notice informing him of the decision and of the reasons for refusal. At the same time that asylum is refused the applicant may be notified of removal directions, or served with a notice of the Secretary of State's intention to deport him, as appropriate. The notice of refusal of asylum will also explain any rights of appeal available to the applicant and will inform him of the means by which he may exercise those rights.

356. A person who is entitled to appeal against refusal of leave to enter may exercise that right only after he has left the United Kingdom, irrespective of his national status, unless:

(i) the person has applied for asylum; or

(ii) the circumstances described in paragraph 354 or 355 above apply,

and the Secretary of State has not issued a certificate under Section 2(1) of the 1996 Act.

379. In addition to the rights of appeal mentioned above, a person who has claimed asylum may, unless paragraph 379A below applies, also appeal under section 8 of the 1993 Act against:

(i) a decision to make a deportation order against him by virtue of section 3(5) of the 1971 Act; or

(ii) a refusal to revoke a deportation order made against him by virtue of section 3(5) or (6) of the 1971 Act; or

(iii) directions for his removal from the United Kingdom given under section 16(1)(a) or (b) of the 1971 Act.

In such circumstances the appeal will be before a special adjudicator who will also consider any appeal under Part II of the 1971 Act.

379A. A person who has claimed asylum may not appeal under section 8 of the 1993 Act if:

(i) a deportation order has been made against him on the ground that it is conducive to the public good; or

(ii) the Secretary of State has issued a third country certificate under section 2(1) of the 1996 Act in respect of his application for asylum and that certificate has not been set aside on appeal.

3 Rights of appeal

Under s 8 of the 1993 Act, an asylum seeker may appeal against the following:

(a) the refusal of leave to enter the UK under the 1971 Act (s 8(1));

(b) any variation of or refusal to vary limited leave to enter or remain in the UK under the 1971 Act (s 8(2));

(c) a decision to make or refuse to revoke a deportation order against him by virtue of s 3(5) or 3(6) of the 1971 Act (s 8(3)); or

(d) directions for his removal from the UK under s 16(1)(a) or (b) of the 1971 Act.

The basis for the appeal in each case is that it would be in breach of the UK's obligations under the 1951 Convention and Protocol relating to the Status of Refugees for the applicant to be removed from or required to leave the UK pursuant to the decision. The appeal is to the special adjudicator, who will also hear any other appeal under Part II of the 1971 Act (para 379). However, a person who has claimed asylum may not appeal under s 8 of the 1993 Act if a deportation order has been made against him on the grounds that it is conducive to the public good, or if the S of S has issued a certificate under s 2(1) of the 1996 Act and that certificate has not been set aside on appeal (para 379A and see p 511 below).

The Asylum Appeals (Procedure) Rules 1996 (SI 1996 No 2070: 'the 1996 Appeal Rules') set out the procedure applicable to asylum appeals. These supersede the Asylum Appeals (Procedure) Rules 1993, which are revoked (s 1(2) of the 1996 Appeal Rules). The 1996 Appeal Rules apply to all asylum appeals whether or not the appeal was instituted before the 1996 Appeal Rules came into force (r 3).

A person may not bring an appeal under s 8 of the 1993 Act unless, before the time of the refusal, variation, decision or directions (as the case may be), he has made a claim for asylum (see para 2 of Sched 2 to the 1993 Act). Thus a person may not bring an appeal unless he makes a claim for asylum before the time of the decision or action against which he is appealing. Earl Ferrers, in promoting this late amendment at the Report stage of the 1993 Bill in the House of Lords, stated that the right course for a person who wishes to claim asylum after a notice of an immigration decision has been served on him is to lodge an application for asylum (HL Debs, vol 543, no 110, col 1186). A claim for asylum should be made to the immigration officer or Home Office. If the application is refused the asylum seeker will be served with a new notice of the decision and will be able to appeal to a special adjudicator at that stage. If there is any ambiguity in the wording of the paragraph, Earl Ferrers, in promoting the Act, disclosed the true intention behind it. Indeed, he went further: he stated that all refused asylum seekers, whatever their immigration status at the time of application or refusal, will have the right to appeal (col 1187). If no appeal is brought in time, the right to appeal ceases to exist (s 8(3A), 1993 Act).

The wording of the paragraph does not restrict the grounds of appeal on which an applicant may rely. It merely ensures that an appeal cannot lie in respect of a decision in relation to an asylum application which has not yet been made. It is clear also that s 8 of the 1993 Act creates a distinct right of appeal which does not in any way restrict other rights of appeal. Nothing in the 1993 Act prevents an applicant who has been refused entry for a temporary purpose claiming asylum after that decision. What he cannot do is to claim, during an appeal against refusal of entry for a temporary purpose, that the appeal should be allowed because he is an asylum seeker (see *Badmus v S of S* [1994] Imm AR 137).

Under s 6 of the 1993 Act the asylum seeker is protected from removal while that claim is being considered substantively. Section 2 of the 1996 Act introduces a significant qualification to s 6 of the 1993 Act. An asylum seeker can be removed without substantive consideration of his claim pursuant to s 2 of the 1996 Act if:

(a) the S of S has certified that the conditions in s 2(1) of the 1996 Act are satisfied; and

(b) the certificate has not been set aside on an appeal under s 3 of the 1996 Act; and

(c) *either* the time for giving notice of appeal under s 3 has expired and no appeal is pending; *or* the asylum seeker is to be sent to a country or territory to which s 2(3) applies (that is, a member state or part thereof, or a country or territory designated by order by the S of S for the purpose of s 2(3)).

However, para 345(2) of the immigration rules limits the power of the S of S to remove an asylum seeker without substantive consideration of his claim. The S of S 'shall not' remove without substantive consideration unless:

(a) the asylum applicant has not arrived in the UK directly from the country in which he claims to fear persecution and has had an opportunity at the border or within the third country or territory to make contact with the authorities of that third country or territory in order to seek their protection; or

(b) there is other clear evidence of his admissibility to a third country or territory.

The special adjudicator will deal with any appeal under s 8 of the 1993 Act against a refusal, variation, decision or direction which the person is entitled to bring under the 1971 Act, on any ground on which he seeks to rely. The special adjudicator may also deal with an appeal under Part II of the 1971 Act against any other decision or action.

The principles set out in s 19 of the 1971 Act as to the jurisdiction of the appellate authorities apply to appeals to the special adjudicator (see para 4(2)(b) of Sched 2 to the 1993 Act). It follows that a special adjudicator must allow an appeal if he considers that the decision against which the appeal was brought was not in accordance with the law or with any immigration rules applicable to the case; or on the grounds that the discretion of the S of S should have been exercised differently, if the case involves the discretion of the S of S. He is entitled to review any determination of a question of fact on which the decision was based. No decision which is in accordance with the immigration rules may be treated as having involved the exercise of a discretion by the S of S by reason only of the fact that he was requested to depart from the rules and refused to do so. However, the special adjudicator is entitled to find that the decision of the S of S is not in accordance with the law if there is a policy which was not properly taken into account by the S of S on the facts found by the special adjudicator (see p 385). In addition, the special adjudicator may make recommendations. There is a right of appeal from the special adjudicator to the IAT, save in the cases discussed below; see p 512.

Bail

Where a person appeals against a decision of type *(a)*, *(c)* or *(d)* on page 499 above, Part II of Sched 2 to the 1971 Act applies in relation to removal directions and bail (by virtue of para 9 of Sched 2 to the 1993 Act). Thus, where a person appeals against any of the determinations mentioned in *(a)*, *(c)* and *(d)* above on Convention grounds, any directions for his removal from the UK previously given by virtue of the refusal shall cease to have effect, and no directions are to be given while the appeal is pending.

Paragraph 29 of Part II of Sched 2 to the 1971 Act makes provision for the grant of bail pending appeal. A person who appeals against a decision of type *(a)*, *(b)* or *(d)* on page 499 above, and who is for the time being detained, may be released on bail under para 29. Thus:

(1) An immigration officer not below the rank of chief immigration officer may release an appellant upon his entering into a recognizance conditioned for his appearance before an adjudicator or the appeal tribunal at a time and place named therein.

(2) A police officer not below the rank of inspector may release an appellant on the same conditions as set out under (1).

(3) An adjudicator may release an appellant on his entering into a recognizance conditioned for his appearance before that or any adjudicator or before the Appeal Tribunal at a time and place named therein. The adjudicator is required to exercise this power, if the applicant so requests, in a case in which the appeal has been dismissed but leave to appeal to the Appeal Tribunal has been given.

(4) The Appeal Tribunal may release an appellant where he has duly applied for leave to appeal to the Appeal Tribunal, on his entering

into a recognizance conditioned for his appearance before the Tribunal at a time and place named therein. Where the Tribunal has granted leave to appeal, the Tribunal is obliged to release the appellant on this basis if he so requests.

The person fixing the bail may impose conditions, and may take sureties (para 29(5)). In Scotland, the appellant would enter into a bail bond rather than a recognizance. Where the adjudicator or tribunal is required or permitted to grant bail, there is a power to postpone taking the recognizance (para 29(6)).

There are procedural provisions about bail applications in r 25 of the 1996 Appeal Rules.

A bail application to an immigration officer or police officer is to be made orally. An application to the appellate authority may be made orally or in writing. A written application must contain a number of detailed particulars (set out in r 25(2)) including the grounds of the application and, where there has been a previous refusal of bail, full details of the change in circumstances since that refusal. The recognizance of an appellant is to be in Form A4, and that of a surety in Form A5 (both forms are in the schedule to the 1996 Appeal Rules).

The 1996 Rules provide that where the appellate authority postpones taking the recognizance, pursuant to para 29(6) of Sched 2 to the 1971 Act, the authority shall certify in writing that bail has been granted (r 25(5)). The person having custody of an appellant shall release the appellant once:

(a) he has received a certificate of the appellate authority that the recognizances of any sureties required have been taken, or is otherwise satisfied that they have been taken; and

(b) he is satisfied that the appellant has entered into his recognizance.

4   The 1996 Appeal Rules

The 1996 Appeal Rules form a comprehensive code of procedure for the conduct of asylum appeals. Part I deals with introductory matters; Part II with appeals to special adjudicators; Part III with appeals to the IAT from a decision of a special adjudicator; Part IV with appeals from the IAT to the CA (or in Scotland the Court of Session); and Part V with matters of general procedure. The 1996 Rules replace the Asylum Appeals (Procedure) Rules 1993. They also incorporate those provisions of the Immigration Appeals (Procedure) Rules 1984 that apply to asylum rules.

(a) Time limits and notice of appeal

A person making an asylum appeal must give notice of the appeal not later than seven working days after receiving notice of the decision against which he is appealing (r 5(1)). By r 42(6), all references in the rules to periods of ten days or less are to be treated as excluding weekends, bank holidays, Christmas Day and Good Friday. There is a special procedure to be followed in 'certified claims' (where the S of S has certified that the claim is one to which para 5 of Sched 2 to the 1993 Act applies, or where the appeal is against a certificate under s 2 of the 1996 Act). In these cases the time limit for giving notice of appeal is two working days, provided that:

(a) the appeal is made under s 8(1) of the 1993 Act (where the applicant is refused leave to enter the UK);

(b) the appellant is in custody in the UK; and

(c) there has been personal service on the applicant of the notice of decision against which he is appealing (r 5(2)).

Notice of appeal may be given by serving on an immigration officer (in the case of an appeal under s 8(1) or (4) of the 1993 Act), or on the S of S (in the case of an appeal under s 8(2) or (3) of the 1993 Act), a form prescribed in the schedule to the 1996 Appeal Rules (Form A1), together with the notice of the decision and reasons appealed against (r 5(3)). If the person wishing to appeal is in custody he may serve the notice of appeal on the person having custody of him (r 5(4)). The immigration officer or S of S must then send to the special adjudicator the documents with which the appellant has served him. He must also send any interview notes and any other document referred to in any decision which is the subject of the appeal (r 5(8)).

There is a special procedure for applicants who appeal from outside the UK under s 3 of the 1996 Act. The time limit in these cases is 28 days after the departure of the ship, aircraft, through train or shuttle train in which the appellant left the UK (r 5(5)). There is a special appeal form for these appeals (Form A1(TC) in the schedule to the 1996 Rules).

When the notice of appeal is not given within the appropriate time limit, it shall be treated for all purposes as having been given within that time limit if the person to whom it was given under the rules is of the opinion that, by reason of special circumstances, it is just and right for the notice to be treated as if given timeously (1996 Appeal Rules, r 5(6)). The special adjudicator shall not extend the time limit for giving notice of appeal except where it is in the interests of justice and he is satisfied that the party in default was prevented from complying with the time limit by circumstances beyond his control (r 41(2); see *Obeng-Atta* (12761)).

This is more restrictive than the provision under the 1993 Rules, now revoked, whereby the special adjudicator could extend time where he considered it necessary in the interests of justice to do so (see r 5(7) and (8) of the 1993 Rules). One issue under r 41(2) is likely to be this: where a time limit is missed because of the fault of an advisor, is this a circumstance beyond the control of the party in default, or is the fault of the advisor to be attributed to the applicant? It is suggested that the provision should be construed strictly, so that the question would be whether the circumstances leading to non-compliance were within the *personal* control of the defaulting party. At any rate, when he instructs professional representatives, an asylum applicant should be entitled to assume that they will act timeously, and their failure to do so should be treated as a circumstance beyond his control.

Needless to say, in view of the restrictive nature of r 41(2), it is now more important than ever for professional representatives to ensure that they comply with the appeal time limits.

(b) No explanatory statement

There is no requirement that the S of S issue an explanatory statement. For a discussion of the significance of such an omission, see the decision of the HL in *Abdi v S of S* [1996] Imm AR 288. The HL (Lord Slynn dissenting) held that there was no duty on the S of S to disclose all the material on which he made his decision that a particular third country was safe. The CA had expressed the hope that it would become the practice for special adjudicators to be supplied with reports such as those prepared by Amnesty International, so that they could exercise their powers to ask for further particulars based on the contents of those reports if they felt the need for more information. The HL did not specifically comment on this point.

(c) Parties and hearing dates

The appellant and the S of S are the primary parties to the appeal, but the UK representative of the UNHCR shall be treated as a party to an appeal upon giving notice to the special adjudicator, at any time during the course of the appeal, that he desires to be treated as a party (r 8(2)). The S of S has a duty to send to the UNHCR all the documents which the appellant has served on the S of S (r 5(7)).

The special adjudicator must serve on the appellant, and the immigration officer or S of S as the case may be, a notice of the date, time and place fixed for the hearing of the appeal. This notice must be served within five working days of receiving a notice of appeal. Once lodged, the notice of appeal may be varied by the appellant by leave of the special adjudicator (r 7).

5   Determination of an appeal

A special adjudicator will determine an appeal no later than 42 days after receiving notice of appeal (r 9, 1996 Appeal Rules). Where the appeal relates to a certified claim the appeal must be determined within ten working days, not 42 (a 'certified claim' being one which the S of S has certified as falling within para 5 of Sched 2 to the 1993 Act, or one where there is an appeal against a certificate issued by the S of S under s 2 of the 1996 Act). However, where the appellant appeals under s 3 of the 1996 Act from outside the UK, the time limit is 42 days, not ten (1996 Appeal Rules, r 9).

(a) Disposal without hearing

A hearing must be held to determine the appeal (r 9(4)), unless it is determined without a hearing under r 35 or is determined summarily under r 36.

Under r 35 there is now a wide range of circumstances in which an appeal may be determined without a hearing. Under r 35(1) it may be so determined if:

(a) the special adjudicator has decided to allow the appeal after giving every other party an opportunity to reply to the appellant's written representations; or

(b) the special adjudicator is satisfied *both* that the appellant is outside the UK or that it is impracticable to give him notice of a hearing, *and* in either case that no person is authorised to represent him at a hearing;

(c) a preliminary issue has arisen, the appellant has been given a reasonable opportunity to rebut the respondent's allegation in writing, and the appellant has either failed to submit a written statement or failed to put forward material that in the special adjudicator's opinion warrants a hearing;

(d) the parties agree in writing on the terms of a determination; or

(e) the special adjudicator is satisfied that the appeal could be disposed of justly without a hearing.

Under r 35(4) and (5), it is not necessary to hold a hearing where the appellate authority is satisfied that the appellant was notified of the hearing date, and is also satisfied that:

(a) the decision appealed against has been withdrawn or reversed and the appellant has been notified in writing to that effect; or

(b) the appeal has been abandoned; or

(c) the decision appealed against has been withdrawn.

In reaching a determination in relation to *(b)*, the special adjudicator can take account of the appellant's conduct (see *Kanayate* (12618)); and in relation to *(c)*, he can take account of the conduct of any party.

(b) Summary determination

Under r 36 an appeal to the special adjudicator or IAT can be determined summarily where it appears that the issues raised on appeal have already been determined at that level in previous proceedings to which the appellant was a party and in which the facts were not materially different. The parties are first to be given an opportunity to make written representations as to why the appeal should not thus be summarily determined.

(c) Promulgation of determination and reasons

The special adjudicator must pronounce the determination and the reasons for it wherever practicable at the conclusion of the hearing. He must send to every party to the appeal written notice of the determination within ten working days of the conclusion of the hearing (r 11(1)). In the case of certified claims, if the adjudicator agrees that the S of S was correct to certify the claim he must pronounce his decision at the conclusion of the hearing and send written notice of his determination to every party to the appeal not later than five working days after the conclusion of the hearing. Every determination must consist of a concise statement of:

(i) the decision on the substantial issues raised;

(ii) any findings of fact material to the decision;

(iii) the reasons for the decisions

(r 2(3)(b)).

(d) Adjournments

Rule 10 deals with the power of a special adjudicator to adjourn an appeal. The special adjudicator shall not adjourn unless satisfied that the adjournment is necessary for the just disposal of the appeal. This imposes a heavy burden on a party seeking an adjournment. The burden is increased by r 10(2), requiring an adjudicator, in considering a request for an adjournment, to have particular regard to the need to secure the just, timely and effective conduct of proceedings. Virtually identical provisions govern the power of the IAT to grant adjournments (r 18). In practice, adjournments should be applied for as far in advance as the circumstances allow. In particular an application for an adjournment as a result of ill health should be supported by medical evidence.

(e) National security

The provision as to national security is in para 5(6) of Sched 2 to the 1993 Act, and is unchanged by the 1996 Act. The effect of this provision is that a person is not entitled to appeal against:

    (a) a refusal of leave to enter;

    (b) a variation of leave which reduces its duration;

    (c) a decision to make a deportation order under s 3(5) of the 1971 Act;
      or

    (d) a refusal to revoke a deportation order,

if the S of S certifies that the appellant's exclusion, departure, or deportation from the UK is in the interests of national security.

Even if the applicant satisfies the definition of 'refugee', he could be refused that status for reasons of national security (*S of S v NSH* [1988] Imm AR 389; *Hussain v S of S* [1993] Imm AR 353).

Whether an applicant who might otherwise be accorded refugee status should be deported on national security grounds is treated by the courts as a decision for the S of S to take, balancing the risk of harm to the individual with the relevant national security considerations. The courts are most reluctant to interfere with such a decision by way of judicial review. The S of S may say that the matters on which he relies in relation to national security cannot be disclosed to the court; it seems at present that in these circumstances the court will treat the decision as, effectively, beyond the reach of judicial review (see *Ex p Chahal* [1995] 1 WLR 526 (CA); [1996] Imm AR 205 (QBD)).

6   The special appeals procedures

The 1993 Act introduced special appeals procedures for certain claims (see para 5 of Sched 2 to the 1993 Act), described in the heading to para 5 as 'claims without foundation'. These special procedures were used mainly in 'third country' cases, but the 1996 Act has extended their scope in two ways. First, s 1 of the Act substitutes a much wider version of para 5 of Sched 2 to the 1993 Act. Secondly, ss 2 and 3 of the 1996 Act make specific provision in relation to third country cases. The 1996 Appeal Rules often refer to 'certified claims': these are cases which the S of S has certified to fall within para 5 of Sched 2 to the 1993 Act, or where he has issued a certificate under s 2 of the 1996 Act.

Although the phrase does not appear in the 1996 Act or the 1996 Appeal Rules, certified claims are often referred to as 'fast track cases' because of the short time limits and special procedures that apply to them.

The scheme of the new version of para 5 is this. The paragraph applies to an appeal if the S of S certifies *both* that:

(a) one of a number of specified matters applies to the claim; *and*

(b) the evidence does not establish a reasonable likelihood that the appellant has been tortured in the country to which he is to be sent.

If, on an appeal to which the paragraph applies, the special adjudicator agrees with the S of S's certification, then there is no further right of appeal to the IAT (new para 5(7)). The heart of para 5 is therefore the various matters which the S of S may certify so as to bring a case within the paragraph. Paragraph 5 may apply to an appeal on any of the grounds mentioned in subss (1) to (4) of s 8 of the 1993 Act—that is to say, it can apply to any asylum appeal (new para 5(1)).

The matters which the S of S may certify as bringing a case within the special procedure are set out below. In *S of S v Munchula* [1996] Imm AR 344 the IAT held that the only power to declare that a 'without foundation' certificate was not made out is a power to declare the claim as 'not without' foundation. The special adjudicator cannot consider whether the decision to certificate is flawed under either s 19(1) or (2) of the 1971 Act because it does not accord with the policy on third countries (see p 466).

(a) Special procedure countries

The provisions on 'special procedure' countries is discussed in Chapter 25, at p 469. Such countries are often referred to as 'white list countries' and are those which the S of S has designated in an order as countries in which it appears to him that there is in general no serious risk of persecution (Sched 2, para 5(2), 1993 Act).

(b) Failure to produce passport, etc

This provision (para 5(3)) applies to a claim if, on arrival in the UK, the appellant was required by an immigration officer to produce a valid passport, and either failed to produce a passport without giving a reasonable explanation of his failure to do so; or produced a passport which was not in fact valid and failed to inform the officer of that fact.

This is a very striking provision. It is well known that asylum seekers often need to travel on false documents (indeed, if they take steps to obtain a valid passport from the country they are leaving then that fact may be treated as an indication that they have no genuine fear of persecution or that they are not of interest to the authorities). Yet an asylum seeker who does this may be subjected to the fast track appeal procedure unless he admits to the falsity of the document on arrival, at a time when it is recognised that asylum seekers may well be prone to deception in order to effect entry to what is seen as a safe haven. An asylum seeker who does this would have to raise his asylum claim at the same time or shortly thereafter (otherwise he would simply be refused entry). This seems therefore to be another measure directed against in-country applicants.

What is also striking is that an applicant cannot escape from the effect of para 5 by establishing that there was a good reason for not informing the officer on arrival that the passport was invalid.

Those who fall within the 'passport' provisions in para 5(3) will have their cases considered on the merits. But they will be subject to whatever special procedure is implemented under para 5(6), and they will have no right of appeal to the IAT. Further, the conduct which brought the asylum seeker within para 5(3) may also affect the view taken of the credibility of his substantive application.

(c) 'Weak/unmeritorious' claims

Sub-paragraph 5(4) is a rag-bag of different types of claim. All they have in common is that for one reason or another they are perceived to be weak or lacking in merit.

There are five headings:

(1) Claims that do not show a fear of persecution for a Convention reason   In effect, this seems to be a refugee law equivalent of treating a case as showing no reasonable cause of action. The danger here is in the way that this provision may affect claims raising controversial legal issues as to the proper interpretation of the Convention. For instance, there must be a risk that cases at the boundary of the 'social group' category, or cases of deserters from military service in fear of punishment, will be certified by the S of S under this head. These cases would then have to be prepared with extreme speed for hearing before the special adjudicator, the only subsequent remedy being by way of judicial review rather than appeal to the IAT. If the S of S uses his powers under this heading too widely, there is a risk that the IAT's role in the development of asylum law will be stultified.

(2) Claims that show such a fear, but the fear is manifestly unfounded or the circumstances that gave rise to it no longer subsist   Advisors will need to be alert to the way in which the S of S uses the provision that 'the [relevant] circumstances no longer subsist'. Often, in decision letters in relation to a particular country, the S of S notes that there may have been human rights violations in the past but the situation has now changed for the better, notwithstanding that reports of independent human rights organisations such as Amnesty International may show that there is still grave cause for concern. This limb of para 5(4) may well be relied on in the future to subject such cases to the special appeal procedure.

This provision therefore makes it especially important that advisors gain access quickly to up-to-date material on the countries with which they deal, so as to be able to challenge the S of S's certificate before the special adjudicator.

(3) Late claims   Paragraph 5(4)(*c*) applies to claims made any time after the appellant:

   (i)   has been refused leave to enter under the 1971 Act;
   (ii) has been recommended for deportation by a court empowered by that Act to do so;
   (iii) has been notified of the S of S's decision to make a deportation order against him by virtue of s 3(5) of the 1971 Act; or
   (iv) has been notified of his liability to removal under para 9 of Sched 2 to that Act.

(4) Fraudulent claims   Paragraph 5(4)(*d*) applies to any claim that is manifestly fraudulent, or where any evidence adduced in its support is manifestly false.

(5) Frivolous or vexatious claims (para 5(4)(*e*))   A similar provision was found in the pre-1996 Act version of para 5. An issue raised in committee in the House of Commons was the purpose this category now serves, given the breadth of the other heads of para 5(4). A Parliamentary Under-Secretary of State for the Home Department (Timothy Kirkhope) responded to the point as follows (HC Committee, 16 January 1996, col 139):

> By reintroducing the category here, we intend—and I am quite open about this—to allow it wider scope than hitherto. We are making our position somewhat clearer than it was in 1993. We intend it to cover repeat and multiple applications which are important ... The term 'frivolous' would apply to a claim that was based on facts that are different from and are wholly incompatible with those cited by the applicant, whether in a previous claim, in contact with the authorities or, indeed, in the same application.

It would apply to claims from manifestly safe countries, such as other European Union states.

The term 'vexatious' would apply when a failed asylum seeker made a repeat claim which did not differ significantly from one which had already been rejected and to multiple claims in several identities.

The phrase 'frivolous or vexatious' does not mean disclosing no reasonable cause of action. There are frivolous or vexatious cases where there is a reasonable cause of action (see *per* Sir Nicolas Browne-Wilkinson in *Blue Town Investment v Higgs & Hill* [1990] 2 All ER 897, [1990] 1 WLR 696). The special adjudicator may therefore look at the evidence of the merits of the case. A case may be frivolous and vexatious either because examination of the facts demonstrates a high probability of failure because the applicant's credibility is manifestly unreliable, and/or because there is an attempt to relitigate decided issues (*Ex p Murida*, unreported, 24 March 1994).

The special adjudicator may disagree with the S of S's certification, or may take the view that there is a different basis for it than that advanced by the S of S. A special adjudicator can take the credibility of the applicant into account to an extent. The Divisional Court, in *R v A Special Adjudicator, ex p Paulino* [1996] Imm AR 122 considered a certificate on this ground issued under the 1993 Act. The court stated:

> If, in the course of that investigation [of oral evidence], it appears to the Special Adjudicator that the applicant's account is unworthy of belief this might justify him in disagreeing with the Secretary of State's certificate and either referring the case back to him for reconsideration of the merits, or finding that the claim is without foundation and dismissing the appeal. It does not follow that want of credibility on the part of the applicant in itself justifies characterisation of his claim as frivolous or vexatious. If the applicant's account is totally incredible on matters which provide the basis for engaging the Convention then his claim can properly be so described. But if his lack of credibility is not so fundamental either because, for example, it only relates to fringe matters or because arguably it does lean on the basis of the claim in our judgment it is not possible for an applicant's claim to be characterised either by the Secretary of State or by the Special Adjudicator as frivolous under section 5(3)(b) [of the 1993 Act].

The suggestion that the proper test was that found in RSC Ord 18 r 19 (which provides for the striking out of pleadings which are an abuse of the process of the court on the ground, among others, that they are frivolous or vexatious) was rejected in *Paulino* on the basis that there are no pleadings in the special procedure, and the facts have to be determined before the question of whether the claim is frivolous or vexatious may arise. However, under the 1996 procedure, oral evidence will often not be available and the analogy is therefore somewhat stronger (see eg, *Somasundaram v Julius Melchior* [1988] 1 WLR 1394).

The expression 'frivolous and vexatious' is also used in the rules of the industrial tribunals in relation to claims which may be struck out (see *Ashmore v British Coal* [1990] 2 WLR 1437), and in relation to costs (see *Marler (ET) Ltd v Robertson* [1974] ICR 72). Arguably, the appeal should not be treated as frivolous or vexatious unless it can be shown to have no prospect of success and to have been brought from an improper motive.

(d) Torture

Paragraph 5(5) is an important escape route from the stringencies of para 5. It applies to a claim if the evidence adduced in support establishes a reasonable likelihood that the appellant has been tortured in the country or territory to which he is to be sent. When certifying that a claim falls under the new para 5, the S of S must certify that para 5(5) does *not* apply. Likewise, it is only if the special adjudicator agrees that para 5(5) does *not* apply that the applicant is excluded from appealing to the IAT (see para 5(7)).

It follows that, under the new Act, when a client has been tortured, evidence of this needs to be submitted at an early stage. It is suggested that in practice the client's own account may well not be sufficient to satisfy the S of S under para 5(5): medical reports should be prepared if at all possible. The Declaration on the Protection of All Persons from Being Subjected to Torture and Other Cruel, Inhuman or Degrading Treatment or Punishment, adopted by the UN General Assembly on 9 December 1975, provides a definition of 'torture'

Article I

1. For the purposes of this Convention, the term 'torture' means any act by which severe pain or suffering, whether physical or mental, is intentionally inflicted on a person for such purposes as obtaining from him or a third person information or a confession, punishing him for an act he or a third person has committed or is suspected of having committed, or intimidating or coercing him or a third person, or for any reason based on discrimination of any kind, when such pain or suffering is inflicted by or at the instigation of or with the consent or acquiescence of a public official or other person acting in an official capacity. It does not include pain or suffering arising only from, inherent in or incidental to lawful sanctions.

2. This article is without prejudice to any international instrument or national legislation which does or may contain provisions of wider application.

However, during the passage of the 1996 Act in Parliament, the responsible minister made clear that the term 'torture' has a wider meaning. Specifically, the minister made no reference to a requirement that torture be conducted by or on behalf of an official. She said:

I have made clear that the term 'torture' can indeed apply to any severe form of physical and indeed psychological abuse deliberately inflicted to cause suffering. I have also made clear that forcible abortion or sterilisation could indeed constitute torture and therefore fall within the scope of the exemption proposed in the amendments I have tabled. (Baroness Blatch, Minister of State at the Home Office, HL *Hansard*, 20 June 1996, cols 494–5.)

(For the full debate during the passage of the 1996 Act see HL *Hansard*, 20 June 1996, cols 476–79, 490–95, 548–9. On torture, see also HL *Hansard* Committee, 23 April 1996, cols 1048–61.)

(e) Cases certified under s 2 of the 1996 Act: third countries

An asylum seeker may be removed from the UK if the S of S has certified that in his opinion three conditions are fulfilled, and, in addition, the certificate has not been set aside on appeal and there are no further rights of appeal to be exercised within the UK (s 2, 1996 Act).

The three conditions are out in s 2(2):

(a) that the person is not a national or citizen of the country or territory to which he is to be sent;

(b) that his life and liberty would not be threatened in that country or territory for a Convention reason; and

(c) that the government of that country or territory would not breach the Convention obligation of non-refoulement in relation to him.

(see p 461).

Where the S of S has so certified, the applicant has a right of appeal against the certificate to a special adjudicator, on the grounds that any of the conditions was not fulfilled at the time the certificate was issued or has since ceased to be fulfilled (s 3(1)). Unless and until such a certificate is set aside on appeal, the applicant is not entitled to pursue any further rights of appeal (s 3(1)(b)). Moreover, there is no right of appeal from the special adjudicator to the IAT against the special adjudicator's refusal to set aside the certificate.

The only route by which such a refusal can be challenged would therefore seem to be to seek judicial review of the refusal.

There is a further important restriction on the right of appeal against the S of S's certificate by virtue of the combined operation of s 2(3) and s 3(2). Section 2(3) applies to any country or territory which is or forms part of a member state or is designated for the purposes of this section in an order made by the S of S. Section 3(2) provides that a person who has been or is to be sent to a country or territory to which s 2(3) applies is not entitled to bring or pursue an appeal under s 3 while remaining in the UK.

In other words, those caught by the combined operation of s 2(3) and s 3(2) will be sent to the relevant 'safe third country' *before* they have the opportunity to pursue an appeal in the UK against the S of S's certificate. That appeal will have to be pursued from outside the UK.

An indication of the countries to be designated under s 2(3) was given by a Minister of State at the Home Office (Baroness Blatch) while the 1996 Bill was in Committee in the House of Lords (HL *Hansard*, 30 April 1996, col 1593):

> There are some countries outside the European Union which have proven and highly developed asylum procedures. It is not sensible that an asylum seeker should be able to delay removal by disputing the safety of Switzerland, for example, any more than it is sensible for an applicant to be able to delay removal by disputing the safety of a European Union member state. The Government believe that an out-of-country appeal is an adequate safeguard for asylum seekers who are to be returned to countries with highly developed and proven asylum procedures. That will be the key criterion for designation under Clause 2. The United States, Switzerland, Norway and Canada meet that condition. Those four countries are candidates for designation under Clause 2.
>
> We will use the designation power under Clause 2 sparingly. We may wish to extend non-suspensive appeals to a country such as Australia ... if we begin to receive asylum applicants who have travelled via that country. But we would not want to use the power under Clause 2 to extend non-suspensive appeals to countries which did not have proven asylum procedures. We do not envisage that we will make frequent additions to the list of countries to which applicants may be removed without a suspensive right of appeal.

The basis of placing a country on the non-suspensive appeal list thus appears to be that it is one of a number of countries with highly developed and proven asylum procedures. Under the Asylum (Designated Countries of Destination and Designated Safe Third Countries) Order 1996 (SI 1996 No 2671), Canada, Norway, Switzerland and the USA are designated for the purposes of s 3(2) of the 1996 Act.

7 Appeal from the special adjudicator to the IAT

(a) Special procedure cases

In these cases there is no right of appeal to the IAT unless the special adjudicator sets aside the S of S's certificate (s 1 of the 1993 Act: see para 5(7) of Sched 2 to the 1993 Act as substituted by the 1996 Act).

(b) Leave

It is necessary to obtain the leave of the IAT in order to appeal (1996 Appeal Rules, r 13(1)). An application for leave must be made not later than five working days after the appellant has received notice of the determination against which he wishes to appeal (r 13(2)). The application is made by serving on the IAT Form A2 (set out in the schedule to the 1996 Appeal Rules), accompanied by the determination against which the appellant wishes to appeal (r 13(3)). The application for leave must be determined within ten working days of its receipt by the IAT (r 13(4)), and if not so determined will be deemed to have been granted (r 13(5)). An application is to be decided without a hearing unless the IAT considers there are special circumstances that make a hearing necessary or desirable (r 13(6)). The IAT must send the parties a notice recording its decision on the leave application, and, if leave is refused, reasons must be given (r 13(7)). On giving leave, the IAT does not have the power to permit the submission of further grounds of appeal after the five-day period in r 13(2) has expired (*Ex p Toprak* [1996] Imm AR 332).

(c) Full hearing

The application for leave to appeal is deemed to be the appellant's notice of appeal, and the grounds may be varied by the appellant with leave of the IAT (r 14(1)). The IAT is to serve notice of hearing on the parties not later than five working days after leave to appeal has been granted (r 14(2)). The parties to an appeal before the IAT are those who were parties before the special adjudicator (r 15(1)); the UK representative of the UNHCR may become a party to the appeal by giving written notice to the IAT that he wishes to be so treated, even if he was not a party before the special adjudicator (r 15(2)).

An appeal is to be decided by the IAT not later than 42 days after the service on the IAT of the appellant's notice of appeal (r 16).

The IAT may if necessary extend the prescribed time to enable it fairly to make the decision (see r 41(1)).

The IAT is required to hold a hearing to decide an appeal, except where an appeal is determined without a hearing in accordance with r 35 or 36 (these rules were discussed above in relation to hearings before a special adjudicator, and they apply equally to appeal hearings before the IAT). The IAT is to determine the appeal itself, unless it considers that it is desirable in the interests of justice or that it would save time or expense to remit the case to another special adjudicator for him to decide the case in accordance with any directions given by the IAT.

The new rules are evidently intended to discourage adjournments, both of hearings before special adjudicators and of hearings before the IAT (see rr 10 and 18). The IAT is not to adjourn a hearing unless satisfied that the adjournment is necessary for the just disposal of the appeal. When considering whether an adjournment is necessary, the IAT is to have particular regard to the need to secure the just, timely and effective conduct of proceedings. Where a hearing is adjourned, the IAT is to consider whether further directions should be given under r 23 (discussed below), and is to give notice orally or in writing to every party to the proceedings of the time and place of the adjourned hearing.

The tribunal is to record the decision on any appeal, and the reasons for it, and is to send to every party to the appeal, not later than ten days after the conclusion of the hearing, written notice of the determination (r 19).

8   Appeals from the IAT

Where the IAT has made a final determination of an appeal, any party may bring a further appeal to the CA (or the Court of Session in Scotland) on any question of law material to that determination (s 9 of the 1993 Act). The appellant must obtain the leave of the IAT, or, if that is refused, of the CA or Court of Session. It appears that a decision of the IAT to remit a case to the special adjudicator is not a 'final determination' for this purpose, as it does not finally dispose of the case, and so the appropriate means of challenging such a decision is by judicial review rather than by an appeal under s 9 of the 1993 Act (see *Ex p Patel* [1996] Imm AR 161).

Applications to the IAT for leave to appeal to the CA or Court of Session are governed by Part IV of the 1996 Appeal Rules. Under r 21, an application to the IAT for leave to appeal is to be made not later than ten working days after the party seeking to appeal has received written notice of the determination (r 21(1)). The application is made on Form A3 (which is contained in the schedule to the 1996 Rules) (r 21(2)). It may be decided by the President or chairman of the tribunal sitting alone (r 21(3)). The tribunal is to decide the application without a hearing unless it considers that there are special circumstances which make a hearing necessary or desirable (r 21(4)). The tribunal is to decide the application and send to the parties to the proceedings written notice of the decision and the reasons for it not later than ten working days after the tribunal has received the application (r 21(5)). (Note also the procedure for appealing to the CA set out at p 399.)

9   General procedure under the 1996 Appeal Rules

Part V of the 1996 Act (rr 22–45) deals with general matters of procedure applicable to appeals to special adjudicators, appeals to the IAT, applications for leave to appeal from the IAT, and applications for bail. References in this Part of the 1996 Appeal Rules to 'the appellate authority' are therefore to be construed as references to the special adjudicator or the IAT, as appropriate.

(a) Directions

The appellate authority has a general power, subject to the provisions of the 1996 Appeal Rules, to regulate the procedure at appeals and to give directions (r 23). Directions may be given orally or in writing after a notice of appeal has been received. Directions may provide for preliminary issues to be determined (see also *Johannes* (12499)); for a pre-hearing review to be held; and for particulars to be furnished. They may require any party to an appeal to file statements of the evidence to be adduced; a paginated and indexed bundle of documents; a skeleton argument (referring to any authorities to be cited and to the relevant passages therein); a time estimate; a list of witnesses to be called; and a chronology.

Directions may also be used to limit the length of oral submissions, the number or length of documents to be produced, the length of oral submissions, and the time allowed for examination and cross examination (for instance by allowing a witness statement to stand as evidence in chief) (see r 23(4)(e)).

It would appear that the power given by r 23(4)(e) to the appellate authority to control the course of the hearing could be used to impose time limits on each stage of the oral hearing. It is therefore increasingly important for those acting for asylum applicants to prepare detailed written witness statements and to use skeleton arguments. This should ensure that essential factual information and legal argument is put before the appellate authority, whatever time limits are imposed in relation to the hearing itself.

The appellate authority has a broad discretion as to how to proceed if directions are not complied with (see r 24). It may treat the party in default as having abandoned its appeal or withdrawn the decision appealed against; or it may proceed with the appeal; or, finally, it may determine the appeal without a hearing under r 35 (discussed above). Clearly, the broad discretion afforded to the appellate authority will need to be exercised judicially and within the context of the rights being litigated. The highest standards of procedural fairness will be required.

(b) Representation

Rule 26 deals with representation. An appellant may act in person or may be represented by counsel or a solicitor, by a person appointed by a voluntary organisation in receipt of a grant under s 23 of the 1971 Act, or (with the leave of the appellate authority), by any other person. The S of S may be represented by counsel, a solicitor, or any officer of his. The UK Representative of the UNHCR may be represented by any person appointed by him for that purpose.

(c) Evidence

General provisions on evidence apply to hearings before both special adjudicators and the IAT. There are also special provisions governing evidence in IAT hearings.

The burden of proof lies:

(a) on any person who asserts that a decision taken under a statutory enactment ought not to have been taken because he is not a person to whom the provision applies (r 31(1)); and

(b) on a person who makes an assertion of fact such that, if it were made to the S of S or an officer for the purpose of any statutory provisions or the immigration rules, the person asserting would be required to establish its truth.

The appellate authority has the power to summon witnesses (using the appropriate form, Form A6 in the schedule to the 1996 Appeal Rules). No person may be required to travel more than 16 kilometres from his residence unless the necessary expenses of his attendance are paid (r 28).

The appellate authority may receive oral, documentary or other evidence of any relevant fact, notwithstanding that such evidence would be inadmissible in a court of law (r 29).

There are important provisions on the power of the appellate authority to require a witness to produce documents. A person may be required to produce any documents in his custody or under his control which relate to any matter in question in the appeal (r 28(1)); but no person may be compelled to give any evidence or produce any document which he could not be compelled to give or produce at trial (r 29(2); see *Petre* (129981)).

In general, every party to an appeal is to have the opportunity to inspect and copy any documentary evidence taken into consideration by the appellate authority (r 30(1); *Ben Guerba* (124641)). There is one important exception to this rule. Where on an appeal it is alleged:

  (a) that a passport or other travel document, a certificate of entitlement, an entry clearance or a work permit, is a forgery; and

  (b) that the disclosure to that party of any matters relating to the method of detection would be contrary to the public interest,

then if supply of a document to that party would involve such disclosure that document shall not be supplied to or made available for inspection by that party (see r 30(2)). What is striking about r 30(2) is that there is no mechanism for the appellate authority to test the assertion that disclosure would be contrary to the public interest. A mere *allegation* to that effect prevents the appellate authority from ordering disclosure.

The IAT may receive in evidence the summary of proceedings before the special adjudicator that (under r 43) is required to be made (r 27(1)). If any party wishes to give evidence to the IAT in addition to that summary, he is required to give written notice to that effect (r 27(2)). The IAT has a discretion to receive or decline to receive such evidence (r 27(3)). Where it chooses to receive evidence (either because a party has applied to adduce evidence, or of its own motion), the IAT may either take the further evidence itself or remit the case to a special adjudicator for the evidence to be taken (r 27(3)(c)).

(d) Hearings

In general a hearing to decide an appeal to a special adjudicator or the IAT is to be held (rr 9(4) and 17(1) respectively), but this is subject to rr 35 and 36 (discussed above), providing for determination without a hearing or for summary determination in certain circumstances.

Hearings are to take place in public (r 32(1)). The appellate authority is, though, required to exclude all members of the public in cases where, in accordance with s 22(4) of the 1971 Act (cases involving the forgery of documents), the appellate authority is required to arrange for proceedings to take place in the absence of a party and his representatives (r 32(2)).

The appellate authority may exclude a member of the public, or members of the public generally, under r 32(3):

(a) at the request of a party; or

(b) where there is behaviour likely to interfere with the proceedings; or

(c) where evidence relating to a non-party is to be given and is of such nature that it ought not to be given in public.

In case (c), the appellate authority may sit in private only if none of the parties requests that it sit in public.

In general, hearings are to be held in the presence of all parties. However, the appellate authority has the power to proceed with a hearing in the absence of an appellant, in four specific cases (set out in r 33(1)):

(a) where the appellant is not in the UK;

(b) where the appellant suffers from a communicable disease or mental disorder;

(c) where by reason of illness or accident the appellant cannot attend the hearing; or

(d) where it is impracticable to give the appellant notice of the hearing and no person is authorised to represent the appellant.

In addition, there is a power to proceed with a hearing in the absence of any party who has been properly notified of the hearing and has not given a satisfactory explanation of his absence (r 33(2) and (3)).

The appellate authority has a power to hear appeals together where they raise common questions of law or fact, or relate to members of the same family, or where for some other reason this course is desirable (r 34). All parties must be given an opportunity to be heard before the appellate authority decides to hear appeals together.

(e) Miscellaneous

A number of functions of the IAT may be performed by the President or a chairman acting alone. These functions are set out in r 37. They consist of any function conferred by Part II of Sched 2 to the 1971 Act (see p 373); any function relating to leave to appeal; and any function of extending time limits under r 41, remitting to an adjudicator under r 17(2), or requiring the attendance of witnesses.

Rule 38 deals with the mode of service of documents. Documents may be sent by post or fax or delivered:

(a) in the case of the IAT, to the secretary to the IAT;

(b) in the case of a special adjudicator, to any person employed as his clerk; and

(c) in the case of the S of S, to the Appeals Support Section of the Asylum Division in the Home Office.

A party to an appeal shall inform the appellate authority of his address for service (r 38(2)), and service at that address is deemed to be good service until the person gives notice of a change of address.

Rule 39 deals with mixed appeals (that is, cases where there is both an asylum appeal under s 8 of the 1993 Act and a non-asylum appeal in relation to other grounds under the 1971 Act). The effect of r 39 is that the asylum appellate authorities are to deal with both appeals, irrespective of which appeal was lodged first.

Rule 40 requires the chief adjudicator to transfer unfinished proceedings from one special adjudicator to another if he is of the opinion that it would not be practicable for the first adjudicator to complete the proceedings without undue delay, or that for some other good reason the proceedings should not be completed by the first adjudicator.

Rule 42 contains a number of detailed provisions as to time. A notice or document that is sent or served under the 1996 Appeal Rules is deemed to have been received on the second day after it was sent (in the case of posting within the UK), or on the fifteenth day after it was sent (in the case of posting from outside the UK). These provisions apply regardless of when, or whether, the document is received. However, under r 42(2), a document sent by post to the appellate authority is deemed to have been received on the day on which it was in fact received.

Any period of time of ten days or less under the 1996 Appeal Rules is to be calculated without including weekends, bank holidays, Christmas Day or Good Friday (r 42(6)).

Any irregularity under the 1996 Appeal Rules before the appellate authority has reached a decision does not render the proceedings void, but the authority is required to take such steps as it thinks fit to cure any resulting prejudice before reaching a decision (r 44).

Clerical mistakes or accidental slips in a determination may be corrected at any time (r 45(1)), and the IAT may correct errors in a special adjudicator's determination after consulting the adjudicator concerned (r 45(2)).

10   Removal and detention of asylum seekers

Under s 6 of the 1993 Act, during the period beginning when a person makes a claim for asylum and ending when the S of S gives him notice of the decision on the claim, he may not be removed from or required to leave the UK. The effect of paras 7, 8 and 9 of Sched 2 to the 1993 Act is that any variation of limited leave to remain is to be stayed pending an asylum appeal; a deportation order is not to be made while an appeal is pending; and removal directions are to be stayed pending any appeal.

However, there is now a significant exception to these safeguards. Section 6 does not prevent a person who has made an asylum claim from being deported if the conditions set out in s 2 of the 1996 Act are satisfied. Section

2 is the new provision governing third country cases. A person may be deported if:

(a) the S of S certifies that the conditions applicable to safe third country cases (set out in s 2(2)) are satisfied; and

(b) his certificate has not been set aside on appeal; and

(c) *either* the time for bringing an appeal has expired, *or* the applicant is to be sent to a member state or a state certified under s 2(3).

The practical effect of these provisions is therefore that where the third country concerned is a member state of the EU, or another state designated under s 2(3), the applicant can be deported and required to pursue any further asylum appeal from the country to which he is sent.

To the extent that s 6 of the 1993 Act has not been modified by s 2 of the 1996 Act, the statements about s 6 made during the passage of the 1993 Act through Parliament remain an important guide to its interpretation. Earl Ferrers, in promoting s 6 in the House of Lords, stated that the intention of the S of S was that anyone who wished to appeal would be able to do so and would be able to stay in the UK for that purpose (HL *Hansard*, 2 March 1993, col 620). Under para 333 of HC 395 an applicant will not be removed from the UK as long as any appeal which he may bring is pending (subject however to para 356, which reflects the terms of s 2 of the 1996 Act).

Earl Ferrers expressed the rule to be that an appeal was pending as long as a further appeal might be brought. By an amendment he introduced, the application of sub-para 5 of para 28 of Sched 2 to the 1971 Act (which would otherwise have been an exception to that rule) was removed in respect of all appeals under the 1993 Act. Earl Ferrers said this:

> We do not intend that restriction [ie Sched 2 para 28(5) to the 1971 Act] to apply to asylum seekers. We intend that every asylum appellant shall be protected from removal for so long as he has an outstanding appeal or, if his appeal is dismissed, for so long as he has the opportunity to bring a further appeal. In other words we want all asylum seekers to be treated in accordance with the general rule on when an appeal is to be regarded as pending, which your Lordships will find set out at s 33(4) of the 1971 Act (HL *Hansard*, 11 March 1993, col 1188).

The Under S of S for the Home Department (Charles Wardle) stated that the intention of the provision is that an appeal shall continue to be treated as pending while an appeal is or may be brought under the 1993 Act (House of Commons Official report, vol 226, no 189, cols 59–60). Thus persons who are refused at the port of entry, or persons whose leave is curtailed at the same time as the refusal of their asylum application, may not be removed until they have had the opportunity of appealing, unless they have signed a disclaimer permitting them to be removed. The applicant may be able to obtain injunctive relief to prevent removal before he has had an opportunity to appeal.

A person may still be detained pending appeal, but only as a last resort when it is believed that he will not comply with the terms of any temporary admission. All personal factors, including an individual's health and dependent relatives, are taken into account when considering detention (Charles Wardle, HL *Hansard*, 12 November 1992, col 55). Where a person has an appeal pending and is detained he may be released on bail either by an immigration officer or by a police officer not below the rank of inspector if the person enters into a recognizance conditioned for his appearance before an adjudicator or the IAT. An adjudicator may release an appellant on his entering into a recognizance for him to appear before another adjudicator at a time and place specified. The person fixing bail may also require sureties.

Part VII

Criminal Offences

Chapter 27

Criminal Offences

1 Offences under the Immigration Act 1971

The criminal offences under the 1971 Act are set out mainly in ss 24, 25, 26 and 27. Briefly, s 24 creates the offence of illegal entry and other generic offences. Section 25 makes it an offence to assist illegal entry and to harbour illegal entrants. Section 26 provides that those who fail or refuse to comply with certain administrative directions under the Act are liable to prosecution. Section 27 makes criminal certain acts committed in connection with the ownership of ships and aircraft or the management of ports.

Except for the offence under s 24(1)(*d*), the offences under ss 24, 25 and 26 are subject to an extended time limit for prosecutions by virtue of s 28(1). An information can be laid within three years of the commission of the offence, as long as it is laid within two months from the date on which evidence on which a prosecution could be based became available to a police officer. This section further provides that for trial purposes an offence may be deemed to have been committed at any place where the alleged offender may be (s 28(3)).

The penal provisions in the 1971 Act are not retrospective and accordingly a person cannot be convicted under the Act as a result of something done before the Act came into force (*Waddington v Miah* [1974] 1 WLR 683).

The new criminal offences in the 1996 Act (see below) will not operate retrospectively. There are no express words to that effect, nor is there a necessary implication in the words used in the 1996 Act.

2 Illegal entry and similar offences

Section 24 is concerned with breaches of immigration control before and after entry by persons who are not British citizens. These are arrestable offences (s 24(2)) and the immigration officers, as well as constables, are given a power of arrest. The only exception is an offence under s 24(1)(*d*) (refusal to submit to a medical examination). All the offences are summary only. The maximum punishment on conviction is a fine at level 5 on the standard scale, presently £5,000, and/or six months' imprisonment. The financial penalty has increased for all summary offences under ss 24, 26 and 27 from level 4 to level 5, by virtue of s 6 of the 1996 Act.

(a) Entry in breach of a deportation order or without leave

Under s 24(1)(*a*), it is an offence knowingly to enter the UK in breach of a deportation order, or to enter without leave. Although the extended time limit applies to this offence (see above), the offence is committed on the day of entry only (*Grant v Borg* [1982] 1 WLR 638 at 646F).

Before the introduction of s 4 of the 1996 Act (see below), the offence was not committed if a person entered with leave obtained by deception, although such circumstances may have given rise to an offence under s 26(1)(*c*) (overstaying after entry). In proceedings for the offence of entering without leave, any date stamp apparently made by an immigration officer on the defendant's passport or travel documents is to be presumed to be a proper stamp unless the contrary is proved (s 24(4)). If proceedings are begun within six months of the alleged illegal entry (but not if proceedings are begun under the extended time limit) the onus of proving that the defendant had leave to enter is on the defendant. Thus if proceedings are begun more than six months after the alleged illegal entry, the defendant is in a more favourable position than if they had been begun within six months, since he does not then have what may be the difficult task of proving positively that he had leave to enter. In *Lamptey v Owen* [1982] Crim LR 42, the Divisional Court held that a defective stamp in the entrant's passport, which did not show, as the prosecution contended, that the entrant had leave to remain only for six months, did not amount to proof that he had committed a s 24(1)(*b*) offence (see below).

(b) Obtaining leave by deception

Section 4 of the 1996 Act inserts a new provision in s 24 of the 1971 Act, creating a separate offence of obtaining leave by deception. A person shall now be guilty of an offence:

> (*aa*) if, by means which include deception by him, he obtains or seeks to obtain leave to enter or remain in the United Kingdom.

The extended time limit provision applies to this subsection and it is also subject to the power of arrest contained in s 24(2). Under that provision a person may be arrested if there is reasonable suspicion that he has committed (*inter alia*) this offence. On what level 'reasonable suspicion' of committing this particular offence will be based remains to be seen. *R v S of S ex p Ghulam Yasin* [1996] Imm AR 62 is an illustration of the potential difficulties in concluding that leave has been obtained or sought by deception. The applicant had applied for and obtained entry clearance for leave to enter as a visitor from his country of residence, Bahrain. He did not use the entry clearance visa immediately but went to Pakistan. There the authorities came to believe he had committed a murder. After obtaining entry to the UK using the visa, he made an application for asylum. He then began working in breach of the conditions imposed and was arrested. The matter was considered by an immigration officer who concluded that the applicant had obtained leave to enter as a visitor by deception, despite the fact that he had validly obtained this original visa, and as a result served him with the notice of illegal entry.

An arrest is unlawful unless there are reasonable grounds for suspecting that the arrestable offence has been committed: *Chapman v DPP* (1989) 89 Cr App R 190.

The offence in s 26(1)(c) is not subject to a power to arrest without warrant, in contrast to the specific offence contained in s 24(1)(aa), which is. It is difficult to forecast how regularly the power of arrest will be used. There are clearly difficulties on many occasions, for example with language, which do not aid the assessment of whether or not there is a deception. The fact that the person will most probably have used some deception to achieve his arrival in the UK may predispose immigration officers to adopt a cynical attitude to the presentation of grave facts which are true. Whether the anxiety that this subsection will provide a sanction to immigration officers who disbelieve those who have genuine cases is misplaced, is yet to be seen.

(c) Overstaying or breach of condition of leave

Section 24(1)(b)(i) makes it an offence for a person who has limited leave to enter or remain in this country knowingly to overstay the time limit, and s 24(1)(b)(ii) creates the offence of knowingly failing to observe a condition of that leave. Neither of these offences is subject to the extended time limit as they are both continuing offences.

If a person had leave to stay for six months and stayed for seven, it would be an offence if he was aware that he was overstaying. The offence is not one of strict liability. If a defendant has mislaid or lost relevant papers and believed that his leave would expire later than it did, the element of 'knowingly' might not be proved beyond a reasonable doubt. In *R v Bello* (1978) 67 Cr App R 288 the defendant contended that his mother's death had so disturbed him that he could not deal with his business affairs and he thought his leave had not expired. The Court of Appeal upheld the conviction on the basis that the defendant had lived a normal life in England in all other respects after his mother's death, and therefore the proviso in s 2(1) of the Criminal Appeal Act 1968 applied. Whether or not a defendant knows he is overstaying the time limit will be an issue to be determined on the facts in each case. Further, there is a distinction between lack of knowledge which is a defence, and ignorance of the law which is not (*Grant v Borg* [1982] 1 WLR 638 at 644B HL). In *Grant v Borg* the HL held that the s 24(1)(b)(i) offence of overstaying can be committed only on the day after the limited leave expires and on no other day. This principle in *Grant v Borg* has been superseded by the 1988 Act. The offence is now a continuing one, but a person cannot be prosecuted more than once in respect of the same limited leave. The provision applies only where leave expired after 10 July 1988. The case is, however, still relevant for Lord Bridge's interpretation of the word 'knowingly'; he observed, at p 646C:

It would be unusual but by no means impossible for an immigrant (as, for example, one who was wholly illiterate) to remain beyond the time limited for his leave but nevertheless to be honestly mistaken in believing that his leave had not expired.

In *Hall* (1985) 81 Cr App R 260 at 264, Boreham J stated that:

Belief, of course, is something short of knowledge. It may be said to be the state of mind of a person who says to himself: 'I cannot say I know for certain that these goods are stolen, but there can be no other reasonable conclusion in the light of all the circumstances, in the light of all that I have heard and seen'.

Where the applicant has a tenable belief that the limited leave was subsisting, this may militate against a finding that he knew he was remaining beyond the limited leave.

The position with regard to the s 24(1)(*b*)(ii) offence of breaching a condition of leave was considered in *Manickavasager v Metropolitan Police Commissioner* [1987] Crim LR 50, where the Divisional Court held that the offence of breach of conditions was a continuing one. While the limited leave remained, so did the condition, producing a continuing obligation to obey.

Where a person is granted limited leave to enter or remain in the UK, the leave may be granted subject to all or any of the conditions contained in para 1, Sched 2 to the 1996 Act. Most significantly, a condition requiring him/her to 'maintain and accommodate himself and any dependants of his, without recourse to public funds' may be endorsed.

(d) Overstaying after entry under s 8(1)

Section 24(1)(*c*) deals with the position of persons who have entered the country legally under s 8(1). Section 8 allows a person who is a member of the crew of a ship or aircraft, who is employed on terms that he will leave the country on the ship or plane that brought him here (or on another ship or plane within seven days of his entry), to enter this country without leave. He is prevented from entering only if he is already subject to a deportation order or was refused entry on his last attempt to enter the UK, or an immigration officer requires him to submit to an examination under Sched 2 to the Act. If such a person, after entering in this way, subsequently fails to leave on his ship or aircraft when it departs, or on another one within seven days of entry, he is guilty of an offence. This offence is subject to the extended time limit, and liability is strict.

(e) Medical examination

It is an offence under s 24(1)(*d*) not to comply with a requirement imposed under Sched 2 to the Act to report to a medical officer of health or to undergo a medical test or examination required by such an officer. Under Sched 2, para 1, an immigration officer has power to require an entrant to whom leave is given to enter the country to report his arrival to a medical officer of health and submit to any such examination as that officer may require. This requirement can be made only on the advice of a medical inspector appointed by the S of S under Sched 2, para 1(2) or, if he is not available, on the advice of a fully qualified medical practitioner. Furthermore, it can be made only if the immigration officer is of the opinion, as a result of that advice, that such an examination is required in the interests of public health.

It should not be an offence under s 24(1)(*b*) to fail to comply with a direction made by an immigration officer in the absence of the necessary medical advice. It is not enough for an immigration officer, simply because an entrant looks unhealthy, to require him to undergo such an examination. The power is clearly aimed at real public health dangers. For example, if someone was diagnosed by a medical practitioner as a possible sufferer from tuberculosis, that would be a proper case for a requirement under para 7. Clearly, clarification of the position would be in the interests of public health. However, if the entrant was diagnosed as suffering merely from a cold, a requirement to undergo a medical examination would not be in the interests of public health. An offence under s 24(1)(*d*), unlike the others created by s 24, is not an arrestable offence. Furthermore, it is a defence to show that there is a reasonable excuse for non-compliance.

(f) Breach of conditions by persons liable to detention or removal

Under s 24(1)(*e*), it is an offence to breach any restriction imposed by virtue of Sched 2 or 3 with regard to residence, employment, or reporting to the police or to an immigration officer. It is a defence if there is a reasonable excuse for the breach. Under Sched 2, para 16 some persons are liable to detention or removal under the authority of an immigration officer. These are persons refused entry, illegal entrants and persons who have arrived in the UK and are subject to examination by an immigration officer under para 2. By virtue of Sched 2, para 21(1), an immigration officer may give a written authority permitting such persons to be admitted temporarily without being detained, or to be released from detention. Paragraph 21(2) provides that such persons shall be subject to conditions concerning residence, employment, and reporting to the police or to an immigration officer. Such conditions are notified to the person in question by the immigration officer.

Under Sched 3, if a deportation order is in force against a person he may be detained by a court or by the S of S. If he is not detained, he is to be subject to such restrictions on residence, employment and reporting to the police as the S of S may from time to time notify to him in writing (para 2(5)).

(g) Ships and aircraft

Section 24(1)(*f*) makes it an offence to disembark in the UK from a ship or aircraft after having been placed on board in order to be removed from the UK. The Channel Tunnel (International Arrangements) Order 1993 (SI 1993 No 1813), Sched 4, para 1(7)(*a*), modifies this section in relation to the Channel Tunnel System so that a person who leaves a train in the UK, having been placed on it for removal, commits an offence. Under Sched 2, para 8, an immigration officer has power to direct various persons (for example, ships' captains and ships' owners) to remove any person who has been refused entry: the S of S has a similar but wider power under para 10. If such directions have been made, an immigration officer may, under para 11, authorise the would-be entrant to be placed on board the relevant ship or aircraft. If that person then disembarks from the ship or aircraft, he is guilty of an offence. Liability for this offence is strict.

(h) Leaving the UK in breach of an Order in Council

By virtue of s 24(1)(g), it is also a strict liability offence to leave the UK or seek to leave the UK through the Channel Tunnel System in contravention of an Order in Council made under s 3(7). This section is a 'tit-for-tat' provision. If any country restricts the right of British citizens to leave that country, an Order in Council may be made prohibiting or restricting citizens of that country who are not British citizens from leaving the UK. This power has not yet been exercised, and presumably will not be exercised except in a serious crisis of international relations. For the purposes of offences in relation to the Tunnel System 'the UK' has an extended meaning (art 5 of the Channel Tunnel (International Arrangements) Order 1993, above). The 'Tunnel System' is defined in s 1(7) of the Channel Tunnel Act 1987.

3 Assisting illegal entry and harbouring

Section 25 creates two separate offences of assisting illegal entry into the UK and of harbouring illegal entrants. The scope of this section has been widened by s 5 of the 1996 Act, which creates two new offences contained in s 25(1)(b) and (c).

(a) Assisting illegal entry

Under s 25(1), it is an offence knowingly to be concerned in arrangements for illegal entry into the UK. The defendant must know, or have reasonable cause to suspect, that the person whose entry he is effecting or assisting is an illegal entrant. The offence is triable summarily or on indictment. If it is tried summarily the maximum penalty is a fine of £5,000 and/or six months' imprisonment. On conviction on indictment the maximum penalty is a fine and/or seven years' imprisonment. This is an arrestable offence, allowing immigration officers to arrest without warrant any person suspected of committing or attempting to commit it, and the extended time limit applies.

Acts falling within s 25(1) are an offence even if done outside this country, if they are committed by a British person belonging to any of the categories of 'British' citizenship under the 1981 Act; see s 4, and Chapter 3.

There are provisions, if a defendant is convicted on indictment, and he is the owner or captain of the ship, aircraft or vehicle used in connection with the offence, for the ship, aircraft or vehicle to be forfeited, subject to certain restrictions (s 25(6), (7)). This provision also applies where the convicted person is a director or manager of a company which owns the ship, aircraft or vehicle in question. In any event, s 43 of the Powers of the Criminal Courts

Act 1973 provides a power of forfeiture which can be exercised in respect of any criminal offence before the Crown Court or the magistrates' court.

A person is not an 'illegal entrant' for the purposes of s 25(1) if:

(a) he is an asylum seeker; and

(b) he does not attempt to seek entry otherwise; or

(c) he does not obtain entry by fraud, such as by the use of false documents; or

(d) he does not obtain entry without documents.

If a person merely disembarks and does not leave the area of the port designated for disembarkation, he is not an illegal entrant (*R v Naillie* [1992] Imm AR 395).

In *R v Singh and Meeuwsen* [1972] 1 WLR 1600 the CA considered whether this offence could be committed despite the fact that the defendants' acts of assisting the illegal entrants were intended to be carried out at a time when the entrants had passed into an area outside the control of the immigration authorities. The entrants had been smuggled in on a ship, hidden inside boilers which were then transported outside the area of the port controlled by the immigration authorities. One of the defendants had intended to drive the immigrants away from the port, and the other defendant was equipped to release them from the boilers. The Court of Appeal held that on the true construction of s 25(1), 'entry into the UK' included helping the entrants to get away from their disembarkation point, so that the defendants had been rightly convicted.

In *Panesar* (1988) 10 Cr App R (S) 457, a sentence of three years for this offence was reduced to two on appeal where the appellant had entered the country with his brother-in-law in the boot of his car and presented a passport on his behalf in a false name. In the case of *Singh and Saini* (1979) 1 Cr App R (S) 90, the CA drew a distinction between those who act for profit and those who commit the offence to help relatives or members of their own community. The appellant had pleaded guilty to the offence of facilitating the entry of an illegal immigrant. Each defendant was sentenced to three years' imprisonment, which was reduced to two years on appeal and the recommendation for deportation made against Singh was set aside.

(b) Assisting asylum claimants

Any person knowingly concerned in making or carrying out arrangements for securing or facilitating the entry into the UK of anyone whom he knows or has reasonable cause for believing to be an asylum claimant commits an offence (s 25(1)(*b*), 1971 Act inserted by s 5 of the 1996 Act). The phrase 'asylum claimant' means a person who intends to make a claim for asylum (within the meaning of the Asylum and Immigration Appeals Act 1993). All the offences in s 25(1) are arrestable by virtue of s 25(3). By subs (1A), the offence is not committed:

(a) by a person who does anything otherwise than for gain, or in the course of his employment by a *bona fide* organisation whose purpose it is is to assist refugees; or (*b*) in relation to a person who has been detained under para 16 of Sched 2 to the Act, or has been granted temporary admission under para 21 of that Schedule;

This offence is made out only where the defendent sought to assist or facilitate 'entry into the UK'. It must also be proved that the defendant had reasonable cause to believe, or actual knowledge, that the person whose entry he assists or facilitates intends to make a claim for asylum within the meaning of the 1993 Act. A 'claim for asylum' is defined in s 1 of the 1993 Act as a claim in respect of which it would be contrary to the UK's obligations under the Refugee Convention (see Chapter 25) to remove the claimant from, or require the claimant to leave, the UK. Article 33(1) sets out that obligation (see p 462). However, a claim is a claim for these purposes only when a person is 'in' a country. The offence would not be made out where a person believed he was assisting a person who intends to make a claim for asylum on arrival at the port of entry. A person who is in detention or on temporary admission has not entered the UK (see s 11, 1971 Act).

Lawyers who assist asylum claimants to gain entry to the UK, if charged with this offence, will have a defence only if they can prove that what they did was in the course of their employment by a *bona fide* organisation whose purpose it is is to assist refugees. The position of those who work for a solicitors' firm without such a purpose is unclear. The fact that there is no requirement in the section that the intention of the asylum claimant be dishonest, or that the means used to assist or facilitate entry be dishonest, highlights the poor drafting of this provision.

(c) Assisting the obtaining of leave by deception

Section 25(1)(*c*) makes it an offence for anyone knowingly to be concerned in making arrangements (or carrying out arrangements) to assist or facilitate a person in obtaining leave to remain in the UK by means 'which he knows or has reasonable cause for believing to include deception'. The means must be part of the arrangements to assist or facilitate obtaining leave to remain. The person making or carrying out those arrangements must believe or have reasonable cause to believe that those means include deception. The deception must be on the part of the person making or carrying out the arrangements or facilitating or assisting the obtaining of leave to remain. It is not clear whether there would have to be clear evidence of dishonesty.

> In determining whether the prosecution has proved that the defendant was acting dishonestly, a jury must first of all decide whether according to the ordinary standards of reasonable and honest people what was done was dishonest. If it was not dishonest by those standards, that is the end of the matter and the prosecution fails. If it was dishonest by those standards, then the jury must consider whether the defendant himself must have realised that what he was doing was by those standards dishonest. In most cases, where the actions are dishonest by ordinary standards, there will be no doubt about it. It will be obvious that the defendant himself knew that he was acting dishonestly. It is dishonest for a defendant to act in a way which he knows ordinary people consider to be dishonest, even if he asserts or genuinely believes that he is

morally justified in acting as he did. For example, Robin Hood or those ardent anti-vivisectionists who remove animals from vivisection laboratories are acting dishonestly, even though they may consider themselves to be morally justified in doing what they do, because they know that ordinary people would consider these actions to be dishonest. (*R v Ghosh* [1982] 3 WLR 110 at p 118).

The experience of the person involved in the arrangements, and the complexity of the arrangements, including the means which are alleged to be dishonest, will play a part in determining whether the defendant had reasonable grounds for believing that the means included deception. The deception in the arrangements will have to be one of the reasons the person obtained leave. It will not have to be the principal cause, as the word 'including' has been used, but it must be proved that the defendant had at least reasonable grounds for believing that the deception could be part of the operative reason for granting leave to remain.

(d) Harbouring illegal entrants or persons in breach of conditions of entry
Under s 25(2), it is a summary offence knowingly to harbour someone whom the defendant believes or has reasonable cause to believe is either an illegal entrant or someone who has committed an offence under s 24(1)(*b*) or (*c*). The maximum penalty is a fine of £5,000 (level 5 on the standard scale) and/or six months' imprisonment. The extended time limit applies to this offence. 'Harbouring' means 'giving shelter' (*R v Mistry, R v Asare* [1980] Crim LR 177). Merely being present when the illegal entrant was sheltered, and engaging him in conversation, is not sufficient to amount to harbouring (*Darch v Weight* [1984] 1 WLR 659). The subsection creates two offences. The first is harbouring a person knowing or believing him to be an illegal entrant. The second is harbouring a person knowing or believing him to be an overstayer. An information which fails to specify which offence is alleged is bad for duplicity (*Rahman & Qadir v DPP* [1993] Crim LR 874).

4   General offences in connection with the administration of the 1971 Act

Section 26 creates a series of summary only offences connected with the administration of the 1971 Act. They are all punishable by a maximum fine of £5,000 (level 5 on the standard scale) and/or six months' imprisonment.

(a) Failure to submit to examination
Under s 26(1)(*a*) it is an offence not to submit to an examination under Sched 2 to the Act. The relevant parts of Sched 2 are para 2, which empowers immigration officers and medical inspectors to examine entrants; and para 3, which empowers immigration officers to examine persons seeking to leave the country in order to establish whether they are British citizens and, if not, who they are.

(b) Failure to provide information or documents
This subsection makes it an offence not to produce information or documents which a person has, if he is requested to produce them in an examination under these provisions. It is a defence both to a charge under this subsection and to a charge under subs (1)(*a*) (above) that there was a reasonable excuse for the refusal or failure.

(c) Misrepresentation
Section 26(1)(*c*) makes it an offence to make, or cause to be made, any misrepresentation to an immigration officer or other person acting lawfully in the execution of the 1971 Act. This would include knowingly making a false statement in an application form under the Act; making an oral statement, for example, to an immigration officer, which the maker did not believe to be true; or presenting a document such as a passport which the person knew contained false information. It covers a statement which is in fact true, but which the maker did not believe to be true. This subsection applies not only to statements made in the course of examinations under Sched 2. It is wide enough to cover tacit representations by conduct. However, it does not go so far as to impose a positive duty of disclosure. The subsection should now be read in conjunction with the offences created by the 1981 Act, s 46 (see p 536 below). The extended time limit for prosecutions applies to an offence under this subsection.

The scope of the phrase 'or other person acting lawfully in the execution of this Act' was considered by the HL in *R v Clarke (Ediakpo)* [1985] AC 1037. It was held that the phrase did not apply to a police officer, even where the officer was investigating a suspected offence under the Act. The 1971 Act confers no duty or power on a police officer to investigate criminal offences committed in contravention of the Act; the police officer's duty to investigate suspected offences arises from the common law. Accordingly, an offence under s 26(1)(*c*) can be committed by a misrepresentation only to a medical officer or some other person (such as a medical inspector), with functions to perform under Sched 2 itself, which will, or may, involve the obtaining of relevant information.

(d) Alteration of, and possession of altered, documents
Under s 26(1)(*d*) it is an offence either to alter any official document issued under the Act (for example, a certificate of entitlement or entry clearance) or to possess any such document or passport which its possessor knows or has reasonable cause to believe is false. It is a defence to a charge under the first limb of this subsection that the alteration was made with lawful authority. The extended time limit for prosecutions applies to the offence. It is also an offence to possess for use a genuine passport with false entries (*R v Zaman* (1957) 61 Cr App R 227, CA). A document is false in this context if it falls within the test in the Forgery and Counterfeiting Act 1981, s 9 (broadly, that it was made or authorised by the wrong person: *R v S of S, ex p Patel* [1986] Imm AR 208).

(e) Failure to complete and produce documents

Under Sched 2, para 3 to the 1971 Act, the S of S is given power to make provision by statutory instrument for the production of landing and embarkation cards. This power was exercised by making the Immigration (Landing and Embarkation Cards) Order 1975 (SI 1975 No 65). Section 26(1)(*e*) makes it an offence, without reasonable excuse, not to complete and produce such a card.

(f) Failure to comply with regulations

Under s 26(1)(*f*) it is an offence without reasonable excuse to fail to comply with regulations made by the S of S under the 1971 Act, s 4(3), as to registration with the police; and under s 4(4) of that Act, as to providing information for hotel records.

(g) Obstruction of relevant officers

Section 26(1)(*g*) creates the offence of obstructing an immigration officer (or other person) acting lawfully in the execution of his duties under the Act. For example, it would be an offence to obstruct a medical inspector acting under Sched 2, para 2(2). It is a defence that there was a reasonable excuse for the action in question (*R v Clarke (Ediakpo)* above).

5 Offences by employers under the 1996 Act

A non-EEA national who wishes to come to the UK to work must be exempted from requiring permission to work; or in possession of a work permit; or qualify under a permit-free immigration category. Section 8 of the 1996 Act creates a series of criminal offences and seeks to place employer/employee relationships on a different footing where there is a question as to the employee's immigration status. An offence will be committed where it is proved that an employer employed a person who has attained the age of 16 and the following conditions are fulfilled:

    (a) the person has not been granted leave to enter or remain in the UK; or

    (b) the person's leave is not valid and subsisting, or is subject to a condition precluding him from taking up the employment.

The S of S intends to make an order specifying conditions in which either offence is not committed (s 8(1)). The burden will be on the defendant to prove, on the balance of probabilities, that he falls within one of these exceptions. A further element is:

    (c) the person is 'subject to immigration control'.

A person is 'subject to immigration control' for the purposes of the 1996 Act if he requires leave to enter or remain in the UK, whether or not he has been given such leave (s 13). The order to be made under this section will need to exempt those on temporary admission whilst an asylum claim is being determined. The practice has been to permit such persons to work if they seek permission six months after such admission.

Each element of the offence must be proved beyond reasonable doubt. There is a defence available to the employer, but it is not available 'in any case where the employer knew that his employment of the employee would constitute an offence under this section' (s 8(3)). It is a defence for the employer to prove, on the balance of probabilities, that:

(a) before the employment began, a document was produced to him;

(b) it appeared to him to relate to the employee;

(c) it was a document of a description specified in an order made by the S of S; and

(d) that document or copy of it (or a record of it) was retained by the employer. The manner of retention is to be specified in an order yet to be made at the time of writing (s 8(2)(a) and (b)).

The following documents will probably be specified and would substantiate a defence: a British birth certificate issued before 1983; a passport showing the holder to be a British citizen; a Certificate of Registration or Naturalisation as a British citizen; a European Economic Area passport or identity document; a travel document endorsed to show that the prospective employee has indefinite leave to remain in the UK or is otherwise entitled to work in this country. Clearly, a National Insurance number or P45 will usually confirm the prospective employee's eligibility to work, although the situation is complicated by the fact that false national insurance numbers are in use. The consultation document, *Prevention of Illegal Working*, November 1995, stated reassuringly that employers would not need to check that the document was authentic and had not been tampered with: 'employers will not be expected to become experts on immigration matters'. To allay any fears, a helpline number was available, providing guidance for employers who have doubts regarding documentation which had been shown to them. The maximum penalty will be a fine not exceeding level 5 on the standard scale, currently £5,000.

The effect of the new provisions may be to inhibit employers from employing persons who may legitimately work in this country. While employers may be encouraged to undertake the necessary checks on all prospective employees, the extra administration to ensure sanctions are avoided may dissuade them from investigating thoroughly the status of potential employees, which may in turn give rise to the unlawful practice of discrimination. Under the section the employer is not required to treat a person less favourably on the grounds of race, so that the section could not form a defence to an allegation of race discrimination if, for example, a black settled person had been required to produce documentation in circumstances in which a white applicant was not required to produce such documentation (see *Hampson v Department of Education and Science* [1991] 1 AC 171).

This offence can be committed by a corporation, and where it is proved that the offence was committed 'with the consent or connivance of or said to be attributable to any neglect on the part of' any director, manager, secretary or other similar officer of the body corporate, that person, as well as the body corporate, shall be guilty of the offence.

There are no specific provisions for procedure under this section. It must be assumed that an information must be laid within six months of the date of the offence (Magistrates' Courts Act 1980, s 127(1) as qualified by s 127(2)(a)) for proceedings to commence. Section 28, which grants an extended time limit for laying an information, does not apply to this section.

It is unclear whether the offence is a continuing one. If the word 'employ' is construed in accordance with s 8(8) as 'employ under a contract of employment', it would appear to be continuous, as a person is employed under a contract of employment for as long as the contract lasts, and not merely when it is concluded. However, the defence and the exception to the defence suggest that the section is concerned with the event of employing the person subject to immigration control. Further, it would not appear to be committed by an employer who employs a person with a work permit which he sees before the employment commences, but continues to employ him after his leave runs out. In these circumstances the employer could rely on the defence in subs (2), and would not fall within the exception to that defence in subs (3) because at the time he employed the person he did not know that doing so would constitute an offence. The offence will be committed from the time the actual employment commenced, but will cease if the person's status changes such that he can work legitimately.

The section use the same definition of 'employment' as appears in the Employment Rights Act 1996. For cases relating to employment in this sense see p 91. The more casual the 'employment' the more difficult it will be for this element to be made out in law. A contract for services is not a contract of employment.

The Code for Crown Prosecutors stipulates a two-stage test to be followed in deciding whether to prosecute:

(a) the evidential test, under which the Crown Prosecutor must be satisfied that there is enough evidence to provide a 'realistic prospect of conviction'. The defence case, and how the prosecution case will be affected by it, must be considered;

(b) the public interest test. If a case passes the evidential test a prosecution will usually follow unless there are public interest factors tending against prosecution which outweigh those in its favour.

It is thought that prosecutions under this section will be rare.

6 Offences by persons connected with ships, aircraft, ports or the Channel Tunnel

Section 27 creates further summary offences which can be committed by captains, owners or agents of ships or aircraft. These are all punishable by a maximum of six months' imprisonment and/or a fine of £5,000.

Under the 1971 Act, Scheds 2 and 3, various detailed provisions are made as to the requirements or directions which can be given to captains of ships and aircraft, and their owners or agents, by immigration officers and the S of S. These requirements or directions concern, for instance, the removal of seamen and aircrews who are not British citizens (Sched 2, paras 12 and 13). Schedule 2 also imposes duties on such persons. For instance, para 27 directs captains of ships and aircraft to ensure that passengers do not disembark without being subject to immigration control.

Section 27(*a*)(i) and (ii) set out the offences which can be committed by captains of ships and aircraft in this context. Section 27(*b*)(i), (ii) and (iii) provide for offences which can be committed by aircraft and ship owners and agents. These include, for example, failure to supply passengers with embarkation cards (s 27(*b*)(iii)). Section 27(*c*) creates an offence of failing to comply with Sched 2, para 26, in connection with 'control areas'. This offence can be committed only by owners or agents of ships or aircraft, persons concerned with managing ports, or the Channel Tunnel concessionaires. The latter commit an offence if they fail without reasonable cause or excuse to make arrangements for the removal of a person from the UK when required to do so by directions given under the 1971 Act. Offences similar to those relating to ships and aircraft are committed in the Tunnel System by train managers and agents operating an international service pursuant to the modifications enacted by the Channel Tunnel (International Arrangements) Order (SI 1993 No 1813), Sched 4, para 1(*g*).

7   Offences under the British Nationality Act 1981

Section 46 of the 1981 Act creates two summary offences. The extended time limit described above in relation to offences under the 1971 Act applies in respect of these offences.

The first offence, under s 46(1)(*a*) and (*b*), is punishable by three months' imprisonment and/or a fine of up to £5,000. It concerns the making of a false statement. The difference is that the statement must be made with the object of procuring something to be done, or not to be done, under the 1981 Act, whereas the offence under the 1971 Act concerns any statement made to persons acting lawfully under the 1971 Act. Two types of statement are caught by the 1981 Act: those which are known by the maker to be false in a material particular, and those which are made recklessly and are in fact false. This is a better drafted provision than that creating the equivalent offence under the 1971 Act, which makes it an offence to make a true statement if the maker does not believe it to be true (1971 Act, s 26(1)(*c*)). The more specific offences in s 24(1)(*aa*) and s 25(1) contain the theme of deception. Integral to such offences is the requirement for intention to deceive on the part of the immigrant. Proof of an intention to deceive does not also prove dishonesty: *O'Connell* (1991) 94 Cr App R 3. The concept of deception was put succinctly by Buckley J in *Re London and Globe Finance Corporation Ltd* [1903] 1 Ch 728 at 732, who stated that 'to deceive is ... to induce a man to believe that a thing is true which is false'.

More recent authorities, however, appear to hold that it is a deception falsely to persuade someone that something may be true. *Metropolitan Police Commissioner v Charles* [1977] AC 177 and *Lambie* [1982] AC 449 were concerned with the fact that the person on whom the deception was practiced was indifferent to whether or not there was a deception, as long as that person suffered no loss. For example, in *Metropolitan Police Commissioner v Charles,* a gaming club accepted cheques from the accused because they were supported by a valid guarantee card. The accused was exceeding his bank's authority, but the gaming club took the view that whether or not the accused was acting without his bank's authority was not their concern. The HL found on these facts that there had been a deception. In the context of immigration offences containing the concept of deception, it would seem that immigration officers will have to provide cogent evidence that an applicant's words, actions, or the absence of either caused the immigration officer to arrive at a determination which was prejudicial to the Home Office. The Court of Appeal held in *Firth* (1989) 91 Cr App R 217 that 'it mattered not whether it was an act of commission or omission'. Thus by omitting to disclose certain facts, a deception may take place.

The second offence under s 46(2) is to fail to comply with regulations on delivering up certificates of naturalisation without reasonable excuse. The maximum penalty is a fine of £2,500. Under the 1981 Act, s 41(1)(f), the S of S make provisions by regulations for the cancellation and registration of certificates of naturalisation of persons deprived of citizenship under the 1981 Act. He may also specify requirements for the delivery up of such certificates. This power has not yet been exercised.

8 Liability to deportation

(a) Under the Immigration Act 1971

Chapter 14 contains a wider discussion of this topic. The present discussion is confined to liability to deportation for criminal offences, dealt with in Part I of the 1971 Act. British citizens are not liable to deportation.

There are two categories of liability to deportation. The first is under s 3(5): a person is liable to deportation if he has entered with limited leave and either breaches a condition of that leave, or overstays. Additionally, para 2 of Sched 2 to the 1996 Act adds a new subsection to the effect that a person is liable to deportation 'if he has obtained leave to remain by deception'. He is also liable to deportation if the S of S deems his deportation to be conducive to the public good, or he is a member of the same family as someone in respect of whom a deportation order is or has been made. The second category is under s 3(6), which provides a further head of liability on conviction for certain offences. The offender must have attained the age of 17, the offence must be one punishable with a sentence of imprisonment, and his deportation must be recommended by the court at the time of sentence. The procedure is contained in s 6 of the 1971 Act.

Section 5 of the Act makes detailed provisions on the making of deportation orders. Schedule 3 sets out the manner in which persons are to be removed from the UK on deportation and makes provision for the detention and control of persons subject to deportation orders. The S of S can make an order for deportation regardless of whether a criminal court has made a recommendation. Even where a recommendation for deportation is made, it is not always acted upon. The power to make a recommendation arises after the requisite formal notice has been given, and is discretionary. The defendant must have been given not less than seven days' notice in writing indicating that he is liable to deportation (s 6(2)), otherwise no order can be made: *R v Omojudi* (1992) 13 Cr App R(S) 346. However, a court may adjourn sentence to allow the requisite notice period to be given. The leading case is *R v Nazari* (1980) 2 Cr App R(S) 84, which sets out the following guidelines as to the relevant matters which the court should take into account when considering whether to make an order recommending deportation.

   (1) The court must consider whether the defendant's continued presence in the UK is to the country's detriment. The more serious the crime, the more difficult it is for the defendant to argue his continued presence is not detrimental.

   (2) The courts are not concerned with the political systems which operate in other countries. Whether a defendant's compulsory return would be unduly harsh due to the regime is a matter for the Home Secretary to consider in each case when deciding whether to act on the recommendation.

   (3) The court must take into acount the effect which an order recommending deportation will have on others who are not before the court and who are innocent persons. For example, where an order would put an innocent spouse in the difficult position of having to choose between going abroad with the deported spouse or remaining in the UK with the children is a situation which should be considered very carefully before a recommendation for deportation is made.

It may be appropriate to make a recommendation for deportation following a conviction even where the person concerned no longer has any ties with his country of origin: *R v Kanapathipillai* (1988) *The Times* 26 March. In the earlier case of *R v Walters*, unreported, 10 August 1977 (*Thomas's Current Sentencing Practice* K1-5H01), however, the recommendation was set aside precisely because, for the 17-year-old appellant, it was considered that the 'consequences would be very severe indeed' if he were to return to a country which he hardly knew even though his grandparents still lived there.

A defendant should be sentenced without reference to his immigration status if the offence is unconnected with his status and the circumstances in which he entered the country. In *Miller v Linton* (1981) 3 Cr App R(S) 171, the CA held that the Crown Court had been wrong to allow the fact that the defendant was an overstayer to influence the exercise of its discretion, and accordingly set aside the recommendation. Even where a defendant is sentenced for an immigration offence, the court is not bound to make a recommendation: *R v Uddin* 27 July 1971 (*Thomas's Current Sentencing Practice* K1-5D01).

In measuring the detriment to the community, the courts look at the gravity of the offence, together with the personal circumstances of the offender. Where a defendant was convicted of a single serious offence of wounding but was otherwise of good character, the CA set aside the recommendation to deport: *R v Compassi* (1987) 9 Cr App R(S) 270. In *R v Kouyoumdjian* (1990) 12 Cr App R(S) 35 the appellant was convicted of fraudulent trading. The CA upheld the recommendation as, even though the appellant had been a man of good character up to the point of his conviction, this offence was very serious, and 'a person who is prepared to carry out this sort of fraud involving very large sums of money is not a welcome visitor to this country'. It follows that where a defendant has persistently offended, the court is more likely to find his continued presence a detriment to the community: *R v Alman*, unreported 8 November 1971 (*Thomas's Current Sentencing Practice* K1-5C01). Where a recommendation for deportation is made it is of 'crucial importance' that the court gives its reasons (*R v Rodney* [1996] CLR 357). Otherwise the recommendation is likely to be set aside by the CA.

The fact that the defendant is reliant on social security is not a matter which amounts to a detriment and is not a factor to be taken into account by the court when deciding whether to make a recommendation: *R v Serry* (1980) 2 Cr App R(S) 336.

(b) Removal and exclusion under the Prevention of Terrorism (Temporary Provisions) Act 1976

Although British citizens are not liable to deportation, they may be liable to removal or exclusion from England, Scotland and Wales (Great Britain) or from Northern Ireland under the provisions of the Prevention of Terrorism (Temporary Provisions) Act 1976, and its successors. The 1976 Act is the successor to the 1974 Act of the same name, passed after the IRA bombings in Birmingham. The purpose of the Act is to enable the authorities to arrest and question persons who are thought to be terrorists and to exclude them from parts of the UK. Under the Act, the relevant S of S may make an order excluding a person from the UK entirely, or from part of it. There is no right of appeal against an exclusion order, although the person on whom it is served may make representations to the Home Secretary within 96 hours. Statutory instruments made under the Act make provision for strict controls at ports of entry.

9 Offences under the Housing Act 1985 and the 1993 Act

A person commits an offence under the Housing Act 1985, s 74 where he:
- (a) has the intention of inducing a local authority to believe in connection with the exercise of its function in relation to homelessness under the Housing Act 1985 that he or another person
  - (i) is homeless or threatened with homelessness;
  - (ii) has priority need; or
  - (iii) did not become homeless or threatened with homelessness intentionally; and

(b) knowingly or recklessly makes a statement which is false in a material particular; or

(c) knowingly withholds information which the authority have reasonably required of him to give in connection with those functions.

Persons who fail to notify a material change in their circumstances also commit an offence under the Housing Act 1985, s 74(3). The offences are punishable by a scale 4 fine, currently £2,500. The 1993 Act applies these provisions to statements made or information withheld with the intention of inducing the housing authority to believe that a person is or is not an asylum seeker or a dependant of an asylum seeker (1993 Act, Sched 1, para 5).

10   Interviews at police stations

Interviews at police stations are conducted under caution. If a person has been detained and is being questioned in connection with immigration matters, silence on his part may be construed as lack of co-operation, and may affect the administrative decision on temporary admission or bail. The provisions of the PACE Codes should be observed both by police officers who may interview the detainee, and by immigration officers if they are investigating a potential offence. Immigration officers in certain circumstances are 'persons (other than constables) charged with the duty of investigating offences or charging offenders'. As a result of s 34(4) of the Criminal Justice and Public Order Act 1994, adverse inferences can be drawn where a person does not provide an explanation at the time of questioning, but later seeks to rely on facts which could have been recounted at the first stage of investigation. Although this provision is more significant where a matter reaches trial, it may weigh heavily with the immigration officers when making the bail decision.

Practitioners attending police stations to give advice should be accredited under the accreditation scheme operating from 1 November 1995. Payment for advice and assistance will not be made unless the advice is given either by a solicitor or by a non-solicitor representative who is registered on the police station register or the immigration register kept by the Legal Aid Board. From 1 February 1997 this requirement will apply also to trainee solicitors. To register, an application to become a probationary representative should be made, and accreditation will take place only when certain approved tests are passed. The board has made it clear that it will not pay for work undertaken by non-registered non-solicitors (see *Legal Action*, November 1995 p 23). The Law Society has published a useful book on immigration advice at police stations, and there is now a training pack for those seeking accreditation.

Appendix A

Visa Requirements

The Appendix to HC 395 provides as follows:

1. Subject to paragraph 2 below the following persons need a visa for the United Kingdom:

    (a) Nationals or citizens of the following countries or territorial entities:

Afghanistan	Ghana	Peru
Albania	Guinea	Philippines
Algeria	Guinea-Bissau	Qatar
Angola	Guyana	Romania
Armenia	Haiti	Russia
Azerbaijan	India	Rwanda
Bahrain	Indonesia	Sao Tome e Principe
Bangladesh	Iran	Saudi Arabia
Belarus	Iraq	Senegal
Benin	Ivory Coast	Sierra Leone
Bhutan	Jordan	Somalia
Bosnia-Herzegovina	Kazakhstan	Sri Lanka
Bulgaria	Kenya	Sudan
Burkina Faso	Kirgizstan	Surinam
Burma	Korea (North)	Syria
Burundi	Kuwait	Taiwan
Cambodia	Laos	Tajikistan
Cameroon	Lebanon	Tanzania
Cape Verde	Liberia	Thailand
Central African	Libya	Togo
Republic	Macedonia	Tunisia
Chad	Madagascar	Turkey
China	Maldives	Turkmenistan
Comoros	Mali	Uganda
Congo	Mauritania	Ukraine
Cuba	Mauritius	United Arab Emirates
Djibouti	Moldova	Uzbekistan
Egypt	Mongolia	Vietnam
Dominican Republic	Morocco	Yemen
Equatorial Guinea	Mozambique	Zaire
Eritrea	Nepal	Zambia
Ethiopia	Niger	The territories formerly
Fiji	Nigeria	comprising the Socialist
Gabon	Oman	Federal Republic of
Gambia	Pakistan	Yugoslavia excluding
Georgia	Papua New Guinea	Croatia and Slovenia.

    (b) Persons who hold passports or travel documents issued by the former Soviet Union or by the former Socialist Federal Republic of Yugoslavia.

    (c) Stateless persons.

    (d) Persons who hold non-national documents.

2.   The following persons do not need a visa for the United Kingdom:

    (a) those who qualify for admission to the United Kingdom as returning residents in accordance with paragraph 18;

    (b) those who seek leave to enter the United Kingdom within the period of their earlier leave unless that leave and for the same purpose as that for which that lease was granted unless it:

        (i) was for a period of six months or less; or

        (ii) was extended by statutory instrument;

    (c) those holding refugee travel documents issued under the 1951 Convention relating to the Status of Refugees by countries which are signatories of the Council of Europe Agreement of 1959 on the Abolition of Visas for Refugees if coming on visits of 3 months or less.

Appendix B

Housing and Social Security

It is outside the scope of this work to give a full exposition of the topic of social security as it affects those subject to immigration control and, as a starting point, advisors are referred to the latest edition of the *Child Poverty Handbook* (Published by the Child Poverty Action Group). In view of the changes effected by the 1996 Act, it is worth setting in context the remarks made on p 61 concerning persons subject to immigration control, and to deal in slightly more detail with the provisions affecting asylum seekers.

Housing

The Minister of State for Social Security, Lord Mackay of Ardbrecknish, stated that the intended result of an order under s 9(2) is that the classes of person subject to immigration control who will be entitled to assistance under the homelessness legislation will consist of refugees (ie persons recognised as such); persons granted exceptional leave to remain; and persons who sought asylum on arrival while their claims are being assessed (see HL *Hansard*, 1 July 1996, col 1219). On 2 July 1996, (HL *Hansard*, col 1309) Lord Mackay gave the list of groups who will be eligible, as above, together with persons who have indefinite leave to remain. Those whom it is intended will not be eligible were identified by Ann Widdecombe on 6 February 1996 (HC Committee, col 553). For the position of recognised refugees and those with exceptional leave to remain, see Chapter 25 and *R v Kensington & Chelsea RLBC ex p Kihara* (1966) *The Times*, 10 July. See also the *Homelessness Code of Guidance for Local Authorities: Supplementary Guidance*, on applications from person subject to immigration control. In *R v S of S for the Environment ex p Shelter and the Refugee Council*, 23 August 1996, Carnworth J held that rights acquired before the 1996 Act in respect of housing are not automatically removed on its coming into force.

Local authorities have duties under the Children Act 1989 which makes the welfare of the child of paramount importance. The Minister made clear that when a local authority is considering a family of persons who are not entitled to housing as a result of the 1996 Act, it has the option of housing the whole family if that is the way in which it feels it can best meet its obligations under the Children Act 1989 (see HL *Hansard*, 2 July 1996, col 1310). He also stated that persons whose applications have been refused might also seek such help while appealing (see HL *Hansard*, 24 June 1996, col 715). This statement distinguishes the relationship of the 1996 Act to the Children Act 1989, from that of the Housing Act 1985 (see *R v Northavon District Council ex p Smith* [1994] 2 AC 402).

In relation to child benefit, the Rt Hon Michael Howard MP, Secretary of State, stated that the s 10 regulation-making powers were not to be used against settled persons (HC *Hansard*, 11 December 1995, col 709). Ann Widdecombe gave the most catholic of assurances concerning the entitlement of persons with indefinite leave to remain. She stated that there was no intention to go any further with the regulation-making powers than with the other regulations on benefits (HC *Hansard* (Committee), 8 February 1996, cols 579–81).

Income support

The Social Security (Persons From Abroad) Miscellaneous Amendments Regulations 1996 (SI 1996 No 30) were introduced on 5 February 1996. However, in *R v S of S for Social Security ex p B* (1996) *The Times*, 27 June (CA)—they were ruled *ultra vires*. Schedule 1 to the 1996 Act reinstated the effect of the regulations. In short, they affect attendance allowance, council tax, disability living allowance, disability working allowance, family credit, housing benefit, invalid care allowance, income support payments on account, and severe disablement allowance. Schedule 1 to the 1996 Act provides in essence that the above regulations, incorporating the amendments to the various benefit regulations entitling persons to the above benefits, should be treated as having effect as if they had been made and come into force on the day the 1996 Act was passed. Income support, payments on account and housing benefit are dealt with in outline below. Lord Mackay of Ardbrecknish stated that once a person is accepted as a refugee he will be able to claim income-related benefits, at the asylum seeker rate, backdated to the start of his application for asylum (HL *Hansard*, 1 July 1996, col 1223).

Regulation 8 of the Persons From Abroad Regulations amends the Income Support (General) Regulations 1987 (SI 1987 No 1967, the '1987 IS Regulations'), regs 21(3), 70(3), (3A), (3B), 71(2). Part IV of the 1987 IS Regulations deals with amounts of benefit for various persons, and reg 17 provides for the amounts of benefit payable. These are subject to regulations providing for applicable amounts in particular cases, reductions in applicable amounts and urgent cases. A claimant's weekly applicable amount is the aggregate of such of the amounts set out in the regulations as apply in his case. There is an amount in respect of himself or, if he is a member of a couple, an amount in respect of both of them, and any child or young person who is a member of his family, except a child or young person whose capital exceeds £3,000. Various applicable amounts are fixed by reg 21 of the 1987 IS Regulations and are set out in Sched 7. An applicable amount of 'nil' applies to a 'person from abroad'.

Regulation 21 contains a definition of 'person from abroad', which extends beyond asylum seekers. The phrase means a person who:

(*a*) has a limited leave as defined in s 33(1) of the Immigration Act 1971 to enter or remain in the UK which was given in accordance with any provision of the immigration rules (as defined in that section) which refers to there being, or to there needing to be, no recourse to public funds or to there being no charge on public funds during that limited leave;

The following persons are not regarded as having a limited leave satisfying the above condition and as a result are not 'persons from abroad'. The person must be a national of:

(1) a Member State,

(2) a state which is a signatory to the European Convention on Social and Medical Assistance (done in Paris on 11 December 1953),

(3) a state which is a signatory to the Council of Europe Social Charter (signed in Turin on 18 October 1961),

(4) the Channel Islands or the Isle of Man, unless, in the case of a national of a state which is a signatory of that European Convention, he has made an application for the conditions of his leave to remain in the UK to be varied, and that application has not been determined or an appeal from that application is pending under Part II of the 1971 Act (appeals).

It is clear that a person may be a person from abroad if one of the other conditions are satisfied, because the conditions are set out as alternatives.

(b) having a limited leave to enter or remain in the UK, has remained without further leave under that Act beyond the time limited by the leave; or

(c) is the subject of a deportation order under s 5(1) of the 1971 Act requiring him to leave and prohibiting him from entering the UK; or

(d) is adjudged by the immigration authorities to be an illegal entrant who has not subsequently been given leave under that Act to enter or remain in the UK; or

(e) has been allowed temporary admission to the UK by virtue of para 21 of Sched 2 to the 1971 Act; or

(f) has been allowed temporary admission to the UK by the S of S outside any provision of the 1971 Act; or

(g) has not had his immigration status determined by the S of S; or

(h) is a national of a Member State and is required by the S of S to leave the UK; or

(i) has been given leave to enter, or remain in, the UK by the S of S upon an undertaking given by another person or persons in writing under the immigration rules to be responsible for his maintenance and accommodation; and he has not been resident in the UK for a period of at least five years beginning from the date of entry or the date on which the undertaking was given in respect of him, whichever date is the later; or

(j) while he is a person to whom any of the definitions in sub-paragraphs (a) to (i) applies in his case, submits a claim to the S of S, which is not finally determined, for asylum under the Convention.

The 'habitual residence' test

The phrase 'person from abroad' also means a claimant for income support who is not habitually resident in the UK, the Republic of Ireland, the Channel Islands or the Isle of Man. This corresponds to the common travel area. In *R v Barnet Borough Council ex p Shah* [1983] 2 AC 309, it was held that there was no substantial difference between 'ordinary residence' and 'habitual residence'. The test there suggested was to this effect: whether a man's abode in a particular place or country has been adopted voluntarily and for settled purposes as part of the regular order of his life for the time being, whether of short or of long duration (and see *F v S* [1991] 2 FLR 349, [1991] Fam Law 312). (See also Social Security Commissioner's Decision CIS/1067/1995.)

However, no claimant shall be treated as not habitually resident in the UK if he is:

(a) a worker for the purposes of Council Regulation (EEC) No 1612/68 or (EEC) No 1251/70 (see p 302) or a person with a right to reside in the UK pursuant to Council Directive No 68/360/EEC or No 73/148/EEC (see pp 302, 306); or *(b)* a refugee within the definition in art 1 of the Convention relating to the Status of Refugees done at Geneva on 28 July 1951 (see p 449); or

  (c) a person who has been granted exceptional leave to remain in the UK by the S of S (see p 486).

A number of cases deal with the meaning of the phrase 'habitually resident'. At the time of writing, the cases of *Sarwar* and *Getachew* (1995) *The Times*, 19 June challenging the *vires* of the regulations introducing this test, are awaiting a decision by the CA.

Urgent cases

Regulation 70 of the 1987 IS Regulations relating to 'urgent cases payments' now provides for certain persons from abroad. To qualify for such a payment a person from abroad must be a person who:

  (a) has, during any one period of limited leave, supported himself without recourse to public funds other than any such recourse by reason of the previous urgent cases provision, and must be temporarily without funds during that period of leave because remittances to him from abroad have been disrupted. He will only obtain an urgent cases payment if there is a reasonable expectation that his supply of funds will be resumed.

  (b) is an asylum seeker;

  (c) is awaiting the outcome of an appeal made under Part II of the 1971 Act (including any period for which the appeal is treated as pending under s 33(4) of that Act);

  (d) is a sponsored immigrant and the persons who gave the undertaking to provide for his maintenance and accommodation have died;

  (e) is subject to a deportation order but his removal from the UK has been deferred in writing by the S of S;

  (f) is a dependant who has been granted permission to remain in the UK pending the removal of a person who is subject to the deportation order;

  (g) is a person who has no or no further right of appeal under the 1971 Act but has been allowed to remain in the UK while an application so to remain is, or representations on his behalf are, being considered by the S of S;

  (h) is adjudged by the immigration authorities to be an illegal entrant who has not subsequently been given leave under the 1971 Act to enter or remain and who has been allowed to remain in the UK with the consent in writing of the S of S;

  (i) is a person to whom temporary admission (within or without the 1971 Act) has been granted or whose immigration status has not been determined, and whose applicable amount would be nil if calculated in accordance with reg 21 of the 1987 IS Regulations;

  (j) is a person other than one who is subject to a direction for his removal from the UK, but whose removal has been deferred in writing by the S of S. This does not apply to a person who has had a deportation order made against him requiring him to leave and prohibiting him from entering the UK.

A person becomes an asylum seeker for these purposes when he submits to the S of S a claim that it would be contrary to the UK's obligations under the Convention for him to be removed from, or required to leave, the UK and that claim is recorded by the S of S as having been made. A person also becomes an asylum seeker when he submits to the S of S on his arrival (other than on his re-entry) in the UK from a country outside the common travel area, a claim that it would be contrary to the UK's obligations under the Convention for him to be removed from, or required to leave, the UK, and that claim is recorded by the S of S as having been made. If a person applies to the wrong officer (say a customs officer rather than an immigration officer) for asylum, the S of S for Social Security's view is that this would be an application 'relating to arrival' (Lord Mackay of Ardbrecknish, HL *Hansard*, 2 July 1996, col 1351). All the applicant needs to do is to state on arrival that he wishes to seek asylum. He does not need to give any further details, in order, for these purposes, to have made a claim for asylum on arrival (see HL *Hansard*, 2 July 1996, col 1183).

A person also becomes an asylum seeker, while present in Great Britain, when the following conditions are satisfied:

(a) the S of S makes a declaration to the effect that the country of which he is a national is subject to such a fundamental change in circumstances that he would not normally order the return of a person to that country; and

(b) he submits, within a period of three months from the day that declaration was made, a claim for asylum to the S of S under the Convention relating to the Status of Refugees; and

(c) his claim for asylum under that Convention is recorded by the S of S as having been made (reg 70(3A)(a)).

A person ceases to be an asylum seeker when his claim is recorded by the S of S as having been finally determined or abandoned. A person also ceases to be an asylum seeker on the date when one of the following conditions is satisfied:

(a) in the case of a claim for asylum which, on or after 5 February 1996, is recorded by the S of S as having been determined (other than on appeal) or abandoned, on the date on which it is so recorded, or

(b) in the case of a claim for asylum which is recorded as determined before 5 February 1996 and in respect of which there is either an appeal pending on 5 February 1996 or an appeal is made within the time limits specified in the Asylum Appeals (Procedure) Rules, on the date on which that appeal is determined.

Urgent cases payments are available to a person only where the notional income he is treated as possessing is not readily available to him; and:

(a) the amount of income support which would be payable but for urgent cases provisions is less than the amount of income support payable by virtue of the provisions of the urgent cases provisions; and

(b) the adjudication officer is satisfied that, unless the urgent cases provisions are applied to the claimant, the claimant or his family will suffer hardship.

Housing benefit

As to the housing provisions see p 543. Lord Mackay set out the government's position on asylum seekers whose cases have been refused and are appealing:

> They would cease to be eligible under the homelessness accommodation and therefore if they have decided against the odds that I have just indicated to remain here and appeal, then they would have to look for other accommodation. For example they might look to the local ethnic community with which they are associated, or to the voluntary sector. If they have children then they can look to the Social Services Department for assistance under the Children Act. (HL *Hansard*, 24 June 1996, col 715).

The 1996 Act, Sched 1, para 3 in effect inserts reg 7A amendments into the Housing Benefit (General) Regulations 1987 (SI 1987 No 1971). A person from abroad who is liable to make payments in respect of a dwelling is treated as if he were not so liable. A 'person from abroad' means a person who has limited leave to enter or remain in the UK which was given in accordance with any provision in the immigration rules relating to

(a) there being, or to there needing to be, no recourse to public funds, or

(b) there being no charge on public funds,

during that limited leave.

Housing benefit is not payable to a person who has no liability to make payments. No entitlement is granted to a person who:

(a) is a national of a European Economic Area State, a state which is a signatory to the European Convention on Social and Medical Assistance (done in Paris on 11 December 1953), a state which is a signatory to the Council of Europe Social Charter (signed in Turin on 18 October 1961), the Channel Islands or the Isle of Man; or

(b) having, during any one period of limited leave (including any such period as extended), supported himself without recourse to public funds other than any previous application of this rule, is temporarily without funds during that period of leave because remittances to him from abroad have been disrupted, provided that there is a reasonable expectation that his supply of funds will be resumed.

Housing benefit may, however, be paid to such a person who has been temporarily without funds for any period, or the aggregate of any periods, exceeding 42 days during any one period of limited leave (including any such period as extended).

The phrase 'person from abroad' also means any person who:

(a) is an overstayer; or

(b) is the subject of a deportation order, being an order under s 5(1) of the 1971 Act requiring him to leave and prohibiting him from entering the UK except where his removal from the UK has been deferred in writing by the S of S; or

(c) is adjudged by the immigration authorities to be an illegal entrant who has not subsequently been given leave under that Act to enter or remain in the UK except a person who has been allowed to remain in the UK with the consent in writing of the S of S;

(d) is a national of a European Economic Area State and is required by the S of S to leave the UK; or

(e) is not habitually resident in the UK, the Republic of Ireland, the Channel Islands or the Isle of Man; or

(f) has been given leave to enter, or remain in, the UK by the S of S upon an undertaking given by another person or persons in writing in pursuance of immigration rules within the meaning of the 1971 Act, to be responsible for his maintenance and accommodation; and he has not been resident in the UK for a period of at least five years beginning from the date of entry or the date on which the undertaking was given in respect of him, whichever date is the later; or

(g) while he is a person satisfying one of the above conditions, but not (e), he submits a claim to the S of S, which is not finally determined, for asylum. Thus a person who is not habitually resident in the UK and who submits an application for asylum will be treated, subject to the provisions set out below, as potentially entitled to housing benefit.

The 'deeming provisions' in respect of EEA nationals which apply to income support also apply to housing benefit.

A person will be treated as a person from abroad if, during any one period of limited leave (including any such period as extended), he supported himself without recourse to public funds other than any such recourse because remittances to him from abroad were disrupted, is temporarily without funds during that period of leave because remittances to him from abroad have been disrupted, provided that there is a reasonable expectation that his supply of funds will be resumed.

A person who is an asylum seeker is entitled to housing benefit. A person is an asylum seeker for this purpose in two situations. First, when he submits, on his arrival (other than on his re-entry) in the UK from a country outside the common travel area, a claim for asylum and that claim is recorded by the S of S as having been made. Second, while he is present in Great Britain, a person becomes an asylum seeker if:

(a) the S of S makes a declaration to the effect that a country of which he is a national is subject to such a fundamental change in circumstances that he would not normally order the return of a person to that country; and

(b) he submits, within a period of three months from the day that declaration was made, a claim for asylum to the S of S under the Convention relating to the Status of Refugees, and

(c) his claim for asylum under that Convention is recorded by the S of S as having been made.

A person ceases to be an asylum seeker:

(a) in the case of a claim for asylum which, on or after 5 February 1996, is recorded by the S of S as having been determined (other than on appeal) or abandoned, on the date on which it is so recorded, or

(b) in the case of a claim for asylum which is recorded as determined before 5 February 1996, and in respect of which there is either an appeal pending on 5 February 1996 or an appeal is made within the time limits specified in the Asylum Appeals (Procedure) Rules, on the date on which that appeal is determined.

Payments on account

Regulation 12 of the Payments on Account, Overpayments and Recovery Regulations 1988 (SI 1988 No 664) makes savings in respect of asylum seekers. If, before 6 February 1996 a person who is an asylum seeker for the purposes of the Council Tax Benefit Regulations, the Housing Benefit Regulations or the urgent cases payments part of the Income Support Regulations, as the case may be, is entitled to benefit under any of those regulations, he continues to be entitled as if the various 'persons from abroad' provisions did not apply to him.

Where a person, in respect of whom an undertaking was given by another person or persons to be responsible for his maintenance and accommodation, claimed benefit to which he is entitled, or is receiving benefit, under those regulations as in force before 6 February 1996, he remains entitled to claim. The same provision is made for attendance allowance, disability living allowance, disability working allowance, family credit, invalid care allowance or severe disablement allowance, until such time as entitlement to that benefit is reviewed under s 25 or 30 of the Social Security Administration Act 1992.

The National Assistance Act 1948

Under s 21 of the National Assistance Act 1948, an asylum seeker may be entitled to residential accommodation, board, and other services, amenities and requisites provided in connection with the accommodation. The local authority has a discretion to make arrangements (with the S of S's approval and 'to such extent as he may direct') for these facilities to be provided to 'persons who by reason of age, illness, disability or any other circumstances are in need of care and attention'. Collins J, in *R v Hammersmith and Fulham Borough Council, ex p M* (1996) *The Times*, 10 October, held that local authorities had a duty to consider whether asylum seekers who had no money with which to support themselves were 'in need of care and attention' within the meaning of s 21(*a*) of the National Assistance Act 1948, as amended, and if they were in need of care and attention to provide the facilities to them. The applicants were destitute because they had failed to apply for asylum on arrival and were therefore ineligible for benefits or housing under the provisions of the 1996 Act. Their only link with the local authority was that they had been sleeping rough or living temporarily in the area.

Collins J focused on the proper meaning of 'in need of care and attention'. The local authority's contention that the applicants needed only money, not care and attention, was rejected. It was because the applicants were deprived of money that they were unable to provide themselves with the basic necessities of life: shelter, warmth and food, and persons in that situation were 'in need of care and attention'. Further, the words 'any other circumstances' were not confined to the physical or mental condition of the person seeking help but were intended to cover unforeseen circumstances and to ensure that a safety net was provided.

It was only Parliament's intention in enacting the 1948 Act, and not the 1996 Act, which was relevant. The purpose of the 1948 Act was to supercede the poor law by ensuring that state benefits, as well as local authority housing and other services, were to be provided for the poor, and subsequent amendments (such as the Children Act 1989 and the National Health Service and Community Care Act 1990) confirmed this aim. The intention underlying the 1996 Act was in any event not frustrated by this interpretation of s 21(*a*). An asylum seeker lawfully in the UK could not have been intended to be left without any means of support; such an intention would have to have been expressly stated on the face of the Act. If satisfied that the applicants had no means of support the local authorities had a duty to assist the applicants.

The protection of the National Assistance Act 1948 will not be available where there are alternative sources of assistance. However, if, as in *Ex p M*, there is evidence that local charities have been overrun and are unable to cope with the demand from asylum seekers, assistance should be made available by the local authority. In addition, the needs of the asylum seeker may have to be assessed under the National Health Service and Community Care Act 1990. Where this is necessary, the local authority should treat the matter as one of urgency, and may be under a duty to provide the facilities on an interim basis if the assessment is deferred. An injunction to enforce these duties may be obtained.

Index